Welfare Consequences of Selling Public Enterprises

A World Bank Book

Welfare Consequences of Selling Public Enterprises

An Empirical Analysis

Ahmed Galal
Leroy Jones
Pankaj Tandon
Ingo Vogelsang

Published for the World Bank
Oxford University Press

Oxford University Press

OXFORD NEW YORK TORONTO
DELHI BOMBAY CALCUTTA MADRAS KARACHI
KUALA LUMPUR SINGAPORE HONG KONG TOKYO
NAIROBI DAR ES SALAAM CAPE TOWN
MELBOURNE AUCKLAND

and associated companies in

BERLIN IBADAN

© 1994 The International Bank for Reconstruction
and Development / THE WORLD BANK
1818 H Street, N.W.
Washington, D.C. 20433, U.S.A.

Published by Oxford University Press, Inc.
200 Madison Avenue, New York, N.Y. 10016

Manufactured in the United States of America
First printing June 1994

The findings, interpretations, and conclusions expressed in this study
are entirely those of the authors and should not be attributed in any
manner to the World Bank, to its affiliated organizations, or to
members of its Board of Executive Directors or the countries
they represent.

Library of Congress Cataloging-in-Publication Data

Welfare consequences of selling public enterprises : an empirical analysis
/ by Ahmed Galal   ... [et al.] ;
with contributions from Fadil Azim Abbas ... [et al.].
    p.   cm.
Includes bibliographical references.
ISBN 0-19-520995-8
1. Privatization—Case studies. 2. Government business
enterprises—Case studies.   I. Galal, Ahmed, 1948–   .   II. Fadil
Azim Abbas.
HD3850.W33   1994
338.9—dc20   93-45504
                                                           CIP

Contents

*Part V. Mexico: Divestiture as an Instrument
of Stabilization*

*Part VI. Cross-Country and Cross-Enterprise Comparisons
and Conclusions*

Foreword

In the past fifteen years, there has been a major shift in thinking about the appropriate role of government in the economic sector. Divestiture of publicly owned enterprises has been at the heart of this shift. From the early privatizations in the United Kingdom and those in developing countries, to the more recent mass sales in the countries emerging from socialism, divestiture of public enterprise has been at the forefront of the policy debate. Although the literature on the subject is extensive, it is by and large theoretical and descriptive. Until now, there has been little empirical work across countries addressing some of the major policy questions that have made privatization controversial in the past—who gains and who loses from divestiture, does it benefit owners and management at the expense of workers and consumers, are privatized firms more efficient?

This study addresses these very difficult questions. Through the use of detailed case studies and carefully constructed counterfactuals, the study identifies the winners and losers from divestiture and estimates gains and losses of sellers, buyers, consumers, workers, and even competitors. This detailed economic analysis moves the divestiture debate beyond theory and anecdote to empirical rigor. The results are in some cases what might have been expected and in others surprising. On the basis of these findings, the book provides concrete policy advice.

Because of the detailed and necessarily focused nature of the analysis, the findings cannot be mechanically transposed to different settings. To do so would misuse the rich detail the study uncovers and, more important, obscure the fundamental links that the book documents between ownership, market structures, institutions, and outcomes. In particular, the analysis, which focuses on one industrial country and three middle-income countries, may not completely reflect factors that have important influences in low-income countries and countries in transition. Nevertheless, the study finds in all but one case that divestiture has provided net welfare gains and that in no case did workers lose out. The study shows that ownership matters but also demonstrates that the accompanying policies have an important influence on the likelihood and magnitude of the benefits from privatization. It offers one of the few instances in this vast literature in which policy advice is based on what demonstrably works and does not work. In doing so, it sets the standard for research in this area in the future.

Michael Bruno
Vice President and Chief Economist
Development Economics
World Bank, Washington, D.C.

Acknowledgments

In an earlier work, Jones, Tandon, and Vogelsang (1990) developed a methodology for evaluating divestiture of public sector enterprises ex ante and proposed that the methodology could and should be used to evaluate the effects of such divestiture thereafter. Ahmed Galal built on this idea, developed a research proposal for the World Bank, shepherded it through to approval, and managed its execution on behalf of the Bank. Leroy Jones served as principal investigator and project leader. This book is the outcome. Each of the four authors took primary responsibility for one country section: Ingo Vogelsang for the United Kingdom, Ahmed Galal for Chile, Leroy Jones for Malaysia, and Pankaj Tandon for Mexico. The two introductory chapters and the two concluding chapters were written jointly.

For the project as a whole, the authors would like to thank the World Bank, which provided primary financing; the Public Enterprise Program of Boston University, which provided secondary financing; the Boston Institute for Developing Economies, which permitted use of its PEPIS5 software; Mary Shirley and John Nellis of the public sector management and private sector development division of the World Bank, who supported the project from its conception and provided invaluable advice and comments; Manuel Abdala, who provided yeoman service in helping to develop the valuation software; Chen Yong Min, who updated the PEPIS5 software for this study; Clemencia Torres, who admirably assisted in software development and provided all computer and analytic support in Washington, D.C.; Andrew Browne and Boyd Gilman, who handled graphics production; and Patricia Regan, who was responsible for esthetics, nongraphics production, and tolerating the authors' foibles.

In the Chilean case, we are grateful to Jorge Marshall, Minister of Economy, who supported the study and provided valuable comments and logistical support; and Raul E. Saez, who, beside contributing to the study, provided field support and valuable insights.

In Malaysia, we are indebted to the economic planning unit of the Prime Minister's Department (especially its privatization wing) which provided the critical initial support, approval, and contacts; the

Socioeconomic Research Unit of the Prime Minister's Department, which provided invaluable support as the collaborating institution; and Shafiee Bohari, Ambikai Phagan, Appana Naidu, and Adnan Mohamed who cheerfully, intelligently, and energetically provided the critical field support. Fadil Azim Abbas coordinated all this work and provided advice and counseling on all things Malaysian, thus playing a facilitating role even beyond his essential role as coauthor.

In Mexico, our principal debt is to the privatization unit in the Ministry of Finance, particularly to Jorge Silberstein, who was the project liaison in the government. He provided not only official sponsorship but also many helpful insights into the privatization program. We also had helpful discussions with Carlos Bazdresch of CIDE and Manuel Sanchez of ITAM. Inder Ruprah, besides contributing to the chapter on Mexicana Airline, provided invaluable advice, assistance, and conversation on all aspects of the project.

In the United Kingdom we benefited from the collaboration with the Department of Applied Economics at the University of Cambridge. Its director, David Newbery, provided valuable insights and criticism while Christopher Doyle and Richard Green participated with field support and as coauthors of three chapters.

Polly Means and Jenepher Moseley meticulously and promptly coordinated the editing and production of the book. Alice Dowsett and Michael Treadway edited it carefully and sensitively.

As if the foregoing list were not long enough, additional case-specific obligations are cited in each chapter.

PART I

Introduction and Methodology

1. Divestiture: Questions and Answers

What happens as a result of public-enterprise[1] divestiture[2] in mixed economies,[3] and why? We attempt in this book to answer this basic question empirically through twelve case studies in four countries—Chile, Malaysia, Mexico, and the United Kingdom—and to draw policy implications.

The importance of the question follows from a fundamental change in the revealed preferences of the world's governments. There has been a marked discontinuity in postwar world economic history: from World War II through the 1970s, and in most subperiods of that era, the public-enterprise sector either expanded or remained the same size in almost all countries; conversely, in the 1980s and early 1990s the sector either contracted or remained the same size in almost all countries.[4]

This change has not gone unnoticed; indeed there is already a burgeoning literature on the subject. Most of this literature, however, is either based on theoretical or political arguments (what the authors predict will happen) or merely descriptive (how the deed was done or could be done). Our approach, in contrast, is resolutely and comprehensively quantitative, derived by comparing the performance of individual enterprises before and after divestiture. We thus complement, but do not replicate, existing empirical work, which is either cross-sectional (comparing different public and private enterprises' performance at a particular point in time) or partial (giving selected indicators of performance), or both (see our survey of the literature below). Chapter 2 elaborates our methodology in some detail, but first we provide an overview by expanding on our basic question.

The Basic Question and Its Subsidiaries

Our basic question is simple: is a country better or worse off when its government divests itself of a public enterprise? That is, what happens as a result of the divestiture: who won, who lost, and how much? In particular, how much does each of the parties affected—the public seller, private buyers, enterprise employees, consumers, and competitors—win or lose? A comprehensive answer is not at all simple, since it requires answers to four subsidiary questions:

- **What happened?** When one compares the periods before and after divestiture, which significant economic variables are seen to have changed? This is the problem of the factual.
- **Why did it happen?** To what extent were these changes attributable to divestiture itself, and to what extent to exogenous changes in the economy or the industry? Or, to put it operationally, what would have happened if the world had evolved as it did in all respects except that the enterprise was not divested? This is the problem of the counterfactual.
- **What will happen?** Many consequences of divestiture, especially those involving planning and investment, emerge only with a considerable lag. Accordingly, cost-benefit calculations need to take into account future differences between actual and counterfactual valuations. This is the problem of projection.
- **What is it worth?** Change generally involves trade-offs: whether from the perspective of the buyer or of the seller, divestiture probably made some things better and some things worse. Deciding whether either party was better or worse off therefore requires both a list of the things each cares about and some weighting system to allow one to add up the net benefits and costs. This is the problem of valuation.

The bulk of each of our enterprise case studies will be organized according to these subsidiary questions. The structure of the book as a whole is as follows. In the rest of this chapter we introduce our approach and describe how it relates to the empirical literature. In the next chapter we describe our methodology in detail. Then follow four sets of case studies, each set devoted to divestiture in a single country: the United Kingdom, Chile, Malaysia, and Mexico. Each set of three case studies is preceded by a background chapter that places the individual divestiture cases in the context of the recent economic history of the country and its public-enterprise sector. After the three case studies, a summary chapter draws conclusions about divestiture in the country in question. The book ends with two chapters that draw on all twelve cases. The first of these is a synthesis chapter, which collects the aggregate evidence on the outcomes of the cases and relates this evidence to some hypotheses about divestiture and the institutional and market conditions surrounding it. The final chapter offers specific policy advice consistent with our findings.

This is a policy-oriented book. But whereas most writers on public-enterprise divestiture start by elaborating on the policies,[5] we proceed the other way around, analyzing outcomes and then proceeding to search for the policies that generated them.

Our main findings lend credence to the conventional view that divestiture is likely to improve economic welfare. However, the sources and distribution of gains show some surprising patterns. We also find that partial divestiture can provide gains that equal those of full divestiture.

Comprehensiveness versus Definitiveness

In framing a study of this sort, one has a choice between making trivial statements with absolute certainty and making important statements with uncertainty. We choose to do both (as well as everything in between).

The problem can be quickly illustrated. The factual question, "What happened to private profits after divestiture?" can be answered quickly and definitively by looking at the enterprise's income statement. Assume there was a dramatic increase in profits. This is at best a starting point for evaluating divestiture, since among other things we also need to know the following:

- To what extent was the increase in profits due to exploitation of market power, and to what extent to improved efficiency? We can begin to sort this out by separating out price and quantity effects, but this is subject to empirical data problems and theoretical indexing problems.
- Assume we conclude that the increase was primarily due to a more generous regulatory pricing regime. Might this price change have occurred even without divestiture? Perhaps, in a liberalizing environment, regulators move toward higher efficiency prices for public and private monopolies alike. The determination hinges on a detailed institutional knowledge of the country's political economy and necessarily involves considerable subjectivity.
- Assume we conclude that the change would not have taken place without divestiture. Then we need to ask to what extent the gains to the producing enterprise were offset by losses to consumers. This requires the determination of demand elasticities, whose measurement will be highly uncertain, as well as controversial judgments on the meaning of consumer surplus.
- Assume we make such judgments. We then need to know to what extent the changes observed will persist into the future. Will the regulatory environment change? Will additional profits mean more investment, relaxation of a capacity constraint, and heightened benefits to consumers in the future? How will demand grow with divesti-

ture, and how would it have grown without divestiture? In short, we need to project an uncertain present into an uncertain future, with attendant potential compounding of error.

Although we ourselves are heroic enough, or foolish enough, to attempt to answer all such relevant questions, many readers may be more judicious. Accordingly, in presenting each case we proceed from the least controversial (the actual) to the more controversial (the counterfactual and projections). In the process we will be moving from measuring the wrong thing perfectly to measuring the right thing imperfectly. Readers who prefer low-variance answers to the wrong question over high-variance answers to the right question may stop at any point. Comprehensiveness has its price.

We now turn from what we did to whom we did it to.

The Sample

We began our selection of cases with some definite preferences about the kinds of enterprises and countries we wished to investigate. However, these theoretical preferences had to be modified in practice.

Sample Selection in Theory

In a world of abundant resources and a large population of divestitures to choose from, we would have selected a stratified random sample of cases. Unfortunately, neither condition was met. On the one hand, intensive case studies are expensive, and the resource constraint limited us to a dozen enterprises. This is much too few to represent adequately even a fraction of the many potential country and enterprise strata. On the other hand, the population from which we had to draw our dozen enterprises was also limited. Divestiture is a comparatively recent phenomenon: many countries had announced divestiture programs by the mid-1980s, but few had executed them to any great extent at the time of our study. Furthermore, none of the countries that had acted had divested a representative sample of their public-enterprise set. For all these reasons, our sample is small and nonrandom by default.

To tease causality out of the limited data, however, we initially planned to:[6]

- Include one industrial country and three developing countries at different levels of income and geographic dispersion, the goal being to see how the results varied with country characteristics
- Within countries, include cases of enterprises operating in both competitive and noncompetitive market structures, to see to what

extent the nature of markets makes a difference to the success of divestiture
• Across countries, examine enterprises within a single sector, to minimize the effect of variations in technology on outcomes
• Select the remaining enterprises so as to reflect variance in other potential causal variables such as size of the enterprise
• Select enterprises divested prior to 1986, since only they would have a sufficient postdivestiture history to analyze.

Sample Selection in Practice

In the end we selected the United Kingdom as the sole industrial country to be examined and Chile, Malaysia, and Mexico to represent the developing countries. Contrary to our intentions, the three developing countries are very similar. As table 1-1 shows, all three are middle-income countries with, in fact, virtually identical GDPs per capita.[7] All were quite well managed in the postdivestiture period. We selected such a nonrandom sample because these were virtually the only developing countries that had actually divested significant numbers of public enterprises by the mid-1980s.[8]

In each of the four countries we then selected three enterprises, whose primary characteristics are shown in table 1-2. In each of three of the four countries we were able to select one telecommunications enterprise and one airline (in one country, Mexico, a second airline was also chosen); the remaining cases include two enterprises from the electricity sector, one trucking enterprise, one gambling enterprise, and one container port. With only three exceptions, the market structures in which the enterprises operated were noncompetitive. Their size varied widely from 400 to 240,000 employees. Their dates of divestiture also varied widely, with the U.K. cases being the oldest and the Mexican cases in particular being more recent than we would have liked.

Table 1-1. *Selected Characteristics of the Countries in the Sample*

Country	Population, 1983		GNP per capita, 1983		GDP growth rate, 1980–90	
	Millions	Rank[a]	Current US dollars	Rank[a]	Percent per year	Rank[b]
United Kingdom	56.3	15	9,180	17	2.5	33
Malaysia	14.9	48	1,870	42	2.5	33
Mexico	75.0	11	2,180	36	–0.9	100
Chile	11.7	54	1,890	41	1.1	77

a. Out of 128 countries.
b. Out of 140 countries.
Source: World Bank Atlas, various issues.

Table 1-2.   *Selected Characteristics of the Enterprises in the Sample*

Country and company	Sector or activity	Market share[a]	Size (number of employees)[b]	Year of divestiture
United Kingdom				
British Telecom	Telecommunications	97	235,000	1984
British Airways	Airline	39	40,800	1987
National Freight	Truck transport	10	24,300	1982
Chile				
CHILGENER	Electricity generation	13	791	1987
ENERSIS	Electricity distribution	95	2,495	1987
Compañía de Téléfonos de Chile	Telecommunications	95	7,240	1988
Malaysia				
Malaysian Airline	Airline	60	10,632	1985
Kelang Container Terminal	Container port	55	797	1986
Sports Toto	Lottery	5	400	1985
Mexico				
Teléfonos de México	Telecommunications	100	50,000	1990
Aeroméxico	Airline	50	11,500	1988
Mexicana de Aviación	Airline	50	12,700	1989

a. Revenue-weighted market share of the divested enterprise in the year prior to divestiture.

b. In the year prior to divestiture.

Source: Enterprise data.

Sample Limitations

Notwithstanding our attempt to select a sample that represents the universe of divested enterprises, the sample is limited in several important ways:

- It does not include countries with relatively low per capita incomes, highly distorted markets, and relatively weak institutional capacity (for example, many of the African countries).[9]
- As already noted, it covers only three cases in relatively competitive markets; it also lacks enterprises producing tradable goods.
- It includes enterprises that were divested very recently.
- In two countries we were congenially but effectively denied access to data for some enterprises that we would otherwise have included.

The first limitation cautions us against applying our findings directly to low-income countries, although many of the results could still carry over. The second limitation may be less problematic, because if divestiture works in noncompetitive markets, it ought to work in competitive ones. In noncompetitive markets there is the potential for positive government intervention, via public ownership or regulation of private owners, to prevent the exploitation of consumers, and it is an open question which of these is superior. In truly competitive markets, in contrast, it is hard to make a case that divestiture can make things worse, and the primary question is then how much can it make things better. The problem is that even if output markets are competitive, the labor, capital, and intermediate input markets may not be. Thus, deleterious welfare effects could still accompany divestiture even into competitive output markets. Precluding enterprises that were divested very recently is problematic to the extent that systematic differences exist between these enterprises and the ones that we selected. Finally, the selective denial of access to enterprise data could have precluded our observing more negative results.

In sum, because our sample is relatively small and nonrandom, sweeping generalizations should be avoided. However, given that many countries and enterprises around the world resemble the cases analyzed, our hope is to shed some light on the following questions:

- What can be expected from making the divestiture decision?
- Under what conditions would such a decision be advantageous to society?

In sum, while selection biases may preclude sweeping *predictions* about what will happen elsewhere, they do not preclude policy *prescriptions* about what to do and what to avoid.

Does Ownership Matter? A Survey of the Literature

This volume is part of a long tradition that attempts to ascertain the difference between public and private ownership. In this section we review this voluminous literature in order to clarify the nature of our own contribution. We begin with theory and proceed to several different classes of empirical attempts to determine whether or not ownership matters.

Theory

There is a huge theoretical literature on public-private differences, drawing on the property rights, transactions costs, contract theory, and public choice traditions, among others.[10] By way of overview, hypothesized differences between public and private enterprises can be assigned to one of two categories:

- *Differences in objectives.* Private enterprises pursue profit; public enterprises may pursue whatever the government wants and is able to finance. This may mean that the public enterprise can promote consumer welfare by not exploiting a monopoly position. On the other hand, it may mean that the public enterprise can instead promote the welfare of politicians by hiring a large number of redundant workers.
- *Differences in constraints.* Even if objectives were identical, public and private enterprises may face different constraints on the pursuit of those objectives. Stories of public enterprises forced to operate with insufficient autonomy (can't pay enough to attract skilled professionals, can't fire unskilled workers, etc.) are legion. Theoretical constraints on the private sector are less commonly cited but are manifest in the frequent claim in poorer developing countries that large, capital-intensive projects require public enterprises because the tiny private sector does not have adequate access to capital.

A particularly important set of public constraints is that on incentives. When property rights are held by the state rather than by individuals, no individual has the incentive to exert the effort to see that resources are used efficiently. This results in high-cost production, among other things. More recently, emphasis has been placed on the constraints on governments' ability to make commitments in an intertemporal framework. This literature argues that a sitting government cannot credibly commit future governments to do or refrain from doing certain things (e.g., not to interfere with the internal operations of enterprises) and that this leads to inefficiently myopic behavior on the part of public-enterprise managers. The most recent strand of theoretical literature, based on principal-agent theory, emphasizes these commitment and incentive constraints that reduce efficiency, but also emphasizes the potential trade-off in terms of objectives (that is, at least in the short run, public enterprises can more easily be made to do what society wants).[11]

In making any such comparisons between public and private, one must of course hold other things equal, varying only the ownership dimension. Perhaps the most important thing to keep constant is market structure. Since most public-enterprise output is sold in monopoly or oligopoly markets, the proper comparison is with regulated private monopolists. These also have efficiency problems. If prices are regulated to allow a fair rate of return, then a private manager has little incentive to control costs. In fact, if that return is higher than the manager's opportunity cost, management has every incentive to overinvest.[12] The reverse problem of underinvestment can occur if the government cannot credibly commit itself to eschew exploitative pricing policies in the future (Levy, Esfahan, Galal, Vogelsang, and Spiller forthcoming). Further, even an unregulated private monopolist could reasonably be expected to take some of the enterprise's profits in the form of increased leisure, thus creating cost inefficiencies akin to those in public enterprises (Leibenstein 1976). One must therefore ask, How much of the problems of public enterprises are due to state ownership and how much to their monopoly positions?

A related element that must be held constant is the size of the enterprise and its ownership structure. In private firms in which ownership is divorced from control, many efficiency-enhancing mechanisms break down (information becomes impacted, incentives are difficult to assign, mechanistic and bureaucratic management is difficult to avoid, capital market monitoring becomes less effective, etc.).[13] Once again we must ask whether the problems of public enterprises are due to their ownership or to their size.

A subjective synthesis of this theoretical literature leads to the following conclusions about the effects of public-private differences:

- Small private enterprises facing competitive output and input markets are unequivocally superior to large public enterprises facing monopoly markets.
- Small public enterprises facing competitive output and input markets can do no better than private enterprises in the same circumstances, but can do considerably worse.
- In large monopoly markets the predictions of theory are ambiguous, depending on the institutional details assumed (how the private sector is structured and regulated, and how the public sector is managed and motivated).

The first statement is of course irrelevant for policy purposes, because it does not reflect a true choice. For the same reason, evidence or arguments in favor of private enterprise that amount to proving this proposition are equally irrelevant. The second proposition justifies mass privatization programs in formerly socialist economies (where one starts with, say, 80 percent of the economy in public hands) but is of minor import in most mixed economies, where the vast bulk of public-enterprise output is sold in imperfect markets (and only 10 percent or so of GDP is in public hands and can potentially be divested). In such economies it is the last conclusion that is critical. But because here the theory is ambiguous we must turn to empirical work.

Public versus Private Comparisons

The oldest and largest body of empirical literature compares different public and private enterprises. At first glance the most striking characteristic of this body of work is its almost laughable diversity of results. Broadly speaking, two sets of conclusions emerge. The first finds private enterprises clearly superior:

> [There is] robust evidence that state enterprises and mixed enterprises are less profitable and less efficient than private corporations. (Boardman and Vining 1989, p. 17)
> There is virtually universal consensus that privatization improves efficiency. (Boycko, Shleifer, and Vishny 1993, p. 1)
> Without exception, the empirical findings indicate that the same level of output could be provided at substantially lower costs if output were produced by the private rather than the public sector. (Bennett and Johnson 1979, p. 59)

A second body of literature draws rather different conclusions. The earliest (to our knowledge) and most influential formulation is that of Caves and Christensen (1980, p. 974).

> Contrary to what is predicted in the property rights literature, we find no evidence of inferior efficiency performance by the government-owned railroad. . . . public ownership is not inherently less efficient than private ownership . . . the oft-noted inefficiency of government enterprises stems from their isolation from effective competition rather than their public ownership per se.

This basic insight on the need to adjust for market structure has since been elaborated on and extended by a large number of authors of individual studies and surveys.[14] Three of the more recent works may be cited as representative:

> The empirical evidence . . . lends only limited support to the hypothesis that SOEs [state-owned enterprises] are less efficient than private firms. The financial results of SOE's certainly show a dismal picture of losses. However, these losses may be a result of social and political demands on the enterprises. In terms of efficiency, these enterprises' performance is much less bleak. As efficient users of resources, they may have done as well as private firms producing the same product in the same country. (Aharoni 1986, p. 215)
> [The evidence] suggests an "edge" for the private sector, but the results vary considerably across sectors. In sectors where there is some evidence of superior public efficiency (electricity and water), there is limited competition or the private firms are highly regulated. Evidence of the greater efficiency of [private companies] appears to be in the delivery of services where governments' subcontracts to the private sector and their monitoring costs—for example, for refuse collec-

tion, fire protection, and non-rail transit—are relatively low. (Boardman and Vining 1989, p. 5)

There is no evidence of a statistically satisfactory kind to suggest that public enterprises in LDCs [less-developed countries] have a lower level of technical efficiency than private firms operating at the same scale of operation. (Millward 1988, p. 157)

How then are the two sets of conclusions to be reconciled? Quite easily, we believe. There are three sets of factors involved. The first set derives from our three theoretical propositions in the previous section. A few of the studies find private enterprise superior for illegitimate reasons, because they compare competitive with monopoly enterprises (see our first proposition). More frequently, they find private enterprise superior for legitimate reasons because they are comparing reasonably competitive enterprises (see our second proposition). Finally, when public and private monopolies are compared, the results are all over the map (see our third proposition).

It is perhaps worth emphasizing that our third proposition does not so much say how public and private enterprises in such sectors are efficient, as how they are *in*efficient. For example, Atkinson and Halvorsen (1986) estimated cost efficiency for a sample of 30 public and 123 private fossil-fueled electricity generating monopolists and concluded that public and private enterprises did not significantly differ in costs, but that both had higher costs than necessary.

Note, finally, that when deciding whether an enterprise is competitive or not, one must consider all relevant markets, input as well as output. For example, in small monopoly markets it has been shown that cost differences favor private firms in cases such as refuse collection (Savas 1974, 1977; Stevens 1978) and fire fighting (Ahlbrandt 1973). Here the monopoly output market is irrelevant, because competitive bidding can be used to select and motivate low-cost private suppliers.

The second set of reconciliation factors involves the variables being used to measure performance. Profit measures typically favor private firms. In part this is due to the public enterprises operating in different sectors from their private comparators, but it persists even in the monopoly environment. A considerable part of this advantage to private firms is due to differences in pricing behavior, however. For example, Moore (1970) found that private U.S. electrical utilities priced more or less at the profit-maximizing level, while public enterprises were well below this level.[15] Productivity measures, on the other hand, do not systematically favor private enterprises but are highly variable or ambiguous for larger, imperfectly competitive industries.[16] This raises the more general point that there are various dimensions to performance, and (to our knowledge) no one has systematically addressed global welfare in terms of both consumer and producer surplus. We shall return to this point later.

A further measurement problem on the efficiency side is that most studies measure *changes* in total factor productivity (TFP). If these are similar in the public and the private sector, it does not necessarily mean that the two sectors are equally efficient, but only that whatever differences exist are neither widening nor narrowing.

The third factor reconciling the various studies of large monopolies is the small-number problem. A country may have only one telephone enterprise and one steel mill. If these are in the public sector in one country but in the private sector in another, it will be difficult to ascribe performance differences to ownership rather than to the different economies and cultures. One major exception is the electricity industry in the United States, where there are large numbers of both private and public enterprises, thus making it a fruitful place to search for public-private differences. An early study of the industry, controlling only for scale of production, concluded that unit costs were lower by a statistically insignificant amount in public enterprises (Yunker 1975). This was a somewhat counterintuitive result at the time and, as was pointed out, could be due to omitted variables. That is, public enterprises might be able to use a lower-cost technology (hydroelectric rather than thermal), receive lower-cost inputs (especially because of tax and interest breaks), have a more beneficial mix of generation and distribution, have a higher-density distribution network, or have other advantages. Subsequent studies tried to correct for these problems, with the result that the public sector advantage persisted, and indeed became larger and statistically significant (for a summary of this literature see Aharoni 1986, pp. 196–97). This literature is widely cited by those who argue that public monopolies can be superior to private, regulated ones. Skeptics, on the other hand, can still argue that none of the studies adequately controlled for everything. The point here is simply that, because of the difficulty of comparing like with like, it is very difficult to prove convincingly the existence of public-private differentials in the case of large monopoly enterprises, even if they are there. This is the third reason for weak, contradictory, or ambiguous results in this realm.

The Divestiture Process

If comparisons of public with private enterprises in large, imperfect markets are thus inconclusive, comparisons of the same enterprise in public and private hands would thus seem a complementary natural experiment. However, this does not remove the problem of comparing like with like, but only relocates it. Instead of comparing different enterprises at the same point in time, we are now comparing the same enterprise at different points in time. Correction still needs to be made for exogenous differences, in this case in the enterprise's environment as it has changed over time. The divestiture wave of the 1980s has provided a fruitful opportunity for expanding empirical investigations into public-private differences.

We divide the resulting literature into two parts. The first group simply describes and analyzes the divestiture transaction. This has received by far the greater attention (to cite but a few examples, see Christiansen and Stackhouse 1987; Leeds 1987, 1988; Wilson 1987; Cook and Kirkpatrick 1988; Lorch 1988; and Vuylsteke, Nankani, and Candoy-Sekse 1988). Typically, this part of the literature describes announced divestiture objectives and how the divestiture was carried out. The description often includes what was sold, to whom it was sold (domestic or foreign investors, workers, the general public, etc.), by what method (public offering, bidding, direct placement, etc.), for how much, and so on. Success is declared when the deal is struck.

This part of the literature is important in its own right; it shows the administrative and political hurdles that have to be overcome in getting divestiture going, and it advises policymakers on how to implement a divestiture program, once a decision to divest has been made. However, it does not attempt, as we do here, to answer the question as to whether divestiture improves welfare or not, nor does it base its advice on a set of empirically tested conditions under which this decision would be advantageous to society.[17]

Partial Measures of Divestiture Success

Several studies have gone beyond an analysis of the nature of divestiture transactions (see, for example, Brittan 1984, Yarrow 1986, Bishop and Kay 1988, Caves 1988, Foreman-Peck and Manning 1988, and Megginson, Nash, and Randenborgh 1992). These may be usefully categorized according to the base against which they compare postdivestiture performance. That is, performance of a divested enterprise can be compared with predivestiture performance of the same enterprise, with other enterprises that were not divested, with other enterprises that were already private, and with foreign enterprises. All these studies largely follow the case study approach and rarely use econometric analysis, because of a paucity of observation points.

Adam, Cavendish, and Mistry (1992) take an intermediate approach between quantitative and process analysis, using country case studies from eight developing countries. Their case studies can be seen as complementing this volume in that they concentrate more on institutional detail but are less quantitative and rigorous. Their comparisons are largely of the same enterprise before and after divestiture.

Among those making international comparisons, of particular note is the study by Foreman-Peck and Manning (1988) that compares the performance of British Telecom with that of five telecommunications enterprises elsewhere in Europe, using TFP as the basis for the comparison. They conclude that "British Telecom is apparently less efficient . . . than [the telecommunications enterprises in] both Norway [where the company is state-owned] and Denmark [where ownership is mixed] but more efficient than [those in] Spain and Italy [where ownership is also mixed]."

Notable among those comparing divested and undivested enterprises is the study by Bishop and Kay (1988), which compares the performance of a number of divested enterprises in the shipping, airline, gas, telecommunications, oil, and automobile industries with undivested enterprises in the coal, rail, steel, and postal sectors in the United Kingdom over the same period. The authors employ several performance indicators, including revenue, employment, profits, profit margins, and TFP. They find that divested as well as undivested enterprises experienced improved performance. They leave the question of causality open to include the business cycle and the threat of divestiture as possible causes.[18]

Megginson, Nash, and Randenborgh (1992) have analyzed the effect of ownership change on performance, using a panel of forty-one enterprises from fifteen countries. Their sample includes enterprises sold through public offerings over the period 1981–89, but no control group of enterprises that stayed in the public sector or were private to begin with. Comparing pre- and postdivestiture data, they find that the change of ownership correlates significantly with higher profitability, better utilization of human and physical resources, enterprise growth, and greater employment.

These and other studies have contributed to a better understanding of the effect of the change of ownership. However, they suffer from several shortcomings. Cross-sectional comparisons are affected by variations in the market structures, regulation, and technology of the enterprises analyzed. Time-series comparisons of pre- and postdivestiture data do not address the counterfactual question. Econometric studies, while capable of deriving generalizable conclusions, miss rich institutional details that only emerge from intensive, detailed case studies. Focusing on historical data, on the other hand, precludes the possibility of capturing the dynamic effects of divestiture, which may accrue only in the future. In this volume, we address these limitations.

Conclusion

In sum, there is a large and growing literature on public-private differences in general and divestiture in particular. For larger enterprises facing noncompetitive markets, this literature gives surprisingly little support to the conventional wisdom that private enterprises generally produce more efficiently than public enterprises. It does not prove that such differences do not exist, but suggests that rather careful methodological techniques are required to reveal them, and then only in the context of particular institutional settings.

We attempt to extend this literature by performing detailed case studies with methods that are global (covering consumer and producer surplus); that explicitly address the distribution of those net benefits to various groups in society; and that attempt to address the counterfactual question of what would have happened in the absence of divestiture. The next chapter explains these methodological features in greater detail.

Notes

1. "Public enterprise" (or state-owned enterprise, or government enterprise, or parastatal) means public production (that is, ownership or internal managerial control of the enterprise is in government hands) for private consumption (that is, output is sold in a market).

2. "To divest" is to get rid of, in this case by sale to the private sector. Divestiture of public enterprises is widely referred to as "privatization." However, in recent years the latter term has been expanded to include everything from mixed public-private hybrids (for example, management contracts or leasing) to anything that makes public entities behave more like private ones (for example, incentive systems), to anything that makes private enterprises behave in practice more like they are supposed to behave in theory (for example, liberalization). In its extreme forms, therefore, "privatization" has come to mean anything that is more private-like, or even (since "private" in this literature is synonymous with "good") any positive economic reform. To avoid confusion, we avoid the use of "privatization" in this volume and prefer "divestiture of public enterprises," or "divestiture" for short.

3. We do not deal with divestiture in former communist regimes, where the concomitant problem of creating markets to divest into raises issues of another order.

4. Such a bold statement obviously must admit important exceptions (for example, the divestiture of British Steel in 1953 or of Korean Airlines in 1968) and qualifications (for example, we restrict the assertion to policy-generated change, recognizing that the public sector can shrink absolutely as a result of recession, and relatively when large public-dominated sectors such as oil production and distribution are hit disproportionately by recession).

5. For a comprehensive description and assessment of such policies see Kikeri, Nellis, and Shirley (1992).

6. For further details regarding the original research plan see Galal (1990).

7. The year 1983 was chosen for the comparison as a year shortly before the big spurt in divestiture.

8. To provide geographic balance we had planned to include Togo rather than Mexico, but we did not receive clearance in time to go ahead. We hope to rectify this in a future project.

9. Nor does it include any previously centrally planned economies, but this was by design, as the problems there are qualitatively different.

10. For comprehensive approaches see Borcherding (1983) and DeAlessi (1982).

11. This literature is reviewed in Laffont and Tirole (1993, chapter 17).

12. This is the Averch-Johnson effect. For a survey of this and other problems with regulation, see Kahn (1992, pp. 49–55).

13. For a survey in the context of privatization see Vickers and Yarrow (1988, chapters 2–4).

14. In addition to those cited below see Borcherding, Pommerehne, and Schneider (1982), Millward (1982), Millward and Parker (1983), Borins and Boothman (1985), and Boyd (1986).

15. Other empirical work on pricing by public and private enterprises in monopolistic industries is sparse. The early work by Peltzman (1971) reaches the conclusion that price structures of public enterprises are less responsive than those of private enterprises to the cost of serving specific customer groups. According to this finding, price structures by public enterprises are bent toward "postage pricing," that is, uniform prices even though costs differ. Hayashi, Sevier, and Trapani (1987) find that publicly owned electric utilities in the United States have generally lower markups than privately owned firms and that they favor industrial customers (which provide an externality to the owning municipalities).

16. For an example of clear profitability differentials combined with ambiguous productivity differences, see Hutchinson (1991); see also Vickers and Yarrow (1988, pp. 141–50).

17. We, too, describe the sale process in the background of each of our country and enterprise cases. In addition, we explore the effect of the sale structure on divestiture outcomes.

18. A further study by Bishop and Thompson (1991) is discussed in chapter 7.

2. Methodology

In this chapter we outline our methodology for answering the basic question posed in chapter 1: What happens as a result of public-enterprise divestiture, and why?

To study the effects of a new economic policy and to properly attribute the observed changes to that policy, it would be desirable to have what statisticians call a "treatment group," in this case of enterprises that have been divested, and a "control group," in this case of enterprises that have not been divested but are otherwise similar to the members of the treatment group. Because the treatment and control groups would differ (ideally) only in that one group was divested and the other was not, any observed differences could, with some justification, be largely attributed to the divestiture. This option, unfortunately, is not open to us. Public enterprises being divested seldom have "twins" that are not being divested; instead they tend to be rather unique—and often monopoly—enterprises. Thus it is difficult, if not impossible, to find a control group against which the performance of the divested enterprises could be compared.

Some might solve this problem by comparing the performance of the enterprise before divestiture with its performance after divestiture and attributing any observed changes to the divestiture. This approach, however, is applicable only in a stationary environment. In reality, economic conditions are constantly changing, and therefore any observed changes in enterprise performance could be driven by changes in the economic environment rather than by divestiture.

The approach we adopt is to compare the performance of the enterprise after divestiture with what that performance would have been had the enterprise not been divested. Thus we construct for each enterprise a counterfactual scenario that serves as our control. The welfare gain (or loss) from divestiture that we will report is then the difference between the level of welfare under divestiture and the level of welfare in our counterfactual scenario.

Scenarios and Projections

Because these concepts are so central to the analysis, it is worth spelling out the principles under which our scenarios and projections are constructed.

The Actual Scenario

We begin the analysis of each case by comparing actual performance before and after divestiture. In most cases we cover five years of public or predivestiture operation and five years of private or postdivestiture operation. The goal is to see if there were any substantial changes in performance, and thereby to identify changes in performance that *may* have been caused by divestiture. We emphasize "may" at this point because we are generally not willing to assume that all the observed changes were caused by divestiture. We represent this case schematically in figure 2-1 by the sharp kink in the "actual" tracing following divestiture.

Figure 2-1.   Performance of a Hypothetical Enterprise under Divestiture and under Continued Public Ownership

Performance variable

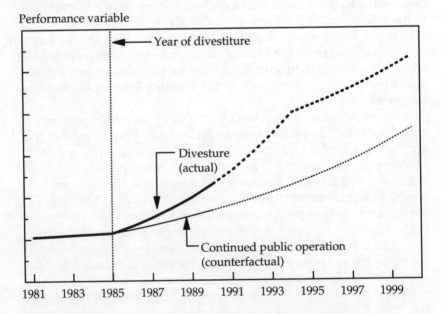

Note: Dashed extensions of curves represent projections into the future.
Source: Authors.

The Counterfactual Scenario

The next step is to move from correlation to causation, from "*may* have been caused" to "*was* caused." The methodological problem is how to decide how much of any change was attributable to divestiture, and how much to exogenous changes in markets or institutions. Given sufficient data, the right way to sort this out would be by statistical regression analysis. Again, however, this option is not open to us because the data are limited. Instead we solve the problem by acquiring a detailed knowledge of each case (including institutional details of the economic environment) and then applying our judgment as to the causes of the observed changes. In general, we adopt a conservative approach in that observed changes are assumed exogenous unless we have strong reason to believe otherwise. Because most of the changes are beneficial, this assumption tends to underestimate the welfare gain due to divestiture, as it forces some divestiture-induced changes into the exogenous category. The set of changes that we deem to have been caused by or that are otherwise associated with divestiture are then, as it were, subtracted out to yield the counterfactual scenario, which describes what would have been the behavior of the enterprise had it not been divested. We represent the counterfactual by the lighter tracing in figure 2-1, with a smaller kink following divestiture, reflecting the judgment that some but not all of the change was due to exogenous factors and would have occurred even without divestiture.

Projections

Our comparison of factual and counterfactual performance over the three- to five-year period for which we have data is useful, but it is incomplete for two reasons. First, the benefits and costs of observed changes persevere into the future and must be considered in any comprehensive calculation. In particular, because we need to aggregate flow items such as future profits together with once-only items such as the sale price, a full projection of flows into the future is essential. Second, many of the benefits of divestiture are dynamic (e.g., improved investment, marketing, and product quality), while others take time to manifest themselves (e.g., organizational change in a large organization), so some changes are not observed in the data period. For both these reasons, we project into the future both the factual and the counterfactual scenarios. Schematically, this step corresponds to the dashed extensions of the actual and counterfactual tracings in figure 2-1. These reflect an assumption that (in this case) the gap will widen at an increasing rate for five years and remain stable thereafter.

Comparing the Scenarios

Having defined the two scenarios in principle, the next task is to estimate the difference in their welfare levels. We do this by estimating the level of welfare for all affected classes of economic agents (buyers, government, consumers, employees, and competitors) in each scenario and then taking the difference between the scenarios. This procedure allows us to calculate not only the aggregate welfare effect from divestiture but also its distribution among the different economic actors.

Because of the level of detail involved, this is not a trivial undertaking, and a complete discussion of the methodological issues involved could occupy several books the size of this one. This chapter therefore provides only an overview of the essential features. Additional details are described in individual chapters, especially the British Telecom case (chapter 4), which is discussed more fully than the other cases in order to illustrate the methodology.

Valuation and Distribution

At the center of each scenario is the calculation of social welfare and its distribution. We begin our detailed discussion, therefore, with our basic approach to valuation. We then provide a more detailed discussion of its implementation in the different scenarios.

Our valuation methodology is in the tradition of applied welfare economics as manifested in the project evaluation literature. We apply it, however, to the *dis*investment rather than to the investment decision. A previous work (Jones, Tandon, and Vogelsang 1990) spells out the details in an ex ante decisionmaking context. Here we apply it in an ex post evaluation context, but the methodologies are essentially the same. Accordingly, we provide here only a brief overview of the essential elements.

The Basic Divestiture Equation

Our basic approach to the evaluation of divestiture involves calculating the difference between two critical numbers: the social value of the enterprise under private operation (i.e., postdivestiture) and the social value of the enterprise under continued government operation (i.e., in the counterfactual scenario). The welfare effect of divestiture consists largely of this difference. The only remaining effect is the one-time effect of the transfer of the sale price from the buyer to the seller (i.e., to the government).

To calculate the social value of an enterprise under either the actual or the counterfactual scenario, we first identify all groups of actors who might be affected by the divestiture of this enterprise. The major groups are as follows: consumers, the government, any other existing shareholders,[2] the buyers, employees, competitors, and the public at large (perhaps in their role as taxpayers). Conceptually, the social value of the enterprise in any scenario is the sum of the welfare levels of each of these groups, or rather the sum of that component of their welfare levels that may be directly influenced by the operations of the enterprise.[3]

In general, the welfare levels under the two scenarios will not be equal. The conduct of the enterprise is expected to change as a result of the sale. On this, opponents and proponents of divestment can agree. On the one hand, private management is said to improve static operating efficiency and dynamic entrepreneurial innovation. On the other hand, private motivation is said to lead to exploitation of consumers, workers, and the environment. In short, there is a trade-off between the possibility that private objectives are less desirable socially, and the possibility that the private sector will pursue these objectives more efficiently. This is what we have termed the fundamental trade-off of divestiture.

If this trade-off is operating, the welfare levels of consumers and employees will be higher in the counterfactual than in the factual scenario, while the buyers and perhaps the government will be better off under divestiture. The net welfare effect of divestiture can then be found by taking the difference between the two social values of the enterprise, which will be the sum of the net changes in the welfare levels of the individual groups. If we denote this change in welfare as ΔW, we can write the preceding sentence in the form of a simple equation:[4]

(1-1) $$\Delta W = \Delta S + \Delta \pi + \Delta L + \Delta C$$

where ΔS (for consumer surplus) represents the welfare effect on consumers, $\Delta \pi$ is the effect on enterprise profits (which includes effects on the buyers, the government, and any other shareholders), ΔL (for labor, its most important component) is the effect on providers of inputs (which also include credit, permits, intermediate goods, etc.), and ΔC is the welfare effect on competitors. This equation therefore says simply that the net welfare impact of divestiture is the sum of the net welfare impacts on each of the groups affected by divestiture.

The profits in equation 1-1 do not all go to one group but rather are distributed between the buyer and seller through payment of the price (which we denote Z) at which the enterprise is sold. Let us consider the way in which profits are distributed. The welfare level of the private buyers after divestiture can be taken as the present discounted value of all future profits of the enterprise that will accrue to them. This amount will then represent the maximum amount the buyers would be willing to pay for the enterprise. The buyers gain to the extent that their maximum willingness to pay (Z_p) exceeds what they actually pay (Z):

$$\text{private buyers' share} = Z_p - Z.$$

In the unlikely event that government negotiators drive such a hard bargain that the buyers gain nothing beyond the opportunity cost of their resources, then $Z = Z_p$; in other words, the buyer gets no part of $\Delta\pi$ and the government gets it all. To the extent that Z falls short of Z_p, the government's share is reduced, so we can write:

$$\text{government's share} = \Delta\pi - (Z_p - Z).$$

We can see from these last two equations why equation 1-1 does include the welfare effects of divestiture on both the buyer and the government, because their sum is simply $\Delta\pi$.

Complications to the Basic Equation

Equation 1-1 is the basic equation for evaluating the welfare effect of divestiture, but it needs modification before being applied. The first modification is to separate out effects that accrue to domestic actors from those that accrue to foreigners. For example, in several of the cases studied, the buying group included some domestic and some foreign buyers. Thus the private buyers' share must be divided into two parts. The fundamental reason for this is that we assume that the domestic government does not care about the welfare of foreigners, and so any welfare effects that accrue to them should be excluded from the net welfare calculation. The same argument applies to the welfare effect on foreign consumers (since many divestitures are of enterprises that sell to foreigners) and on foreign competitors, where there is international competition in the enterprise's markets. When this is done, we will have divided up equation 1-1 as follows:

$$\Delta W = \text{domestic welfare effects} + \text{foreign welfare effects}.$$

The next modification has to do with the use of welfare weights. The moment we have divided the total welfare effect into its domestic and foreign components, a case can be made that we need different welfare weights for the different components. Foreign welfare effects should be assigned a weight of zero, to indicate that we do not care about welfare effects on foreigners, while domestic effects should receive a normal weight of one. But we need not stop there. Within the domestic component of welfare, there are situations in which it can be argued that the different subcomponents should carry different weights. For example, a staple of the project evaluation literature is the notion that a dollar of government revenue may be worth more than a dollar of the numeraire consumption good by a factor termed the government revenue multiplier (λ_g).[5] What is less widely recognized is that a dollar of profits can also be worth more than a dollar of consumption, so that there is also a private profit multiplier (λ_p) that is greater than unity.[6] Further, under certain conditions, each of these multipliers may instead be less than one (i.e., revenues or profits may be less valuable than consumption). The fundamental idea here is that, when an economy is highly distorted (as captured in note 6 by the cases of distortionary taxes and capital market imperfections), the different components of welfare may require different weights, and increasingly so as the level of distortion in the economy grows. Fortunately, three out of four of our case countries—Chile, Malaysia, and the United Kingdom—have economies that could be deemed relatively undistorted, and so we have been able to ignore the problem of welfare weights. The fourth country, Mexico, was in severe fiscal crisis during the 1980s, and so there was a need to acknowledge this in the government revenue multiplier. A more detailed discussion of this consideration is deferred to chapter 19.

In most of our cases, therefore, we make one key modification to equation 1-1, which is to divide the welfare effects into domestic and foreign components. Computing the unweighted net welfare effect gives us the world welfare effect from divestiture. This gives a measure of the total gains (or losses) available for distribution. Assigning a weight of zero to the foreign welfare effects yields the domestic welfare effect, which may be the key variable of interest to a typical government policymaker. In each of our enterprise cases we will report separately the domestic and total welfare effects, plus their distribution among the different groups of economic actors identified above.

Calculation of the Components of Welfare

The basic strategy in calculating the different components of welfare is to construct a simple model for each of the relevant product markets in which the enterprise operates and then to calculate each of the welfare components in each market. Aggregating the results over the product markets and across time (by discounting) gives us the required estimates for each welfare component.

Figure 2-2, which illustrates a simplified version of a market,[7] gives some hint of the process. Assume that the enterprise is earning revenues of some particular amount from the sale of the commodity whose market is being illustrated. The first task is to determine the components of revenue, namely, the quantity sold and the price. Cost information is then needed to estimate the profit, which is price minus average cost times the quantity. This is shown in the figure as "profit of enterprise." Next the profits of competitors and of foreign producers are similarly estimated. In this example we have assumed that competitors have slightly lower average variable costs (AVC) than the divested enterprise. Similarly, we can estimate the profits of the enterprise and of competitors in export markets (shown to the left of the vertical axis in the figure).

Figure 2-2.   Welfare Gains and Losses in a Typical Divestiture Scenario

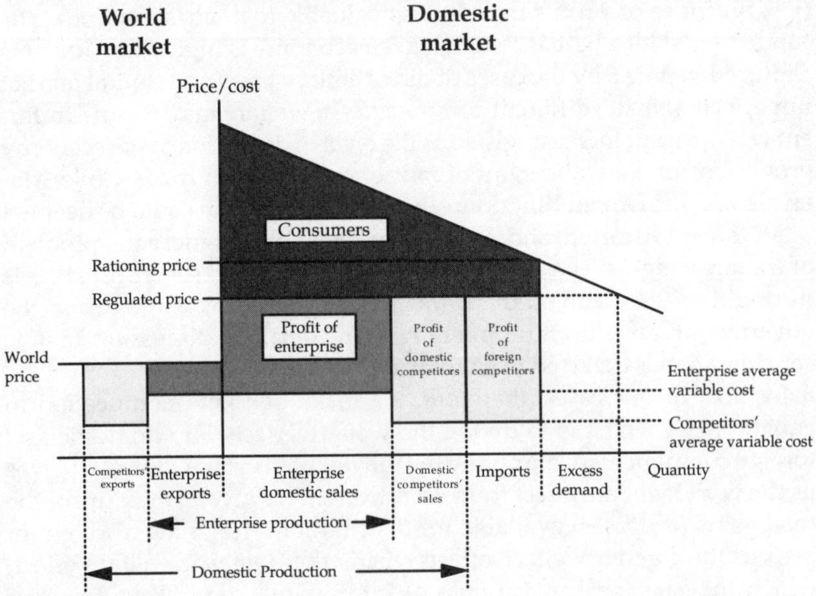

World   Domestic
market   market

Price/cost

Consumers

Rationing price

Regulated price

Profit of
enterprise

Profit
of
domestic
competitors

Profit
of
foreign
competitors

World
price

Enterprise average
variable cost

Competitors'
average variable cost

Competitors   Enterprise   Enterprise   Domestic   Imports   Excess   Quantity
exports   exports   domestic sales   competitors'   demand
                                                sales

◀── Enterprise production ──▶

◀────── Domestic Production ──────▶

Note: For simplicity, the figure ignores indirect taxes, shadow prices, and the welfare
cost of nonprice rationing. "Enterprise" refers to the public enterprise in question.

Included in the cost data is information on the size of the work force and
the average wage paid, which allows us to calculate any welfare impact
on workers.

We turn now to consumers. We use consumer surplus as our measure
of consumer welfare. Therefore, we need to specify a demand curve,
starting with the point on the curve at which consumers presently find
themselves. If the market is free, then total sales and the price at which
those sales are taking place define the relevant point on the demand
curve. If, however, price is regulated (as it is in many of our cases), we
know that the observed price and quantity do not reflect a point on the
demand curve. We then need to estimate the level of excess demand at
the regulated price to yield a point on the demand curve. Information
on (or informed assumption about) the elasticity of demand, combined
with an assumption of linearity, then allows us to trace the demand curve
itself. Consumer surplus is then measured by the area below the demand
curve and above the price, as shown in the figure, if rationing is done by
a mechanism that mimics price rationing. In reality, rationing is hardly
likely to be so perfect. We have therefore generally assumed random
rationing, which would yield an area slightly different from that shown.

A note regarding the assumption of linear demand is in order. As is clear from figure 2-2, the assumption of linearity can significantly bias the measure of consumer surplus if the true demand curve is not linear, because consumer surplus under a nonlinear demand curve may encompass considerably more (or less) area, particularly in the region close to the vertical axis. However, because we will ultimately be taking the *difference* in consumer surplus between the two scenarios, the area of consumer surplus close to the vertical axis will be canceled out. Thus the assumption of linearity is much more innocuous than might appear at first glance (and really amounts to a very normal first-order approximation).

Although the figure does not show any of the flows accruing to the government, we of course also calculate any tax revenues, whether indirect (such as excise or value-added taxes) or direct (corporate profits taxes). In this way we will have calculated the welfare impact of divestiture on all the major groups of economic agents: buyers, competitors, workers, consumers, and the government.

Two further complications deserve mention. First, many public enterprises produce a variety of products that are related to one another, and these interrelationships need to be taken into account. To the extent possible we have attempted to do this. Particularly on the demand side, we model the several markets simultaneously. For example, in the telecommunications enterprises in our sample (British Telecom, Teléfonos de México, and Compañía de Teléfonos de Chile), the revenues from rentals and from metered calls (whether local or long distance) are clearly related. It would be erroneous to calculate consumer surplus for each of these categories and simply add them up. Rather, we calculate the consumer surplus from the different categories of calls and then *subtract* the payments for rentals. The implicit model is one where the rental activity itself yields no direct utility; utility arises from calls, and the rental fee is a lump-sum payment that reduces net surplus from the calling activity. Of course, being able to receive as well as initiate calls does yield some benefit, and we have accounted for this separately through an allowance for call externalities. The point is not to review here all the multiproduct demand adjustments we have made (many will be spelled out in individual cases, particularly the British Telecom case), but only to point out that this is an issue that has received our attention.

On the cost side, we have less success to report. In most cases we have been unable to separate out the costs of production for the different products; indeed, typically the enterprises themselves are unable to effect such an allocation. We have therefore generally ignored multiproduct adjustments on the cost side, instead treating the whole cost structure as a single activity (with its component parts, of course, such as labor, materials of various kinds, and energy).

The second complication has to do with the dynamic aspects of firm behavior after divestiture, particularly with reference to projections into the future. We defer discussion of this until the section on "Projections" below.

The Actual Scenario

We turn now to a somewhat more detailed discussion of the actual and counterfactual scenarios and of the projections of both. The actual scenario is the one that actually occurs, that is, the one in which the enterprise is divested and enters the private sector. We begin each of our case studies with the least controversial part of the analysis, namely, comparison of the behavior of the enterprise before and after divestiture. The objective is to form as complete a picture as we can of the trends operating in the enterprise prior to divestiture and of the changes that have occurred since then. To this extent, our approach is similar to the standard approach adopted in any case study. The difference in our approach is that the resulting picture of the enterprise is formed not merely impressionistically, through a series of interviews and perhaps a limited analysis of published enterprise accounts, but rather through a highly detailed and exhaustive study of all the quantitative material we were able to gather on the enterprise. This material naturally includes the enterprise accounts, but usually we were able to dig deeper and gather more detail than is typically available in the income statement and balance sheet. Further, we do not take the published numbers at face value; instead we translate all enterprise accounts (which follow accounting conventions and definitions, which sometimes vary from country to country) into their economically meaningful counterparts.

We therefore use interviews with enterprise officials (which we undertook in all cases) to help in interpreting the findings of our quantitative analysis, rather than to reach impressions of the enterprise's behavior. Naturally, interviews are not always reliable, because enterprise officials may answer questions strategically rather than straightforwardly. However, because our primary source of information is our own quantitative analysis, this potential problem is not a problem at all for us.

In what follows, we provide some detail on our selection of the key variables to be examined and how information on these variables was obtained.

From Enterprise to Economic Accounts

The first step in the quantitative analysis of enterprise performance for each case study is to create a time series of economically meaningful data for the enterprise. Our strategy is to use the enterprise accounts themselves to the extent possible, augment these with exogenous data where necessary, and then convert the resulting information to economic accounts using national income and wealth accounting methodology. Using an existing software package,[8] we do the following:

- We enter complete income statement and balance sheet details,[9] taking care to ensure that the data for each year are internally consistent, and that the data are consistent from year to year. This approach has obvious advantages in terms of accuracy, but more importantly it reflects the fact that every entry has economic content that must be explicitly considered. We exercise quality control by questioning every entry and ensuring consistency within any given year and over time.
- We enter additional exogenous data (such as interest rates and various commodity-specific inflation factors) as well as additional data from the enterprise not usually entered in the financial statements (such as prices and quantities of major inputs and outputs). The intent here is to put more detail and economic content into the data. For example, the income statement will often simply have an entry for "revenue," possibly broken down further into a few major revenue categories. Our goal is to break down total revenue into as many categories as possible—say, five to ten major product groups. Then we decompose revenue from any one source—for example, international long distance calls in the case of a telecommunications enterprise—into its price and quantity components. Thus, in this example, we might have total number of calls placed, or total number of minutes, multiplied by an average price per call or per minute. The same sort of price-quantity breakdown is carried out on the input side, including capital inputs. This step is crucial in constructing constant-price data, because we then have commodity- or input-specific price series.
- We then convert the enterprise accounts into economic accounts by mapping all entries in the income statement into a production and distribution of surplus statement, and changes in all entries in the balance sheet into an economic flow-of-funds statement, from which wealth accounts can then be created.

Calculation of Variables

We now explain the methodology behind some of the more important economic variables thus calculated.

PROFIT: PUBLIC VERSUS PRIVATE. We use the familiar concept of private profit as a measure of returns to the shareholders of the enterprise. From the social point of view, however, private profit does not adequately reflect the performance of the enterprise. For this purpose, therefore, we use a modified notion of profit, or quasi rents (the return to fixed capital), defined as follows:

$$\text{public profit} = X - II - W - R - rK^w$$

where X is the value of output, II is the value of intermediate inputs, W is employee compensation, R is factor rentals, and rK^w is the opportunity cost of working capital.

We refer to this modified notion of profit as "public profit" (the return from fixed capital to all of society's claimants) to distinguish it from conventional private profit (returns to the equityholders only). Public profit differs from private profit in three ways. First, in addition to returns to equityholders, it includes returns to debtholders (interest) and government (direct and indirect taxes); these flows, usually regarded as costs to the enterprise, are not subtracted out. Second, to correspond to the economic concept of quasi rents, public profit excludes nonoperating returns (e.g., from sale of assets) and deducts the opportunity cost of working capital (interest forgone on working capital used). Third, it is measured gross of the depreciation allowance, because we are measuring the return to fixed capital and therefore should not consider the cost of that capital.

CURRENT VERSUS CONSTANT PRICES. All of the data are presented in terms of both current and constant prices; the constant-price series is obviously the key one for performance. It is here that our careful work in constructing the economic tables of the enterprise pays rich dividends. Whereas conversion to constant prices usually involves deflating all current prices by the same consumer price index or GDP deflator, we are able to use specific price data (inflation adjustors) for each category of output or input.[10] We therefore end up with a far more meaningful set of constant price data.

FIXED CAPITAL. The stock of fixed capital is measured using the perpetual inventory method. Annual flows for various asset classes[11] are taken from changes in the balance sheet and aggregated over time, adjusting for asset-specific inflation, deterioration, and disposals. Rather than construct a fixed capital series by deflating the "plant and equipment" entry in the balance sheet by some easily available deflator, as is usually done, we painstakingly attempt to reconstruct the entire time pattern of investment in each of several classes of fixed capital. Thus, as far as possible, we divide up each year's investment into each of the asset classes and then, for each year, decompose each investment figure into its price and quantity components. This produces a much more accurate picture of the "quantity" of each type of capital, primarily through the use of deflators specific to that type of capital. Frequently there are quite wide differences in inflation rates for different asset classes, and our procedure captures the effects of those differences.

REAL PUBLIC PROFITABILITY AND PRODUCTIVITY. Having constructed constant-price time series for all the relevant variables, we are in a position to examine the performance of the enterprise. We use two measures of performance, very similar to one another but answering slightly different questions.

The first of these, total factor productivity (TFP), is familiar in the literature. TFP is the ratio of the benefits generated by the enterprise to its incurred costs, including the opportunity cost of fixed capital (rK^f):

$$\text{TFP} = \frac{\text{benefits}}{\text{all costs}} = \frac{X}{II + W + R + rK^w + rK^f}.$$

The idea here is to divide the quantity of output by the quantity of inputs (although prices enter in through the weighting mechanism). In the formula, r is the opportunity cost for both fixed and working capital, although in practice we generally use different values for r in these variables. The other variables are as previously defined.

The second measure of performance, which we call public profitability, will be less familiar to most readers. It is obtained by dividing public profit (or quasi rents) by the stock of fixed capital to which it is a return. Thus, public profitability is a rate-of-return measure. When calculated in real terms, it is functionally very similar to TFP, as can be seen from its formula:

$$\text{public profitability} = \frac{\text{benefits} - \text{variable costs}}{\text{fixed costs}} = \frac{X - II - W - R - rK^w}{K^f}.$$

Note that exactly the same variables appear in this formula as in that for TFP; only their arrangement is different. Public profitability relates net benefits (in the numerator) to the capital in place that made them possible, whereas TFP is a ratio of benefits to all costs, including that of fixed capital. Conceptually, therefore, TFP is a better measure of long-run performance, when the enterprise is free to choose its level of fixed capital. Public profitability, however, is a better measure in the short run, when the level of fixed capital can be taken as invariable.[12] As it turns out, it does not matter much on which measure we focus, because, as our empirical work demonstrates, the two indicators generally tell identical stories. Our main goal is to estimate the level of operating efficiency in the enterprise before and after divestiture, and each measure captures the general trend in this variable.

CONSUMER SURPLUS. Of course, TFP and public profitability capture only efficiency effects that accrue to the enterprise. From the social point of view, another important element of performance is the impact of the enterprise's activity on consumers, which we measure through the traditional consumer surplus measure. Consumer surplus is notoriously difficult to measure, and it tends to be very large relative to the other components of social welfare if demand is inelastic. For both these reasons we discuss our methods of calculating consumer surplus in more detail in chapter 4, as part of our discussion of British Telecom, an enterprise that operates in markets with generally inelastic demand. Here we note that for most of our analysis we need only consider *changes* in consumer surplus for small or modest price changes. In these cases we either approximate consumer surplus changes by the previous period's quantity times the price change (this is known as the Slutsky compensation), or we take a first-order, linear approximation of the demand curve derived from our knowledge of one point on the curve and from an estimate of demand elasticity.

OTHER RETURNS. Other returns go to other producers or to owners of inputs. An estimate of the former falls out of our market picture, as was illustrated in figure 2-2. The latter category of return, especially rents accruing to labor, is important but difficult to quantify. Such rents depend strongly on the current state of the labor market in the country in question. We have not attempted to derive a unified approach to measuring these rents. Thus, the method used differs slightly from country to country and sometimes for different cases within a country.

The Counterfactual Scenario

Recall that our basic approach calls for comparing the actual (and projected) performance of the enterprise after divestiture with the counterfactual: performance as it would have been observed had the enterprise never been divested. In constructing our counterfactual scenario, our basic approach has been to assume that it will be similar to the actual scenario unless we have strong reasons to believe otherwise. The key therefore is to search for apparent differences in performance between the divested enterprise and its undivested counterpart.

In other words, whereas thus far we have looked for *correlations* between conduct and divestiture, the next step is to look at the *causation* of those correlations, so as to exclude from the counterfactual those aspects of the behavior of the enterprise that may be attributed to divestiture. For example, how much of any improvement in labor productivity is due to exogenous changes in technology and the economy, and how much to changes in decisions that would not have been made in the absence of divestiture? Ideally, with abundant data one would use econometric analysis to answer this question. Such an approach, however, is out of reach for our purposes given the multitude of dependent variables and the small number of observations. In its place we have adopted a case study approach, using judgment to construct scenarios of what would have happened in the absence of divestiture. Given our goal of evaluating net benefits, it is both necessary and sufficient to answer the above questions by comparing the counterfactual with the actual.

Determining causation is harder than determining correlation, to say the least. Accordingly, our methodologies become considerably more heterogeneous, varying from country to country, from enterprise to enterprise, and from variable to variable. One common thread is that we do *not* try to estimate a bottom-line counterfactual (such as public profitability) directly. Rather, we work with subsidiary variables, estimating prices and quantities of outputs commodity by commodity and estimating costs by type, and then letting these accumulate to the bottom line. Aside from this, our sample enterprises and industries vary so much in detail that we have had to customize our detailed approach for each case. Accordingly, here we only outline the general approach and leave the details to the cases themselves:

- Ideally, one would like to be able to compare similar divested and undivested enterprises in the same industry in the same country, thereby eliminating cross-country and cross-industry effects. Such comparators, however, are generally not available.
- Instead we look at similar enterprises in other countries (particularly for evidence on technological change). An example of this is comparing telecommunications enterprises both within and outside our sample of case studies.
- We also look at dissimilar enterprises (undivested public enterprises) in the same country for evidence on counterfactual behavior. For example, the financial constraints on British Rail and the U.K. electricity industry after the divestiture of British Telecom can be taken as prima facie evidence of the kind of financial constraints that British Telecom might have faced in the absence of divestiture.
- We compare predivestiture with postdivestiture trends of various variables and try to relate the observed changes to conditions other than divestiture. In particular, we try to make adjustments for changing macroeconomic conditions (especially by adjusting demand trends).
- We use information on specific variables, such as demand elasticities or technical coefficients (input-output ratios), to calculate the counterfactual from our factual observations.
- We take guidance from findings by others on empirical regularities and from enterprise insiders about specific events that may have shaped outcomes. For example, such information has helped us decide whether the expansion of investment by British Telecom after divest-

iture was due to overcapitalization or to the previous suppression of needed replacement and modernization.

To summarize: any observed change in the conduct and performance of an enterprise can have many causes, divestiture being only one of them. We construct counterfactuals in order to isolate the effect of divestiture from all other effects. The counterfactual, in effect, compares the divested enterprise with itself, but in its undivested form. In addition, the number of case studies in this volume permits us to compare the divested enterprise with other divested enterprises in other industries in the same country and with divested enterprises (possibly in the same industry) in other countries. Wherever possible, we also draw upon data on enterprises remaining in the public sector. These comparisons with other enterprises are partly done in each individual case study and help us construct counterfactuals; more comprehensive comparisons are done across all the cases in chapters 23 and 24.

It is important to raise a caveat here. Because of the way they are constructed, the counterfactual scenarios are necessarily subjective and therefore open to criticism and even disbelief. Their subjectivity cannot be helped; it is in the very nature of the case study approach. Obviously we believe in each case that the counterfactual we have constructed is the most reasonable one possible, and we are willing to defend it vigorously. In particular, we base our subjective judgments not merely on a couple of interviews but also on a thorough quantitative analysis of as much relevant data as we could find. Nevertheless, to allow for the possibility of errors of judgment, we perform sensitivity analysis on all our assumptions. This takes two forms. First, we examine the sensitivity of our results to changes in assumed values of all the relevant parameters, such as demand elasticities and discount rates. Second, and perhaps more important, we examine separately the impact of each of our key assumptions on what defines the counterfactual. For example, perhaps the "true" counterfactual involves slower labor productivity growth, a lower rate of investment, and lower prices. We separately calculate the final welfare effect of each of these key differences. This allows the reader who believes, say, that the assumption of lower prices is unreasonable to then arrive at a bottom line free of that assumption. In this way, different scenarios for the counterfactual can be examined easily.

Projections

The world does not end at the termination of the data period, and therefore neither can our story. The benefits and costs of divestiture continue into the future and must be incorporated into the analysis. In particular, the welfare effect of divestiture consists of a combination of one-time effects, such as the payment of the purchase price by the buyers to the government, and flows that continue indefinitely into the future, such as profits, tax payments, and consumer surplus. We are interested not only in adding up these different effects to get a single estimate of the welfare impact of divestiture, but also in comparing the sale price with the stream of future returns in order to examine whether the sale price was at least equal to the discounted net present value of future dividends and taxes had the enterprise not been sold. To cut off the analysis at some arbitrary point in time, whether it be the present or even five or ten years into the future, would render meaningless any attempt to add up such effects or to make any judgment on the adequacy of the sale price. Incorporating the future is therefore inescapable.

One way to incorporate future effects would simply be to assume that the situation in the last year of our data period will persist indefinitely into the future. If all the relevant variables have converged to steady-state equilibrium by the end of the data period, this is perfectly appropriate, and the projections will simply be the end-of-period flows divided by an appropriate discount factor. However, it is highly unlikely that the system will have reached equilibrium so quickly. Actually projecting the future is therefore essential.

There are two quite different future effects that need to be captured:

- Behavior may change: like battleships, enterprises with tens of thousands of employees and millions of dollars worth of fixed capital do not turn on a dime. Some of the benefits of divestiture may take years to manifest themselves.
- The world may change: even if conduct is unchanged, changes in the economic environment may exacerbate preexisting cost-benefit differentials. For example, differentials in cost efficiency become more expensive if demand accelerates.

Thus our task in projecting the future costs and benefits of divestiture is to project as realistically as possible how the world might change over the foreseeable future, how behavior might be different in the divested enterprise, and how these changes add up in determining the net effect of divestiture on the enterprise and on the economy.

Obviously, projecting the future is a risky business at best. We cannot hope to make precise and accurate predictions over any significant length of time. We attempt no predictions at all of future changes about which only speculation is possible at present. Rather, we do perform trend extrapolations of the relevant variables, such as inflation and discount rates, real demand growth, and productivity growth. Combining these in an essentially linear model of the enterprise allows us to capture future effects of divestiture that are small now but may grow over time. Thus the basic strategy of the projections is to identify the forces that were already in place at the end of our data period and then to project their effects into the future so as to allow their interactions to play themselves out.

As with the data period, we need both actual and counterfactual numbers for the projection period; thus both scenarios are projected out. Again we use the conservative assumption that any differences between actual and counterfactual trends require a specific justification.

Although all our projections are done in terms of economically meaningful variables and the aggregate welfare change is thereby determined, in the end it is necessary to reconvert to standard (accounting) enterprise accounts to obtain insight into the distribution of the welfare change. For example, fixed capital formation is typically a function of an incremental capital-output ratio and the quantity of output, with capital measured using the perpetual inventory method. For welfare purposes, this is all we need to know to determine the capital costs of future expansion. However, the owners' share is further dependent on the tax deductibility of depreciation and interest, which transfers some of the cost of the investment to the government in the form of reduced tax revenue. To capture these effects it is necessary to translate the projected economic variables into projected balance sheets and income statements. This we do for both scenarios. Although the projections must extend conceptually far into the future, as a practical matter we introduce a time horizon of either five or ten years, assume that the system is in equilibrium at that point, and then use simplified shortcuts to capture further effects.

The Bottom Line

Our basic approach, therefore, is to project how the enterprise will perform in the future and how it would have performed had it not been divested. We combine our projections with the observed data and the simulations for the counterfactual for the data period. This gives us a complete time series for both scenarios, starting at divestiture and extending into the indefinite future. The difference between the two time series then gives us the effect of divestiture. We follow the methodology outlined under "Valuation and Distribution" above to obtain all the key variables of interest. In particular, we estimate the total welfare impact of divestiture and then decompose this estimate in two important ways: first between domestic and foreign actors, and then, within each of these categories, between the different classes of actors, such as consumers, buyers, the government, workers, competitors, and others. In this way, we are able to identify who gained and who lost by divestiture, and by how much.

By and large we have tried to be conservative in our assumptions so as to provide a lower bound on the welfare effect of divestiture. For example, we are conservative in our growth estimates. Insofar as private output exceeds public (as it usually does), underestimation of growth rates would tend to lead to an underestimate of the benefits of divestiture. Similarly, when we observe a change in the behavior of the enterprise following divestiture, we attribute that change to divestiture only if we can argue with reasonable certainty that such an attribution is justifiable. Again, because most observed changes tend to be beneficial ones, this leads to an underestimation of the benefits of divestiture.

One final word about the use of hypothetical counterfactuals and of projections. Critical readers may be tempted to dismiss the results as having too little basis in hard data. We can be sympathetic to this argument, but we cannot accept it. As we argued in the introduction to this chapter, the use of a counterfactual is the closest we can get to a sound methodology; comparing the divested enterprise with totally different nondivested enterprises or with itself prior to divestiture would be simply unacceptable. Similarly, as we have argued, *not* to use projections, thereby ignoring future effects, would be a far greater sin than any we are guilty of. Thus we have attempted to do as good a job as possible in an environment with just a few data points; the alternatives were worse. And we offer the skeptical reader, through our sensitivity analysis, the option to pick and choose among our assumptions. Ultimately, of course, it is for the reader to decide what there is to learn from our case studies, to which we now turn.

Notes

1. In a number of cases, the government was not the sole owner of the enterprise being divested but only a majority shareholder.

2. We use the word "directly" here to emphasize that we calculate only direct or first-round effects. In the economics jargon, our approach is a partial-equilibrium one.

3. For simplicity we use single-period notation. Each term should be thought of as the discounted net present value of a stream. For the ugly way of doing it, see Jones, Tandon, and Vogelsang (1990).

4. The argument is relatively straightforward. Assume that public goods or other targets of government expenditure exist and must be financed by taxes. Taxes impose a deadweight welfare loss or excess burden, meaning that at the margin a dollar of taxes results in a loss of consumption of more than one dollar. Therefore, any revenue to the government that allows taxes to be reduced by one dollar restores more than one dollar of consumption, and λ_g is greater than unity.

5. Assume that capital income is taxed or that other distortions in markets for capital or entrepreneurship drive a wedge between the return to capital and the present value of the consumption stream it generates. Then, insofar as profits are used for investment, λ_p also exceeds unity.

6. We leave out nonprice rationing, indirect taxes, shadow prices, and the like. For these details see Jones, Tandon, and Vogelsang (1990) as well as some of the case studies.

7. The package we used is the Public Enterprise Performance Information System (PEPIS), originally developed and used in performance contracting in Pakistan, the Republic of Korea, Venezuela, and India.

8. Including supporting statements such as details of sales, cost of sales, and other supporting tables. This corresponds to a thirty- to forty-page financial statement circulated internally rather than the two or three pages usually presented in annual reports, and it includes such esoterica as adjustments for previous years and transfers to other accounts.

9. Technically, we have used discrete Divisia indexes with continually changing weights.

10. These typically include buildings, civil works, machinery, vehicles, and furnishings and fixtures.

11. Alternatively, public profitability could be used to evaluate the performance of public-enterprise managers who do not have discretion over the level of fixed capital at their disposal, for example because investment decisions are made by the central government.

PART II

United Kingdom: Selling the Crown Jewels of an Industrial Economy

3. Divestiture in the United Kingdom

During the 1980s the United Kingdom under the government of Prime Minister Margaret Thatcher implemented an extensive and highly influential program of public-enterprise divestiture. Although the share of GDP divested was less than in some other Western countries, such as Chile, and far less than that now being attempted in Eastern Europe, the U.K. divestiture program has provided a role model for other countries to follow. The U.K. divestiture program is large both in absolute scale (involving over 6 percent of GDP) and in terms of the size of the enterprises divested, which include British Airways, British Gas, British Petroleum, British Telecom, and the regional electricity enterprises. The range of assets divested has also been wide, involving such diverse activities as housing, manufacturing enterprises, transport service enterprises, energy industries, telecommunications, and catering services, among others. Divestiture has also been accompanied by deregulation and the implementation of innovative regulatory instruments.

The U.K. divestiture program has been described and analyzed in a number of books[1] and in many journal and newspaper articles. Our approach differs from all of these in that we try to perform in-depth quantitative analyses of individual divestiture cases. Out of the many U.K. divestitures we have chosen three: British Telecom, British Airways, and National Freight.

These three divestitures are fairly well spread across the history of the divestiture program to date. National Freight's divestiture in 1982 was among the very first; British Telecom's occurred two years later, and it was the first large utility to be sold; British Airways was sold in 1987, although its divestiture had been planned early on. We chose not to examine any more recent divestitures because we wanted to have enough data in each case to be able to observe the performance of the enterprises following divestiture.

Our case studies also span a fairly wide spectrum in terms of size and market structure. National Freight is the United Kingdom's largest road freight business and operates in competitively structured markets. However, National Freight is small compared with British Telecom, which still holds a virtual monopoly in U.K. telecommunications network services. British Airways lies between National Freight and British Telecom in size and market structure. Nevertheless, it is one of the world's largest airlines and has market power in all routes involving the two major London airports.

In this chapter we continue with a description of the general features of public enterprises and their divestiture in the United Kingdom. In the next section we briefly discuss U.K. government control over public enterprises from the time it emerged in the mid-1960s to the beginning of the divestiture program. We then describe the origins of the divestiture program under Prime Minister Thatcher. Next we provide an overview of the U.K. economy during the 1980s, intended as a backdrop to the divestiture program, which is analyzed in the final section.

Government Control of Public Corporations

In the United Kingdom there are three main types of public ownership. First, an enterprise may be operated as a department of state, directly controlled by the central government as part of the civil service. Second, an enterprise may be organized as a company as defined by the Companies' Acts but have all or the majority of its shares owned by the central government, as, for example, in the case of Cable and Wireless before 1983. Third, an enterprise may have the intermediate status of a public corporation, owned entirely by the state but a legal entity in its own right. A public corporation differs from a civil service–controlled entity in that it is allowed to borrow from private sources on its own account and to maintain its own reserves.

A public corporation is answerable to Parliament and ultimately to the voters. The senior management or board of each public corporation is appointed by the relevant minister of state. Before 1979 policy guidelines for public corporations were contained in a number of White Papers and acts of Parliament. The common theme of both is that public corporations, including the postal service, should act in the interests of the public.

The main guidelines affecting the behavior of the nationalized industries in the United Kingdom were set out in the 1967 and 1978 White Papers. Among other things, the guidelines spelled out financial targets, investment criteria, and pricing rules. Additional operating rules came from the introduction of external financing limits (EFLs)[2] in 1975. The relationship between the public corporations and the government evolved, over the late 1960s and through the 1970s, from one of relatively decentralized control through arm's-length regulation to one of more centralized control. This centralization arose because of the increased emphasis the government began to place on macroeconomic stabilization. As the government was experiencing serious fiscal difficulties in the mid-1970s, the prospect of greater control over the expenditures of the public corporations, which form part of the U.K. government accounts, became very attractive. The conflicting priorities between microeconomic and macroeconomic objectives seemed to contribute to the difficulties of managing public corporations. By the end of the 1970s, however, the mood had changed, and the Conservative government elected in 1979 called for radical reform.

The Conservative Government of 1979

A Conservative government was elected in May 1979 and committed itself to a radical reshaping of the U.K. economy. Foremost on the agenda was to "roll back the frontiers of the state," to quote a party slogan of the 1979 campaign. In their manifesto the Conservatives promised to undertake some divestiture of state assets. Three enterprises would be denationalized: British Aerospace, British Shipbuilders, and the National Freight Company.[3] The manifesto also stated that the Conservatives would liberalize the workings of the bus industry. Rather surprisingly in retrospect, the party placed little emphasis on the denationalization and liberalization proposals in the manifesto.

The Conservative government strengthened the monetarist policies initiated by the previous, Labour government and embarked upon policies aimed at encouraging private enterprise and reducing the scale of state intervention. At the beginning of the 1980s privatization itself was not high on the government's agenda, but it is clear from the following statement that the government was nevertheless unfavorably disposed toward the nationalized industries:

We have to manage the nationalised industries that we have inherited. We have to reduce the range of such industries by selling part of the shares of some to the public. . . . [W]e should wherever possible introduce competition into the nationalised industries. (Sir Keith Joseph, speech at the October 1979 Conservative party conference)

In the early 1980s the government honored the divestiture pledge in its 1979 manifesto; this marked the beginning of what was to become known as the privatization program. Privatization was seen as having two principal components: denationalization, which we call in this volume divestiture; and liberalization, which means exposing enterprises to more competition. Conservative governments and politicians over time developed a strong set of arguments in support of privatization. These included, in particular, expanded freedom of choice for consumers, increased economic efficiency, breaking the power of public sector trade unions, improved government finances, broader share ownership, and increased employee interest in the well-being of their divested enterprises.

The Performance of the U.K. Economy during the 1980s

To get a better understanding of the performance of the divested enterprises during our observation period, 1980 to 1990, we need to analyze the performance of the U.K. economy over the same period.[4] Economic policy in the United Kingdom since May 1979 has been designed by a succession of Conservative governments. All of these governments have been strident advocates of the free market, and their economic policy has been aimed at lowering inflation while at the same time promoting conditions designed to stimulate growth in output and employment. The policies have largely been medium-term in scope and have been specified annually. In the early 1980s the emphasis was on reducing the growth rate of the money supply, by targeting broad money aggregates, and on lowering public sector borrowing. More recently the focus has shifted toward nominal GDP growth and the exchange rate.

The policies have been partly successful, as can be seen from table 3-1. Initially, in 1980, real GDP increased by 2.3 percent, but the next year, following the imposition of stringent monetary growth targets, there was a dramatic fall in real GDP of 3.9 percent. Over the period 1980–90, growth in real GDP averaged a little over 1.9 percent per year. After the recession year of 1981, growth in real GDP averaged a little over 3 percent per year for the remainder of the decade. This represented the United Kingdom's longest sustained period of economic growth since the 1960s and reversed the deterioration experienced throughout the 1970s. The growth in GDP occurred largely in the services sector, whereas manufacturing output initially declined, only reattaining its 1979 level in 1984. Since 1984, manufacturing output has experienced relatively high rates of growth, but in 1990 growth declined significantly. Average annual growth in manufacturing output over the whole period was about 1.2 percent.[5]

Retail price inflation jumped at the beginning of the period from 9.7 percent in 1979 to 19.1 percent in 1980. This jump was caused mainly by an increase in the value added tax (VAT) from a range of 10 to 12 percent to a new uniform rate of 15 percent. Inflation declined from 1980 onward to a low of 2.4 percent in mid-1986 but thereafter followed an upward trend: from 3.8 percent in 1988 to 5.2 percent in 1989 and 5.4 percent in 1990. Over the period, government borrowings gradually fell, and be-

Table 3-1. *Changes in Selected Economic Indicators, United Kingdom, 1979–90* (percent per year)

Year	GDP [a]	RPI [b]	Services earnings [c]	PPI [d]	Output per person [e] Whole economy	Output per person [e] Manufacturing	GDCF [f]	Base rate [g]	Rate of return [h] Non-manufacturing [i]	Rate of return [h] All industries [j]	Rate of return [h] Telecom-munication [k]	Rate of return [h] BT [l]
1979	—	9.7	—	—	—	—	—	—	—	—	16.5	—
1980	2.3	19.1	—	14.6	1.5	1.7	3.2	14.9	—	13.6	—	14.2
1981	-3.9	12.7	—	2.3	-1.6	-4.1	-8.6	15.3	—	13.9	21.4	17.7
1982	2.0	11.0	10.5	13.1	3.9	9.3	-6.3	13.3	—	13.8	18.3	21.2
1983	3.1	5.0	9.8	5.1	4.7	7.9	7.5	11.1	13.2	15.4	22.5	20.2
1984	3.1	5.2	5.1	7.2	2.6	6.9	4.8	9.3	14.2	16.6	18.4	17.7
1985	3.1	5.5	7.3	9.6	1.5	4.0	8.7	10.8	15.3	17.3	19.5	18.3
1986	1.6	2.8	7.7	-5.5	0.0	0.3	0.0	12.0	16.1	17.9	21.3	19.5
1987	3.8	4.0	7.7	-0.1	0.7	6.6	2.6	10.5	16.4	—	21.5	20.0
1988	5.8	3.8	8.8	1.8	3.4	6.3	13.6	9.3	15.5	—	24.2	20.7
1989	3.0	5.2	6.3	6.4	3.0	5.5	14.1	11.4	—	—	39.7	20.8
1990	1.6	5.4	8.9	2.9	—	0.8	1.5	14.4	—	—	—	21.2
Averages [m]												
1980–84	1.3	10.6	10.2	8.5	2.2	4.3	0.1	12.8	13.7	15.0	20.1	18.2
1985–90	3.2	4.4	7.8	2.5	1.7	3.9	6.8	11.4	15.8	17.6	24.2	20.1
1980–90	1.9	7.9	7.6	5.2	1.9	4.2	3.7	12.0	15.1	15.6	23.0	19.2

— Not available.

a. At factor cost; average estimate in first quarter (Q1) 1985 = 100; b. Retail Price Index, all items, 1985 (Q1) = 100; c. Average real earnings in the services industries, 1985 (Q1) = 100; d. Producer Price Index of materials and fuel purchased by manufacturing industry, 1985 (Q1) = 100; e. 1985 (Q1) = 100; f. At November 1979 and June 1980; g. Average short-term interest rate at London clearing banks; the minimum was 7.5 percent in May 1988 and the maximum 17 percent between November 1979 and June 1980; h. Rates of return are computed on a historical cost basis before interest and taxation; i. Nonmanufacturing; based on a sample of the United Kingdom's 500 largest firms; j. Excluding oil and gas; k. Telecommunications (British Telecom, Cable and Wireless, and Racal Vodaphone; 1987 figure is an estimate); l. British Telecom; rates of return are calculated by averaging the figures appearing in company reports published over the calendar year. All the figures are evaluated over the financial year (second quarter to first quarter); m. Averages are calculated omitting unavailable data points.

Source: *Bank of England Quarterly Bulletin*, November 1987; *Business Monitor*, Department of Trade and Industry; Datastream; *Economic Trends Annual Supplement* 1989 and June 1990.

tween 1987 and 1991 the fiscal accounts were in surplus. In 1990–91, however, the size of the surplus fell dramatically.

The annual rate of growth in real earnings in the service industries over the period 1980–90 averaged 7.6 percent. Growth in labor productivity over the whole 1980–89 cycle was relatively high in comparison with the 1970s but was broadly in line with the long-term trend. For the economy as a whole, productivity growth averaged 1.9 percent per year between 1980 and 1989, and in manufacturing the figure was 4.2 percent. It has been estimated that growth in total factor productivity was more than double that of the 1970s, reaching a rate of about 1.5 percent per year in the later years of the period. Unit labor costs for the whole economy rose on average by 5.8 percent per year between 1980 and 1989.

Gross domestic capital formation (GDCF) grew in real terms by 3.2 percent in 1980, but during the recession of 1981 it fell by 8.6 percent; this deterioration continued in 1982, when GDCF fell by a further 6.3 percent. From 1983 onward GDCF growth was usually positive, except possibly in 1986, and it reached a peak of 14.1 percent in 1989. Most investment took place in the services sector, and it was only toward the end of the 1980s that investment in manufacturing increased appreciably.

Profitability, measured as rate of return on a historical cost basis, was relatively low from 1980 to 1982, averaging 13.6 percent for all industries, excluding oil and gas. The latter figure is lower than that attained at the depth of the last serious recession in 1975: for the years 1974–76 the average rate of return for all industrials was 16.7 percent. After 1982 profitability improved: between 1983 and 1986 it averaged 16.8 percent for all industrials, and for the largest nonmanufacturing firms it averaged 15.1 percent between 1983 and 1988. Profitability continued to increase throughout the latter half of the 1980s but began to slow down markedly at the end of the 1980s.[6]

Other features of the U.K. economy over the period are as follows. In the early 1980s there was a sharp rise in the number of unemployed, but from 1987 until 1989 unemployment dropped sharply. It then increased slightly in 1990–91. The balance of payments on the current account was in surplus until 1987 but substantially in deficit thereafter.

Overall macroeconomic policy was deflationary in the early 1980s, and economic growth deteriorated. From about 1982 onward the state of the economy gradually improved. Between 1983 and 1989 growth was relatively rapid, averaging 3.4 percent per year. Growth reached a peak of 5.8 percent in 1988, coinciding with a preelection period during which monetary policy was relaxed considerably, with the base rate (the average short-term interest rate offered by London clearing banks) falling to 7.5 percent for a while, its lowest level in the 1980s. This relaxation in policy precipitated excessive growth in expenditure, and the economy began to overheat and inflation to accelerate. In response to the increase in inflation, monetary policy was tightened, and the base rate was increased to 15 percent. Economic growth subsided at the end of the 1980s, and in 1990 it stood at only 1.6 percent. In effect, 1980–90 followed a cyclical pattern, with a severe recession in 1981, relatively rapid growth between 1983 and 1989, and a sharp reduction in growth at the end of the decade. A severe recession set in again in 1990.

U.K. Divestiture since 1980

The range of enterprises held by the U.K. public sector at the beginning of the 1980s was remarkable. Besides operating a number of enterprises with natural monopolistic characteristics, such as gas distribution, electricity generation and supply, rail transport, and water supply, the government owned enterprises manufacturing ships, steel, computers, silicon chips, offshore oil rigs, airplanes, automobiles, and electronic goods; it operated bus services, postal services, airlines, coal mines, ports, and specialist medical financial services, and it managed health and education services. This shows that the scope of the government's interests within the U.K. economy was extremely wide. Many of the enterprises owned by the government participated in fragmented markets.

The divestiture of many of these public enterprises during the 1980s was dramatic. Since the election of the Conservative government in 1979, the policy of privatization has changed the ownership structure of the U.K. economy markedly. By 1990 over thirty major enterprises valued at over £27 billion and employing nearly 800,000 people (around 3.3 percent of the work force) had been transferred to the private sector (Parker and Hartley 1991). A total of seventy-five enterprises had been divested by the end of 1990. The share of GDP generated by state-owned enterprises, which had stood at 11.5 percent in 1980 (Vickers and Yarrow 1988), was down to less than 5 percent in 1990. Only a handful of enterprises remained fully in the public sector at the beginning of the 1990s, the most prominent being the postal service, British Coal (coal extraction), and British Rail (rail and parcel delivery services). Nevertheless, all of the latter have experienced some deregulation and exposure to competition.

The U.K. privatization program gathered momentum in the early 1980s, following the divestiture of British Aerospace in February 1981. Between December 1979 and the divestiture of British Telecom in November 1984, the government realized £2.9 billion in gross receipts from the divestiture of nineteen enterprises.[7] Of these, twelve were sold privately rather than through public offerings. The divestiture of two enterprises alone accounted for around 32 percent of gross sales receipts;

these were Britoil (first issue November 1982, for £549 million) and Enterprise Oil (in June 1984, for £392 million), both of which were sold by tender and were undersubscribed. The British Aerospace offer raised less in gross receipts (£150 million) than the sale of either oil enterprise, but it was seen as a success by the Conservative government because the issue was oversubscribed. The British Aerospace divestiture convinced the Conservative government that a massive privatization program could reap substantial political benefits.

Following the divestiture of British Telecom, the U.K. government realized that size and monopoly power were not obstacles to the success of a privatization program. This led the government to embark on a vigorous divestiture program. The major sales in the second half of the 1980s (excluding second and third issues of previously divested enterprises such as British Telecom) were British Gas (£5.4 billion; all figures are in gross terms) in December 1986, British Airways (£900 million) in February 1987, Rolls-Royce (£1.4 billion) in May 1987, British Airports Authority (BAA) plc (£1.3 billion) in July 1987, British Steel (£2.5 billion) in December 1988, the ten water holding companies of England and Wales (£5.2 billion) in November 1989, and the twelve regional electricity enterprises (£5.2 billion) in November 1990. These sales put the grand finale on a decade of public-enterprise divestiture.

Notes

This chapter was written by Christopher Doyle and Ingo Vogelsang.

1. Most notably by Kay and Thompson (1986), Vickers and Yarrow (1988), and Bishop and Kay (1988).

2. An EFL places a constraint on the annual change in the net indebtedness of a public corporation to the government; it is therefore a way of controlling the cost of new capital investment and working capital increases not financed by internally generated revenues. EFLs are still imposed and are typically set about eighteen months prior to the end of the financial year to which they will apply.

3. The term "denationalization" refers specifically to the disposal of state assets to the private sector. By the mid-1980s the term "privatization" was being widely used to encompass both denationalization and liberalization. This is discussed further in the next section.

4. Data in this section are from the *Economic Trends* Annual Supplement 1989, *Economic Trends* June 1990, Green (1989), Maynard (1989), and the country economic surveys of the United Kingdom prepared by the Organization for Economic Cooperation and Development (1987/88 and 1988/89). The data are for financial years, that is, from the second quarter of one calendar year through the first quarter of the next. Some additional data are contained in the appendix.

5. This is the view expressed by the Organization for Economic Cooperation and Development (see note 4) and by Maynard (1989).

6. See *Bank of England Quarterly Bulletin*, May 1989, and issues of *Business* magazine from the period.

7. We have ignored the divestiture of British Petroleum (BP) in these statistics. That divestiture stretches across two political regimes, and for consistency we are focusing on the Conservative regime only. The first tranche of issued share capital was divested in June 1977 by a Labour government, for financial rather than ideological reasons. The Labour government, however, retained a 51 percent holding in the enterprise. The Conservative government divested a further 5 percent of the issued share capital in November 1979 (raising £290 million gross) and a further 7 percent in September 1983 (generating £566 million gross). The remaining government-held shares were divested in October 1987, raising £7.2 billion gross.

4. British Telecom

There are several reasons why British Telecom (BT) makes an excellent basic case study to illustrate our methodology:

- **Timing**. The enterprise was divested in the winter of 1984, long enough ago to have generated several years of performance data since divestiture, but not too long ago to make it impossible to find performance data for the period before divestiture.
- **Telecommunications**. This is an industry of prime importance throughout the world. All countries that have not yet done so are confronted with the decision as to whether to divest their telecommunications sectors.
- **Policy issues**. BT's divestiture was accompanied by an interesting set of regulatory policies that other countries may consider adopting in one way or the other.
- **Success story**. The BT divestiture is a celebrated case that has been criticized and analyzed by others. This allows us to contrast our methodology with other analyses.

The Conventional Wisdom

Around 1980, BT was seen as an overstaffed and badly organized public enterprise, using technologically and physically outdated capital equipment, short on investment, and with long lists of new customers waiting for phone connections. Divestiture, market liberalization, and a new regulatory scheme were all proposed as ways of substantially improving BT's performance. It was hoped that after divestiture BT would become highly profitable, become more responsive to customer needs, slash costs by reducing its work force by 5,000 per year (Beesley and Laidlaw 1989), increase investment, and be forced to lower prices for long distance (including international) services. Other government objectives included a reduction in the public sector borrowing requirement (PSBR),[1] a widening of share ownership, increased employee participation, and better labor relations.

BT's performance since its divestiture has been analyzed by a number of economists, politicians, regulators, and financial analysts, who largely agree on the following:

- BT has been fairly successful in terms of financial performance, although it has so far not been very lucky in its acquisition and diversification policy (including its acquisitions of Mitel and McCaw Cellular Communications Inc.). The U.K. director general of telecommunications found that BT's overall rate of return after 1984 was increasingly on the high side compared with other industries. As a consequence, he tightened the price regulation formula *RPI - X* (the retail price index minus a productivity adjustment factor) in 1988 by successively increasing X and by increasing the scope of price regulation.
- BT's principal U.K. competitor, Mercury Communications, by concentrating on a small market niche and by taking a long time to install capacity, has for a number of years been less of a challenge to BT than most observers had expected. In line with this initial disappointment, the half-hearted U.K. approach to competition in telecommunications has been heavily criticized by Beesley and Laidlaw (1989) and Vickers and Yarrow (1988).
- For the first five years after divestiture, BT kept general price levels for its regulated products below the legal limit (Johnson 1989).
- BT has rebalanced its rates by increasing local rates, access charges, line rentals, and private circuits relative to long distance and international rates. Although this seems to have come as a surprise to the general public, it was fully in keeping with the expectations of experts such as Littlechild (1983).
- There were some initial problems with the quality of BT's services. Both BT's management and the U.K. Office of Telecommunications (OFTEL) attributed these to labor unrest, but others (e.g., Vickers and Yarrow 1988) pointed to a link between tight *RPI - X* regulation and product quality. The problems have also been attributed to reductions in the labor force in 1980–84 (J. Wilby, British Telecom, personal communication).[2]
- Beesley and Laidlaw (1989, p. 40) have argued that, as late as 1989, BT still had 75,000 too many employees (by international standards). This observation seems in line with BT's chief executive's own assessment in 1990, when he initiated a major reorganization and layoff program.
- BT's improvements in financial terms and in productivity performance (total factor productivity, or TFP) started to materialize around 1982–83, before divestiture. This turnaround has been explained by the general change in the U.K. business climate around that time; a general perception among public enterprises in the United Kingdom

that they had to shape up for eventual divestiture;[3] and liberalization in the U.K. telecommunications sector, which preceded divestiture by two years.

Although our quantitative analysis is compatible with these findings, we hope to surprise the reader by shedding new light on the sources of BT's change and on the total value of BT's divestiture and its distribution.

Background

Telephone services first became available in the United Kingdom in 1878, provided by private companies and municipalities. To create an integrated national network, in 1912 the government granted the Post Office a statutory telecommunications monopoly. In 1969, in an attempt to promote decentralized decisionmaking, the Labour government converted the Post Office into a public corporation. In 1980 the Post Office renamed its telecommunications division British Telecom and started to publish completely separate accounts. In 1981 BT was formally vested as a public corporation in its own right. Following an announcement of its intentions in July 1982, the government sold 51 percent of the enterprise's shares to private shareholders in November 1984.

Simultaneously with the corporatization and eventual divestiture of BT, the government was also loosening its monopoly position. In 1981, three important steps were taken:

- Firms were allowed to compete with BT in the customer premises equipment market.
- Firms were permitted to provide value added network services on lines leased from BT.
- Other companies were invited to apply for licenses to build and operate alternative networks.

In 1982, Barclays Merchant Bank, British Petroleum, and Cable and Wireless formed a consortium called Mercury Communications, which subsequently obtained a license to provide competing telecommunications services. Mercury, which became a wholly owned subsidiary of Cable and Wireless in 1984, has since built a small network and is increasingly providing competition to BT, particularly in the business sector. BT and Mercury enjoyed a government-sanctioned duopoly from 1983 to 1991. As a result of a government review of the duopoly policy in 1991, other consortia have been awarded licenses to operate new mobile and cordless telephone services in the 1990s.

Despite all this, BT still dominates the U.K. market. Its share of revenues from operating switched services was an estimated 96.2 percent in 1989, having declined only slightly from the 1980 figure of 99.8 percent.

In other network services BT had an estimated revenue share of 95.5 percent in 1989, whereas the figure in 1980 was 99.8 percent.

Telecommunications Economics

BT is a multiproduct firm. Its main outputs, comprising over 90 percent of its total revenues, are telecommunications network services. In addition, it sells (or rents out) customer premises equipment, such as telephone sets and private automatic branch exchanges, and a variety of other outputs related to communications, such as consulting services and telephone directories. We have aggregated BT's different outputs into the following major categories:

- Business rentals
- Residential rentals
- Local calls
- Long distance calls less than 56 kilometers
- Long distance calls over 56 kilometers
- International outgoing calls
- International incoming calls
- Apparatus supply
- Private circuits
- Miscellaneous outputs.

Quantities for business and residential rentals are the numbers of rented connections as published in BT's annual reports over the whole period 1980–90. The revenues and derived prices, however, include a share from connection charges incurred by moving or receiving the initial connection.

For all the call categories, business and residential customers are combined. Prices for domestic local and long distance telephone calls can move in different directions. There is a standard price per unit for all types of calls. This unit price buys a specific length of calling time differentiated by time of the week and distance of call. Thus, BT can change its calling prices by adjusting the price per unit or by adjusting the length of calling time allowed per unit. The interaction of these types of price changes makes it difficult to calculate price changes for distance categories, where calls within these categories differ by length and time of the week. Thus, we have had to construct a composite commodity for each of these categories. Prices have been calculated for such a composite "representative telephone call" from disaggregated published price data.

We have differentiated between outgoing and incoming international calls because BT adds the full revenues that it receives for incoming calls from foreign telephone carriers to its international telephone revenues and claims its payments (known as accounting rates) as costs of outgoing calls.

The category "apparatus supply" refers to terminal equipment. Apparatus is a set of very heterogeneous and differentiated products (domestic private automatic branch exchanges and telephones, sales, maintenance, and rentals). Until 1981, BT enjoyed a dominant position as a buyer of such equipment from manufacturers and as a retail supplier to its customers. Part of this retail supply was done jointly with exchange line rentals. Since 1981 other suppliers have entered the market, gradually weakening BT's dominant position. We judge the apparatus market today as quite comparable to that for computers and consumer electronics.[4]

The "private circuits" category has been one of the fastest-growing services in telecommunications. Private circuits consist of lines leased from BT by business customers. The "miscellaneous outputs" category includes all other sources of revenue, including domestic telegraph and telex, cellular service, directories, value added network services, consulting, and Mitel (which manufactures private automated branch exchanges). Intragroup sales are also netted out here.

Demand for most of BT's telecommunications services is fairly price-inelastic. However, the elasticities differ distinctly for different services. They tend to be lowest for rentals and local telephone calls. Within the calling categories, elasticities tend to increase with distance (and price). Elasticities for private circuits appear to be quite high, in part because the public network is a close substitute. For many of BT's services, demand curves shift outward substantially over time, as consumer incomes increase and new telecommunications applications are introduced.

Consumption externalities are important in telecommunications. Positive externalities are associated with the fact that a call provides potential benefits to both the caller and the person called. For example, the addition of new subscribers to the network increases the usefulness of the system to existing users, who do not, however, have to pay for this added benefit. These same new subscribers cause negative externalities if the additional calls result in network congestion.

We have no good cost information on any individual telecommunications services. Hence, we refrain from making specific cost assignments.

Pricing Policy

Before divestiture, BT followed government pricing policies, which meant that prices had to reflect long-run marginal costs and cover accounting costs, including the opportunity cost of capital. For the main network services, BT used two-part tariffs, consisting of a quarterly rental charge for a connection and a user fee. Peak-load pricing was used to reflect lower demand in the evenings and on weekends. Residential users paid lower prices than business users, to encourage more subscribers.

Following the oil price shock of 1973, the government attempted to control inflation by holding down prices, but the resultant losses were deemed intolerable. In 1975 telephone charges were raised an average of 75 percent, and BT returned dramatically to profitability. The steep price increases were met with criticism, however, as they were interpreted as indicating the exploitation of monopoly power. When investments were dearly needed in the early 1980s, the government believed that the only effective response was the eventual abolition of the monopoly and the divestiture of BT.

In light of this concern with monopoly pricing, and despite the fact that new entry of telecommunications providers was contemplated, it was recognized as essential that BT's prices be regulated after divestiture. The United States was seen as the only country with experience in regulating privately owned telecommunications companies, and regulation there had taken the form of a ceiling rate of return. The U.K. government, however, rejected this form of regulation as too difficult to implement and prone to cost inefficiencies. Instead, a form of direct price regulation was adopted, which has come to be known as the *RPI* - X form of price cap regulation.

Price cap regulation puts a ceiling on the average price increase for a certain basket of services. The services originally included in the basket were those in which BT enjoyed a complete or effective monopoly: exchange line rentals for business and residential users, and all dialed calls originating and terminating in the United Kingdom. In 1984 these two categories yielded approximately half of BT's revenues. Excluded were connection charges, apparatus, calls from public call boxes, private circuits, data communications services, and international services. The inclusion of private circuits in 1989 and international services in 1991 increased the scope of price cap regulation to two-thirds of BT's revenues.

Under the regulation, the average price for the basket of included services is to rise by no more than the retail price index (RPI) minus a factor designated X, to be determined by OFTEL, to reflect the long-term declining trend in costs due to technological progress in the telecommunications industry. For the years 1984–89 X was set at 3 percent per year. For 1989–91 it was increased to 4.5 percent per year. The inclusion of international services in 1991 brought it to 6.25 percent, and for 1993 to 1997 it has been set at 7.5 percent per year (for the separate basket of "private circuits" X was set at zero from 1989 onward). Thus, at an inflation rate of about 4 percent, BT was actually obliged to reduce prices for 1992–93 by more than 2 percent on average. Within the basket, until 1993 BT was free in principle to rebalance prices. It formally agreed not to raise rental charges more than 2 percent per year above the rate of inflation.

Investment and Borrowing

At the end of fiscal 1970, the telecommunications division of the Post Office had outstanding loans of £1.76 billion, against fixed assets whose net book value was £2.14 billion. Heavy borrowing continued through the early 1970s, as is seen in table 4-1, with the self-financing ratio reaching a trough in 1974 at 36.9 percent. By 1977 outstanding loans stood at £3.88 billion.

During 1978–83 BT had failed to meet government targets for reductions in the real cost of production. According to Beesley and Laidlaw (1989) these targets had been set at 5 percent per year, whereas real cost reductions of only 2.8 percent were achieved. On the other hand, BT met the financial targets set for 1977–84 in all years but 1980 and 1981.

In the late 1970s and early 1980s BT's investment policy apparently was crippled by external financing limits (EFLs) that were imposed on BT and other public enterprises in order to reduce the PSBR. In 1979–81 BT invested US$2,746 million per year, compared with US$5,190 million by the (equally large) France Télécom and US$5,091 million in telecommunications investments by the (slightly larger) Deutsche Bundespost (Organization for Economic Cooperation and Development 1988). What is not clear is whether the financing limitations reduced or increased BT's real unit costs of output at that time. EFLs may have increased unit costs because modern, cost-saving capital equipment could not be purchased. Or EFLs may have reduced unit costs because excess capacity during the 1979–81 slump was less severe than other-

Table 4-1. *Changes in Indebtedness, British Telecom, 1971–83*
(millions of pounds sterling)

Year	Gross borrowing	Repayments	Net borrowing	Self-financing ratio (percentages)
1971	221.9	29.5	192.4	51.0
1972	277.7	29.5	248.2	53.7
1973	405.0	29.5	375.5	38.6
1974	322.9	29.5	293.4	36.9
1975	565.4	29.5	535.9	39.8
1976	302.7	32.7	270.0	92.4
1977	244.8	36.6	208.2	109.2
1978	0.0	48.1	−48.1	113.9
1979	112.0	284.9	−172.9	106.1
1980	59.1	237.5	−178.4	79.2
1981	94.9	170.3	−75.4	111.9
1982	302.3	174.7	127.6	88.8
1983	43.0	184.0	−141.0	125.0

Source: BT data.

wise. Almost certainly the EFLs had adverse long-run effects on unit costs.

It is worth noting why the investment constraint on BT may have been particularly damaging to its efficient operation. Because of mistakes or miscalculations made many years earlier, BT was in need of extensive modernization. During the 1970s, as telephone capacity in the United Kingdom was being doubled, 57 percent of new exchange capacity used the totally antiquated Strowger technology, and 28 percent used the also-obsolete Crossbar technology. It was only in 1976 that the first semielectronic exchange was installed. Thus at this point there was an urgent need to undertake large-scale investments to upgrade the capital equipment of BT, but the enterprise was constrained by the newly imposed EFLs.

The pressure to reduce the PSBR was cited as one of the justifications for divestiture. Divestiture was beneficial in this regard in two ways. First, the sale proceeds reduced the need to borrow. Second, the future borrowings of the divested enterprise would no longer be included in the PSBR. It appears that the removal of the EFLs on BT was one of the most significant effects of divestiture on the enterprise.

In the early 1980s, under pressure from BT, the government agreed to allow the enterprise to issue bonds. However, this initiative ran into legal and other problems in distinguishing the bond issue from public borrowing. In 1982 the issuing of the bonds was overshadowed by the intention to divest BT.

Labor and Labor Relations

At the end of 1970, BT's approximately 240,000 workers were represented by seven unions, the largest of which was the Post Office Engineering Union (POEU) with 118,000 members. BT's management was under pressure to cut costs, because of the generally tight budgetary situation and because of criticisms that BT was less efficient than its international counterparts. However, little headway toward reducing staffing was made in talks with the unions. In 1981, management unilaterally announced a plan to reduce the work force by 15,000 over a five-year period. This plan was put into effect in 1982, and by 1985, through attrition and voluntary retirement, the work force had been cut from 250,000 to 235,000.

Divestiture has not changed the basic structure of labor relations. Workers continue to be represented by several unions, with the POEU, which changed its name in 1985 to the National Communications Union (NCU), still in the lead. Bargaining between the company and the unions remained difficult, and there has been at least one industrial action (in 1987). Nevertheless, agreements have been reached calling for large wage increases, in return for changes in working practices that allow the company greater flexibility in labor allocation decisions. Thus it appears that progress has been made in adapting the work force to changed practices in the telecommunications industry—something BT had been unable to achieve prior to divestiture.

What Happened?

In this section we try to find out what changed in the course of (as distinct from "as a result of") divestiture by examining various partial indicators of enterprise performance. The analysis is partial in three distinct ways. It is partial temporally in that it only examines an eleven-year period (1980–90), covering five years before divestiture and six years after. It is partial methodologically in that it only considers what actually happened, ignoring what would have happened in the absence of divestiture. Finally, it is partial analytically in that it looks at a hodgepodge of costs and benefits without specifying the trade-offs necessary to reach a summary judgment of performance.

Each of these three limitations will be removed in subsequent sections. In the process, we will be moving from measuring the wrong thing perfectly to measuring the right thing imperfectly. This section, therefore, although intended as a starting point for the analysis, may also serve as an ending point for those who prefer low-variance answers to the wrong question over high-variance answers to the right question.

Profit and Profitability

PUBLIC AND PRIVATE PROFIT. A natural place to start is with the bottom line of the income statement, which we call private profit (dividends plus retained earnings). As shown in figure 4-1, private profit was roughly £500 million in 1980 and 1981, then doubled to about £1 billion, where it remained nearly unchanged through 1985, after which it rose smoothly to £1.9 billion in 1990. There are thus two turning points to explain: one corresponding to the announcement of divestiture and the other lagging its implementation by one year. Looking only at private profit, one might conclude that the announcement of divestiture caused a one-time jump in performance, whereas its execution initiated a dynamic process of steady improvement in a previously static world. Such a conclusion would be unwarranted.

Although private profit is a useful measure of return to the equityholder, we are interested in the return to all of society's resources, which we call public profit. As also shown in figure 4-1, public profit tells a quite different story, showing essentially a continuous linear trend with no pronounced flattening across the pre- and postdivestiture periods. Why is the public profit trend unchanged when the private profit trend shows

Figure 4-1.   Public and Private Profit at Current Market Prices, British Telecom, 1980–90

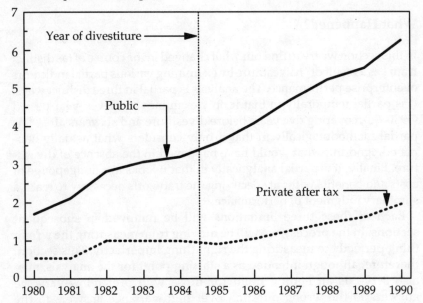

Source: Authors' calculation from BT annual reports.

a kink? The answer is that the total size of the pie (public profit, or quasi rents) has grown fairly smoothly, but its distribution has not. This can be seen in figure 4-2, which decomposes the total surplus (or return to capital). The discontinuity in private profit in 1984–85 was obviously due primarily to the introduction of direct taxes, which in turn was due not to divestiture but to alterations in the national tax code.[5] The 1982 discontinuity is explained by two factors:

- In 1982 the total surplus rose by £694 million; two-thirds of this increase was passed through to private profit (interest and depreciation were essentially fixed, and only indirect taxes rose proportionately). The 30 percent rise in total surplus thus translated into a 131 percent rise in private profit, on the usual residual multiplier principle.
- In 1983 a £257 million rise in public profit was more than eaten up by increases in other distributions. In particular, a rise in the implicit depreciation rate from 8.8 percent to 10.6 percent chewed up £193 million. A 9.3 percent rise in total surplus thus translated into a 3 percent fall in net return to equity. This demonstrates why private profit is not a good performance measure.

That is, in 1982 there was an exceptionally large increment in the size of the pie, and equityholders got the biggest piece of that increment. In 1983 there was a normal increment, but this was absorbed elsewhere.

In sum, inspection of current profit and its distribution yields three discontinuities accompanying divestiture. Two of these clearly cannot be attributed to divestiture, namely, the effects of the introduction of direct taxes and changes in average depreciation rates. The third—the high rate of growth of public profit in 1982—remains a candidate for further investigation.

CURRENT AND CONSTANT PROFIT. Figure 4-3 shows public profit and its derivation at constant market prices. Two points are noteworthy. First, there is an intriguing trend change: at constant prices public profit declines somewhat from 1980 to 1982, then rises at a fairly steady rate through 1990. Second, this trend change was not due primarily to a change in output (which grew at a more or less constant rate over the entire period), but to a change in costs. From 1980 through 1982, both intermediate inputs and labor grew slightly faster than output. There-

Figure 4-2. Return to Capital at Current Market Prices, British Telecom, 1980–90

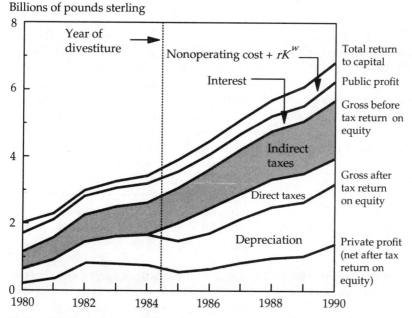

Billions of pounds sterling

Note: rK^{W}, opportunity cost of working capital.
Source: Authors' calculations from BT annual reports.

Figure 4-3. Public Profit at Constant Prices, British Telecom, 1980–90

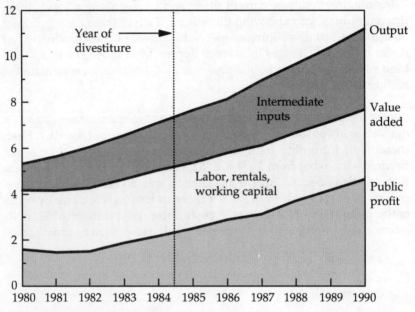

Source: Authors' calculations from BT data.

after, intermediates grew at about the same rate as outputs, but through 1990 the quantity of labor input stayed more or less constant.[6]

In sum, there was a major discontinuity in performance in 1982, due primarily to an increase in real output per worker and secondarily to a stabilization of intermediate requirements per unit of output. These results are important and will be elaborated upon below. Consideration of return alone, however, is misleading without simultaneous inspection of that to which it is returned, namely, capital stock.

FIXED CAPITAL. In contrast to the inconspicuous changes in profit, the discontinuities in fixed capital formation (figure 4-4) are dramatic.[7] At constant prices fixed capital formation was essentially stable in the predivestiture period, but it rose at an average rate of 16 percent per year thereafter.

The impressive discontinuity in the flows naturally gets diluted in the corresponding stock of fixed capital, which is ten times larger and also includes deterioration. However, at constant prices, there is still a hefty difference between the predivestiture annual average growth rate of 4.7 percent and the postdivestiture rate of 7.4 percent.[8] This upward shift in fixed capital formation is potentially an extremely important change in conduct accompanying divestiture, and the reasons behind it will be a focus of our analysis below.

PROFITABILITY AND PRODUCTIVITY. Combining the numerator (profit) and the denominator (capital stock) yields the true bottom line of this section, namely, return to fixed capital, or profitability. As figure 4-5 shows, although the private and current price public versions diverge, neither shows any marked upward trend change around the time of divestiture. The constant-price story is considerably more interesting. Here there is a dramatic turning point, but it occurs in 1983 rather than 1985. That is, from 1980 through 1982 public profitability at constant prices decreased (from about 12 percent to about 11 percent); thereafter it increased steadily by almost 1.5 percent a year to a 1990 level of about 20 percent.

As explained in chapter 2, the purpose of the constant-price public profitability measure is conceptually identical to that of the total factor productivity (TFP) indicator. They differ only in specification: that is, what goes into the numerator as opposed to the denominator, how variables are measured, and which numeraire is selected.

Figure 4-4. Gross Fixed Capital Formation, British Telecom, 1980–90

Billions of pounds sterling

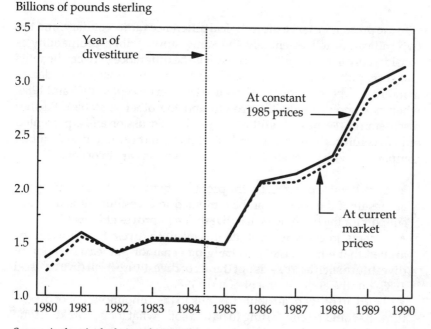

Source: Authors' calculations from BT data.

Figure 4-5.   Private and Public Profitability, British Telecom, 1980–90

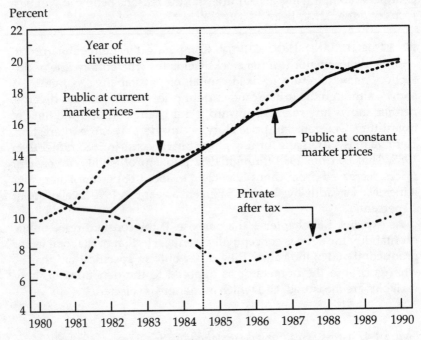

Percent

Source: Authors' calculations from BT data.

In the present instance the technical differences are secondary, and the two indicators tell essentially the same story. Public profitability is considerably more volatile,[9] because it is the difference between benefits and costs rather than their ratio. However (as can be seen most clearly in figure 4-6), both series rise and fall in tandem (except in 1985 and 1986, when one shows negligible growth and the other is stable). Further discussion of TFP thus adds little to the earlier discussion and is presented only to comfort those more familiar with this indicator and to facilitate comparison with other studies. Four observations are in order:

- First, the sharp reversal of the profitability trend in 1983 is an important result: if the change can be attributed to divestiture, it is dramatic support for the hypothesis that divestiture improves efficiency.
- Second, in order to attribute this event to divestiture, it has to be argued that what matters in changing behavior—at least in a partial divestiture such as BT's—is not the act of divestiture itself (in BT's fiscal 1985) but the announcement of it (in 1982).
- Third, in order to attribute the kink to the announcement of divestiture, it would be comforting to have a somewhat longer prekink time series (see below for evidence extending the time series).

• Fourth, in order to see the kink it was necessary to eliminate price effects and focus on real or quantity effects. The fact that prices and quantities move differently will surprise no one, but it does suggest that there may be a positive return to further investigation of price versus quantity effects.

PRICE AND QUANTITY DECOMPOSITION. Table 4-2 decomposes changes in public profit (and its components) into price and quantity effects. For each variable, the table reports three pieces of information: how much the value of the variable itself changed over the previous year (in absolute rather than percentage terms); how much of that change would have occurred if only prices had changed; and how much would have occurred if only quantities had changed.[10]

For example, consider the 1989 public profit triplet near the lower right-hand corner. Public profit rose by £173 million between 1988 and 1989, but prices moved against BT to such an extent that it would have lost £299 million had quantities not changed in the company's favor to the tune of £472 million. Contrast this with 1981 (in the lower left-hand corner), when prices moved overwhelmingly in BT's favor, offsetting

Figure 4-6. Year-to-Year Changes in Total Factor Productivity and Real Public Profitability, British Telecom, 1981–90

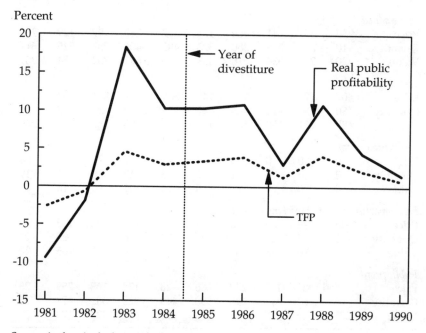

Percent

Source: Authors' calculations from BT data.

negative quantity effects. These two extreme differences suggest an important trend accompanying the announcement of divestiture. That is, public profits increased every year both before and after divestiture. However, this was accomplished by quite different mechanisms: in 1981 and 1982 it was due primarily to favorable price effects, and thereafter to positive quantity effects.

Where did these changes in the bottom line originate? Table 4-2 shows that the change clearly stems primarily from output pricing. Output price increases generated roughly £800 million for BT in both 1981 and 1982—that figure is double the highest level, and quadruple the average,

Table 4-2. Decomposition of Public Profit Trend into Price and Quantity Effects, British Telecom, 1981–90
(millions of 1985 pounds sterling)

Year	1981	1982	1983	1984	1985	1986	1987	1988	1989	1990
Output										
Price	766	814	182	–35	242	187	194	209	126	369
Quantity	229	341	487	534	535	547	843	690	747	891
Value	949	1,155	669	449	777	734	1,037	899	873	1,260
Less intermediate inputs										
Price	36	163	223	29	106	–104	–91	10	–4	119
Quantity	239	222	112	154	212	58	437	157	223	272
Value	275	385	335	183	318	–46	346	167	219	391
Value added										
Price	730	651	–41	–64	136	292	285	199	129	250
Quantity	–10	119	376	380	323	488	406	533	525	619
Value	720	770	334	316	459	780	691	732	654	269
Less wages										
Price	407	176	177	166	143	389	163	324	293	182
Quantity	80	55	–19	–6	–42	–32	40	–35	67	87
Value	487	231	158	160	101	357	203	289	360	269
Less rented factors										
Price	0	0	0	0	4	1	7	10	10	4
Quantity	0	0	0	71	6	23	17	–18	6	19
Value	0	0	0	71	10	24	24	–8	16	23
Less opportunity cost of working capital										
Price	–23	–8	–85	10	54	–70	–17	28	125	40
Quantity	–15	2	82	20	29	53	26	1	–20	–21
Value	–38	–6	–3	30	84	–17	8	28	105	20
Public profit										
Price	346	483	–132	–239	–66	–28	132	–163	–299	23
Quantity	–75	62	311	295	330	443	325	585	472	535
Value	271	546	179	56	264	416	457	422	173	557

Source: Authors' calculations from BT data.

seen in subsequent years. In contrast, intermediate inputs exhibit no discernible trend, with price changes paralleling the general rise of wholesale prices, and quantities increasing at a somewhat more modest rate than output.

The labor trend ("Wages" in table 4-2) is distinguished for its lack of dramatic kinks. Representatives of labor often oppose divestiture as inimical to the interests of workers, but this result is not apparent in the BT record. To be sure, the largest wage increment was in 1981, and both 1981 and 1982 saw significant work force expansions; however, 1986, 1988, and 1989 all saw substantial wage increases as well, and the work force expanded in 1987 and 1989.

In sum, what needs to be explained here is not the existence of a kink but the absence of one. In both periods, rising labor costs—due much more to increased wages than to increased employment—added considerably to BT's costs, typically consuming about half of the surplus generated at the value added level.

Rented factors are negligible at BT and may be ignored. The exogenous price component of working capital moves both with the interest rate and with the general price index. The quantity component of working capital exhibits no notable trend.

In sum, both before and after divestiture BT generated substantial additional revenues from sales each year, and it used those funds for roughly equal increments in intermediate inputs, labor, and profits. The major difference was that, before the announcement of divestiture, the revenue boost came primarily from raising prices; thereafter it came primarily from increasing real output.

Finance

By "financial" behavior we refer primarily and conventionally to the way in which investment is financed and to the differential returns (costs, from the enterprise's point of view) to the various sources of funds—that is, with the liabilities and net worth side of the balance sheet, and associated flows. In fact, because we are looking for evidence of change, we will concentrate on the flows in the form of sources of funds. We also include secondarily, and less conventionally, the management of nonoperating assets (these are quantitatively negligible at BT, peaking at £166 million pounds, or 1.4 percent of total revenues, in 1988). We begin with a description of the one major financial event—the restructuring of the enterprise prior to sale.

Divestiture is often facilitated by financial restructuring or "cleaning up the balance sheet." Usually, this takes the form of a debt-equity swap in which the government takes some debt off the enterprise's accounts and thus raises the net worth of the enterprise by the same amount. The government's debt portfolio falls, but, as a first approximation, its equity portfolio rises by the same amount (assuming no behavioral change in the firm and 100 percent government debt and equity positions). However, and also as a first approximation (abstracting from uncertainty, interest rate differentials, and tax considerations), private willingness to pay will rise by the same amount, and if this increase is actually extracted in the sale price, the government is made whole. Viewed in this light, a debt-equity swap is nothing but a little accounting juggling, which raises the sale price to a politically acceptable level without major economic consequences.

Prior to the sale of BT, a number of actions were taken which, taken as a whole, amounted to such a debt-equity swap:

- **Debt for debt**. The government wrote off a £2.79 billion loan and forgave a pension fund obligation of £1.25 billion. In return, the government received two pieces of paper: £2.75 billion in "unsecured loan stock" and £0.75 billion in "preference shares." We treat both as debt instruments, because they earn a fixed rate of return, convey no voting rights, and are senior in claims on earnings to equity shares.
- **Debt for equity**. When the four debt-for-debt transactions are netted out, BT's debt fell by £540 million, and owned reserves rose by an equivalent amount.
- **Equity for equity**. The government was issued £1.5 billion worth of shares—a paper transaction that reduced one component of net worth (reserves) while raising the other (paid-in capital) by an equivalent amount.

Figure 4-7 gives a breakdown of total sources of funds, which reveals the following points:

- One obvious change associated with divestiture is 1985's debt-equity swap, which appears as a £540 million equity inflow offset by an equivalent debt outflow. The two flows cancel, as there was no net inflow of funds in this period.
- A second change is the jump in the use of the non-interest-bearing debt in the three years following divestiture. This is due to the introduction of direct taxation and dividends and the need to build up a year-end reserve to pay those obligations.
- An important nonchange is that (except in 1985) the preeminent source of funds was internal (retained earnings and depreciation allowance). That is, both before and after divestiture, BT was able to more than finance its growth from sale revenues. In fact, in four of the ten years the enterprise actually retired more debt than it acquired, and in the other years net debt acquisition did not account for more than 20 percent of total sources of funds.

Figure 4-7. Sources of Funds, British Telecom, 1981–90

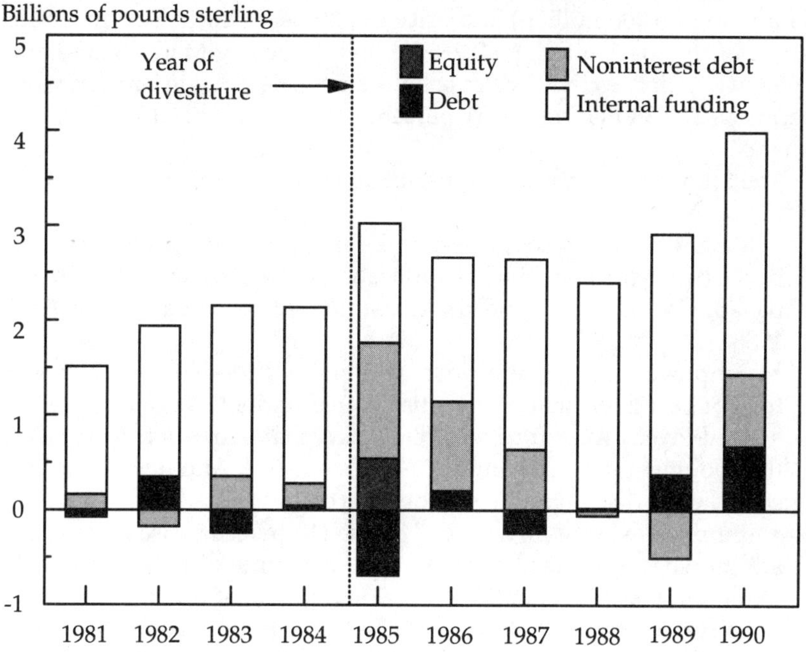

Billions of pounds sterling

Source: Authors' calculations from BT annual reports.

• Another nonchange, which follows directly from the first, is a precipitous decline in the debt-equity ratio.

Fiscal Effects

The impact of the divestiture of BT upon the U.K. treasury can be divided into two parts. First is the price received for the shares it sold. Our calculations show that the net price for 51 percent of the enterprise (in March 1985 pounds sterling) was £3,588 million. Second, an impact that has received much less attention but is potentially more important is the flow of funds to the treasury that occur on an ongoing basis. The principal components of this flow are taxes and the government's share of BT's dividends. Also included are interest on and repayment of government loans and transactions relating to the government's preference shares. The net impact of this flow is sizable. Our calculations show a sharp jump in flows to the treasury, from about the £450 million level to approximately the £1,500 million level within less than three years after divestiture (detail is provided below). We discuss first the sale transaction itself and then its fiscal effect.

Nominally, the sale of 50.2 percent of BT's issued share capital consisted in the U.K. government offering for sale 3,012 million shares (out of a total of 6,000 million) at a price of 130 pence each. This made the value of the share offering £3,916 million. Choosing March 1985 as the reference point, we have calculated the net sale price in present value terms as £3,588 million for 51 percent of the enterprise (3,059 million shares).[11]

The following points are important in arriving at this figure:

- Payment for the shares was to be made in three installments: 50 pence per share at the time of application in November 1984, 40 pence payable in June 1985, and the remaining 40 pence payable in April 1986.
- Employees of the enterprise were offered 54 shares each free. A total of 12 million shares were distributed under this offer.[12]
- Employees were further offered two shares free for every share they bought, up to a maximum of 154 free shares. Another 27.6 million shares were distributed free under this offer.
- Employees were offered a 13-pence (10 percent) discount on any additional shares they bought up to a maximum of 1,600 shares. The reduction was to be applied to the final payment due in April 1986, which would accordingly be only 27 pence. Under this offer, 84 million shares were sold at the discounted price.
- As an incentive to buyers to hold their shares long-term (thereby minimizing downward pressure on the stock price), two schemes were offered. Buyers could choose between a share bonus scheme and a bill voucher scheme. Under the share bonus scheme, investors holding their shares for three years would receive one free share from the government's holdings for every ten shares they held, up to a maximum of 400 free shares per investor. Under this scheme, 47 million shares were distributed free by the government in December 1987. These were in addition to the 3,012 million shares in the public offering and caused a reduction in the government's holding from 2,988 million shares to 2,941 million. Under the bill voucher scheme, investors who held their shares for certain specified periods received vouchers worth £18 each that could be used toward their telephone bills. About 1.1 million vouchers were issued, mostly in 1985. These vouchers amounted to a cash payment from the government to the investing public totaling about £21 million.

Thus, of 3,059 million shares sold (3,012 million shares in the initial offering and 47 million pursuant to the bonus share scheme):

- 39.6 million were distributed free in November 1984.
- 84 million were sold at a 10 percent discount.

- 2,888.4 million were sold at full price.
- 47 million were distributed free in November 1987.

Aggregating the various receipts, we find the government received £3,842 million net. Subtracting the transactions costs yields £3,693 million net. These nominal receipts took place over a period of three years. Discounting at a nominal rate of 12 percent yields a net present value of receipts in March 1985 of £3,588 million.

In the five years prior to divestiture, the only flows of funds occurring between BT and the treasury were interest on loans held by the Secretary of State (roughly £300 million annually), the occasional repayment of part of the principal, and value added tax. The company was paying no corporate income tax, nor was it paying any dividends. Leaving aside the value added tax (which has a very stable trend; see table 4-3), the net annual flow to the treasury was on the order of £450 million (table 4-3 and figure 4-8).

After divestiture there were two dramatic changes.[13] The first is that BT started paying sizable amounts of corporate income tax (in the range of £750 million to £850 million). This change is due at least in part to a change in the tax law in 1984 that reduced the deductibility of depreciation as an expense, and in part due to the increased profitability of the company. To what extent the jump in tax payments is attributable to divestiture is therefore not entirely clear. The second dramatic change is

Table 4-3. Fiscal Flows, British Telecom, 1980–90
(millions of pounds sterling)

Flow	1980	1981	1982	1983	1984	1985	1986	1987	1988	1989	1990
Direct taxes	0	0	0	0	0	535	743	754	833	858	767
Government share of dividends	0	0	0	0	0	117	224	252	279	309	350
Preferred shares redeemed	0	0	0	0	0	0	0	250	250	250	0
Preferred dividends	0	0	0	0	0	41	63	57	38	2	0
Interest on government debt	295	285	298	302	290	337	336	328	321	318	307
Repayment of government loans	182	11	–107	112	154	44	61	53	23	85	92
Total	477	296	191	414	444	1,074	1,427	1,694	1,744	1,822	1,516
Value added tax	338	434	536	588	636	705	777	842	916	996	1,155

Source: Authors' calculations from BT data.

that the company paid steadily increasing dividends (of which the treasury receives just under half). In 1990 the treasury's share of dividends was £350 million. In short, the fiscal flow to the treasury went up dramatically after divestiture, by roughly £1 billion per year. This combined effect of taxes and dividends therefore is much larger on a present value basis than the sale price for the company.

The bottom line on fiscal flows may be summarized as follows:

- The government received £3,588 million (in March 1985 present value terms) in sale revenues.
- In addition, actual annual cash flows from BT to the treasury increased dramatically after divestiture.
- However, the bulk of the increase was due to an exogenous tax increase, and the remainder derived from changes in productivity and in pricing and investment decisions described earlier.

In sum, there is no evidence of change in conduct in the fiscal flows. Nor is there evidence (yet) that the government on balance came out ahead fiscally. To reach that conclusion one has to consider the flows

Figure 4-8.   Fiscal Flows, British Telecom, 1980–90

Billions of pounds sterling

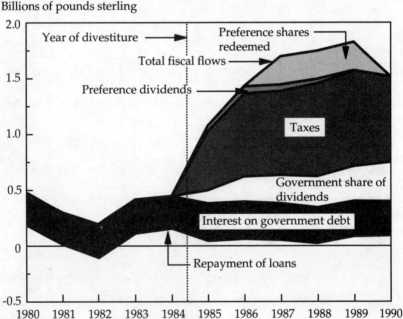

Note: A positive flow is from BT to the government.
Source: Authors' calculations from BT data.

forgone: the £540 million in debt forgiven and the dividends, interest, and taxes that would have accrued to the government in the absence of divestiture.

Effects on Consumer Welfare

How have consumers been affected by the divestiture of BT? The simplest way to answer this question is to look at relative prices. As we have already seen at the aggregate level, relative output prices rose in 1981 and 1982 and fell thereafter. Accordingly, it comes as no surprise that consumers were worse off (as measured by changes in consumer surplus)[14] in 1981 and 1982 and better off in each year thereafter (see the bottom line of table 4-4).

As usual, disaggregation yields a rather more complicated story, with some changes helping consumers even in 1981–82 and some hurting them even in later years (table 4-4). In particular, the relatively small positive aggregate effects in 1983 and 1985–87 are due to a mixture of positive and negative effects, with the latter slightly predominating, whereas for 1987–89 a moratorium by BT on (nominal) price changes in the RPI - X basket resulted in more uniform consumer benefits across services. To make sense of this diversity, consider figure 4-9, which divides BT's revenues into two categories: long distance services (domestic calls at distances greater than 56 kilometers, and all international calls, totaling approximately 40 percent of revenues),[15] and all other services (including especially rentals,[16] local calls, and miscellaneous outputs, totaling approximately 60 percent of revenues). The assumption in aggregating these two groups is that *within* them prices move almost in the same proportions.[17] As can be seen, *between* the categories prices behaved similarly in 1981 and 1982 but diverged thereafter. The change in consumer surplus in long distance services turned positive a year earlier (in 1983) and remained positive at a quite stable level thereafter. "Other services" shows a much more variable behavior, with consumer surplus actually declining in 1986 and 1987. In fact, for these other services the good years did not fully offset the bad years until 1990.

In sum, to the extent consumer surplus can be used as a measure of consumer welfare, consumers in the aggregate have done better every year since the announcement of BT's divestiture, but consumers of long distance services have done considerably better in all years, whereas consumers of local and other services have barely broken even over the whole period. This price restructuring in favor of long distance service in the wake of telecommunications reform will look familiar to observers of the breakup of American Telephone and Telegraph Co. (AT&T) in the United States. Whether or not the causation is similar will be discussed in the next section.

Table 4-4. *Changes in Consumer Surplus, British Telecom, 1980–90* (millions of pounds sterling)

Type of service	1980	1981	1982	1983	1984	1985	1986	1987	1988	1989	1990
Business rentals											
Real price	64.0	76.4	96.0	105.9	99.2	96.2	100.0	103.0	100.0	93.0	90.0
Change in price	n.a.	12.4	19.6	9.9	-6.7	-3.0	3.8	3.0	-3.0	-7.0	-3.0
Change in consumer surplus	n.a.	-43.6	-69.9	-36.0	25.4	12.2	-16.9	-14.0	15.0	36.7	16.8
Residential rentals											
Real price	47.3	52.8	57.6	59.5	56.5	55.0	57.1	58.9	57.4	53.4	51.6
Change in price	n.a.	5.4	4.8	1.9	-2.9	-1.6	2.2	1.8	-1.6	-4.0	-1.7
Change in consumer surplus	n.a.	-79.9	-72.9	-29.4	46.9	27.4	-39.9	33.6	30.4	82.3	37.9
Local calls											
Real price	6.1	6.7	7.3	7.9	7.6	7.6	7.6	7.9	7.6	7.0	6.6
Change in price	n.a.	0.5	0.6	0.7	-0.3	-0.1	0.1	0.3	-0.3	-0.5	-0.5
Change in consumer surplus	n.a.	-90.0	-104.6	-115.4	54.5	15.3	-12.6	4.1	82.0	138.0	126.4
Long distance calls less than 56 kilometers											
Real price	21.9	24.4	24.5	24.2	23.3	24.0	25.4	26.9	25.3	23.5	21.9
Change in price	n.a.	2.5	0.1	-0.3	-0.9	0.7	1.5	1.4	-1.5	-1.8	-1.7
Change in consumer surplus	n.a.	-28.6	-0.9	4.1	12.0	-9.8	-24.8	24.9	31.5	42.5	46.3
Long distance calls over 56 kilometers											
Real price	71.8	79.4	83.2	69.7	65.9	61.0	56.3	47.8	43.0	40.0	36.8
Change in price	n.a.	7.6	3.8	-13.5	-3.9	-4.9	-4.8	-8.4	-4.8	-3.0	-3.2
Change in consumer surplus	n.a.	-165.6	-86.1	319.8	99.8	135.1	148.3	89.8	185.6	131.2	155.3

International outgoing calls											
Real price	7.1	6.8	6.4	5.4	4.7	4.6	4.7	4.7	4.5	4.1	3.8
Change in price	n.a.	−0.4	−0.4	−1.0	−0.7	−0.1	0.1	−0.0	−0.2	−0.4	−0.3
Change in consumer surplus	n.a.	41.8	51.7	148.4	125.2	28.0	−22.7	7.0	47.8	122.6	121.4
International incoming calls											
Real price	2.2	2.0	2.7	3.3	3.0	2.8	2.4	2.2	1.9	1.5	1.5
Change in price	n.a.	−0.2	0.7	0.6	−0.3	−0.1	−0.4	0.2	−0.3	−0.3	−0.0
Change in consumer surplus	n.a.	23.9	−101.2	−100.2	61.6	27.1	101.3	1.5	95.9	108.9	8.4
Apparatus											
Real price	9.9	11.3	12.8	13.3	12.9	12.9	13.4	13.8	13.7	13.2	13.0
Change in price	n.a.	1.3	1.5	0.5	−0.4	−0.0	0.5	0.4	−0.1	−0.5	−0.3
Change in consumer surplus	n.a.	−93.1	−123.5	−48.5	43.3	0.9	−52.1	36.6	5.4	41.1	21.4
Private circuits											
Real price	83.7	88.6	99.7	110.5	106.0	108.4	119.7	132.3	143.9	133.9	133.0
Change in price	n.a.	4.9	11.0	10.9	−4.5	2.4	11.2	12.6	11.7	−10.0	−0.9
Change in consumer surplus	n.a.	−12.7	−29.8	−29.7	14.7	−7.8	−38.8	−60.3	−57.0	60.1	5.4
Miscellaneous[a]											
Real price	98.9	104.7	107.8	106.5	106.0	107.5	107.7	107.4	107.2	106.2	104.0
Change in price	n.a.	5.8	3.1	−1.3	−0.5	1.5	0.2	−0.3	−0.3	−0.9	−2.2
Change in consumer surplus	n.a.	−16.0	−10.5	4.7	2.1	−6.3	−1.1	2.2	2.2	7.7	20.3
Total change in consumer surplus	n.a.	−463.8	−547.8	117.8	485.4	221.9	41.6	127.0	440.7	771.4	559.5

a. Includes telex, cellular records, yellow pages, etc.

Source: Authors' calculations from BT data.

Figure 4-9. Changes in Consumer Surplus, British Telecom, 1981–90

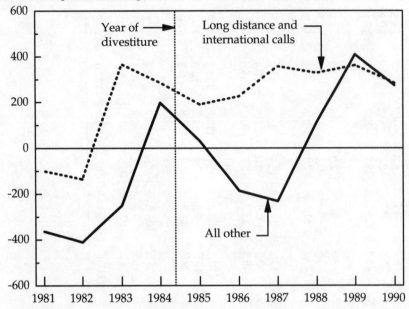

Millions of pounds sterling

Source: Authors' calculations from BT data.

Consumer surplus alone, however, does not tell the whole story. The most important consumer concern, besides price, is quality of service. Quality has many dimensions, not all of which are quantifiable. There can be no doubt that, because of technical improvements, telephone calls have become clearer in recent years, calling connections have become faster, and many new services have been added on. However, the most essential and quantifiable aspect of quality continues to be availability of service. Availability is impaired when a call does not get through, when a line or a telephone needs repair, when there are no functioning public pay phones around, or when a customer cannot subscribe to the service at all. The last of these appears to be the most important in terms of variation over time and in some sense is the most important aspect of quality. We therefore concentrate on this aspect of BT's service quality.[18]

Table 4-5 provides the relevant data. The first data column shows the number of customers waiting for a telephone connection at the end of BT's fiscal year (the backlog),[19] and the second the average waiting time. From these two series of numbers it appears that this dimension of quality was at its worst in 1980, improved steadily to 1984, and then suffered a decline to 1987, followed by a recovery that has once again brought BT close to the best levels of 1984. This picture agrees with the popular perception that quality suffered a decline for several years following divestiture.

Whether this view of company performance is entirely appropriate can be questioned. In particular, the backlog and average waiting time do not make any adjustment for the level of demand. The "peak performance" of the mid-1980s is at least partially explained by the fact that demand was relatively low in that period. By the same token, the very large backlog in 1980 was due at least in part to very heavy demand in the period 1978–80. To try to quantify this idea, table 4-5 also lists the number of new connections or installations made each year, as well as the sum of the backlog and new connections, which we label "demand." The demand column thus reports the total number of installations that could have been made in that year had connections been provided instantaneously. We see that, at its trough in 1983, demand was half the level of 1989. The last column of the table calculates the proportion of demand that was actually met. This shows the same basic trend as our earlier crude quality measure: improvement from 1980 to 1984, some deterioration to 1987, followed by recovery to 1989; however, the adjustment for the level of demand makes the swings less dramatic and indicates that performance in 1989 actually surpassed its previous peak in 1984.

In sum, there is some parallel between our relatively crude quality measures and consumer surplus movements for local services. We do find some deterioration in quality in the early years after divestiture, followed by improvements that have offset the bad years.

Table 4-5.   Demand and Waiting Time for New Connections, British Telecom, 1980–89

Year	Backlog (thousands of connections)	Average waiting time (days)	New connections (thousands)	Demand (thousands)	Proportion satisfied (percentages)
1980	550	71	1,231	1,781	69.12
1981	342	51	821	1,163	70.59
1982	185	28	553	738	74.93
1983	153	21	459	612	75.00
1984	90	12	626	716	87.43
1985	140	18	692	832	83.17
1986	200	26	733	933	78.56
1987	220	29	647	867	74.63
1988	210	26	949	1,159	81.88
1989	125	15	1,089	1,214	89.70

Source: Authors' calculations from BT data.

Summary

Our search for quantifiable changes associated with divestiture yields four primary conclusions:

- **Quantity effects.** Global measures of real quantitative or productivity effects (i.e., real quasi rents per unit of capital and TFP) show a distinct turning point from decline to improvement after 1982. However, the origins of this discontinuity were localized, being largely due to a sharp and continuous increase in output per worker.[20]
- **Price effects.** In 1981 and 1982, improvements in nominal quasi rents were overwhelmingly due to favorable relative price movements. Thereafter, price effects were either negative or small and positive. Once again, this global change can be traced to a single primary source, namely, the level *and* structure of output prices.
- **Investment effects.** Real gross fixed capital formation was stagnant through 1984 and then took off, suggesting a release in an investment constraint.

In short, the quantitative evidence suggests only three clear and significant behavioral changes associated with divestiture, namely, in output pricing, labor productivity, and fixed capital formation. Although these changes are important, so also is the complementary proposition:

- **Noneffects.** For most primary variables, the story is one of continuity before and after divestiture. That is, most things either did not change significantly or changed as a result of factors clearly exogenous to the divestiture exercise.

If these results are accepted, then we have simplified our task considerably. In the difficult task of searching for counterfactuals, we need only worry about three variables. Furthermore, while we must still project all variables (under both factual and counterfactual scenarios), our results will not be very sensitive to projections that apply to both sides equally.

Why Did It Happen?

The causes of two of the correlations to be explained—pricing and the investment constraint—are readily traceable to government policy decisions, so that we need "only" specify what policies would have been pursued had divestiture not gone through. There being no purely objective way of answering such a question, we attempt to tell a reasonable counterfactual story and then rely on sensitivity analysis to establish its robustness. In explaining the 1982 discontinuity in productivity, in contrast, we have to ascertain causation as well as quantify it.

In the remainder of this section we deal with the three discontinuities in turn. Although we assume that nothing else changes independently, everything changes dependently: price changes result in changes in output, intermediate input levels, profits, retained earnings, borrowing, interest payments, and so on. Chapter 2 specified the assumed technical relationships governing these dependent reactions and thus completes our description of the counterfactual.

Investment Effects

Investment is the simplest part of our counterfactual story. The change here was due to BT being released from constraints imposed by the PSBR during a period of fiscal stringency. In the absence of divestiture, the constraint would eventually have been relaxed in any event, as the fiscal situation improved and deteriorating service led to the exercise of political voice. An analysis of borrowing behavior at other U.K. public enterprises that were not divested (notably the electric power sector and British Rail) leads us to assume, in our base counterfactual, that the constraint would have been relaxed two years later than it actually was.

We have discussed in some detail the impact of the PSBR and the associated EFLs on BT's investment program. The budgetary crunch in the mid-1970s led to the imposition of limits on the amount public corporations could borrow. BT turned from heavy borrowings in the period 1970–77 to a situation where it was borrowing less than it was repaying on earlier loans (see figure 4-1). This was at a time when BT's investment needs were growing more critical, as its capital stock was severely antiquated and in need of modernization.

The pressure to modernize had grown so great that in 1981 the government agreed in principle to permit BT to issue performance-related bonds—the so-called Buzby bonds—and in 1982 it allowed BT to raise funds by issuing a telecommunications bond in return for keeping price increases below the rate of inflation. Thus it is possible that the EFL constraint would gradually have diminished. We observe, however, that BT did not vigorously seize this opportunity to embark on its modernization program. It could be argued that, because divestiture was also announced in 1982, management was distracted by this major restructuring, and that the investment program might have been initiated otherwise. However, we do not see any evidence that the kind of investment program actually undertaken by the newly private BT from 1985 on would in fact have occurred under continued government ownership.

In short, there is persuasive evidence that divestiture led to an effective relaxation in the investment constraint. Quantification is a bit more difficult, involving three separate issues: first, how long would the investment constraint have persisted? second, how quickly and completely would investment have recovered? and third, how would other variables have responded to differences in fixed capital formation? We consider these in turn.

Several facts are germane to the persistence question. First, the U.K. fiscal deficit turned to a surplus in 1987–88. Second, investment at other U.K. public enterprises, such as those in the electric power sector, began to recover in 1989. Third, in our counterfactual run, BT is able to pay dividends to the treasury from 1985 onward. These amounts could have been invested instead. Fourth, BT spent £80 million on the acquisition of Mitel in 1986–87, which it most likely would not have done under continued public operation. Accordingly, we assumed an initial two-year lag, with fixed capital formation unchanged at real 1985 levels through 1987. However, this created substantial output constraints, which we hypothesize would have led to sufficient public outcry that the constraint would have been released. Accordingly, we impose a more modest investment counterfactual at approximately 50 percent of the difference between the 1985 level and the actual private levels achieved in 1986.

The next issue is, How long would the adjustment process have taken? Would a hypothesized public BT have immediately made a huge investment and caught up with the actual divested BT? Or would it have adjusted over several years? Or would it have maintained the previous level of investment and never caught up? We assume that, once the constraint was released, BT would eventually have made the investments necessary not to let supply fall further behind demand. This means that only part of the loss associated with the constraint persists beyond 1986 and 1987. We believe this is a fairly conservative estimate: in fact, under continued government ownership investment might well have lagged considerably more.

The final question is whether other variables would have been affected. For example, if capital investment is labor saving, then keeping the investment constraint in place would have resulted in higher labor costs in 1986 and 1987. However, the trend in labor productivity does not show any clear impact of the investment constraint, so we eschew any such effect in our base run.

Price Effects

In 1985 the *RPI* - X pricing formula was imposed on BT. This leads us to pose three counterfactual questions:

- Would the *RPI* - X formula have been imposed in the absence of divestiture, or would it have been business as usual?

- If the formula had not been imposed, how would the *level* of prices have differed from that under divestiture?
- For a given level of prices, would the *structure* of prices have differed because of differing incentives and realms of discretion?

The answer to the first question is easy. No other U.K. public enterprise has thus far had price cap regulation imposed on it. For the U.K. electricity generation and distribution industries, similar reforms were adopted only in conjunction with divestiture plans in 1990. We conclude that the RPI - X formula would not have been adopted in the absence of divestiture. Nor (and this is of relevance to the "realm of discretion" issue raised below) would OFTEL have been created.

Before 1985, prices for all of BT's outputs were constrained either by market forces or by political considerations. BT had financial targets but no official rate-of-return bands that would have triggered automatic price increases if targets were exceeded, or decreases if there were revenue shortfalls. However, prices were generally increased after BT had achieved low rates of return for some time. Between 1960 and 1984 such changes occurred about ten to fifteen times for most of the services that are currently under price caps. The price changes were generally clustered in particular years, notably 1967–68, 1972–73, 1975, and 1980–81. This indicates that price changes were generally made when achieved rates of return were getting substantially out of line with target returns. In addition, adjustments often did not succeed all the way, so that repeated price changes occurred within a year. Divestiture in connection with the RPI - X price regulation seems to have made price changes much more regular.

Further, the X in the RPI - X formula is likely to change every three to five years. These changes will at least in part be influenced by any difference between BT's actual rate of return and the cost of capital. The main difference between RPI - X regulation and rate-of-return regulation, then, is that the former allows for a longer regulatory lag. With the RPI adjustment, the regulated firm can for some time cope with input price inflation. With the X adjustment, consumers can stay happy even if nominal prices increase.[21]

We conclude that the counterfactual story is one of less frequent price changes, which, for a given cost structure, would have been close over time to the RPI - X average. However, the less frequent price changes impose an economic loss, because consumers would have been equating marginal benefits to prices that were too high in some periods and too low in others.

As explained below, it is our view that BT's price structure has moved in the direction of more efficient (and profit-maximizing) price ratios. Prices of service elements where demand elasticity is low (such as rentals and local calls) have been raised relative to service elements where the demand elasticity is higher (such as long distance calls).

How does BT's pricing compare with telephone rates charged abroad? A comparison with the United States for 1989 yields the following picture. In the United States, quarterly rental charges are about the same as installation charges, whereas BT's installation charges are about four times as high as its quarterly rental charges. In the United States, local call rates are very low compared with long distance rates. Within long distance rates, distance-related rate increases are very low. For BT, the difference between local and long distance rates is much less pronounced than in the United States, whereas within long distance the difference between shorter and longer distances is greater. Differences due to peak-load pricing are more pronounced for BT than in the United States. The two last effects are probably due in part to the distortionary local access charges in the United States and in part to excess capacity in the U.S. trunk networks. In total, call charges for BT are probably slightly lower relative to fixed charges than for the United States. Overall, one may conjecture that BT's price structure is currently more efficient than the U.S. price structure.[22]

Other than for the United States we have little information about actual foreign rate structures as opposed to changes in rate structures. However, with the possible exception of Greece, the United Kingdom (that is, BT) was the only one of the twelve European Community countries that made a major move toward a more efficient telephone price structure during the 1980–87 period. BT increased local call rates and installation charges, kept monthly rentals and calls of intermediate length about constant, and substantially reduced long distance and international rates. Almost all other countries underwent the opposite structural change with respect to installation charges and rental rates (Mansell 1990), increasing the latter relative to the former. BT's direction of change from local to long distance rates was followed by five countries, whereas five other countries actually increased long distance relative to local rates.

To what extent is BT's change in rate structure attributable to divestiture? It has been suggested to us in personal communication and by the literature (e.g., various OFTEL publications and Vickers and Yarrow 1988) that under continued public ownership there would probably have been much less of a tendency to increase local and reduce long distance and international rates. Against this view one could argue that BT might well have restructured its telephone tariffs under continued public ownership in a manner similar to that under divestiture. The basis for this conjecture lies in BT's pricing history from 1960 to 1980 and thereafter. During the 1960–80 period BT's residential connection charges increased by 450 percent, quarterly rental charges increased by 217 percent, local call rates by about 750 percent, and long distance call rates by about 330 percent. The last of these increases is probably exaggerated, because it is for operator-assisted long distance calls only. The numbers do, however, clearly indicate that BT did some restructuring of tariffs during the 1960–80 period and that this followed the same basic pattern as from 1980 to 1987. In particular, BT increased charges for local calls relative to long distance calls and relative to rental charges. In the early 1980s, before divestiture, BT continued this restructuring. This may have occurred in anticipation of emerging network competition that would probably have forced BT sooner or later to further reduce long distance rates relative to local rates.[23]

BT would probably have kept international rates about where they were at the end of our observation period. There are three reasons for this: competition from Mercury, international trends, and fairly low political priority for reducing rates on international calls. Because of political opposition to such steep increases, rental rates and prices for private circuits would probably not have been increased as much as they were.

Our pricing counterfactual therefore reflects the following assumptions:

- There are some outputs for which BT sets prices according to the market (apparatus and miscellaneous services) or in an unconstrained profit-maximizing fashion (international outgoing and incoming calls). For all these services we assume that actual and counterfactual prices coincide.
- Prices for private circuits actually increased dramatically in the 1984–89 period. The main reason is that they were previously subsidized but thereafter could be priced freely. Here we assume that under continued public operation BT would have attempted to increase prices, but that consumer lobbies would have reduced the actual increases to 7 percent per year.
- All other prices fell under the original RPI - X formula. For the counterfactual we assume instead that the level of these prices would have been adjusted downward if BT's overall rate of return on fixed assets (at book value) exceeded 20 percent. These prices would have been adjusted upward if BT's overall rate of return on fixed assets fell below 16 percent. In the counterfactual run the first price increase was triggered in 1987 and was immediately followed by a price decrease, and then steady prices for a five-year period.
- Under the counterfactual we assume no price restructuring among the basic service categories. There are two reasons for this. First, BT's actual price restructuring resulted in consumer outrage, which is easier for a divested enterprise to deal with than for the government as the owner of a public enterprise. Second, other European countries were not doing this kind of restructuring at that time. Hence, there was no foreign example to point to.

- Constraints on pricing accompanied by constraints on capital formation are likely to lead to excess demand. We assume that excess demand occurred, in particular during 1986–87 but to some extent also thereafter. This was most pronounced for telephone line rentals and for the various calling categories, where we would predict congestion to continue to some extent.
- Under the counterfactual we expect that BT's market share would have declined by more than in the actual case for apparatus, private circuits, and miscellaneous services. These are the areas where BT as a public enterprise would have had a distinct disadvantage.[24]

Quantity Effects

In the previous two subsections the cause of the kink was clear and we had only to quantify the counterfactual. In the present case, however, the causation is in question. Recall from figure 4-6 that TFP declined in 1981 and 1982 but thereafter improved in every year, albeit at a decreasing rate. Was this change endogenous, due to the announcement of divestiture freeing and/or motivating employees to work more efficiently, or was it exogenous, due to economic recovery returning the firm to a long-run steady-state rate of technological progress? To answer this question, we examine time-series and cross-section data in turn.

EVIDENCE FROM BT'S HISTORY. The question is whether 1982–83 marked a major turning point or the end of a little bump. Part of the answer obviously resides in what went on before. Unfortunately, a time series linking the 1970s and the 1980s is difficult to construct because of data incompatibilities. Before BT's separation from the Post Office in 1980, the two institutions' accounts were commingled, and therefore it is not possible to put together a complete and reliable time series. Getting a handle on intermediate inputs and capital stock is particularly difficult, on outputs and labor less so. Accordingly, we proceed from consideration of highly imperfect measures of the right thing (TFP) to only moderately imperfect measures of the wrong thing (labor productivity).

Several other studies of TFP at BT have been performed, but none overlaps the 1970s and 1980s. The best available study prior to the 1980s is that of Foreman-Peck and Manning (quoted in Kwoka 1990), whose 1965–80 time series is linked to ours and displayed with the GDP growth rate in figure 4-10.[25] To the extent this linkage is justifiable, note the following:[26]

- TFP growth rates are, on average, not wildly dissimilar in the two periods: 1.65 percent from 1965 through 1980 (Foreman-Peck and Manning 1986) versus 2.05 percent from 1981 through 1990 (our estimate).

Figure 4-10. Year-to-Year Changes in Overall Productivity, British Telecom, and Gross Domestic Product, United Kingdom, 1965–89

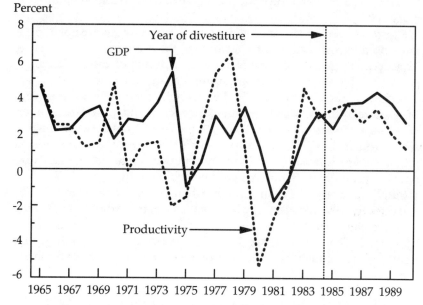

Source: Authors' calculations from BT data and U.K. Annual Abstracts of Statistics, various years.

- During the earlier period there appears to have been an increase in the variance around a clearly declining trend, whereas in the latter period the variance decreased around a stable or slightly declining trend.
- However, both the variance and the trend in TFP growth rates in both periods correlate highly with the GDP growth rate, with the former leading the latter by one period and with greater variance.[27]

Viewed in this light, the 1982 turning point no longer looks like a structural response to institutional change but appears to be part of normal historical variation. One obvious hypothesis is that BT appears to lose more than proportionally going into the recession and gain more than proportionally coming out.

To generate a more consistent and longer time series of performance, we constructed three different indices of labor productivity, each using the same measure of labor input[28] but different measures of output. Our own measure of real output per worker uses the quantity index of output from our study but is available only for 1980–90. The "calls per worker" measure uses the total number of inland calls as the measure of output. Since long distance calls, international calls, and other services have been growing faster than inland calls, inland calls tend to grow more slowly than real output. Accordingly, we include a comprehensive indicator, which we call "deflated revenue per worker," using deflated nominal BT revenue.[29]

Figure 4-11 shows that the levels of the three measures are not dissimilar, and all grow significantly faster than the economy as a whole. As expected, things are somewhat messier in terms of rates of change, shown in figure 4-12. There are a number of anomalies in the data, especially in the earlier years. In the first half of the 1970s we find very little correlation between output per worker and calls per worker, whereas in the second half of the 1970s the correlation between the two series is quite strong. Under both series it is hard to escape the conclusion that the changes in labor productivity experienced during the 1980s are not very different from the changes that occurred during the 1970s. Nor is the post-1982 level of changes higher than that experienced in 1976–78, nor does the 1983 recovery appear to have been more dramatic than the 1976 recovery. Thus, the major result of the previous section is clearly reinforced. That is, the sharp improvement in the early 1980s at first glance appears much more like a recovery from recession than a change

Figure 4-11. Trends in Labor Productivity, British Telecom, and Gross Domestic Product, United Kingdom, 1970–90

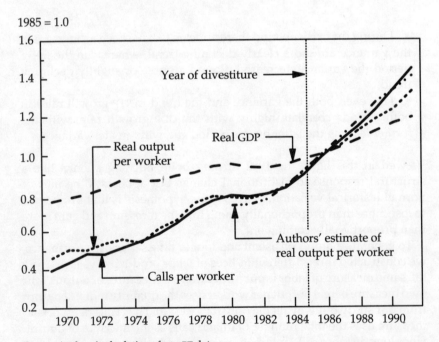

1985 = 1.0

Source: Authors' calculations from BT data.

Figure 4-12. Year-to-Year Changes in Labor Productivity, British Telecom, and Gross Domestic Product, United Kingdom, 1971–89

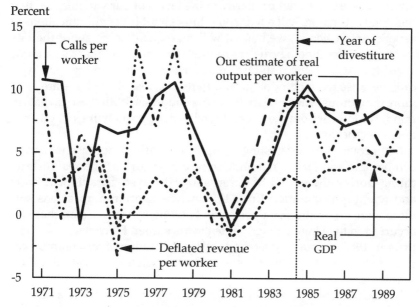

Source: Authors' calculations from BT data and U.K. Annual Abstracts of Statistics, various years.

in structure associated with divestiture. However, the link between real GDP and BT's labor productivity changes over the whole period is statistically very weak. In particular, contrary to our expectations, the change in BT's number of calls has been quite unrelated to GDP growth ratios. Examination of the international experience will shed additional light on this relationship.

EVIDENCE FROM ABROAD. Even if performance were unchanged before and after divestiture, one could still argue that divestiture was successful if it avoided what otherwise would have been a decline. This would be the case, for example, if opportunities for productivity improvement have dwindled over time, as technological change has slowed or as some stock of potential improvements has been exhausted. One way to examine this hypothesis is to look at BT's productivity performance from a comparative cross-company or cross-country perspective.

Alas, no very good comparator is available: there is nothing else in the United Kingdom of comparable size (Mercury had less than 2 percent of BT's sales in 1989), and cross-country comparisons are fraught with incompatibilities. We will nevertheless compare BT with AT&T and

Deutsche Bundespost (DBP), bearing in mind the many intervening economic, historical, and institutional differences. As usual in international comparisons of this sort, we hope that most of the country-specific differences are reflected primarily in the levels of our variables, so that their rates of change will tell us something about telecommunications in general. In particular, we hope it will reveal something about the rate and nature of technological progress and the impact of macroeconomic variables. At best, the resulting comparisons must be interpreted with care, because the methodological differences described above are even more dangerous when one looks across countries. With these caveats in mind, we look at both partial and total factor productivities in international perspective.

DBP provides an interesting comparison with BT because its size is comparable[30] and it has not undergone any major institutional restructuring during the period of observation. It stayed a traditional posts and telegraph operation until 1989, when telecommunications services were separated from posts and banking services, a step that had occurred in the United Kingdom ten years earlier. However, as with BT prior to 1980, accounting methods allow separation of telecommunications from postal operations, subject to the usual joint cost allocation problems.

In contrast, AT&T is interesting because it underwent a drastic institutional change in 1984. Previously a unified private regulated company, it was split up into eight separate companies. AT&T also differs from BT in having been vertically integrated into the manufacturing of telephone equipment and in having faced competition at an earlier stage. The pre-1984 AT&T was many times as large as BT, with four times the number of employees and ten times the assets by value. After 1984 AT&T consisted of the former equipment manufacturing arm, long distance telecommunications services, and Bell Laboratories. This is still a larger and rather different animal than BT. In addition, there are seven regional Bell operating companies, each of which is somewhat smaller but still quite comparable to BT in size and type of operations. Our data cover the combined total, equivalent to the old AT&T.

Figure 4-13 displays TFP changes for BT, AT&T, and DBP from 1965 onward.[31] An immediate impression is that volatility in productivity changes is not a function of institutional change. BT's volatility was already apparent from our prior exposition, but table 4-6 shows that the U.S. company's volatility has been nearly as pronounced, and DBP's even greater. Crandall (1989) reports a deterioration of U.S. productivity in 1984–85 as a result of AT&T's divestiture. We suspect that part of this trough is a measurement artifact due to nearly US$5 billion in write-offs of telephone equipment (telephones) by AT&T. Since 1983 DBP appears to have experienced somewhat lower TFP increases than BT, but the five years reported after 1982 are too few to make much out of this observation.

Figure 4-13.   Year-to-Year Changes in Total Factor Productivity, AT&T, British Telecom, and Deutsche Bundespost, 1965–89

Percent

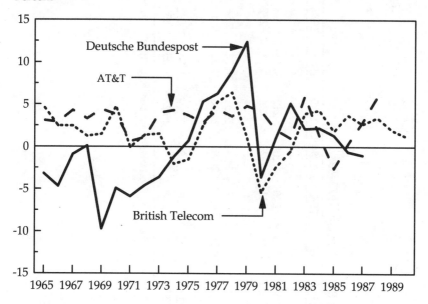

Source: Authors' calculations from BT data; Christensen (1981), Crandall (1989), and Elixmann (1989).

Interestingly, DBP's productivity shows the same trough as BT's around 1980. However, this does not correspond to German recession or even to world recession, and the AT&T series is also not obviously correlated with U.S. macroeconomic activity. The hypothesis of BT productivity correlating with macroeconomic activity is therefore weakened. Further, BT output changes do not correlate with changes in U.K. GDP.

In short, the international data suggest a high degree of volatility in TFP, a lack of correlation with macroeconomic activity, an apparent absence of any strong nonstationary trend, and a virtual coincidence of the averages in TFP changes across these three countries over a period of more than twenty years. This would further confirm the hypothesis that the productivity changes observed for BT as a result of divestiture are insignificant, or at least not demonstrable from the quantitative record. In addition, long-run TFP changes in this industry across countries are likely to be caused by the same factors. We conjecture that these factors relate to technical change and induced changes in consumer demands. However, from changes in TFP that follow equal stationary trends we cannot infer TFP levels. BT may have higher or lower TFP levels than the others to begin with.

Table 4-6. Employment and Output, Deutsche Bundespost and British Telecom, 1979–89

Quantity	1979	1980	1981	1982	1983	1984	1985	1986	1987	1988	1989
Number of employees (thousands)											
Deutsche Bundespost	190	195	200	204	205	208	212	214	216	216	216
British Telecom	246	251	252	246	241	235	236	234	237	244	246
Number of lines (millions)											
Deutsche Bundespost	19.23	20.85	22.09	23.03	23.86	24.92	25.91	26.72	27.56	28.41	29.40
British Telecom	17.38	18.20	18.75	19.21	19.84	20.55	21.26	21.91	22.16	23.95	25.01
Number of inland calls (billions)											
Deutsche Bundespost	19.10	20.95	22.50	23.85	25.08	26.06	27.19	28.52	29.72	29.82	31.00
British Telecom	19.86	20.18	20.81	21.40	22.69	24.50	26.22	28.05	30.30	33.63	36.98

Note: Figures for Deutsche Bundespost are by calendar year; those for British Telecom are by fiscal year minus one (e.g., "1979" is April 15, 1979 to April 4, 1980).

Source: Deutsche Bundespost and BT data.

Although some cross-country comparisons of TFP levels are available (Foreman-Peck and Manning 1986), the comparability problems for inputs and outputs are formidable. Easier comparisons are possible in terms of simple input and output data. These allow us to derive some simple partial productivities.

Table 4-6 compares personnel in telecommunications services at DBP with BT's personnel for 1979–89. Although the personnel level at DBP remained below that at BT in all years, the difference shrank over time. If we relate personnel to output variables, we see that the number of telephone lines supplied by DBP was about 20 percent higher on average, but the lead first expanded and then shrank. The total number of inland calls at DBP was higher than at BT until 1987, but BT built a lead of nearly 20 percent in 1988–90. Thus, based on numbers of calls, labor productivity at DBP appears to have been about 25 percent higher than at BT in 1980, but this difference shrank to zero by 1989. As usual, partial productivities are only part of the story. From the investment patterns over the last fifteen years it appears that BT has been using less (or less costly) capital inputs than DBP. Capital inputs are hard to measure and difficult to compare across countries.[32] It may well be that DBP had to pay higher prices for the same capital equipment. This is quite likely to hold for standard equipment and for labor-intensive construction work.[33] At the same time the larger number of lines supplied by DBP is a sign of genuinely higher capital intensity than at BT. Overall, the labor productivity trends for 1980–89, showing higher increases after 1982 for BT than for DBP, are in line with the TFP trends.

Summary

BT shows a clear improvement in productivity at the time of the announcement of divestiture. However, time-series and international comparisons of telecommunications productivity performance both cast strong doubt on the hypothesis that this improvement was due to institutional change. We conclude that there is no convincing quantitative evidence that BT productivity has been enhanced by divestiture through 1990 (improvements since 1990 will be discussed below). Accordingly, in our base counterfactual run we assume no behavioral change in technical coefficients.

Given the primary changes noted above, most of the derivative changes follow from basic economic and accounting identities. One other change worth noting is that we assume BT would not have acquired Mitel under continued government ownership. As a result, BT's miscellaneous outputs (and their export share) are larger under the actual than under the counterfactual scenario. Our bottom-line evaluation is hardly affected by this.[34]

What Will Happen?

The telecommunications industry is undergoing such massive changes in technology and market organization that the only certainty about the future is that dramatic changes will occur, dooming to failure any attempt at accurate prediction. In our projections, therefore, we have not attempted to forecast how markets or technologies are going to change. Rather, we have taken the existing frameworks used to analyze the data period 1980–90 and have made assumptions about growth rates and parameter values that seem reasonable. In other words, we have prepared our projections *as if* no dramatic changes were going to take place, on the theory that how the divested enterprise and the undivested enterprise might react differently to such changes is impossible to predict.

Our approach is therefore as follows. For each output category, we have made assumptions about how demand will grow over time. To capture the effect of divestiture, we have assumed that demand growth is outside the control of BT. However, BT's response may be quite different under private than under public ownership (for example, because of different pricing strategies). Therefore, the prices and quantities supplied may be different. These projections yield estimates of revenues for the actual (private ownership) and counterfactual (continued public ownership) cases. We also make assumptions about how unit costs will change over time, resulting in projections of costs for the two cases. We then summarize the resulting trend in quasi rents.[35]

Revenues

Besides assuming demand growth to be exogenous, we have assumed a constant 6 percent inflation rate in the projection period, so that nominal demand for each type of output grows by that factor also. The projection period starts in 1991 because our data input for actual data was terminated in 1990.

For real-demand growth we assume that traditional network services reach a steady-state growth rate by 1995, whereas new services, such as value added network services and cellular telephones, are assumed to grow at faster rates.

We assume that some differences between the public and private cases creep in with respect to market shares. We assume that, in all rental and calling categories, market shares remain unchanged.[36] However, for apparatus we assume that BT's market share declines at a 4 percent rate under private operation and at a 5.88 percent rate under public operation. These rates correspond to a reduction in BT's market share by 2015 to 22 percent under private operation and 15 percent under public operation. The difference is due to the assumed greater aggressiveness of the private enterprise.

Finally, we needed to make assumptions about the levels of capacity for the various outputs in the two cases. We assume essentially no capacity constraints in either case. However, we assume that the slight excess demand existing in 1991 will persist throughout the projection period. In relative terms this assumption carries less and less importance over time.

For our price projections we were initially constrained in the private case by the implications of the RPI - X price cap with X set at 4.5 percent. In 1991 (fiscal 1992), BT received a new price cap with X set at 6.25 percent, good until 1993 (fiscal 1994). The new cap now includes international telephone services, whose prices are initially reduced by 10 percent. As for the regulated network outputs, for 1991–95 we have applied a plausible version of X = 4.5 with a subsequent switch to X = 6.25. From 1996 onward we assume real rental prices remain unchanged, while real prices in the various calling categories decline at 3.5 percent per year.[37] We have made plausible assumptions for the other categories, with technological progress and competition pushing real prices down.

For the public case our projections are a hybrid of two mechanisms. In part, prices are assumed to adjust to meet the profitability targets, as for the period 1985–90. In part, prices also reflect competitive pressures, in which case they match the prices in the private case.

Costs

For both the private and the public cases we assume that nominal input prices will rise by 6 percent per year (in other words, zero real change). We assume that the loan rate, the opportunity cost of working capital, and the discount rate remain constant at 15 percent (9 percent in real terms).

The driving force behind input requirements is technological progress, which we believe to be primarily of the labor-saving and the capital-saving variety. We have assumed that per unit requirements of intermediates, inventories, and working capital remain unchanged throughout the period, for both cases. Changes have been assumed, however, for the capital and labor requirements. The incremental capital-output ratio is assumed to decline by 1 percent per year in both cases, reflecting continued technological progress in the telecommunications industry.

The change in labor productivity is a key assumption. In 1991 BT announced its intention to reduce its work force by 30,000 by 1994. That this reduction in work force did not come sooner is explained by the argument that it took management some time after divestiture to plan a reorganization. We assume this reduction in work force to be feasible without any adverse effects on output.[38] Further, we assume that no corresponding work force reduction would have taken place in the counterfactual case. This may be regarded as an extreme assumption, but it seems justified in light of the fact that BT management before divestiture had repeatedly attempted, without success, to reach agreements with the labor unions that would have introduced greater flexibility in labor allocation. After divestiture, however, management was able to reach such agreements quickly (see above).

Although the quantity of labor does not decline dramatically in the public case, we do implicitly assume some partial improvement in the labor efficiency parameter. We assume that labor productivity improves by 5.3 percent per year throughout the period in both cases. In the private case the impact of the work force reduction is to reduce labor costs per unit of output during the first three years by 11.4 percent, or roughly 4 percent per year. After 1993 the labor cost per unit then increases at a rate of 0.7 percent per year.

Summary

The revenue and cost projections come together in our projections of quasi rents. Annual quasi rents in the private case are projected to grow from £3.8 billion in 1990 to £21.2 billion in 2015, for an annual nominal growth rate of 7.1 percent. Quasi rents in the public case are projected to grow from £3.4 billion in 1990 to £18.3 billion in 2015, for an almost equal nominal growth rate of 7 percent per year.

Projections of all other variables also follow from the projections of basic prices and quantities. Thus, for example, the price and quantity projections for outputs give rise to projections of consumer surplus. The profit projections yield projections of direct taxes and dividend payments. Dividend payout rates have been assumed to maintain relatively stable debt-equity ratios. All of these derivative projections are discussed in the next section.

Finally, a word on robustness. Making projections is more art than science. Thus it might be thought that these estimates of future variables are not terribly reliable. Although this may hold for the raw variables, it is less important a reservation for the variables we are most concerned with, namely, the *differences* between revenues (consumer surplus, etc.) in the private case and in the counterfactual case. These differences will be much less sensitive to our specific assumptions, and we therefore place a correspondingly greater reliance on them.

What Is It Worth?

In the previous sections we observed that as a result of divestiture some variables went in one direction and others in the opposite. Here we net out these differences to determine the bottom line. Were the net benefits positive or negative, and how were they distributed? Our answers can be summarized in five propositions (table 4-7 and figure 4-14):

• Although not much changes as a result of divestiture, what does change is sufficient to make the world better off by about £10 billion and the United Kingdom better off by £9 billion (all figures are net present values in 1985 pounds sterling). This is less than 2 percent of the total discounted welfare generated by BT, but it is about two-thirds of BT's private value.
• Private buyers do well for themselves, paying £3,750 million (£1.19 per share) for stock worth about £7,470 million (£2.85 per share), for a net gain of £3,720 million. Out of these total gains, £1 billion goes to foreign shareholders, leaving £2,720 million for U.K. nationals.
• Government is less of a winner, coming out £2,250 million ahead.
• Consumers, on the other hand, are better off by £4,150 million.[39] Although this is a large number, it is only about 0.8 percent of the total discounted consumer surplus generated by BT's outputs.
• BT's erstwhile competitors lose from divestiture, although the amount is relatively small (£120 million) and not terribly robust.

Table 4-7. *Distribution of Welfare Gains and Losses from Divestiture, British Telecom*
(millions of pounds sterling)

Economic actor	Private operation	Public operation	Difference
Government			
Taxes	12,135	10,131	2,004
Net quasi rents	7,146	10,493	−3,348
Net sale proceeds (cash)	3,592	0	3,592
Total	22,872	20,625	2,247
Employees	0	0	0
Private domestic shareholders			
Diverse	2,722	0	2,722
Concentrated	0	0	0
Foreign shareholders	999	0	999
Competitors	963	1,083	−121
Subtotal	27,556	21,708	5,848
Consumers	511,589	507,438	4,151
Total	539,145	529,146	9,999

Source: Authors' calculations.

Figure 4-14.   Distribution of Welfare Gains and Losses from Divestiture, British Telecom

Billions of pounds sterling

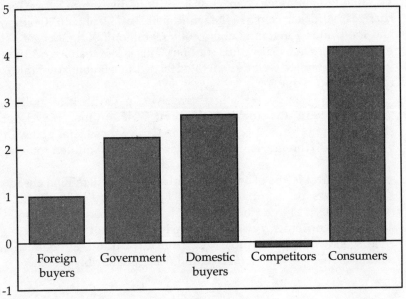

Source: Authors' calculations.

- In terms of intertemporal distribution of welfare effects, the actual data period (1985–90) comes out with a modest net gain (£705 million). The first five-year projection period (1991–96) shows a large positive balance of £2,855 million as the increase in labor efficiency kicks in. The final period shows the greatest effects in total (£6,595 million), despite discounting. However, since this period is three times as long as the previous one, the annual effect is less than half that for 1991–96.

In short, the BT case does not really illustrate what we have elsewhere termed the fundamental trade-off of divestiture in a noncompetitive market (Jones, Tandon, and Vogelsang 1990, pp. 74–75). That is, on the one hand, the divested firm operates with greater efficiency,[40] producing benefits for society. On the other hand, constrained by the RPI-X formula, it does not exploit market power to a greater extent. In the present case, the benefits outweigh the costs.

These bold assertions are of course subject to many qualifications, which we will enumerate in the balance of the chapter.

Change in Profit

The change in profit from the divestiture of BT may be summarized as follows:

	1985 present value (millions of pounds sterling)
Net change in welfare	9,999
Plus transaction costs	158
Gross change in welfare	10,157
Less change in consumer welfare	4,151
Change in producer welfare	6,006
Less change in competitors' profits	−121
Change in BT profits	6,127

This change in profits is distributed as follows:

	Private	Public	Total
Profits after tax	7,471	−3,348	
Plus taxes	0	2,004	
Plus/less sales price	−3,750	3,750	
Net profits	3,721	2,406	6,127
Percentage share	61	39	

Note the following major points:

• As a result of divestiture, profits in the telecommunications industry rise by about £6,000 million, but about £120 million of this comes at the expense of BT's competitors, creating a £6,120 profit increment for BT.
• If one looks at profits only, the government suffers a net loss of £1,344 million, while £7,470 million goes to the private buyers. Note that this only applies to the postsale flows.
• The sale price (£3,750 million), however, reverses the sign, with the government now getting a positive share (£2,406 million).

In short, the structure of the deal gave the private buyers the rights to 120 percent of the ensuing incremental cash flows. However, after paying the government £3,750 million for the right to this stream, they netted about 60 percent of the profit increment whereas the government got about 40 percent. The private buyers may have been overcompensated, but the government certainly did not do badly.

We noted above that BT's oligopolistic competitors suffered a small but significant loss from divestiture. How did this come about? In seven sectors the market was assumed to be either monopolistic or perfectly competitive, and in neither case could BT behavior alter the returns to other firms in the same market. However, BT operated in three oligopolistic markets: apparatus, private circuits, and miscellaneous outputs.[41] In such markets BT's behavior can affect competitors in two different ways. First, there is a market share effect: reduction in BT's market share can lead to a reduction in BT's quasi rents but (at the same market price) to an increase in quasi rents accruing to BT's competitors. The amount of the latter is affected by the difference in costs between BT and the expanding competitors. Second, there is a market price effect: BT's divestiture could raise the market price, reducing consumer surplus but at the same time increasing the quasi rents of BT's competitors (at given market shares).

For all three sectors the market share effect dominated. As a result of divestiture BT retains a higher market share than under continued public operation. Hence, oligopolistic quasi rents enjoyed by BT's competitors would have been higher in the counterfactual than in the actual case.

Change in Consumer Surplus

Consumers as a group, as we noted earlier, are the big winners from the divestiture of BT. In present value terms they are better off by about £4,150 million (in 1985 pounds sterling).

Although this potential improvement is attributable to more aggressive cost reduction by the divested BT, matters are not as simple as the Introductory Economics monopoly diagram would suggest. For one thing, many of BT's product prices are regulated by the *RPI* - X price cap. In fact, this type of regulation produces a differentiated result in terms of protecting consumers.

Almost all the consumer surplus change comes from three product categories: business rentals, residential rentals, and long distance calls greater than 56 kilometers.[42] But whereas consumer surplus *losses* from rental charges are very much higher in the private case, consumer surplus *increases* for the long distance category are also very much higher. Note that all these prices are within the *RPI* - X basket, and in that sense they are all regulated. But because BT is permitted, under the regulatory rules, to restructure prices within the basket, our estimate is that substantial restructuring has taken and will continue to take place. The rental category, characterized by very inelastic demand, suffers substantial price increases, whereas the long distance category (with greater elasticity and subject to competition) enjoys price decreases. On balance, we find that the effects on consumers of price decreases dominate the effects of price increases as BT moves to being a more profit-oriented firm.

If we believe that business users account for somewhat more than half of all long distance calls, so that somewhat more than half the consumer surplus derived from that category accrues to them, then we can conclude that business users as a group are affected less in a welfare sense by divestiture than are residential users. The reason is that the loss in consumer surplus for residential rentals is very much greater than the loss from business rentals, whereas the gains from lower long distance prices are divided more in favor of business users. Thus, the average residential consumer is quite possibly a net loser from divestiture. In this light, the decision by the Thatcher government to widen share ownership to all sections of society could be seen as a mechanism to compensate consumers and encourage their acquiescence in the divestiture and the price changes that resulted.

Change in Labor Rents

We have no hard quantitative evidence that rents to labor (if any existed) changed with BT's divestiture. There are three potential sources of changes in labor rents. First, BT could have hired (or laid off) more employees than otherwise, and there is a rent differential between working for BT and not. Second, BT could have paid its workers more (or less) for the same amount of effort after divestiture than it otherwise would have. Third, BT employees could have received special deals in BT shares. There is some quantitative evidence on all three of these sources.

First, in 1990 BT started to reduce its work force substantially, in particular by laying off managers. Severance pay, however, made all this redundancy voluntary, so that we do not see any measurable loss in labor rents here. Second, there has been a slight increase in pay per BT employee relative to U.K. wage and salary trends in general. The difference, however, is too small relative to plausible increases in the average qualification of BT workers to allow the conclusion that rents to labor increased.

Third, BT employees received £56 million in share discounts and free shares. In addition, employees gained £1.66 per share on 84 million discounted shares purchased. Employees also bought an undocumented number of undiscounted shares. Thus, employees bought substantially more than five times as many shares as did the average U.K. citizen. Because it is unclear how many of these they would have purchased had they not been employees, we can only conjecture that BT employees gained £150 million to £200 million by becoming BT shareholders.

Sensitivity Analysis

Two general principles underlie our sensitivity results. The bad news is that our welfare measures are rather small residuals of rather large numbers. For example, welfare changes by about £10 billion on sales whose 1985 net present value totals nearly £150 billion. Relatively small differences in the big primary numbers can result in quite large differences in the small residuals. Conditions such as this tend to provoke sensitivity avoidance behavior.

The good news is that for our most important results we are differencing V_{sp} against V_{sg} , and that most changes that have a big effect on one also have a big effect on the other and so net out. Accordingly there are two distinct sets of sensitivity variables: those that have a symmetrical effect on the actual and the counterfactual, and those that have an asymmetric effect. In the important latter group are our three base counterfactual assumptions. In the unimportant former group are practically all the other variables.

How much of the welfare change is due to each of the three principal behavioral changes? Our answer to this question can be summarized as follows:

- The change in the pricing regime with the private exploitation of market power has almost no net effect on consumer welfare. In contrast, there is a large transfer to the government due to additional taxes and a smaller loss of quasi rents. This says that RPI - X pricing improves efficiency over cost-plus pricing.
- The investment constraint, in marked contrast, is considerably less important. Consumers are hardly better off by the expanded output, but the public benefits through the network externality.
- Enhanced labor productivity has a substantial positive welfare effect by itself (£6,885 million) because of the reduced costs.
- In addition, enhanced labor productivity is responsible for a substantial cross-product term with pricing, which primarily benefits consumers (£3,570 million). That is, lower labor costs, with some prices being cost sensitive, yield lower prices, which benefit consumers. Adding the effect of enhanced labor productivity to the effect of pricing (or vice versa) reduces the net incremental effect of each of these by more than 50 percent.
- Interacting investment constraints with pricing also primarily benefits consumers but has a small incremental effect over pricing alone.
- The investment constraint has almost no additional net effect when added to the combined effect of labor productivity and pricing.

As discussed in an earlier section, telephone line rentals may be viewed as services in their own right or as inputs to calls, which then are viewed as the only services desired by consumers. Under the first view (which in practice is followed by BT and OFTEL), one can argue that there is a separate consumer surplus derived from installing and renting a line and that this consumer surplus is in addition to the consumer surplus from making calls. Under the second view, the fee for line installation and the rental fee are simply the fixed part of a two-part (or nonlinear) pricing scheme for telephone calls. Calculating and adding up consumer surpluses for rentals and calls then involves double counting. Instead, one should either count only the consumer surplus for rentals (which takes into account the expected costs and benefits of calling) or the consumer surplus for calling minus the rental charges.

Of course, in a perfect quantitative analysis both views have to yield the same result. The first view is correct as long as the cross-elasticities between rentals and calls are accounted for. The second view is correct if option demand and benefits from incoming calls are accounted for.

Since we have highly incomplete information about demands, we have tried to make calculations incorporating both views. In our base case we totally ignore the consumer surplus from rentals but deduct rental charges from the total consumer surplus for calls. We also add the 50 percent externality to the consumer surplus for calls (including a 0.5 weight for incoming international calls). In a second run we treat demands for calls and demands for rentals as separate commodities with additive consumer surplus and add the network externality of 50 percent of consumer surplus for rentals. This has two major effects. First, the size of consumer surplus is increased by about 90 percent and the externality by about 150 percent under both the actual and the counterfactual. Second, the difference (the discounted welfare gain from divestiture) is reduced by nearly £3,000 million. The net consumer surplus change remains positive, however. The main reason for the difference is that, in the base case, price increases on rentals and connection charges under divestiture only count with their expenditure and not with an additional loss of Harberger triangles.

We have also analyzed the sensitivity of our results to other parameters, with the following notable results:

- For the government revenue multiplier, an increase from 1.01 to 1.3 results in roughly a 12 percent increase in $V_{sp} - V_{sg}$.[43] The surprising feature of the private revenue multiplier is that the elasticity has the same sign as that of the government revenue multiplier and about three times its value. Since, if anything, we would expect both revenue multipliers to be greater than one, our estimate of the welfare change is likely to be conservative.
- For the government discount rate an increase from 15 percent to 16 percent would lead to a reduction in $V_{sp} - V_{sg}$ of about 12 percent. However, we believe that our government discount rate (9 percent real) is already on the high side.
- A 1 percent per year increase in the private capital-output ratio leads to a 6 percent increase in $V_{sp} - V_{sg}$. This result makes sense, given that the public capital-output ratio remains the same as the private.

- An increase in private labor efficiency from 1.05 to 1.06 results in roughly an 80 percent increase in $V_{sp} - V_{sg}$, whereas a similar increase in the public labor efficiency turns it negative.
- An increase in the public profit target from 20 percent to 21 percent results in an increase in $V_{sp} - V_{sg}$ of roughly 4 percent. This means that an increase in prices under continued public operation makes divestiture look better.
- Interestingly, an increase in the public dividend payout ratio makes divestiture moderately less attractive.
- As expected, an increase in prices by the divested BT in the projection period reduces the positive welfare effects of divestiture.
- V_{pp} is most sensitive to private pricing, labor efficiency, the capital-output ratio, the rate of capital deterioration, and disposal of capital.

Overall, the sensitivity analysis shows that our results are most sensitive to realistic changes in the labor productivity differential between private and public operation.

Summary

Our review of the quantitative record suggests that, as a result of the divestiture of BT:

- Operating efficiency did not change before 1991. There was an earlier distinct turning point from decline to improvement in BT's productivity after 1982. However, considerations of longer time-series and international comparisons make it highly unlikely that this was due to institutional change of any sort, let alone the announcement effect of divestiture. In contrast, downsizing of the labor force beginning in 1991 is making a significant contribution to operating efficiency.
- The level and structure of output prices changed as a result of a change in the regulatory environment.
- The level of fixed capital formation rose sharply in the first three years after divestiture. Real gross fixed capital formation was stagnant through 1984 and then took off, because of a release in an investment constraint.
- Most other variables either did not change significantly or changed as a result of factors clearly exogenous to the divestiture exercise.
- What did change was sufficient to make the world better off by £10 billion and the United Kingdom better off by £9 billion (net present value in 1985 pounds sterling). This is equivalent to almost £20 billion in 1992 pounds sterling, or US$30 billion.
- The distribution of the welfare gain comes as close to a Pareto improvement as possible. Only BT's competitors were identified as

(minor) losers. Other probable minor losers were some residential and business consumers adversely affected by relative price changes within BT's bundle of outputs.

Notes

This chapter was written by Ingo Vogelsang, Leroy P. Jones, and Pankaj Tandon, with Manuel A. Abdala and Christopher Doyle. The authors are grateful for explanations of data and facts to William P. Kember, D. P. Savill, Nicolas Sullivan, and Jonathan Wilby of British Telecom; Peter Culham of OFTEL; and Jack Summerscale of Barclays de Zoete Wedd.

1. The PSBR is the total borrowing at the end of the fiscal year needed to cover the central government's own budget deficit and the financial deficits of local authorities and public corporations, plus government lending to the private sector.

2. Vickers and Yarrow (1988) hypothesize that the RPI - X regulation amounts to rate-of-return regulation in disguise. That could in the long run lead to employment of excessive capital relative to labor. We hypothesize that quality of telecommunications services tends to be labor intensive in the short run but capital intensive in the long run. A waiting list for connections can be reduced by employing more technicians, but the network has to be adapted to the new connections as well.

3. See Bishop and Kay (1988). A convincing explanation for the "shaping-up effect" is given by Caves (1990), who argues that reputation effects in the market for managers and the credible threat of retrospective punishment after divestiture may lead to the loss of rents by labor and management before competitive pressure is actually exerted.

4. International trade in telephone equipment has gained in importance over the last decade. As far as we know, however, apparatus that is internationally traded by BT or its subsidiaries is contained in our miscellaneous category.

5. The Finance Act of 1984 included a Reaganesque trade-off of lower corporate tax rates for lower deductions. In particular, the allowance for capital expenditures in the first year dropped from 100 percent to 25 percent. One result—recognized in the enterprise's sale prospectus—was that BT would begin paying taxes in 1985.

6. BT's 1991–93 labor force reduction will be discussed below. For reasons of confidentiality, BT was unwilling to provide us with any breakdown by type of worker. Accordingly, our nominal labor series is nothing more than total employee compensation, and our real series is simply total employment.

As a sensitivity test, we assume that BT workers received wage increases at the mean level of all U.K. workers and use this to deflate values to obtain a quality-adjusted estimate of quantity. Our story of increasing labor productivity thus seems relatively robust. It is likely that BT substituted high-skilled for low-skilled workers, but unless both groups then received far lower than average wage increases, our absolute results will not be materially affected.

7. Note that the relationship between current and constant flows is sometimes contrary to expectations here, because the price of telecommunications equipment declined in some periods.

8. For capital we use the perpetual inventory method benchmarked to BT's 1987 technical revaluation. This implies a rate of price increase for BT's capital goods that is considerably lower (by 5 percentage points per year from 1980 to

1990) than for capital goods in the economy as a whole; this is perfectly reasonable given technical progress in the telecommunications industry. Sensitivity analysis to the rate of inflation and of deterioration of capital goods gives no evidence of a change associated with divestiture. Instead we have only differing estimates of the rate of technical progress, and this does not affect our comparative divestiture story.

9. The variance of the TFP series is 0.007, compared with 0.05 for public profitability (after converting the latter to a comparable index, with 1985 = 100).

10. The cross-product effect (changing prices on changing quantities) is arbitrarily allocated to the pure effects in proportion to those pure effects.

11. This result is quite close to calculations for the National Audit Office (reported by Vickers and Yarrow 1988, p. 182), according to which the net proceeds—after accounting for discounts, other incentives, and transactions costs—were £3,600 million. This calculation disregards the time value of money.

12. Much of the detail in this section is derived from a letter from David Savill of BT to Christopher Doyle, dated 3 April 1990.

13. The company continued to pay interest on outstanding loans and is also repaying loans, so that this flow has continued at roughly the £400 million level. Some temporary fiscal flows occurred during 1987–89 as the company paid preference dividends on £750 million worth of preference shares, which it has now redeemed. Thus this element of flow has stopped.

14. Interpreting the change in consumer surplus is difficult when demand is shifting. In later sections this is generally not a problem, because most of the ambiguous attributions cancel out of our V_{sp} - V_{sg} calculations. Here, however, we include only the unambiguous portion of the change (change in real price times previous year's quantity) as a first approximation. This is known as the Slutsky compensation (Varian 1984, p. 144).

15. In this case we have included consumer surplus accruing to receivers of incoming international calls, on the assumption that this is equal to the consumer surplus accruing to the foreigners placing the calls. In the remainder of this study consumer surplus for incoming calls is halved and treated as an externality for domestic consumers.

16. Here we have treated rentals as commodities demanded in their own right. Later we will treat the demand for rentals as derived from the demand for calls.

17. The only cases where this assumption is violated slightly, and temporarily, are prices for international outgoing calls (in the first category) and for private circuits (in the second).

18. In addition, the available evidence suggests that the quality variation in rates of call completion and in speed of repair service runs parallel to that in telephone line installation. For the years after divestiture, OFTEL has added some indicators of service quality, such as numbers of customer complaints or percentages of customers satisfied with BT's services. Since these measures are not available for the years before divestiture, we decided not to use them here.

19. For the years after 1983 these are constructed from numbers on waiting times for new lines. We did not allow for any grace period before counting unfilled orders. Hence our numbers appear to be quite high compared with official statistics, which only start counting the waiting period after four or eight weeks. The rounding in the years 1984 and later indicates that these are our estimates.

20. A secondary source was stabilization of the ratio of intermediate inputs to outputs, which had previously been rising. This sharpened the turning point but contributed nothing to the continued trend of improvement.

21. For a discussion of the properties of price cap regulation, see Vickers and Yarrow (1988) and Vogelsang (1988).

22. We have neglected here new developments in the United States, such as optional calling plans and special offerings for business customers.

23. Although, without divestiture, Mercury might have received a less favorable interconnection agreement with BT, and thus might initially have become even less competitive than it did in actuality.

24. For the different call categories we have neglected Mercury's market share, which was very small during this period with the possible exception of international phone calls and private circuits. In fact, at least until 1991 Mercury was operating in a market niche, serving almost exclusively large-business customers, to which BT, because of its pricing restrictions, could not respond, and it therefore concentrated its efforts on the remaining customers.

25. GDP calendar-year levels are converted to BT fiscal-year levels by simple 0.75/0.25 averaging. Using quarterly data would give a better approximation.

26. Any such conclusion is of course justifiable only so far as it is legitimate to link the two TFP series. There is room for doubt on this score because TFP measures can vary wildly with assumptions.

27. An obvious anomaly is 1970. Available data do not allow us to double-check Foreman-Peck and Manning's results, however.

28. Labor inputs were here taken as the average number of workers reported as employed by BT (or by the Post Office in telecommunications) at the beginning and the end of each fiscal year. In our basic calculations we adjust these figures by converting part-time employment to full-time equivalents and deducting labor devoted to own-account construction. For the longer time series this is not possible, so we use the unadjusted series in this section.

29. Total BT revenues are deflated by the telecommunications (called communications or post and telecom prior to 1976) price index implicit in the consumer expenditure series in United Kingdom, Central Statistical Office, various issues.

30. For lack of sufficient data we could not do a comparison with France Télécom. Employment at both has been in the 200,000-to-250,000 range over the relevant period. Note, however, that France Télécom had a remarkable turnaround in the 1980s (Duch 1991).

31. We construct data series for BT as above, that is, splicing the Foreman-Peck and Manning series to our own. Data for AT&T are from Christensen (1981) and Crandall (1989), and those for DBP from Elixmann (1989).

32. For example, starting in 1982 BT was no longer capitalizing customer connections. Thus, BT's investments from this period onward would appear to be smaller by the amount invested in such connections. In our report we have adjusted BT's investment in customer connections for 1980 and 1981 to concur with practice in later years. We do not know how foreign telecommunications companies treat customer connections. Therefore comparisons of assets and investments may be tricky.

33. DBP has for a long time financed some equipment suppliers (e.g., Siemens AG) that were protected from competition. During the 1980s BT used between 10 percent and 15 percent of its work force for own work capitalized. The equivalent figure for DBP appears to be similar. We were able to calculate this number for

1987 and 1988, when it was 13.9 percent and 14.3 percent, respectively. Higher wages in Germany then could translate into higher capital costs.

34. BT's performance was actually worse as a result of the Mitel acquisition, which contributed neither to profits nor to domestic consumer surplus.

35. Since this country study was published in early 1991, we have tried to incorporate some developments in 1991 and decided to leave out others, such as the further sale of the government's shares in BT in 1991 and 1993. This has no impact on our bottom line results and very little impact on the distribution of gains and losses.

36. This appears to be unfair to Mercury and to BT's potential new competitors for network services, which almost certainly will gain large market shares over time. Rather than reduce BT's assumed market share for these categories, however, we chose to constrain the growth rates of its residual demands.

37. The new pricing regime with $X = 7.5$ percent, to go into effect in BT's fiscal 1994, was agreed upon after our case study was completed. We have tried to be conservative in our estimation of the effects of divestiture.

38. BT in actuality achieved this reduction by the end of fiscal 1992 and accomplished a further 40,000-worker reduction during fiscal 1993. Thus, our assumption again proved conservative. This was counterbalanced by an actual reduction in output growth.

39. We include here both the impact on direct consumers and the value of network externalities. Note also that we did not count consumer surplus from rentals, but only that from calls minus the cost of rentals. The reason is that the demand for rentals is derived from the demand for calls. The price of rentals, therefore, affects consumer surplus as does the fixed part of a two-part tariff. The network externality effect has also been captured through calls rather than through rentals. Thus, we have neglected any option value from renting a telephone line.

40. We use the term "efficiency" broadly here to include a variety of things, including both static productivity gains and dynamic timing of investment and pricing decisions, as will be explained below.

41. We purposely neglected BT's shrinking market share in the miscellaneous outputs category. Competitors' quasi rents for these outputs are therefore zero in our calculations. Such quasi rents could be quite substantial, but they are notoriously hard to quantify.

42. In four categories consumer surplus does not change at all, indicating that prices are assumed to be the same under both the actual and the counterfactual.

43. The effects of such a large discrete change cannot, of course, be estimated adequately using an elasticity. However, it may give a sense of the rough magnitude.

5. British Airways

Many state-owned airlines around the world are candidates for divestiture. Of potential relevance to them is the case of British Airways (BA), which by the time of its divestiture in February 1987 was a flourishing enterprise—less than six years earlier it had recorded an operating loss equal to 5 percent of turnover. The case of BA could also provide valuable lessons for the divestiture of public enterprises in other oligopolistic industries.

BA is the dominant airline in the United Kingdom and has been since its foundation. Its main business, which provided nearly 90 percent of its fiscal 1992 turnover of £5.2 billion (BA's fiscal year begins 1 April), is in scheduled flights carrying both passengers (81 percent of revenue) and freight (8 percent). It has a route network covering about 160 destinations, most of which are served from London's Heathrow Airport, BA's main base. BA carries more international passengers on scheduled flights than any other airline in the world, although the four largest U.S. airlines' domestic passengers make these airlines larger than BA overall.

Before divestiture, and especially around 1980, BA had the reputation of an enterprise with too many staff, massive excess capacity, and occasional substantial losses. Economists, politicians, regulators, and financial analysts have studied BA's performance after the announcement of divestiture. What emerges is some agreement about the nature of that performance and some divergence on its attribution. First, BA was highly successful financially. While in this respect the divestiture of BA is conventionally viewed as a major success, the remarkable turnaround in BA's performance occurred between the announcement of divestiture in 1979 and its consummation in 1987. Second, BA has succeeded in the marketplace by establishing a reputation for quality of service and by expanding at a healthy rate. Third, BA has had fairly peaceful labor relations, even as it has reduced its work force. Fourth, the success has been related to the announcement of divestiture rather than to divestiture itself; the appointment of Sir John King (now Lord King of Wartnaby) as chairman; and the magic year 1983, which brought a turnaround in most U.K. public enterprises that had not yet been divested (see Bishop and Kay 1988).

Background

In the following sections we trace the historic background of BA, airline economics, and pricing policy and regulation.

History

BA can trace its origins back to the world's first daily international scheduled service, operated between London and Paris by Aircraft Transport and Travel, Ltd., beginning on 25 August 1919. The company that is now BA has had a varied history of mergers and acquisitions. The airline under its current name was the result of a merger in the 1970s between the United Kingdom's two publicly owned dominant carriers, British Overseas Airways Corporation and British European Airways.[1] Both these corporations had had mixed fortunes during the 1950s and 1960s. British Overseas Airways Corporation introduced the world's first jet airliner, the Comet, in 1952, but had to withdraw it from service after three crashes in the next two years, and the company frequently recorded losses.

In 1969 the Edwards Committee, which had been established in 1967 to consider the future of U.K. aviation, recommended combining the two airlines under a State Airline Holdings Board, although it did not advocate an operational merger. It also recommended encouraging the private sector to create a "second force" airline, so that the United Kingdom could always have a choice when designating airlines for international routes. This airline was created in 1970 when Caledonian Airways took over British United Airways to form British Caledonian (BCal). BCal was given a number of international route licenses, although it remained far smaller than BA and financially much weaker. The British Airways Board was created by the 1971 Civil Aviation Act and became the holding corporation for British European Airways and British Overseas Airways Corporation in April 1972. In January 1973 it was decided that the entire airline should trade under the single name of BA, and the subsidiary corporations were dissolved in April 1974.

Although it was a public corporation accountable to a minister of state, from the beginning BA stated that its "primary objective is to conduct its affairs on strictly commercial lines" (BA 1973, p. 10). At first, BA suffered from the problems of having to merge two organizations and eliminate duplication. These problems were not helped by the way in which the two corporations were to continue as separate divisions within BA, each controlling its own marketing and operations. The problems were recognized in an April 1977 reorganization of the airline into four divisions covering commercial operations, flight operations, engineering, and planning. Throughout the period, the British Airways Board's objective was to rationalize the operations of BA without resorting to layoffs (BA 1973, p. 17), a policy that would have fitted well with political constraints even if it was not dictated by them. During the 1970s, BA had a reputation for overstaffing, low productivity, and poor labor relations: strikes caused the loss of £11 million in operating profits in fiscal 1975 and £40 million in fiscal 1978.

In 1978 a team led by Roy Watts, who became chief executive in June 1979, produced a corporate plan. The Watts plan recognized that BA was badly overstaffed. It highlighted the fact that BA produced only 122,000 available tonne-kilometers per employee, compared with an average in 1976 of 208,000 available ton-kilometers per employee for a sample of eight other airlines (BA 1978), and that BA's earnings were correspondingly low. BA's aircraft fleet was also aging, and many of its airplanes would fail the noise regulations to be introduced in 1986.

The Watts plan hoped to solve these problems by volume growth, in the expectation that the industry's historical growth rates would continue. If BA could carry 30 million passengers in 1986, compared with 16 million in 1978, while keeping its staff and fleet size fairly constant (with larger-capacity wide-bodied jets), it could solve its productivity problems without large-scale layoffs. The plan assumed that BA would be able to achieve this growth, given a favorable industry environment, by appropriate marketing aimed at capturing a larger share of the leisure trade. The huge investment in new fleet was expected to cost £2.4 billion, but the planners expected that £1.5 billion would be available from BA's own cash flow. The plan was detailed and internally consistent, although it was optimistic in assuming growth of 90 percent by 1986, given that government forecasts were for a rise in passenger numbers in the United Kingdom of between 42 and 78 percent during the period (Green 1978). Unfortunately, the oil price rise of 1979 and the ensuing recession destroyed the assumptions on which the Watts plan rested.

In April 1979, during the general election campaign, the Conservative party revealed a plan to sell some of the government's shareholding in BA to the private sector, to create a mixed private and public enterprise similar to British Petroleum. In July, with the Conservatives now in office, Trade Secretary John Nott formally announced this plan and introduced the Civil Aviation Bill to transform BA from a public enterprise to a company suitable for sale. The time required for legislative approval meant that selling any shares would be impossible until autumn 1980 at the earliest, and this target was soon amended to autumn 1981. However, by that time BA's profits had taken a disastrous turn for the worse.

The 1979 oil shock had doubled the price of aviation fuel, while the slump in the U.K. economy had reduced the number of domestic and scheduled international passengers. Operating profits fell from £76 million in fiscal 1979 to £17 million in fiscal 1980, and as demand continued to fall, BA suffered an operating loss of £102 million in fiscal 1981, with an overall loss of £141 million. Volume was falling, costs were rising, and fares on the North Atlantic routes, BA's most important market, were being cut in response to the challenge of Laker Airways.

Sir John King became chairman of BA in February 1981. A survival plan announced in September spelled the formal end of the 1978 Watts strategy of expansion: a number of routes were cut; cargo-only services were ended; and some subsidiary companies and assets, such as a flying training college, were sold. Large-scale layoffs were announced and generous severance terms offered: employment had already fallen from 57,741 in March 1979 to 52,310 in March 1981, but was down to 43,200 a year later and reached a low of 36,794 in March 1984. Although the first of these reductions occurred before King's appointment, the subsequent reductions were more drastic.

The immediate impact of the recovery plan was a small operating profit and huge writedowns in fiscal 1982. BA's results in fiscal 1983 were much better, and by late 1983 it was expected that BA would be divested in early 1985. However, by this time BCal had started a lobbying campaign alleging that a divested BA would dominate the U.K. airline industry to an unhealthy extent. BCal suggested that BA should transfer its domestic flights to U.K. regional airlines and sell BCal one-fifth of its routes and planes for £200 million, which would reduce BA's share of scheduled services among U.K. airlines from 83 percent to about two-thirds. Transport Secretary Nicholas Ridley responded to this suggestion (and to counterarguments from BA) by announcing that the Civil Aviation Authority (CAA) would review the prospects for competition among U.K. airlines and come up with recommendations.

This announcement started a period of lobbying, although BA was fairly quiet until the CAA produced its report (United Kingdom, CAA 1984) in July. The CAA recommended that BA be reduced in size, shedding its routes to Zimbabwe and Saudi Arabia, all its scheduled services from Gatwick Airport, and its European services from provincial U.K. airports. These routes would be given to BCal and other airlines; the CAA calculated that the changes would cost BA 7 percent of its revenues. BA responded forcefully: employees wrote to their members of Parliament, ministers were lobbied, and BA's case was pressed through the news media. On 5 October Ridley announced that BA would have to give up its Saudi Arabian routes but would receive BCal's South American routes (which had been losing money) in return (United Kingdom, Department of Transport 1984). This decision, a victory for BA, seemed to clear the way for divestiture. In November 1984, however, the sale was postponed because BA was threatened with legal action for alleged collusion against Laker Airways, a low-cost carrier that had gone bankrupt in 1982. These actions were settled out of court in summer 1985, but the sale was again postponed in March 1986 while the United Kingdom and the United States negotiated services between the two countries. After the skirmishes over BA's market power, the airline was finally divested on 30 January 1987, nearly eight years after the first announcement and six years after Lord King's appointment.

Later in 1987 an event of almost equal importance took place: BA acquired BCal, its main U.K. rival. BCal had been in a weak financial position throughout the 1980s, and the 1984 CAA review had been intended to strengthen it (United Kingdom, CAA 1985). The smaller route exchange imposed by the government should have added £18 million a year to BCal's profits (United Kingdom, Department of Transport 1984), but the Saudi Arabian routes declined in importance just as BCal took them over, and thus the exchange did not help BCal.

In July 1987 BA and BCal announced an agreed merger at a proposed price of £237 million for actual BCal net assets valued at £278 million at the time of the transaction. The airlines argued that the alternative would be that a foreign company would buy BCal, which could result in it losing its international route licenses, and that "synergies" between the two enterprises would allow them to reduce BCal's costs and run its operations profitably. The airlines claimed that this potential for cost reductions was what prompted the high sale price, rather than any desire on the part of BA to gain BCal's route licenses and benefit from reduced competition.

The merger was referred to the Monopolies and Mergers Commission, which approved the bid in November 1987 (United Kingdom, Monopolies and Mergers Commission 1987). BA had agreed to give up 5,000 landing slots at London's Gatwick Airport, where most of BCal's operations were based, and to surrender several of BCal's European route licenses where both airlines had previously been operating. Scandinavian Airlines Systems (SAS) meanwhile offered £110 million for a 26 percent stake in BCal, with the aim of creating a twin hub network based at Gatwick and Copenhagen. BA had earlier reduced its bid, but this viable alternative plan forced it to raise its price to £246 million, and it gained control of BCal as of 31 December 1987. Fees of £7 million, reorganization expenses of £90 million, and the cost of absorbing net liabilities of £10 million meant that BCal cost BA a total of £353 million.

Airline Economics

Table 5-1 shows recent growth in air travel in the United Kingdom between 1977 and 1989 in terms of numbers of passengers. The number of passengers grew at 7.3 percent per year, so that if the average distance flown per passenger followed the world trend, the U.K. market grew slightly faster than the world average in terms of passenger-kilometers. The early 1980s were a lean period for the industry. In the United

Table 5-1. Airline Passengers in the United Kingdom, 1977–89
(passenger miles)

	International		
Year	Scheduled	Nonscheduled	Domestic
1977	23.4	10.9	5.6
1978	26.9	11.8	6.6
1979	28.7	12.4	7.6
1980	28.8	13.3	7.5
1981	29.0	14.8	7.0
1982	27.8	16.5	7.3
1983	28.2	18.1	7.4
1984	30.8	20.4	8.2
1985	33.7	19.2	8.8
1986	34.5	22.9	8.9
1987	39.9	26.7	9.7
1988	44.3	27.1	10.8
1989	48.4	26.9	11.8

Source: CAA data.

Kingdom, in contrast to the rest of the world, international nonscheduled services continued to expand through the recession (and only fell in 1986, when trans-Atlantic traffic was low), while scheduled services suffered a small absolute fall and a long period of very little growth. Domestic services grew faster than the more regulated international scheduled services, as in the world as a whole, but the rate of growth in the United Kingdom (a geographically relatively small market for domestic services) was well below the world average.

An airline's cost per available seat-kilometer (ASK) depends on the characteristics of its routes. On a short flight, the high costs of heavy fuel consumption at takeoff, airport charges, and the engineering checks that must be performed after every flight can only be spread over a relatively small number of kilometers, giving a much higher average cost. Short-haul aircraft spend more time on the ground being prepared for the next flight than do long-haul ones, so that BA's long-haul Boeing 747s averaged more than 4,300 flying hours apiece in fiscal 1990, while its short-haul Boeing 737s averaged fewer than 2,600 hours. This means that the depreciation costs of the short-haul aircraft must be spread over a smaller number of kilometers. BA's cost was 7.5 pence per ASK on its European routes in fiscal 1990, against a cost of 3.7 pence per ASK on its intercontinental routes (these figures are derived from BA's own accounts). Comparisons of airlines' costs per ASK must therefore take the length of their routes into account.

Careful scheduling is needed to obtain the maximum number of passengers on each flight and to use aircraft as intensively as is profitable. During the 1980s, airlines increasingly attempted to solve this problem by the use of hub and spoke systems. They decreased the number of direct flights between minor airports while concentrating on providing good services to a hub airport, with convenient connections along other spokes to the passengers' final destinations. The hub airports become busier as a result, and the others less crowded, but passengers can be better served if a frequent connecting service replaces an infrequent direct service.

The main motive for changing to a hub and spoke system is to raise the load factor on an airline's services, for this is one of the crucial determinants of the relationship between revenues and costs. In Europe many airlines have long operated a kind of hub system simply by basing the majority of their flights at their country's main international airport, and BA is a prime example of this, with 70 percent of its passengers traveling through London's Heathrow Airport, and 25 percent of them changing flights there. The importance of having a comprehensive network is shown by the fact that, in 1980, 64 percent of the passengers who arrived at Heathrow on a BA flight and changed flights there remained with BA, while BA only picked up 36 percent of passengers who changed flights after arriving on a different airline (even though very few of them would leave Heathrow on the airline they arrived with; United Kingdom, CAA 1984, appendix 7).

A major competitive factor for BA is congestion at Heathrow, BA's main base. The demand for takeoff and landing slots at Heathrow greatly exceeds the supply, and a committee made up of representatives of the airlines that use the airport allocates the slots. The committee generally allows each airline to continue using the slots it has used in the past, and airport charges are based on the British Airports Authority's costs rather than on the value of the slot to the user. This gives incumbent airlines a privileged and potentially very valuable position. Bishop and Thompson (1990) found that charter passengers were paying 5 percent more for flights via Gatwick to the Mediterranean in 1987 than via uncongested airports. Since charter passengers are generally very price sensitive, a higher markup might be expected for scheduled flights at Heathrow, especially on the more expensive classes.[2]

One other important factor is the change in the way that airlines have financed their costly fleets. In the past almost all aircraft were owned by the airlines that operated them, or rented under finance leases that transferred ownership of the aircraft to the airline over the term of the lease. Airlines have rarely been able to finance their fleet acquisitions from their past earnings, and this has given them debt-heavy capital structures. Since the early 1980s BA has increasingly obtained its aircraft on operating leases, under which the leasing company retains ownership of the aircraft; this eliminates the debt that would otherwise appear on BA's balance sheet. Some of these leases are for fixed terms, but others can be extended, giving BA a great deal of flexibility.

Pricing Policy and Regulation

International scheduled air transport is one of the most highly regulated, or rather cartelized, industries in the world. Airlines are usually required to notify governments of the fares that they intend to charge, often for prior approval, and are generally granted exemption from any antitrust legislation to set these fares through the conferences of the International Air Transport Association. On many routes the airlines pool their revenues, which is often justified as a means of allowing them to offer a mixture of peak and off-peak flights without being at a competitive disadvantage. BA was a party to twenty-one such pooling agreements in 1987 (United Kingdom, Monopolies and Mergers Commission 1987, paragraph 2.20), although BA states that "the aggregate amounts paid and received by BA under these arrangements are not material" (BA 1987). This statement, which presumably applies to BA's network as a whole, is not inconsistent with significant net revenue transfers on particular routes.

Travel between European Community countries is currently being liberalized. An initial package agreed on in 1987 (Vincent and Stasinopoulos 1990) allowed an airline to expand its capacity on any route, unless its home country would then have more than 55 percent of the capacity on that route (the threshold was increased to 60 percent in October 1989). Entry restrictions on many routes were eased, with dual designation (two carriers per country allowed) on routes above a certain size (250,000 passengers initially, but now on any route with at least 180,000 passengers per year). The agreement also included automatic governmental approval for various categories of discount fares, and "fifth freedom" rights (the right to carry passengers not passing through the carrier's home country). Subject to various conditions involving nondiscrimination, airlines' commercial agreements on fares, timetables, and other matters are still exempt from Community competition rules. Beginning in 1993, all European airlines are allowed to fly any route within the Community, including domestic routes, subject to common licensing requirements.

International charter flights, which carried 30 percent of U.K. air passengers in 1989, have not been as closely regulated. They are not usually covered by bilateral agreements, and airlines usually apply directly to the governments involved for permission to fly. Ease of entry varies between markets; for example, between the United Kingdom and the Mediterranean countries access is generally easy and charter flights have a high market share. Charter regulations were relaxed during the 1970s, and advanced booking charters now allow cheap travel without the need to belong to an affinity group.

Within the United Kingdom, the CAA is responsible for the industry's economic and technical regulation, including deciding which U.K. airline to designate under bilateral agreements and issuing domestic route licenses. During the 1970s the CAA's policy was fairly restrictive. For example, CAA guidelines stated that it would "not normally license new short-haul scheduled services that will . . . make [existing efficiently operated services competing directly or indirectly] less than fully remunerative" (United Kingdom, CAA 1978, p. 11).

The CAA gradually relaxed this policy during the 1980s. By 1985 it was "ready to license competing services by British Airlines even at the risk of some impairment of an existing British service" (United Kingdom, CAA 1985, paragraph 3), and entry to domestic services is now practically free, except for services from London's Heathrow Airport. Domestic fares need only be filed with the CAA, which retains the right to disapprove them, but "whenever possible the Authority will allow market forces to set or influence the levels of fares and rates for air transport" (United Kingdom, CAA 1985, paragraph 15).

Special traffic distribution rules applied at Heathrow from 1977 to 1991 because of the congestion there. Whole-plane charters were banned, and airlines that had not been operating from Heathrow before 1977 were not allowed to fly there. The Secretary of State for Transport had to authorize any new domestic services. In spring 1991 two ailing U.S. carriers sought to sell their Heathrow routes to stronger rivals that did not have landing rights, and the U.K. government decided to end the ban on new airlines to accommodate the newcomers. Other airlines have also started to use Heathrow, most notably Virgin Atlantic Airways, a niche carrier with routes to the United States and Japan. So that Virgin could use its flying rights, BA was forced to give up a number of landing slots at Tokyo. BA's profits may be seriously affected by the opening up of Virgin's main base.

What Happened?

This section examines the quantitative aspects of what happened before and after divestiture.

Profit and Profitability

The 1980s started with a slump for BA. As shown in figure 5-1, private profit (dividends plus retained earnings) deteriorated rapidly from 1980 to 1982, when BA was recording an overall loss of nearly £450 million. The fiscal 1982 results showed a small operating profit of £12 million, despite the depressed world market, but BA announced extraordinary provisions of £426 million. A report by Price Waterhouse had recommended that BA make provision for as many future costs as possible (Campbell-Smith 1986, p. 30); thus BA charged layoff provisions of £198.8 million and a supplementary depreciation of £208 million to the fiscal

Figure 5-1. Public and Private Profit, British Airways, 1980–90

Millions of pounds sterling

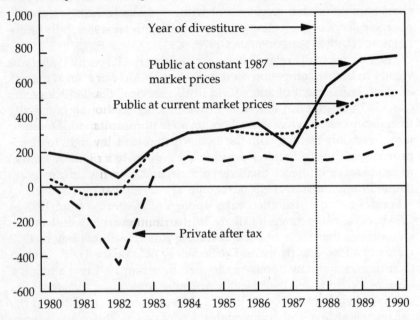

Source: Authors' calculations from BA data.

1982 accounts. The huge net loss for that year, which gave BA a negative net worth of £257 million, was therefore partly the result of accounting practices. The enterprise had estimated future severance costs at £98 million, of which £44 million was written back to reserves in fiscal 1984 and 1985.[3]

The writedown of the aircraft fleet reflected the depressed market for secondhand aircraft at the time, since BA's aircraft are written down to a residual resale value, rather than to zero, over their estimated lives. This was also partially reversed by a revaluation of £107 million in 1984, although that revaluation was to take account of other factors, mainly the effect of a rise in the value of the dollar, the currency in which most aircraft are traded, and the revaluation was credited to BA's reserves to offset the increase in the sterling value of the dollar loans used to buy the aircraft.

Private profits improved in 1983 by more than £500 million and in 1984 by another £116 million. BA did not significantly exceed the profit level reached in 1984 until 1990, and actually made substantially lower profits in 1985, 1987, and 1988. Looking only at private profit, one is likely to agree with Bishop and Kay (1988) that BA followed the bandwagon of public and divested U.K. enterprises that had a positive turnaround in 1983. The question is whether this conclusion can be extended to other performance measures.

As also shown in figure 5-1, public profit tells a slightly different story, with a much less dramatically decreasing trend from 1980 to 1982 and a somewhat less dramatic turnaround in 1983 and 1984. From 1985 to 1990 the changes in public and private profit sometimes have different signs. Also, there is a clearly visible improvement in 1988, after divestiture, and one year earlier than the improvement in private profits. The sources for the differences between public and private profit are shown in figure 5-2, which decomposes the total surplus (or return to capital). Depreciation jumped £225 million in 1982 but fell back to 1981 levels in 1983. An antitrust settlement in the Laker Airlines case led to a negative transfer of £33 million in 1985. Interest payments peaked in fiscal 1984. Direct taxes remained low from 1980 to 1987 because of loss carryforwards from 1980 to 1982.

In sum, current public profit and its distribution exhibit one obvious trend change in 1983 and a less visible trend change in 1988, after divestiture.

Figure 5-2. Return to Capital at Current Market Prices, British Airways, 1980–90

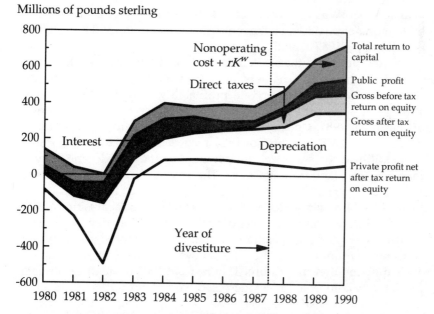

Millions of pounds sterling

Note: rK^w, opportunity cost of working capital.
Source: Authors' calculations from BA data.

Figure 5-2 also shows public profit at constant market prices. Two points are noteworthy. First, public profits at constant prices declined substantially more from 1980 to 1982 than did public profits at current prices (even though not as dramatically as private profits); but the turnaround in fiscal 1984 was partially reversed in 1987, which in terms of public profit at constant prices turned out to be the third-worst year in the decade. The years 1988 to 1990 then witnessed a second and even stronger turnaround than that from 1982 to 1984, with 1990 recording the best performance in the decade. This second turnaround started in 1988 (rather than in 1989 as for private profit). Second, both turnarounds were not caused primarily by a change in output (which contracted during 1982–84 but grew strongly during fiscal 1986 and 1988–90), but by a change in costs. From 1980 through 1982 intermediate input costs rose while output contracted, and labor contracted slightly less than output. In fiscal 1984 both intermediate inputs and labor contracted while output expanded. Thereafter, intermediates grew at about the same rate as output, but the quantity of labor input increased more slowly.

In sum, BA suffered from major slumps in performance in 1982 and 1987, followed by recoveries starting in 1983 and 1988.

The variations in gross fixed capital acquisition (figure 5-3) are dramatic. At constant prices capital formation paralleled the trend in public profits during 1980–82, but continued to deteriorate in 1983. It was quite variable during 1984–90, with a generally upward trend and a distinct peak in 1988. While this peak reflects the acquisition of BCal with £363 million (in nominal terms), the remaining £500 million still represents a doubling over 1987 capital formation.

Relating profits to the stock of capital yields the main performance measure of this section, namely, return to fixed capital, or profitability. As shown in figure 5-4, private profitability exhibited the expected strongly negative turn during fiscal 1982 and then rebounded strongly during fiscal 1984. Unexpectedly, private profitability again declined during fiscal 1988 and did not fully recover in 1989 and 1990. Public profitability at current prices did not undergo the 1988 decline but was relatively constant from 1984 on. The reason for the disappointing private and current price profitability performance is the substantial increase in the denominator, in particular through the acquisition of BCal in fiscal 1988 (and in the private profit case is possibly due to writeoffs connected with the acquisition of BCal). The constant-price story is considerably more optimistic. This shows a dramatic upward turn in 1988, the year after divestiture! That is, from 1982 through 1986 public profitability at constant prices increased, from about 2.3 percent to about 19.1 percent. Thereafter it decreased to 11.6 percent in 1987 and then increased dramatically to a 1988 level of more than 27 percent, reaching nearly 30 percent in 1989 (followed by a slight decline to 28 percent in

Figure 5-3. Gross Fixed Capital Acquisition, British Airways, 1980–90

Millions of pounds sterling

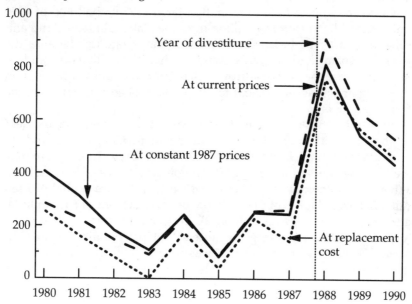

Source: Authors' calculations from BA data.

1990). If the 1988–90 change can be attributed to divestiture, it supports the view that divestiture improves efficiency.[4]

Finance

BA had three main sources of finance in the public sector. Public dividend capital (PDC) was intended to be the equivalent of a private company's equity, paying an agreed dividend that would at least equal the interest that would have been paid had the money been lent from the National Loans Fund. Loans from the National Loans Fund were a second alternative in the enterprise's early years, although BA took out only two small loans after 1976 and had repaid all loans by 1984. The third alternative, which the government increasingly encouraged as its finances came under strain in the mid-1970s, was to borrow abroad. The treasury gained because the loan was outside the U.K. financial system and helped it keep within its targets.

BA was initially meant to have a debt-equity ratio of between 35-65 and 50-50, although the £65 million of PDC it inherited in 1972 gave it a ratio of 67-33. BA followed this policy until 1976, by which time it had £280 million of PDC and a debt-equity ratio of 39-61. Extra PDC was issued at a rate of £10 million a year from then until fiscal 1982, although this was grossly insufficient to maintain the desired debt-equity ratio, given the airline's performance. At its founding BA had PDC of £65 million and other borrowings of £188 million. By March 1977 BA had PDC of £290 million, had borrowed £84 million from the National Loans Fund and £134 million from abroad (at its own exchange rate risk because the treasury scheme had not yet begun),[5] and had £20 million outstanding in finance leases and other borrowings. In 1979 BA wrote off £160 million of PDC in an agreed settlement to the problem of cost overruns on the Concorde supersonic jet.

By March 1981, BA's PDC had been reduced to £170 million, the debt to the National Loans Fund had declined to £34 million, and BA had covered foreign loans of £524 million (as the scheme closed to new loans), other foreign loans of £110 million, and leases of £114 million. When BA plc took over in March 1984, it had a share capital of £180 million, covered loans of £445 million, uncovered loans of £327 million, and finance leases of £129 million. To this point the treasury had guaranteed all of BA's borrowings, because a public corporation (in the U.K. sense of a state-owned enterprise) was an arm of the government. This guarantee probably allowed BA to borrow at lower interest rates than

Figure 5-4. Private and Public Profitability, British Airways, 1980–90

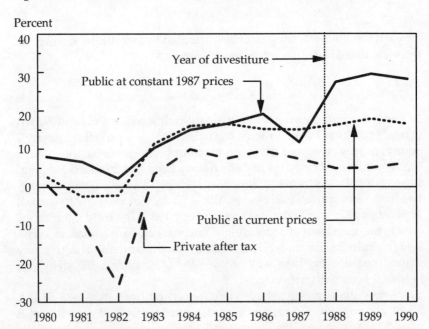

Source: Authors' calculations from BA data.

Figure 5-5. Sources of Funds, British Airways, 1981–90

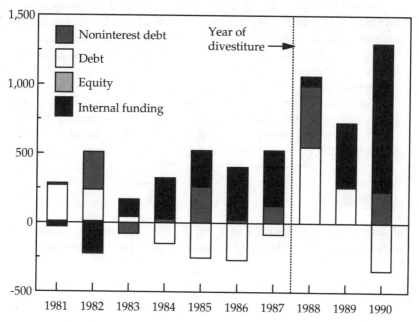

Millions of pounds sterling

Legend:
- Noninterest debt
- Debt
- Equity
- Internal funding

Year of divestiture →

Source: Authors' calculations from BA, various years.

other airlines in the private sector and enabled it to survive as a going concern in the early 1980s, when its liabilities exceeded its assets and it was technically bankrupt. Shortly after divestiture, in March 1987, BA had covered foreign loans of £89 million, other foreign loans of £133 million, and finance leases of £75 million; this represented a large decrease in the enterprise's indebtedness and a change in the mix of loans.

Figure 5-5, which presents total sources of funds, reveals turning points in 1987 (upward) and 1989 (downward). The breakdown of sources reveals the following points:

- In only three years was debt the primary source of finance. In 1981 and 1982 this was because of the enterprise's lack of profitability, and in 1988 it was because of the need to finance the acquisition of BCal.
- After 1983 (except for 1988) the main source of financing was internal (retained earnings and depreciation).
- The consequence was a precipitous decline in the debt-asset ratio from 1983 through 1987 and in 1990 (figure 5-6). The interruption in 1988 of the 1983–90 trend was caused by the acquisition of BCal.

- What is not apparent from the figures is that, at the time the prospectus was written in 1987, 41 out of 163 aircraft were leased on operating leases. Of these, 25 were extendable leases that could be converted to finance leases after six years, giving BA the option of purchasing the aircraft at no further cost. By March 1990, 72 out of 224 aircraft were financed by operating leases, 61 of them extendable. All the new aircraft acquired since the divestiture were on operating leases, with the exception of 8 Airbus A320s. The catalyst for this change appears to have been the need to add to the airline's short-haul fleet in 1983, at a time when the treasury was opposing extra public investment, and BA's debt-equity ratio was far too high for an easy flotation. A leasing deal arranged that summer allowed BA to acquire 14 Boeing 737s, circumventing treasury restrictions and financial market worries (Campbell-Smith 1986, pp. 95–102).

Fiscal Effects

The impact of the divestiture of BA on the U.K. treasury can be divided into two parts. First and most obvious is the price received for the shares

Figure 5-6.   Debt-Asset Ratio, British Airways, 1980–90

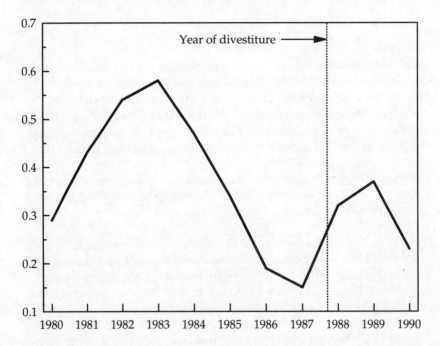

Source: Authors' calculations from BA, various years.

sold. Our calculations show that the net price for 100 percent of the enterprise (in February 1987 pounds sterling) was about £815 million. Second, an impact receiving much less attention, but potentially more important, is the flow of funds to the treasury that occurs on an ongoing basis. The principal components of this flow are taxes, and its net impact is sizable. We discuss first the sale transaction itself and then its fiscal effect.

The plan was to sell 720 million shares at a price of 125 pence each, of which 65 pence was payable at once and 60 pence six months later. U.K. financial institutions were initially allocated 45 percent of the shares, BA employees and the U.K. public were allocated 32 percent, foreign investors were allocated 20 percent, and the government retained 3 percent for use in incentive schemes. The issue to the public was oversubscribed by thirty-two times, and clawback provisions changed the allocation of shares, so that the public took 45 percent, U.K. institutions took 36 percent, and foreigners took 16 percent. The opening price on 11 February was 118 pence per partly paid share, falling to 109 pence at that day's close—a premium of 68 percent on the first installment.

The first-day premium on the shares represented a rise in the enterprise's value of £317 million. The government had planned for a rise of just under half that amount to have a successful issue, but the remainder was caused by a misreading of investors' sentiment about the enterprise (the government had initially presented it as an opportunity for experienced shareholders rather than for first-time buyers), and a rise in the general level of share prices between the announcement of the offer price and the start of dealings in BA shares (according to a National Audit Office report). Between the issue and June 1990 (before the Gulf crisis affected stock markets), BA generally outperformed the FT-Actuaries All-Share Index. The index rose by 23 percent during the period, while BA rose by 75 percent from the offer price and 28 percent from the first-day price (adjusted for the second payment), which suggests that the first-day price was sensible.

The actual net proceeds of the original issue are estimated to have been £858.5 million. The sale was of 699 million shares worth £873.2 million at the issue price. Employee discounts and free shares reduced this by £14.7 million. The government retained 3 percent of the shares to use as a loyalty bonus to small shareholders, and in May 1987 it estimated that it would need to use £13.1 million worth of these to satisfy the bonus (one share for every ten to a maximum of 400 extra shares). The remaining shares were to be sold, which was estimated to give a premium on the offer price of another £6.7 million. In the event, the government only issued 6.8 million bonus shares, sold some others (of its original 21.6 million shares), and continued to hold 3.2 million shares. If all the shares originally retained for the bonus are valued conservatively at £1.25 (in 1987 pounds sterling), whatever the price at which they are disposed of, then the 14.8 million shares can be valued at £18.5 million, giving total proceeds of £877.1 million.

The estimated transaction costs to the government came to £33.9 million (costs borne by BA and the costs of departmental administration are not included in the figures cited, which come from the National Audit Office, United Kingdom, 1987/88). Thus, the government's net receipts add up to £843.2 million. If one discounts to 30 January 1987 all receipts and costs to the U.K. government of the sale, then the net proceeds are reduced by another £25 million to £30 million, to about £815 million.

Annual fiscal flows are presented in figure 5-7. In the seven years prior to divestiture, the flows of funds between BA and the treasury consisted of small amounts of interest on loans held by the secretary of state (roughly £1 million annually), occasional payment and repayment of part of the principal, equity capital infusions, and value added and corporate income taxes. Except in 1980, the enterprise was paying no dividends. Leaving aside the value added tax, the net annual flow to the treasury was roughly £5 million.[6] The exception was 1984, when BA repaid £42.7 million in debt to the National Loans Fund.

Figure 5-7.   Fiscal Flows, British Airways, 1980–90

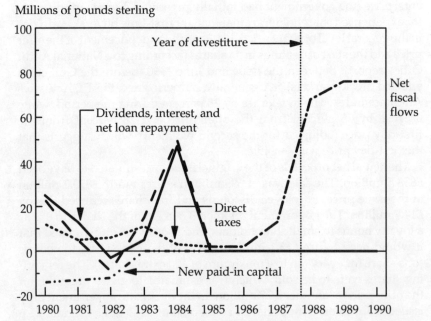

Millions of pounds sterling

Note: A positive flow is from BA to the government.
Source: Authors' calculations from BA, various years.

After divestiture, BA started paying sizable amounts of corporate income tax (in the range of £70 million to £80 million). This happened at least in part because of a change in the tax law in 1984 that reduced the deductibility of depreciation as an expense, and in part because of the enterprise's increased profitability. To what extent divestiture caused the jump in tax payments is therefore not entirely clear. In short, after divestiture the fiscal flow to the treasury rose some £60 million in the first year.

To reach the conclusion that the BA divestiture substantially enhanced U.K. fiscal flows, one has to consider the flows forgone, that is, dividends, interest, taxes, and other flows that would have accrued to the government in the absence of divestiture. This will be taken into account later.

Effects on Consumer Welfare

How has the divestiture of BA affected consumers? The simplest way to answer this question is to look at the trends in BA's prices. Table 5-2 compares BA's overall output prices during 1980–90, deflated by the consumer price index. Clearly, during 1981–85 BA's price increases exceeded the rise in the consumer price index, while during 1986–89 they stayed below it. In nominal terms, during the whole period prices for scheduled intercontinental flights increased least (69 percent), and those for scheduled U.K. and European flights increased most (95 percent). Prices for charter and other services were also on the high side (rising 92 percent and 83 percent, respectively). If one leaves out unusually high increases in prices for charter flights and unusually low increases in prices for scheduled intercontinental flights from 1980 to 1981, then charters become the service with the lowest increases from 1981 to 1990 (19 percent), while scheduled intercontinental flights (58 percent) are comparable with U.K. and European flights (65 percent) and other services (53 percent). By deemphasizing charter services, BA was building on higher-quality and higher-price services. The effect on consumer welfare of such quality shifts is hard to judge. Year-to-year comparisons indicate that, on the basis of pure price changes, consumers of BA's services lost surplus heavily in 1983, when BA was recovering financially. Starting in 1985, consumer surplus increased every year, especially in 1988.[7]

Summary

The question "What happened?" has three primary answers in terms of quantifiable changes in BA's behavior and performance around the time of divestiture:

Table 5-2. Real Price Changes and Consumer Surplus, British Airways, 1980–90

Category	1980	1981	1982	1983	1984	1985	1986	1987	1988	1989	1990
Scheduled U.K. and European flights											
Real price	0.84	0.89	1.02	1.15	1.19	1.04	0.99	1.07	0.98	0.89	0.88
Change in Price	n.a.	0.05	0.13	0.14	0.04	-0.15	-0.04	0.08	-0.09	-0.09	-0.01
Consumer surplus	n.a.	-38.00	-97.00	-97.00	-26.00	113.00	41.00	-77.00	101.00	103.00	15.60
Scheduled intercontinental flights											
Real price	0.37	0.35	0.35	0.39	0.40	0.41	0.38	0.36	0.34	0.34	0.33
Change in Price	n.a.	-0.02	0.00	0.03	0.01	0.01	-0.03	-0.02	-0.03	0.00	0.00
Consumer surplus	n.a.	64.00	-3.00	-118.00	-43.00	-40.00	112.00	81.00	134.00	-7.00	27.00
Air tours and charter services											
Real price	0.22	0.32	0.32	0.29	0.29	0.29	0.28	0.25	0.27	0.25	0.23
Change in Price	n.a.	0.10	0.00	-0.03	0.01	0.00	-0.01	-0.03	0.01	-0.02	-0.02
Consumer surplus	n.a.	-49.00	1.00	23.00	-4.00	4.00	5.00	32.00	-14.00	11.00	15.00
Other services											
Real price	0.51	0.55	0.61	0.67	0.67	0.62	0.60	0.63	0.57	0.51	0.50
Change in Price	n.a.	0.03	0.06	0.06	0.01	-0.05	-0.02	0.03	-0.06	-0.06	-0.01
Consumer surplus	n.a.	-18.00	-33.00	-33.00	-3.00	18.00	9.00	-10.00	20.00	25.00	5.00
Aggregate											
Real price	0.86	0.88	0.92	1.00	1.04	1.00	0.95	0.94	0.88	0.84	0.83
Change in Price	n.a.	0.02	0.04	0.08	0.04	-0.04	-0.06	-0.01	-0.06	-0.04	-0.01
Consumer surplus		-41.00	-132.00	-226.00	-76.00	114.00	168.00	26.00	241.00	132.00	62.00
Memorandum: consumer price index	0.71	0.79	0.86	0.90	0.94	1.00	1.04	1.07	1.13	1.22	1.32

n.a. Not applicable.
Source: Authors' calculations from BA data.

- **Quantity effects**. Global productivity and productivity surplus measures (real quasi rents per unit of capital and total factor productivity) show a dramatic positive turnaround in 1983. A major productivity slump in 1987 was followed by a recovery in 1988.
- **Price effects**. BA's output prices increased most dramatically during 1980–82, the years with the highest rate of inflation. They only decreased across the board in 1986 and to some extent in 1988. In real terms, prices increased in all years from 1980 to 1984 and decreased in all years from 1985 to 1990.
- **Investment effects**. Real gross fixed capital formation declined steadily during 1980–83 from £400 million to £100 million, then had a bumpy increase to about £250 million in 1987, jumping to above £800 million in 1988 and then declining to £440 million in 1990. Even if one omits the acquisition of BCal, the jump in 1988 is still impressive, and the subsequent decline appears minor. Thus, divestiture was clearly followed by growth in fixed capital formation and acquisition.

In sum, the quantitative evidence suggests only two clear and significant behavioral changes that could possibly be associated with divestiture, namely, positive turnarounds in 1984 and 1988 for productivity and public profits at constant prices and for fixed capital formation. The change in direction of real output prices in 1985 and the reduction in real gross fixed capital formation in fiscal 1990 appear to have been unrelated to divestiture.

Why Did It Happen?

How can we explain the correlations we found between BA's performance and divestiture? Two features make the answer particularly difficult. First, our data suggest that there were two major turnarounds in BA's performance, during fiscal 1984 and 1989, that have to be explained. Second, the timing of the turnarounds does not provide clear clues related to divestiture. The first turnaround occurred years after plans for BA's divestiture were made public, but before the actual divestiture took place, whereas the second turnaround coincided as much with divestiture as with the acquisition of BCal. Thus, for the first turnaround we have to explain that the phenomenon was not simply caused by the business cycle or some other condition exogenous to BA. If we find that it was caused by some endogenous factor, then we have to relate this factor to the announcement of divestiture. For the second turnaround we also have to be able to exclude external causal factors and to explain that the acquisition of BCal would not have happened under continued public operation of BA. Rather than consider the changes in investment, price, and quantity components at once for the entire 1980–90 period, we therefore prefer to explain the two major positive turnarounds separately.

The 1983–84 Turnaround

Recall that BA's performance in terms of private profit, public profit at constant prices, and total factor productivity deteriorated substantially during 1980–82. In 1980 real fixed capital formation was still at exceedingly high levels, indicating that BA was in the midst of a major aircraft fleet expansion program that was viewed as a means of reducing past overstaffing. In 1980 oil prices accelerated, and the airline industry, despite (or because of) rising output prices, experienced a slump in output quantity. BA's dismal performance in 1981 and 1982 can thus be traced to continued overstaffing combined with overinvesting. Hence, the 1983–84 turnaround starts from a deep valley in performance.

INVESTMENT EFFECTS. It appears fairly obvious that BA experienced overinvestment in 1980, so that the overall load factor fell from 64.6 percent in 1980 to 60.7 percent in 1981. This was the largest drop in any year between 1971 and 1990 (however, the 1981 load factor was still higher than in any year before 1979). The question is whether this situation was any different from that of other airlines, domestic or foreign.

Given the extent of overcapacity, BA had little need for additional investment, and therefore investment constraints, if any, would not have been binding. BA's gross capital formation remained low until 1987. This was in line with moderate output growth and an increase in load factors. Thus, unless BA's output would have grown more under the prospect of continued public operation, there is no reason to suspect that investment would have occurred at a substantially different level. However, after paying for a larger wage bill, even the low level of net capital formation experienced might have required substantially more external financing (or government subsidies).

PRICE EFFECTS. During 1980–82 output prices increased substantially, but as noted earlier, these increases were not enough to keep pace with input price increases. This seems to have been a phenomenon that BA shared with other airlines. The world's airlines as a group suffered operating losses from 1980 until 1982, and their operating profits averaged less than 3.5 percent of revenue between 1977 and 1988, before taxation and interest payments.

A comparison of average prices charged (per revenue tonne-kilometer) by BA and BCal (see table 5-3) shows that in 1980 (BA fiscal year 1981) prices were almost the same for both airlines (33.0 pence for BA versus 33.5 pence for BCal). However, thereafter BA's prices (and operating costs before depreciation) increased at a much faster rate until 1984, when BA's average price reached 48.3 pence versus 42.7 pence for BCal. The years 1985 and 1986 saw larger price increases for BCal, while BCal's price decline in 1987 was catastrophic against BA's almost steady prices. A

Table 5-3. *Average Prices and Costs, British Airways and British Caledonian, 1980–89*

Year	Prices		Costs	
	BA	BCal	BA	BCal
1980	33.0	33.5	31.2	30.5
1981	37.0	35.0	37.2	32.4
1982	39.1	35.5	37.1	34.1
1983	44.6	40.4	39.0	36.9
1984	48.3	42.7	40.5	38.4
1985	50.5	45.1	42.4	40.4
1986	50.0	45.8	44.4	41.6
1987	49.8	41.9	44.5	38.8
1988[a]	53.0	n.a.	46.4	n.a.
1989[b]	52.4	n.a.	44.7	n.a.

n.a. Not applicable.

a. BA figures partially include BCal.

b. BA figures fully include BCal.

Source: *International Airline Statistics*, various years, with adjustments made for BA's fiscal year.

comparison of price and cost increases shows that BCal was doing comparatively much better than BA in 1981, while BA was doing better from 1983 on.

In its pricing of outputs, the question is whether under continued public operation BA would have charged prices different from those under anticipated divestiture. We strongly believe that BA had been aiming for profit-maximizing prices and would have done the same under continued public operation, for two main reasons. First, given the large share of foreigners among BA's customers, the U.K. government would have had little reason to induce BA to charge prices below profit-maximizing levels. Second, even profit-maximizing prices, over the long run, have not led to excessive profits in the airline industry in general.

However, if one compares price and quantity growth at BA with that at BCal during 1980–87, one is led to believe that BA did change its pricing policy. During this period BA's prices grew, on average, by 6.1 percent compared with BCal's 3.2 percent price rise. Against this, the growth rate of operating costs (before depreciation) was 5.2 percent for BA versus 3.5 percent for BCal. Thus, BA apparently moved to higher-cost outputs (shorter distances and more service) relative to BCal but, in addition, enjoyed a net price increase (or cost decrease) over BCal. The conjecture that there have been net price increases relative to BCal is confirmed by the differential rate of expansion in the quantity of output. Output (in revenues per tonne-kilometer) grew at an average rate of 9.4 percent for BCal compared with 1.7 percent for BA. In contrast, the merged BA-BCal experienced a decrease in nominal prices and unit operating costs in 1989 over 1988 in terms of revenue tonne-kilometers. This suggests a structural output effect of the BCal merger on BA, and supports the conjecture that price and cost differences between BA and BCal before 1988 were due to differences in output structure.

QUANTITY EFFECTS. As stated earlier, BA's public profitability and total factor productivity increased during 1983–86 and 1988–89 but declined in 1981, 1982, and 1987. The question is, Were the 1983–86 improvements endogenous, caused by the announcement of divestiture, or exogenous, attributable to macroeconomic recovery? To answer this question we examine time-series and cross-sectional data in turn.

The main intertemporal question is whether the years 1983–85 mark an extraordinary recovery compared with the cyclical fluctuations that went on before. Unfortunately, data deficiencies prevent us from constructing a time series linking the 1970s and 1980s. Some partial indicators are, however, available from the literature. Hutchinson (1991) calculated growth rates in labor productivity for BA for 1970–75 at 0.9 percent per year, for 1976–81 at 8.1 percent, and for 1982–87 at 9.3 percent. (Hutchinson's numbers on BA's labor productivity are not quite compatible with those of Bishop and Thompson 1991, who report an average increase of 7.4 percent per year for 1970–80.)

Considering that 1981 and 1982 were low-productivity years, this indicates only minor improvement after 1982, while the period 1976–81 shows a real takeoff compared with 1970–75. Additional information provided by Hutchinson on capital-labor ratios makes the 1982–87 period look relatively worse, because the capital-labor ratio during this time increased by 10.7 percent per year compared with decreases of 0.5 percent for 1976–81 and 8.4 percent for 1970–75. Thus, Hutchinson's analysis indicates that from 1983 on BA was simply getting back onto its own long-run productivity trend. However, BA's crisis management is likely to have accelerated this process substantially.

BA's improvement in productivity would say little about the success of divestiture if BA's performance relative to other airlines simultaneously declined. The only comparable U.K. airline at the time was BCal, which experienced substantial difficulties. We would therefore rather compare BA with some other European airlines, all of which are fully or partly state owned.

A comparison of BA's total factor productivity on European routes with that of four other European airlines (Air France, KLM, Lufthansa, and Swissair) shows BA improving from third to second place between 1981 and 1986 (Encaoua 1991, pp. 121–22). Air France is first in both years. However, in 1981 it was 23.6 percent ahead of BA, but in 1986 it was only 4.9 percent ahead. According to Encaoua, all five airlines had a bad year in 1986 (BA's fiscal 1987) and a good year in 1984. The other years were a mixed bag.

BA shows a clear improvement in profitability and productivity during 1983–85. To some extent, time-series data of airline productivity performance lend support to the hypothesis that causation was specific to BA crisis management, but domestic and international comparisons do so more clearly. We conclude that there is convincing quantitative evidence that BA's performance improved during 1983–85 (subsequent improvements will be discussed later). Now, which factors specific to BA can be made responsible for the turnaround?

In 1981 Sir John King was appointed chairman to turn BA's performance around. His strategy was to reduce both the work force and capital expansion. Although the turnaround can be attributed to King's appointment, whether it can be attributed as an announcement effect of divestiture is questionable. The coverage in *The Economist* (e.g., 7 April 1979, p. 89, and 9 September 1979, p. 102) makes it plain that the government had planned to (partially) divest BA by 1981 or 1982, and that BA's management supported this. That announcement definitely did not lead to a performance improvement. Rather, immediately after the announcement performance deteriorated because of overinvestment and continued overstaffing.

It was the new management team under King that reduced overstaffing directly and turned the company around using a strategy of cost cutting rather than raising output. Hence, if one wants to attribute the 1983–84 improvement to the announcement, one might as well do so for the 1980–82 downturn. However, as the Monopolies and Mergers Commission (1987) put it, "Lord King of Wartnaby was appointed chairman, with the remit of returning the company to profitability and preparing it for privatisation." It is apparent from this that King took on the task as chairman with the clear understanding that BA would be divested. Thus, if the appointment of King can be attributed to divestiture, and the turnaround to the appointment of King, then the turnaround can be attributed to divestiture. There is, therefore, a high probability for a counterfactual without King and without the 1983–85 turnaround. However, other U.K. public enterprises in desperate situations have been able to attract executives of King's caliber and have been able to lay off large numbers of workers without the threat of divestiture. Most notable is the appointment of Ian McGregor as chairman of British Steel and later of the National Coal Board, and the layoffs at these two enterprises as well as at British Rail (these layoffs are documented in Bishop and Kay 1991).

The 1988–89 Turnaround

There is another reason not to stylize the 1983–84 turnaround into a major proof of a strong positive announcement effect. While the change during 1983–86 was dramatically positive, BA's productivity in 1986 exceeded its 1980 level by only 8 percent, and then declined in 1987.

A similar point can be made about the 1988–89 turnaround. Without the 1987 deterioration the 1988–89 turnaround would have been less visible. The bad year from April 1986 to March 1987 runs parallel to a decline in airline travel worldwide, especially across the Atlantic (this is also evident from Encaoua 1991). BA's prospectus (p. 39) reports a 21 percent decline in revenue passenger-kilometers on the North Atlantic routes in the first quarter of fiscal 1987, during which BA did not adjust its capacity. This contributed to the drop in the overall load factor from 68.0 in 1986 to 67.0 in 1987, although part of this was caused by expansion of short-haul capacity.

The investment effects of the 1988–89 turnaround are the simplest part of our story. BA was divested at a time when the public sector borrowing requirement had already largely ceased to be a stringent constraint. The only investment that we postulate as a result of divestiture was the purchase of BCal. We believe that this would not have taken place under continued public operation of BA, but the reason for this belief is not an investment constraint on BA's part. Given that private buyers were available, the government of Prime Minister Margaret Thatcher, on ideological grounds, would not have allowed a state-owned BA to take over its private competitor.

We cannot be sure about the exact extent to which BA's enormous gross fixed capital formation in 1988 and 1989 was influenced by the BCal acquisition. However, assume that there is a remainder that would have had to be financed under continued public operation. This could fairly easily have been accomplished, given that the U.K. fiscal deficit turned to a surplus in 1987–88; that investment at other U.K. public enterprises (e.g., in the electric power sector) began to recover in 1989; and that, according to our counterfactual run, BA would have been able to pay dividends to the treasury from 1987 on. The amounts could have been invested instead.

To what extent are changes in BA's rate level and rate structure attributable to divestiture? To begin with, note that two changes about divestiture might trigger price changes. The first is that BA would become free of government objectives to sacrifice profits in exchange for consumer benefits. The second is that BA's acquisition of BCal would reduce competition in the airline market. We have already disposed of the first argument in our discussion of the 1983–84 turnaround. Thus, we now have to show what the effect of the BCal acquisition on prices has been, if any.

One strong hypothesis is that BA would probably have kept rates from 1987 to 1990 about where they actually ended up. This was the Monopolies and Mergers Commission's basic prediction when it approved the BA-BCal merger. Three reasons support this conjecture: first, the regulation of domestic rates and the dependence of international rates on bilateral agreements; second, the existence of legal entry barriers and airport congestion at Heathrow and Gatwick; and third, the contestability of airline markets. We discuss these reasons in turn.

The United Kingdom had deregulated domestic rates by 1985, long before the acquisition of BCal. International bilateral agreements were still important but only governed about half the routes in which BA and BCal used to compete directly. Clearly, bilateral agreements are likely to have some cartel effects. We nevertheless judge that the scope of regulation and bilateral agreements during 1987–90 would not have prevented all or most of BA's international prices from being lower if BCal had continued to be independent.

Legal entry barriers have increasingly lost importance in aviation. Domestically in the United Kingdom they had been abolished by 1987 and were not binding on BCal for most of the routes in which it was competing with BA. The more intriguing question concerns airport congestion. To dispose of this argument, we really would have to show that Gatwick and Heathrow were not fully constrained during all of 1987–90. One way to make this point is to show that traffic increased without an increase in capacity. In reality, major expansions at Heathrow had been largely completed by 1987, while at Gatwick new capacity was added in stages from 1987 on (United Kingdom, Department of Transport 1985). Traffic at Heathrow increased from 308,000 to 368,000 movements, and at Gatwick from 174,000 to 189,000 movements during 1987–90 (United Kingdom, Department of Transport forthcoming). Whereas before the expansion Heathrow had virtually no excess capacity, it must have had some when the new terminal came on stream. Gatwick was less constrained to begin with, and its traffic grew by less than the capacity expansion.

The contestability hypothesis states that it is not actual competition alone but equally potential competition that determines the price in markets with no entry barriers. Aside from congestion, other entry barriers appear to exist that make airline markets noncontestable. This has been shown repeatedly in the literature and is now widely acknowledged (see, for example, Morrison and Winston 1987, and Hurdle and others 1989).

To sum up, the only reason with substance why the BA-BCal merger might not have influenced rates is airport congestion. To the extent that congestion posed no binding constraint on the combined output of BA and BCal, the question therefore remains how prices would have been set in the absence of the merger. First, we have no information on direct competition in charter flights. Note here that BA was not and is not the dominant charter airline in the United Kingdom, and BCal was only 40 percent of BA's size in charters. This market was and remains reasonably competitive. Hence, any price effect of the BCal acquisition on the charter airline market is unlikely. Second, we can dismiss the notion that BCal would have had an effect on market prices on scheduled routes where it did not compete directly with BA (dismissal of contestability and of network pricing). Third, we assume Cournot competition in equilibrium for those markets in which BA and BCal competed before the merger and that were not subject to price regulation or bilateral agreements.[8] For scheduled flight services we come up with a 0.4 percent price differential between the actual and the counterfactual.[9] Prices for charter and other services appear to have been unaffected by divestiture.

BA shows some improvement in productivity at the time of divestiture. As mentioned above, productivity increases in the years 1983–86 resulted mostly from a decrease in the quantity of inputs, while outputs were flat or declining. In contrast, large output increases accompanied the 1988 and 1989 productivity increases. These output increases can be traced largely to BA's acquisition of BCal. Furthermore, when the 1987 productivity slump is ignored, the extra improvement in productivity in 1988 appears to be small and fully attributable to the BCal acquisition. Through the merger with BCal, BA actually grew by less than the former size of BCal. This is partly because the merged enterprise had to give up slots, and partly because of the relative price increase. According to our estimates, the revenue difference between the actual situation and the counterfactual in 1989 (the first full year after the merger) is £600 million, rather than BCal's premerger revenues of £750 million. The corresponding difference in the number of employees is 5,400, compared with 7,700 BCal employees before the merger. This difference can be used as the basis for a counterfactual estimation of the merger's effect on BA's productivity.

Other than that, we conclude that there is no convincing quantitative evidence that BA's productivity through 1990 was enhanced by the 1987 divestiture.

Counterfactual Scenarios

We have argued that the appointment of a successful top manager in 1981 and the 1983–84 turnaround would likely have happened without the plan for BA's eventual divestiture. Our base counterfactual therefore ignores any announcement effects and looks only at changes that occurred in direct connection with divestiture. In addition, we briefly report on an alternative scenario that helps us evaluate a possible announcement effect from the measures Lord King and his management team took from 1982 on.

Accordingly, in our base counterfactual run, we assume very little behavioral change in technical coefficients. The main behavioral effects of divestiture here stem from the acquisition of BCal.

The base counterfactual assumes three major differences from what actually happened. First, BCal's assets, liabilities, routes, employees, and so on would not have been added to BA, but would instead have been used elsewhere. Here we assume that BCal would have continued to exist, either independently or merged with another, possibly foreign, airline. Second, without the merger, BA would have kept prices slightly lower than it actually did. We assume that the effect of the merger on prices was restricted to scheduled flight services and amounted to a 0.4 percent price differential. Third, without the merger, BA would have had less incentive and opportunity to increase labor productivity.

In the alternative counterfactual scenario we assume that BA's work force reduction between 1982 and 1984 would have been much less drastic, and we trace the consequences of this difference. In addition, we assume the BCal acquisition would not have occurred.

What Will Happen?

The airline industry has been undergoing such massive changes in market organization and has been so affected by world politics that its long-run outlook is highly uncertain. The outlook of any single firm in this market is more uncertain still. In our projections, therefore, we have taken the existing frameworks used to analyze the data period 1980–90 and have made assumptions about reasonable growth rates or parameter values. The main purpose is not to predict the future, but rather to derive present discounted values for the main variables.

To facilitate comparison between the private and public cases, we have assumed the same exogenous long-run demand growth of 4 percent per year for the actual situation and for both counterfactual cases (note, however, that BA's 1990 annual report still quoted a consensus of predictions for 6 percent annual growth of the airline industry through the 1990s). In addition, we have assumed a constant 6 percent inflation rate in the projection period, so nominal demand for each output grows by that factor also.

To make quantity projections and to achieve counterfactual output quantities, we made assumptions about (real) price elasticities of demand for BA's four outputs. These assumptions reflect our reading of the relevant economics literature. For scheduled U.K. and European flights we assumed an elasticity of 1.1, for intercontinental flights of 1.2, for air tours and charters of 1.5, and for miscellaneous services of 1.0.

Regarding prices we assumed that, in line with our conservative bias, the estimated price differential of 0.4 percent for scheduled flight services would persist over time. As concerns price changes over time, an assumed real price decrease of only 0.2 percent per year after 1990 reflects our conviction that major real price decreases cannot continue forever.

For both the private and the public cases we assumed constant real input costs other than labor after 1990, plus a constant opportunity cost of working capital, a discount rate of 15 percent (or 9 percent in real terms), and a constant loan rate of 12 percent (or 6 percent in real terms).

The driving force behind input requirements is technological prog-ress, which we believe to be primarily labor saving. We have assumed that the per unit requirements of intermediate inputs, inventories, and working capital remain unchanged throughout the period for both cases. We have, however, assumed changes in labor requirements.

BA reduced its work force by more than 4,000 in 1991–92. Although the quantity of labor has not declined dramatically, we take this as indicative for the current private sector management of BA, and therefore we implicitly assume some improvement in the labor efficiency parameter resulting in a 1 percent annual reduction in real labor costs after 1990 in the private case. In the public case, we assume that real labor costs per unit of output would have been stationary during 1988–90 and would decline by 1 percent per year thereafter.

What Is It Worth?

In this section we determine the bottom line on net benefits, and we examine whether they were positive or negative and how they were distributed.

Given our base scenario assumptions, we can summarize the answers in six propositions (table 5-4 and figure 5-8):[10]

• Although changes from divestiture went in both directions, society reaps a net gain of £680 million (in 1987 pounds sterling). If this were converted into a perpetual annual flow (at a real interest rate of 9 percent), it would be 2 percent of BA's 1987 revenues. About £125 million of the net gain goes to foreigners, while about £550 million stays in the United Kingdom.

• Private buyers do well for themselves, paying about £875 million (£1.22 per share) for stock worth £1,650 million (£2.29 per share), for a net gain of about £770 million. Of this gain, about £83 million goes to BA employees.

• The government is less of a winner, coming out about £315 million ahead.

• Consumers, in contrast, are worse off by about £325 million, which, however, is only 0.6 percent of the present value of consumer surplus generated in BA's markets. (Foreign consumers lose approximately an additional £190 million [in 1987 pounds sterling] that has not been included in our other calculations.)

• Although output prices went up, BA's erstwhile competitors lose about £85 million from divestiture. However, we believe that compet-itors actually gain, because the negative number results from quasi rents that would have accrued to the former BCal (or its potential other acquirers) and are now shifted to BA.

- In terms of intertemporal welfare change, the data period (1987–90) comes out with a loss of £150 million (including transaction costs), and the first five-year projection period (1991–96) shows a moderately positive balance of £200 million, as less financing is required. The final period shows the remaining gain of about £630 million. The negative outcome for the data period is entirely explained by additional financing, in particular of BCal's assets. Although these assets are financed in the data period, their productive benefits occur largely during the first five years of the projection period.

The bottom-line results under the alternative counterfactual scenario (not shown) differ from those in the base scenario mainly by an increase in the net gain to society of about £240 million, from £680 million to about £920 million (in 1987 pounds sterling), with virtually all the increase going to the government in the form of higher taxes (£130 million) and less reduction in quasi rents (£110 million).[11]

Our base value of V_{pp} of about £1,650 million is almost exactly equal to BA's highest stock market value in January 1993. Considering that V_{pp} is a 1987 present value, one may be surprised that it is so close to BA's

Table 5-4. Distribution of Welfare Gains and Losses from Divestiture, British Airways
(millions of pounds sterling)

Category	Private operation[a]	Public operation[b]	Difference
Government			
Taxes	5,123	4,776	346
Net quasi rents	502	1,376	−874
Net sales proceeds (cash)	843	0	843
Total	6,468	6,153	316
Employees	0	0	0
Private domestic shareholders			
Diverse	646	0	646
Concentrated	0	0	0
Foreign shareholders	126	0	126
Competitors	892	976	−84
Subtotal	8,131	7,128	1,003
Consumers	49,278	49,600	−323
Total	57,409	56,729	680

a. BA and BCal combined.
b. BA only.
Source: Authors' calculations.

market assessment at the time of this writing. It is also much higher than BA's actual market assessment right after divestiture. In our view, the main reason for the difference lies in the applied discount factor. Our base case scenario shows BA only earning normal rates of return over the long run. We do, however, assume steady-state conditions in the future without major interferences such as the Persian Gulf war. Clearly, we could have done a risk adjustment in the private discount rate for BA's profits. An increase in the nominal private discount rate from 15 percent to 20 percent reduces V_{pp} to £1,177 million, slightly below BA's market valuation on the first trading day in 1987. However, our main emphasis has been on the welfare effects rather than on the stock market. We therefore have assumed away uncertainty and risk aversion.

Compared with other industries, BA has been paying fairly high average wages and salaries. For example, between 1980 and 1987 the average remuneration of BA employees was 35 percent higher than that of the average British Telecom employee, and 65 percent higher than that of the average National Freight employee. Although differences in qualifications and responsibilities can explain a large portion of the difference, one might expect that any involuntary layoffs at BA from

Figure 5-8.   Distribution of Welfare Gains and Losses from Divestiture, British Airways

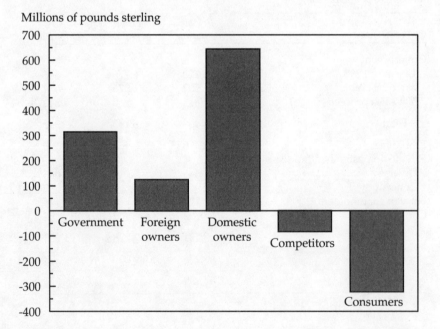

Millions of pounds sterling

Source: Authors' calculations.

divestiture would reduce labor rents. In our base case scenario we postulate no causal relationship between divestiture and the BA layoffs in the early 1980s. However, we have to consider the layoffs of 4,600 employees in fiscal 1992 and 1993. For these layoffs BA has put aside £97 million in severance pay. This comes to slightly more than £20,000 per employee. We believe that this amount is enough to compensate for most or all labor rents lost through layoffs.

The difference in average employee remuneration between BA, on the one hand, and British Telecom and National Freight, on the other, widened during 1980–84 and shrank thereafter. This indicates that BA's divestiture has not created any sizable new labor rents through wage and salary increases.

Labor rents were, however, created through the sale of shares to BA employees at the time of divestiture. Eligible employees and pensioners received a total of £14.7 million in discounts and free shares. In addition, they were given the opportunity to buy more shares at divestiture than were ordinary U.K. citizens. The total amounted to about 9.5 percent of BA's shares at the time. One can argue that as citizens they would have bought some amount of shares anyway. However, 94 percent of the eligible employees made use of the offer, whereas fewer than 2 percent of the general population became shareholders. Hence, we believe that £14.7 million plus about 9 percent of the remaining total shareholder gain of £757 million (772 minus 14.7) accrues to employees, giving them a total of £83 million.

Conclusion

The quantitative evidence on BA's performance suggests two clear and significant behavioral changes that could possibly be associated with divestiture, namely, positive turnarounds in 1984 and 1988 for productivity and fixed capital formation. We believe that two events can explain these two main turnarounds. The 1984 turnaround is based on cost-cutting and possibly on output-improving measures taken by BA under its new chairman, Lord King. Lord King's appointment itself could be related to the announcement of BA's divestiture, but we remain uncertain about this causal link.

The 1988 turnaround is closely linked to BA's acquisition of BCal and the synergies realized through this merger. We firmly believe that the merger would not have occurred without BA's divestiture.

Our base counterfactual traces only the consequences of the government's sale transaction and the effects of the BCal acquisition. In addition, our alternative counterfactual scenario takes into consideration that announcement effects could have occurred during 1982–86.

Our review of the quantitative record suggests that as a result of the divestiture of BA:

• BA acquired BCal in December 1987, resulting in some improvement in operational efficiency and some increase in BA's market power.

• BA improved its performance during 1982–87 through massive layoffs during 1982–84. This improvement could be attributed to the announcement effect of divestiture.

• Changes after 1987 were sufficient to make society better off by £680 million at 1987 prices. If one includes changes made between 1982 and 1987 as an announcement effect of divestiture, the net gain increases to £919 million.

• BA's divestiture was almost a Pareto improvement, with some overall losses for consumers and possibly for BA's competitors.

Notes

This chapter was written by Ingo Vogelsang and Richard Green with Manuel Abdala. The authors would like to thank Roger Maynard of British Airways for supplying them with data.

1. From 1960 on, other U.K. airlines were allowed to operate scheduled flights, but none came close to the size of the state carriers.

2. This assumes that the convenience of using Heathrow is worth more, relative to the fare, for the more expensive classes than for charter travelers.

3. Differences between our numbers and BA's published income statement and balance sheet result from our spreading out provisions for severance pay over the 1982–85 period.

4. As explained in chapter 2, the total factor productivity indicator and public profitability at constant prices tell essentially the same story. In BA's case, public profitability is considerably more volatile because it is the difference between benefits and costs rather than their ratio. However, both series rise and fall in tandem.

5. Between 1977 and 1981 the U.K. treasury operated an exchange cover scheme, under which BA could borrow in dollars in the United States and then swap the dollar loan for an existing one with the treasury.

6. During 1980–85 BA paid, on average, £3 million per year in direct taxes to foreign governments. This number was reduced to £1 million during 1986–89 and increased to £5 million in 1990.

7. Consumer surplus change here has been calculated by multiplying the price change by the quantity sold in the previous period (the Slutsky compensation). By neglecting the effects of demand elasticities, the Slutsky compensation is a conservative approximation that underestimates improvements in consumer surplus and overestimates deteriorations.

8. We assume here that other firms' market shares do not change as a result of the merger. Under this assumption the other firms have to experience marginal cost increases along with output reductions (see Farrell and Shapiro 1990 on the problem of relating price increases to mergers). If oligopolistic competition between airlines is of the Bertrand type, the price effects of the BA-BCal merger will depend on the change in joint capacity and its effects on the marginal cost of the marginal suppliers. Similarly, if BA can be viewed as a dominant firm and the other firms as the competitive fringe, the price effect would depend on the merger's effect on the marginal cost of the marginal firms. In the case of domi-

nance at a hub, an increase in the price differential between BA and its remaining rivals at Heathrow and Gatwick is likely (see Borenstein 1989). If the combined BA-BCal has less market share than the two individual enterprises had before the merger, then it is questionable whether the market share increase of (foreign) competitors benefits the United Kingdom.

9. Our numbers are derived by calculating implicit price-cost margins from unit cost and revenue tables provided in Encaoua (1991). The resulting price effect is small enough to be considered conservative. In fact, BA's price differential over BCal before the merger indicates that there is some product differentiation that we are unable to capture in our model. For the effect of mergers on prices in differentiated product markets see Willig (1991, pp. 281–312).

10. We have also conducted sensitivity tests of the relative impact of various variables on the profit and welfare change from the BA divestiture. Unsurprisingly, BA's private valuation, V_{pp}, is most influenced by output pricing, capital disposal, and capital deterioration rates. In addition, our bottom-line welfare results are fairly sensitive to changes in BA's output pricing (relative to input prices) and the real discount rate.

11. What needs some explanation is why BA employee rents remain the same as under the base case scenario. Recall that BA reduced its work force drastically during 1982–84. Accordingly, the difference under continued public operation between the base case and the alternative counterfactual scenario in the number of employees between 1982 and 1987 is 30,000 employee-years. However, BA paid £167 million in severance pay to employees leaving the enterprise or retiring early. This severance would have paid for 12,000 employee years or 40 percent of the total remuneration. In our view, 40 percent is a generous estimate of the rents to BA employees at the time. Hence, we believe that virtually no employee rents were lost as a result of the reduction in BA's work force.

6. National Freight

NFC plc, formerly the National Freight Consortium plc, is the holding company for a number of transport and other companies. As a holding company, NFC supplies central direction to its operating companies but delegates most decisions to them. This decentralization of decisionmaking (also practiced when NFC was in the public sector) makes the U.K. road transport industry very different from the typical, fairly monolithic, nationalized industry. Road freight transport is a fragmented industry. It is also a major one: turnover in the United Kingdom equaled 8.7 percent of that country's GDP in 1989, and the industry is similarly important in most other countries, so that a major state-owned transport enterprise is a good candidate for divestiture.[1] NFC is also of great interest because, for most of the 1980s, 80 percent of its shares were reserved for past and present employees of the group and their families, who still own the majority of shares, although the company is now quoted on the London Stock Exchange. NFC's employee buyout was almost unique in the history of public-enterprise divestiture, and the company believes strongly that its worker-shareholders have created a much more successful company because they own it.

The 1982 employee buyout of NFC has been celebrated as a surprising success. Before divestiture, NFC's outlook was bleak. Around 1980 in particular, NFC was overstaffed, short on investment, and losing money. After divestiture the company grew in output but continued for some time to shrink in employment.

Hopes and expectations for NFC's divestiture were not high after the government produced reports saying that it would not be possible to find a willing buyer. On the other hand, NFC was operating in competitive markets. Also, for a number of years NFC had been a financial drain on the government. Hence, it was a prime candidate for divestiture.

There appears to be wide agreement among economists, politicians, regulators, and financial analysts about NFC's performance since divestiture. First, NFC has been extremely successful in terms of its financial performance, although this may have been helped by its inheritance of valuable real estate, which could be disposed of in a booming real estate market. Second, NFC has been successful in its output markets and has expanded rapidly. Third, labor ownership has worked: NFC has had peaceful labor relations even as it has reduced its work force and increased productivity. Fourth, the company's new owners have made enormous capital gains (over 10,000 percent in less than ten years).

This chapter will not overturn any of these conclusions. However, our quantifications may change the conventional view about the distribution of the benefits.

Background

The following sections trace the history of National Freight in the context of the freight industry in the U.K. as well as labor relations in the NFC.

History

The motor freight transport industry in the United Kingdom has almost always been highly fragmented. The industry became significant only after the first world war released many ex-service vehicles, and many demobilized servicemen became self-employed owner-drivers. There were few entry barriers, either legal or financial, and few economies of scale for many types of operation at the level of the firm, so that a pattern of many small firms was established and has tended to remain (Mackie, Simon, and Whiting 1987). Concern over safety—and for the railway companies' profitability as they lost business to the road haulers—led to the creation of a system of operator licensing in 1933, intended to ensure standards and restrict entry. To carry goods for "hire or reward" an operator had to demonstrate "proof of need," but this was not required for a firm wishing to carry its own goods. "Own-account" haulage was therefore boosted by the licensing system, even after the 1953 Transport Act made entry easier by requiring those objecting to a license application to prove that there was no need for the service.

The licensing system failed to protect the railways' freight business. The railways carried 26 percent less general merchandise in 1937 than in 1913, despite the overall rise in activity. Growth in road transport since 1953, both in absolute terms and relative to rail, has been substantial, and there was also a significant shift away from own-account to hire-and-reward haulage during the 1960s, when carriers' licensing became easier, but before it was replaced by operator licensing (requiring only technical competence) in 1970.

In 1948 the Labour government nationalized many of the long distance road haulage firms under the British Transport Commission, but many of them were returned to the private sector by the subsequent Conservative government between 1952 and 1956. British Road Services (BRS) ran those that remained in the public sector, competing against the private haulers. In 1962 all the publicly owned nonrail transport businesses were brought under the Transport Holding Company, which bought some other businesses from the private sector, encouraged by the 1964–70 Labour government.

The 1968 Transport Act created the National Freight Corporation,[2] which was charged with integrating road and rail services throughout the country. NFC comprised the road freight transport companies of the Transport Holding Company (which were profitable), two shipping companies (one of which was sold and the other closed in 1971), and two former divisions of British Rail (which were both money losers). Freightliners Ltd., in which British Rail retained a 49 percent stake, was the recently established rail terminal and road haulage part of the railway's freight container activities and was expected to become profitable as it matured. National Carriers Ltd. was the new name for British Rail's division of road parcel carriers, which was massively unprofitable: its revenues in 1968 were about £25 million and its losses £20 million—as far as could be gathered, since British Rail did not give it separate accounts. National Carriers' 25,000 staff were transferred to NFC but remained members of the railway unions, covered by railway pension schemes, which would cause problems later. The government realized that absorbing National Carriers would cause problems for the new corporation, and it allocated up to £60 million in grants over five years, to cover losses and interest payments on the corporation's debt. NFC was set up with £99 million of fixed-interest debt and no equity, which would later mean that trading profits were often converted into overall losses. NFC's other inheritance from National Carriers was a "dowry" of property, often occupying prime sites. This was intended to be some compensation for the enterprise's other problems, and it started NFC in the property business.

The burden of interest payments was a heavy one for NFC and kept the group from making an overall profit in more than two of its first nine years, although it only traded at a loss in the recession years between 1974 and 1976. This burden was reduced by the 1978 Transport Act, which wrote off £53 million of NFC's debt (leaving £100 million) and provided a £15 million grant for capital expenditure. The legislation also returned the profitable Freightliners business to British Rail. As a result of the restructuring, NFC made an overall profit of £10 million in 1979.

The idea of divesting NFC was first mentioned in 1977 in "The Right Track," a Conservative party policy document on transport, which proposed the sale of part of NFC to create a "BP solution" (British Petroleum Co. plc had been for many years owned partly by the government and partly by private shareholders). This solution was the subject of a *Daily Telegraph* article in March 1979, which was immediately noted by the NFC board (McLachlan 1983), and the Conservative election manifesto of April 1979 confirmed that party policy was "to sell shares in the NFC to the general public in order to achieve substantial private investment in it." During the election campaign the corporation analyzed some of the possibilities for a sale, none of which looked particularly promising. The profitable divisions might be sold piecemeal or as a group, but either scheme would leave an unprofitable rump, and the board would resist any breakup. Selling the corporation as a whole would be more acceptable to the board, but it knew that the government would find it difficult to sell the enterprise except for much less than its net asset value, meaning that NFC's financial prospects would first have to improve.

When the Conservatives won the election, NFC began to work toward a divestiture, advised by the merchant bank J. Henry Schroder Wagg & Co. (Schroders), which also acted for the government. Schroders soon confirmed that a mid-1981 flotation was the earliest possible, and that they would have preferred a later date. On 21 June U.K. Transport Secretary Norman Fowler confirmed that he was considering methods of meeting the commitment in the party's manifesto, and that he "preferred . . . to retain the NFC in the form in which it is broadly constituted at present" (*Hansard*, 21 June 1979). The Transport Bill published in November and passed in June 1980 enabled him to turn NFC into a public limited company and to sell its shares as he thought fit. National Freight Company Ltd. took over the assets and liabilities of the National Freight Corporation on 1 October 1980, when the corporation's debt of £100 million was extinguished.

At this stage, however, a flotation of shares was rapidly receding into the distant future. The general recession of 1980 greatly reduced NFC's turnover and profits, and therefore the valuation that the stock market would place on the enterprise. Equally important was the loss of the enterprise's largest contract, with the British Rail Express Parcels Service. British Rail was losing money on this service and obtained permission to end it in September 1980. NFC made a profit on the contract, which represented 7 percent of its turnover, and its loss caused NFC to incur restructuring costs of £25 million (McLachlan 1983, p. 34). Schroders soon announced that a flotation would be impossible before 1982, and the prospects better in 1983. Against this background of delay imposed largely by external factors, a group of senior executives, led by Peter Thompson, deputy chairman and chief executive, began to investigate the possibility of a management buyout. In the first months of 1981 the idea of a buyout open to all employees was born and presented to the board and the Department of Transport. Insiders would be willing to buy the enterprise without waiting for an audit to show profitable results, as a flotation would require; this would allow an earlier sale. The concept of an employee-owned company would also be politically attractive, it was felt. The hope was that employees who owned shares in their company (for it was to be a shareholder-owned company, not a cooperative) would work harder, producing better results. In April 1981 the Department of Transport gave its approval to proceed toward a sale, and the consortium was publicly announced on 18 June 1981. Negotiations on the sale price for the enterprise were concluded on 15 October. One problem faced during this period was that the U.K. Companies' Acts made it illegal for a company to use its assets as security for a loan with which to purchase its own shares. Barclays Merchant Bank was willing to lend to the consortium on an unsecured basis but would have required 40 percent of its equity in return; this was acceptable to the consortium, but it would have greatly preferred to restrict the bank's share to below 20 percent. The Companies' Act of 1981 changed the law so that assets of subsidiary companies could be used as security, subject to various declarations by their directors, and mortgages were taken on 250 properties owned by the operating subsidiaries, worth a total of £76.5 million, during November.

The formal offer of shares in the consortium was made in January 1982. The sale would succeed only if a large number of employees, most of whom had never considered buying shares before, invested in the consortium, and its leaders considered good communications with its work force vital. After a slow start, the offer was eventually oversubscribed by 12.5 percent, and larger applications had to be scaled down when the subscription period closed on 16 February. The sale was formally completed on 19 February 1982.

Between 1982 and 1989 NFC was practically unique, as a limited company with most of its shares restricted to what Sir Peter Thompson (he was knighted in 1984) called the "NFC family" of employees, past employees, and their families. With these restrictions, the consortium's shares could not be floated on the stock exchange, and special arrangements had to be made to allow dealings in them. A special NFC share-dealing trust organized four dealing days each year. A "fair price" per share was established by an independent valuer and publicized shortly before each dealing day; those eligible could then apply to buy or sell shares through the trust. The value of the shares rose fairly steadily, after taking account of a number of share splits intended to help widen ownership.

As the value of the consortium's share capital rose, the directors feared that the demand for shares from new employees would become insufficient to absorb the supply as the older workers, who had bought many shares cheaply in 1982, began to sell those shares (Thompson 1990, p. 168). They decided that this meant that a stock market flotation was inevitable, and the important question was how best to retain NFC's special character. To make a takeover harder, the consortium's articles of association were changed to limit the maximum shareholding to 8 percent of the issued shares. If a shareholder wished to exceed this limit (which would be essential in a takeover bid), a general meeting of the consortium would be required to change the articles, and at this meeting employee-owned shares would count double.

NFC decided against a flotation of new shares, because a price for the shares would have to be set in advance, but it arranged a so-called introduction to the stock exchange, in which trade in the existing shares of a company starts on a given day. No price had to be set in advance, as the market makers would soon determine a price, as they did with their existing share portfolios. This route reduced the costs the NFC would have to bear.

The board did not want too much of the "family" shareholdings to be sold once the shares were on the stock exchange, and it arranged a rights issue immediately before the introduction, to raise £50 million. Existing shareholders were offered one share for every eight they already held, but at the deeply discounted price of £1.30 (a trading price of £2.10 was expected; the valuation on the last dealing day had been £1.85). The mechanism for selling some shares at a profit to finance the acquisition of the holder's remaining allocation was carefully explained, since a major aim of the issue was "to make sure that the existing investors did not sell too many of their base load [of shares]" (Thompson 1990, p. 189). An investor who had committed the average individual shareholding of £700 in 1982 would make £2,800 by selling the rights issue shares.

When trading opened on 6 February 1989, the price settled at around £2.60 per share, much higher than expected. The "family" shareholders did reduce the proportion of shares that they held but continued to control the company; they still control it as of this writing and are expected to do so for many years at the current rate of selling.

The company's structure, which, with some movement between groups and some new groups created during the period, had lasted NFC for seventeen years, was changed in 1989. NFC is now organized in four divisions, each of which contains all the NFC companies in its special product lines. Whereas in the past foreign companies formed a separate group, NFC now attempts to offer an international service. The largest division in terms of turnover is Home Services, which contains the moving companies. Transport, the second largest division, includes BRS in the area of contract haulage, the more specialized Tankfreight, BRS Automotive (a car transporter company), Waste Management, and the Lynx parcels business. The third core division is Logistics, which includes companies that offer distribution services, mostly to the retail sector. In terms of personnel, Transport is the largest division, followed by Logistics and Home Services. The fourth division, Travel and Property, is not considered to be a core business sector and is much smaller than the other three (at 4 percent of turnover, but 16 percent of operating profits in 1989–91).

Transport Economics

In the absence of price and entry regulation, motor freight transport is an inherently unconcentrated industry. The technology of trucking and warehousing is fairly simple. In contrast to railroads, roads usable for trucking are freely available (except for gasoline and vehicle taxes). Thus, entry is cheap and easy. Economies of scale are exhausted at fairly low firm sizes in haulage, while in storage and terminal operation they may gain some relevance at the local level.[3] In recent years economies of scale may have gained more importance, as freight companies have come to solve more logistical problems for their clients and thus can offer faster and more extended services. Although in many instances the transport of a particular commodity between two given points might be considered a separate market, this view is not economically reasonable because trucks can easily be moved from one location and one commodity to another. Freight transport is not a single, indivisible industry; its numerous parts vary enormously. Flexibility is therefore essential for a successful transport company.

It has been contended that road transport is an industry subject to at times "destructive" competition. This has been linked to the relative ease of entry, which in time of severe recession may lead to entry by jobless entrepreneurs. To the best of our knowledge there exists no empirical evidence to substantiate this contention. Entry into trucking is easy, but so is exit. Trucks have a short life span and an almost perfect resale market. Nevertheless, to the extent that swings in supply and demand are seen as a threat, road haulage companies try to hedge against the accompanying risks by signing long-term contracts with shippers.[4]

Given the competitive nature of the industry, we assume in our analysis below that NFC has virtually no power over prices and, in the long run, should earn only a competitive return on its investments.

Labor and Labor Relations

The NFC's relations with its unions have long been generally cordial—a sign of the times was that, in November 1974, a new BRS parcels branch at Deptford was opened by J. L. Jones, MBE, general secretary of the Transport and General Workers' Union (NFC 1974) But they were also complex, with ten unions representing the three main negotiating groups (one represented all three groups) and another 5,000 workers covered by other bargaining machinery.

From 1969 to 1980 NFC reduced its labor force gradually by 50 percent, from 66,000 to 33,000; then in 1981 alone it cut its work force by nearly 30 percent, to 24,000. From 1984 onward employment at NFC was on a gradual rise, reaching almost 34,000 in 1991.

The Transport and General Workers' Union (TGWU), representing 85 percent of the enterprise's manual workers, opposed the sale at the time, and three of the four other unions were lukewarm, treating it as the least objectionable method of privatization, if privatization was inevitable. Yet many individual union members bought shares in the company. Bradley and Nejad (1989) sampled employees of BRS (Southern) in 1984 and found that one TGWU out of every three in the sample owned shares by that date. This was significantly different from the pattern among members of other unions and among nonunionized staff, where roughly three out of five were shareholders (there were actually more shareholders among members of the other unions than among the nonunion staff). Bradley and Nejad also found that managers and clerical employees, staff at small depots, and employees who were homeowners were more likely to invest, and they ascribed this finding to better information: homeowners were likely to be more familiar with the sort of financial package involved in buying shares, and the other classes were likely to have more knowledge of NFC's prospects than drivers who worked mostly on their own and had little contact with managers at large depots.

The analyses in the next two sections show the extent to which employee ownership, among other factors, changed NFC's performance after divestiture.

What Happened?

In this section we provide a quantitative description of NFC's development from 1977 to 1987. This period covers about five years before and five years after divestiture. To maintain the ability to analyze the five years before divestiture in detail, we sacrifice detail on the actual years after 1987, which are covered briefly in the section that presents our projections.

Profit and Profitability

Given the alleged private success of NFC's buyout, we start with private profit.[5] As shown in figure 6-1, the years 1977–82 were on average unprofitable; persistent profitability returned in 1983, and profits grew from that point onward. Growth occurred at decreasing rates from 1983 to 1985, but 1986 marked a strong increase followed by an almost equally strong increase in 1987.

As figure 6-1 also shows, public profit (at current market prices) tells essentially the same story. In particular, it shows the same turnaround in 1983 as does private profit (note that the kink appears in 1982, but the turnaround is in 1983). The only difference is that public profit in 1986–87 traces a convex upward curve, whereas the curve is concave for private profit. Figure 6-2 decomposes the total surplus. It shows in particular

Figure 6-1. Public and Private Profit, National Freight, 1977–87

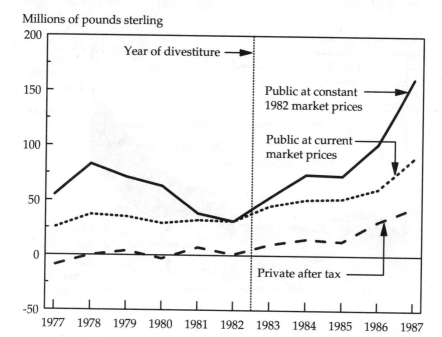

Millions of pounds sterling

Source: Authors' calculations from NFC data.

that most of the difference between private and public profit is accounted for by depreciation and debt service; direct taxes played no role through 1983 and only a small role thereafter.

Figure 6-1 provides two striking observations on public profit and its derivation at constant market prices. First, the period starts with an intriguing reversal: at constant prices public profit increased by 50 percent in 1978, then declined steadily from 1979 through 1982. The steady rise in public profit at constant prices from 1983 to 1987 is substantially more impressive than the movement at current prices. The 1987 level of the former is almost double that of 1978.

In sum, all three measures of profit show a major turnaround in performance in 1983. We found this to be due primarily to an increase in real output per worker and an expansion of output.

The variations in fixed capital formation (figure 6-3) are even more pronounced than the changes in profit. Much of this variation stems from two strong outliers (1978 and 1986), when fixed capital formation declined relative to trend, and the dramatic increase starts concurrently with that for public profit at constant prices.[6] Otherwise, fixed capital formation was constant from 1977 to 1982 and thereafter tripled in the

Figure 6-2.   Return to Capital at Current Market Prices, National Freight, 1977–87

Millions of pounds sterling

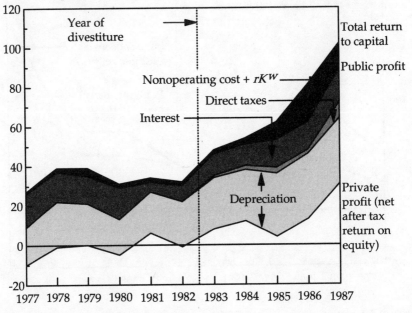

Source: Authors' calculations from NFC data.

five years from 1982 to 1987. The same series at constant prices shows essentially the same picture but at a somewhat lower level.

Changes in profits are easier to interpret when they are related to one of their primary causes, capital. Hence, an important summary performance measure is return to fixed capital or profitability. As figure 6-4 shows, all three measures of profitability show a kink around the time of divestiture. However, the private and the current-price public versions show a minor turnaround already in 1981. In contrast, the story for public profitability at constant prices is one of a pronounced turnaround in 1983. We have two waves, the first one peaking in 1978 and the second in 1984. That is, from 1978 through 1982, public profitability at constant prices fell by more than half (from about 28 percent in 1978 to about 11 percent in 1982); thereafter it increased to a local peak of almost 26 percent in 1984, but reached a global peak of 45 percent in 1987.

NFC's changes in total factor productivity (TFP) have been surprisingly small but somewhat volatile (figure 6-5). TFP decreased sharply from 1978 to 1982, then increased moderately for two years, decreased slightly in the next year, and increased once again in 1986 and 1987. Overall TFP in 1987 was only some 13 to 15 percent above its level in 1977 (the difference depends on which of three methods is used to calculate the capital cost component of TFP: the opportunity cost of the capital stock, enterprise profit, or depreciation plus the opportunity cost). This is substantially less than the overall increase in public profitability, which more than doubled. However, as can be seen clearly in figure 6-5, TFP and public profitability at constant prices rose and fell in tandem (except for 1980, when TFP showed a decrease and public profitability a slight increase).

Government Finance

The financial impact of the divestiture of NFC on the U.K. treasury can be divided into two parts. First and most obvious is the price the government received for the shares sold. The second impact stems from the flow of funds to and from the treasury that occurs on an ongoing basis. The principal components of this flow before divestiture were interest payments on government loans and new government grants (equity). Since divestiture they have been mostly taxes. We first discuss the sale transaction itself and then its fiscal effect.

Figure 6-3. Gross Fixed Capital Acquisition, National Freight, 1977–87

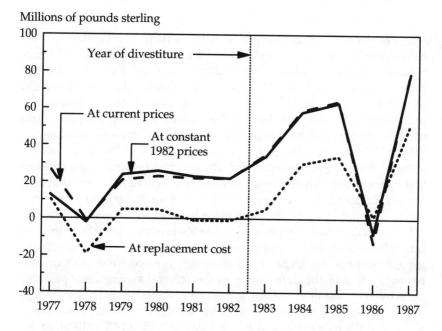

Millions of pounds sterling

Source: Authors' calculations from NFC data.

Figure 6-4.   Private and Public Profitability, National Freight, 1977–87

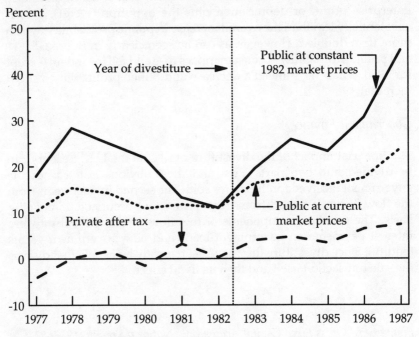

Source: Authors' calculations from NFC data.

The financial package finally negotiated, which was close to what the consortium originally wanted, involved a purchase price of £53.5 million, of which £7.5 million consisted of equity and the remaining £46 million was financed as debt. A syndicate of banks also provided a £30 million short-term credit facility as working capital for NFC. Employees of NFC had to raise at least £2.5 million in cash, or else the banks would not provide credit for their purchase of shares. The banks also demanded at least 17.5 percent of the equity in the form of special "B" shares, which allowed them to appoint a director. The consortium arranged a package that offered every employee an interest-free loan of £200, repayable in weekly installments over a year, in order to buy shares, and most retail banks considered applications for other loans to buy shares generously.

Divestiture is often facilitated by financial restructuring or "cleaning up the balance sheet," and NFC was no exception. Prior to the sale of NFC, the government was to pay the enterprise's pension fund £48.7 million to cover some of the deficiencies in the scheme arising from past underprovision; the government agreed to cover other deficiencies on a pay-as-you-go basis. These pension payments have often been used to argue that the true price paid for NFC was only about £5 million, or the net proceeds of the sale. Such arguments ignore the fact that these payments related to liabilities that had been incurred before 1975 and should be seen as a belated acknowledgment that the corporation's true profitability in those years was overstated (although government decisions were responsible for much of the original underfunding). The payments were not concerned with NFC's current or future performance but represented a liability that would have had to be met somehow. Had the divested enterprise been required to fund the pensions, it would have inherited a burden from the past that would have impeded its performance, without changing the incentives for management. In other words, the £48.7 million pre-1975 underfunding had not been carried on NFC's balance sheet as a liability for any length of time—it was only discovered in March 1980, and a provision for it in NFC's balance sheet of £21.6 million was made on 30 September of that year. By paying the amount out of the sale proceeds, the U.K. government made the balance sheet numbers correspond to the enterprise's actual liabilities. The government could also have corrected the balance sheet at an earlier date to reflect the actual liabilities.[7] In any case, if one assumes that the government eventually would have had to step in to pay for these deficiencies, then the purchase price should not be reduced by this use of funds.[8]

Figure 6-5. Year-to-Year Changes in Total Factor Productivity and Real Public Profit, National Freight, 1978–87

Percent

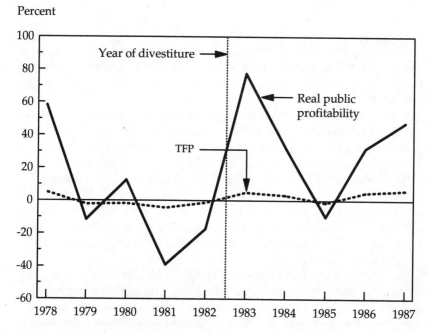

Source: Authors' calculations from NFC data.

Figure 6-6.   Fiscal Flows, National Freight   1977–87

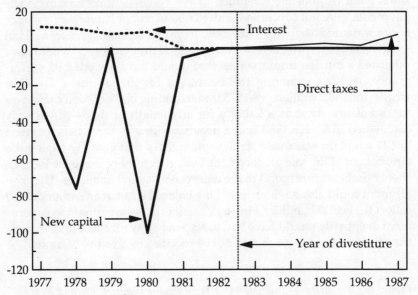

Millions of pounds sterling

Note: A positive flow is from National Freight to the U.K. government.
Source: Authors' calculations from NFC data.

The post-1975 underfunding was not covered by the agreement. But in fact it disappeared during the 1980s, in the face of lower inflation and better investment performance than the actuaries had predicted.

In the five years prior to divestiture, the only flows of funds between NFC and the treasury were interest on loans held by the secretary of state (roughly £10 million annually) and transfers from the treasury to NFC (in varying amounts: £30 million in 1977, £76 million in 1978, none in 1979, £100 million in 1980, and £5 million in 1981). The enterprise was paying no corporate income tax, nor was it paying any dividends. We disregard NFC's payment of value added tax (VAT) because we believe that NFC's divestiture has had no effect on the total VAT collected by the U.K. government. The net annual flow to the treasury averaged on the order of £35 million (figure 6-6).

Since divestiture, NFC has been paying sizable amounts of corporate income tax, in the range of £8 million in 1987 and averaging £21 million in 1988–91. This is a consequence of the increased profitability of the company. Taxes did not start to increase until long after NFC returned to profitability, largely because of loss carryforwards. To what extent the jump in tax payments is "due" to divestiture is not entirely clear because profits might have increased in any case.

The bottom line on fiscal flows looks like a big bonanza for the government:

- The government received £53.5 million (in February 1982 pounds sterling) in sale revenues and paid £48.7 million into NFC's retirement fund, for a net cash position of £4.8 million.
- The annual net cash flow position of the treasury vis-à-vis NFC improved by roughly £40 million (figure 6-6).
- The bulk of this improvement was due to the discontinuation of transfers from the treasury to NFC.

Effects on Consumer Welfare

How have consumers been affected by the divestiture of NFC? NFC is the largest or one of the largest firms in most of the markets in which it operates. However, in all of its markets NFC is subject to competition. The question is whether competition is sufficiently fierce that NFC has little or no effect on the market price. Having consulted the literature and discussed this issue with experts in the field, we conclude that NFC's influence on market prices is negligible. This does not mean that we believe consumers do not benefit from a decrease in NFC's costs or an improvement in NFC's quality of service. Rather, we believe that by far the larger share of such improvement is captured in an increase in NFC's (public) profit.

One could argue that NFC has a small but significant effect on prices in its markets. In this case, because of NFC's relatively small market share there would be a leverage effect, and consumer welfare would be affected to a much larger extent (by a multiplier of one divided by NFC's market share). We have no way of measuring this effect. However, in terms of overall welfare (social surplus) the effect will be negligible because it is accompanied by an almost equal and opposite change in competitors' profits.[9]

Summary

Our observation of quantifiable changes in the five years before and after NFC's divestiture yields four primary conclusions:

- **Quantity effects.** Real quantitative or productivity changes (real quasi rents per unit of capital and TFP) show a major turnaround for NFC in the year following divestiture. This turnaround is even more impressive and steadier than the turnaround in private profits for which the NFC divestiture is so well known.

- **Investment effects**. Real gross fixed capital formation was stagnant through 1982 and then took off, suggesting a release of an investment constraint. However, there was a major interruption of this positive trend in 1986.
- **Fiscal flows**. The U.K. government's fiscal flow position vis-à-vis NFC improved vastly after divestiture.
- **Noneffects**. Output price effects are not measurable, given that NFC operates in competitive industries, and given that we have no direct way of measuring NFC's quantities of output.

Our next task is to explain these results, in particular the change in productivity, the removal of the investment constraint, and the fiscal improvements for the U.K. government.

Why Did It Happen?

The NFC spent the 1970s as a public enterprise attempting a badly needed rationalization, and its results reflected this. By the time of the employee buyout in 1982, although trading conditions were extremely depressed, NFC had rationalized the majority of its operations and had been fairly successful in its move toward more specialized services with higher yields. It is not surprising that subsequent years, when the economy was buoyant, produced good results. The company's share performance has been extremely successful, but it should be remembered that the consortium started life with seven times as much debt as equity, which contributed to the magnitude of the subsequent rise: had the consortium started with a capital structure consisting of 100 percent equity (an unlikely counterfactual under the circumstances, of course), the performance of its equity, although still good, would have been less spectacular.

It is revealing, however, to see that NFC performed comparatively well in 1990–92, despite a severe economic downturn in the United Kingdom. The enterprise had been badly affected by previous recessions, but the change in service mix, together with the group's international acquisitions (described below), strengthened it during the easier years of the late 1980s.

Investment Effects and NFC's Drain on the Treasury

Two reasons can be given for NFC's takeoff in investment.[10] First, after divestiture NFC could use innovative financing techniques and build on its banking connections. Second, a favorable business climate and output growth necessitated additional capacity.

One can argue further (as we do below) that NFC's productivity performance has been better under divestiture than it would have been under continued public operation. Lower productivity would have generated less internal funds for investment under continued public operation. However, the structure of the employee buyout actually increased NFC's debt. Also, we believe that, at least for a number of years, NFC would not have paid any dividends under continued public ownership. As a result of these factors, a publicly owned NFC could have financed the same investment from 1982 to 1985 without funds from the government and without a larger increase in debt than actually occurred.

Since the main fiscal flow change upon NFC's divestiture was the discontinuation of new government capital and the forgiveness of government debt, one could argue that this was simply caused by the act of selling NFC. However, as we have just seen, it is quite likely that the U.K. government would, for some time, not have had to pump further money into a publicly owned NFC (we assume that the government would still have paid for the pre-1975 pension fund deficiency).

Price Effects: NFC's Dealings in Real Estate

There have been worries about NFC's activities in the property market. The company inherited a large number of freight depots when it was founded, and it was expected that many of them would prove unneeded as rationalization proceeded. The 1976 report was explicit, stating that "the dowry on which National Carriers relied for its reinvigoration was its property, especially in the urban areas" (NFC 1976, p.7). When the buyout was negotiated, the consortium was "able to tempt [Barclays Merchant Bank] with the potential value of our inner city sites . . . although, in all honesty, during the depression of 1981 no-one realized how valuable they were to become in the boom years of the 1980s" (Thompson 1990, p. 81). At first these property sales were entered in the accounts as extraordinary items, but from 1975 on they were put in the main body of the income statement. This unusual step boosted profits at a time when they were badly needed—the NFC would have incurred a loss instead of a profit in 1981, just before the flotation, if property sales had been excluded (Thompson 1990, p. 121).

The treatment of property sales in this way was justified by the volume of property available for disposal, and the NFC certainly continued to find sites to sell through the 1980s. Table 6-1, taken from NFC's accounts, shows the balance between property disposals and investment in land and buildings.

It can be seen that, although disposals generally exceeded new investment until 1983–84, NFC did invest a considerable amount in land and buildings during the period, and it would be difficult to support a claim that essential facilities have been so run down as to harm the group's performance. The group's property division has also become involved in entrepreneurial property development, which proved extremely prof-

Table 6-1. Changes to Land and Buildings, National Freight, 1972–89

Year	Profit on disposals	Net book value[a] of disposals	Total value of disposals	Additions by NFC	Acquisi-tions (mergers)	Total added
1972	5.1	1.1	6.2	3.1	0.0	3.1
1973	6.4	1.3	7.7	4.9	0.0	4.9
1974	1.3	0.9	2.2	8.4	0.0	8.4
1975	5.4	1.9	7.3	6.0	0.0	6.0
1976	6.4	2.3	8.7	3.0	0.0	3.0
1977	1.7	13.1	14.8	6.6	0.0	6.6
1978	4.6	2.3	6.9	6.2	0.0	6.2
1979	4.6	2.3	6.9	6.2	0.0	6.2
1980[b]	6.1	1.7	7.8	8.1	0.0	8.1
1981	7.7	3.0	10.7	4.9	0.0	4.9
1981–82[c]	8.3	3.8	12.1	3.9	0.0	3.9
1982–83	11.6	4.3	15.9	4.4	0.1	4.5
1983–84	4.7	3.5	8.2	0.7	10.1	10.8
1984–85	6.5	4.6	11.1	1.7	20.0	21.7
1985–86	4.1	3.3	7.4	3.3	3.6	6.9
1986–87	3.3	3.7	7.0	10.8	40.1	50.9
1987–88	6.1	8.4	14.5	13.8	6.4	20.2
1988–89	16.5	11.9	28.4	17.1	13.5	30.6

a. At historical cost until 1986, when properties were included in the accounts at valuation.

b. In 1980 NFC changed its financial year to begin in October. Data in this line are for January to September.

c. Data in this line are for the thirty-two-week period from the February 1982 takeover to the end of the financial year in October.

Source: NFC, *Annual Report*, 1972 to 1988–89, and other NFC data.

itable in the late 1980s, although the results became less favorable in the 1990–92 downturn.

Some major questions that remain are whether all this would have happened under continued public operation, and what the effect of the property deals has been on NFC's performance. Clearly, under continued public operation NFC would have started out owning the same property, which it could have continued to use for its operations, left idle, or sold off. In our view it is quite likely that, in an effort to increase its capital base, NFC would have sold off the property under continued public operation. Making this assumption for the counterfactual is quite conservative and will make divestiture look worse than it actually was.

The effect of property sales on NFC's performance is twofold. Theoretically, in terms of productivity they should be quite neutral, while on the financial side they should generate additional funds. In our practical calculations, however, property sales are part of miscellaneous output, the quantity of which is determined by dividing sales revenues by a price index. Property sales influence our productivity figures to the extent that property inflation differs from the sum of price change and productivity change of miscellaneous output. Property sales thus enhanced our productivity measure in 1978 and 1980, heavily reduced it in 1984, and slightly reduced it in 1985–87.[11] As a result, our treatment of property sales makes productivity look worse after divestiture than it actually was.

Quantity Effects

Recall from figure 6-5 that TFP increased in 1978, 1983–84, and 1986–87 but declined in 1979–82 and 1985. The productivity decreases in 1979–82 were largely due to output decreases that were accompanied by smaller input decreases (with the exception of the decrease in labor in 1981), whereas the productivity increases in 1983–87 were mostly due to a smaller increase in the quantity of inputs, while outputs were increasing. Although the 1978 increase undoubtedly was not due to an announcement effect of divestiture, the question is whether the later improvements were due to the employee buyout freeing and/or motivating employees to work more efficiently, or to economic recovery leading to higher growth rates and fuller capacity utilization.

   We try to answer this question by comparing the discovered changes with NFC's historical performance and with performance in the rest of the freight haulage industry. Unfortunately, a lack of data prevents us from constructing a TFP time series linking the 1970s and 1980s. However, we can perform some comparisons on partial productivities. In particular, we can construct labor productivities for NFC from 1969 to 1989, relating the enterprise's annual revenues (deflated by the retail price index for transport and vehicles) to its average number of employees.

   This time series is plotted in figure 6-7. During its first decade, 1969–79, NFC's labor productivity increased by 33 percent, compared with 120 percent in its second decade, 1979–89. According to the figure, the takeoff in labor productivity occurred in 1981, one year before divestiture. This contrasts with our finding on TFP, which took off in 1983, the year after divestiture. Figure 6-8 compares the 1977–87 change in labor productivity just described with the change in TFP and with the change in labor productivity derived from our PEPIS data base. On a year-to-year basis these three productivity changes appear to be quite different from each other (in fact, both labor productivity series are closer to the TFP series than to each other). Cumulatively, however, the change in each of the two labor productivities is very close, at about 70 percent (70 percent for PEPIS and 72 percent for the alternative), whereas the total TFP change amounts to only about 14 percent.[12] This means that other partial productivities must have improved by substantially less than labor productivity. In fact, the ratio of deflated revenues to NFC's fleet capacity for

Figure 6-7.   Labor and Overall Productivity, National Freight, 1969–89

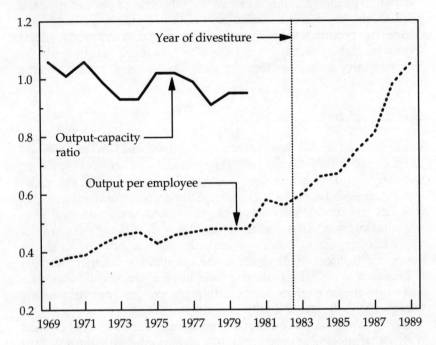

Source: Authors' calculations from NFC data.

1969–79 suggests that during the 1970s capital productivity may actually have declined.

With these pieces of information we have a basis to conjecture that NFC's TFP stagnated during the 1970s and only took off around the time of divestiture. The precise timing, however, remains somewhat unclear as far as labor productivity is concerned. Interestingly, under both labor productivity series we observe an increase in 1981, at the time that NFC lost a major portion of its revenue through cancellation of the British Rail parcels service contract. Since, unlike labor productivity, TFP deteriorated in 1981, it must be true that NFC was able to reduce its labor inputs more quickly than its other inputs, in particular capital. In fact, the capital-output ratio recorded a steep increase in 1981.

Two main differences between NFC and the U.K. road haulage industry in general stick out. First, in 1979, 1981, and 1982 NFC's output dropped relative to industry output. About half of the 1981 difference of 10 percent in industry tons hauled (or 14 percent in industry ton-kilometers) is explained by NFC's loss of the British Rail contract. The remainder is due to either deliberate shrinking or loss in competitiveness. Second, after 1983, NFC's output grew substantially faster than industry output under both measures, and that was before NFC's huge output expansion in 1988. This expansion paralleled the increase in fixed capital formation but without the 1986 slump. Overall, these observations are compatible with a major quantitative turnaround of NFC as a result of divestiture.

Summary Explanation for the Turnaround after Divestiture

There is ample anecdotal evidence about the interest that NFC's worker-shareholders take in their company. Management has put a high priority on communication with its workers and has used a variety of publications and meetings to keep the work force informed. Company policy is not to distinguish between shareholders and nonshareholders when considering promotions or layoffs, and managers do not necessarily know which employees are shareholders in any case. In the sample taken by Bradley and Nejad (1989) in 1984, shareholders were significantly more likely to feel proud of the company's progress and to agree with statements that shareholders had an incentive to cooperate with management and work harder, but substantial minorities of both shareholders and nonshareholders disagreed.

Figure 6-8.   Year-to-Year Changes in Productivity, National Freight, 1978–87

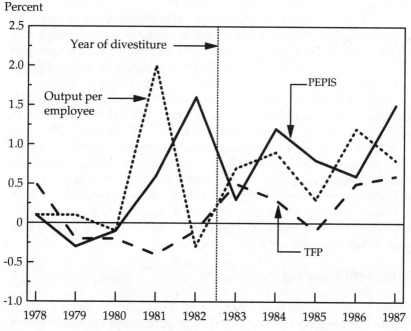

Percent

Source: Authors' calculations from NFC data.

Shareholders and nonshareholders also had different perceptions of the success of the buyout and of how it had affected their job security, but Bradley and Nejad found no evidence that this was affecting industrial relations adversely by creating an "us versus them" culture between shareholders and nonshareholders.

We find that this characterization of incentives for increased labor productivity is compatible with the quantitative evidence. There may be some disagreement as to when precisely NFC started to improve its productivity substantially, and the increase in labor productivity definitely led the increase in TFP. Hence, there may have been an announcement effect. Clearly, however, NFC's productivity and output increases after 1982 were higher than for the U.K. road haulage industry in general. This leads us to believe that NFC's expansion and productivity improvements can be attributed to divestiture.

Base Counterfactual

As in all of our case studies the number of plausible counterfactual stories is large. We restrict ourselves to one base case counterfactual, and we have performed sensitivity analyses to capture deviations from the base case. However, there may be other, totally different counterfactuals that cannot be captured through sensitivity analysis. Our base case counterfactual assumes that a publicly owned NFC would have continued to perform in a manner similar to that before divestiture. That means that our base case is characterized by trend extrapolation of productivity improvements, whereas the divestiture scenario is characterized by kinks. In particular, we did not assume that NFC would have been broken up and sold piecemeal. Although that was considered, we believe that NFC's management would have successfully resisted such a move.

Three major differences from what actually happened are assumed in our base counterfactual story. First, we assume that labor productivity increases in 1983–87 would have followed the 1977–82 trend. This means an improvement of 4 percent per year, substantially below the 7 percent improvement actually achieved. Second, we assume that there would not have been an employee profit-sharing scheme. Profit sharing started in 1986. Hence we assume that in 1986 and 1987 wages would have been 1 percent lower than in the actual case. Third, NFC restructured its balance sheet after divestiture. We assume that under continued public operation this would not have happened.

What Will Happen?

In our projections we have taken the existing frameworks used to analyze the data period 1977–87 and have made assumptions about growth rates and parameter values that seem reasonable. Our approach is as follows.

For the 1988–90 period we use actual data from NFC's annual reports for revenues, costs, assets, equity, debt, and the like. Our counterfactual for this period comes from an extrapolation of the 1982–87 counterfactual, but amended by the influence of what actually happened.

For the years after 1990 (until 2012) we have made assumptions about how the quantity demanded and price for each output category will grow over time. This is related to projections for the road haulage industry's demand growth in general, but is not necessarily the same. Our projections yield estimates of revenues for the actual and counterfactual cases. We also make assumptions about how unit costs will change over time, which yield the projections discussed below. We then summarize the implications.

Revenues

In 1988, 1989, and 1990 NFC's revenues increased by 36 percent, 18 percent, and 9 percent, respectively. The huge increase in 1988 was largely due to the acquisition of Allied Van Lines. For 1988–90 we assumed that, under the counterfactual, NFC would have had the same domestic sales as it actually had. However, for international sales we assumed that the 1987 share in total sales is preserved. The rationale here is that NFC needs some international business as part of its operations. However, the enormous expansion that the acquisition of Allied Van Lines represents would not have occurred, according to our base counterfactual.[13] The assumption is actually quite conservative, since there were major foreign acquisitions between 1982 and 1987, and the public sector NFC did not buy companies abroad after its unfortunate purchases in Europe in the early to mid-1970s (sold soon afterward at a loss). Our counterfactual then shows revenue growth rates of 14 percent, 8 percent, and 7 percent in 1988, 1989, and 1990, respectively.

To facilitate comparison between the private and the public cases, we have assumed the same exogenous 2 percent domestic output growth per year for the actual and the counterfactual cases for the years after 1990. In contrast, for international sales we assumed 3 percent demand growth for the private case and 2 percent demand growth for the counterfactual public case. These are fairly conservative growth projections, much below NFC's growth rate over the decade 1980–90 (8.1 percent), but slightly above the 1977–87 growth rate (1.6 percent). Assuming a 2 percent long-run annual growth rate for the U.K. economy, this assumption corresponds to a unitary income elasticity for NFC's domestic outputs. In addition, we have assumed a constant 6 percent inflation rate in the projection period.

Regarding NFC's prices, we took the actual prices for 1988–90 and assumed a real price decrease of 0.2 percent per year thereafter.

Costs

For both the private and the public cases we assumed that nominal unit costs for most inputs would rise by 6 percent per year, leaving real input costs unchanged. We further set the opportunity cost of working capital, the discount rate, and the loan rate constant at 15 percent (or 9 percent in real terms).

In 1988 NFC experienced a huge improvement in labor productivity concurrently with a large deterioration in the input coefficient for intermediate inputs. The main reason for this cost shift lies in the inclusion of Allied Van Lines, which NFC operates on a commission basis. Thus, virtually all the costs added by Allied are intermediate inputs; there is hardly any extra labor. These shifts in coefficients are not followed in the counterfactual.

The driving force behind the long-run input requirements is labor-saving technological progress. We have assumed that the per unit requirements of intermediates, inventories, and working capital remain unchanged throughout the period for both cases. Changes have been assumed, however, for labor requirements.

Although the quantity of labor actually declined dramatically in 1982–90, we implicitly assume only a slight reduction in real costs of labor per unit of output of 1 percent per year throughout the 1991–2012 period in both the private and the public case. However, the relative differences in labor costs between the two cases remain at their 1987 level.

Summary

The revenue and cost projections come together in our projections of profits. Annual quasi rents (including taxes) in the private case are projected to grow from £54 million in 1987 to £490 million in 2015. Quasi rents (including taxes) in the public case are projected to grow from -£8 million in 1987 to £475 million in 2012. The peculiar development of quasi rents over time is shown in figure 6-9, which provides for a positive turnaround for the counterfactual case only after 1988.[14] The dip in 1986–88 is explained by two factors: first, a deterioration in output prices relative to productivity improvements, which, in particular in 1988, lag more and more behind the private case, and second, the lack of non-operating income in the counterfactual case (actual nonoperating income soared in 1987 under divestiture).

Projections of all other variables also follow from the projections of basic prices and quantities. Thus, profit projections yield projections of

Figure 6-9. Projections of Quasi Rents, National Freight, 1977–93

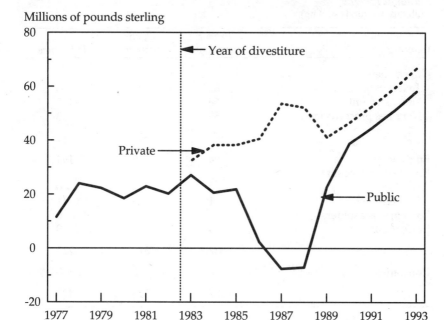

Source: Authors' calculations from NFC data.

direct taxes and dividend payments. Dividend payout rates have been assumed to maintain relatively stable debt-equity ratios.

What Is It Worth?

In previous sections we observed specific aspects of NFC's performance as a result of divestiture. Here we determine the bottom line. Were the net benefits positive or negative, and how were they distributed?

The answers can be summarized in three propositions (table 6-2 and figure 6-10):

- Although they are smaller than expected, the changes resulting from divestiture leave U.K. society better off by about £225 million (in 1982 pounds sterling). If we converted this amount to a perpetuity it would be about 4 percent of NFC's 1982 revenues.[15]
- Private buyers did well for themselves, paying £8 million for equity shares worth £242 million, for a net gain of £234 million. This gain is split between employees and their families (£193 million) and other shareholders (£41 million). Purchasers of £46 million worth of NFC debt neither gain nor lose.[16]

Table 6-2.   Distribution of Welfare Gains and Losses from Divestiture, National Freight
(millions of pounds sterling)

Category	Private operation	Public operation	Difference
Government			
Taxes	182	135	48
Net quasi rents	68	179	–112
Net sales proceeds (cash)	53	0	53
Total	303	314	–11
Employees	194	0	194
Private domestic shareholders			
Diverse	0	0	0
Concentrated	41	0	41
Foreign shareholders	0	0	0
Competitors	0	0	0
Subtotal	537	314	223
Consumers	0	0	0
Total	537	314	223

Source: Authors' calculations.

- The government, on the other hand, is slightly worse off, by £11 million.

These bold assertions are subject to many qualifications and are based on aggregation of data from various sources. In the rest of this section we raise a few of these issues and end with four primary conclusions.

We show V_{pp} to be equal to £288 million. This amount is for the sum of £46 million in debt and £7.5 million in equity. Assuming that the debt was worth its par value in 1982 when NFC was divested, we can set our calculated value for the share capital at £242 million. How does that compare with NFC's share value of £1,133 million at the time we finalized our numbers in September 1991? Out of NFC's current share capital, £54.5 million was raised on 1 October 1988. Discounting the remaining share capital back to 1982 at 15 percent, we get £298 million.[17] This is fairly close to £242 million. However, the relevant figure to compare with NFC's current value is the discounted present value of quasi rents and additional financing generated from 1991 onward. That turns out to be only £101 million, or roughly one-third of NFC's current market value discounted to 1982. Thus, our projection remains considerably less optimistic than the current stock market valuation. Interestingly, this is so even though we generate high and growing returns to capital over the years.

Why did the U.K. government sell an enterprise of this value at such a low price? The answer could lie in pessimistic projections in 1982 or in deliberate underpricing. The government probably underestimated the effect of a change in the business cycle on NFC's property values. However, that can only explain a small part of the company's success. To the extent that employee ownership has enhanced NFC's productive performance since divestiture, the government probably had no chance to receive a substantially higher price for its NFC shares at the time of divestiture. It appears that, at the time, management and employees were unable to raise substantially more money than they actually did for acquiring the enterprise.

The five-year data period (1983–87) shows an overall welfare gain of £64 million. The first five-year projection period (1988–93) shows a moderately positive balance of £17 million, as less operating quasi rent accrues. The final period accounts for the remaining large gain of £141 million. On an annual discounted basis the first five years clearly provide the largest gain, while the second five years are the least favorable. The major reason for this shift is that NFC's actual expansion in 1988–90 was less favorable than the 1982–87 expansion.

Figure 6-10. Distribution of Welfare Gains and Losses from Divestiture, National Freight

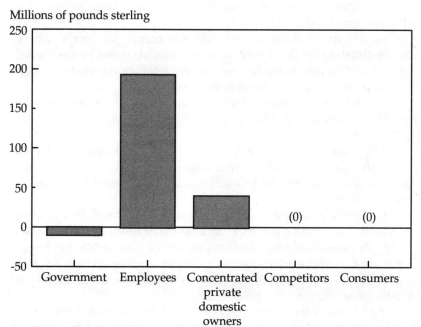

Source: Authors' calculations.

We argued above that NFC employees and their families realized a net present value gain of nearly £200 million on account of their share ownership. Are there any other gains or losses in labor rents to report as a result of divestiture? Two items come to mind.

First, NFC laid off large numbers of employees in 1980 and 1981. Could these layoffs be viewed as announcement effects of divestiture? We do not believe this to be the case. The layoffs occurred during a major slump in demand for road haulage in the United Kingdom in general. For NFC in particular the 1981 layoffs were largely the result of the loss of the British Rail contract. Even if one believes that the layoffs are related to divestiture, it is not clear that a major rent loss is involved. The laid-off NFC employees received severance pay. Although this pay appears to have been substantially less generous than that offered by British Airways around the same time, it probably covered most of the NFC employees' rent, given that they received 50 percent less pay than British Airways employees on average. We conclude that labor rents were not reduced by any divestiture-related layoffs.

Second, NFC employees received income under a profit-sharing scheme starting in 1986. We ascribe to this a pay difference of 1 percent in 1986 and 1987. If this difference were maintained forever, it would lead to a discounted rent differential between the actual and the counterfactual of about £20 million. However, in a competitive labor market it is unlikely that such a differential can be maintained over any long period of time. We therefore refrain from making any adjustment in total labor rents for this factor.[18]

A sensitivity analysis shows that our results are conservative, underestimating the likely welfare improvement caused by the divestiture of NFC. Our results are, however, fairly sensitive to realistic changes in labor productivity and possibly in output prices.

Our search for quantifiable changes associated with divestiture covers the 1977–87 period. It yields four primary conclusions:

- Major improvements in NFC's productivity performance started the year after divestiture. This turnaround is more impressive and steadier than the turnaround in private profits for which the NFC divestiture is so well known.
- Real gross fixed capital formation was stagnant through 1982 and then took off, suggesting a release in an investment constraint. There was a partially unexplained major interruption of the positive trend in 1986.
- Consumer price effects are not measurable, given that NFC operates in competitive industries, and given that we have no direct way of measuring NFC's output quantities.
- As a result of the divestiture of NFC, society was made better off by £223 million (in 1982 pounds sterling). Surprisingly, the government came out losing £11 million.

Comparisons with NFC's history before divestiture and with the road haulage industry in the United Kingdom as a whole suggest that NFC's performance improvement was indeed caused by divestiture.

Notes

This chapter was written by Ingo Vogelsang and Richard Green. The authors are grateful to A. J. Morrish, M. D. R. Sweet, B. Waddingham, and the editors of *Motor Transport* for providing data on NFC and the road haulage industry, and to Manuel A. Abdala, A. Browne, and B. Gilman for valuable assistance in using the data.

1. NFC's value added is approximately 40 percent of its turnover. Hence, the trucking industry is likely to contribute about 3.5 percent to U.K. GDP.

2. This was succeeded by the National Freight Company Ltd. in 1980, which was acquired by the National Freight Consortium plc in 1982. The consortium changed its name to NFC plc in 1989. The initials NFC will be used throughout this chapter; the particular organization that they stand for will depend on the date.

3. For recent evidence on the possible existence of economies of scale in U.S. trucking see Keeler (1989).

4. Where possible, the NFC group wanted to operate under the security of long-term contracts, sometimes providing a fleet in the customer's livery to provide the benefits of a dedicated transport operation without the managerial bother of running an own-account transport division. Contract hire provided 18 percent of the group's revenues by 1979, and 32 percent by 1986.

5. This is defined as dividends plus retained earnings from operations. Starting almost from zero, in 1985–87 nonoperating returns, especially the "other income" category and release of provisions (reserves accumulated for contingencies), have become important as a source of funds. Correspondingly, in the last few years there has been an increasing use of funds for nonoperating assets. Capital gains from the sale of real estate are treated as operating returns to the extent that this is one of NFC's ongoing activities.

6. About half of the reduction in 1978 is accounted for by the divestiture of Freightliners to British Rail, and a major portion of the 1986 reduction is accounted for by a reduction in the acquisition of assets through the purchase of other companies. Being lumpy by nature, the acquisition of outside companies naturally fluctuates from year to year.

7. If one reduces the purchase price by the £48.7 million, one should also reduce it further by the £100 million in debt forgiven by the government on 1 October 1980 (after the decision in principle to divest).

8. A relevant point in this connection may be that NFC's 1982 annual report lists £26.2 million in reserves resulting from the fact that NFC's net assets exceeded the purchase price by that amount. However, the value of a company can be smaller than net assets if expected profits are low and assets cannot be liquidated easily.

9. An increase in industry profits, however, can be competed away through entry and expansion of high-cost firms. An eventual decrease in industry profits can be avoided through exit.

10. Other than the lumpiness of investment in the acquisition of new companies we have no explanation for the reduction in fixed capital formation in 1986.

11. Profits from property disposal show no trend change after divestiture. There is a marked increase only in 1988–89.

12. The enormous increase in labor productivity in 1988 can in our view be attributed mostly to the change in NFC's output mix due to the acquisition of Allied Van Lines.

13. Thus, we assume that the major difference in investment between the actual and the counterfactual concerns NFC's investments abroad. These were quite substantial in 1987, with the acquisition of Dauphin Distribution Services and later with the acquisition of Allied Van Lines, both in the United States.

14. One can argue that the crisis situation simulated by our counterfactual for 1987 and 1988 could have led to a breakdown of NFC as a public enterprise. In this case the future net benefits of the counterfactual would vanish. On the other hand, a liquidation of NFC's assets at that time would have made the government whole, and other firms could have taken over NFC's operations. In that sense the alternative counterfactual would not necessarily have come out much worse than our base case. See also note 15.

15. If, under continued public operation, NFC had been eventually shut down in 1988, the gain from its actual divestiture would increase by at most £100 million. The bulk of this benefit accrues to the government. See also note 14.

16. However, they win to the extent that they simultaneously held shares in NFC (recall that the lending banks were also shareholders).

17. This leaves out dividends paid by NFC in the meantime. The 15 percent discount rate corresponds to about 16.5 percent when dividends are taken into account.

18. One could argue that employees, as the main shareholders, could try to exploit nonshareholder employees by reducing wages in favor of dividends. This would not work in the long run because the disadvantaged employees would leave. It would also deteriorate the work climate. Conversely, workers as shareholders could water down the ownership rights of fellow shareholders by increasing wages and salaries at the expense of dividends. This is always a fear of creditors and outside shareholders under labor shareholding. The profitability of this strategy depends on the labor share in equity compared with the fraction of workers owning shares. At least initially, with an 82.5 percent labor share in equity, this could not have been a profitable strategy. Moreover, this strategy would hurt the share price in addition to the reduction in current dividends.

7. Summary: United Kingdom

The U.K. divestiture program of the 1980s arose because of a decline in the efficacy of government management of public corporations. Over the 1970s this became especially acute, with successive governments facing conflicts between macroeconomic and microeconomic objectives. The macroeconomic pressures diminished the availability of investment funds and exerted pressure for monopoly pricing; both these results were in direct conflict with underlying microeconomic principles. This ultimately led to the introduction of a large-scale divestiture program.

The U.K. approach to divestiture over the 1980s, however, was not a carefully controlled and preplanned program. It commenced with the sale of various (relatively) small state-owned enterprises operating in competitive markets and was not a major feature of the political agenda in 1980. At the beginning of the 1980s the electorate was more interested in being offered tax cuts than in buying shares in a massive divestiture program. Following the sale of British Aerospace in 1981, however, attitudes changed and privatization became a central issue on the political agenda. This led eventually to the sale of large public utilities, once thought to be immune. Overall the program has been an evolving one, with mistakes being remedied through time.

The U.K. divestiture program has had considerable influence on similar programs elsewhere in the world. Many of the companies (merchant banks, stockbrokers, law firms, advertising agencies, etc.) involved in the U.K. program have since played an active part in divestitures throughout the world. The program as it evolved over the 1980s, which became referred to simply as "privatization," was of considerable size and scope and led to the implementation of innovative regulatory mechanisms. By the early 1990s the scale of the public sector in the United Kingdom had fallen by over 50 percent, and preparations are now under way for the divestiture or further deregulation of the remaining state-held productive assets (British Coal, British Rail, and the postal service).

Elsewhere in the world governments have looked to the United Kingdom to draw lessons for their own divestiture programs.

Lessons from the U.K. Cases

Certain commonalities and differences among the three U.K. cases set them apart from cases in other countries. The commonalities clearly dominate the emerging picture: all three of the enterprises in our case studies are in service industries involving network services. Quantification here is difficult because quantities of service output are notoriously hard to measure, and costs are often impossible to assign to individual services. On the other hand, services are interesting because they represent a growing part of the economy in most countries and because they tend to pose intriguing regulatory problems. The latter is particularly true for British Telecom (BT) and British Airways (BA).

All three U.K. cases demonstrate the productivity enhancement that typically accompanies a substantial reduction in the work force. In the cases of BA and NFC most of this happened before divestiture, and one can argue to what degree it can be attributed to divestiture: in the case of BA, maybe; in the case of NFC, almost certainly not. In the case of BT the substantial reduction in employment started six years after divestiture. In all three cases the labor force reductions were paralleled by either output reductions (BA and NFC) or a decline in the growth rate of output (BT). Even though generous severance pay was provided, employment reductions have generally been highly profitable for the companies.

All three cases witnessed major expansions in fixed capital formation after divestiture. This too turned out to be beneficial for all three in terms of productivity and profitability. Since divestiture of the three enterprises occurred at different times, with differing degrees of fiscal stringency in the U.K. treasury, the takeoff in capital expenditure is not in all cases the result of a relaxation of an investment constraint. For NFC and BT the expansion in investment after divestiture occurred at a time when the U.K. government purse was very tight and investment by public enterprises was severely limited. This was not so for BA, however, which started a major expansion in 1987 and 1988.

In all three cases management was not changed as a result of divestiture. However, one can argue that new management was brought in to enable the divestiture of BA. Also, management at BT changed shortly after divestiture as a result of the retirement of the chief executive officer, to be replaced by an internal successor. In the cases of NFC and BA, top management was instrumental in influencing the way divestiture occurred.

All three cases resulted in ownership structures that leave no controlling interest with any individual or firm. Only in the case of NFC was there a major shareholder (Barclays Bank), and the remaining share capital was concentrated by type of owner (labor and management and their families) but widespread among individuals.

All three cases come close to achieving Pareto improvements and leave only minor losers. Since BA and BT are firms with market power, it comes as no surprise that the losers in their cases include their competitors and some consumers. What is surprising is the smallness of the losses, which come close to vanishing in rounding errors. Since NFC operates in a competitively structured industry, neither competitors nor consumers can be identified as losers. In NFC's case it is only the government for which we calculate a small loss, tempered, however, by a large public relations gain from the financial success of NFC as a labor-managed firm. NFC may also be seen as a loss leader in the government's divestiture program.

In terms of divestiture strategy the three U.K. cases differ. BT's was a well-planned and smoothly executed divestiture. Some other divestiture options were sacrificed to achieve this smoothness. In particular, BT was not split up and sold piecemeal. In contrast, NFC's divestiture was in danger of being dragged out indefinitely because of the enterprise's financial and operational difficulties. NFC's management seized on the government's embarrassment at this situation and proposed a quick divestiture solution. Thus, the lack of government strategy was compensated by management's readiness to step in. BA's divestiture, in a similarly difficult postponement, shows that such a situation can be turned to the government's advantage if postdivestiture management is chosen right away.

The three cases include a (virtual) monopolist (BT), an oligopolist (BA), and a competitive enterprise (NFC). Surprisingly, in terms of our bottom line, we find no clear relationship between the welfare effect of divestiture and market structure in the U.K. cases: relative to its sales in the year of divestiture, BT shows the largest gain, followed by NFC and then BA. This ordering is unaffected by an inclusion of benefits from the prior restructuring of BA between 1981 and 1987.

The Comparative Performance of Public and Divested Enterprises

Our analysis has not focused on the behavior of enterprises that remained in the U.K. public sector over the 1980s. There is some work by others that allows us to draw a picture, however. This work is important because it generates the background against which to measure the success of individual divestiture cases. Bishop and Kay (1988 and 1991) have provided some performance indicators of divested public enterprises and of those that remained owned by the state in the United Kingdom.

As shown in table 7-1, Bishop and Kay (1991) provide estimates of total factor productivity (TFP) for eight U.K. enterprises for 1979–90. Three of these enterprises have remained publicly owned (British Coal, British Rail, and the postal service), two were divested very late in the decade (British Steel, in December 1988, and Electricity Supply, in December 1990), while three were divested somewhat earlier (British Telecom in November 1984, British Airports Authority in July 1987, and British Gas in December 1986). There appears to be no discernible pattern of relationships between TFP change and ownership change. In fact, if anything the biggest improvement between the two periods occurs for British Coal and British Rail. Had both these enterprises been divested in 1983 and shown the same performance improvement, one would have pointed to them as major successes of divestiture. On the other hand, one can argue that these enterprises had been doing particularly badly in 1979–83, so they started from a low base. Similarly, the vast improvement of British Steel over the whole decade is partly explained by the miserable shape it was in before.

Nevertheless, it appears clear that during the 1980s state-owned enterprises in the United Kingdom substantially changed their behavior. What stands out is that these enterprises were allowed to reduce employment by amounts that are large even by the standards of privately owned firms. It has to be borne in mind, however, that these firms operate in stagnating or declining industries, so that output was falling simultaneously (by less than labor in the cases of coal and steel, and by more than labor in the case of rail). It appears that the remaining state-owned

Table 7-1. *Year-to-Year Changes in Total Factor Productivity at Selected Public Enterprises, United Kingdom, 1979–90*

	Average annual change (percentages)		
Enterprise	1979–90	1979–83	1983–90
British Airports Authority	1.0	–1.6	2.6
British Coal	2.6	–0.8	4.6
British Gas	1.0	–1.0	2.2
British Rail	1.2	–2.9	3.7
British Steel	6.4	4.6	7.5
British Telecom[a]	3.5	3.0	3.7
Electricity supply[b]	1.5	–0.3	2.6
Post Office	2.3	1.7	2.7
Average	2.4	0.1	3.7

a. Our own calculations indicate average total factor productivity increases of 0.6 percent for 1980–83 and 3.2 percent for 1983–90.

b. CEGB and regional electricity boards.

Source: Bishop and Kay (1991).

enterprises are in stagnating sectors (the postal service has grown, but slowly), while divested enterprises have been expanding.

Hence, inferences from table 7-1 have to be drawn with a lot of caution. Clearly, however, the remaining state-owned enterprises in the United Kingdom during the 1980s improved their efficiency and laid off employees on a large scale.

Conclusion

Welfare gains from our three U.K. divestitures are comparatively small because, at the same time, performance of the remaining state-owned enterprises improved considerably. Thus, the very fact that we have found consistent gains is remarkable.

Each of the three cases has peculiarities that make it stand out as a learning experience for others. The BT case shows the benefits of skillful regulation and the beneficial effects of a relaxation of investment constraints. The BA case shows the benefits of tough and cost-saving management. The NFC case shows that good management can go hand-in-hand with employee ownership.

We have found all three U.K. divestiture cases to have been successful. Particularly with respect to BT this might be seen as contrasting with Vickers and Yarrow's (1988) view that the U.K. government could have done better. However, our counterfactual in each case was not the perceived best available alternative policy but rather continued public operation. At the same time our case studies are compatible with an emerging view that divestiture in the United Kingdom was successful in a climate of new entrepreneurial spirit and long-lasting boom after a severe recession. One may speculate that divestiture has itself contributed to this spirit and prosperity, but that was not the topic of our partial analysis.

PART III

Chile:
Selling Efficient Public Enterprises in Well-Regulated Markets

8. *Divestiture in Chile*

Paul E. Sigmund (1990) has written, "In no country in the world, not even in Margaret Thatcher's Britain, has privatization been carried as far as it has in contemporary Chile." This is particularly true in that divestiture in Chile was part of an overall transformation of the economy; it was pursued as early as 1974 and continued in two major waves through 1990; it covered enterprises in competitive and monopolistic markets; it used almost all divestiture methods known to date; and it had its successes and pitfalls along the way.

Because of its significance, Chile's experience has been the subject of extensive analysis. However, no systematic attempt has been made to assess the welfare effects of divestiture in Chile at the microeconomic level. The following three case studies attempt to fill this gap. First, however, this chapter briefly reviews the Chilean divestiture experience over the past two decades, to provide a context for the microeconomic analysis. In addition, the chapter sheds some light on how to implement an overall divestiture program, as opposed to selling a particular enterprise.

The Macroeconomic Context

Divestiture affects and is affected by the environment in which it is carried out. On the one hand, fiscal stringency and mounting foreign debt often provide the primary motivations to divest. Economic growth and nondistorting policies increase the prospects that divestiture will be beneficial to society. On the other hand, divestiture can ease the fiscal and foreign debt crises in the short run, and it may provide an impetus for growth in the medium term. Therefore, a natural starting point is to elaborate on the macroeconomic environment in which divestiture took place in Chile.

Stabilization and Structural Reform: 1974–81

Soon after its seizure of power in September 1973, the military government of General Augusto Pinochet began to pursue a fundamentally different economic development strategy from that which had prevailed during President Salvador Allende's administration between 1970 and 1973. In the new strategy, market forces and the private sector were to be the main agents for growth. Accordingly, the government introduced a number of stabilization and structural reforms, which between 1974 and 1981 included:

- Reducing the role of the state through restrictive fiscal policy, divestiture, and forcing public enterprises to be self-financing
- Foreign trade liberalization, which included the elimination of all quantitative restrictions on imports by 1976 and the reduction of tariffs from an average ad valorem rate of 94 percent with a large dispersion to a flat rate of 10 percent in 1979 (there was also an opening up of the capital account)
- Deregulation of the financial market, which meant freeing interest rates, lowering legal reserve requirements, and phasing out quantitative controls on lending
- Tax reform, which included the establishment in 1975 of a flat 20 percent value added tax and the revision of corporate and income taxes
- Labor market reform, under which unions were banned and wage adjustments left to market forces (in 1979 a new labor law was introduced, outlining the rules for dismissals and hiring and reintroducing collective bargaining and full wage indexation).

The new regime's stabilization efforts initially slowed the economy down, after which it began to recover and then expand. GDP dropped by almost 13 percentage points in 1975 but grew at a rate well above 3.5 percent through 1981. During the same period inflation declined from triple-digit levels to less than 10 percent in 1981. The fiscal deficit disappeared and the current account deficit declined. These results led some observers to term this period the "Chilean miracle."

Crisis and Stabilization: 1982–84

In 1982 Chile's GDP fell by 14 percent, and unemployment rose to 18 percent. Net inflows of foreign credit fell sharply in 1981 and dried up in 1982. The central bank lost a significant amount of reserves in an effort to support the exchange rate, which had been fixed since 1979. The current account deficit rose to over 10 percent of GDP. The crisis led to widespread bankruptcies and prompted the government to take over some fifty previously divested banks and commercial enterprises.

This deep recession was the result of a number of policies. Fixing the exchange rate to control inflation while opening up the capital account contributed to a significant inflow of unguaranteed long-term credit, which increased the external debt to 69 percent of GDP by 1982. Ironically, domestic inflation was higher than world inflation, in part because of full wage indexation. Meanwhile, currency appreciation, higher real interest rates (which exceeded 30 percent per year), and the poor supervision of the financial sector (which weakened the quality of loans) all eroded the competitiveness of the country's tradable goods sector and led to a current account deficit of 14.5 percent of GDP in 1981. Further aggravating the situation were a number of external factors, including a sharp increase in oil prices, a fall in copper prices, and a surge in international interest rates.

In response to the crisis the government abandoned the fixed exchange rate policy, and in 1983 it put a ceiling on the current account deficit and restricted the level of domestic expenditures. The government also negotiated the amortization of external debt and obtained fresh funds to cover interest payments. In the process, however, the central bank absorbed bad loans by providing massive subsidies to debtors in dollars.

Adjustment and Recovery: 1985–90

Facing sluggish economic growth in 1985 (2.4 percent), high unemployment (16.4 percent), and low saving and investment rates (5.4 and 13.9 percent, respectively), the government decided to embark on even deeper economic reforms. It tightened domestic expenditures, devalued the peso, and devised mechanisms to reduce the size of the foreign debt. The central bank authorized debt-equity swap operations, and new loans were obtained from the International Monetary Fund and the World Bank. At the same time, import tariffs were lowered and a more ambitious divestiture program was initiated. As a result, a new phase of sustained and accelerated growth began in 1986. Both the fiscal and the current account deficits decreased. Exports grew rapidly, while the foreign debt declined. Inflation decreased, and in 1989, for the first time in a decade, unemployment returned to single-digit rates. Investment also increased, reaching 20 percent of GDP by the end of the decade.

In short, the Chilean economy witnessed two deep recessions in the last two decades, in 1974–75 and in 1982–83. However, the country's structural reforms were deep enough to enable the economy to survive the crises and to have an impact on the economy.

Divestiture and Public-Enterprise Reform

Divestiture and public-enterprise reform were important ingredients in Chile's reform program, and it is to these we now turn.

The Extent of Divestiture

The Chilean public-enterprise sector consists of three distinct groups. One group of enterprises was created by law to provide a wide array of goods and services such as railroads, postal and telegraph services, water and sewage, port services, air transport, petroleum extraction and refining, copper refining, public ground transportation, trading in agricultural products, shipping, television, pharmaceuticals, and insurance. Each of the enterprises within this group fell under the jurisdiction of the relevant technical ministry. A second group of enterprises was created by the Corporación de Fomento de la Producción (CORFO), the state institution created in 1939 to foster economic development. CORFO enterprises operated in the steel, petroleum, and electricity sectors, among others. Finally, a third group of enterprises came into being through a wave of nationalizations in the 1970–73 period, when Allende's administration adopted a policy of income and asset redistribution. The nationalized firms included, for example, the copper mines,[1] Chilectra (an electricity generation and distribution holding company), and Compañía de Teléfonos de Chile (CTC; the local telephone services company). The government purchased the shares of almost all commercial banks,[2] and it intervened in 259 additional enterprises without acquiring their ownership.

The three groups of public enterprises accounted for 39 percent of GDP in 1973, up from 14 percent in 1970. They numbered 498 in all in 1973, including those enterprises in which the government had intervened without acquiring them; this was up from 64 in 1970 (table 8-1). The public-enterprise sector dominated not only public utilities, mining, and telecommunications but also the manufacturing and banking sectors.

The first wave of divestiture started in 1974. It began with the return of the 259 "intervened" firms to their private owners, followed by the sale of over 200 enterprises and banks. Even though this round of

Table 8-1. Number, Employment, and Output of Public Enterprises, Chile, Selected Years, 1965–89

Indicator	1965	1970	1973	1980	1989
Number of enterprises	—	64.0	498[a]	43.0	27.0
Employment as a share of work force (percent)	—	4.6	5.6	3.2	1.0
Value added as a share of GDP (percent)					
Including CODELCO	14.2	—	39.0	24.1	15.9
Excluding CODELCO	—	—	—	—	6.6

— Not available.
a. Includes enterprises in which the government intervened but that it did not acquire.
Source: Luders (1990) and authors' calculations for value added excluding CODELCO.

divestiture excluded large firms, natural monopolies, and firms created by law, the number of divested firms was large enough to reduce the public-enterprise sector as a proportion of GDP to 24.1 percent in 1981, from 39 percent in 1974.

Beyond the sale of enterprises, the government contracted out to the private sector such services as public education, trash collection, and the tending of public parks. And in 1981 it reformed and sold the social security pension system, replacing the public pay-as-you-go pension system with one based on individual pension savings accounts.

As noted above, this wave of divestiture was partially reversed in the early 1980s, when the government had to take over some fifty banks and firms. The 1982 recession spread defaults throughout the economy. In December 1981 the government intervened in two important banks and six smaller financial institutions. The economic situation worsened through 1982, and the financial crisis culminated in January 1983 with government intervention in five banks, the closing of three more, and the direct government supervision of another two. According to Arellano (1983), these ten institutions represented 45 percent of the capital and reserves of the financial system.

Intervention in banks meant the takeover of a large number of other enterprises, either because the banks were their most important creditors or because they were related through ownership. Among those that were taken over for the first time were four pension funds, the largest two of which also belonged to the two largest conglomerates. These two pension funds had, in December 1982, 50.7 percent of the workers and employees affiliated with the new pension system and 57.5 percent of the system's accumulated pension funds.

As the economy recovered in subsequent years the government resold these banks and enterprises. More important, in 1985–90 it embarked on a second wave of divestiture, which was qualitatively and quantitatively more significant than the first. This time divestiture included some of the largest corporations producing tradable goods (e.g., Soquimich, IANSA, and CAP), enterprises in telecommunications (CTC and ENTEL), electricity (e.g., Chilectra and ENDESA), and, toward the end, water and sewage services. This wave of divestiture reduced the share of public enterprises in GDP to 15.9 percent by 1989. If the copper company CODELCO is excluded, the share drops to a modest 6.6 percent. The number of public enterprises fell to twenty-seven in the same year.

Public-Enterprise Reform

The reform of public enterprises paralleled Chile's macroeconomic adjustment and divestiture. The process started immediately after the military takeover by eliminating labor redundancy. In mid-1974 the government issued a decree requiring a number of non-CORFO public enterprises to reduce their personnel by 20 percent before the end of 1975. It created the "New Entrepreneur Plan" to provide laidoff workers a new source of income. Other enterprises were encouraged to reduce their work forces. As a result, employment decreased in almost all large public enterprises by 1979. In some cases the decrease was significant; for example, employment was cut by 49 percent at ENDESA and EFE (the state railways), and 55 percent at the national airline LAN-Chile.

CORFO then instructed its enterprises to pursue "goals and procedures similar to those of a private company." Managers were notified that their enterprises would be expected to finance their own operating costs and debt service. Responsibility for financing of investment and for borrowing came under the Ministry of Finance, which instructed the enterprises to get rid of any unnecessary assets and stocks, improve their billing procedures, search for new sources of financing, and reduce personnel when required. Public utilities (water, electricity, gas, and telephone), for example, were ordered to apply to public sector entities the same rules of service suspension for unpaid bills as were applied to the private sector. Transfers to public enterprises became the exception rather than the rule. Other elements of favorable treatment toward public enterprises such as income tax and import duty exemptions were also eliminated. In addition, since CORFO enterprises had always been joint stock corporations—with some even having minority private shareholders prior to 1970—they were subject to the same regulations and information disclosure rules that applied to private corporations in the same category.

Self-financing would not have been possible, however, if pricing policies had not been changed. Thus, the government dramatically increased the prices public enterprises could charge; these prices had eroded in the period 1970–73. It then freed the prices of tradables and established the basis for setting tariffs for nontradables (e.g., electricity and telecommunications in 1982, and water and sewage in 1989; see the next three chapters for details of the regulatory framework for the electric power and telecommunications sectors).

In parallel, public enterprises increasingly faced intense competition. As quantitative restrictions on imports were eliminated and import tariffs reduced, firms producing tradable goods had to compete internationally. In the noncompetitive sectors the government eliminated entry barriers, for example in transportation. In addition, it divided a number of large public enterprises into independent companies; for example, the holding company Chilectra was divided into two electricity distribution companies and one generating company in 1981.

As a result of these reforms the operating performance of most public enterprises improved.[3] As shown in table 8-2, revenues as well as taxes and transfers increased substantially in relation to GDP after 1973, while expenditures fell. The overall deficit of the public-enterprise sector prac-

*Table 8-2. Summary of Operations of Public Enterprises, Chile,
Selected Years, 1970–89*
(percentages of GDP)

Item	1970	1973	1979	1983	1986	1989
Current revenues	16.9	16.2	27.0	29.5	35.4	28.1
Current expenditures	15.9	24.0	17.6	18.5	22.6	15.5
Net savings	1.0	–7.8	9.4	11.0	12.8	12.6
Taxes and transfers	1.2	1.9	8.3	8.6	9.1	11.5
Net capital revenues	0.0	–0.1	0.2	–0.1	0.5	0.7
Capital formation[a]	4.2	2.5	1.9	2.6	4.7	2.5
Deficit	4.4	12.4	0.6	0.3	0.5	0.7

a. For 1970 and 1973, capital revenues are net of capital expenditure. For the other years, capital formation includes capital expenditures.

Source: For 1970, 1973, and 1979: Larraín (1988); for 1983 and 1986: Larrañaga and Marshall (1990); for 1989: Ministry of Finance data.

tically vanished. (The decrease in current revenues as a percentage of GDP after 1986 is the result of the second divestiture program.)

Implementation of Divestiture

In the first wave of divestiture in the 1970s, CORFO established a bidding policy according to which both domestic and foreign investors could participate. Offers could be made in domestic or foreign currency, and the general method of payment was an initial down payment with the balance to be paid in inflation-indexed installments at annual interest rates ranging from 8 to 12 percent. Real assets equivalent to 150 percent of the debt had to be provided as collateral. CORFO could, if it chose, declare that none of the bids was acceptable and enter into direct negotiations with potential buyers.

CORFO followed the above procedures in selling enterprises in which its equity share exceeded 10 percent. Where its stake was lower it auctioned off the shares through the stock market. By 1978, of the sixty-nine enterprises for sale in which CORFO had more than a 51 percent interest, fifty had been sold. The buyers were domestic corporations in forty-seven cases, foreign investors in ten, individual domestic investors in twenty-one, enterprise employees in sixteen, and a cooperative in one case (CORFO 1978). From 1974 to 1978 the proceeds from these sales amounted to US$699 million at 1990 prices.

Although the design and implementation of the divesture program seemed appropriate, the events of the early 1980s proved them otherwise. According to Marshall and Montt (1988) and Larraín (1988), the reason for the failure of divestiture and the government takeover of some divested enterprises and banks is as follows. The sale typically started with a highly leveraged purchase of a financial company from CORFO, which was then used to bid on other industrial companies. Although participants in auctions and bids had to present detailed financial statements, accounting practices at the time did not call for the consolidation of balance sheets. As a result, groups with very small capital bases managed to gain control of large volumes of assets. According to Arellano (1983) and Foxley (1988), by June 1982 bank loans to related enterprises represented more than 15 percent of outstanding loans in most cases, more than 20 percent in a number of banks, and even more than 40 percent in the case of Chile's second largest private bank.

In the second divestiture episode (1985–90) the process improved significantly. CORFO's council would decide what percentage of an enterprise would be sold, by what method, at what price, and to whom. Only prequalified investors could participate. When the enterprise was to be purchased by a conglomerate, cash payment was required. Perhaps more important, the government had by then introduced several institutional and regulatory reforms, which, as the next chapters will illustrate, proved critical in ensuring better corporate governance and performance of firms. The most important of these are the following:

- *Bank regulations.* After the banking system was recapitalized and had recovered from the 1981–83 crisis, a new banking law was enacted in 1986. Among the changes introduced was a restriction on doing business with related parties (for a detailed description of the reforms in the banking system after the crisis see Ramírez 1989).
- *Regulation of joint stock companies.* This regulation tightened the rules for disclosure of transactions between related companies, stock purchases and sales, financial statements, penalties for publishing false or misleading information, and the use of inside information.
- *Regulation of natural monopolies.* This regulation included the enactment of new regulatory regimes for the electricity and telecommunications sectors in 1982, as elaborated in the next three chapters.
- *Regulation of pension funds (mutual funds) and insurance companies.* These regulations placed limits on how much pension funds could invest in the securities of one issuer or related issuers; specified the rules for disclosure of information about capital, net worth, and technical reserves; and expanded the power of the regulatory institution.

Within this improved framework, CORFO sold a number of important enterprises, generating for the treasury the equivalent of US$1.4 billion (at 1990 prices) between 1985 and 1989. Table 8-3 provides a breakdown of the methods of sale and the first buyers of the key enterprises sold during this period. The enterprises were frequently sold through a combination of stock market offerings, public auctions, and direct sales.

Pension funds emerged as important institutional investors. Foreign investors participated actively, in part by purchasing shares in the stock market, but mostly through the debt-equity swap program started by the central bank in 1985. Workers acquired shares of their companies in almost all cases, which they financed by using their severance benefits in advance, benefits obtained in collective bargaining, profit sharing or paid vacations, or loans from the enterprise itself, CORFO, or the banks. They paid a price equal to the average closing price on the stock market, sometimes with a time lag. As share prices were rising, this lag afforded them an implicit discount. In other cases, they received explicit discounts.

The Aftermath

In sum, Chile reduced the size of its public-enterprise sector in relation to GDP from 39 percent in 1973 to 16 percent in 1989 (6.6 percent if the largest remaining public enterprise, CODELCO, is excluded). Divestiture was carried out in the context of turning the Chilean economy into one of the most open in Latin America, but one in which the regulatory role of the state became stronger.

To be sure, the Chilean journey on the road of divestiture was not always smooth. In the 1970s the government paid inadequate attention to the who, the how, and the when of divestiture. This led to a concentration of ownership, overindebtedness, and eventually (during the crisis of the early 1980s) the return of several divested firms and banks to the government. In contrast, by the time the second round of divestiture was under way in the mid-1980s, the economy was well functioning and appropriate regulations were already in place.

This rich experience has generated a number of interesting studies, some of which have already been mentioned. Other studies (e.g., Marcel 1989, Hachette 1988) have investigated the aggregate effect of divestiture on the government budget, saving, investment, and employment. However, nowhere could we find any systematic analysis of the microeconomic effects of divestiture that carefully identified the overall change in economic welfare and the consequences of this change on all important economic actors (buyers, government, consumers, workers, and competitors). The next three chapters address these questions by analyzing cases of divestiture in three Chilean industries: electricity generation, electricity distribution, and telecommunications. The ultimate objective of this analysis is twofold: first, to determine whether divestiture made Chile better or worse off, and, second, to identify the conditions that made the outcome positive, so that other countries might attempt to simulate these conditions in their own divestiture programs. The results of the three cases are then summarized in chapter 12.

Table 8-3. *Methods of Divestiture and Buyers of Major Divested Enterprises, Chile, 1985–89*

Enterprise	Sector	Method of divestiture	First buyers
CAP	Steel	Stock market	Various investors
		Direct sale to workers	Own workers
CHILGENER	Electricity	Stock market	Various (including foreign) investors, pension funds
		Direct sale to workers	Own workers
CHILMETRO	Electricity	Stock market	Various investors, pension funds
		Direct sale to workers	Own workers
CHILQUINTA	Electricity	Stock market	Various investors, pension funds
		Direct sale to workers	Own workers
CHILEFILMS	Filmmaking	Auction	Domestic investor
CTC	Telecommunications	Stock market	Various investors, pension funds
		Direct sale to workers	Own workers, public sector employees
		Auction	Foreign investor
ECOM	Data processing	Direct sale to workers	Own workers
EDELMAG	Electricity	Direct sale to public	Small regional investors[a]
ELECDA	Electricity	Direct sale to public	Regional investors[a]
		Direct sale to public	Various investors
		Stock market	Small investors
		Expropriation settlement[b]	Domestic investor
EMEC	Electricity	Auction	ENDESA employees
EMEL	Electricity	Direct sale to workers	Regional investors[a]
EMELARI	Electricity	Direct sale to public	Public sector employees
		Direct sale to workers	Small investors
		Expropriation settlement[b]	Regional investors[a]
ELIQSA	Electricity	Direct sale to public	Public sector employees
		Direct sale to workers	Various investors
		Stock market	Small investors
		Expropriation settlement[b]	EMEL
EMELAT	Electricity	Auction	ENDESA employees
		Direct sale	

Company	Sector	Method of sale	Buyers
ENAEX	Explosives	Auction	Foreign investor
ENDESA	Electricity	Direct sale	FAMAE (an enterprise of the Chilean army)
		Stock market	Various investors, pension funds
		Direct sale to workers	Own workers, public sector employees
ENTEL	Telecommunications	Expropriation settlement[b]	Small investors
		Stock market	Various investors, pension funds
		Direct sale to workers	Own workers, Chilean army
IANSA	Sugar	Expropriation settlement[b]	Small investors
		Direct sale	Sugar beet producers, own workers
ISE Generales	Social security	Stock market	Various (including foreign) investors
		Stock market	Various investors
ISE Vida	Social security	Direct sale to workers	Own workers
Laboratorio Chile	Laboratories	Stock market	Not available
		Stock market	Various investors, pension funds
LAN-Chile	Airline	Direct sale to workers	Own workers
		Stock market	Various investors
		Direct sale to workers	Own workers
PEHUENCHE	Electricity	Auction	Various (including foreign) investors
		Direct sale to workers	Own workers
PILMAIQUEN	Electricity	Subscription of new shares	ENDESA
PULLINQUE	Electricity	Auction	Foreign investor
SACRET	Finance	Auction	Unidentified investor
Schwager	Coal	Direct sale to workers	Own workers
		Stock market	Various investors, pension funds
		Direct sale to workers	Own workers
Soquimich	Chemical and mining	Expropriation settlement[b]	Small investors
		Stock market	Various investors, pension funds
		Direct sale to workers	Own workers
TELEX-Chile	Telecommunications	Auction	Foreign investor

a. These companies were partially sold to the general public only in the region in which the enterprise is located. This was called "regional popular capitalism."
b. In 1987 a law was passed to settle the claims of farm owners who had been expropriated during the Allende administration.
Source: CORFO, Memoria Anual, various years; Marcel (1989); Valenzuela (1989).

Notes

This chapter was written by Ahmed Galal and Raul E. Sanz.

1. Already in 1967, however, the government had started the acquisition of 51 percent of the country's largest copper mines, in a process called "Chileanization."

2. Before 1970 there was only one publicly owned commercial bank; by 1973 CORFO owned more than 50 percent of the equity of fourteen banks and a minority share in another five. Of seventeen commercial banks in operation in September 1973, fourteen were administered by CORFO, thus giving it effective control over the financial system (see Larraín 1988).

3. ENACAR, a state coal company, and EFE have continued to lose money.

9. CHILGENER

In most developing and even in some industrial countries, electricity enterprises are owned by the state. Ownership and regulatory functions are merged in the same government agency or agencies, and the generation, transmission, and distribution of electricity are vertically integrated.

This preference for government ownership, merging of control and regulatory functions, and vertical integration seems to rest on the presumption that market-based solutions will produce a suboptimal supply of electricity in the short and the long run, for several reasons. First, electric projects require lumpy investment, asset specificity, and a long gestation period, which only governments can easily afford. In part, governments can afford to invest in large-scale electric projects because they are large savers, but another reason is that the social discount factor is lower than the private one, because governments can spread risk over the entire population. Second, the distribution of electricity is characterized by economies of scale, which produces natural monopolies whose regulation under private ownership is by no means problem-free, even in industrial countries. Finally, reliable provision of electricity requires investment planning, stand-by capacity, and coordination of operation, all of which are perceived to be easier to handle if electricity enterprises are publicly owned, because public ownership presumably reduces the problem of information asymmetry. This presumption rests on the premise that public-enterprise managers work less hard than their private-enterprise counterparts to keep enterprise information away from government agencies.

Chilean policies in the electricity sector since the early 1980s contrast with this paradigm on all counts. First, the government established the National Commission of Energy (CNE by its Spanish abbreviation) as an autonomous regulatory agency in 1978, assigning the ownership function to the government holding company, the Corporación de Fomento de la Producción (CORFO). Second, it broke up the country's vertically integrated electricity enterprises into separate generation and distribu-

193

tion enterprises. Third, it issued a new regulation in 1982 that based pricing on marginal cost and clarified other rules of the sector's operation. Finally, it culminated these reforms with the divestiture of most of the country's state-owned electric power enterprises. These features uniquely qualify the Chilean divestiture experience to address the general question as to whether market or quasi market solutions are capable of producing satisfactory results in the electricity sector.

This chapter analyzes the divestiture experience of CHILGENER S.A., which is typical of electricity generating enterprises in Chile in that it underwent all the reforms outlined above. The enterprise was incorporated in 1981. While under public ownership it operated on a commercial basis, and it had to abide by the 1982 regulatory scheme. Its ownership was transferred to the private sector in 1987. Therefore, the analysis of CHILGENER should enable us to answer the following interesting questions:

- How well does a commercialized and regulated public enterprise in the electricity generating sector perform?
- Under such circumstances, does divestiture still lead to welfare improvement?

Background

CHILGENER's primary mission is to generate, transmit, and sell bulk electricity. Until 1981 the enterprise operated as an integral part of Chilectra S.A., which, as a government holding company, also managed CHILQUINTA and CHILMETRO.[1] Together, the three units comprised a vertically integrated operation for the generation, transmission, and distribution of electricity.

In 1981 CHILGENER experienced the first of two institutional shocks when it was incorporated as a separate enterprise. However, it remained a subsidiary of Chilectra until 1986, when the latter was dissolved. The second shock came when its ownership was fully transferred to the private sector by January 1988.

Whether public or private, incorporated or not, CHILGENER's installed generating capacity remained virtually constant in the 1980s, at 597 megawatts. The enterprise began building a new hydroelectric plant (Alfalfal) in 1986, which came on stream in 1991. This plant added a generating capacity of 160 megawatts (or a mean annual electric energy generation of 820 gigawatt-hours), a 220-kilovolt transmission line, and a command, control, and data acquisition system.

Excluding Alfalfal, CHILGENER has sixteen thermal and hydroelectric generating units; over 85 percent of this capacity is thermoelectric. This has implications for the company's cost structure. In general, there is an inverse relationship between the fixed and the variable costs of generating electricity. As shown in table 9-1, the estimated fixed costs of gener-

Table 9-1. Fixed and Variable Costs of Electricity Generation, Chile, 1989

Type of generator	Fixed costs (U.S. dollars per installed kilowatt)	Variable costs (U.S. cents per kilowatt-hour)
Hydroelectric	1,000–2,000	0
Thermoelectric steam (coal fired)	900–1,100	2–4
Thermoelectric steam (oil fired)	800–1,000	2–4
Thermoelectric diesel	300–900	—
Gas turbine (oil fired)	300–500	9

— Not available.
Source: CNE (1989).

ating hydroelectricity are relatively high, but the associated variable costs are practically zero. Conversely, while the variable costs of generating electricity using thermal plants are considerably higher than for hydroelectric plants, the associated fixed costs are lower.

In addition to generating electricity, CHILGENER operates a transmission system 254 kilometers in length. It operates and maintains several substations. It also owns a wharf on the Pacific coast, which it uses for loading and unloading coal; the company subcontracts this installation's excess capacity, for example to CODELCO.

Market Characteristics

CHILGENER is one of eleven electricity generating enterprises in Chile. In addition, a number of industrial and mining companies produce electricity for their own use, selling the residual for public consumption. In 1989 the company owned 14 percent of the country's installed generating capacity, which represented 17 percent of that in the Central Interconnected System (SIC). In turn, the SIC accounts for about 80 percent of Chile's installed capacity.[2]

An enterprise's share of installed capacity does not, however, necessarily translate into a corresponding market share in electricity generation. Table 9-2 shows that, although the supply of electricity in the SIC has been on the rise, CHILGENER's share fluctuated between 8 and 26 percent during the period 1980–89. The lack of correlation between installed capacity and electricity generation stems from the existing regulatory setup in Chile, which is designed to minimize the overall cost of supply while promoting competition among generating enterprises. In this setup:

- Enterprises compete for the approval of the regulatory agency to establish new projects. Selection is made by the CNE on the basis of a least-cost investment program.

Table 9-2. Gross Electricity Generation in the Central Interconnected System (SIC), Chile, 1980–89
(gigawatt-hours)

Enterprise	1980	1981	1982	1983	1984	1985	1986	1987	1988	1989
ENDESA	5.8	6.3	7.1	7.5	7.7	8.7	6.7	7.3	7.4	6.6
CHILGENER	2.4	2.4	1.5	1.6	2.1	1.5	1.2	1.0	2.2	3.9
COLBUN	0.0	0.0	0.0	0.0	0.0	0.0	2.9	2.9	2.5	2.0
Others	0.2	0.2	0.2	0.3	0.3	0.4	0.4	0.7	0.8	0.8
Self-supplying	1.2	1.3	1.1	1.2	1.3	1.2	1.2	1.3	1.3	1.3
Total	9.6	10.1	9.9	10.6	11.4	11.8	12.5	13.2	14.3	14.7
Memorandum: CHILGENER market share (percent)	25	23	16	15	18	12	9	8	15	26

Source: ENDESA (various years).

- Once installed, the decision to operate certain plants is made by the Economic Load Dispatch Center (ELDC), which permits the operation of the plant with the lowest marginal cost among all generators at any given point in time to satisfy demand.
- Meanwhile, enterprises decide individually to conclude supply contracts with clients, up to the limits of their capacity.[3] Norms for enterprise capacity are also set by the ELDC.
- Enterprises producing at less than capacity fulfill their contractual obligations by purchasing the deficit from the system. Given that excess generation by one enterprise is absorbed by another, the system is continuously in equilibrium.

Overall, generating enterprises in the SIC are run as if they were a multiplant firm, irrespective of ownership. At the center of all this is the role played by tariffs, competition, and regulatory institutions. These issues are elaborated below.

The Regulatory Framework

The General Law of Electric Power of 1982 embodies the regulatory rules governing the sector in Chile.[4] Some features of this law have been mentioned. A few additional features are elaborated below, with the focus on electricity generation. The regulatory aspects of electricity distribution are discussed in the next chapter.

TARIFFS. Prices for sale of electricity to distribution enterprises are regulated, not because of economies of scale in electricity generation, but because prices to end users are themselves regulated. These prices are set on the basis of short- and long-run marginal costs. The long-run marginal cost is calculated by CNE for the least-cost investment program to meet peak demand, using a computer programming model. Tariffs are revised twice a year, taking into account differences in locations. If necessary, they are modified in the interim on the basis of an indexation formula for water reservoir levels and cost components such as fuel.

Spot prices for exchange among generating enterprises are set by the ELDC on the basis of short-run marginal cost at the substation of origin. To ensure price stability, spot prices are calculated into the future, taking into account parameters acceptable to all participants, including reservoir levels, prices of coal and of oil, demand, and so on.

Finally, tariffs for major consumers—defined as those with installed capacity above 2 megawatts—are not regulated. Suppliers have to compete in this segment of the market, which accounted for 52 percent of total consumption in 1989. Regulation stipulates the automatic adjustment of regulated tariffs whenever they deviate from these unregulated tariffs by more than 10 percent. By law, negotiated tariffs must be made public.

COMPETITION. To ensure adequate competition among generating enterprises, any producer can gain access to any consumer through the transmission system by paying "wheeling" charges. These charges are based on the short-run marginal cost or the average incremental cost of transmission, or are negotiated. Self-generation is encouraged, subject to prespecified technical standards. Entry is also permitted subject to CNE scrutiny.

REGULATORY INSTITUTIONS. CNE advises the government on tariff formulation and investment planning. It also oversees the implementation of regulation and acts as an arbitrator in disputes. Its high-ranking board is presided over by a representative of the president of Chile. Its members include the ministers of defense, economy, finance, mining, and planning and the chief administrator of CNE. The CNE administrator is assisted by a small but well-qualified staff.

The Ministry of Economy is entrusted with the power to approve tariffs on the basis of CNE proposals. It also monitors, through the superintendent of electricity and fuels, compliance with the regulations and procedures regarding installations and services. Finally, it attends to customer complaints regarding service or tariffs.

The daily operation of the ELDC, including setting spot prices for exchange among generating enterprises, is left to a commission whose members are representatives of the generating enterprises themselves. For this reason the ELDC is often referred to as the "generators' club." The ELDC was established in May 1985. It operates under a set of rules designed and enforced by CNE, the objective of which is to ensure equal access to the system, fair competition, and safety and reliability of the supply of electricity.

In sum, the regulatory setup in Chile combines a high degree of coordination and elements of competition. Coordination is intended to guarantee the supply of electricity at the lowest marginal cost possible. Competition is intended to pressure generating enterprises to reduce marginal cost. While implementing the regulation is entrusted to an autonomous regulatory agency, the daily operation of the dispatch center is left to the generating enterprises themselves (for a fuller description of the system see Bernstein 1988).

Divestiture

Having established a regulatory framework, the government of Chile, beginning in the mid-1980s, pursued a strategy of withdrawing gradually from owning electric power enterprises (table 9-3). This policy was consistent with the market-oriented approach pursued by the government since 1974 and contrasts with previous policies toward the sector, which beginning in 1940 featured a steady increase in government participation, first through CORFO, then through ENDESA, and after 1970 through Chilectra.

The divestiture of CHILGENER began in October 1985, when Chilectra announced it would sell 30 percent of the enterprise. In the next two months the parent enterprise offered CHILGENER's employees the option of receiving 50 percent of their severance payments in advance if they invested at least 80 percent of that sum in shares of the enterprise. The

Table 9-3. *Government Shares of Enterprises in the Electricity Generation Industry, Chile, 1982–89*
(percentages of total)

Enterprise	1982	1983	1984	1985	1986	1987	1988	1989
CHILGENER	100.0	100.0	100.0	95.2	64.6	35.0	0.0	0.0
ENDESA	98.3	98.3	98.3	98.3	98.3	90.7	90.7	90.7
COLBUN	n.a.	n.a.	n.a.	n.a.	98.2	98.2	98.2	98.2
PEHUENCHE	n.a.	n.a.	n.a.	n.a.	97.0	31.1	33.6	0.0
EDELNOR	—	—	—	—	—	—	0.0	0.0
PULLINQUE	—	—	—	—	—	—	0.0	0.0
PILMAIQUEN	—	—	—	—	—	—	0.0	0.0
EDELEAYSEN [a]	n.a.	n.a.	n.a.	n.a.	n.a.	92.0	89.6	89.6
EDELMAG [a]	n.a.	n.a.	n.a.	n.a.	n.a.	87.6	0.0	0.0

— Not available.
n.a. Not applicable.
a. Also distributes electricity; part of ENDESA prior to 1987.
Source: Ale and others (1990).

option of receiving the remaining 20 percent in cash provided workers with an added incentive to act upon the offer. As a result, 84 percent of them purchased a total of 4.2 percent of the enterprise's equity, as shown in table 9-4. The value of the shares was derived from the average price on the stock market in the last two weeks prior to the offer.

In April 1986 Chilectra was liquidated and the ownership of CHILGE-NER transferred to CORFO. Since CORFO already owned 99 percent of Chilectra, this transaction did not entail any financial transfers. Thereafter, CORFO continued the divestiture process by offering shares on the stock market. As a result, the private sector gained control of the enterprise (65 percent) in 1987. By January 1988 the company was 100 percent privately owned and controlled, with foreigners owning 41 percent.

The sale of CHILGENER took effectively a little over two years to complete. The enterprise was sold to a diverse group of domestic and foreign buyers, including pension funds, other financial institutions, employees, and other individuals. Whether sold on the stock exchange or directly to workers, the shares were priced as they were valued by the stock market. The government neither offered nor agreed to any tax exemptions or debt relief, nor did it undertake any physical, financial, or labor restructuring prior to the sale. CHILGENER continued to operate under the same regulatory scheme after divestiture.

What Happened?

What was the effect of divesting CHILGENER? Our attempt to address this question begins by measuring the enterprise's performance before and after divestiture. We measure performance in terms of profitability,

Table 9-4. Ownership Structure, CHILGENER, 1982–90
(percentages of total)

Shareholders	1982	1983	1984	1985	1986	1987	1988	1989	1990
Public									
CORFO	0.0	0.0	0.0	0.0	64.6	35.0	0.0	0.0	0.0
Chilectra	100.0	100.0	100.0	95.2	0.8	0.0	0.0	0.0	0.0
Total	100.0	100.0	100.0	95.2	65.4	35.0	0.0	0.0	0.0
Private domestic									
Pension funds	0.0	0.0	0.0	0.0	13.2	26.8	26.2	36.7	31.1
Employees	0.0	0.0	0.0	4.2	5.2	4.9	4.9	1.8	1.5
Others	0.0	0.0	0.0	0.6	16.3	33.4	27.7	15.9	19.5
Total	0.0	0.0	0.0	4.8	34.7	65.1	58.8	54.4	52.2
Private foreign	0.0	0.0	0.0	0.0	0.0	0.0	41.3	45.6	47.8

Source: CHILGENER (various years).

productivity, and fiscal and consumer effects for the period 1982–90. In subsequent sections we examine the causes of this performance, project the future performance of the enterprise and what it would have been without divestiture, and estimate the welfare impact of divestiture.

Profitability and Productivity

We begin with an analysis of CHILGENER's recorded profits, output, and investment before and after divestiture.

PROFIT: PUBLIC VERSUS PRIVATE. Figure 9-1 shows that after-tax private profit increased dramatically following the divestiture of CHILGENER. The turning point occurred in 1988, when profit almost doubled its 1986 level, rising from 3.0 billion Chilean pesos (Ch$) to Ch$5.5 billion. Results in subsequent years only reinforced this trend, as profit reached Ch$11.0 billion in 1990. The notable decline in profit in 1987 was due primarily to an avalanche and mudslide into the Colorado River, which destroyed a 29-megawatt hydroelectric plant and damaged some of the installations at Alfalfal.

Figure 9-1.   Public and Private Profit at Current Market Prices, CHILGENER, 1982–90

Billions of pesos

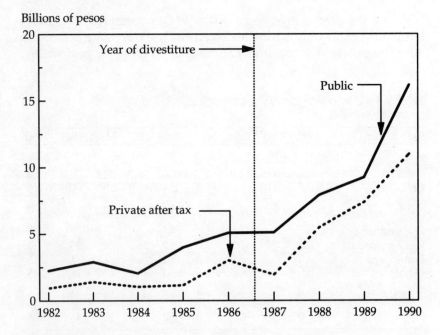

Source: Authors' calculations from CHILGENER data.

Figure 9-2. Public Profit at Constant Market Prices,
CHILGENER, *1982–90*

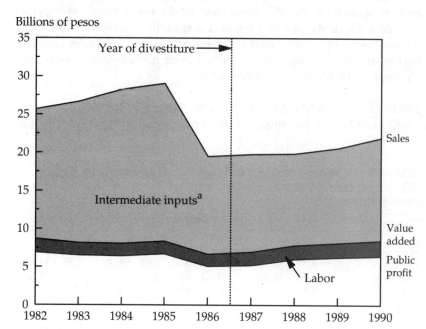

Billions of pesos

a. Includes purchases for resale.
Source: Authors' calculations from CHILGENER data.

A similar conclusion can be derived from inspecting the trend in public profit (quasi rent or producer surplus), also given in figure 9-1. Starting from Ch$5.1 billion in 1986, public profit more than tripled in 1990, reaching Ch$16.5 billion.

As quasi rent went up, so did the returns to equityholders (in the form of dividends and depreciation), debtholders (in the form of interest), and government (in the form of taxes). Further calculations indicate, however, that the lion's share of the increment accrued to equityholders.

In short, the analysis of public and private profit at current prices gives an impressive picture of improved performance in the post-divestiture period. If this improvement is attributable to divestiture, it strongly supports the hypothesis that divestiture promotes profit-maximizing behavior. However, to reach such a conclusion, further analysis is warranted.

PUBLIC PROFIT: CURRENT VERSUS CONSTANT. Our next step is to eliminate the effect of prices by calculating public profit at constant prices. Constant prices were derived from information provided by CHILGENER, in which the values of outputs and inputs are decomposed into their quantity and price components. The results, given in figure 9-2, are most illuminating. Unlike the decline in quasi rent at current prices in 1984 and its stagnation in 1987, inspection of the trend at constant prices reveals a sharp decline in 1986 and a smooth recovery in 1987. The contrast between public profit at current and at constant prices suggests that additional mileage can be gained from further decomposing the changes into price and quantity effects.

PRICE AND QUANTITY DECOMPOSITION. Table 9-5 decomposes public profit (and its components) into how much each variable changed in

Table 9-5. Decomposition of Public Profit Trend into Price and Quantity Effects, CHILGENER, 1982–90
(billions of pesos)

Change in	1983	1984	1985	1986	1987	1988	1989	1990
Output								
Price	3.55	2.25	6.38	6.81	3.62	6.79	9.75	14.64
Quantity	0.40	0.90	0.50	−11.69	0.27	0.13	1.09	2.84
Value	3.95	3.15	6.88	−4.88	3.89	6.92	10.84	17.48
Intermediate inputs								
Price	2.58	2.60	4.14	2.42	3.17	4.61	7.54	6.07
Quantity	0.68	1.03	0.35	−8.19	−0.01	−0.89	0.68	2.33
Value	3.26	3.63	4.49	−5.78	3.16	3.72	8.22	8.41
Wages								
Price	0.21	0.32	0.37	0.01	0.49	0.21	0.62	1.46
Quantity	−0.03	0.02	0.04	−0.02	0.04	−0.02	0.05	0.32
Value	0.17	0.34	0.42	−0.004	0.53	0.19	0.67	1.79
Rented factors								
Price	0.0	0.0	0.0	0.0	0.0	0.0	0.0	0.0
Quantity	0.0	0.0	0.0	0.0	0.0	0.0	0.0	0.0
Value	0.0	0.0	0.0	0.0	0.0	0.0	0.0	0.0
Working capital								
Price	−0.07	0.06	0.06	−0.12	0.05	0.09	0.51	0.32
Quantity	−0.06	−0.03	−0.02	−0.06	0.11	0.12	0.10	−0.06
Value	−0.13	0.03	0.03	−0.18	0.16	0.21	0.61	0.26
Public profit								
Price	0.84	−0.74	1.81	4.50	−0.09	1.88	1.07	6.78
Quantity	−0.19	−0.12	0.14	−3.42	0.13	0.92	0.26	0.24
Value	0.65	−0.86	1.94	1.08	0.04	2.80	1.34	7.02

Source: Authors' calculations.

Figure 9-3. Gross Fixed Capital Formation, CHILGENER, 1982–90

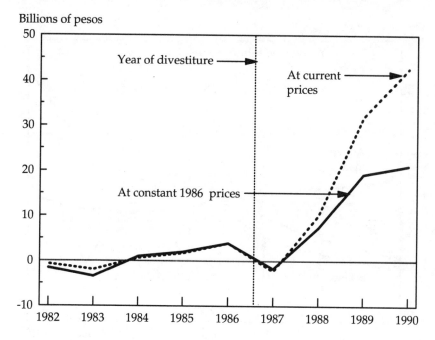

Source: Authors' calculations from CHILGENER data.

absolute terms over the previous year, how much of that change would have occurred if only prices had changed, and how much would have occurred if only quantities had changed. Table 9-5 shows that, if 1984 is excluded, prices moved in favor of CHILGENER throughout the period analyzed. In contrast, the quantity effects were positive more frequently and significantly during the period of private ownership. That is, in both periods CHILGENER generated substantial annual incremental revenues. The main difference was that prior to divestiture the boost came largely from price increases, and thereafter from a combination of price and quantity increases, except in 1990.

Changes in the components of quasi rent originated primarily from changes in sales and intermediate inputs, including purchases of electricity for resale. The net effect of both variables mirrors the price and quantity decomposition of public profit just indicated.

The changes in employment, although modest, are intriguing. As can be seen from table 9-5, the number of employees declined under public ownership in 1983 and 1986, supporting the assertion that publicenterprise managers in Chile have had the autonomy to deal with workers as work conditions required. On the other hand, the number of employees increased under private ownership (except in

Figure 9-4. Fixed Operating Assets, CHILGENER, *1982–90*

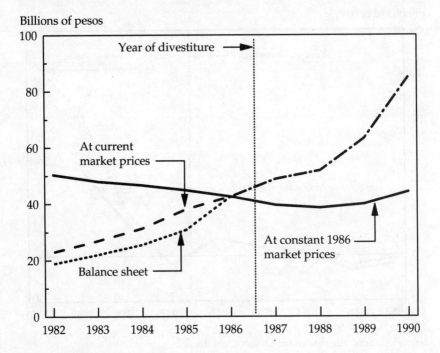

Source: Authors' calculations from CHILGENER data.

1988), which negates the hypothesis that divestiture inevitably threatens workers.

Changes in wages are equally revealing. Under both regimes they increased to cope with inflation. The modest wage increase in 1988 was due to partial indexation of a two-year contract agreed to in 1986. Once again, there is no evidence that divestiture hurt workers. Finally, the opportunity cost of working capital generally increased over time as CHILGENER increased its activity. Nevertheless, its share in total cost is relatively modest—a finding that calls for no further exploration.

FIXED CAPITAL. Absolute changes in output, profit, and other variables convey more meaningful information when related to fixed capital or other relevant denominators. Thus, we look next at fixed capital formation and capital stock, which are also important in their own right.

As shown in figure 9-3, gross fixed capital formation was fairly stagnant under public ownership until 1985. It then picked up in 1986, increasing sharply thereafter, especially in 1988 and 1989. This pattern was interrupted by a notable decline in 1987, caused, as noted above, by the avalanche in that year.

Increased fixed capital formation is normally expected to lead to an increase in the total capital stock. However, inspection of figure 9-4 indicates the opposite: fixed assets at constant prices in fact declined in the first two years under private ownership. The reason is that the Alfalfal project was still in progress five years after its inception, and this points in turn to the long gestation period electric generating projects require. In contrast, the balance sheet value of fixed operating assets at current prices increased over time. Notice that the balance sheet value and our estimate of the market value of fixed assets are almost identical. The reason is that Chilean firms, including CHILGENER, adjust their fixed operating assets annually for inflation and deterioration, following the perpetual inventory methodology. The divergence between the revalued and the balance sheet value of capital stock in the earlier period is due to an adjustment on our part to reflect retroactively the effect of a comprehensive technical revaluation undertaken by the enterprise in 1986.

PROFITABILITY. Figure 9-5 fits the pieces together. It shows (together with further calculations) that private profitability at current prices improved under private ownership. In relation to revalued capital, it averaged 9.8

Figure 9-5. Private and Public Profitability at Current Market Prices, CHILGENER, 1982–90

Percent

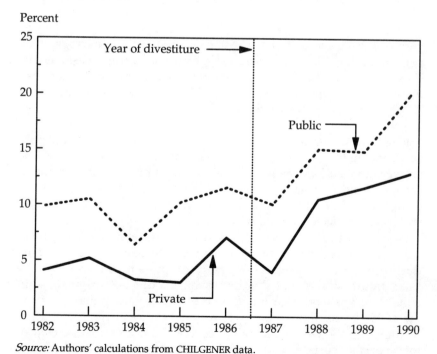

Source: Authors' calculations from CHILGENER data.

Figure 9-6.   Real Unit Costs of Operation, CHILGENER, *1982–90*

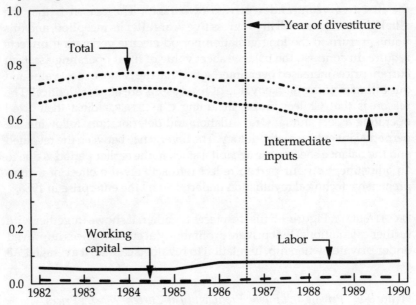

Source: Authors' calculations from CHILGENER data.

percent during the period 1987–90, compared with an average of 4.6 percent during 1982–86. Figure 9-5 (again with further calculations) similarly shows that public profitability at current prices increased under private ownership, averaging 15.1 percent, whereas it averaged 9.7 percent under public ownership.

PARTIAL VERSUS TOTAL PRODUCTIVITY. Does improved private and public profitability at current prices mean improved productivity? The answer obviously depends on whether the improvement was due to changes in output relative to input prices or to changes in output relative to input quantities. To sort out one from the other, we examine next unit costs and total factor productivity (TFP).

We start with average variable cost. Figure 9-6 exhibits an improvement (i.e., a decline) in the ratio of variable costs to output value during the period of private ownership, despite a reversal in 1990. The same figure shows that this improvement did not originate with either labor or working capital, both of which hardly changed from their 1986 levels. Rather, the improvement can be attributed to intermediate inputs, which generally accounted for about 70 percent of total variable costs. The bulk of these inputs consisted of electricity purchased for resale, and coal. In recent years, the consumption of coal alone has accounted for over 80 percent of total intermediate inputs, as CHILGENER's production-to-sales ratio increased significantly (97 percent in 1990). Thus, the decline in intermediate inputs can be traced to greater efficiency (reduced consumption of coal per gigawatt-hour of electricity generated), which is an important point because it testifies to improved management.

Compared with average variable cost, real and nominal fixed unit costs in relation to generated output declined even more sharply after divestiture, as can be seen from figure 9-7. This result is not surprising, given that CHILGENER's plant factor increased from 50 percent in 1985 to 83.4 percent in 1989. (Plant factor is defined as the kilowatt-hours generated by a given plant over a certain period of time divided by its maximum load—its capacity—during the same period.) That is, in recent years, the company's capacity utilization has increased without the capital stock increasing, and this has had the effect of reducing average fixed cost. Recall, however, that the decision to operate a given plant is exogenous to generating enterprises in Chile.

When variable and fixed costs are integrated into TFP, an overall measure of productivity, the results still favor the private-ownership

Figure 9-7. Average Capital-Output Ratios, CHILGENER, 1982–90

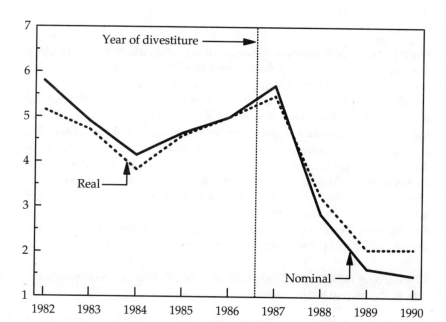

Source: Authors' calculations from CHILGENER data.

Figure 9-8. Total Factor Productivity and Real Public Profitability,
CHILGENER, 1982–90

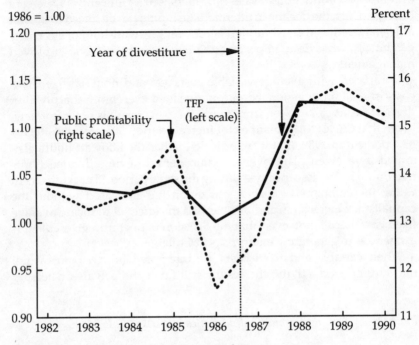

Source: Authors' calculations from CHILGENER data.

period. As figure 9-8 shows, this conclusion holds whether productivity is measured by TFP or by public profitability at constant prices. The question is: By how much did productivity improve?

Calculated using the geometrical average, the productivity differential is estimated at 2.8 percent per year. When calculated as a simple average, the differential is much higher, amounting to 6.5 percent per year. The large divergence between the two measures is due to the convexity of the TFP curve under public ownership and its concavity under private ownership. For this reason, the geometrical average, which only captures the contribution of two observations, is misleading; the simple average, which captures the contribution of all observations, is more appropriate. Thus, we conclude that the productivity differential between public and private operation is 6.5 percent per year.

SUMMARY OF PROFITABILITY AND PRODUCTIVITY. This analysis yields the following primary conclusions:

- Divestiture was associated with a higher rate of return on revalued capital, nearing 10 percent in 1990. This rate of return compares favorably with an average rate of return of less than 6.0 percent for a large sample of developing countries (see World Bank 1991). It also compares favorably with a real interest rate of 7 percent on three-month deposits in Chile. This suggests that marginal cost pricing can provide producers with adequate incentives to expand. Hence, the fear of underinvestment, often expressed by skeptics of divestiture, may not be well founded.

• Divestiture was also associated with improved efficiency, which, if due to divestiture, lends support to the hypothesis that change of ownership increases productivity.

• Finally, divestiture was associated with a surge in investment, which, again, if attributable to divestiture, is consistent with the hypothesis that divestiture relaxes a resource constraint.

These are important changes. However, we still need to ask whether they would have occurred in the absence of divestiture. Before turning to this question, however, let us first examine in preliminary fashion the effect of CHILGENER's divestiture on the government's budget and consumers.

Fiscal Effects

From the Chilean treasury's perspective, two important considerations are the sale price and the annual flow of funds between CHILGENER on the one hand and CORFO and the treasury on the other. Both elements are considered below, although we defer judgment on the fiscal impact of divesting CHILGENER to the concluding section of the chapter.

PROCEEDS FROM THE SALE. The proceeds from selling CHILGENER, expressed at December 1987 prices, amounted to Ch$12.6 billion, or the equivalent of 20 percent of the company's net worth in the same year. Brokerage fees were very modest, accounting for less than half of a percent of the sale proceeds. Clearly, however, the comparison between sale price and net worth is inappropriate: buyers pay far more attention to the prospects of the company and alternative investment opportunities. In addition, governments ought to compare the lump sum gain from sale plus taxes from private operation with the net revenues that would have been received had public ownership continued.

ANNUAL FLOWS. To provide a flavor of what the Chilean government traded CHILGENER for, figure 9-9 gives a breakdown of the annual flow of funds between the enterprise and the treasury before and after divestiture. On a net basis, there is a clear indication that the treasury now receives less resources from the company than it would have absent divestiture, even though corporate taxes increased under private opera-

Figure 9-9.   Fiscal Flows, CHILGENER, *1982–90*

Billions of pesos

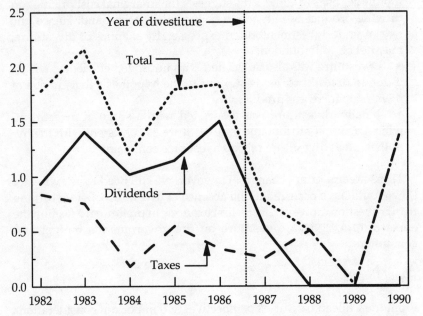

Source: Authors' calculations from CHILGENER data.

tion except in 1989. But this is not a surprising result for two reasons. First, the government is no longer entitled to receive dividends. Second, when it was a public enterprise, CHILGENER did not impose a burden on the treasury—the enterprise received no subsidy, equity, loans, or preferential treatment. The absence of such transfers, which are common to public enterprises in many other countries, reflects the long-standing tradition in Chile of operating public enterprises as if they were privately owned. As indicated in chapter 8, they have long been instructed to maximize profit and be self-financing. Further, their managers have had adequate autonomy to make important operating decisions, in return for which they have been held accountable to the government as the owner.

Effects on Consumer Welfare

From the perspective of Chilean consumers, the divestiture of CHILGENER is arguably neutral. Even though the company has a significant market share, it is in no position to exercise monopoly or oligopoly power. In the market for major industrial clients it has to compete with other generating enterprises. Major clients have the options of self-generation or finding alternative sources of supply. In the medium run they even have the option of using sources of energy other than electricity. In the market for exchange of electricity among generating enterprises, tariffs are set on the basis of marginal cost, irrespective of the terms of the contracts negotiated with clients and irrespective of ownership. Thus, CHILGENER is essentially a price taker. As such, it cannot by itself affect the price charged to consumers, whether it is publicly or privately owned. Hence, no further analysis of consumer surplus is pursued in the rest of this chapter.

Summary

In this section we have analyzed a bundle of partial performance indicators before and after divestiture. The primary conclusions are that divestiture was associated with improved profitability and productivity and increased investment; that no judgment can be made as yet as to whether the fiscal incidence of divesting the enterprise was negative or positive; and that the divestiture of CHILGENER has had no significant effect on consumers, largely because the company is a price (and in fact a quantity) taker.

Why Did It Happen?

The counterfactual story in the case of CHILGENER is one of continuity of the past. However, two positive correlations deserve further investigation: that between divestiture and TFP changes, and that between divestiture and increased investment.

Where did CHILGENER's productivity changes originate? Were they due to changes in sector characteristics, the regulatory setup, or the level of economic activity? Or were they due to behavioral changes caused by divestiture? Would investment have increased even without divestiture? Would it have increased at the level observed under private ownership? These are the questions addressed in this section. The objective is to explore causality, which, although important in its own right, also enables us to identify the counterfactual parameters. The latter are particularly important because we are ultimately interested in comparing the actual and projected performance of the divested CHILGENER with what it would have been without divestiture.

Elsewhere we hypothesized that changes in performance can be attributed to four distinct sets of factors: changes in ownership, changes in sector characteristics, changes in macroeconomic conditions, and changes induced by sale conditions (Galal 1990). To explore whether these factors influenced performance changes, we proceed by a process of elimination: if performance changes cannot be attributed to A,

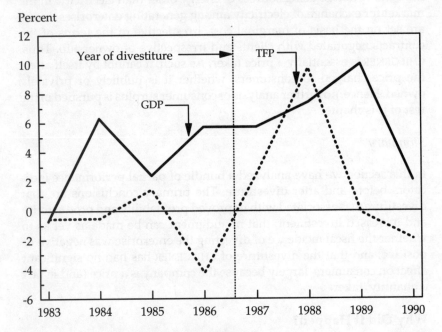

Figure 9-10. *Year-to-Year Changes in Total Factor Productivity at* CHILGENER *and Gross Domestic Product in Chile, 1983–90*

Source: Authors' calculations from CHILGENER data.

they must be attributed to B or C; if they cannot be attributed to B, they must be attributed to C. For the surviving hypotheses the issue collapses to finding supporting evidence.

Nonsurviving Explanatory Variables

Our search for causality begins by eliminating those explanatory factors that seem to matter little or not at all. Factors in this category are the conditions of sale, the state of macroeconomic activity, and regulation of the electricity generating sector.

As noted above, the sale of CHILGENER left the enterprise's market structure unchanged. It involved no tax exemptions or debt relief. It imposed no restrictions on hiring, firing, or wage setting other than those observed by all enterprises in Chile. Further, it entailed no physical, labor, or financial restructuring. Therefore, there is no evidence to support the hypothesis that sale conditions contributed to the changes in performance.

As for the state of macroeconomic activity, it can be seen from figure 9-10 that there is a strong positive correlation between Chile's GDP growth rate and TFP changes during the period of private ownership. Therefore, it is tempting to conclude that the changes in TFP are due, at least in part, to the business cycle—economic expansion increased demand, thus capacity utilization, and thus productivity, whereas economic contraction had the opposite effect. However, the same figure shows a very weak correlation between the two variables during the public-ownership period, which suggests that the explanation must lie elsewhere.

Can CHILGENER's improved productivity be attributed to changes in the regulatory framework? This argument would particularly hold if the regulatory setup had changed before divestiture in such a way as to pressure enterprises to be more efficient. As already noted, however, CHILGENER operated under the same regulatory framework before and after divestiture. Thus, no change in the enterprise's performance can be explained by changes in the regulatory setup either.

Surviving Explanatory Variables

Where, then, did the TFP changes originate? Two competing and equally compelling explanatory variables remain: the "system's cycle" and the change of ownership.

THE SYSTEM'S CYCLE. In Chile, the supply of electricity is planned such that a new project comes on stream every few years. Given the country's large hydroelectric potential, new projects have systematically used hydroelectric technology, as can be seen from table 9-6. As they begin operation, the marginal cost of generating electricity using thermal technology becomes too high. Enterprises that use thermal technology, such as CHILGENER, are then instructed by the ELDC to operate less

Table 9-6. *Actual and Planned Generating Capacity in the Central Interconnected System (SIC), Chile*

Plant or enterprise	Owner	Capacity megawatts	Date completed or scheduled
Antuco	ENDESA	300	1981
COLBUN	COLBUN	400	1985
Machicura	COLBUN	90	1985
Alfalfal	CHILGENER	160	1991
Canutillar	ENDESA	144	1991
Pehuenche	PEHUENCHE	500	1991
Curillinque	ENDESA	75	1994
Pangue	ENDESA	400	1995

Note: All plants are hydroelectric.
Sources: ENDESA (1989), CHILGENER (1990), CNE (1989).

intensively, and they incur higher average fixed costs as a result. Between the coming on stream of new projects, however, as demand increases while supply remains constant, these enterprises are instructed to operate increasingly intensively, incurring lower average fixed cost. They thus tend to go through a profit cycle. Therefore, to the extent that improved profitability and productivity follow the coming on stream of a new project, these changes can be attributed, at least in part, to the system's cycle.

CHILGENER was affected by the coming on stream of COLBUN in 1985. The system's cycle was thus in a favorable phase for CHILGENER in the late 1980s, and this, combined with a drought between 1988 and 1990 that reduced the system's hydroelectric capacity, make it hardly surprising that the enterprise's plant factor increased from 50.0 percent in 1985 to 83.4 percent in 1989. As capacity utilization increased, fixed unit costs declined, as we have seen, leading to improved productivity. Therefore, we cannot reject the system's cycle hypothesis as an important determinant of the productivity improvement experienced by CHILGENER in the postdivestiture period.

OWNERSHIP CHANGE. Does this conclusion mean that the change of ownership made no difference? In theory, transferring ownership to the private sector should reduce the principal-agent problem, which, although common to large private and public corporations, is more prevalent under public ownership for reasons explained elsewhere in this volume (especially chapter 23). Managers of private firms, to a greater extent than public managers, are expected to strive to maximize profit and minimize X-inefficiency. Therefore, the question is whether there is any evidence that they did so in the case of CHILGENER after divestiture.

Thus far, the most significant and concrete manifestation of such behavioral changes within the enterprise is the dramatic decline in the consumption of coal per gigawatt-hour of output, noted earlier. Interviews with management, regulators, and government officials suggest that the divestiture of CHILGENER brought about a number of additional changes. To cite but a few examples:

- The new board of directors replaced top management with a seemingly more dynamic team.
- A new corporate plan was drawn up in 1989, focusing on diversification; this was followed by a reorganization of the company.
- As a result, CHILGENER now uses its wharf not only to import coal for its own use but also to serve third parties.
- In addition, a new contract has been negotiated with workers, allowing them a share in profits and linking compensation to individual performance.

Therefore, it seems reasonable to conclude that the change in owner-ship contributed partly to CHILGENER's improved productivity. The question is, By how much?

It is difficult to determine precisely the separate contributions of the change of ownership and of the system's cycle to improved productivity. Yet given that fixed costs account for a large proportion of total costs, and given that changes in fixed unit costs are essentially beyond the control of management, it can be safely assumed that the bulk of the change in productivity is due to the system's cycle rather than to the change of ownership. Accordingly, and arbitrarily, we will conserva-tively assume that divestiture contributed a mere 1.5 percent (out of the total 6.5 percent estimated above) to productivity. To satisfy readers who find this assumption implausible, the bottom-line results will be esti-mated under two additional scenarios: one in which the full improve-ment in productivity is attributed to the change of ownership, and another in which the full improvement in productivity is attributed to the system's cycle.

Investment

Another question is whether investment would have increased at the same pace had CHILGENER continued to be publicly owned. The answer is a simple yes. The only investment project undertaken under pri-vate ownership thus far has been the Alfalfal project, which was con-ceived, approved, and begun prior to divestiture. Financing (in the form of a loan from the Inter-American Development Bank) was also arranged under public ownership. Therefore, we conclude that there is no evidence as yet of a change in investment behavior that can be attributed to divestiture.

Summary

Our search for causality leads us to three primary conclusions:

- CHILGENER's improved productivity is overwhelmingly attribut-able to increased capacity utilization, which is due in turn to what we have referred to as the system's cycle. Given that capacity utilization is determined exogenously, divestiture cannot be credited with this improvement.
- Nevertheless, there is some quantitative and qualitative evidence to support the conclusion that divestiture contributed, albeit mod-estly, to the productivity improvement. The most notable manifesta-tions of this kind so far are the dramatic decline in the consumption

of coal per unit of output and the use of the company's wharf to serve third parties.

- In contrast, there is no evidence to support the hypothesis that divestiture relaxed the resource constraint, thus increasing investment.

What Will Happen?

Projecting an uncertain future inevitably involves a margin of error. The room for error is even greater in the present context because we also need to quantify how CHILGENER would have behaved had it continued to be publicly owned. To reduce the margin of error we follow CHILGENER's own most recent projections, in part because they reflect the recent performance of the company and its plans, and in part because the underlying assumptions seem consistent with most forecasts of the electricity sector in Chile. At the end of this section we test for the credibility of our estimates.

Private Projections

According to CHILGENER officials at the time of our study, the prices at which it sells electricity were expected to decline in real terms around 1991–92 and around 1995–96 and then stabilize.[5] The two downturns were expected to follow from the coming on stream of the new projects listed in table 9-6. Given this level of prices, sales will vary between self-generation and purchases from other enterprises. On the cost side, average variable cost were expected to decline sharply in real terms in 1991–92, then rise. The initial decline was expected to result from the low cost of operating Alfalfal. The rise thereafter is due to having to operate the thermoelectric plants more intensively.

CHILGENER's projections assume that no new power plants will be built.[6] Further, the company intends to fully repay all outstanding interest-bearing debt by 2006. It assumes a depreciation rate of 3 percent and a dividend payout ratio of 75 percent at maximum. Further, it assumes an interest rate of 9 percent on foreign loans and a real interest rate of 10 percent on domestic loans.

Public Projections

In estimating the counterfactual we deviate from the above assumptions in only two respects. First, under the base case scenario we assume, for the same level of output, that public total average cost would have been higher than projected for private operation by an efficiency differential of 1.5 percent. This assumption is derived from the productivity analysis and discussion of causality above. Second, starting from the premise that CHILGENER would have had to meet the same financial obligations whether publicly or privately owned, we assume that the government would have had to give up its dividend policy of capturing 100 percent of profit in order to maintain a debt-equity ratio of 1.0. This ratio has been the enterprise's policy throughout.

Credibility of Projections

Under the foregoing assumptions, the net present value of CHILGENER is estimated at Ch$42.5 billion as of December 1990.[7] As table 9-7 shows, our estimate of the enterprise's value is only 12 percent lower than the value of the firm on the stock exchange.[8]

Several explanations of the divergence are plausible. The capital market is imperfect. Our estimate might be inaccurate. Or we now have more information than was available to investors at the time of divestiture. Or investors may have viewed the government's initial announcement that it would only sell 30 percent of the enterprise as a signal of continued public ownership. Whatever the explanation, the important point is that the two estimates are not wildly different, which lends credibility to our projections.

What Is It Worth?

What are the bottom-line results of divesting CHILGENER? Who won? Who lost? And how much did they win or lose?

Base Case Scenario

We first estimate a bottom line for our most plausible scenario, in which a modest productivity differential is attributed to divestiture.

WELFARE EFFECTS. Under this scenario, in which 1.5 percent out of the total 6.5 percent productivity gain is credited to divestiture, the divestiture of CHILGENER improved world welfare by Ch$4.0 billion, in net present value terms at 1987 prices. The change in welfare is calculated as the difference between the social value of CHILGENER under the actual

Table 9-7. *Estimates of Net Present Value, 1987 and 1990*
(billions of pesos)

Estimate	At December 1990 prices
Authors	42.5
Stock market	47.9

Source: Authors' calculations and data from the Santiago stock exchange.

scenario (private operation) and that under the counterfactual scenario (continued public operation).[9] After the share of foreigners is netted out, divestiture improved domestic welfare by Ch$1.3 billion, again expressed in net present value terms at 1987 prices. The change in domestic welfare represents 7 percent of the private value of CHILGENER, and that of world welfare 21 percent of the same denominator. The perpetual annuity equivalent of the change in world welfare is estimated at 2.1 percent of the enterprise's 1986 sales, and that of domestic welfare at 0.7 percent.[10]

WINNERS AND LOSERS. A breakdown of the winners and losers is given in table 9-8. In terms of net present value at 1987 prices:

- CHILGENER's shareholders, domestic and foreign, are the biggest winners, realizing a total of Ch$6.6 billion in additional profits. This is the difference between their maximum willingness to pay for the enterprise (Ch$19.1 billion) and the price they actually paid (Ch$12.5 billion).
- Among buyers, Chilean shareholders other than employees gain Ch$3.8 billion, and employees Ch$0.1 billion. Foreign shareholders come out Ch$2.7 billion ahead.

Table 9-8. Distribution of Welfare Gains and Losses from Divestiture in the Base Case, CHILGENER
(billions of pesos)

Economic actor	Private operation (V_{sp})	Public operation (V_{sg})	Gains from divestiture ($V_{sp} - V_{sg}$)
Government			
Taxes	8.3	8.0	0.3
Net quasi rents	0.0	15.4	−15.4
Net sale proceeds	12.5	0.0	12.5
Debt takeover	0.0	0.0	0.0
Others	0.0	0.0	0.0
Total	20.9	23.4	−2.7
Employees	0.1	0.0	0.1
Private domestic shareholders	3.8	0.0	3.8
Consumers	0.0	0.0	0.0
Total	24.8	23.4	1.3
Foreign shareholders	2.7	0.0	2.7
World	27.4	23.4	4.0

Note: Figures are estimated 1987 present values.
Source: Authors' calculations.

Table 9-9. *Distribution of Welfare Gains and Losses from Divestiture under Alternative Scenarios*, CHILGENER
(billions of pesos)

| | Productivity differential ascribed to divestiture | | |
Economic actor	None	All	Partial[a]
Government			
Taxes	0.0	1.3	0.3
Net quasi rents	–19.1	–2.3	–15.4
Net sale proceeds	12.5	12.5	12.5
Debt takeover	0.0	0.0	0.0
Other	0.0	0.0	0.0
Total	–6.6	11.5	–2.7
Employees	0.1	0.1	0.1
Private domestic			
shareholders	3.8	3.8	3.8
Consumers	0.0	0.0	0.0
Total	–2.7	15.4	1.3
Foreign shareholders	2.7	2.7	2.7
World	0.0	18.0	4.0

Note: Figures are 1987 present values.
a. This scenario ascribes 1.5 percent of the total 6.5 percent improvement to divestiture.
Source: Authors' calculations.

- In contrast, the Chilean treasury and CORFO are left Ch$2.7 billion poorer than they would have been in the counterfactual scenario. Under continued public ownership they would have received Ch$15.4 billion in net quasi rents, plus Ch$8.0 billion in taxes. With divestiture, they receive only the sale price (Ch$12.5 billion) and Ch$8.3 billion in expected future taxes. The fiscal loss represents 22 percent of the sale price.

Alternative Scenarios

In an alternative scenario in which divestiture is credited with no efficiency gains, welfare does not change with divestiture, as the first column of table 9-9 shows. Public CHILGENER is as good as private CHILGENER. The only difference is that government now forgoes Ch$19.1 billion in net quasi rents, in return for sale proceeds of Ch$12.5 billion. This makes the fiscal impact of selling the enterprise negative by 53 percent of the sale price.

Alternatively, in a scenario where divestiture is credited with the full gains in productivity (second column of table 9-9), world welfare improves by Ch$18.0 billion and domestic welfare by Ch$15.4 billion. Under this scenario the government forgoes Ch$2.3 billion in net quasi rents but receives Ch$13.8 billion from the sale proceeds and taxes. On a net basis this translates into a positive fiscal effect of 92 percent of the sale price.

Summary and Lessons

The primary conclusions of this case study of the divestiture of CHILGENER are the following:

- Divestiture correlated with higher profitability (at current and at constant prices), improved productivity, and increased investment.
- The improved profitability was due in part to marginal cost pricing and in part to increased capacity utilization. Both factors are not divestiture-specific. Rather, they are determined by the regulatory setup in Chile.
- Nevertheless, part of the productivity improvement was due to behavioral changes caused by divestiture, the most notable manifestations of which thus far are the decline in the consumption of coal per unit of energy generated and the use of the wharf to serve other parties.
- There was no increase in investment due to divestiture. The only project under way was initiated under public ownership.
- Nothing else has changed. However, the gains in productivity were large enough to make the divestiture of CHILGENER welfare-improving by Ch$4.0 billion, the equivalent of 21 percent of the private value of the enterprise.
- Private shareholders were the biggest winners, making Ch$6.6 billion, of which foreigners made Ch$2.7 billion.
- The Chilean government came out Ch$2.7 billion poorer, making the fiscal impact of divesting CHILGENER negative by 22 percent of the sale price.

The analysis of CHILGENER lends support to the hypothesis that divesting electricity generating enterprises is advantageous to society even where:

- Public enterprises in the power sector operate as if they were private firms, including abiding by the regulatory rules.
- Those rules are based on marginal cost pricing, competition, and coordination of operation and investment.
- Regulation is enforced by an independent regulatory body equally across enterprises, irrespective of ownership.

The analysis also suggests that the welfare gains from divestiture may accrue at a fiscal cost, even where the sale involves no concessions to sweeten the deal. This trade-off underscores the importance of clarifying the objective of divestiture up front. Finally, although the analysis falls short of ascertaining whether divestiture would have improved welfare in the absence of effective regulation and relatively well run public enterprises, it supports the general conclusion that quasi-market solutions in the power sector are capable of functioning relatively well. This is an important result since Chilean policies in this sector contrast with those of most countries. As noted at the outset, Chile relies on private ownership and regulation; most other countries rely on public ownership, vertical integration, and centralized decisionmaking.

Notes

This chapter was written by Ahmed Galal. The author is grateful to Juan Antonio Guzman, general manager of CHILGENER, and Juan Alberto Fernandez, chief of its planning and development office, for their cooperation and helpful discussions; and to John Besant-Jones for commenting on an earlier draft.

1. Chilectra dates back to 1921. It was later sold, along with several electric companies in the central zone of Chile, to the South American Company. Under the latter, each company operated as an autonomous entity until their consolidation in 1936. In subsequent years Chilectra took over several other electricity companies in the same zone of concession, which enabled it to serve the current region V (which includes Valparaiso and Viña del Mar) and the metropolitan area of Santiago, or approximately half the population of Chile. Chilectra was dissolved in 1986, leaving the ownership of its subsidiaries to CORFO.

2. Chile has four interconnected systems: the SIC, the Norte Grande Interconnected System, the Interconnected System of AYSEN, and that of Punta Arenas. The SIC is the most important.

3. Firm capacity is defined as the maximum power its generating units can contribute during the peak period of the system with a reliability exceeding 95 percent. The peak period is defined as an important block of high-demand hours.

4. Previously, electricity companies operated under DFL no. 4, which went into effect in 1959.

5. The price projections are based on an annual growth rate of demand of 5.5 percent, a world oil price of US$18 per barrel, a coal price of US$58 per ton, domestic inflation of 25 percent per year, external inflation of 4 percent per year, and devaluation of the currency following a crawling peg rule.

6. A few projects are being considered. However, neither the company nor we include any of these projects in the analysis, because they will have to compete for the approval of CNE, and the outcome of that competition is uncertain.

7. Assuming a real discount rate of 10 percent for the period 1991–2014, since all values are expressed in constant 1990 prices. For the period 1987–90 all values are in current prices; thus, we apply actual nominal discount rates.

8. Note in addition that CHILGENER was sold over a period of approximately two years. During this period share prices (at constant 1987 prices) increased. As a result, the government was able to capture part of this appreciation. Interestingly enough, these government gains came at the expense of foreign sharehold-

ers, who purchased most of their shares in January 1988, paying a price 7 percent higher than the average real price at which the enterprise was sold.

9. To convert all flows to their corresponding social values, we assumed that all prices in Chile sufficiently approximate their opportunity cost. Thus, we set all shadow multipliers equal to one.

10. The perpetual annuity equivalent is obtained by multiplying the change in welfare by the discount factor (10 percent), then dividing by annual sales.

10. ENERSIS

ENERSIS S.A. has a concession to distribute electricity in the metropolitan area of Santiago, Chile. The enterprise is a natural monopoly because electricity distribution is characterized by economies of scale. Despite this monopoly position, the government sold 62 percent of its ownership to the private sector in 1986, after having introduced a regulatory regime in 1982.

These features make ENERSIS an intriguing case to analyze for several reasons:

- As a regulated private monopoly, it allows an examination of the effect of changing ownership under a theoretically unpredictable outcome; private monopolies are likely to be more efficient than public ones but are simultaneously expected to exercise their monopoly power and capture regulators. Therefore, the net effect on society is uncertain.
- Prior to divestiture the enterprise operated as if it were privately owned. Its management was instructed to maximize profit, and it had the autonomy to pursue this objective, in return for which it was held accountable for its results. In keeping with a Chilean policy that is most unique in the developing world, ENERSIS then had to abide by the same regulatory rules applied to other distribution enterprises, whether public or private. Under such conditions, the question is whether private ownership can still make a difference.
- The combination of these two features allows us to address a dilemma often encountered by policymakers, namely, whether to allow a public enterprise to operate as a regulated private monopoly or to operate it as a reformed and regulated public monopoly.

The case of ENERSIS differs from that of CHILGENER, analyzed in chapter 9, in two main respects. On the one hand, ENERSIS is the sole distributor of electricity in Santiago, whereas CHILGENER is one of many competing electricity generating companies in Chile. On the other hand, ENERSIS enjoys economies of scale; CHILGENER does not. Thus, the analysis in this chapter complements that of the previous one. Together, both chapters make it possible to address more fully the general question as to whether or not quasi-market solutions and private ownership are capable of producing satisfactory results in the electricity sector.

Background

Throughout most of its long history as a subsidiary of Chilectra S.A., Chilectra Metropolitana (the company that is now ENERSIS) operated as a private firm. The enterprise became publicly owned in 1970, when the government of President Salvador Allende nationalized most of the productive sector in Chile, as recounted in chapter 8. This policy was short lived for many enterprises. The planned divestiture of Chilectra Metropolitana was announced in 1985. By 1987 the company was 100 percent privately owned.

Between 1970 and 1981 the enterprise operated under the umbrella of Chilectra S.A., a government holding company that also owned CHILGENER and CHILQUINTA. The three subsidiaries comprised a vertically integrated enterprise in the generation, transmission, and distribution of electricity. In 1981 the government decided to incorporate the three enterprises. This strategy, in hindsight, achieved three objectives. First, it facilitated the process of tariff setting by avoiding the joint cost problem. Second, it enhanced competition, in particular among generating companies, where economies of scale do not exist. Third, it made divestiture relatively easier because finding buyers is generally easier for smaller enterprises than for large ones.

Under private ownership, the shareholders of Chilectra Metropolitana amended its statute in November 1987, extending the company's mission to include the management of and investment in electricity-related activities. To this end, they formed ENERSIS as a holding company on 1 August 1988. This company currently controls Distribuidora Chilectra Metropolitana and four smaller firms.[1] Diversification was carried out primarily by expanding existing departments to serve third parties.

Demand and Cost Structure

Three characteristics distinguish the demand faced by ENERSIS. First, even though the company is one of twenty-five electricity distribution companies in Chile, it alone faces the demand for electricity in the metropolitan area of Santiago. This regional monopoly is dictated by the economies of scale inherent in electricity distribution technology. Second, demand in the company's area of concession grew at an annual rate of 5.2 percent during the period 1982–90. This average conceals significant sectoral variations, however. As table 10-1 shows, while consump-

Table 10-1. *Prices and Sales by Type of Customer, ENERSIS, 1982–90*

Customer	1982	1983	1984	1985	1986	1987	1988	1989	1990
Residential									
Price[a]	5.7	6.5	7.7	11.0	13.3	15.9	19.4	24.4	34.0
Sales volume[b]	1,037	961	1,041	1,038	1,054	1,098	1,124	1,207	1,232
Value of sales[c]	5,906	6,290	8,033	11,390	14,004	17,442	21,802	29,463	41,875
Commercial									
Price[a]	5.5	6.3	7.2	10.2	11.9	14.0	17.1	22.0	31.1
Sales volume[b]	440	443	475	495	535	577	621	678	679
Value of sales[c]	2,415	2,775	3,405	5,061	6,371	8,070	10,615	14,887	21,109
Industrial									
Price[a]	4.0	4.5	4.9	6.9	7.9	9.4	11.9	15.1	21.2
Sales volume[b]	793	849	1,000	1,070	1,216	1,353	1,486	1,648	1,668
Value of sales[c]	3,164	3,807	4,934	7,337	9,553	12,651	17,717	24,854	35,433
Other									
Price[a]	4.2	5.2	5.8	8.2	9.7	11.6	14.3	18.7	26.5
Sales volume[b]	505	498	532	526	558	584	612	621	596
Value of sales[c]	2,103	2,570	3,097	4,316	5,419	6,767	8,772	11,589	15,809
Total									
Price	4.2	5.0	5.6	8.0	9.7	11.1	14.2	17.7	27.4
Sales volume	2,775	2,751	3,048	3,129	3,363	3,612	3,843	4,154	4,176
Value of sales	13,588	15,442	19,469	28,104	35,347	44,930	58,906	80,793	114,226

a. In pesos per kilowatt-hour.
b. In gigawatt-hours.
c. Price times sales volume, in millions of pesos.
Source: ENERSIS data.

225

tion by the industrial sector grew faster than the average (at 9.8 percent per year), consumption by the commercial sector grew at a rate closer to the average (5.6 percent per year), and that by the residential sector at a rate below the average (2.3 percent per year). In 1990 the share of each group in total consumption was as follows: the industrial sector accounted for 40 percent, residential customers for 30 percent, and the commercial sector for 16 percent. The remaining 14 percent was shared by the agricultural sector, government, and the transport sector.

Finally, demand for electricity fluctuates between peak and off-peak periods. This feature makes ENERSIS in effect a multiproduct firm, even though electricity is a homogeneous product. Furthermore, it raises a question about how demand is modulated in Chile to ensure efficiency in consumption. This point will be discussed below. Suffice it to mention here that present regulation offers consumers a range of tariff options ex ante, which vary between peak and off-peak periods. Ex post, it is possible to classify customer groups by revealed preferences, as shown in table 10-1. This classification is useful for measuring the changes in consumer surplus following divestiture, as will be seen later.

As for the cost structure of electricity distribution, it depends, inter alia, on the extent of economies of scale, the price the distributor pays for electricity purchased from generating companies, and the losses incurred in the process of transmitting electricity to end users. In the Chilean context, ENERSIS enjoys the largest economies of scale of any electricity distributor because the company serves the most densely populated area in the country. Like other distribution companies, it pays regulated prices for its purchases of bulk electricity.[2] Finally, the company incurs technical losses (i.e., from inefficiencies inherent in the conduction of electricity over distance) and losses from theft and unbilled use. As table 10-2 shows, the sum of both types of loss as a proportion of total electricity purchases peaked at 22.4 percent in 1983 and bottomed at 14.2 percent in 1989. The recent decline in losses (due in part to technological improvements in monitoring) has an important bearing on allocative efficiency, as will be analyzed later in this chapter.

The Regulatory Framework

ENERSIS operates under the General Law of Electric Power, enacted in 1982. The law aims at providing producers adequate incentives to expand and operate efficiently, protecting consumers from monopoly exploitation, and rationalizing electricity consumption. To this end it specifies how concessions are granted, how tariffs are formulated, and who enforces the regulation and settles disputes. These issues are elaborated below (see chapter 9 for a discussion of the regulatory rules governing electricity generating companies in Chile).

Table 10-2. *Purchases, Sales, and Losses of Electricity,* ENERSIS, *1982–90*

Year	Purchases[a]	Sales	Losses	Losses as a share of purchases (percent)
1982	3,329.1	2,773	547.7	16.5
1983	3,557.6	2,751	799.6	22.4
1984	3,782.8	3,048	728.6	19.3
1985	3,938.5	3,129	802.6	20.4
1986	4,249.5	3,363	887.4	20.9
1987	4,512.9	3,612	894.1	19.8
1988	4,741.2	3,843	891.1	18.8
1989	4,853.4	4,154	689.7	14.2
1990[b]	4,896.3	4,176	719.8	14.7

a. Sales plus losses do not add up to purchases because the latter includes self-consumption, which has accounted historically for 0.2 percent of purchases.
b. In the medium term, ENERSIS expects losses to persist at 12.5 percent of purchases.
Source: ENERSIS data.

Because economies of scale are involved, the regulation allows enterprises to compete for licenses to distribute electricity; the awardees must then abide by the established regulatory rules. One of these is that distribution companies are obliged to supply electricity to clients upon demand. At the same time, the regulation authorizes electricity enterprises to request financial contributions from consumers requiring new connections. These contributions can be reimbursed in the form of equity, bonds, electricity, or any other mutually agreed form of repayment.

Tariffs are regulated only for consumers with installed capacity of less than 2,000 kilowatts; tariffs for larger users are negotiated. Where tariffs are regulated, consumers are offered several alternative tariffs and billing plans, facing which each modulates his or her own demand. Those whose electricity use causes the system to expand (i.e., those whose demand is large and coincides with the peak demand of the system) pay a higher (capacity) price. Those whose use does not cause the system to expand pay a lower (energy) price, based on short-run marginal cost. The options vary by voltage and according to peak—defined as 6 p.m. to 11 p.m. (1800 to 2300 hours), May to September, except for weekends and holidays—and off-peak periods.

Regulated tariffs to final consumers have two components: bulk tariffs (known in Chile as node prices) and distribution costs. Node prices are set by the National Commission of Energy (CNE) on the basis of the short-run or long-run marginal costs of producing and transmitting electricity. Distribution costs are calculated for 1 kilowatt-hour at peak and off-peak periods for an ideal firm. They include three elements: the cost of investment, operation, and maintenance; the cost of administration, billing, and other consumer-related activities; and losses of electricity.

CNE calculates node prices twice a year, in April and October. It negotiates distribution costs (and thus retail tariffs) with the distribution companies every four years. In the interim, distribution companies are allowed to adjust these tariffs for changes in node prices, the copper price index, the wholesale price index, wages, and the import price index.

At the time of our study, retail tariffs had been last negotiated in 1988. The cost proposals made by different distribution enterprises, those prepared by CNE, and those finally agreed to are presented in table 10-3. The following observations may be made:

- Distribution companies vary significantly in the extent to which they enjoy economies of scale. However, since regulated tariffs take the size of the firm into account, the benefits from economies of scale are transmitted to consumers.
- The tariffs agreed to in 1988 were closer to CNE estimates than to the enterprises' proposals. This occurred because the regulation includes a conflict resolution rule, according to which failure to reconcile cost differentials results in taking one-third of the enterprise estimate and two-thirds of the CNE estimate in the tariff calculation.
- Since regulated tariffs prevail for four years, enterprises can internalize any efficiency gains in the interim.[3] However, these are temporary gains because the regulators are likely to transfer them to consumers in the next round of tariff negotiation.

Three institutions are responsible for implementing the regulation. CNE is the most important. It advises the government on tariff formulation and investment decisions. The Ministry of Economy approves tariffs, based on CNE's proposals. The superintendent of electricity and fuels monitors compliance with regulations and procedures regarding installations and services.

Divestiture

Private sector participation in the ownership of ENERSIS first appeared in 1983, following the 1982 regulation, which, as noted, authorized electricity enterprises to request reimbursable financial contributions from consumers. ENERSIS took advantage of this provision, reimbursing some customers with shares at book value. Thereafter the shares began to be traded on the Santiago stock exchange.

The divestiture of the enterprise gained momentum in 1985, when Chilectra decided to sell 30 percent of its shares. Shares were first sold to the enterprise's employees, in several tranches. Employees were offered the option of using their legal severance payment in advance. Over 90 percent of them acted upon the offer. In 1986 the process intensified, as

Table 10-3. *Proposed and Agreed Distribution Costs for Electricity Tariffs
in Chile for 1989–92*
(pesos per kilowatt per month)

Area	Proposed by CNE	Proposed by enterprises	Agreed
Area 1[a]			
High tension			
Investment	342.6	529.1	404.8
Operation	143.9	268.9	185.6
Total	486.5	798.0	590.4
Low tension			
Investment	838.2	1,234.6	970.3
Operation	342.7	504.9	396.8
Total	1,180.9	1,739.5	1,367.1
Area 2			
High tension			
Investment	452.8	406.8	419.5
Operation	335.1	514.8	395.0
Total	760.9	921.6	814.5
Low tension			
Investment	779.4	838.4	799.1
Operation	475.6	992.2	647.8
Total	1,255.0	1,830.6	1,446.9
Area 3			
High tension			
Investment	1,026.4	931.0	994.6
Operation	407.7	839.0	551.5
Total	1,434.1	1,770.0	1,546.1
Low tension			
Investment	742.9	1,110.0	865.3
Operation	528.9	1,009.0	688.9
Total	1,271.8	2,119.0	1,554.2

a. Only ENERSIS falls within area 1, which corresponds to the Santiago metropolitan
area.
Source: CNE data.

can be seen from table 10-4, with further sales of shares on the stock
market. As a result the private sector acquired a 62 percent majority stake
in the company. In August 1987 the company became 100 percent
privately owned.

The ownership structure of ENERSIS in 1990 was such that two-thirds
of the shares were split almost equally between the company's employ-

Table 10-4.   Proceeds from Sale of ENERSIS, *1985–87*

| Date | Number of shares sold (thousands) | Revenue (millions of pesos) | | Average price per share (pesos) | |
		At current prices	At constant prices[a]	At current prices	At constant prices[a]
August–December 1985	1,031	894	1,310	866.8	785.7
January–August 1986	2,789	2,824	3,585	1,012.6	1,014.8
September 1986	507	521	661	1,027.2	1,008.3
October 1986	943	993	1,242	1,052.8	1,065.7
November 1986[b]	367	385	475	1,050.0	1,295.0
November 1986	150	187	230	1,248.0	1,539.0
December 1986	266	355	230	1,331.1	1,330.0
January 1987	326	509	431	1,559.9	1,728.6
February 1987	79	147	606	1,859.9	1,804.3
June 1987[b]	346	569	172	1,645.0	1,724.0
July 1987	1,392	3,293	626	2,365.3	2,072.6
August 1987[b]	2,359	4,118	3,563	1,752.2	1,633.5
Total	10,547	14,795	17,299		

a. December 1987, deflated by the consumer price index.
b. Sold directly to employees in exchange for severance payments.
Source: ENERSIS and CORFO data.

ees and pension funds. The remaining third was owned by a variety of private enterprises, other financial institutions, and individuals. Workers were able to acquire such a large share of the company in part by using their severance benefits, but also in part by creating an investment company, which was able to mobilize additional resources thanks to active management participation.

Two final observations are worth noting. First, even though all transactions were concluded through the stock market, table 10-4 indicates that workers paid less than the trend in share prices, which translates into an implicit subsidy. This result followed from keeping the offer price constant at a time of rising share prices. Second, because the share prices were rising on the stock market, the government was able to capture part of the appreciation by selling the enterprise over a period of time, rather than in one shot.

What Happened?

How did the divestiture of ENERSIS affect domestic and world welfare? We begin to answer this question by measuring the performance of the enterprise before and after divestiture (1982–90), focusing on its operation and its impact on consumers.

Profitability, Productivity, and Finance

We first examine the enterprise's financial results and productive efficiency in the years before and after divestiture.

PROFIT: PUBLIC VERSUS PRIVATE. As measured by private profit after tax, the performance of ENERSIS surged following the transfer of its ownership to the private sector. As figure 10-1 shows, company profits were 1.9 billion Chilean pesos (Ch$) in 1982; after a sharp decline in 1983, profits increased steadily, especially in 1989 and 1990, reaching Ch$31.6 billion in 1990.

On a trend basis, two obvious kinks can be detected: one downturn during the period of public ownership (1983) and one upturn during that of private ownership (1989). Enterprise reports attribute the downturn in 1983 to exogenous factors: higher input and lower output prices, both of which are regulated. In contrast, company reports attribute the upturn in 1989 to improvements in efficiency. Neither assertion can be verified at this stage.

Figure 10-1. Public and Private Profit at Current Market Prices,
ENERSIS, 1982–90

Billions of pesos

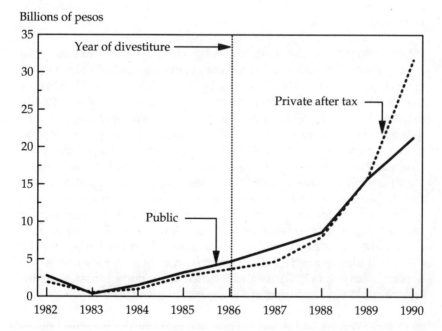

Source: Authors' calculations from ENERSIS data.

Private profit is particularly important to private shareholders. But to society as a whole, public profit (quasi rent or producer surplus) is a more appropriate measure of the contribution of all resources. On this score, figure 10-1 shows that society did better under private ownership as well (except in 1990). However, the two kinks identified above persist.

One surprising observation is that private profit was larger than public profit in 1990. Usually the reverse is true, because public profit is a measure of all returns from operation to capital, whereas private profit is the return to equityholders alone. This paradox can be explained by the significant increase in net nonoperating income, which amounted to Ch$19.6 billion in 1990. In turn, the surge in net nonoperating income was due to the unusual return on the company's investment in other divested enterprises, especially ENDESA, where its share in equity stood at 11.4 percent in 1989 and 12.1 percent in 1990. On a total investment of Ch$54.9 billion in 1990, ENERSIS made Ch$4.3 billion in dividends and Ch$31.4 billion in capital gains. The rate of return on this investment was a reasonable 11 percent, but the capital gains were an unusually high 69 percent.[4]

In short, the analysis of current profit shows that divestiture was associated with a significant improvement in public and private profit. The turning point (1989) occurred two years following divestiture. If this improvement is attributable to divestiture, it lends support to the hypothesis that private ownership improves profitability, which may also mean improved efficiency. However, further analysis is required to reach such a conclusion.

PUBLIC PROFIT: CURRENT VERSUS CONSTANT. To abstract from the price effect we calculate quasi rent at constant prices (figure 10-2).[5] Inspection of this figure yields two observations. First, while the 1983 and 1989 kinks persist, producer surplus at constant prices otherwise exhibits a steady increase over the period of public and private ownership. Second, neither the 1983 downturn nor the 1989 upturn can be fully attributed to price movements. In 1983 intermediate inputs, which constitute about 70 percent of total costs, grew faster than output. In contrast, intermediate inputs fell in 1989 (as electricity losses declined from 18.8 percent in 1988 to 14.2 percent in 1989), and output diversification increased.

These are important findings. The steady increase in quasi rent at constant prices suggests that ENERSIS was relatively efficient under public as well as private ownership—an issue we explore further below. The second finding poses the counterfactual question as to whether the decline in losses of electricity and the increase in output from diversification would have occurred in the absence of divestiture.

PRICE AND QUANTITY DECOMPOSITION. To examine the price and quantity effects, shown in table 10-5, reconsider quasi rent in the two excep-

Figure 10-2.   Public Profit at Constant Prices, ENERSIS, *1982–90*

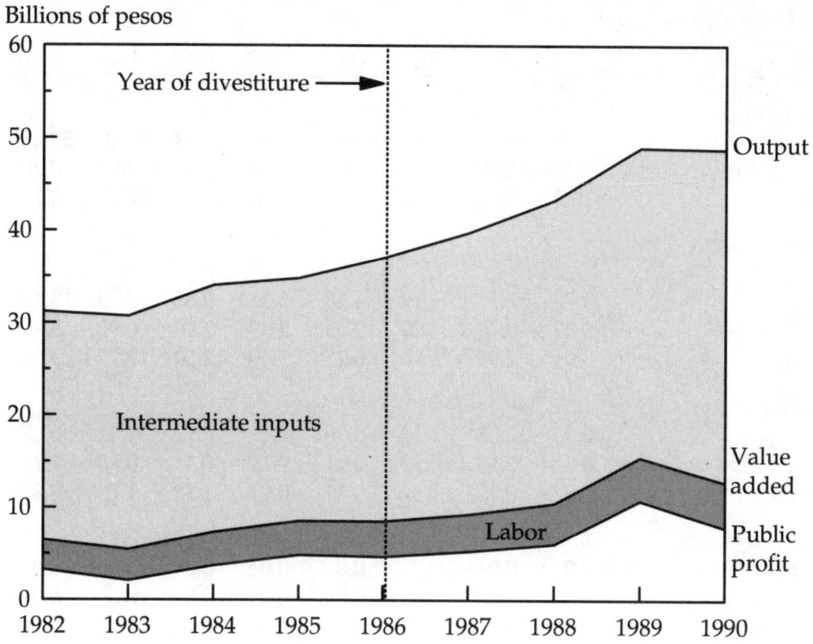

Billions of pesos

Source: Authors' calculations from ENERSIS data.

tional years, 1983 and 1989. In 1983 quasi rent declined by Ch$2.5 billion, about 80 percent of which (Ch$2.0 billion) was due to unfavorable price changes. However, the quantity effect was also negative. In contrast, the sharp increase in public profit in 1989 was caused by a significant quantity improvement.

More generally, 1983 and 1989 were exceptions to a trend in which prices moved in favor of ENERSIS throughout the period analyzed. However, the boost in the postdivestiture period came from a combination of price and quantity increases (except in 1990).

The changes in the components of public profit stem mostly from changes in output and intermediate inputs. Excluding 1983, the net price effect of both was positive under both regimes, especially in 1990. The net quantity effect was similarly positive in all years, except for 1983 and 1990.

The changes in wages followed a distinct pattern. Under public operation they increased every other year, as contracts were negotiated with partial indexation. Under private operation not only did wages increase, but so did employment. The increase in employment negates the hypothesis that divestiture inevitably involves a reduction in the labor force. The significant increase in wages in 1990 was due to a

Table 10-5.   Decomposition of Public Profit Trend into Price and Quantity Effects, ENERSIS, 1982–90
(billions of pesos)

Change in	1983	1984	1985	1986	1987	1988	1989	1990
Output								
Price	2.21	2.54	8.49	5.57	7.46	11.69	18.38	35.46
Quantity	–0.22	1.85	0.49	1.97	2.92	4.43	8.99	–0.28
Value	1.99	4.39	8.98	7.54	10.38	16.12	27.38	35.19
Intermediate inputs								
Price	3.72	2.12	6.19	4.18	5.31	9.63	16.79	18.49
Quantity	0.23	0.79	–0.29	2.03	2.09	2.96	0.97	5.30
Value	3.95	2.91	5.90	6.21	7.40	12.60	17.77	23.80
Wages								
Price	0.53	–0.02	1.19	–0.001	0.77	0.93	1.42	5.07
Quantity	0.04	0.18	0.13	0.11	0.14	0.45	0.28	0.24
Value	0.57	0.15	1.33	0.11	0.91	1.38	1.70	5.30
Rented factors								
Price	0.0	0.0	0.0	0.0	0.0	0.0	0.0	0.0
Quantity	0.0	0.0	0.0	0.0	0.0	0.0	0.0	0.0
Value	0.0	0.0	0.0	0.0	0.0	0.0	0.0	0.0
Working capital								
Price	–0.10	0.14	0.13	–0.26	0.10	0.10	0.58	0.45
Quantity	0.0	0.009	–0.04	0.004	0.05	0.03	0.13	0.19
Value	–0.10	0.15	0.09	–0.26	0.15	0.13	0.71	0.64
Public profit								
Price	–1.94	0.31	0.98	1.65	1.28	1.02	–0.40	11.45
Quantity	–0.49	0.87	0.68	–0.17	0.64	0.98	7.60	–6.01
Value	–2.43	1.19	1.66	1.48	1.92	2.01	7.20	5.45

Source: Authors' calculations.

decision by the company's board to pay workers additional compensation if profit as a proportion of net worth exceeded 20 percent, which did in fact occur.

Finally, changes in the quantity of working capital were too small to affect total costs or quasi rents.

FIXED CAPITAL. These observations do not reveal the real bottom line; one should relate all returns to the factor of production presumed to receive them, namely, capital stock. Given that the enterprise's additional investment was relatively modest in relation to its capital stock, we note (in figure 10-3) that fixed operating assets at current and at constant prices exhibit a steady increase throughout the period analyzed. More-over, since ENERSIS, like other Chilean enterprises, revalues capital using the perpetual inventory methodology, market and book value assets correlate closely.

PROFITABILITY. Dividing private and public profit by the revalued capital stock gives the profitability ratios reported in figure 10-4. This figure (together with further calculations) shows a dramatic improvement in performance under private ownership. Under the latter, private profit-ability in relation to net worth and revalued capital averaged 18.8 and 23.1 percent, respectively. The corresponding five-year averages of the two indicators under public ownership stood at 6.7 and 8.6 percent, respectively. Similarly, public profitability at current prices in relation to revalued capital averaged 22.3 percent under private ownership, com-pared with a five-year average of 10.7 percent under public ownership. At constant prices, the same figure also shows that public profitability improved under private ownership, averaging 21.8 percent versus 11.7 percent under public operation.

Figure 10-3. Fixed Operating Assets, ENERSIS, 1982–90

Billions of pesos

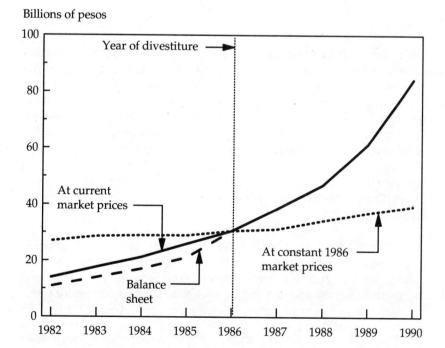

Source: Authors' calculations from ENERSIS data.

Figure 10-4. Private and Public Profitability, ENERSIS, *1982–90*

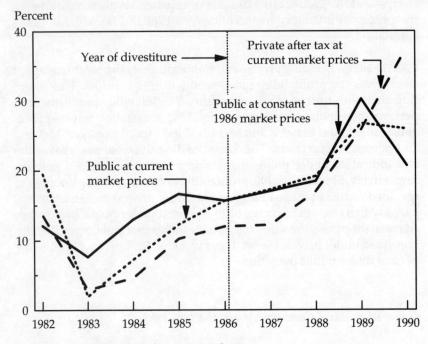

Source: Authors' calculations from ENERSIS data.

The significant increase in profitability following divestiture derives in part from an increase in output prices relative to input prices. However, it also derives from a reduction in losses of electricity, output diversification, and increases in nonoperating income. The benefits from reduced losses are arguably temporary for two reasons. First, opportunities to reduce them further diminish over time. Second, the regulators are likely to capture these benefits when tariffs are next revised. The same logic applies to nonoperating income to the extent that the benefits are due to a one-time capital gain. In contrast, the benefits from output diversification are likely to persist over time, as will the normal returns on venture capital.

PARTIAL VERSUS TOTAL PRODUCTIVITY. Improved profitability at constant prices means improved productivity. To explore the productivity question further we calculate a number of indicators, beginning with labor and capital productivity and concluding with total factor productivity (TFP).

Inspection of figure 10-5 supports the previous findings; that is, with the exception of the downturn in 1983 (and, for capital productivity, in 1985) and the surge in 1989, labor and capital productivity improved steadily under both public and private operation. However, these results have to be interpreted with caution for two reasons. First, they suffer from the well-known problems of partial indicators (as explained in chapter 2). Second, they are based on the assumption that output equals sales. For ENERSIS, however, output is not equal to sales because of losses of electricity from theft and nonbilled use.

To address both problems, we calculate TFP and its annual change (ΔTFP/TFP) over the period 1982–90. TFP is measured as a quantity index of output to inputs, following the procedure outlined in chapter 2. Output is defined here as the sum of sales and electricity consumed for free; the latter is evaluated at market prices paid by residential customers, since most free consumption of electricity is reportedly by this group. The results (together with public profitability at constant prices) are reported in figure 10-6. The story they tell is the one already told in figure 10-5.

FINANCE. Finally, we analyze ENERSIS's sources and uses of funds. This analysis complements that of profitability and productivity. Its importance lies in the fact that the financial position of an enterprise affects its ability to grow and to furnish working capital for itself, and ultimately affects its productivity. In the case of ENERSIS, it is also important because of the significant changes in nonoperating assets.

Figure 10-5. *Average Labor and Capital Productivity,* ENERSIS, *1982–90*

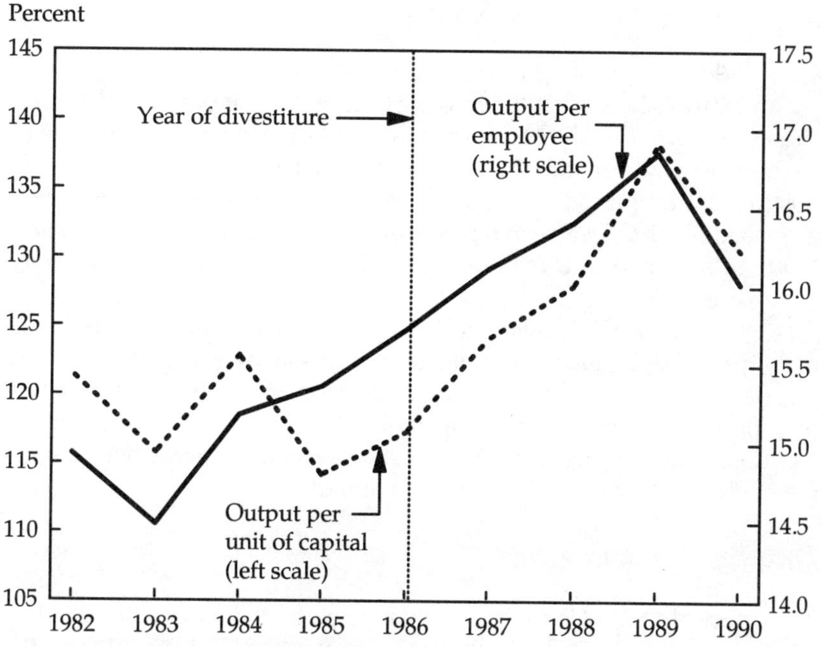

Percent

Source: Authors' calculations from ENERSIS data.

Figure 10-6.   Total Factor Productivity and Real Public Profitability,
ENERSIS, 1982–90

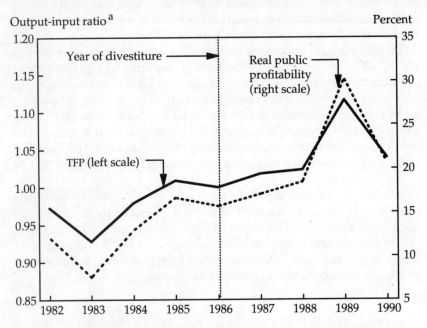

a. At constant 1986 prices.
Source: Authors' calculations from ENERSIS data.

Figure 10-7 shows ENERSIS's uses of funds for the period 1982–90. It shows that, whether the enterprise was public or private, it used most of its funds for investment in its own operation. The main difference in the postdivestiture period is that the company, as already noted, invested more heavily than before in nonoperating assets, especially in 1989 and 1990. As it turned out, the returns on this investment were extremely rewarding.

ENERSIS under public ownership generated most of its resources internally, primarily because of the government's insistence that public enterprises be self-financing. Under private operation the company has maintained a high self-financing ratio. However, it also contracted a significant amount of debt in 1989. As internally generated funds increased in 1990, some of the debt was retired.

Effects on Consumer Welfare

The effect of ENERSIS's divestiture on consumers depends on whether and how much it caused movements in real prices and in output quantity and quality. Consumers are better off the lower the real price, the greater the quantity produced, and the better the quality of that production.

As a first approximation we calculate the changes in consumer surplus (ΔCS) for all customers, except those consuming electricity for free, as:

(10-1) $$\Delta CS = Q_{t-1} \cdot (P_t - P_{t-1})$$

where P refers to the real price, Q represents quantity sold, the subscript t refers to the current year, and the subscript t-1 to the previous year (this is known as the Slutsky compensation). For free consumption we measure ΔCS as:

(10-2) $$\Delta CS = P_{t-1} \cdot (Q_t - Q_{t-1}).$$

That is, consumers of electricity for free are worse off the greater the reduction in the quantity of losses, evaluated at last year's price.

In the aggregate, consumers were worse off under private operation, as figure 10-8 shows. This observation applies to consumers charged a

Figure 10-7. Uses of Funds, ENERSIS, 1983–90

Billions of pesos

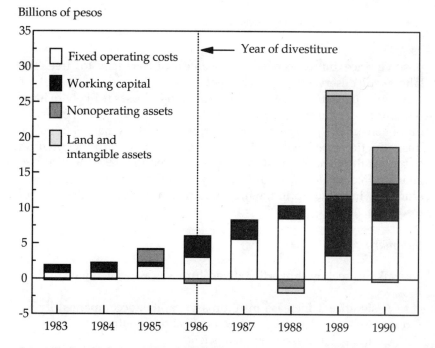

Source: Authors' calculations from ENERSIS data.

Figure 10-8. Changes in Real Consumer Surplus, ENERSIS, *1983–90*

Billions of 1986 pesos

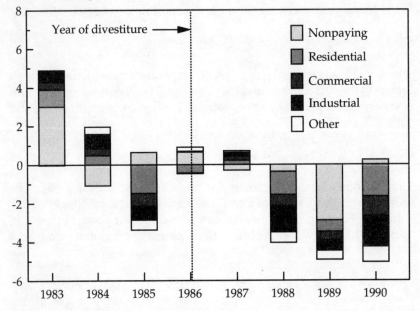

Source: Authors' calculations from ENERSIS data.

positive price, but especially to consumers of electricity for free. The latter result deserves further comment.

As will be discussed below, the reduction in losses is likely to have two effects in the future. First, it is likely to mean lower prices for those consumers charged positive prices, as the regulators translate this reduction into lower tariffs in the next round of tariff negotiation (which at the time of our study was scheduled for 1992, the tariffs to go into effect in 1993). Second, society should benefit from improved efficiency in consumption, which would lead to a better allocation of resources.

Summary

Overall, this section shows that divestiture was associated with:

- A significant increase in returns to capital, accompanied by reduced losses of electricity and diversification of output
- Continued improvement in efficiency
- Increased returns from nonoperating assets, mainly from investing in ENDESA.

Divestiture was also associated with a decline in consumer surplus, especially for users of electricity free of charge.

Why Did It Happen?

Correlation is not equivalent to causation. Only in the rare event where all other things remained equal save the change of ownership would it be reasonable to attribute the above changes in performance to divestiture. Other things do not usually remain equal. The economy booms or slows down. Market structure and regulatory rules change. The sale process itself may alter the conditions under which the enterprise operates. Thus, it is important to ask the counterfactual question, Would the observed discontinuities have occurred in the absence of divestiture?

Nonsurviving Explanatory Variables

The conditions of the sale are the easiest explanatory factor to dispose of in the case of ENERSIS. The sale left the enterprise's market structure and regulatory framework unchanged. It provided no concessions to alter the incentive structure, such as tax exemptions or debt relief. It did not change the enterprise itself: no presale physical, financial, or labor restructuring was undertaken. In short, no significant changes in performance can be attributed to the sale conditions.

Can performance changes be attributed to changes in sector characteristics? Following divestiture there was no shift in government policy toward the electricity sector. ENERSIS continued to operate in the same area of concession, and its operation continued to be governed by the same regulatory rules. Thus, no significant changes in performance can be attributed to sector characteristics either.

Can the changes be attributed to the state of macroeconomic activity? The hypothesis runs as follows: a booming economy causes expansion of demand and increased sales, thus greater utilization of existing resources, and hence productivity improvement.[6] To explore this possibility, we plot in figure 10-9 TFP changes against GDP growth rates over the period 1983–90. Two observations are noteworthy:

- Negative TFP changes correlate strongly with economic downturns (for example, in 1983, 1985, and 1990), and positive ones with economic recovery (for example, in 1984, 1987, and 1989), at times with a one-year lag (for example, in 1986 and in 1988). Therefore, the relative changes in productivity are arguably the product of the business cycle rather than of ownership change.[7]
- If 1983 and 1990 are excluded, TFP improved under public and private ownership alike, which supports the perception that ENERSIS

Figure 10-9. Year-to-Year Changes in Total Factor Productivity, ENERSIS, *and Gross Domestic Product, Chile, 1983–90*

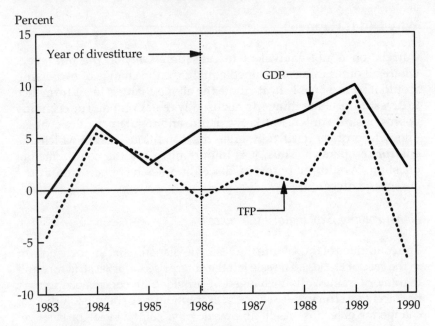

Source: Authors' calculations from ENERSIS data.

was relatively well run as a public enterprise, too. This finding lends support to the secondary hypothesis, that reforming public enterprises and regulating them, rather than divesting them, can improve efficiency. ENERSIS, like other public enterprises in Chile, faced a hard budget constraint. It had to abide by a relatively well conceived and implemented set of regulations. Its objectives were not clouded by noncommercial goals. Its managers were relatively autonomous in making operational decisions, in return for which they were held accountable to demanding owners.

Surviving Explanatory Variables

Does that mean that divestiture made no difference? Not quite. Productive efficiency aside, other things have changed: electricity losses went down, prices increased, output diversification went up, and nonoperating returns escalated enormously. These changes have had consequences for ENERSIS, consumers, and the Chilean treasury. They also have had repercussions on allocative efficiency. If neither sale conditions, nor sector characteristics, nor the state of economic activity are responsible for these changes, it can be argued that they are attributable to divestiture. The general plausibility of this argument stems from the views expressed by management, regulators, and government officials that ENERSIS, now more than before, behaves as a profit maximizer. It also derives from observed changes within the company, which reflect an increased concern for profit.[8] To cite but a few examples, compensation has been linked to profitability; the composition of the work force has improved (by increasing the number of college-educated employees); and the company has undergone an organizational change to cope with expansion.

Apart from the general plausibility of the ownership argument, it is still valid to ask whether the specific changes observed after divestiture would have occurred had ENERSIS remained publicly owned.

LOSSES OF ELECTRICITY. It could be plausibly argued that ENERSIS would have reduced its losses from theft and nonbilled use under continued public ownership, because the enterprise had created a department for this purpose as early as 1983. However, table 10-2 suggests that the effort intensified, with significant results, under private ownership. Therefore, although we concede that losses would have eventually declined under the counterfactual, the rate of decline would have been slower than that achieved following divestiture.

PRICE EFFECTS. Given that ENERSIS's prices are regulated, it could also be argued that the changes in these prices are attributable to the regulation, not to divestiture. However, this is an oversimplification. Regulated tariffs are derived in part from actual losses. Therefore, to the extent that losses would have been higher under continued public ownership, prices would have also been higher.

To illustrate this point, recall that the actual price under private operation (P_p) was calculated as:

$$(10\text{-}3) \qquad P_p = P^* \left[1 + \tfrac{1}{3}\, \alpha\, (L^* - L_p)\right]$$

where P^* is the price agreed to between CNE and ENERSIS, excluding losses of electricity; L^* is losses as estimated by CNE; L_p is losses as estimated by ENERSIS; the coefficient $1/3$ refers to the differential allowed by the regulation in case of dispute; and α represents the weight of losses in total purchases of electricity for distribution. Similarly, the counterfactual price (the price under continued operation as a public enterprise, or P_{pe}) would have been estimated as:

$$(10\text{-}4) \qquad P_{pe} = P^* \left[1 + \tfrac{1}{3}\, \alpha\, (L^* - L_{pe})\right].$$

Substituting equation 10-3 in equation 10-4 and solving for P_{pe} yields:

$$(10\text{-}5) \qquad\qquad P_{pe} = P_p \left[1 + \tfrac{1}{3}\,\alpha\,(L_{pe} - L_p)\right].$$

Therefore, as long as $(L_{pe} - L_p) > 0$, P_{pe} would have been greater than P_p.

OUTPUT DIVERSIFICATION. It is true that the diversification of output following divestiture took place primarily by expanding existing departments in the company to serve third parties. However, in view of the past behavior of ENERSIS (and other public enterprises in the same sector), it is likely that the expansion would not have materialized in the absence of divestiture.

NONOPERATING EFFECTS. Three reasons lead us to believe that nonoperating investment would not have occurred under the counterfactual scenario. First, if ENERSIS had enjoyed excess profit, the likelihood is high that the government would have captured it in the form of dividends and taxes. Second, in the unlikely event that retained earnings were permitted, past management behavior suggests that funds would have been invested in low-risk and highly liquid projects with modest returns. Third, in view of the limitation imposed by the government on public-enterprise borrowing in the past, it is unlikely that the enterprise would have borrowed to invest in nonoperating assets.

Summary

Except for the gain in productive efficiency, which we attribute to the business cycle, we conclude that ENERSIS's changes in performance are the product of divestiture. Therefore, for the counterfactual scenario we hypothesize that:

- Losses from theft would have been higher.
- Thus tariffs would have been higher.
- Output diversification would have been lower.
- Nonoperating investment, and thus revenue, would have been lower.
- Other things would have continued more or less the same as before.

These are critical differences, which will be incorporated in building the counterfactual projections in the next section.

What Will Happen?

This section projects the performance of ENERSIS as a private company and what that performance would have been without divestiture. By relaxing the constraint imposed by the short time horizon of actual postdivestiture experience, these projections make it possible, as will be seen in the next section, to answer a wider range of questions than has been possible thus far.[9]

Operating Revenue and Cost

In estimating operating revenue and cost we make the following assumptions:

- Demand is exogenous, irrespective of ownership. Overall demand will grow at its historical trend of 5.2 percent per year.[10] Demand of residential customers will grow at 3.2 percent per year, that of commercial customers at 5.2 percent, that of industrial customers at 7 percent, and others at 3.9 percent.
- Under private operation electricity losses will decline further to reach 13.0 percent by 1993 (11.0 percent for technical reasons and 2.0 percent because of theft). Thereafter they will remain constant at 12.5 percent. Under the counterfactual, it is assumed that these losses would have declined at their historical trend (between 1984 and 1986) of 5.0 percent per year during the period 1987–90, declining thereafter at 8 percent until they reached the private level.
- Revenue from diversification will increase in proportion to output, using for private projections the technical coefficient of 1990, and for public projections the technical coefficient of 1986.
- Under private operation, tariffs are adjusted downward in 1993 and in 1997, allowing, respectively, 13.5 and 12.5 percent for electricity losses. (Recall that tariffs were revised in 1988 on the basis of 18 percent for losses.) Where tariffs are estimated, and given demand shifts, quantity sold is derived residually. Under the counterfactual, tariffs are adjusted downward every four years, starting in 1988, until losses fall to their level under private projections. Given demand shifts and tariffs, quantity sold is estimated endogenously.
- As for operating costs, we assume that intermediate inputs, wages, and the opportunity cost of working capital increase in proportion to output under both scenarios. The only difference concerns the ratio of intermediate inputs to output sold, which is adjusted by the percentage of losses corresponding to private and public operations.

Investment, Finance, and Nonoperating Income

Under both scenarios, ENERSIS is assumed to invest sufficiently to meet demand. Investment is derived from the historical average and decremental capital-output ratios, which were estimated at 0.78 and 0.988, respectively. It is also assumed, under both scenarios, that ENERSIS will maintain a ceiling debt-equity ratio of 1.0. Given depreciation, the financing gap is closed by borrowing, provided the debt-equity ceiling is not binding. Otherwise, the assumption of a dividend payout ratio of 100 percent is relaxed.

The projection of net nonoperating income deserves careful consideration because of its importance in this case. As noted above, the company made Ch$19.6 billion in 1990. This figure consists of Ch$12.2 billion profit on its investment in ENDESA (of which Ch$8.0 billion was capital gain), Ch$2.7 billion in interest on receivables, Ch$1.9 billion from sales of assets and materials, and Ch$2.8 billion from miscellaneous sources. Our projection under private operation assumes that net nonoperating income will remain constant in relation to nonoperating assets and receivables, albeit with some adjustment. We exclude the sale of assets and materials as well as the capital gains following their full amortization in 1994. For the public-ownership projections, nonoperating income is assumed to remain constant in proportion to nonoperating assets and receivables, but at its level of 1986.

Results

Under these assumptions, our estimate of the company's net present value, expressed in 1990 prices, is Ch$147.8 billion. The corresponding value of the company on the stock market was Ch$174.4 billion at the end of 1990. Thus, our estimate is only 15 percent lower than the 1990 market valuation. The modest divergence between our estimate and that of the market is probably due to a temporary surge in market valuation arising from the unusual capital gains from investment in ENDESA, as can be seen from figure 10-10.

What Is It Worth?

What, then, has been the effect on shareholders, government, consumers, competitors, and citizens of the divestiture of ENERSIS? Where did the change in welfare come from?

The divestiture of ENERSIS improved world welfare by Ch$18.5 billion and domestic welfare by Ch$16.3 billion; both of these figures are expressed in net present value terms at 1987 prices. The gain in world welfare represents 31 percent of the private value of ENERSIS, and that of domestic welfare 27 percent of the same denominator. As a proportion of the enterprise's 1986 sales, the annual component of the perpetuity equivalent of the gain in world welfare is estimated at 5.0 percent, and that of domestic welfare at 4.4 percent.

Figure 10-10. ENERSIS *Share Prices and Chilean Stock Price Index,*
1986–90

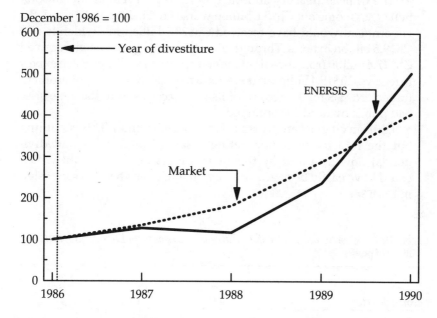

December 1986 = 100

Note: The market index used is the IGPA index of prices on the Santiago stock exchange.
Source: Santiago stock exchange data.

Winners and Losers

Who were the winners and losers from the divestiture? Table 10-6 gives
a breakdown of the welfare effects by recipient. In net present values at
1987 prices:

- ENERSIS's shareholders, domestic and foreign, are the biggest winners, realizing gains of Ch$42.9 billion. This is the difference between
the price they paid for the enterprise (Ch$17.3 billion) and their
maximum willingness to pay (Ch$60.3 billion), assuming they fully
anticipated all realized gains at the time of purchase.
- Of this gain, employees, in their capacity as shareholders, gain
Ch$13.9 billion, which corresponds to their share in total equity (32
percent). Foreign shareholders gain Ch$2.2 billion, corresponding to
their share in equity of 5.2 percent in 1990.
- Ordinary (paying) consumers are better off by Ch$17.5 billion, as
the reduction in electricity losses was translated into lower prices.
However, the same reduction in losses makes nonpaying consumers

of electricity worse off by Ch$9.8 billion. On the whole, consumers are better off by Ch$7.7 billion.

• The Chilean treasury and the government development corporation CORFO come out Ch$5.6 billion worse off. Had it not divested, the government would have received Ch$28.9 billion in dividends and Ch$9.5 billion in taxes. Through divestiture, the government received Ch$17.4 billion from the sale of the enterprise. In addition, it can expect to receive Ch$15.4 billion in taxes. On a net basis, then, the government traded ENERSIS for 85 percent of its total receipts from the enterprise had public ownership continued.[11]

• Chilean citizens are worse off by Ch$26.3 billion. This is nothing but the returns on nonoperating assets (capital gains and dividends) now acquired by the shareholders of ENERSIS, but which could have easily been acquired by other citizens had they invested in ENDESA.

Table 10-6. Distribution of Welfare Gains and Losses from Divestiture, ENERSIS (billions of pesos)

Economic actor	Private (V_{sp})	Public (V_{sg})	Gains from divestiture $(V_{sp} - V_{sg})$
Government			
Taxes	15.4	9.5	5.9
Net quasi rents	0.0	28.9	−28.9
Net sale proceeds	17.4	0.0	17.4
Debt takeover	0.0	0.0	0.0
Others	0.0	0.0	0.0
Total	32.8	38.4	−5.6
Private domestic shareholders			
Employees	13.9	0.0	13.9
Pension funds, others	26.8	0.0	26.8
Total	40.7	0.0	40.7
Consumers			
Paying	2,772.7	2,755.2	17.5
Nonpaying	22.1	31.9	−9.8
Total	2,794.8	2,787.1	7.7
Citizens	−26.3	0.0	−26.3
Total domestic	2,841.9	2,825.6	16.3
Foreign shareholders	2.2	0.0	2.2
World	2,844.1	2,825.6	18.5

Note: Figures are discounted net present values as of 1987.
Source: Authors' calculations.

Table 10-7.   *Effects of Divestiture on Welfare by Origin,* ENERSIS
(billions of pesos)

| | | Consumers | | | | |
Origin of welfare change	Share-holders	Paying	Non-paying	Citizens	Govern-ment	Total
No change	–17.3	0.0	0.0	0.0	17.3	0.0
Output diversification	4.6	0.0	0.0	0.0	0.8	5.4
Losses	4.9	17.4	–9.8	0.0	0.6	13.1
Nonoperating income	9.5	0.0	0.0	–12.2	3.7	0.0
Capital gains	12.3	0.0	0.0	–14.1	1.8	0.0
Total effect	13.9	17.4	–9.8	–26.3	–5.6	18.5

Note: Figures are expressed as 1987 present values.
Source: Authors' calculations.

Origins of the Change in Welfare

Where did the change in welfare come from? Table 10-7 gives a break-down of the contribution of each behavioral assumption to the bottom line. In the first row divestiture is assumed to bring about no behavioral changes. In the following rows we add the effect of each behavioral change, ending with the results of the base case.

Where divestiture is assumed to bring about no behavioral changes, welfare remains unchanged. The government sells the enterprise to the private sector for Ch$17.3 billion. The transaction cost is too small to make any difference.

The benefits from output diversification accrue mainly to the share-holders. But as profits go up, the government receives more in taxes. Consumers are left unaffected because of the competitive nature of the markets in which these products are produced and sold.

Reducing losses of electricity enhances welfare, albeit with multiple effects. It obviously affects nonpaying consumers of electricity ad-versely. However, their losses are more than compensated by the gains to paying consumers, producers, the government, and society. Paying consumers benefit as the regulators translate the reduction in losses into lower prices. Producers save the cost of providing electricity for free. The government receives more taxes as profits go up. Society as a whole gains from better allocation of resources and more-efficient consumption of electricity.

Nonoperating income and capital gains appear in table 10-7 as returns to the shareholders of ENERSIS, but also as losses to citizens. The argument for this treatment is that, had ENERSIS not invested in ENDESA, somebody else would have. Thus, nonoperating income is a mere transfer of re-sources. A possible counterargument is that the company undertook a risky investment, for which it should be rewarded socially. This may be so in some cases. In the present case, however, most observers would not consider investment in ENDESA risky.

Summary and Lessons

Our conclusions may be summarized as follows:

- The divestiture of ENERSIS correlated with a surge in profitability, a significant decline in losses of electricity due to theft, improved productivity, diversification of output, and escalation of nonoperating investment.
- Of these changes, the reduction in losses, output diversification, and the increased returns from nonoperating investment were directly attributable to divestiture.
- The combined effect of these changes on welfare was positive, representing 31 percent of the private value of the enterprise, or, in terms of the annual component of the perpetuity equivalent, 5.0 percent of 1986 sales.
- The gains in welfare accrued mostly to private shareholders, including employees, but gains also accrued to consumers.
- However, the government and Chilean citizens as a group were worse off.

The examination of ENERSIS's divestiture lends support to the following hypotheses:

- Divestiture promotes profit-maximizing behavior. In the case of ENERSIS, the behavioral changes manifested themselves in a reduction in losses from theft, diversification of output, and exploitation of investment opportunities in the rest of the economy.
- Divesting monopolies in well-regulated markets limits their ability to exercise their market power and improves resource allocation. In the present case, regulation had the effect of translating the reduction in losses from theft into lower prices, which benefited some users, while leaving nonpaying consumers of electricity worse off. However, the loss in consumer surplus resulting from reducing electricity losses is not the typical story of a private monopolist exploiting market power. Rather, it is a story of resource reallocation, the outcome of which is a positive welfare gain (not a deadweight loss) to society.
- Reforming and regulating public enterprises improves efficiency. This is evident from the relative efficiency of ENERSIS under public ownership.

- The net benefits of divestiture accompanied by effective regulation can outweigh the net benefits from reforming and regulating public enterprises. Therefore, the policymaker's dilemma is resolved in this case in favor of divestiture and regulation.

Coupled with the analysis of CHILGENER in chapter 9, the analysis of ENERSIS lends support to the general proposition that market-based solutions and private ownership in electricity are capable of producing even better results than the alternative policy of public ownership and vertical integration.

Notes

This chapter was written by Ahmed Galal. The author is grateful to Marcos Zelberberg, general manager of Chilectra Metropolitana, and his staff for their cooperation and insightful discussions, and to John Besant-Jones for commenting on an earlier draft.

1. The four companies are SYNAPSIS S.A., a computer and data processing company; Inmobilaria Manso de Velasco S.A., a real estate management, maintenance, and construction company; Distribuidora de Productos Eléctricos S.A., which trades in energy-related equipment; and Compañía Eléctrica del Rio Maipo S.A., a small electricity distribution company within the same zone of concession as ENERSIS.

2. Given that tariffs for bulk electricity are regulated, distribution companies tend to conclude long-term contracts with generating companies to ensure stability of supply and appropriate technical specifications.

3. For example, ENERSIS was allowed 18 percent for losses in 1988. In fact, the company was able to reduce its losses below this level.

4. Recognizing the unusual nature of the capital gains, ENERSIS only recorded Ch$8.0 billion out of this total in the income statement of 1990. The remainder was to be amortized over the next four years.

5. Constant prices, here and elsewhere, are derived from information provided by ENERSIS, in which the values of outputs and inputs were decomposed into their quantity and price components.

6. Observing that the performance of both divested and undivested enterprises improved in the United Kingdom, Bishop and Kay (1990) posed, without resolving them, two possible explanations: the improvement was due to the state of the economic activity or to the "the threat of divestiture."

7. Note that the performance of ENERSIS, as well as that of other firms in Chile, whether private or public, must have benefited from the general characteristics of the macroeconomic policies of that period. See chapter 8 for elaboration.

8. Recall that managers (and workers) now own part of the company. Therefore, even though the top management has remained largely unchanged, it is not surprising to observe an increased concern for profit.

9. Recall, for example, that calculating the fiscal impact of divestiture requires comparing the sale price plus taxes from private operation with government revenues forgone over an extended period through the giving up of ownership.

10. For an estimated income elasticity of electricity consumption of 1.2, this implies a GDP growth rate of about 4.2 percent per year, which is well within the realm of possibility for Chile. See CNE (1986) for an estimate of income and price elasticities.

11. The negative fiscal effect is in fact smaller than reported by the extent to which reduced losses from theft means higher value added tax revenues.

11. Compañía de Teléfonos de Chile

Traditionally, the sale of state-owned telecommunications enterprises has been viewed as a mere transfer of public to private monopolies, leading to uncertain and possibly negative effects on welfare. But since the mid-1980s government withdrawal from direct participation in this sector has come to be viewed as an opportunity to improve efficiency, modernize technology, and mobilize fresh capital to meet excess demand—witness, for example, the recent divestiture of telecommunications enterprises in Chile, Mexico, Argentina, and Venezuela. The empirical question is whether private ownership (with regulation) is more advantageous to society than public ownership. This chapter attempts to answer this question by analyzing the welfare consequences of divesting Compañía de Teléfonos de Chile (CTC).

Compared with the other Chilean enterprises we examined, CTC offers a number of distinctive economic, technological, and institutional characteristics. The enterprise operates in an industry characterized by rapid technological progress, economies of scale and scope in production, and externalities in consumption. These features raise a host of questions. For example, what is the effect of ownership change on technological innovation, which is often embodied in capital? Since marginal cost pricing in the presence of economies of scale creates a deficit, and thus underinvestment, how is this problem being addressed in Chile? If tariffs were to deviate from marginal cost pricing to avoid a deficit, would they be set on the basis of the welfare-maximizing rule of inverse elasticity and nonlinear pricing models? Further, given economies of scope and sunk costs, are incumbents able to undercut newcomers, at least in certain segments of the market?

On the institutional front, CTC also offers a number of interesting features. First, the ownership of the enterprise has changed from private (prior to 1970) to public (through 1987) to private once again (since 1987). Even more interesting, under private ownership the controlling shareholders have always been foreigners. The question is whether foreign ownership is always associated with the divestiture of large (relative to the domestic capital market) enterprises whose technology is changing rapidly. Second, not only did the government of Chile sell CTC, which dominates the market for local network services, but it also divested the Empresa Nacional de Telecomunicaciones (ENTEL), which dominates the market for long distance services. Because each company stands to gain from penetrating the market of the other, it is of particular interest to explore whether there are behavioral differences between public and private duopolies. Another interesting characteristic of CTC is that it shares the telecommunications sector with a number of the other divested enterprises examined in this volume, which should enable us to conduct interfirm comparisons across countries.

Background

Telephone services were introduced in Chile by the Compañía de Teléfonos de Edison as early as 1880. In 1927 International Telephone and Telegraph Corp. (ITT) acquired the company, which in 1930 was incorporated as CTC. CTC continued to operate under private ownership until 1971, when the Chilean government intervened in its operation.[1] In 1974 CORFO (the Chilean state holding company) acquired ITT's share, despite the otherwise market-oriented approach of the government at that time. Government majority ownership continued through 1987, somewhat longer than for other natural monopolies, for example in the electricity distribution sector. By February 1988 the private sector had acquired 86 percent of the enterprise's equity. Thus, the ownership of the enterprise went full circle, beginning with and ending in (foreign) private ownership.

Throughout its history CTC has been the main carrier of telecommunications services in Chile, owning approximately 95 percent of all telephone lines in the country. By concession, which was renewed in 1982 for 50 years, the enterprise provides local telephone services in about 77 percent of the national territory, serving approximately 92 percent of the population. It also has a concession to provide national long distance services in Santiago and Valparaiso, where about 50 percent of the population resides.

CTC has expanded considerably in recent years. As table 11-1 shows, whereas the number of new lines increased at an annual rate of only 5 percent in the 1970s, it increased at an annual rate of 10 percent in the 1980s. The number of telephones per 100 inhabitants increased by only 32 percent between 1970 and 1980, from 4.1 to 5.4, respectively. In the 1980s telephone density doubled, reaching 8.9 telephones per 100 inhabitants in 1990. The degree of automation and digitalization also increased, reaching 99.6 percent and 64 percent of all lines, respectively,

Table 11-1. Selected Growth Indicators, Compañía de Teléfonos de Chile, 1970–90
(thousands unless specified otherwise)

Indicator	1970	1975	1980	1985	1986	1987	1988	1989	1990
Installed lines	258	340	407	550	585	615	634	800	1,059
Lines in service	241	305	360	505	528	548	592	646	812
Telephones	353	434	550	719	749	770	820	895	1,096
Telephones per 100 inhabitants	4.1	4.7	5.4	6.4	6.6	6.7	7.0	7.4	8.9
Automation (percentages of total)	86.5	89.0	92.1	95.5	96.1	98.0	98.5	99.3	99.6
Digitalization (percentages of total)	0.0	0.0	0.0	34.1	36.8	36.0	37.9	51.1	64.0
Pending applications	3	12	114	151	219	230	236	284	308

Source: CTC (1990).

in 1990. Moreover, the company expanded into activities whose tariffs are unregulated—for example, public telephones, cellular telephones, and private telephone systems and equipment—by means of several subsidiaries.[2] As a result, the share of its revenue from unregulated services in total revenue went up from 16 percent in 1982 to 25 percent in 1990.

Market Characteristics

Even though CTC increased the number of new lines by 72 percent from 1987 to 1990 alone, the market for telecommunications services in Chile is far from saturated. In fact, the number of pending applications has been rising, as table 11-1 shows. This rise may be due to increased expectations on the part of the applicants of actually getting a phone, and to the company's improved ability to meet these applications. Nevertheless, the demand gap is expected to persist through 1996, even if CTC fully implements its current expansion plan.

A second characteristic of the market for basic telecommunications services in Chile is that it is highly concentrated. As already noted, CTC dominates the market for local services, accounting in 1989 for 94 percent of the total. The remaining 6 percent was shared by Compañía Telefónica del Sur (3.5 percent), Compañía Manufacturera de Equipos Telefónicos (1.0 percent), Compañía Telefónica Manquehue (0.8 percent), Comuna de los Condes (0.4 percent), and Compañía de Teléfonos de Coyhaique (0.3 percent). ENTEL, on the other hand, dominates the market for international long distance services and, to a lesser degree, the market for national long distance services. CTC transfers about 21 percent of national long distance traffic by means of a digital microwave link between Santiago and Valparaiso, in operation since December 1988.

By comparison, the market for complementary services is less concentrated and is growing rapidly. For example, in the market for cellular telephones, CTC has to compete with CIDCOM in the metropolitan area of Santiago and in region V, which includes Valparaiso and Viña del Mar. (By regulation, only two concessions to provide cellular telephones may overlap.) In the markets for facsimile, telex, telegraph, and data transmission, the company faces considerable competition, for example from TELEX-Chile and VTR. Nevertheless, CTC's sheer size, sunk cost, institutional presence throughout the country, and service and maintenance capabilities still place the company in a favorable position vis-à-vis both established competitors and newcomers.

The final important characteristic of the market for telecommunications services in Chile is that it is in a state of flux. Following the divestiture of CTC and ENTEL, each company is attempting to penetrate the traditional market of the other. On the one hand, CTC applied in 1989 for concessions to provide national and international telecommunications services through satellite links throughout Chile and fiber optic links to the Santiago-Valparaiso and Santiago-Temuco markets. These concessions, if granted, would have immediate adverse repercussions on ENTEL. Not surprisingly, ENTEL filed a complaint, arguing that granting such a concession would provide CTC with a monopoly. At the time of our study the dispute was awaiting resolution by Chile's supreme court. ENTEL, on the other hand, applied in April 1989 for concessions to provide local services in certain business sectors of Santiago. In response, CTC filed an objection, arguing that the telecommunications law does not allow a concession holder to carve out a specific area within an existing concession. This case is also still pending. However both cases are resolved, the emergence of these disputes illustrates the changed nature of the relationship between the two firms under private ownership. Under public ownership the two enterprises resolved their conflicts, when any occurred, through their common owner. Under private ownership conflicts have escalated and are being resolved through the courts. This is an important change in behavior, deserving of a thorough investigation in its own right.

The Regulatory Framework

The state of development of the telecommunications sector in Chile today is partly the product of signals provided by the regulatory setup, which has evolved over time. Before 1982, CTC operated under Decree Law no. 4 of 24 July 1959. Under this regime CTC was supposed to receive prices high enough to provide it with a 10 percent rate of return on revalued capital. The Tariff Commission—composed of the General

Director of Electric Services as president; representatives of CORFO, the Institute of Chilean Engineers, and the Production and Trade Confederation; and an appointee of the president of Chile—had the mandate to approve these tariffs. In practice, tariffs were often adjusted on political grounds and frequently failed to keep up with inflation. There was cross-subsidization in favor of consumers of local services. Investment was relatively modest, and pending demand was increasing.

In 1977 the government abolished the Tariff Commission and issued Decree Law no. 1,762, establishing the Undersecretariat of Telecommunications, SUBTEL, as part of the Ministry of Transportation and Telecommunications. SUBTEL was granted the responsibility of designing and supervising all policies and technical norms pertaining to the telecommunications sector. It soon became apparent, however, that changing the institutional setup alone was insufficient; the rules of the game had to be changed, too.

In 1982 the government issued the General Law of Telecommunications (Decree Law no. 18,168), which followed closely that for electricity. This law emphasized competition in the provision of services. It placed no limits on the number of enterprises that may be granted concessions in a given geographical area, except for technical reasons. It left the decision on whether a given market is competitive or not to the Fair Trade Enforcement Office, one of two antitrust agencies in Chile. This commission ruled that local and long distance services (excluding public telephones and cellular telephony) are not competitive. Thus, their tariffs had to be regulated on the basis of marginal cost, as provided in the law.

Although this law was an improvement over previous arrangements, it was short on the details of implementation, especially regarding tariffs. Moreover, SUBTEL was still a growing institution and lacked sufficient regulatory experience. Since CTC and ENTEL were still publicly owned, these shortcomings meant in practice that tariffs were simply negotiated between the two enterprises, SUBTEL, and the Ministry of Economy. These negotiations resulted in maintaining cross-subsidization and keeping tariffs in line with inflation.

In 1987 there occurred a significant modification of and additions to the General Law of 1982 (other modifications have followed since). The most important addition concerned tariffs, which were now to be calculated on the basis of the long-run marginal cost of each service and geographical area, taking a hypothetical efficient firm as a base. Where economies of scale are present, tariffs are adjusted upward to ensure that enterprises are self-financing. These adjustments are introduced in such a way as to minimize distortions and to generate the enterprise's rate of return, following the capital asset pricing model. That is:

$$R_i = R_{rf} + \beta_i (R_p - R_{rf})$$

where R_i is the rate of return on the revalued capital of enterprise i, R_{rf} is the rate of return on risk-free assets, β_i is enterprise i's systematic risk, and R_p is the rate of return on a diversified investment portfolio. R_{rf} is defined as the rate of return on a saving account at the Banco del Estado de Chile. R_p may under the law be drawn from international data, provided it does not fall below 7 percent. Once approved, tariffs remain effective for the next five years, adjusted in the interim every two months by the inflation index for each service. Disputes are settled by a committee of three experts, one nominated by each party and the third by mutual agreement.

Recognizing that the implementation of the new rules would take time, the 1987 law allowed enterprises one year to come up with tariff proposals. CTC and ENTEL prepared such studies, and a new tariff structure became effective as of January 1989 (table 11-2). For CTC the ideal firm was defined to have 760,000 lines, to provide regulated services only, to use a digital system, to be fully automated, to operate with 6.7 workers per thousand lines, and to incur no cost for interconnections. The rate of return allowed was 12 percent on revalued capital (based on an 8 percent risk-free rate and a 4 percent risk premium; ENTEL meanwhile was allowed a 14 percent rate of return).

The new tariff structure will gradually eliminate the allocation fees and cross-subsidization between local and long distance services. It provides enterprises adequate incentives to expand and operate efficiently. Meanwhile, it avoids the problem of excessive investment, known to follow from the fair rate of return, primarily because the costs are derived from an ideally efficient firm.

Divestiture

CORFO announced that it would sell 51 percent of CTC in 1986. The sale process began in 1987, when the government offered CTC's employees

Table 11-2. Regulated Tariff Schedule for Telephone Service, Chile, 1990–93
(September 1989 base rate = 100)

Service	1990	1991	1992	1993
Local metered service				
Monthly charge	123	138	154	171
Variable charge	100	100	100	100
Local flat rate service	114	125	136	147
National long distance	80	74	65	65
International long distance	100	100	100	100
Allocation fee	62	25	12	0

Source: CTC data.

Table 11-3. Ownership Structure, Compañía de Teléfonos de Chile, 1982–90
(percentages of total)

Shareholders	1982	1983	1984	1985	1986	1987	1988	1989	1990
Public									
CORFO	92.2	92.2	92.2	92.1	89.5	75.0	14.2	2.9	0.1
Private domestic									
Pension funds	0.0	0.0	0.0	0.0	0.0	7.6	7.7	11.6	11.6
Employees of CTC	0.0	0.0	0.0	0.0	0.0	6.4	4.3	3.2	3.2
Others[a]	7.0	7.0	7.0	7.1	9.8	10.2	23.5	31.9	25.8
Total	7.0	7.0	7.0	7.1	9.8	24.2	35.5	46.7	40.6
Private foreign									
Bond Corp.	0.0	0.0	0.0	0.0	0.0	0.0	50.1	49.2	0.0
Telefónica de España	0.0	0.0	0.0	0.0	0.0	0.0	0.0	0.0	43.4
Others	0.8	0.8	0.8	0.8	0.8	0.8	0.1	1.2	16.0
Total	0.8	0.8	0.8	0.8	0.8	0.8	50.3	50.4	59.4

a. Includes public employees.
Source: CTC (various years).

50 percent of their severance payments in advance on the condition that they invest 80 percent of the sum in shares in the enterprise. Eighty-four percent of the employees elected to participate in the offer, acquiring 6.4 percent of the enterprise by the end of 1987. Workers were guaranteed that the value of their shares would not fall below their entitled severance payment at the time of retirement. In the same year pension funds also acquired 7.6 percent of the enterprise. In total the private sector held 25 percent (table 11-3).

In August 1987 CORFO invited domestic and foreign investors to bid for 30 percent of the enterprise under two conditions: first, the bidder had to commit itself to subscribe in new shares so that its final percentage of ownership would eventually reach 45 percent, and second, the awardee had to buy more than 10 million "B" shares of CTC.[3] The first condition was intended to ensure expansion, and the second to allow the new equityholders a voting majority in decisionmaking.

CORFO received three bids, from Bond Corp. (a New Zealand corporation), Telefónica de España, and a local communications holding company. Bond Corp. won the bid in January 1988, albeit with some controversy.[4] Subsequently Bond purchased additional shares, which increased its stake to 50.1 percent of CTC's subscribed capital stock. Because CTC's bylaws forbid any single shareholder from holding more than 45 percent of the total stock, Bond had to sign a "deconcentration agreement" in October 1988, agreeing to reduce its participation to 45 percent by October 1992.

In April 1990 a subsidiary of Telefónica de España, Telefónica Internacional Chile, acquired Bond's stock in CTC for US$392 million. Telefónica had previously purchased 20 percent of the voting stock of ENTEL. As a result, the Preventive Commission (the other Chilean government agency involved in antitrust enforcement) ruled that Telefónica had to give up its equity interest in one company or the other on the grounds that its ownership of both companies would adversely affect competition in the long distance market. Telefónica appealed this ruling, arguing that what counts is the behavior of companies in the marketplace, not their equity structure. At the time of the study this case was awaiting resolution by the supreme court.

In 1989 CORFO began to sell its remaining shares in CTC to public sector employees, including those in the armed forces. Participation in this offer entitled employees to purchase additional shares, to be paid for in quarterly installments over four to six years at annual real interest rates ranging between 2 and 4.5 percent; this compared with an average real market interest rate of 8.86 percent in 1989, which implies a subsidy. As a result, the number of shares held by workers (inside and outside the firm) reached 11.5 percent in 1989.

Summary

This background provides the following insights:

- Under public ownership CTC expanded somewhat, but a large demand gap persisted. To mobilize additional resources, the government announced in 1986 that it would sell 51 percent of CTC, and in 1987 it laid down the foundations for the formulation of prices.
- Because CTC is a relatively large enterprise, the government had to sell it by public bid, placing no limitation on foreign participation, but requiring that the bidders commit themselves to inject new equity and to implement an agreed investment program.
- Improvements in regulation notwithstanding, the regulatory setup in Chile is still evolving. The most important challenge facing the regulators today concerns entry, which was fueled by the sale of CTC and ENTEL to the private sector.

What Happened?

Has the sale of CTC affected the enterprise's performance, and what have been the effects on consumers and on the enterprise's sellers and buyers? As in other cases we begin to answer this question by analyzing the actual performance of the enterprise over the period 1982–90.

Profit and Profitability

PROFIT: PUBLIC VERSUS PRIVATE. Under public ownership CTC's profit after tax (private profit) fluctuated and was even negative by Ch$3.1 billion in 1982 and Ch$1.9 billion in 1985. Following divestiture, profits immediately doubled, from Ch$8 billion in 1987 to Ch$15.7 billion in 1988. By 1990 profits had more than quadrupled from their 1987 level. More generally, figure 11-1 shows that the period of public ownership was characterized by a series of unsuccessful takeoffs. Under private ownership, on the other hand, profits improved significantly and steadily. A turning point occurred in 1986, before the actual divestiture, which implies a positive announcement effect. Nevertheless, the more dramatic improvement (in 1988 and beyond) coincided with actual private operation.[5]

Further inspection of figure 11-1 yields two additional conclusions. First, unlike the trend in private profit, that of quasi rent (or public profit) was rather smooth during the public-ownership period. This means that the 1982 and 1985 losses were due to nonoperating activities, which were in this case due to shifts in government foreign exchange policy.[6] The

Figure 11-1. Public and Private Profit at Current Market Prices, Compañía de Teléfonos de Chile, 1982–90

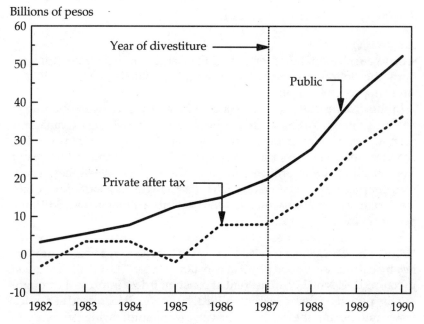

Billions of pesos

Source: Authors' calculations from CTC data.

Figure 11-2. Public Profit at Constant Market Prices, Compañía de Teléfonos de Chile, 1982–90

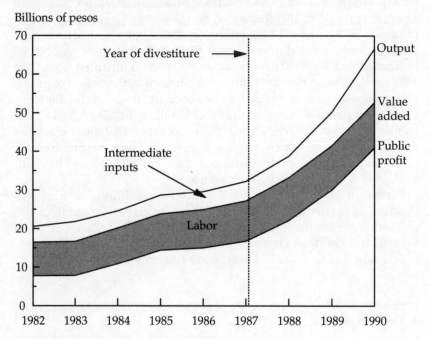

Source: Authors' calculations from CTC data.

second conclusion, however, is that the trend in public profit still supports the notion that private ownership coincided with a significant surge in producer surplus.

In short, divestiture was associated with a surge in private and public profit. Although this conclusion is obvious, its underlying explanations are not. Performance changes either for "good" or for "bad" reasons. The changes are "good" for society as a whole where, for example, they result from productivity improvement. They can be "bad" when they result, for example, from increased prices. To disentangle the good from the bad we construct, in the balance of this section, a number of additional performance indicators.

PUBLIC PROFIT: CURRENT VERSUS CONSTANT PRICES. We begin our journey by calculating public profit at constant prices.[7] The results are given in figure 11-2. Notably, quasi rent at constant prices improved throughout the period analyzed, except in 1983. However, it increased at a much faster rate during the period of private ownership, owing primarily to an increase in the quantity of output. Thus, recent improvements in quasi rent at current prices are not fully attributable to changes in tariffs.

PRICE AND QUANTITY DECOMPOSITION. To examine the price and quantity effects more fully, we decompose, in table 11-4, quasi rent and its components into these two effects. The findings are most revealing. On the output side, CTC benefited from favorable price changes under public as well as under private operation. However, the enterprise increased the quantity of output more significantly under private ownership; in fact, the change in output quantity in 1990 was more than nine times the corresponding change in 1987. As output grew, so did intermediate inputs. Yet on a net basis

Table 11-4. *Decomposition of Public Profit Trend into Price and Quantity Effects, Compañía de Teléfonos de Chile, 1982–90*
(billions of pesos)

Change in	1983	1984	1985	1986	1987	1988	1989	1990
Output								
Price	2.58	2.22	4.73	4.50	7.02	3.78	10.88	8.21
Quantity	0.60	1.70	3.02	0.79	2.86	8.50	17.02	27.80
Value	3.18	3.92	7.75	5.29	9.88	12.28	27.91	36.01
Intermediate inputs								
Price	0.35	0.54	1.04	0.73	1.08	0.88	1.92	4.84
Quantity	0.51	−0.43	0.30	−0.16	0.45	0.59	5.05	10.21
Value	0.85	0.10	1.34	0.56	1.53	1.47	6.97	15.05
Value added								
Price	2.23	1.68	3.70	3.77	5.94	2.90	8.96	3.38
Quantity	0.10	2.14	2.71	0.95	2.40	7.91	11.97	17.58
Value	2.33	3.82	6.41	4.73	8.35	10.81	20.94	20.96
Wages								
Price	0.07	0.093	1.35	2.02	2.79	1.57	4.31	8.34
Quantity	0.07	0.18	−0.005	0.30	0.39	0.47	−0.28	0.50
Value	0.13	1.12	1.35	2.32	3.18	2.04	4.02	8.75
Rented factors								
Price	0.06	0.09	0.14	0.13	0.21	0.16	0.33	0.54
Quantity	−0.02	0.06	0.07	0.10	0.05	0.08	0.18	0.07
Value	0.04	0.15	0.21	0.22	0.26	0.24	0.50	0.61
Working capital								
Price	−0.09	0.12	0.11	−0.26	0.10	0.13	1.16	1.10
Quantity	0.03	0.03	0.008	0.01	0.03	0.41	1.00	0.30
Value	−0.06	0.16	0.12	−0.24	0.14	0.54	2.16	1.40
Public profit								
Price	2.19	0.54	2.09	1.88	2.84	1.04	3.17	−6.61
Quantity	0.03	1.85	2.64	0.54	1.93	6.95	11.08	16.81
Value	2.22	2.39	4.73	2.42	4.77	7.99	14.25	10.20

Source: Authors' calculations.

Figure 11-3.   Gross Fixed Capital Formation, Compañía de Teléfonos de Chile, 1982–90

Billions of pesos; 1986 = base

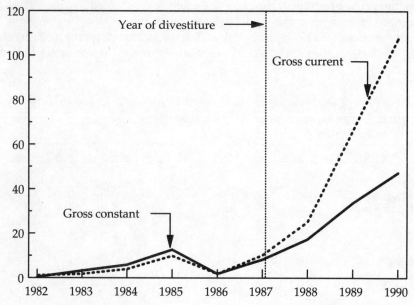

Source: Authors' calculations from CTC data.

(measured by value added) the increase in quantity is still impressive, amounting in 1990 to more than seven times the change in 1987.

Wages under both regimes increased systematically, in part to cope with inflation and in part because the trade unions have been relatively strong. Similarly, new hiring was kept to a minimum, even under public ownership. The main difference is that the two phenomena are more pronounced in the postdivestiture period. In the last negotiation (in 1990) with twenty-one unions—made up of nine bargaining groups and representing 7,200 nonexecutive employees—the company agreed to a real increase in wages of 13 percent over two years, intending at the same time to reduce the number of workers per thousand lines in service from 10.6 in 1990 to 6.7 in 1996. Whether this target would have been feasible under continued public ownership is an important counterfactual question, which we revisit below.

Changes in factor rentals and the cost of working capital are too small to warrant further investigation. The important point, which can be seen from the decomposition of public profit itself, is that the overall effect of prices on CTC was positive during the entire period analyzed, except in 1990. In contrast, only the private period was characterized by an impressive increase in quantities.

FIXED CAPITAL. The impressive increase in output was due to an even more impressive increase in investment. CTC's initial plan for 1988–92 contemplated a capital expenditure of Ch$401 billion, of which Ch$214.6 billion had already been spent by December 1990. As a result, gross fixed capital formation skyrocketed, as shown in figure 11-3. By comparison, gross fixed capital formation had stagnated under public ownership, except in 1985. Naturally, as investment increased in the latter period, so did fixed operating assets.

From the counterfactual perspective, the critical question is whether CTC would have been able to raise sufficient funds to undertake such a massive expansion program. If not, relaxing the resource constraint may turn out to be the most important effect of divesting the enterprise, with potentially significant repercussions on consumers, government, and CTC itself (see "Why Did It Happen?" below).

PRIVATE VERSUS PUBLIC PROFITABILITY. Thus far we have employed a set of performance indicators expressed entirely in absolute terms. To neutralize the effect of size we now derive a set of relative performance indicators, beginning with private and public profitability. As shown in

Figure 11-4. *Private and Public Profitability, Compañía de Teléfonos de Chile, 1982–90*

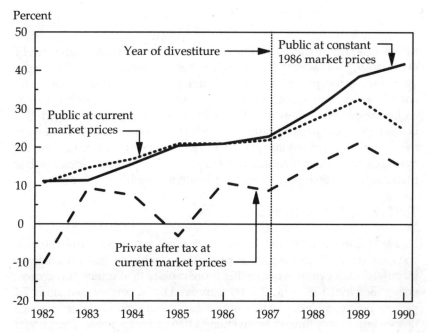

Source: Authors' calculations from CTC data.

*Figure 11-5.   Total Factor Productivity and Real Public Profitability,
Compañía de Teléfonos de Chile, 1982–90*

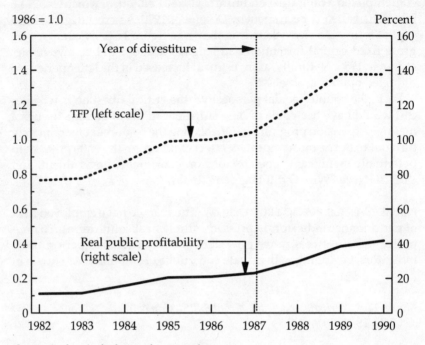

Source: Authors' calculations from CTC data.

figure 11-4, the results still favor the divestiture period. Under public ownership, profitability in relation to net worth averaged 4.5 percent per year during the period 1982–87. Under private ownership the corresponding three-year average was 14.3 percent. Similarly, public profitability at current prices in relation to revalued capital averaged 17.7 percent per year under public ownership, compared with a three-year average of 28.0 percent under private ownership. At constant prices, the averages for public profitability stood at 17.3 percent under public ownership and 36.6 percent under private ownership.

Total Factor Productivity

Figure 11-5 presents the results for TFP changes and public profitability at constant prices. These results support the conclusion that productivity improved under private ownership more rapidly than under public ownership. Between 1982 and 1987 TFP improved by 36 percent, averaging 7.2 percent per year. Under private ownership TFP improved almost as much (32 percent) in only three years, averaging 10.6 percent per year. Thus, under private ownership CTC surpassed its productivity record under public ownership by an annual average efficiency differential of 3.4 percentage points. A major reason for this improvement is the much faster growth in capital than in labor, which not only improved labor productivity but also enabled the company to benefit from expansion in other areas.

Finance

As noted, the boost in CTC's performance originated primarily from expansion. Expansion depends in turn on the availability of funds. Thus, it is useful to complement the above analysis by looking at CTC's sources of funds over the period 1982–90.

CTC's sources of funds are given in figure 11-6. Between 1983 and 1986 the bulk of these resources came from depreciation and the enterprise's own reserves. Thereafter new equity surfaced as an important source of finance. In fact, between 1986 and 1990 the enterprise issued 477.3 million new shares, which represents 132 percent of the enterprise's number of shares in 1986. Of these shares, Bond Corp. acquired 204.6 million in 1988 for Ch$30.0 billion, and the American Depository and the International Finance Corporation undertook the underwriting of 110.5 million shares on the New York stock market in 1990.

Figure 11-6. Sources of Funds, Compañía de Teléfonos de Chile, 1983–90

Billions of pesos

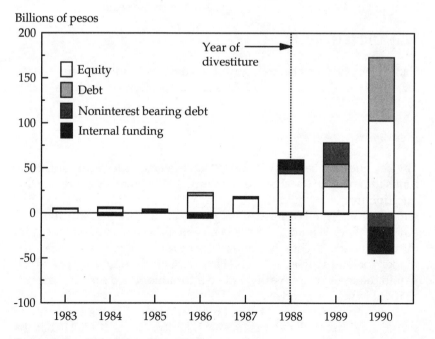

Source: Authors' calculations from CTC data.

These equity injections created a ripple effect. They enabled CTC to mobilize additional debt, domestically and abroad. In turn, the acquired resources enabled the enterprise to expand. Expansion itself generated more funds internally. In addition, the infusion of equity had a positive effect on CTC's capital structure. The critical issue here, which we address next, is whether the mobilization of such resources would have been feasible in the absence of divestiture.

Summary

The analysis of CTC's performance yields the following primary results:

- Under public ownership, profits after tax fluctuated, becoming negative in 1982 and 1985. The 1982 and 1985 losses were caused essentially by shifts in government foreign-exchange policy, namely, a significant devaluation in 1982 and the elimination of the system of foreign exchange differentials.
- In contrast, divestiture paralleled a significant improvement in after-tax profit and producer surplus. These improvements were due in part to favorable relative prices. For the most part, however, they originated in a surge in investment, output diversification into non-regulated value added services, and improved productivity.
- In turn, the surge in investment was caused by the infusion of fresh capital in the course of selling CTC to the private sector.

Why Did It Happen?

Can divestiture be credited with the changes in investment behavior, tariffs, and productivity? This is the question we address in this section.

Investment

The key question here is, Would CTC have been able to secure sufficient funds to expand in the absence of divestiture? We may disaggregate this question further: Would the government have provided the enterprise with new equity? Would it have given up its 100 percent dividend payout policy? Would CTC have been able to borrow sufficiently to fill the demand gap? Would the enterprise have attempted to penetrate the market for long distance services? Finally, given the necessary resources, would the enterprise have diversified into value added services as much as it did in private hands?

Our short answer is that it is highly unlikely that the government would have given the enterprise new equity. Nor is it likely that the government would have given up its 100 percent dividend payout policy. However, given that CTC's debt-equity ratio was relatively low (65 percent in 1987), the enterprise would probably have been able to borrow in substantial amounts, up to a ratio of 1.25. (This had been the enterprise's debt-equity ceiling for some time.) In addition, it would have capitalized, where possible, on the legal provision that allowed it to request reimbursable financial contributions from customers requiring new connections.[8] Finally, we argue that CTC would not have invested in long distance services, nor would it have been able to expand into value added services as much as it did under private control.

These assertions are based on past government behavior vis-à-vis CTC and on CTC's own behavior. During the last ten years of its ownership of CTC, the government did not provide the enterprise with any equity injections, nor did it convert any debt into equity. Further, CORFO systematically insisted on capturing 100 percent of profit after taxes in the form of dividends. In fact, the story of 1985 is most revealing. In that year the demand gap was growing, and the need for new investment was apparent. But the enterprise was likely to lose money. Out of concern for dividends, CORFO insisted that CTC change its financial year to 18 months (spanning the second half of 1985 and the whole of 1986), so that some dividends could be collected in advance.[9]

There are several reasons to doubt that CTC would have invested in the market for long distance services. First, both CTC and ENTEL were owned by CORFO, which therefore may not have cared which enterprise made more money (ENTEL was divested in 1988). The Planning Ministry would have tended to approve investment for the enterprise's traditional market. Finally, the two enterprises would probably have continued to maintain a friendly relationship rather than the rivalrous one that emerged under private ownership. Thus, we are persuaded that neither CTC nor ENTEL would have attempted to penetrate the traditional market of the other.

Finally, we also doubt that a public CTC would have followed the diversification strategy pursued by the private CTC. Our main reason is that the enterprise would have first allocated its scarce resources to network expansion, treating value added services as a residual.

The implications of these arguments are as follows:

- Investment would have increased under public ownership as it had in the past, thanks to additional borrowing, reimbursable financial contributions, and depreciation. However, in the absence of new equity, the increase in investment would have been relatively modest compared with that under private ownership. That is to say, divestiture released the resource constraint.[10]
- In any case, the public CTC would not have invested in fiber optic and satellite technologies, thus leaving the long distance market to ENTEL.

Tariffs

Would the government have changed the telecommunications law in 1987 had CTC not been divested? Would the new tariff structure have been the same? Our response to both questions is yes, for three main reasons:

- The government of Chile has consistently attempted to improve regulations when they have proved to be less than effective. This is evident from its more successful effort in the electric power sector, discussed in chapters 9 and 10. It is also evident from the government's repeated attempts to improve the regulation of the telecommunications sector itself. In fact, the government is currently considering revising some aspects of the 1987 regulatory structure to correct for some shortcomings.
- Past regulatory reforms were applied to public and private enterprises alike—one of the distinguishing characteristics of Chilean regulatory policy.
- Where reforms were introduced, they were generally derived from economic principles, especially regarding tariff formulation. In fact, the 1982 law stipulated that pricing would be based on marginal cost. There is no reason to believe that the 1987 regulatory reform would have been an exception.

Productivity

Would the productivity improvements observed after divestiture have materialized in the absence of divestiture? Our answer to this question is no: even if we were persuaded that divestiture brought about no behavioral changes within CTC, it did increase investment, which has positive implications for productivity.

To elaborate, any case for crediting divestiture with no efficiency differential would have to rest on the following grounds. Productivity improved before and after divestiture, as figure 11-7 shows. Where productivity changed, it correlated closely with GDP growth rates, as also shown in figure 11-7. Finally, the sale of the enterprise left its management and workers largely unchanged. Thus, by this argument, no efficiency improvement should be attributed to divestiture.

The case for the alternative hypothesis, that divestiture did enhance productivity, is more persuasive. It rests on the following grounds:

- Even though productivity improved on a trend basis before and after divestiture, its rate of change was higher under private ownership by 3.4 percentage points (the average annual differential over three years).

Figure 11-7. Year-to-Year Changes in Total Factor Productivity, Compañía de Teléfonos de Chile, and Gross Domestic Product, Chile, 1983–90

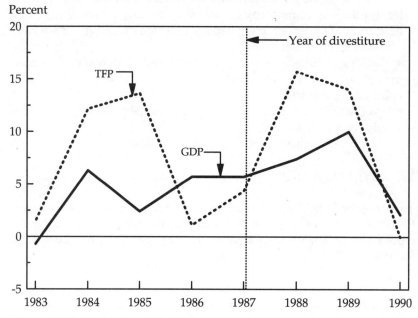

Source: Authors' calculations from CTC data.

- This result is closely linked to the surge in investment in recent years, which has introduced more-efficient technology and economies of scale.
- Expansion in turn will enable the company to reduce the number of employees per thousand lines in service from 10.6 in 1990 to 6.7 in 1996.
- The divested CTC expanded into value added services; this expansion, given excess demand in basic network services, would not have materialized otherwise.

Therefore, even if we assumed that divestiture caused no behavioral changes within the enterprise, the strong likelihood that investment would have been lower under continued public ownership suggests that labor productivity would have been lower as well.

Summary

In the absence of divestiture, we conclude that:

- Investment would have been limited to CTC's ability to generate funds internally, to borrow within the limits of a debt-equity ratio of

1.25, and to request reimbursable financial contributions from customers requiring new connections.

- The enterprise would not have invested in long distance services, leaving such investment to its sister enterprise ENTEL. (The assumption here is that if the government had not divested CTC, it would not have divested ENTEL either.)
- Lacking sufficient resources to meet pending demand, the enterprise would not have expanded as much as it did into nonregulated value added services.
- Productivity would have been lower, largely because expansion would have been slower.
- Tariffs (and other variables) would have been the same.

What Will Happen?

To assess the long-run effects of CTC's divestiture, this section projects the performance of the divested enterprise and what that performance would have been without divestiture. Our general procedure is as follows:

- Until demand is satisfied, projections are supply-driven. Supply depends on availability of funds, which are constrained in turn by depreciation and retained earnings, the room for borrowing, and new equity. Once excess demand is satisfied, we assume that the company will invest sufficiently to meet normal demand shifts.
- Given supply and tariffs (and thus revenue), costs are derived proportionately.
- Finally, under both scenarios, we assume the same depreciation and direct and value added tax rates.[11] All projections are at constant 1990 prices.

Investment

Projected private investment is derived from CTC's 1990 investment plan for the period 1991–96. According to this plan, the company contemplates a total capital expenditure of Ch\$441 billion, 89 percent of which will be devoted to the expansion of new lines, 9 percent to services whose tariffs are unregulated (e.g., public phones, cellular telephony, and other value added services), and the rest to national and international long distance service. Given that the company has no concession as yet in long distance service, we simply assume that it will sell this component of the investment program to a third party at cost.[12] Financing is assumed to come from depreciation and retained earnings, borrowing at a real interest rate of 9 percent, and supplier credits. We assume a dividend payout ratio of 80 percent, provided the debt-equity ceiling of 1.25 is not binding to execute the investment program. Otherwise we reduce the dividend payout ratio to 60 percent.

Had CTC remained publicly owned, we assume that the enterprise would have expanded its basic network and associated services, as it had in the past. We allow maximum financing, short of new equity other than contributions from customers requiring new connections, and assume that the enterprise would not have attempted to penetrate the traditional market of ENTEL. Finally, for reasons discussed in the previous section, the dividend payout ratio is assumed to be 100 percent of profit after tax.

On the basis of these assumptions, the private CTC is dramatically different from the CTC that would have emerged had it continued publicly owned. Under private operation CTC is expected, between 1990 and 1996, to increase the number of lines in plant from 1.0 million to 1.8 million, the number of lines in service from 0.8 million to 1.6 million, the number of telephones from 1.1 million to 2.1 million, the share of automated equipment in the total from 64 percent to 100 percent, and the share of equipment digitalized from 64 percent to 84 percent.[13] Full implementation of the plan is expected to eliminate excess demand by 1996. Thereafter the company expects demand to require the addition of 74,000 lines per year.

In contrast, an undivested CTC would have probably increased the number of lines in service from 0.7 million in 1990 to 0.9 million by 1996, which at that time would only represent half the capacity of the firm under private ownership. A backlog of phone applications would have persisted. Unable to satisfy demand for basic network services, the enterprise would not have expanded as much into value added services. That is, investment in public and cellular phones, facsimile machines, and data transmission systems would also have been relatively modest.

Revenue

Under both scenarios we apply the tariff schedule given in table 11-2 to regulated activities through 1993. Thereafter we assume that tariffs will remain constant in real terms.[14] For activities whose tariffs are unregulated, we assume that prices will remain constant at their level of 1990.

To project quantities we allocate the number of lines in service under each scenario to residential and commercial customers, distinguishing subscribers in the "per call" from those in the "flat rate" system. For the former we estimate the total number of calls using the 1990 average of 2,550 calls per line per year. In the long distance market, we similarly estimate quantities by multiplying the number of lines in service by the 1990 averages of 220 calls per line per year for national long distance service and 170 minutes per line per year for international long distance service.

Given the tariff structure, which is common to both scenarios, and the total number of calls, which differs substantially, we estimate revenues for the two scenarios as follows:

- For local service we multiply the schedule of fixed charges by the estimated number of lines in service, and the variable charge by the estimated number of calls.
- For national and international services we also multiply the tariff schedule by the estimated number of calls, keeping CTC's share in total revenue (with ENTEL receiving the remainder) at its level of 1990.
- We assume that, for each scenario, revenue from other sources will increase in proportion to investment in other activities.

Costs

Under both scenarios we assume that operating costs will grow in proportion to the average number of lines in service; the only exception is the labor requirement per line. In projections for the firm under private ownership we assume that CTC will reduce the number of workers per thousand lines in service from 10.6 in 1990 to 6.7 by 1996, owing in principle to expansion. For the counterfactual scenario we assume that the enterprise would also have reduced the number of workers per thousand lines, but only at the historical rate of decline between 1978 and 1987. This translates into an average of 12.2 workers per thousand lines in 1990 and 10.1 in 1996.

Table 11-5. *Alternative Estimates of the Net Present Value of Compañía de Teléfonos de Chile, 1988 and 1990*

Estimate	Billions of pesos		Millions of dollars	
	1988	1990	1988	1990
Authors' estimate of private CTC	116	295	473	875
Bond Corp. and Telefónica de España	138	294	554	871
Stock market valuation	98	223	400	661
Actual sale price	59	n.a.	241	n.a.
Authors' estimate of valuation under public operation	60	131	245	389

n.a. Not applicable.
Source: CTC, Santiago stock exchange data, and authors' estimates.

Results

On the basis of the above assumptions, the private calculus[15] of the net present value of CTC under private operation is estimated at Ch$116 billion in 1988 and Ch$295 billion in 1990. These estimates are compared in table 11-5 with the valuation implicit in Bond Corp.'s and Telefónica's bids for the enterprise, its value on the Santiago stock exchange, the actual sale price, and our estimate of CTC's value had the enterprise continued to be publicly owned.

OUR ESTIMATE VERSUS BIDDERS' IMPLICIT VALUATIONS. Our estimate of CTC's value in 1988 is 16 percent lower than the valuation implicit in Bond Corp.'s purchase price. However, our estimate in 1990 is virtually the same as that implicit in Telefónica's purchase price. Thus, we feel quite comfortable about our projections.

OUR ESTIMATE VERSUS STOCK MARKET VALUATION. The stock market valuation of CTC has been consistently lower than our estimate and the estimates implicit in Bond's and Telefónica's bids for the enterprise. This suggests that the capital market in Chile is relatively imperfect.

OUR ESTIMATE OF PRIVATE CTC VERSUS OUR ESTIMATE OF PUBLIC CTC VERSUS THE ACTUAL SALE PRICE. Our estimate of the value of CTC under private operation is almost twice that for the enterprise had it continued under public ownership. How can this result be explained? Simply put, our estimate of the private value of CTC represents the maximum the private sector was willing to pay, fully recognizing the enterprise's potential. On the other hand, our estimate of the public value of the enterprise summarizes the effect of continuing public behavior. Thus, it represents the floor price below which the government would not have been willing to sell the enterprise and still make money.

Table 11-6. Proceeds from Sale of Compañía de Teléfonos de Chile, 1985–90

Year	Number of shares sold (thousands)	Value (millions of pesos)		Price per share	
		In current pesos	In constant 1988 pesos	In current pesos	In constant 1988 pesos
1985	1,656.7	58.5	98.1	35.3	59.2
1986	8,159.3	539.7	811.1	66.1	99.4
1987	17,062.7	3,298.0	3,800.5	193.3	222.7
1988	204,438.3	36,565.6	40,341.3	178.9	197.3
1989	8,407.9	1,387.2	1,327.2	165.0	157.9
1990	95,144.3	15,698.8	12,930.3	165.0	135.9
Total	334,869.0	57,547.8	59,308.4	171.9	177.1

Source: CTC (various years).

What about the near symmetry between the floor price, given in table 11-5, and the actual sale price, detailed in table 11-6? At face value, the similarity suggests that the government did no more than break even, with the private sector fully internalizing the gains from turning the company around. That is, the fiscal impact of divesting CTC is revenue neutral in the long run. This conclusion is unwarranted because we have not yet taken into account the streams of taxes under both regimes, which we do in the next section. Until then we defer judgment on the budgetary impact of divesting CTC.

What Is It Worth?

What was the effect of divesting CTC? Table 11-7 presents the bottom-line results of our analysis. In terms of net present value as of 1988:

- Chilean welfare is enhanced by Ch$574 billion. This is the difference between the social value of CTC under private operation and its social value had it continued publicly owned. This is a substantial change: it represents about five times our estimate of the private value of CTC, and the perpetual annuity equivalent is about 145 percent of the company's 1987 sales.
- World (national and international) welfare is also enhanced, by Ch$612 billion. Foreigners are expected to gain the equivalent of Ch$39 billion, while still leaving Chileans considerably better off.

In other words, the divestiture of CTC provides an instance where divestiture with regulation is superior to public ownership with regulation. It also offers an example of foreign participation creating a positive-sum game in which both nationals and foreigners can benefit.

Winners and Losers

Who are the recipients of the positive change in overall domestic welfare? As table 11-7 also shows:

- Consumers are the biggest winners, gaining Ch$516 billion, or 90 percent of the total improvement in domestic welfare.
- CTC's domestic shareholders are expected to come out Ch$8 billion ahead; within this group, CTC's employees realize Ch$5 billion.
- ENTEL, the provider of long distance services, gains Ch$16 billion.
- The Chilean government is expected to come out Ch$33 billion ahead, equivalent to 28 percent of our estimate of the private value of the company.

These distributional effects merit elaboration.

Table 11-7. Distribution of Welfare Gains and Losses from Divestiture, Compañía de Teléfonos de Chile
(billions of pesos)

Economic actor	Private operation (V_{sp})	Public operation (V_{sg})	Gains from divestiture ($V_{sp} - V_{sg}$)
Government			
Taxes	40	15	25
Net quasi rents	-2	49	-50
Net sale proceeds	58	0	58
Debt takeover	0	0	0
Other	0	0	0
Total	97	64	33
Private domestic shareholders			
Employees	5	0	5
Pension funds, others	14	11	3
Total	19	11	8
Consumers	1,104	588	516
Competitors	43	27	16
Citizens	0	0	0
Total domestic	1,263	690	574
Foreign shareholders	39	0	39
World	1,301	689	612

Note: Figures may not sum to totals because of rounding.
Source: Authors' calculations.

CONSUMERS. What makes the Chilean consumers the biggest winners? In general, divestiture benefits consumers if it reduces real prices, increases the supply of services, or improves their quality. We argued that CTC's divestiture did not change tariffs one way or the other. However, it will increase the stock of installed lines in service by more than 160 percent between 1988 and 1996. The divested enterprise will also provide a variety of value added services.[16] Not surprisingly, the effect of divestiture on consumers is overwhelming, accounting for 84 percent of the total change in welfare.[17]

Did divestiture improve the quality of services? The indicators in table 11-8 suggest otherwise. On the positive side, the private CTC reduced the percentage of calls receiving no answer. The company also appears to be more responsive to customer complaints, as can be seen from the decline in the percentage of problems corrected within twenty-four hours. Nevertheless, the proportion of completed calls has declined, that of busy signals has increased, and the number of reported problems per year has

Table 11-8. Quality of Service Indicators, Compañía de Teléfonos de Chile, 1982–89
(percentages of total unless specified otherwise)

Indicator	1982	1983	1984	1985	1986	1987	1988	1989
Calls completed	63.4	64.3	65.0	65.9	63.1	60.6	57.6	56.2
Calls engaged	26.3	25.4	26.0	25.1	26.8	27.9	30.4	31.0
No answer	8.9	9.1	8.0	8.1	8.3	8.2	7.7	7.9
Problems								
Thousands per year	816	813	865	821	810	838	754	883
Percent corrected within 24 hours	71.0	75.8	77.1	79.1	68.6	66.8	77.7	70.6

Source: CTC data. The data are from a sample of local calls in the Santiago metropolitan area.

stagnated. These developments mean that our estimate of the effect of divesting the enterprise on consumers is somewhat overstated. It is difficult to say by how much, given the significant increase in capacity, but it is doubtful that the modest deterioration in the quality of services is sufficient to alter the main finding substantially, let alone reverse it.

DOMESTIC SHAREHOLDERS. Under private operation, domestic shareholders—mainly pension funds, CTC employees, other public employees, and hundreds of small investors—are better off as a group by Ch$19 billion. This is a net rather than a gross gain since we subtracted from it the price paid to purchase shares. Under the counterfactual scenario private domestic shareholders would also have been better off,[18] but by only Ch$11 billion. Therefore, on a net basis, domestic shareholders are better off following divestiture by Ch$8 billion. In addition, the composition of the beneficiaries following divestiture is quite different from that under public ownership.

ENTEL. Under both scenarios ENTEL benefits from the expansion of CTC. Expansion of the local network not only generates additional revenue for the provider of local services, but also increases access to, and thus demand for, downstream activities. The additional net quasi rent to ENTEL depends on the magnitude of network expansion and the rate of return allowed by regulators.

Since divestiture caused a substantial expansion in CTC, ENTEL emerges, as expected, as one of the beneficiaries. We estimate ENTEL's gains at Ch$16 billion, using a rate of return on capital of 14 percent (the maximum rate permitted by the regulators). One qualification is in order: to the extent that the private CTC penetrates the long distance market, these gains may be overestimated, as CTC will be able to internalize some of the gains. (It seems likely that Chile will introduce a multicarrier system soon.)

GOVERNMENT. Had the government kept CTC public, it would have received Ch$49 billion in dividends and Ch$15 billion in taxes. Following divestiture, the government received Ch$58 billion in sale proceeds, net of transaction costs. In addition, the treasury is expected to receive Ch$40 billion in taxes from the divested enterprise. Thus, the fiscal impact of divesting CTC is a positive 28 percent of our estimate of the private value of the company.

This is an interesting result because it contrasts with our findings in the cases of CHILGENER and ENERSIS, where the fiscal impact of divestiture was negative. How can this difference be explained? We believe that the method of sale may have made a difference. We know that CTC was sold in part through public bids, whereas CHILGENER and ENERSIS were essentially sold on the stock market. In turn, public bids may have increased the potential competition for the enterprise among large investors who can afford to evaluate it more thoroughly than small investors can. If this explanation holds, it implies that selling enterprises through public bids, allowing foreigners to participate, can enhance government revenue.

Origins of the Change in Welfare

So far we have discussed what happened to the size of the pie and the distribution of the increment in welfare. The question here is, Where did the change in welfare come from?

We decompose in table 11-9 the relative contributions of the changes brought about by divestiture to the change in welfare. The following points are noteworthy:

- Expansion of the basic network contributes the greatest share to welfare enhancement, with benefits accruing to consumers, competitors, and shareholders.

Table 11-9. Origin of the Change in Welfare, Compañía de Teléfonos de Chile

Behavioral difference	Contribution (billions of 1988 pesos)	Percentages of total
Increased investment	384	62
Diversification	190	32
Improved labor productivity	38	6
Total	612	100

Source: Authors' calculations from CTC data.

- Diversification into value added services ranks next, impacting once again mostly on consumers, shareholders, and the government.
- Labor productivity contributes modestly to the change in welfare, largely because the telecommunications industry is capital intensive.

Summary and Lessons

Our analysis of CTC yields the following primary conclusions:

- Divestiture brought about a massive infusion of foreign and domestic capital, and it increased the room for borrowing. As a result, the company will more than double its capacity between 1988 and 1996, further expand into a variety of value added services, and enhance labor productivity.
- These are dramatic changes, which will enhance domestic welfare by Ch$574 billion, or about five times our estimate of the private value of the company; the perpetual annuity equivalent of this figure is 145 percent of CTC's 1987 sales.
- Given tariff regulation and expansion, consumers will benefit the most from divestiture; their gains alone account for 84 percent of the total change in welfare.
- But domestic and foreign shareholders, competitors, employees, and the government also benefit.

In short, the divestiture of CTC is Pareto-improving, making everybody better off without making any one else worse off. Notwithstanding this impressive result, the divestiture of CTC and ENTEL has had several other effects. Most notably:

- It fueled competition between the two companies, resulting in an attempt by each to penetrate the traditional market of the other. In response, Chile is now considering the introduction of a multicarrier system in the long distance market. The effect of the new system on welfare is difficult to assess at this stage, but to the extent that it enhances competition it may further improve welfare.
- It posed new challenges to the ability of existing antitrust rules and institutions to resolve disputes that may not have surfaced otherwise. A case in point is Telefónica de España's ownership of 45 percent of CTC and 20 percent of ENTEL, which if left unaddressed may adversely affect competitive behavior.

The story of CTC lends support to the following hypotheses:

- Divestiture releases the resource constraint, especially at times of fiscal stringency. In the case of CTC it especially mobilized foreign capital, which was necessary because the company is large in relation to the domestic capital market.

• As a result, divestiture alleviates excess demand in basic infrastructure services, such as telecommunications, which are vital to economic development. For this to occur, however, the Chilean government had to insist that the buyers commit themselves to an ambitious investment program.

• Foreign participation can be rewarding to the foreign investors as well as to the host country, provided effective regulation is in place.

• In the absence of effective regulation, private ownership in and of itself is insufficient to meet excess demand. This is evident from the period 1959–71, during which CTC was privately owned but nevertheless did not expand sufficiently.

• Divestiture promotes profit-maximizing behavior. In the case of CTC the behavioral changes are most apparent in the company's attempt to diversify output, expand into new markets, and, while generously paying workers, demand higher productivity.

• Finally, divestiture does not necessarily hurt workers. On the contrary, in the case of CTC they came out winners.

To conclude, selling public telecommunications monopolies, even to foreigners, can create a positive-sum game in which all parties can benefit. However, the CTC case suggests that, if the transaction is to be mutually beneficial, governments are well advised to insist, during the sale negotiation, that the new owners undertake an investment program to meet excess demand, in return for which the government should be willing to commit itself to maintaining an appropriate and stable regulatory regime, particularly regarding tariffs.

Notes

This chapter was written by Ahmed Galal and Clemencia Torres. The authors are grateful to Oscar Marquez and other staff of CTC for their cooperation, to Felipe Montt for his advice and counsel, and to Manuel Abdala for helpful comments.

1. The term "intervened" is used in Chile to mean government control of the enterprise, but not ownership.

2. CTC has six subsidiaries: CTC-ISAPRE (formed in 1987), which provides health care for the group's employees; CTC-Cellular (1988), which provides portable cellular telephone services; CTC-Negocios (1988), which trades in goods related to telecommunications activities; CTC-Transmisiones Regionales (1989), which provides installation and equipment for long distance telecommunications services; CTC-Servicios (1988), which provides legal, financial, tax, computer, and real estate advisory services; and CTC-Operaciones Telefónicas (1988), which specializes in telecommunications infrastructure.

3. CTC's equity is composed of two series of shares, "A" and "B." The A shares were originally held by CORFO. Minority private shareholders owned B shares.

The only difference between the two types of shares is that the B shares can elect one member of the company's board even though they represent less than one-seventh of the company's equity.

4. The Chilean General Accounting Office refused to approve the sale to Bond Corp. on the grounds that it had offered to increase CTC's equity by a smaller number of shares than CORFO required from other bidders. As a result, CORFO decided to declare that none of the bids was satisfactory and went on to offer the shares in a direct sale under the same conditions as the original open bid. Almost immediately, the shares were sold to Bond Corp. In addition, the board of directors of CTC approved the sale of 10,440,204 B shares to the Bond group. This sale was challenged in court by a group of private shareholders because it would give Bond a majority on the board. The court rejected the complaint, finding that CORFO's procedure of selling the shares directly, bypassing the General Accounting Office decision, was legal.

5. Announcing the sale of a public enterprise may have a positive effect on performance if it entails appointing new management, as happened in the United Kingdom, or if it motivates management and workers to get their act together. Conversely, the announcement can be demoralizing if it is perceived by management and workers as threatening. None of these conditions seems to have been present in the case of CTC.

6. In 1982 the government devalued the peso by 88 percent; this move hit CTC hard because 90 percent of its debt was denominated in foreign currency. In 1985 the government announced that it would no longer provide enterprises with preferential foreign exchange to settle their foreign debts. Thus, the market value of the central bank's debt to CTC plummeted, and this led to nonoperating losses. This practice was of course applied not only to CTC but also to other public and private firms.

7. Constant prices, here and elsewhere, are derived from information provided by CTC, in which the values of outputs and inputs were decomposed into their quantity and price components.

8. Up to a maximum of 49 percent of total equity if government was to retain public ownership, provided private customers were willing to finance as much of the new connections.

9. In a normal calendar year, dividends are paid in four installments (in April, July, October, and January) on the basis of anticipated profits after taxes.

10. Skeptics may argue that the government could have relaxed the resource constraint without selling CTC. The counterargument is that governments face a hard budget constraint, violating which can generate adverse macroeconomic effects, reduce the country's creditworthiness, or both. Alternatively, if the government had decided to shuffle resources around, giving, for example, more resources to CTC, it would have deprived another project of those resources. Either course would have been costly to society.

11. Direct taxes, which were 15 percent at the time of our study, were scheduled to decline to 10 percent starting in 1993. Value added taxes, on the other hand, were reduced in 1987 from 20 percent to 16 percent.

12. Even if CTC were permitted to operate in the long distance market, this component of the investment program would be too modest to have a significant impact on our projections.

13. This plan is a revised version of the 1988–92 plan, in which CTC contemplated a total expenditure of Ch$401 billion, of which it had implemented Ch$214.6 billion by December 1990.

14. That assumption need not hold. In fact, regulators in the United Kingdom and Mexico follow the *RPI - X* formula, which allows for a decline in real tariffs. See the case studies of British Telecom (chapter 4) and Teléfonos de México (chapter 19) in this volume for further details.

15. As opposed to the social calculus, in which one should take into account the effect of divestiture on all important economic actors (e.g., consumers), adjust for price distortions, and net out transfers.

16. Expansion into value added services is particularly important given the trend in the telecommunications business around the world, which is marked by a relative contraction in "POTS" (plain old telephone service) and an expansion into "VANS" (value added network services). For further details see *The Economist* (1991).

17. We calculated the change in consumer surplus by estimating the area under the demand curve for residential and commercial customers, using the variable charge for local calls and price elasticities of -0.18 for residential customers and -0.20 for commercial customers. From these estimates we subtracted the fixed charges (i.e., connection and installation fees) and the fixed component of the two-part tariff. Further, we used a shadow multiplier of 1.5 to account for externalities in consumption, resulting from the ability not only to place calls but to be called as well. Lacking the necessary information, we did not calculate any consumer surplus for long distance services, even though CTC provides such services in a segment of the market.

18. These include essentially the shareholders who held 10 percent of the enterprise's shares prior to divestiture, plus a few customers who would have purchased shares when they received new connections.

12. Summary: Chile

The divestiture of CHILGENER, ENERSIS, and CTC improved domestic and world welfare. This conclusion holds despite the differences in structure of the markets in which the three enterprises operate, and despite the fact that all three were relatively well run public enterprises. As can be seen from figure 12-1, however, the magnitudes of the gains vary from case to case.[1] The welfare changes in the two electricity cases (CHILGENER and ENERSIS) were modest compared with that in the case of CTC. Do these welfare changes exhibit characteristic distributional patterns? Do they systematically originate from improved productivity? What factors explain them: markets, institutions, the sale structure?[2] Finally, what conclusions can be drawn from the Chilean cases?

Decomposition of Welfare Changes

Only in CTC did all parties gain and none lose. At CHILGENER and ENERSIS, although most actors benefited, others lost. The effect of divestiture on the main actors is summarized in figure 12-1 and elaborated below.

- **Buyers**. Foreigners participated in the purchase of equity of all three enterprises. In no case did they lose, but neither did Chilean investors. In the case of CTC, foreigners gained substantially, but domestic actors gained several times as much.
- **Government**. In contrast, the Chilean government lost in two of the three cases (CHILGENER and ENERSIS), although by small amounts. Thus, the gains in overall welfare accrued at a fiscal cost.
- **Consumers**. Despite the monopoly position of ENERSIS and CTC, the gains to producers did not occur at the expense of consumers. On the contrary, in the divestiture of CTC consumers gained by a substantial margin from the company's subsequent expansion. At ENERSIS, some consumers were made worse off by the reduction in theft of electricity, but others gained even more as reduced costs meant lower regulated prices.

285

Figure 12-1. Summary of Winners and Losers from Divestiture, Chile

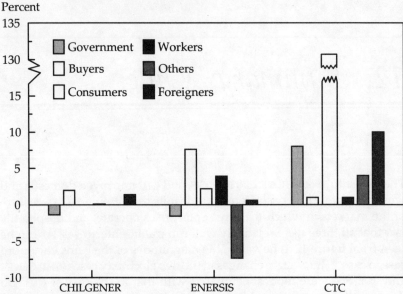

Note: Gains and losses are the annual component of the perpetuity equivalent of the welfare change, expressed as a percentage of annual sales in the last predivestiture year. *Source:* Authors' calculations.

- **Workers.** Workers gained in all three cases through participation in ownership and appreciation of the shares they acquired. The gains were particularly substantial at ENERSIS, where management and workers acquired a large share of the enterprise. Meanwhile there were no layoffs because the enterprises were not overstaffed to begin with.
- **Competitors.** No major effect on competitors is detected except in the case of CTC, whose expansion benefited ENTEL, the company providing complementary long distance services.

Origins of the Change

The changes in welfare originated from different sources, the most important of which are shown in figure 12-2 and summarized below:

- **Productivity.** Divestiture improved the productivity of CTC and CHILGENER. At ENERSIS productivity also improved but not beyond its historical trend. The gains in productivity at CHILGENER came from better management of existing resources, whereas at CTC they were derived largely from increased investment.
- **Investment.** The divestiture of CTC relaxed the resource constraint, leading to a doubling of capacity in five years to meet pending de-

Figure 12-2. Summary of Sources of Welfare Change from Divestiture, Chile

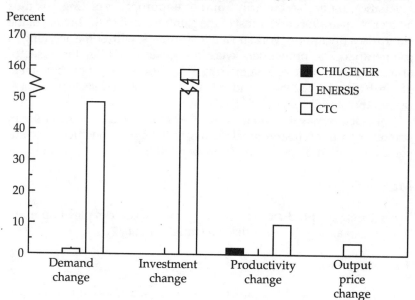

Percent

CHILGENER
ENERSIS
CTC

Demand change Investment change Productivity change Output price change

Note: Gains and losses are the annual component of the perpetuity equivalent of the welfare change, expressed as a percentage of annual sales in the last predivestiture year.
Source: Authors' calculations.

mand. In the cases of CHILGENER and ENERSIS divestiture did not cause any dramatic change in investment behavior.

• **Prices.** Despite the market power enjoyed by CTC and ENERSIS, the only change in output prices due to divestiture was at ENERSIS, where better management reduced electricity theft. Otherwise regulation prevented the exploitation of consumers in the telecommunications and electric power sectors.

• **Endogenous demand expansion.** Divestiture induced a number of market-expanding activities, mainly through the creation of new subsidiaries where synergies were present. For example, CTC introduced a series of new value added services, and ENERSIS began to sell electrical equipment and provide a number of electricity-related services.

• **Nonoperating performance.** Only ENERSIS realized significant returns and capital gains from financial investment.[3] These gains are not considered welfare improving, given that other citizens would otherwise have made them.

In sum, the divestiture of the three Chilean enterprises created a positive-sum game in which Chile and the world were better off than before. The origin of the gains varied from one enterprise to another but came primarily from investment, improved productivity, and product diversification, and secondarily from more appropriate pricing, and thus better resource allocation. Most of the gains accrued to the buyers of the enterprises (including workers) and consumers, with some accruing to competitors. The only losers were the government (in the cases of CHILGENER and ENERSIS, by a moderate amount), a subset of consumers of electricity (in ENERSIS), and citizens, who otherwise would have reaped the capital gains made by ENERSIS.

What factors may explain these results? In general, the answer lies in market conditions, institutional factors, and the way in which the companies were sold. These issues are elaborated below.

Market Factors

In particular, the product, labor, and capital markets can play important roles in explaining these results. How might that be?

The Product Market

Two of the three Chilean enterprises operate in noncompetitive markets. CTC has a virtual monopoly in the market for telecommunications network services, and ENERSIS is the sole provider of electricity in Santiago. Only CHILGENER operates in a relatively competitive market structure. Nevertheless, welfare improved in all three cases. This result negates the conventional wisdom that private monopolies exercising their market power will reduce consumer surplus. In addition, it underlines the effectiveness of regulation in the Chilean economy, as elaborated below.

If effective regulation prevented potential losses to consumers, it is also worth noting that the government altered the market structure of the electric power and telecommunications sectors prior to divestiture. In the electric power sector the government separated generation from distribution. In the telecommunications sector it freed entry and encouraged competition in all markets, except in instances where a case was made through the antitrust commission to the contrary. As a result, increased competition may have precluded us from observing losses to consumers and may have alleviated the burden on regulators.

Finally, divestiture itself is causing market structures to change. In the telecommunications sector the divestiture of CTC and ENTEL led each to attempt to penetrate the traditional market of the other. As a consequence, the government is now considering a change in its policy in the long distance market in favor of a multicarrier system. To the extent that the new system will enhance competition and improve welfare, the positive effects of divesting CTC and ENTEL may be even greater than reported here. In the electricity sector the opposite phenomenon is emerging. ENERSIS acquired some 10 percent of the shares of ENDESA, causing concern that ENDESA may favor ENERSIS in granting access to transmission lines. If that should happen, the positive welfare improvements from divesting ENERSIS would be overstated. Both problems are now being addressed by the government.

One reason why consumers did not lose in the cases involving monopolies in electricity distribution and local telephone services is the effectiveness of the long-run marginal cost pricing regime adopted in Chile, first in the electric power sector and then in telecommunications. This regime is based on the projected future costs of a hypothetical efficient firm. It offers enterprises a fair rate of return, using the capital asset pricing model. Prices remain in effect for five years, during which they are adjusted automatically for inflation. The regime thus provides enterprises with incentives to be more efficient and to expand. Meanwhile it protects consumers from potential exploitation.

Price and entry regulations are not, of course, sufficient to ensure an effective regulatory regime. Credibility of government commitment and the existence of safeguarding institutions to prevent opportunistic government behavior are also important. These issues are addressed briefly later in this chapter.

The Labor Market

There are several reasons why workers were not hurt by the divestiture of their enterprises in the three cases analyzed. First, there were no layoffs. Chile had already restructured the labor force in its public enterprises in the 1970s, which meant that at the time of divestiture these enterprises operated more or less with the labor force they needed. Second, divestiture did not cause wages to deteriorate. On the contrary, at CHILGENER and ENERSIS the new owners introduced profit-sharing schemes to motivate workers. Finally, workers acquired equity shares in all three cases and a controlling stake at ENERSIS. As a result, they benefited from rising profits and share appreciation.

It can, of course, be argued that these benefits may have been offset in part by increased effort on the workers' part. After all, private owners would not tolerate the slack that may have existed under public ownership. But even if this is so, it is not clear whether greater effort on the part of workers is necessarily associated with lower utility (for a discussion of this point see chapter 15).

The Capital Market

All three enterprises' shares were already being quoted on the stock market before divestiture. In that sense the existence of a capital market facilitated valuation and thus the sale transaction. Thereafter, the trading of shares on the stock market undoubtedly helped enhance Chile's capital market development.

Following divestiture, the capital market may also have provided a mechanism of corporate governance in two ways. First, fluctuations of share values on the stock market may have provided the owners a signal as to how management was doing, prompting corrective action. Second, stringent borrowing criteria, especially in international capital markets without implicit government guarantees, may also have persuaded management to shape up.

To be sure, the capital market in Chile is still limited and somewhat imperfect. This may partly explain why such a large enterprise as CTC was sold through public bids that involved foreigners. It may also explain why CTC and subsequently ENERSIS have resorted to raising capital abroad.

Summary

The role of markets in explaining the welfare changes in the Chilean cases can be summarized as follows:

- The positive results at CHILGENER support the proposition that divesting public enterprises in competitive markets can be beneficial. Moreover, the positive results at CTC and ENERSIS suggest that effective regulation can prevent monopoly exploitation of consumers, and that divestiture can produce substantial gains through expansion.
- Market structures are not always to be taken as given; they can be influenced by government policy and by divestiture itself. Government can increase competition by splitting large enterprises into smaller units. Divestiture produces more aggressive behavior, the impact of which on competition is uncertain.
- Divestiture is likely to benefit workers where labor reforms have already been introduced. The gains may follow from greater employment opportunities, profit sharing, and/or equity participation.
- The existence of capital markets makes divestiture easier, but divestiture in turn undoubtedly enhances capital market development. Moreover, capital markets can play a positive role in helping shareholders monitor management.

Institutional Factors

The structure and behavior of Chilean institutions were also important to the outcome of the three divestiture cases.

The Principal-Agent Relationship

One of the reasons why the changes in welfare were relatively modest in the case of CHILGENER and ENERSIS is that the two enterprises did not suffer from problems often observed in public enterprises. The principal (the government) did not force managers (the agents) to pursue multiple and conflicting objectives, nor did it deprive them of operational freedom, including the freedom to set selling prices, except in cases of monopoly. In the latter, prices were set by the regulators on the basis of well-specified formulas, irrespective of ownership.

Although CTC operated under similar conditions, the enterprise faced a resource constraint, which precluded adequate expansion to meet demand. The scarcity of resources followed from the tight fiscal policy imposed by the government on most public enterprises for macroeconomic and other reasons (including the ideological position that the state should only play a subsidiary role in economic activity). Had the enterprise been able to expand as much as needed to meet pending demand, the welfare effect of divesting CTC would have also been relatively modest.

Perhaps the most remarkable observation about the Chilean cases is that divestiture improved welfare at all, given the limited room for turning these companies around. How did private ownership make the difference? Profit maximization and better incentives seem to have led management to improve X-efficiency at CHILGENER by diversifying coal supplies, using coal more efficiently, and using the company's port facility to serve third parties. At CTC, management diversified into value added telecommunications services. At ENERSIS, even though efficiency did not improve beyond its historical trend, management reduced losses of electricity and invested aggressively in profitable companies elsewhere. Accordingly, even where public enterprises are relatively efficient, private ownership may still improve the principal-agent relationship, with positive results.

Regulatory Institutions

The positive results in the Chilean cases also reflect the effectiveness of regulatory institutions in providing enterprises with adequate incentives; their credibility led the private sector to invest as massively as it did. Meanwhile regulation also seems to have been effective in protecting consumers. Several factors appear to account for these results. In both the electric power and the telecommunications sectors:

- The regulation clearly specifies the rules of entry and pricing, which are applied to all enterprises, irrespective of ownership. Moreover, the regulation provides clear procedures for settling disputes. In the telecommunications sector, for example, disputes over tariffs are settled by a three-person arbitration committee.

• The regulation itself and the agencies responsible for it (CNE for electricity and SUBTEL for telecommunications) were introduced well before divestiture.

• Perhaps more important, details of the regulatory rules are contained in the laws themselves, which are difficult to change in Chile, given the country's political institutions (a fragmented legislature and a weak presidency) and its independent judiciary system (for more on this point see Galal 1994).

Summary

Our analysis of the role of institutional factors in explaining the welfare effects of divestiture in the Chilean cases suggests that:

• Even where the principal-agent relationship in public enterprises is least problematic, divestiture can enhance profit-maximizing behavior and incentives, with positive implications for society.

• Effective and credible regulatory institutions can prevent monopolies from exploiting consumers and provide producers adequate incentives to invest in such asset-specific utilities as telecommunications.

Sale Structure

The way in which divestitures were structured in Chile often had a favorable influence on their outcomes.

Ownership versus Control

In the three Chilean cases the government relinquished 100 percent of its shares, and thus control of the enterprise, to the private sector. That meant that the private sector owners have had the freedom to bring about the behavioral changes expected of them. Evidently this freedom has led to improved productivity, increased investment, and the other favorable results we have found.

Of course, the government could have transferred control without selling a majority of its shares, as happened, for example, in some cases in Mexico (see chapters 18 to 22). Moreover, it could have exercised its control differently even if it had retained a majority of the shares, as the Malaysian cases (see chapters 13 to 17) demonstrate. These variations were not observed, however, in the three Chilean cases.

Prior Restructuring

In none of the Chilean cases did the government undertake major investments prior to divestiture for the purpose of facilitating the sale of the enterprises. On the contrary, in selling CTC the government sought and obtained a commitment from the primary buyers to bring in fresh capital to finance needed expansion, and this expansion in turn brought about the most significant positive welfare effects in the entire sample.

On the surface, it also seems that the government did not undertake any legal, labor, or market restructuring of the three enterprises prior to divestiture. That is not the case, however, when a longer time horizon is considered. In commercializing the operation of its public enterprises in the mid-1970s, the government instructed managers to get rid of redundant workers, creating at the same time a fund to ease the cost of their adjustment. Similarly, in the early 1980s the government increased competition in the electricity and telecommunications sectors by splitting up large enterprises in the former and allowing free entry in the latter. These reforms clearly paid off, as evidenced by the modest gains to society from divestiture in Chile compared with those in other cases in this book.

The Sale Transaction

Chile phased each of the three divestitures over a two-year period on average, combining several sale mechanisms including share offerings on the stock market, bidding, and direct sale to workers. The government allowed foreign participation, primarily because some of the enterprises were quite large relative to the domestic capital market. In its direct sales to workers, the government offered no share discount in the majority of cases and in fact made no special provision for employees other than allowing them to use their severance pay in advance.

Overall, the process was more transparent, better phased, and more carefully scrutinized (especially in the choice of the buyers) than the country's earlier divestiture process. These features apparently led to favorable results.

Summary

The positive welfare improvements in the Chilean cases are correlated with:

- Full transfer of ownership and control to the private sector
- A commitment by the private sector buyers to meet demand, in return for which the government committed itself to provide appropriate regulation
- Significant public-enterprise reform prior to divestiture.

Conclusions

The Chilean cases demonstrate that selling public enterprises can be beneficial to society whether the enterprises operate in competitive or noncompetitive markets, and even where the enterprises are relatively efficient. The cases also demonstrate that these gains are contingent on what policymakers do, especially regarding competition, regulation, and sale structure.

A number of other specific conclusions are worth underlining. First, the positive results at ENERSIS and CTC support the conclusion that the net benefits from divesting and regulating monopolies can outweigh the net benefits from reforming and regulating the same monopolies while keeping them public. This is an important result because Chilean policies in the electricity and telecommunications sectors contrast with those of most countries: Chile relies on private ownership and regulation, whereas most countries rely on public ownership and centralized decisionmaking. The Chilean success story can be traced to enterprise restructuring to enhance competition, effective regulation, and then divestiture. Failing this, divestiture may not necessarily have a favorable outcome. In fact, CTC performed rather poorly under private ownership between 1930 and 1971 (for details see Galal 1994).

Another important conclusion from the Chilean cases is that, even where divestiture leaves behavior within the enterprise largely unchanged, it can release the resource constraint. In the case of CTC, divestiture mobilized foreign capital, which led to a doubling of capacity in five years. This outcome was possible because the Chilean government structured the sale of CTC so that the buyers agreed to an ambitious investment program, in return for a government commitment to an "appropriate" regulatory framework.

Notwithstanding these positive results, the analysis of the Chilean cases also suggests that divestiture may accrue at a fiscal cost, even where the sale involves no concessions to sweeten the deal. This trade-off underscores the importance of clarifying the objective of divestiture up front. Moreover, the analysis also suggests that divestiture poses continuous challenges to policymakers. In the Chilean cases, the sale of CTC and ENTEL fueled rivalry between the two companies. Similarly, the participation of ENERSIS (an electricity distribution company) in the ownership of ENDESA (an electricity generation company) is causing concern that anticompetitive behavior may develop. However, Chile already has in place the necessary antitrust rules and institutions to resolve such disputes.

In short, divestiture is capable of bringing about significant welfare gains to society, provided that society adopts welfare-enhancing policies. Chile has adopted such policies and reaped the benefits, especially in its divestiture efforts of the 1980s. The Chilean success story thus serves as a model for other countries to emulate.

Notes

This chapter was written by Ahmed Galal.

1. Welfare change is measured as the annual perpetual component of welfare change relative to sales in the year prior to divestiture.

2. As recounted in chapter 8, Chile divested its public enterprises into an environment conducive to efforts to improve efficiency. Chile liberalized its markets (for domestic production and imports) and generally pursued sound macroeconomic management, which meant that divested and undivested enterprises alike faced greater pressure to operate more efficiently. These issues are not explored further below.

3. This occurred primarily through ENERSIS' investment in the equity of ENDESA, the largest electricity generating enterprise in Chile, whose divestiture took place in 1990.

PART IV

Malaysia: Divesting for Growth and Equity

13. Divestiture in Malaysia[1]

Divestiture is well suited to an economy in which growth and profit maximization are paramount. But what if the country is equally concerned with social goals, including the redistribution of wealth? Can divestiture be carried out in such a country? What changes, if any, must be introduced to the exercise? Do the changes amount to watering down the original objectives and effects of divestiture? If so, is divestiture really necessary for such a country?

Malaysia's answers to the above questions are especially germane for two reasons. First, the country's most important public policy between 1971 and 1990, the New Economic Policy (NEP), stressed both growth and equity distribution. Second, Malaysia has implemented a policy of divesting government entities since 1983. These two policies are described in turn.

The New Economic Policy

Ethnic Malays (or Bumiputra) constitute the majority of the Malaysian population and therefore control its democratic political institutions. Political power, however, does not translate into economic power: in 1970 the Bumiputra held only 1.9 percent of corporate assets. The NEP was therefore designed to redress the imbalance between political and economic power. A major goal was to increase the Bumiputra share of assets to 30 percent by 1990. To further this goal the government created a host of public enterprises: financial institutions to hold shares on behalf of the Bumiputra, entrepreneurial organizations to set up new firms and eventually transfer shares to the Bumiputra, financial and support organizations to help private entrepreneurs, and standard government enterprises managed by Bumiputra. The government has had considerable success in increasing the Bumiputra share of assets, largely at the expense of foreigners.

Features of the Divestiture Policy

The government first announced the divestiture policy in 1983. The policy had the following objectives (Malaysia, Government of, 1984, pp. 22–23):

- To increase the private sector's role in the development of the economy.
- To reduce the financial burden on the government of maintaining extensive and expensive services.
- To improve the level of productivity and efficiency of the services and enterprises that would be divested.

These features were elaborated as follows (Malaysia, Government of, 1984, p. 22):

A new departure in the direction of the strategy to encourage greater private investment in the economy will be required if the private sector is to be revitalized and to assume a much bigger development role. The progressive and selective privatization of Government services and investments will be part of the new strategy to increase the role of the private sector in the development of the economy. There are various forms of privatization depending on the extent of ownership that is retained by the Government when the existing service is privatized. Privatization can be complete when the entire ownership and control of the existing service or interest is sold off and transferred to the private sector. Partial privatization implies that the transfer of ownership is not complete and only a portion of the Government's ownership interest is transferred to the private sector. Privatization can be selective when a Government agency divests only a part of its services to the private sector. Commercialization, involving the adoption of certain commercial practices, can be a phase in privatization while the encouragement of greater private sector participation in the provision of new services will enhance the scope and extent of the private sector in the economy. In its broader form, privatization can encompass various aspects of private sector participation in the economy and seeks to promote the influence of market forces, the enhancement of opportunities for private entrepreneurship and the encouragement of greater competition in economic activities. The ultimate objective of privatization is the reduction of the size and presence of the Government and, conversely, the need to expand the role of private enterprise in the economy.

All this is quite standard and could have been part of the divestiture plans of almost any country. More noteworthy is the emphasis on equity.

The policy contained promises that the government would carry out divestiture without adversely affecting the interests of consumers, employees of the divested bodies, the Bumiputra, or the nation as whole. As spelled out by the government (Malaysia, Government of, 1984, p. 23):

> Privatization will be implemented within the context of the NEP and it must be stressed that it will not negate the NEP. Increasing opportunities for ownership participation, jobs and business to Bumiputra and other Malaysians, are expected to be generated by privatization. The substantial assets and other interests of the public sector which will be privatized will provide the basis for further corporate growth of the Bumiputra private sector and these will undoubtedly provide ample opportunities for Bumiputra, at various levels and scale of operation, to share in the benefits arising from privatization. The Government will also ensure that the ownership conditions will be implemented with flexibility on the privatized enterprises as it will be important to ensure that ownership imbalances between Bumiputra and other interests are further reduced.
>
> Efforts will be taken to ensure that the benefits of privatization will be widely shared. The interests and welfare of the employees affected by privatization will be adequately taken into account before the services are privatized. As a substantial proportion of the services that are proposed to be privatized will be basic services, the Government will make the necessary arrangements with the private sector acquiring the basic services to ensure that the level of prices charged to the consuming public, especially the lower income groups, will not be unduly high or unfair. The Government will, therefore, take the responsibility for ensuring that privatization will be implemented with the maximum advantages to the nation.

Another distinctive characteristic of the Malaysian strategy was an explicit recognition of partial divestiture as an option (Malaysia, Government of, 1991, p. 13):

> Privatization is defined as the transfer to the private sector of activities and functions which have traditionally rested with public sector. This definition applies to enterprises already owned by the Government and to new projects which normally have been implemented by the public sector. In effecting such transfers, three essential organization related components are involved, viz., management responsibility; assets (with or without liability) or the right to use assets; and personnel . . . privatization must involve the transfer of at least one of the components.

The divestiture policy was part of a set of new policies aimed at increasing productivity and growth in both the public and the private sectors and increasing the private sector's role in economic development. The policies ranged from establishing "Malaysia Incorporated" to introducing the Look East Policy and the National Agricultural Policy, and from absorbing Islamic values in administration to installing punch clocks in government offices.

Reaction to the Divestiture Policy

The announcement of the privatization policy took the public and the civil service by surprise. The very term "privatization" was new to them, and there was widespread ignorance in the months following the announcement about the manner in which the government would implement the policy. There was, however, little doubt about the government's political commitment, which stemmed from a long-simmering dissatisfaction with the performance of public enterprises. Among the dissatisfied parties were Dr. Mahathir Mohamad, who had expressed his views long before he became prime minister in 1981, and the top echelon of the Economic Planning Unit (see Mohamad 1970; Malaysia, Government of, 1985, pp. 66–68; Wahab 1987; Al-Haj and Yusof 1988).[1] The government did not make the empirical basis for the dissatisfaction public, but the feeling was given widespread credence because of the views of the prime minister and his top advisers on the subject.

One of the immediate results of the ignorance of various segments of society about the utility of divestiture was resistance to it. Civil service unions for one, especially CUEPACS (the Congress of Unions of Employees in the Public and Civil Service) and those representing workers at the Kelang Port Authority (who were concerned about the possible negative effects of the planned divestiture of the port's container terminal), came out strongly against it (for details see Havelka and Havelka 1990, pp. 200–02). Concerned individuals also criticized the policy. The most strident criticism, published in a 1989 book, revolved around the following points (Jomo 1989):

- As an alternative to divestiture, the public sector could be run more efficiently, as some public enterprises had demonstrated. Also, divestiture would not provide a miracle cure for all the problems, especially the inefficiencies, associated with the public sector, nor can divested enterprises guarantee that the public interest will be most effectively served by their taking over public sector activities. In addition, by diverting private sector capital from making productive new investments to buying public sector assets, economic growth would be retarded rather than stimulated.

- Greater accountability of and more effective control over the public sector would ensure greater efficiency in achieving the public and national interests while limiting public sector waste and borrowing.
- The government would only be able to divest profitable or potentially profitable enterprises and activities, because the private sector would only be interested in those.
- Divestiture would not resolve the fiscal problem, because the public sector would lose income from the more profitable public sector activities and would be stuck with financing the unprofitable ones. This would undermine the potential for cross-subsidization within the public sector.
- Divestiture tends to affect adversely the interests of public sector employees and the public, especially the poor, to which the public sector is supposed to be more sensitive.
- Divestiture would give priority to maximizing profits at the expense of social welfare and the public interest, except on the rare occasions when the two coincided. Thus, for example, only profitable new services would be introduced rather than services needed by the people, especially the poor and the politically uninfluential.
- Divestiture exercises in Malaysia might not even pretend to achieve their alleged objectives—supposedly to increase Bumiputra wealth and business opportunities—by invoking NEP restructuring considerations. With increased competition from the Bumiputra, except in those cases where new owners can arrange for collusion with the Bumiputra, political influence and connections would probably play a more significant role in business.

In addition to all these criticisms, political parties, including components of the ruling party (the National Front) and even the United Malays National Organization also expressed their concern that divestiture might slow down the restructuring programs of the NEP.

The Implementation of Divestiture

The barrage of criticism notwithstanding, the Malaysian government implemented its divestiture policy with vigor. By the end of 1990 it had succeeded in divesting 106 government entities and activities: 11 departmental activities, 10 new projects, 1 activity of a statutory body, and 84 government enterprises (Malaysia, Government of, 1989, pp. 19–20; 1991, pp. 57–59). The most common mode of divestiture was sale of equity (72 entities or activities); followed by management contracts (15); build-operate-transfer arrangements (8);[2] sale of assets (3); lease arrangements (2); lease and sale of assets (2); management buyouts (2); and build and operate arrangements (2 entities; Malaysia, Government of, 1989, pp. 19–20; 1991, pp. 52–59). The vast majority of activities divested were commercial and manufacturing operations (82), followed by infrastructure and utility construction (10), with various other types of activities making up the rest (Malaysia, Government of, 1989, pp. 19–20; 1991, pp. 52–50).

In terms of protecting the Bumiputras' interests, seventy of the divestiture projects involved the transfer of government enterprises to Bumiputra companies. Complete details on the projects are unavailable, but at least in the case of the major ones (e.g., Sports Toto Malaysia, Malaysian Airline Systems, Malaysian International Shipping Corporation, Kelang Container Terminal, and Syarikat Telekom Malaysia), the government took steps to ensure that a portion of shares sold were allocated to Bumiputra individuals, companies, or trust agencies.

Issues to be Explored

By international standards, the divestiture program was clearly a remarkable achievement, both in the number of activities divested and in the protection of Bumiputra interests. However, certain questions remain to be answered.

First, in most cases divestiture was carried out with little or no change in management or the work force. In certain cases the government did not even decrease the amount of control it exerted over the divested entities. Therefore, one must ask whether improvements in the performance of such entities can be attributed to divestiture.

Second, most of the divested entities were already in Bumiputra hands in the sense that state-administered Bumiputra trust agencies owned them. Transferring their ownership to other Bumiputra individuals, companies, or trust agencies such as Permodalan Nasional Berhad did not increase the total share of the Bumiputra in corporate wealth. One must therefore ask what the net gain in Bumiputra holdings was.

Third, in those cases that involved monopolistic activities, such as container services and telecommunications enterprises, divestiture has not changed their monopolistic character. Thus an important question is whether or not the divested enterprises exploited their position at the expense of consumers.

Fourth, in the major cases listed above, ultimate control remains in government hands. The government is directly or indirectly the majority shareholder or holds a "golden share" with certain special rights or privileges. The question is whether or not such partial divestiture really makes a difference in performance.

The three case studies that follow address these issues and others. A concluding summary chapter provides a synthesis of the answers.

Notes

1. Fadil Azim Abbas wrote this chapter.

2. Al-Haj and Wahab were, at different times, the directors-general of the Economic Planning Unit. The report by the government called for greater government control over the budgets of public enterprises, in particular the nonfinancial public enterprises. These views were only expressed after the 1983 announcement on divestiture, but they correctly expressed feelings prevalent before 1983.

3. This required the private company to construct a facility, normally an infrastructural or utility project, operate it for a period, and then return it to the government.

14. Malaysian Airline Systems

Malaysian Airline Systems Berhad (MAS) has a virtual monopoly in scheduled domestic service in Malaysia and is also a major player in international service in the region. In 1985 and 1986, both domestic and foreign share placements reduced the central government's status from that of dominant shareholder to a minority shareholder. However, government agencies, including state authorities and public enterprises, retained a majority holding, and the federal government also retained a specially privileged "golden share."

In comparison with other divestitures worldwide, the case of MAS then has three major distinguishing features. First, institutionally it is a case of partial financial divestiture. It is financial in that the government traded shares with diversified private buyers for cash, but yielded little of its control over the enterprise; it is partial in that only about a third of the shares left the public sector. Second, economically the firm's domestic and international operations have distinctly different commercial opportunities, regulatory constraints, political importance, and welfare impact. Thus, how divestiture affected behavior across the two markets is of particular interest. Third, foreigners are affected by the divestiture in three distinct roles: as buyers of part of the enterprise, as consumers of its services, and as competitors on international routes. Accordingly, the distinction between domestic and world welfare changes is critical in this case.

Background

History

MAS is endowed with great genes, having descended from the same parent which spawned that acknowledged leader of the airline industry, Singapore Airlines.[1]

Both airlines' origins date to the 1937 formation of Malayan Airways Limited, which only began actual operations in 1947. Subsequent events followed major political changes in the region. In 1963 the Federation of Malaysia was formed, and the airline changed its name to Malaysian Airways, subsequently absorbing Borneo Airways, which had hitherto operated in the states of Sabah and Sarawak on the island of Borneo. In 1965 Singapore left Malaysia, but the two governments continued as business partners, changing only the airline's name, to Malaysia-Singapore Airline.

The marriage did not last, however. The conflicting interests of the two governments, especially on the issue of balance between domestic and international routes, led them in 1971 to agree to a divorce and the formation of separate national airlines. As a result, in 1972 the Malaysian government incorporated MAS and gave it the following official objectives:

- To provide the people of Malaysia with an efficient and profitable air transport system that enhances the standing of the nation and the policies of its government
- To develop an efficient domestic service within Malaysia that directly links eastern and western Malaysia and contributes to the economic and social integration of the country as a whole
- To provide simultaneously competitive and profitable international services that support Malaysia's trade, tourism, and other activities
- To contribute to national aspirations and foster an organization that is in harmony with the government's multiracial objectives.

Institutional Characteristics

In pursuit of these conflicting objectives, the following arrangements were imposed on MAS:

- Appointments to the board of directors of MAS were made by the government or with its concurrence. In practice, board members were top civil servants from the ministries of Transport and Finance, the Department of Civil Aviation, the state governments of Sabah and Sarawak, and prominent business people and professionals from the private sector.
- The government also appointed the chairman of the board and the managing director.
- The Department of Civil Aviation and the Ministry of Transport regulated the operations of MAS in terms of airport expansion in Malaysia, the acquisition of landing rights abroad, air and airport safety, and so on.
- The government guaranteed all loans and credit facilities granted to MAS.

- The government's consent was required for all major purchases by MAS and other major decisions, including increases in domestic fares, disposals of substantial assets, and amalgamations, mergers, and takeovers.
- The government would compensate MAS for losses incurred on its rural air services in the event that the enterprise's profits were less than 15 percent of its share capital. (Rural airline services are provided by small, often single-engine aircraft and are a very small proportion of total sales. This provision thus does not reflect an automatic subsidy on the bulk of domestic routes.)

Market Characteristics

MAS operates in two distinct spheres: a monopolistic domestic market and an oligopolistic international market. In 1985 the domestic market accounted for almost half of passenger trips, but only a quarter of revenue. The tension between the competing needs of these two markets was manifest in both the 1972 split from Singapore Airlines and the objectives set for MAS. The same tension will be an important element of our analysis.

In the international arena MAS, although bound to abide by the broad guidelines suggested by its organizational objectives, was generally free from government intervention in setting prices, choosing destinations to serve, and establishing service standards. Its decisions on these matters were mainly determined by the pursuit of profit under imperfect market conditions. These imperfections manifested themselves in three ways:

- As protectionism, in the form of demands for reciprocal landing and other rights
- As joint service agreements with other airlines to operate an equal number of flights between two selected cities, charge the same ticket prices, and share the revenues earned (by 1985 MAS was carrying out joint flights with Thai International on two routes and with Singapore Airlines on two other routes—this is obviously a nice solution from the oligopolists' point of view but potentially detrimental to consumer interests)
- As an unnatural monopoly, with MAS enjoying virtual sole carrier rights to transport Malaysian pilgrims to Saudi Arabia to perform the Hajj each year, based on an ongoing contract with the Malaysian Pilgrims Management and Fund Board.

If MAS's international markets fell considerably short of the competitive ideal, its domestic markets were even less competitive. MAS had a virtual monopoly on all routes covering points within Malaysia, including those in the interior of Sabah and Sarawak. The government, however, retained the right to control prices in pursuit of social objectives. The regulatory regime was simplicity itself: from 1983 through 1990 the government did not allow any domestic price increases.

In sum, MAS represents a standard case of public-enterprise cross-subsidization, in which profits in one imperfect market (international) are used to subsidize losses in another imperfect market (domestic). Additional details of the market structure and its consequences will emerge as we proceed.

Divestiture

MAS and the Ministry of Transport took the initiative to divest MAS shares. The consultants' report on the proposed divestiture was completed in January 1985, the cabinet approved the proposal in August of that year, and the following month the prospectus was presented to the public. The share offering took the following form (see table 14-1). Thirty-five million (existing) ordinary shares were reserved for government-approved Bumiputra institutions by way of private placement; 70 million new ordinary shares were issued, with 17.5 million reserved for

Table 14-1. Evolution of Shareholding, Malaysian Airline Systems, April 1979–October 1986

		Flow of shares		Stock of shares	
Date	Event	Number of shares (millions)	Price (M$)	Shares outstanding (millions)	Percentage held by the federal government[a]
April 1979	n.a.	n.a.	n.a.	70	90
September 1985	Bonus issue (4-for-1 stock split)	210	0.0	280	90
October 1985	Sale of government shares	35[b]	1.8	280	78
October 1985	New issue	70[c]	1.8	350	60
October 1986	Sale of government shares	63[d]	4.5	350	42

n.a. Not applicable.

a. Excluding 5 percent each held by the Sabah and Sarawak state governments.

b. To Malaysian institutions.

c. Including at least 17.5 million to MAS employees, who may have picked up more from the general issue.

d. Including 35 million to the Brunei government, with the balance going largely to foreigners.

Source: MAS data.

the employees of MAS and its subsidiaries; the balance were made available to Malaysian citizens, Malaysian companies, societies incorporated in Malaysia, and Malaysian institutions, after reserving 3.0 million shares for an approved institution. All the shares had a par value of M$1.00, but sold at M$1.80.

To ensure government control of critical operating decisions, a golden share was created. The most important feature of this share is that it allows the government to appoint six directors to MAS's board of directors, the chairman, and the managing director. The golden share does not carry any rights to vote at general meetings, but it does entitle the holder to attend and speak at such meetings. Certain matters—in particular, the alteration of specified articles of association of MAS; any substantial disposal of assets; and any amalgamation, merger, or takeover—require the special shareholder's prior consent. The special shareholder also has the right to require MAS to redeem the golden share at par at any time.

The public offering received a subscription of M$717 million; that is, it was oversubscribed by 6.6 times, with the excess demand among Bumiputra applicants allocated by lottery. MAS was listed on the Kuala Lumpur stock exchange in late 1985, and its shares traded at prices ranging from M$1.92 to M$3.10 during the first six months of listing. Since then they have acquired a reputation as blue chips. In 1987 a second tranche of 20 percent of MAS stock was sold to foreigners at M$4.50 per share.

The divestiture had the following effects:

- The government's share of MAS stock decreased from 90 to 42 percent by November 1986.
- The sale of 35 million existing ordinary shares generated gross revenues of M$63 million for the government, while the sale of 70 million new ordinary shares yielded gross proceeds of M$126 million for MAS. The second sale to foreigners, at a considerably higher price than the first, yielded an estimated M$283 million.
- The institutional relationship between MAS and the government described earlier remained essentially unchanged. The special shareholder provision was a clear demonstration of the government's intention to retain control over MAS. There was, however, one important exception: the government would stop guaranteeing MAS loans and credit facilities.

What Happened?

This section compares MAS's performance before and after divestiture to examine what happened in the course of divestiture. The extent to which this correlation is causal is deferred until the next section.

Figure 14-1. Public and Private Profit at Current Market Prices, Malaysian Airline Systems, 1981–90

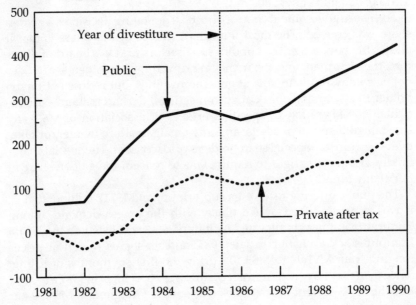

Source: Authors' calculations from MAS data.

Profit and Profitability

PUBLIC VERSUS PRIVATE PROFIT. A natural place to start is with the bottom line of the profit-and-loss statement, which we refer to as private profit (dividends plus retained earnings). As shown in figure 14-1, private profit was negligible or negative from 1981 through 1983, then rose to about M$100 million, where it remained through 1987, and thereafter grew steadily to more than M$200 million in 1990. There are thus two turning points in private profit to be explained: an improvement following the announcement of divestiture and a deterioration following its implementation. These changes in performance, however, may not necessarily be caused by divestiture. There are many reasons for this, but the first is that private profit measures the wrong thing. The rest of this section undertakes a series of measurement adjustments to try and obtain a better measure of the impact of divestiture on national welfare.

The first problem is that while private profit is a useful measure of return to the equityholder, we are really interested in the return to all of society's resources, which we call public profit. As explained in more detail in chapter 2, public profit differs from private profit in three ways:

first, in addition to returns to equityholders, it includes returns to debtholders (interest) and government (direct and indirect taxes); second, to correspond to the economic concept of quasi rents, it excludes nonoperating returns and deducts the opportunity cost of working capital; and third, to correspond to cost-benefit methodology and avoid the use of accounting depreciation rates, profit is measured gross of the depreciation allowance.

As figure 14-1 also indicates, public profit tells a dampened story, being closer to trendless both before and after divestiture (the announcement increment and the implementation decrement remain but are less dramatic in percentage terms). The reason for the discrepancy is that the total size of the pie (public profit or quasi rents) has grown more smoothly than has its distribution. This can be seen in figure 14-2, which decomposes the total surplus (or return to capital). For example, note that the differences from 1981 through 1983 are largely due to rising distributions to debtholders (interest payments) and increases in the allocation of earnings to depreciation reserves.[2]

In sum, inspection of current profit and its distribution yields only minor discontinuities accompanying divestiture. Private profit turned

Figure 14-2. Return to Capital at Current Market Prices, Malaysian Airline Systems, 1981–90

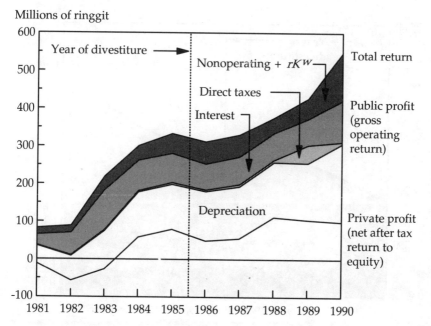

Millions of ringgit

Note: rK^W = opportunity cost of working capital.
Source: Authors' calculations from MAS data.

up markedly with the announcement of divestiture, and public profit somewhat less so. In contrast, the execution of divestiture coincided with a slight drop in performance. This is, of course, nowhere near the end of the story, because we need to look at many other things, including inflation and capital.

CURRENT VERSUS CONSTANT PROFIT. Public profit and its derivation at constant market prices are shown in figure 14-3. Two points are noteworthy. First, the trend is now quite different: we now see that performance—as measured by public profit—improved dramatically from 1981 through 1983 and then leveled off. Second, the improvement in the early years was caused by output rising more rapidly than in later years, which, coupled with roughly stable input coefficients and partially offset by rising labor costs, created a magnified growth of the residual bottom line.

Consideration of returns alone is misleading without simultaneous inspection of that to which they are returned, namely, capital stock.

Figure 14-3. Public Profit at Constant Market Prices, Malaysian Airline Systems, 1981–90

Millions of ringgit

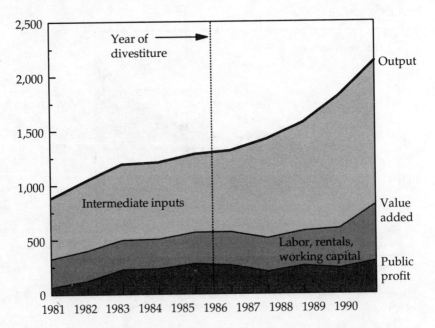

Source: Authors' calculations from MAS data.

Figure 14-4. *Gross Fixed Capital Formation, Malaysian Airline Systems, 1981–90*

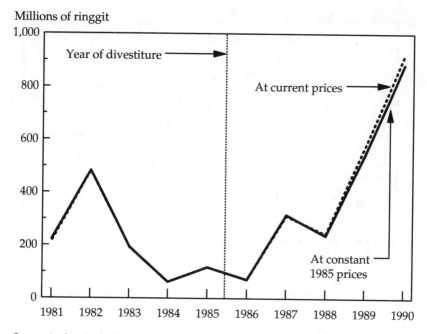

Source: Authors' calculations from MAS data.

FIXED CAPITAL. In contrast to the changes in profit, the discontinuities in fixed capital formation (figure 14-4) are dramatic. At both current and constant prices, fixed capital formation declined precipitously from 1982 through 1984, was then stable at a low level just prior to and just after divestiture, and finally took off dramatically.

The impressive discontinuity in the flows naturally becomes diluted in the corresponding stock measure (not shown), which is ten times larger and includes deterioration. However, real operating assets (at replacement cost) grew at a compound annual rate of only 4 percent from 1983 to 1986, but thereafter grew at more than 16 percent. This upward shift in fixed capital formation is potentially an extremely important change in conduct accompanying divestiture, and in the section on "Why Did It Happen?" we will focus on its causality.

PROFITABILITY. Combining the numerator, profit, with the denominator, capital stock, yields the true bottom line of this subsection, namely, the return to fixed capital, or profitability. As shown in figure 14-5, private profitability and public profitability at current prices show a similar trend of improvement following the announcement of divestiture, a slight dip

Figure 14-5. Private and Public Profitability, Malaysian Airline Systems, 1981–90

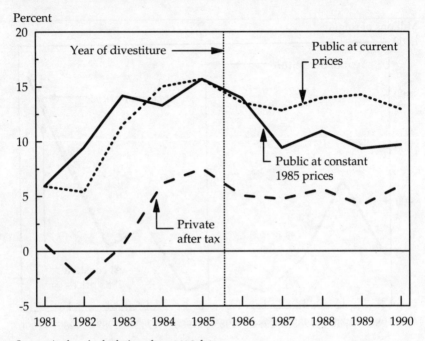

Percent

Source: Authors' calculations from MAS data.

at divestiture, and stability thereafter. Public profitability at constant prices makes divestiture look even less beneficial, eliminating the announcement effect and increasing and prolonging the decline after divestiture.

We have thus far identified three kinks associated with divestiture: a dramatic rise in fixed capital formation, a decline in productivity,[3] and a change in the relative price structure (since real and nominal profitability trends differ). This last observation requires additional investigation, which we shall conduct after issuing a warning against drawing premature conclusions.

PRICE AND QUANTITY DECOMPOSITION. Table 14-2 decomposes changes in public profit (and its components) into price and quantity effects. For each variable, the table reports three pieces of information: how much the value of the variable itself changed over the previous year (in absolute, not percentage, terms), how much of that would have occurred if only prices had changed, and how much would have occurred if only quantities had changed.[4]

As an example, consider the 1990 public profit triplet in the lower right-hand corner of the table. Public profit rose by M$68.2 million between 1989 and 1990, but prices moved against MAS to such an extent that it would have lost M$28.6 million if quantities had not changed in the airline's favor to the tune of M$96.8 million. Contrast this with 1987, when relative prices moved overwhelmingly in MAS's favor, offsetting negative quantity effects.

Examine the following points:

- At the broadest level (public profit), there is no clear trend in relative prices, but quantities are negative only in the two years immediately following divestiture.

Table 14-2. Decomposition of Public Profitability into Price and Quantity Effects, Malaysian Airline Systems, 1982–90
(millions of ringgit)

Component	1982	1983	1984	1985	1986	1987	1988	1989	1990
Output									
Price	18.1	39.8	41.5	–22.0	–15.3	–3.5	44.5	78.7	89.1
Quantity	144.1	143.2	14.4	84.6	19.8	101.9	145.8	240.4	50.0
Value	162.9	183.0	55.8	62.5	4.5	98.3	190.3	319.1	439.1
Less intermediate inputs									
Price	28.9	0.6	–45.4	–10.2	–7.5	–80.7	9.9	21.2	89.8
Quantity	84.2	53.2	5.4	17.2	26.3	132.8	98.5	177.2	82.6
Value	113.1	53.8	–40.1	6.9	18.7	52.2	108.4	198.3	172.3
Equals value added									
Price	–10.1	39.2	86.9	–11.8	–7.8	77.1	34.6	57.5	–0.6
Quantity	60.0	90.1	9.0	67.4	–6.4	–30.9	47.3	63.2	267.4
Value	49.9	129.2	95.9	55.6	–14.2	46.2	81.9	120.7	266.8
Less wages									
Price	34.4	8.0	12.3	18.0	5.4	8.4	27.1	22.8	21.5
Quantity	14.3	–2.2	–1.3	11.9	3.6	7.6	2.6	17.8	59.6
Value	48.7	5.8	11.0	29.9	9.0	16.1	29.7	40.6	81.1
Less rented factors									
Price	–0.9	0.8	1.0	–0.7	–2.1	–1.4	1.7	2.8	2.2
Quantity	–3.5	–8.5	4.5	0.3	7.3	–0.8	4.0	28.5	108.4
Value	–4.5	–7.8	5.5	–0.4	5.3	–2.2	5.7	31.3	110.6
Less opportunity cost of working capital									
Price	–7.3	14.0	0.1	1.9	–8.4	–6.0	–7.6	3.6	4.3
Quantity	1.1	0.8	0.4	0.5	5.6	2.6	1.5	0.8	2.6
Value	–6.2	14.8	0.5	2.4	–2.8	–3.4	–6.1	4.4	6.8
Equals public profit									
Price	–36.3	16.4	73.5	–31.0	–2.8	76.1	13.4	28.3	–28.6
Quantity	48.1	100.0	5.4	54.8	–22.9	–40.4	39.2	16.0	96.8
Value	11.8	116.4	78.9	23.8	–25.7	35.7	52.6	44.3	68.2

Source: Authors' calculations from MAS data.

Figure 14-6.   Average Variable Costs, Malaysian Airline Systems, 1981–90

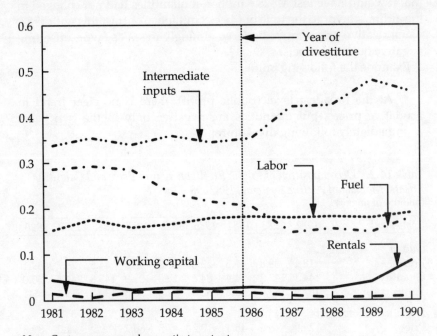

Note: Costs are expressed as a ratio to output.
Source: Authors' calculations from MAS data.

- Output, however, shows a dramatic trend, with relatively modest price effects but quantities rising sharply at the beginning of the period, flat in the middle, and growing rapidly thereafter.
- Intermediate input quantities largely track output, suggesting fixed coefficients, with price increases surprisingly moderate except for the impact of fuel prices, which fell substantially in 1984 and 1987 and rose dramatically in 1990.
- Labor shows steady price increases from 1983 onward (there was a major wage hike of 10 percent in 1982), averaging 4 percent per year, with the number of workers growing substantially only in 1990.
- Working capital shows only small changes, but these are largely caused by prices, because the interest rate varied widely, from a high of nearly 10 percent in 1985 to a low of less than 3 percent in 1988.

Two summary observations follow from these price and quantity decompositions. First, the only significant kink around divestiture is the takeoff in the quantity of output. Whether this was caused by better marketing, relaxation of an investment constraint, macroeconomic recovery, or something else will be a major concern of the next section.

Second, a notable feature of the MAS case, even though it represents continuity rather than change, is the enterprise's ability to stay out of the red despite output price increases being constrained to 2 percent annually during a period when inflation was averaging 3.1 percent. In part this was because MAS's input prices—especially labor and fuel—rose at less than the general rate of inflation, and in part because efficiency improved.

UNIT COSTS. The changing efficiency relationships can be expressed as ratios of particular inputs to outputs, either nominal or real—that is, as unit costs. We will first consider variable costs and then fixed costs in the form of capital-output ratios.

Average variable costs (nominal inputs over real outputs) are shown in figure 14-6. First note the cost structure. Labor and fuel are the two largest individual cost categories, each consuming a fifth or a sixth of revenues. However, the most important category is miscellaneous intermediate inputs, a highly diverse bundle of goods and services.

Inspection of the trend for kinks yields little that is remarkable. Falling fuel prices reduced the unit cost of fuel during the first two-thirds of the

Figure 14-7. *Unit Costs at Constant Prices, Malaysian Airline Systems, 1981–90*

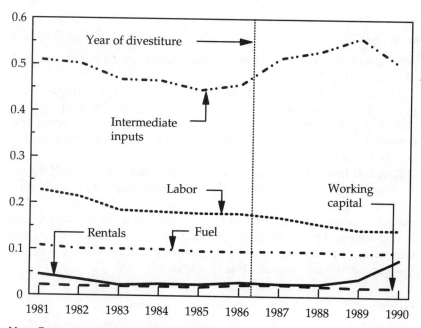

Note: Costs are expressed as a ratio to output.
Source: Authors' calculations from MAS data.

Figure 14-8. Average Capital-Output Ratios, Malaysian Airline Systems, 1981–90

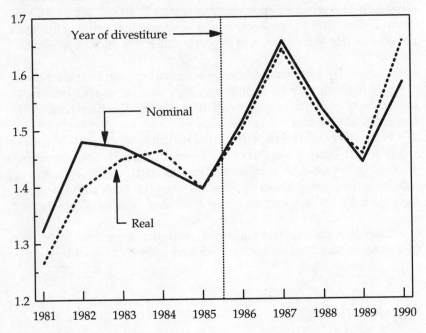

Source: Authors' calculations from MAS data.

period, and rentals substituted for intermediate inputs at the very end of the period.

Taking out the effect of changing input prices as well, figure 14-7 presents real unit costs (real inputs divided by real outputs), or technical coefficients. While again no kink is evident (except the substitution effect mentioned above), labor productivity does show a steady improvement.

Real and nominal average capital-output ratios are shown in figure 14-8. In sharp contrast to the variable unit cost series, these fixed unit costs show a marked turn for the worse following divestiture. That is, the extra capital generated a less than proportional rise in output. This is not necessarily a bad thing, so long as the present value of the incremental return is above the opportunity cost over the life of the investment. We will evaluate this trend later.

Finance

By financial behavior we refer primarily and conventionally to the way in which investment is financed and to the different returns (costs from the enterprise's point of view) to the various sources, that is, to the liabilities and net worth side of the balance sheet and associated flows. As we are looking for evidence of change, we will concentrate on the flows in the form of uses and sources of funds. Under the financial rubric we also, less conventionally, include the management of nonoperating assets.

Figures 14-9 and 14-10 present real and nominal uses and sources of funds. Interpretation is clouded by the anomalous peak and trough in 1989 and 1990, respectively. MAS took out a large volume of loans in 1989 to buy financial assets, which it then liquidated in 1990, using some of the proceeds to acquire capital and some to reduce debt. The resulting kinks are presumably due to the arbitrariness of the fiscal year and the term structure of existing debt: shift the fiscal year by six months and the kinks would go away.

If we make the foregoing adjustment, we may note the following:

- Internal corporate savings were the largest source of funds except in 1982, when MAS borrowed heavily, and in 1985, when divestiture resulted in an infusion of new equity.

Figure 14-9.   Uses of Funds, Malaysian Airline Systems, 1982–90

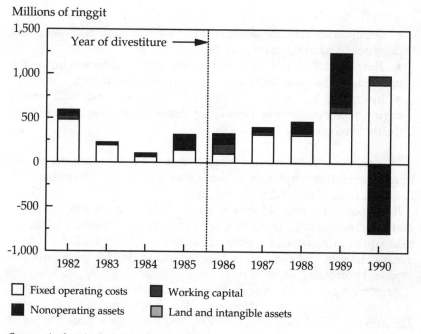

Source: Authors' calculations from MAS data.

Figure 14-10.   Sources of Funds, Malaysian Airline Systems, 1982–90

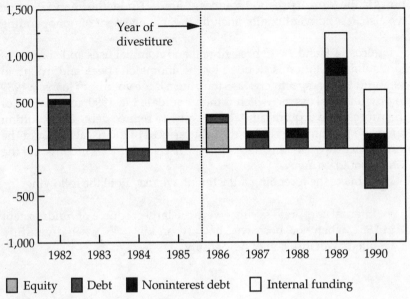

Millions of ringgit

Year of divestiture

☐ Equity   ■ Debt   ■ Noninterest debt   ☐ Internal funding

Source: Authors' calculations from MAS data.

- On the uses side, the dominant feature is the fall and rise in the purchase of fixed operating assets.
- The same fall and rise do not appear as a surge of borrowing on the uses side in 1987 and 1988, which is somewhat surprising.
- Instead of borrowing, MAS financed the 1987 and 1988 capital acquisitions primarily by liquidating financial reserves accumulated during its constrained years.

In sum, the investment constraint appears to have taken the strong form of precluding buying (even using the firm's own funds) rather than the weak form of precluding borrowing.

If we look at sources of funds as a stock rather than as a flow, we see that a decreasing reliance on debt after 1982 caused a marked fall in the debt-equity ratio, which fell from a peak of about 5.0 in 1982 and 1983 to a steady level of 1.3 from 1986 on (after adjusting 1989 for the anomalous year-end borrowing noted above).

Another aspect of financial performance is nonoperating returns. Not much of interest appears here (other than a one-time jump in capital gains on the sale of used assets in 1990), and thus they are not discussed further.

Why Did It Happen?

In the previous section we identified three major changes that were contemporaneous with divestiture: increased investment, declining productivity, and changing relative prices. In this section we examine the extent to which these changes were caused by divestiture. A complete answer to the question of causation requires an explicit statement of the counterfactual, namely, what would have happened in the absence of divestiture.

The Investment Constraint

The investment story is quickly told. In the early to mid-1980s,[5] MAS wanted to expand, and with load factors approaching—and eventually exceeding—the international industry standard of 70 percent, there is a prima facie case that it should have expanded. The government, however, apparently concerned with the fiscal shortfall and the balance of payments deficit, would approve neither domestic nor foreign borrowing. In the wake of the announcement of divestiture, however, the government did begin to approve expansion proposals.

Note three institutional features of this story:

- Managerial behavior did not change. The same set of MAS managers pushed for expansion before and after divestiture.
- Managerial autonomy did not change. The government still had the final say by virtue of any one of three independently sufficient conditions: holding a clear and substantial plurality of shares directly;[6] holding a majority of shares indirectly;[7] and holding a single golden share.[8]
- What did change was the way in which the government exercised its decisionmaking power. Before divestiture it said no; thereafter it said yes.

The critical question is whether or not the change in decisionmaking was due to divestiture, with the government taking the view that, as a "private" entity, MAS should now be allowed to make investment decisions on a purely commercial basis: if MAS wants to borrow and the banks are willing to lend without a government guarantee, then that is MAS's business. It is the unanimous view of those interviewed at MAS and elsewhere that the government did see matters in this light.

The primary competing hypothesis is that changes in the macroeconomic environment relaxed the government's fiscal constraints, and that the government would have allowed MAS to resume investment even without divestiture. This hypothesis is refuted by three arguments. First, although inflation was under control by 1985, the country then plunged into a recession, and the fiscal and balance of payments deficits persisted. Second, other large utilities—especially the telephone system—remained constrained in their investment activity until much later. Third, we can find no one in Malaysia—including some of those involved in the decisionmaking process at MAS—who believes this version of events.

We therefore accept the hypothesis that the investment constraint would not have been relaxed in the absence of divestiture. However, given prior behavior at MAS, subsequent behavior with other public enterprises, and common logic, it is reasonable to assume that, even without divestiture, the government would have eventually released the investment constraint as macroeconomic conditions improved.

The quantitative issues of how much later and how released are, of course, subject to considerable uncertainty. Relevant facts are that the real GDP growth rate rose to 5 percent in calendar year 1987 (largely MAS's fiscal 1988) and to 9 percent in calendar year 1988, and the current account balance turned positive in 1987. Accordingly, for our basic counterfactual scenario we assume a three-year lag; that is, the capacity actually added in 1986 would not have been added until 1989 without divestiture. A further counterfactual question is whether or not, once the constraint was released, MAS would eventually have caught up. Stylized facts of international public-enterprise life are that periodic national fiscal crises result in periodic curtailment of public-enterprise investment. We model this in our base counterfactual by assuming arbitrary five-year cycles, with counterfactual public capital stock catching up to private capital stock linearly over three years, then being held to replacement levels for two years, with the cycle then repeating itself.

Declining Productivity

To what extent can the decline in productivity following divestiture be attributed to divestiture? Two alternative sources of change must be considered. First, there is obviously an exogenous macroeconomic impact following from the Malaysian recession of 1985–86. Second, there is the less obvious endogenous impact of the investment constraint in a monopoly market. These possibilities are analyzed in turn.

MACROECONOMIC IMPACT. In a recession, demand and real output fall, and with significant fixed inputs, total inputs fall less than proportionately and productivity declines. Several factors make this unconvincing as an explanation of the decline at MAS:

- Recall from table 14-2 that, while productivity declined during the recession, recovery did not follow: levels remained roughly constant from 1987 through 1990.
- As shown in figure 14-11, the number of passengers carried did not decline with the recession but grew at a reduced rate: domestic traffic declined marginally, but the larger international load continued to rise in both 1986 and 1987.
- If we take into account other inputs and use revenue weightings, the impact of the recession on output is even less evident (see the output quantity index in table 14-2). The annual real growth of output was 3.5 percent from 1983 to 1985, rising to 5.2 percent from 1985 to 1987.[9]

We need to look elsewhere for the decline in productivity, which means looking at inputs. Figure 14-12 shows clearly that in 1986 and 1987 both fixed and variable real inputs grew more rapidly than real output (it is the relative slopes that matter here, not the levels). The figure is less useful in gauging the relative importance of the two inputs.[10] In fact, the impact of the variable input rise is five times that of the fixed inputs. That

Figure 14-11. Domestic and International Ridership, Malaysian Airline Systems, 1981–90

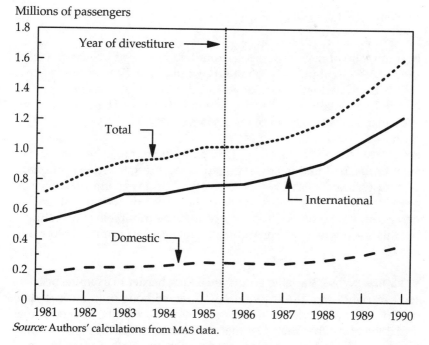

Millions of passengers

Source: Authors' calculations from MAS data.

Figure 14-12. Quantities of Output and of Variable and Fixed Inputs, Malaysian Airline Systems, 1981–90

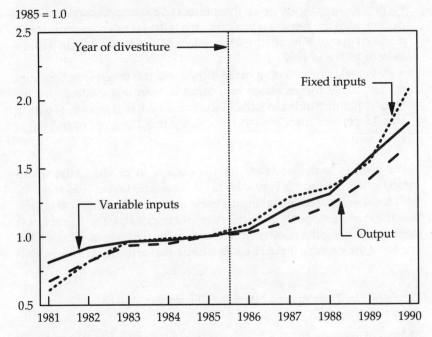

Source: Authors' calculations from MAS data.

is, if the ratio of fixed inputs to output had remained unchanged from 1985 to 1987, real public profitability would have been only 1 percent higher than it actually was. However, if the ratio of variable inputs to output had remained unchanged, it would have been 5 percent higher. We consider the two types of inputs in turn.

FIXED INPUTS. The examination of fixed inputs is straightforward. Recall from figure 14-8 that the average capital-output ratio surged dramatically in 1986 and 1987. This was not caused by any change in efficiency or technology, but by the relaxation of the investment constraint already described. Its impact on productivity is thus attributable to divestiture, but this is a downstream consequence and not a new primary behavioral change.

VARIABLE INPUTS. Variable inputs are a little harder to examine because we can only carry the exploration so far without running into data confidentiality problems. Recall from figure 14-7 that the only real variable input other than fuel that rose relative to real output in 1986, and especially in 1987, was intermediate inputs. Further pinpointing of the change is not possible without releasing proprietary information. However, we are allowed to report (based on detailed accounts made available by MAS) that well over half of the nominal increase came in just two areas: passenger services that were contracted out (primarily meals) and advertising and promotion (also largely carried out by third parties).

The fact that the increase is largely in business services creates a technical problem, because our price index for this category is economy-wide and may or may not accurately reflect the prices for the particular types of services consumed by MAS, and hence our derivation of a real increase may be inaccurate. However, MAS sources confirm that there was a real push toward improving business services at the time.

If this was indeed the case, what interpretation should be put on the increased expenditure? Was it a good thing or a bad thing? Was divestiture responsible? We confess that we have no good evidence on either score, but our informed judgment is that it was a good thing. Investments in the quality of service and in marketing could have a major future return by helping to fill the (by this time) rapidly expanding MAS fleet. We also believe that divestiture was not responsible, except as another indirect consequence of the relaxation of the investment constraint, which created the expanding capacity that needed to be filled.

Note that it is the second judgment that is critical for our analysis, because if the increased expenditure would have occurred anyway, it does not matter whether it is good or bad. Our judgment is once again based on interviews.

SUMMARY OF REASONS FOR DECLINE IN PRODUCTIVITY. In sum, we can draw two conclusions. First, one part of the decline in productivity was caused by a rise in capital relative to output, and four parts were caused by a rise in nonfuel intermediate inputs, largely passenger services and advertising. Second, neither change was attributable to divestiture, except as an indirect consequence of the relaxation of the investment constraint. Critics who would like to show a greater impact of divestiture might well focus on the rise in marketing expenditures. We, however, shall proceed on the assumption of no internal behavioral change.

Improving Relative Prices

Recall that, after divestiture, relative prices turned in MAS's favor. However, this was largely because of falling fuel prices in 1987, a clearly exogenous event. International output prices are likewise independent of divestiture, set by MAS within the loose cartel structure of IATA (the International Air Transport Association). Prices of intermediate inputs are exogenous. This leaves domestic fare structures and wage rates as possibly affected by divestiture.

As noted earlier, domestic fares rose by 25 percent in 1983 and were then held constant for the remainder of the period under review. Management—before and after divestiture—continually requested price increases, but these were denied, most recently in 1991. Although continuity is thus evident in the periods before and after divestiture, we need to ask whether this uniformity will continue.

A priori theorizing can run either way. On the one hand, one could argue that private shareholders will create greater pressure on the government to create profits when other market conditions are unfavorable, thus implying that domestic price increases will be more generous under private operation. On the other hand, one could argue that national airlines set prices so as to use profits in protected domestic markets to cross-subsidize unfair competition with private carriers in international markets, thus implying that price increases will be more generous under public operation.

In the case of MAS there is not much evidence either way. It might be thought that since no domestic price increases were granted in the two years before divestiture or in the six years after, behavior would be identical under both regimes. However, corporate conditions in the period after divestiture never matched those in the period before divestiture. The 1983 price increase followed a drop in return to equity (dividends plus retained earnings, divided by net worth) from 3.5 percent in 1981 to -24 percent in 1982. After divestiture, returns never fell below 15 percent. The question is, How low must earnings fall before triggering a domestic price increase, and how will this differ between public and private regimes?

Our answer for the base counterfactual is based on two premises:

• The public interest of the federal shareholders, reinforced by the 10 percent combined share of Sabah and Sarawak (the two states located off peninsular Malaysia, and thus particularly sensitive to domestic airfares), will preclude domestic price increases so long as some lower-bound level of profits is maintained. If profits fall below that level, domestic fares are raised discontinuously to achieve some target level. This holds true under private and public regimes alike.

• The private interest of private shareholders, however, will operate to ensure a higher lower-bound and a higher target rate under private operation.

For illustrative purposes we therefore set the public lower bound at zero (based on actual behavior during 1981–82), the private lower bound at 5 percent, and the public and private targets at 15 and 20 percent, respectively. The 15 percent band may seem excessive, but the 25 percent jump late in fiscal 1983 led to a return to equity of 35 percent in 1984.

Conclusion

In the previous section we saw that not much changed at the time of divestiture. In this section we have seen that much of what did change was not attributable to divestiture, and that what did change was in the regulatory environment and was not internal to the firm. This judgment about the relative unimportance of divestiture is reflected in MAS's 1986 annual report: the two-page chairman's statement does not mention divestiture; the four-page director's report details the share issue, but says nothing about public and private participation, asserting that "This issue was made to provide additional funds to meet the Company's capital expenditure on aircraft fleet expansion" (MAS 1987, p. 61). The "Highlights of the Year" section does devote one paragraph to divestiture. This paragraph is reproduced below, together with another paragraph given equal emphasis in the report (MAS 1987, p. 99):

The balloting of 52.5 million MAS shares for public subscription on 6 November 1985 marked a new era in MAS development: the national carrier went private, the first government agency to do so under the Malaysian government privatization program. The shares for public subscription was part of the overall issue of 70 million shares—of which 17.5 million were reserved for MAS employees system wide. On 16 December 1985, MAS shares were listed under the Industrial Index of the Kuala Lumpur Stock Exchange.

On 4 March 1986 new uniforms for the female inflight and ground front line staff were launched in a colorful ceremony in conjunction with a cabin crew graduation held in the new MAS Headquarters Building. Our Chairman, YM Raja Tan Sri Mohar and his deputy, YB Datuk Sulaman Sujak, were among the dignitaries who witnessed the glittering occasion. The new uniforms, marking the first change since 1977, features, besides winter attire, the basic sarung kebaya tailored from batik fabric with "cempaka" flower designs against a "kelara" weave pattern.

The implication that privatization had the same importance as a change of stewardess uniforms is either an understatement or an overstatement. It is an overstatement of the importance of privatization if one believes that the investment constraint would have been loosened anyway, that marketing expenditures would have increased in any event, and that there would be no future differences in pricing policy. It is an understatement if one believes the reverse. We are in the latter camp and will proceed to evaluate the welfare implications of these two changes. The uniform change is nonetheless a useful reminder of the comparatively modest internal changes that accompanied MAS's form of divestiture.

In sum, although not much changed internally as a result of divestiture, a good deal changed externally, in the form of relaxed investment and pricing constraints.

What Is It Worth?

Who should care about MAS's divestiture, and why? As shown in table 14-3:

- Consumers (domestic and foreign) should care the most, as they gain a total of M$2,606 million (this and all subsequent figures are in 1985 net present values) from divestiture, equivalent to roughly a quarter of one year's total sales. However, these gains all accrue to foreigners—domestic consumers actually lose M$590 million.[11]
- The Malaysian government should care, as it comes out about M$1 billion ahead, or roughly enough to pay for one year's federal expenditures on health care.[12]
- Buyers of MAS stock (foreign and domestic, including employees) also should care, as they paid a total of M$406 million for shares worth M$1,037 million, for a gain of M$631 million, or 155 percent.[13] Approximately one-quarter of this accrues to foreigners.
- Foreign competitors—primarily Singapore Airlines and Thai International—should care, because they gain the equivalent of M$169 million.
- Overall, the bulk of the gains (nearly 80 percent) accrue to foreigners.

These bold assertions will be amplified and qualified below, but first we note three unique characteristics of the results as a whole:

- Divestiture is sweet (in the sense of Pareto efficient) in that in the aggregate (that is, looking only at functional groups such as consumers and not at their domestic and foreign breakdown), everybody wins and nobody loses. The actors listed above are made better off without anyone else being made worse off.
- That there is a net gain is unsurprising, since our two counterfactuals are responsive to two of the most basic principles of economic policy: get prices "righter," and invest where the benefits of investing seem likely to exceed the costs.
- That no functional group loses is surprising but attributable to the offsetting effects of the two different changes: pricing reform makes consumers a lot worse off, but they are more than compensated by the

Table 14-3. *Distribution of Gains and Losses from Divestiture, Malaysian Airline Systems*
(millions of ringgit, 1985 present values)

Economic actor	Private operation	Public operation	Gains from divestiture
Domestic			
Consumers	22,269	22,859	−590
Government			
Taxes	2,163	1,705	458
Net quasi rents	1,011	834	177
Share sales (less transaction cost)	401	0	401
Debt subsidy or takeover	0	0	0
Others	0	0	0
Total	3,575	2,539	1,036
Shareholders			
Diversified	397	0	397
Concentrated	0	0	0
Employees	79	0	79
Total	476	0	476
Miscellaneous			
Employees (as inputs)	0	0	0
Competitors	0	0	0
Providers	0	0	0
Citizens	0	0	0
Total domestic	26,320	25,398	922
Foreign			
Consumers	19,128	15,932	3,196
Shareholders	155	0	155
Competitors	1,219	1,050	169
Others	0	0	0
Total foreign	20,502	16,982	3,519
Total	46,821	42,380	4,442

Source: Authors' calculations.

expansion of capacity from the investment reform; shareholders, in contrast, are made a little worse off by the investment change, but they are more than compensated by the pricing change.

The last observation leads to a general organizing principle: in the case of MAS, understanding the impact of the pricing and investment regimes independently is quite easy, but their interaction is occasionally opaque. Accordingly, we proceed by describing the two regimes independently.

This has the further advantage of informing those who might believe one of our counterfactual stories, but not the other.

The Identity Regime

Table 14-4 provides an overview of the next few sections by showing various values of MAS under each of four different regimes. The left-hand column assumes that nothing changes as a result of divestiture (the identity regime), the next two columns display the impact of pricing and investment changes independently, and the last column gives our basic story (summarized above) of both investment and pricing changes.

Table 14-4. Regime Comparisons, Malaysian Airline Systems
(millions of ringgit)

Value		Price =	Public	Public	Private	Private
		Investment =	Public	Private	Public	Private
V_{pp}						
Production			2,649	2,668	3,431	3,526
Financial			−2,248	−2,379	−2,382	−2,489
Total			400	289	1,049	1,037
V_{sp}						
Production			30,271	31,806	31,046	31,677
Financial			−4,744	−5,285	−4,994	−5,352
Total			25,527	26,521	26,052	26,325
V_{sg}						
Production			30,271	30,225	30,271	30,225
Financial			−4,828	−4,828	−4,828	−4,828
Total			25,443	25,398	25,443	25,398
$V_{sp} - V_{sg}$						
Production			0	1,580	744	1,451
Financial			84	−457	−166	−524
Total			79	1,118	604	922
Distribution						
Consumers			0	4,572	−895	2,606
+ Government			1	−70	925	1,036
+ Buyers, etc.			−6	−117	643	631
+ Competitors			0	169	0	169
+ World welfare change			−5	4,554	673	4,442
= Foreigners			−84	3,436	70	3,519
= Domestic welfare change			79	1,118	604	922

Source: Authors' calculations.

The identity regime assumes that the divestiture accomplished nothing and that the divested MAS behaves exactly the same as if it had not been divested. As such, it serves as the baseline of our analysis. Note only the following:

- Since nothing material changes as a result of divestiture, the only world welfare impact is the loss of the transaction costs of executing the sale, which we estimate at M$5 million.
- Under business as usual, our calculations show the private value of the firm (V_{pp}) to be M$379 million, which is equivalent to a per share value of M$2.38. This is not dramatically above the actual price set for the initial offering (M$1.8). Given the usual discount for initial public offerings, the initial share price was not unreasonable for the firm as it had traditionally been run.
- Although aggregate welfare does not change, its distribution does. Domestic shareholders who bought at the low initial price would have gained M$79 million, while (mostly) foreign shareholders who bought at the higher second-round price of M$4.5 would have lost M$84 million.
- Given the losses to foreign shareholders, domestic welfare would actually have been enhanced under this regime. Recall that this is simply a hypothetical baseline: it is, of course, unlikely that foreigners could have been induced to pay M$4.5 per share under these conditions.

The Pricing Regime

Recall our basic pricing assumption that international fares are set exogenously, but domestic fares are adjusted to maintain profitability within a target band. Under public operation that band is 0 to 15 percent, but under private operation we conjecture that it would rise to 10 to 25 percent. Under the pure pricing regime (column three in table 14-4), investment is held constant at the identity level, where significant excess demand is present. Accordingly, quantities do not respond to the changing domestic prices; there is only a reduction in unfulfilled demand. The primary distributional results are as follows:

- As expected, consumers lose substantially (M$895 million) from the higher prices. Only domestic routes are affected, so domestic consumers bear virtually all the loss (the small foreign loss of M$70 million is from foreigners taking domestic flights).
- As also expected, shareholders and the government gain from the higher prices (M$643 and M$925 million, respectively).
- Unexpectedly, however, the first two effects do not offset one another. Under the conditions described (rising prices with fixed capacity and excess demand), one would have expected a precisely

offsetting transfer of surplus from consumers to producers. However, as can be seen, there is a net gain in domestic welfare. Why?

• Part of the explanation is that some of the consumer loss accrues to foreigners, who are given zero weight in the domestic welfare calculation. However, foreigners are only a small part of the domestic market, and, in any event, world welfare also rises.

• The bulk of the explanation comes from a sometimes neglected reason for getting prices righter, namely, the welfare costs of rationing. With excess demand, rationing is required. If this is done by any mechanism other than willingness to pay, welfare is reduced, as people whose demand for travel is weaker are accommodated at the expense of those with stronger demand. In this environment, raising prices reduces the welfare costs of rationing and creates a net gain for society.[14] Under our assumptions, the resulting net gain in welfare is M\$673 million.[15]

• Competitors are unaffected, as the price changes only affect domestic markets, where there is no competition.

In sum, under the pure pricing regime, divestiture shifts quasi rents from consumers to producers, but the gains exceed the losses. Recipients of quasi rents—the government and shareholders—gain more than consumers lose, but consumers' losses are substantial.

The Investment Regime

The second consequence of divestiture at MAS was relaxation of the investment constraint. The divested enterprise is hypothesized to invest so as to meet demand, given prices. The public enterprise, in contrast, is periodically prohibited from investing by federal fiscal concerns. In a few years, the constraint is relaxed and the public enterprise catches up to the divested enterprise, only to start falling behind again thereafter. That is, public capacity does not diverge continuously from private capacity, but rather lags during the early part of a five-year cycle, then catches up fully.

The pure investment regime is somewhat impure in that domestic prices are not held constant across the public and private stories; rather, regulatory regimes are held constant. That is, both enterprises are assumed subject to the same 0 to 15 percent band, but this results in somewhat different price structures because of the different levels of investment, revenues, and costs. The goal is to see what happens as a result of relaxing the investment constraint without changing the pricing rules.

Unlike the pure price regime, the investment change affects international markets, so we must specify the competitive response of other carriers. As already noted, the bulk of MAS's international revenues are from highly imperfect markets, with entry restricted by reciprocal allocation of landing rights. Although there is a continuum of imperfections, we capture the essence of the structure as a weighted average (40 percent and 60 percent, respectively) of two extreme international markets, one of which is competitive and the other of which is a cooperative duopoly. For the competitive sector think of the long haul from Kuala Lumpur to London. The competition comes from the consumers' alternative of dropping down to Singapore and taking any carrier they like from there. On such routes there are no rents accruing to competitors, and there is no consumer surplus. For the cooperative duopoly, think of MAS's and Singapore Airlines' sharing of the traffic on the Singapore–Kuala Lumpur route. The question then is, If MAS cannot expand on this route, does Singapore Airlines take up the slack or not? Given the secrecy of the relevant agreements, we confess to some uncertainty on this issue. Our assumption, however, is that for relatively short lags of a few years such as we are positing, the Malaysian government will not agree to an expansion of slots unless MAS is in a position to maintain its share. Accordingly, the investment constraint also affects the competitors on these routes, and the amount of revenue to be shared falls. Rising load factors take up some of the slack, but the competition also loses from the constraint and gains from its removal.

Shown in column two of table 14-4, more important distributional consequences of such an environment are as follows:

- Consumers—both domestic and foreign—prosper because of the expansion of capacity.
- In contrast, recipients of quasi rents—shareholders and the government—are losers, essentially because the allowed average rate of return on the extra investment is less than the cost of debt to fund it.
- Competitors gain, because additional profits in the duopoly routes are not offset (as at MAS) by pricing policies in domestic markets.

In sum, expanding investment without changing the pricing regime is good for consumers, but bad for those who have to foot the bill.

The Divestiture Regime

Putting the two pure regimes together yields the base results described at the beginning of this section and shown in column four of table 14-4. The losses to consumers from higher prices are more than offset by the gains from higher investment levels, and the losses to producers from higher investment are more than offset by the gains from higher prices. The two sets of policies interact to produce a cyclical pattern. Only two additional points require emphasis at this point. First, domestic consumers still come out behind because they pay the entire bill in terms of higher prices, but receive only a portion of the benefits in terms of expansion of capacity. Second, shareholders are essentially indifferent between the pure pricing regime and the joint regime, as in either case they are guaranteed the same high rate of return on their investment and will pay the same for that return whether at a lower or a higher level of activity.

Summary and Lessons

The facts of the MAS case, interpreted through the twin lenses of theory and judgment, have led us to the following conclusions on the consequences of the MAS version of divestiture:

- Absolutely nothing discernible changed within the enterprise. Responses to the external environment were unchanged.
- Outside the enterprise, absolutely nothing changed in the government's power to intervene in MAS's decisions. What did change was the way in which the government chose to exercise this discretion.
- In particular, the government got both investment and prices "righter" in that economic factors played a larger and political factors a smaller (although still far from negligible) role in deciding outcomes.
- As a result of the new investment decisions, consumers gained at the expense of capitalists (the government and private shareholders), while the change in pricing had the opposite impact. The net impact was positive for both groups, however. Competitors also gained, so world welfare increased.
- A considerable portion of the gains leaked to foreign shareholders, consumers, and competitors, however, so that domestic welfare gains were only about a fifth of the total.
- In particular, domestic consumers were net losers, as they paid all the costs of the higher prices but received only a fraction of the benefits of the expanded investment.

The following hypotheses on divestiture are consistent with the MAS case but, of course, not proved by it:

- Partial financial divestiture is a largely cosmetic exercise, in the sense that the government's power to intervene is unchanged.
- Partial financial divestiture can nonetheless be beneficial if the introduction of private shareholders shifts the exercise of government discretion in the direction of more economically rational decisions. The fact that these same decisions *could* have been taken without divestiture is irrelevant if they *would* not have been taken.

- When divesting enterprises with market power, the regulatory regime is critical. Market power allows consumers to be exploited for political ends under public operation and for capitalist ends under private operation. Constraining this exploitation is essential under both regimes.
- In optimizing the regulatory regime, careful attention must be given to the leakage of benefits to foreigners.

Notes

This chapter was written by Leroy Jones and Fadil Azim Abbas with Yong-Min Chen. In addition to those listed at the beginning of this volume, the authors would like to acknowledge the cooperation received from the following individuals at Malaysian Airline Systems: Tan Sri Abdul Aziz Rahman (managing director), Noor Amiruddin Nordin (manager, research and data), and S. Supiah (manager, accounts).

1. The material in this section is based largely on Danker (1981), Malaysian International Merchant Bankers Berhad (1985), Malaysia, Government of (1989), and MAS (various years).

2. The most glaring difference is the 1989 tax bump, which was caused by exhaustion of accumulated investment write-offs. The 1990 rise in nonoperating returns was caused by a one-time jump in gains on used aircraft sold during the period.

3. Public profitability in real terms attempts to measure the efficiency relationship between real inputs and real outputs, as does productivity.

4. The cross-product effect (changing prices on changing quantities) is arbitrarily allocated to the pure effects in proportion to those pure effects.

5. Decisions made from 1981 or 1982 through 1984 or 1985 and affecting fixed capital formation from 1983 through 1986.

6. The government's residual 42 percent share would suffice for control of most corporations with diversified private shareholders, but, to be on the safe side, there is an additional proviso precluding anyone but the government or its agent from "holding shares representing more than 10% of the issued shares or from exercising more than 10% of the total voting rights" (MAS Articles of Association, Article 66).

7. The state governments of Sabah and Sarawak held 5 percent each throughout the period, which made for a government majority when added to the federal government's 42 percent. In addition, various public enterprises held shares, which were thus ultimately controlled by the government; for example, for most of the period Permodalan Nasional Berhad held about 8 percent.

8. Recall that, among other things, the golden share allowed the government to appoint six of the eleven directors.

9. As also shown in table 14-2, prices did fall somewhat during the recession, but this does not affect the productivity index (except insofar as relative price changes affect the weighting).

10. This is in part because capital stock changes are dampened when we calculate profitability by taking an average of beginning and ending stocks, and in part because the variable inputs are differenced whereas the fixed inputs are a ratio.

11. Gains to foreign consumers include both their gains as international passengers and their losses as domestic passengers. The same holds true for domestic consumers.

12. Our estimate of the gain is M$1,036 million; 1985 federal expenditures on health care totaled M$1,097 million (World Bank 1988, vol. III, table 3.2, p. 34).

13. Buyers (largely domestic) paid M$1.8 per share for 105 million shares in fiscal 1986, and mostly foreign buyers paid M$4.5 per share for another 63 million shares in fiscal 1987. Discounting to our base year of fiscal 1985 yields M$406 million.

14. The standard objection to this line of reasoning is that effective demand is a function of income, and that giving commodities to the poor at the expense of the rich creates not a loss but a gain. This is valid when talking about rice, but we feel comfortable in ignoring it for airline travelers, who are typically, if not exclusively, well into the top half of the income distribution.

15. Recall our emphasis in chapter 2 on the limitations of assuming a linear demand curve. In general, this is acceptable because we are working at the margin and differencing the results. Here, however, we are not working at the margin, and a nonlinear demand curve would yield quite different results. If the real demand curve were concave to the origin, the losses from rationing would be considerably greater. Accordingly, our estimate of the gains is conservative.

15. *Kelang Container Terminal*

"They sold the gold mine and kept the coal mine," was how one union leader described the deal in which the Malaysian government divested 33 percent of the revenues and 56 percent of the profits (revenue and profits for 1983 from ASEAM Bankers Malaysia Berhad 1984, pp. 28–36), but only 13 percent of the labor force[1] in selling the container operations of Kelang Port Authority (KPA). Kelang is Malaysia's principal port, serving the capital region. The first distinguishing characteristic of this case, therefore, is that it is a special case of divestiture by horizontal dis-integration, in which the government breaks up a multiproduct enterprise prior to sale. This is widely recommended as a means of fostering competition where some of the product markets are potentially competitive and thus clearly belong in the private sector, and others are not and therefore require public ownership or regulation. This case is special in that what was sold was not the most competitive activity, but the most lucrative one. There is, of course, nothing wrong with selling a gold mine if one gets enough in return. The analytical question then is, How much did the government receive compared with what it gave up?

In the Kelang Container Terminal (KCT) case, the sale of the gold mine was considerably more benign than it might have been because it was kept largely within the family, with the husband keeping roughly half and most of the rest going to the wife. That is, a second distinguishing feature of the KCT case is that only about 10 percent of the shares were actually sold to the private sector. The remainder went to other public enterprises, so the government only relinquished a small fraction of the revenues from its "gold mine." This is not necessarily a mere cosmetic change, because while the government retains ownership, the way it is exercised may be quite different than before: indirectly held public enterprises are often accorded considerably greater autonomy than those directly controlled. The analytical question here is whether or not this change in the form of public ownership generates positive efficiency benefits that exceed the transaction cost and the leakage to private (in this case foreign) minority owners.

Regardless of the impact on efficiency, distribution among ethnic groups was affected because the Bumiputra Investment Foundation, a financial intermediary that managed unit trusts for ethnic Malay investors, ultimately owned the bulk of KCT shares that went to public enterprises. The third distinguishing characteristic of the case, therefore, is that New Economic Policy (NEP) interests were fostered through an increased share of container revenues passing through to the Bumiputra.[2] The analytical question here is, How much did the Bumiputra gain?

A fourth characteristic is that while the sale promoted horizontal dis-integration, it also fostered vertical integration: the dominant partner (80 percent) of the dominant buyer (of 51 percent of KCT) is Kontans Nasional Sendirian Berhad, which is the dominant firm in the downstream four-firm oligopoly that handles all container transport out of the port. The analytical question here is whether or not the resulting linkage between KCT and Kontans Nasional Sendirian Berhad reduces downstream competition.

The final distinguishing characteristic is the unique role of labor. In all countries, unions are potential losers from divestiture and typically oppose sale. In the Kelang case the unions became (ex post) supporters of the divestiture of KCT and even more ardent advocates of the divestiture of the balance of KPA. The reason is not hard to find: transferred workers received an immediate raise of 20 percent, an increment that has since risen to as much as 50 percent. Spouses of neighbors who were and were not transferred are not reluctant to point out the differences to their unionized husbands. Analytically, the question is whether the government gained anything from this windfall transfer, either economically in the form of enhanced motivation and efficiency, or politically in the form of enhanced labor support for future divestitures (Kelang was the first Malaysian sale).

Background

The history of KCT dates back to 1973, when KPA added container services at Port Kelang to its existing port services.[3] Under the KPA three units provided container services: the Container Terminal Department, the Container Mechanical Engineering Department, and the Container Security Section. Services included four major types of operations— dockside, dock to container stacking yard, container stacking yard, and container stacking yard to consignee—as well as a variety of ancillary services.

Under KPA management, container traffic grew steadily (table 15-1). Even though service charges for using the container terminal remained unchanged over the entire predivestiture period, the container terminal accounted for one-third of KPA's revenues and more than half of its

Table 15-1. *Throughput, Market Share, and Growth Ratio of Traffic, Kelang Container Terminal, 1980–89*

Category	1980	1981	1982	1983	1984	1985	1986	1987	1988	1989
Port Kelang throughput (thousands of FT)										
Conventional	7,725	7,512	8,021	8,488	8,520	8,296	7,990	8,242	9,714	11,009
Containerized	2,221	2,375	2,523	3,046	3,837	4,166	4,313	4,932	6,154	7,297
Total	9,954	9,887	10,544	11,534	12,357	12,462	12,303	13,174	15,686	18,306
Market share of containers (percentages)	22	24	24	26	31	33	35	37	39	40
Average annual compound growth rates (percent)				1980–84		1984–86		1986–89	1981–89	
Conventional				3.2		-0.6		9.9	4.0	
Containerized				11.0		16.9		15.0	14.1	
Total				5.0		3.9		10.1	7.0	

Source: KCT data.

profits (ASEAM Bankers Malaysia Berhad 1984, pp. 28–36). In the midst of this considerable achievement, the Malaysian government decided in 1983 that it would embark on a policy of divestiture. In 1984 it announced that KCT would be the first unit to be divested under this program. The decision was attributed to the prime minister himself.

Divestiture

The process of divestiture was long and difficult, lasting more than two years (November 1983 to March 1986), and can be summarized as follows:

- KPA incorporated KCT on 30 October 1985 as its wholly owned subsidiary.
- KPA then awarded KCT a twenty-one-year license to operate the container terminal.
- KPA then sold 51 percent of KCT shares to Konnas Terminal Kelang Sendirian Berhad (KTK) for M$56.9 million. The sale only involved movable equipment and did not include the wharves, the container stacking area, or land, because of the legal complexities of transferring title to such publicly owned properties. KTK was selected from among six bidders, all of which were joint ventures between Malaysian and foreign interests. KTK was a joint venture of Kontans Nasional Sendirian Berhad (80 percent) and P & O Australia (20 percent). P & O was a private company with long experience in container terminal management as well as in shipping, stevedoring, and cold storage facilities. Kontans Nasional Sendirian Berhad, a road container transport company licensed to haul containers to and from Port Kelang and any point in peninsular Malaysia, was in turn owned by the Bumiputra Investment Foundation (82 percent), the Malaysian International Shipping Corporation (7.5 percent), the National Corporation (7.5 percent)—all government owned and/or controlled enterprises—and others (3 percent). The sale was effected on 17 March 1986.
- The lease, like the license, was for a period of twenty-one years. It required KCT to pay KPA an annual rental of M$17 million, with a 10 percent increase every three years. Furthermore, three months after the sale, KCT had to begin paying 2.5 percent over operating costs for firefighting and security services provided by KPA. KCT also had to bear the financial costs of routine maintenance and depreciation of the leased equipment, and was to make an additional payment of M$150 per container if the annual throughput were to exceed 335,000 twenty-foot-equivalent container units (TEUs). Finally, KCT was responsible for making major repairs to the leased facilities and for purchasing new capital equipment.

- KCT absorbed all employees of KPA who were directly involved in operating the terminal. They were afforded terms no less favorable than those they had enjoyed under KPA; guaranteed employment with KCT for at least five years (subject to the normal reasons for termination, such as showing a gross lack of discipline or having reached retirement age); and assured of enjoying accrued pension benefits earned while working for KPA. Workers were given the option of staying with KPA or, if they joined KCT, to continue working at KPA pay scales. All chose to transfer to KCT on KCT's terms.
- To protect national interests, KPA retained price-setting authority. In addition, the government amended the Port Authorities Act to allow the prime minister to withdraw the use of any port service in the event of a public emergency or in the interests of public safety.
- The government originally envisaged that KCT shares would be sold publicly on the Kuala Lumpur stock exchange. The plan was to offer 35 percent of the shares to the general public and 5 percent to KCT employees, with KTK retaining 40 percent and KPA 20 percent. As of 1991, this had not been done.

Institutional Characteristics

KPA was a typical public corporation. As an authority it was financially autonomous and had its own specialized staff. Financial autonomy meant that it was empowered and expected to raise funds for its activities and that it had to pay corporate taxes. Having its own staff meant that it had the power to hire and fire its staff and that they were not transferable to other government agencies. KPA was primarily responsible to the Ministry of Transport, with control also exercised by other government agencies (namely, the Ministry of Finance, the Economic Planning Unit, and the Selangor State Secretariat) represented on the board of directors and the management committee. In addition, KPA sought advice and feedback from several other government agencies, users' associations, chambers of commerce and industry, and political parties through its Port Consultative Committee (KPA 1983, pp. 4–8). These arrangements indicate that despite the legal authority given to KPA under the Port Authorities Act, its management was very much circumscribed by various government bodies. How different was KCT?

KCT is legally a private limited company, but it remains public in the sense that government entities own 90 percent of its equity. A nine-member board of directors guides KCT in the performance of its functions. Four of these, including the chairman and deputy chairman, are from Kontans Nasional Sendirian Berhad; one represents P & O Australia; and the four others represent KPA, the Treasury, the Ministry of Transport, and the Economic Planning Unit.[4] Clearly, KCT remains subject to govern-ment authority should the government choose to exercise it.

In terms of management, since its incorporation KCT's underlying policy has been asserted to be a compelling desire to operate as a commercial entity. According to its present chief executive officer, "As a commercial entity we have ... to conduct our affairs in a business like manner and to try and inculcate the same business approach in our work-force" (*Straits Shipper*, 5 March 1991b, p. 5).

KCT's management policy is reflected in the goals it set after taking over the container terminal, namely, ensuring the effective deployment of workers and machines; increasing dockside equipment; providing labor with better working conditions, higher wages, and improved benefits and incentives and generally treating labor as the most import-ant factor in the organization; and improving work systems (including changing and improving operational procedures relating to ship and box transport), developing direct-user relations, enhancing employees' skills, and restructuring the organization (*Straits Shipper*, 5 March 1991b, p. 5; 18 March 1991c, p. 7).

Perhaps the best testimony to the propriety of KCT's management policy is that the enterprise's employee union officials largely concur with and support the steps management has taken. This is not to say that they do not have any grievances, but rather that the grievances (wages should be higher and the government's plan to list KCT on the stock exchange should be expedited) are separate issues and do not reflect a rejection of the productivity improvement sought by management (authors' discussion with union officials, June 1991).

Market Characteristics

KCT has a monopoly on container traffic in and out of the capital region. Competition is provided by conventional cargo at KPA and by container traffic at Singapore and, within Malaysia, at Pasir Gudang in the south, Penang in the north, and Kuantan in the east. The magnitude of the competition from the other ports is indicated by a 1985 estimate that 50,000 TEUs flowed through Singapore to the Kelang service area, or about 20 percent of that moving through Kelang itself (ASEAM Bankers Malaysia Berhad 1984, p. 26).

The extent of competition from conventional cargo is suggested by the trend in container versus conventional cargo flowing through Port Kelang. As shown in table 15-1, container traffic averaged 36 percent of total tonnage cleared through the port from 1980 through 1989. How-ever, from 1981 to 1989 container traffic grew at more than twice the rate of conventional cargo (14 percent versus 4 percent a year). The market share of containers rose from 22 percent in 1980 to 40 percent in 1989.

What Happened and Why?

Coincident with divestiture in March 1986, KCT's performance improved markedly. As shown in figure 15-1, public profitability at current market prices grew at an annual average compound rate of only 1.9 percent from 1981 to 1986, but at a rate of 11.6 percent from 1986 to 1990.[5] These improvements occurred despite unfavorable price movements in both periods. Taking away these price effects therefore further enhances the performance story: public profitability at constant market prices grew at an annual average compound rate of 4.7 percent in the period before divestiture and at 17.7 percent after divestiture.

The divestiture of KCT thus correlates with a distinct positive kink in performance. The question is how much of this relationship is causal.[6] To answer this question, we first note that the accounting source of the kink is in the numerator (public profit) rather than the denominator (fixed assets). The latter was roughly stable from 1982 to 1987 and then began to rise significantly, indicating that it did not contribute to the kink but retarded performance (in the accounting sense) thereafter. It follows

Figure 15-1. Private and Public Profitability, Kelang Container Terminal, 1981–90

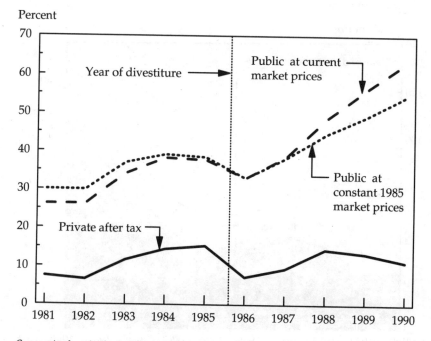

Source: Authors' calculations from KCT data.

that improved performance was caused by a rise in profits that first preceded and then exceeded the increase in the capital stock.

Output

The composition of public profit is given in figure 15-2 at current prices. Note that performance clearly tracks output, with labor and intermediate inputs rising far less rapidly than output. This is equally true before and after divestiture, with the 1983 and 1984 output surges yielding substantial gains in profits.

It follows that if we can explain output changes, we can explain much of the performance changes. To what extent was the increased output due to the endogenous consequences of divestiture and to what extent to exogenous demand shifts?

PRICE EFFECTS. How much of the output change was due to changing prices? Figure 15-3 shows that the answer is a simple, surprising, and dramatic "none." The only price change during the entire period was a decrease in free storage time from seven to five days late in 1986. We

Figure 15-2. *Public Profit at Current Market Prices, Kelang Container Terminal, 1981–90*

Thousands of ringgit

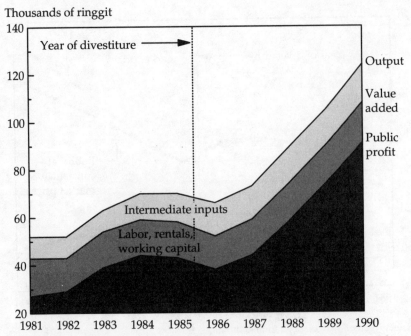

Source: Authors' calculations from KCT data.

Figure 15-3. Decomposition of Output into Price and Quantity Effects, Kelang Container Terminal, 1983–90

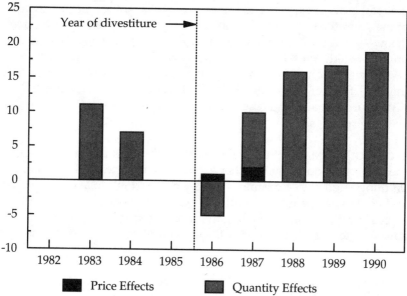

Thousands of ringgit

Note: Data are at current market prices.
Source: Authors' calculations from KCT data.

translate this into a 28.6 percent increase in the price of storage, which in turn caused a 3.9 percent increase in the price of total output spread over 1986 and 1987 (on the arbitrary assumption that average storage time was seven days). Output changes were therefore virtually all on the real side.

ALTERNATIVES. What then caused the real output changes? There are six relevant possibilities:

- Exogenous increased demand for cargo services
- Exogenous deterioration in services by competitors, which increased Kelang's share of the market
- Actions by KCT to increase the demand for cargo services—actions that would not have been taken without divestiture
- Actions by KCT to increase the demand for cargo services that would have been undertaken even without divestiture
- Actions by KCT to increase market share that would not have been taken without divestiture
- Actions by KCT to increase market share that would have been undertaken even without divestiture.

We dismiss the second possibility out of hand: the primary competitors are in Singapore, and the staff we interviewed at KPA were not aware of any significant changes there. We also dismiss the third and fourth possibilities on the grounds that transport charges are a small fraction of the total costs of exports and imports, port charges are a small fraction of that, and the improvements in service quality at Kelang—described below—were only a fraction of that. Furthermore, some part of any impact would have happened without divestiture, so any counterfactual is still smaller. Therefore, as a first approximation, we may assume that the total flow of cargo into Kelang's service area was unaffected by divestiture. What then is the relative importance of the first, fifth, and sixth alternatives?

EXOGENOUS DEMAND SHIFTS. The first possibility is indeed a certainty, the only question being whether exogenous demand shifts explain everything. Figure 15-4 examines this by comparing Malaysian real GDP and container quantity (output) indexes. The results provide surprisingly strong support for the hypothesis that endogenous factors played a major role. Quantities moving through the terminal before divestiture

Figure 15-4.   Output at Kelang Container Terminal and Gross Domestic Product, Malaysia, 1981–90

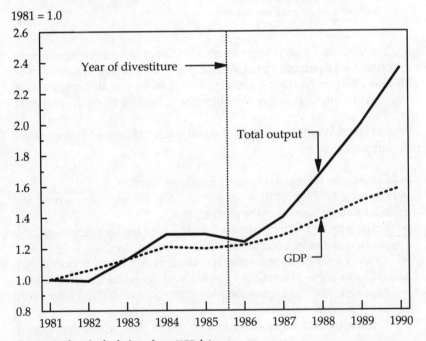

1981 = 1.0

Source: Authors' calculations from KCT data.

grew at a rate very close to the real GDP growth rate; thereafter they grew considerably faster. It is, of course, possible that something discontinuous happened on the demand side to shift the historical relationship, but we know of no such event. What might have happened internally?

ENDOGENOUS MARKET SHARE. Many people believed that conditions at the terminal in the early 1980s were of concern to the consumer. A Malaysian scholar (Salleh n.d., p. 5) writes, "By the early 1980's . . . there was mounting concern that if conditions did not improve, Port Kelang might be blacklisted by international shippers." He also notes (p. 3), "The facility was suffering from excessive congestion. There was continuous complaint about low productivity, pilferage had reached disturbingly high levels and security was lax by international standards." According to a World Bank paper (Levy and Menendez 1989, p. 6), "In the late 70's and early 80's, the operating efficiency of the container terminal was rated as poor by the shipping companies, although KPA was able to show some improvements by the mid 80's."

Concern about the impact of this performance on Malaysian trade prospects was one of the factors that placed the container terminal at the head of the divestiture list. An impressive analysis of the problems and a list of proposals to rectify them was one of the factors that led to the selection of the winning bidder for the terminal. The winner noted that (Kontans Nasional Sendirian Berhad and P & O Australia 1989, pp. 3–5):

> Operating systems in respect of receiving and delivery, terminal yard, ship planning and ship working are inadequate to enable the terminal to operate at optimum efficiency levels. . . . Current productivity levels within the terminal are well below the levels achieved at major competitive ports in the region. . . . Equipment downtime is high, there is a lack of pre-planning and co-ordination and equipment drivers lack expertise and motivation. . . . There is no formalized planned maintenance program. . . . Equipment downtime is high due to lack of skill and understanding of the equipment by the drivers. . . . Inexperience and certain inefficiencies of third parties have contributed to the low levels of productivity. The parties concerned include customs, freight forwarders, consignees, consignors and in some cases inland haulers and immigration. . . . There is no evidence of a detailed and well planned marketing strategy which will attract new business and retrieve lost cargo to the port.

Management reforms implemented after divestiture quickly altered consumers' perceptions. The London-based Trio Consortium of major shipping lines annually evaluates container port performance. In 1985, Port Kelang was eleventh of the fifteen rated ports. Its ranking improved quickly to seventh in 1986, sixth in 1987, and fourth in 1988, before

Figure 15-5.   Performance at Kelang Container Terminal and Seven Other East Asian Ports, 1985–89

Average crane moves per hour

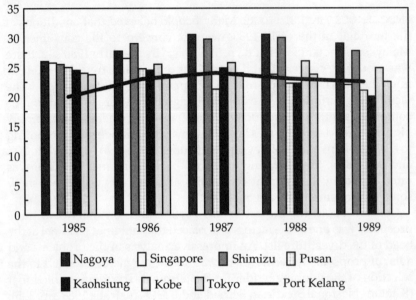

■ Nagoya   ☐ Singapore   ▨ Shimizu   ☐ Pusan

■ Kaohsiung   ☐ Kobe   ☐ Tokyo   ──── Port Kelang

Source: Mohamed (1990).

dropping back to seventh in 1989 and sixth in 1990 (first two years reported in Havelka and Havelka 1990, p. 204; subsequent years as reported by KCT). Even in the last year, Port Kelang rated higher than Bremerhaven, Hamburg, Hong Kong, Jeddah, Kaohsiung, Le Havre, Pusan, Rotterdam, and Southampton.

The basis for these rankings is primarily time, which is money for capital-intensive shipping companies. One standard measure of time is crane moves per hour. This indicator is used in figure 15-5 to compare Kelang's performance with that of some other East Asian ports. Kelang shows a rapid rise to a plateau of performance comparable with international standards by 1987.

In sum, improvements in container operations appear to have contributed significantly to increased market share for Kelang. This occurred partly at the expense of conventional cargo at Kelang, and partly at the expense of both container and conventional cargo handled by competing ports, principally Singapore.

INVESTMENT AND CAPACITY. Generating additional demand is one thing; meeting it is another. Figure 15-6 compares actual and projected throughput with existing and maximum capacity and reveals the following:

- Inherited capacity (35,000 TEUs) was in excess of both projected and actual demand through 1988.[7] Thereafter, additional investment and other improvements were required.
- Maximum theoretical capacity (constrained by wharf and yard size) as estimated in 1984 and 1985 was 500,000 TEUs, representing a level of demand that was projected to be reached in 1992 but was actually achieved in 1990.[8]
- A 41 percent expansion of capacity was therefore required to service 1990 demand, and this was successfully accomplished.

COUNTERFACTUAL OUTPUT. KCT's output achievements were clearly impressive. For divestiture analysis, however, the critical question is how much of this would have been accomplished anyway under continued KPA operation. KPA, after all, was hardly a static operation and showed significant improvements during the first half of the 1980s. As was shown in figure 15-4, output increased substantially from 1982 to

Figure 15-6. Actual and Projected Capacity and Throughput, Kelang Container Terminal, 1981–90

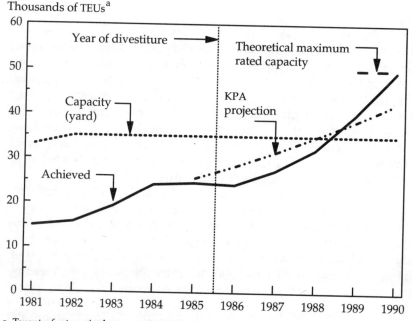

Thousands of TEUs[a]

a. Twenty-foot equivalent container unit (TEU).
Source: Kontans Nasional Sendirian Berhad and P&O Australia (1985, p. 35).

1984, before being curtailed by the Malaysian recession of 1985–86. There were also significant gains in handling time from 1981 through 1983.

Accordingly, what we want to incorporate into our counterfactual scenario is continued gains in output at Kelang in the absence of divestiture, but at a slower rate than what actually occurred. How much slower? There is no definitive way to choose the counterfactual growth rate, but for our base run we use KPA's own projected growth rate of about 10 percent (though from the lower 1986 actual level rather than the projected level shown later in table 15-2). We further assume that KPA could have financed and implemented the investment programs necessary to achieve this expansion, given that it had already ordered a major expansion.

Turning to output projections, we use the actual 1986–90 growth rate under KCT operation (17 percent) and continue the 10 percent rate under KPA operation. A critical choice comes in deciding what to do after the present capacity limit of 800,000 TEUs is achieved. We simply cap capacity at that level (although we do allow actual output to exceed rated capacity because of an efficiency increment described below). However, additional container capacity will have to be built thereafter. A further major gain from divestiture will accrue if this is accomplished by an organization whose performance is influenced by KCT, if not by KCT itself. Since we do not credit such a gain, our estimates are conservative.

Inputs

Although output growth was the most important source of improved profitability at KCT, productivity gains also played a role. This is apparent from figure 15-7, which for 1986–90 shows public profit rising more rapidly than real output (23.7 percent versus 17.2 percent per year) because the real quantities of labor and intermediate inputs grew more slowly (3.3 percent and 4.9 percent, respectively). (The semilogarithmic scale of the figure allows us to interpret equal slopes as equal percentage changes and steeper slopes as faster growth.) The question is whether or not these changes are causally related to divestiture.

The basic data for our search are set out in table 15-2. It decomposes all value changes into their price and quantity components. By way of illustration, consider the bottom triplet for public profit. The bottom line shows annual changes in the value of surplus, while the two lines above show how much of each was due to price and quantity changes. With minor exceptions in 1982 and 1987, the price line is negative, meaning that on balance prices moved against the enterprise, with input prices rising more than output prices. Furthermore, in general, small negative price effects were more than offset by large positive quantity effects. For

Figure 15-7. *Public Profit at Constant Prices, Kelang Container Terminal, 1981–90*

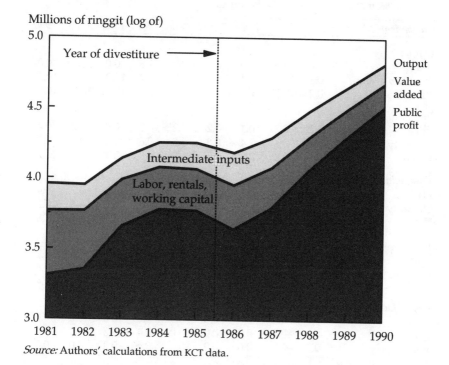

Source: Authors' calculations from KCT data.

example, in 1990 nominal surplus grew by M$15.3 million, but this would have been M$17.8 million had relative price changes not nicked the company to the tune of M$2.5 million. We now investigate labor and intermediate inputs in more detail.

LABOR. First consider the wage component of table 15-2:

- Quantities are measured in terms of hours worked, including overtime. This explains the considerable annual variance in quantities despite a relatively stable work force.
- In marked contrast to other inputs and outputs in a low-inflation economy, price effects dominate quantity effects.
- Price increases were particularly noticeable after divestiture, with average total worker compensation rising at an annual compound rate of 12 percent. Deflating by the consumer price index gives real wage gains of 10 percent per year.
- In sum, by 1990 workers were paid 78 percent more per hour in nominal terms (60 percent more in real terms), put in 6 percent more

*Table 15-2. Decomposition of Public Profitability Trend into Price
and Quantity Effects, Kelang Container Terminal, 1982–90*
(base = 1986, millions of ringgit at market prices)

Component	1982	1983	1984	1985	1986	1987	1988	1989	1990
Output									
Price	0.0	0.0	0.0	0.0	0.8	1.8	0.0	0.0	0.0
Quantity	–0.3	10.7	7.4	0.0	–4.7	7.7	15.9	16.7	19.5
Value	–0.3	10.7	7.4	0.0	–3.9	9.5	15.9	16.7	19.5
Intermediate inputs									
Price	–0.2	0.2	0.1	–0.2	–0.2	0.2	0.9	0.7	0.4
Quantity	–0.3	0.1	2.4	0.8	1.5	0.6	1.2	0.0	1.3
Value	–0.6	0.2	2.5	0.5	1.3	0.8	2.1	0.7	1.7
Value added									
Price	0.2	–0.2	–0.1	0.2	1.0	1.6	–0.9	–0.7	–0.4
Quantity	0.1	10.6	4.9	–0.8	–6.1	7.1	14.7	16.6	18.2
Value	0.3	10.4	4.8	–0.5	–5.2	8.7	13.8	16.0	17.8
Wages									
Price	0.3	0.3	0.9	1.2	3.0	1.3	0.9	1.1	2.1
Quantity	–0.5	0.3	0.1	–0.3	–0.8	0.3	0.7	0.8	0.4
Value	–0.2	0.6	1.0	0.8	2.2	1.5	1.7	1.9	2.4
Rented factors									
Price	0.0	0.0	0.0	0.0	0.0	0.0	0.0	0.0	0.0
Quantity	–0.4	–0.1	0.0	0.0	0.0	0.4	–0.3	0.0	0.0
Value	–0.4	–0.1	0.0	0.0	0.0	0.4	–0.2	0.0	0.0
Opportunity cost of working capital									
Price	–0.2	0.0	0.2	–0.4	–0.2	–0.5	0.1	0.2	0.0
Quantity	0.0	0.1	0.1	0.1	0.1	0.0	0.0	0.1	0.1
Value	–0.1	0.0	0.3	–0.3	–0.1	–0.5	0.2	0.3	0.1
Public profit									
Price	0.1	–0.4	–1.3	–0.6	–1.9	0.8	–2.1	–2.0	–2.5
Quantity	0.9	10.3	4.8	–0.5	–5.4	6.4	14.2	15.7	17.8
Value	1.0	9.9	3.5	–1.0	–7.3	7.2	12.2	13.8	15.3

Source: Authors' calculations from KCT data.

hours, and produced 76 percent more in comparison with the end of
the KPA period.

To place the wage increases in perspective, it is useful to compare total
employment costs per worker at the container terminal and at KPA as a
whole. This is done in figure 15-8. Curiously, although terminal compensation rates closely matched those of KPA from 1981 through 1983, they
began to diverge substantially not in 1986, but in 1984. We do not know
whether this divergence is due to data errors, some sort of predivestiture

attempt to gain union support, or some other factor. Nonetheless, the size and growth rate of the gap are impressive. By 1990, average compensation was 83 percent higher at KCT, roughly corresponding to the union claim that compensation was twice as high in 1991. Nominal annual growth rates from 1985 to 1990 were 3.1 percent at KPA compared with 12.3 percent at KCT.

Did worker compensation at KCT increase more than at KPA as a result of heightened worker incentives and productivity, or as a result of workers being bribed for labor peace by providing a share of increased rents whose origins were elsewhere? The initial sharp jump in the wage bill in 1986, combined as it was with a reduction in hours worked and output, can only be interpreted as a bribe (or a down payment on future productivity gains). Thereafter, however, there were dramatic productivity gains. We have already noted the dramatic increases in output per worker, and will shortly note reductions in repair and maintenance costs as well. However, it is illuminating to go behind these statistics to take a brief look at the underlying change in labor relations.

We had a delightful and informative meeting with five union leaders at KCT, who began by making the following points:

Figure 15-8. Average Total Compensation per Worker, Kelang Container Terminal and Kelang Port Authority, 1981–90

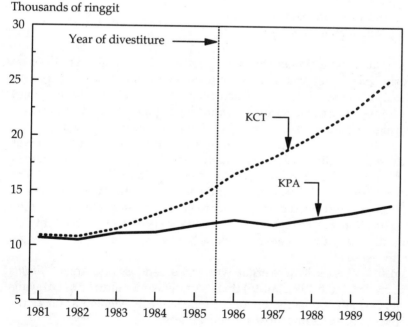

Thousands of ringgit

Source: KCT data.

- Sure, we're making 50 percent more now, but
- We're working twice as hard, and our pay should be even higher to reflect that; also,
- Other benefits have decreased (among other things, pension and housing loan conditions are less favorable, and medical leave has been curtailed).

In short, the leaders were doing their job as advocates for the workers they represented. The bottom line, however, was unambiguous. No one seemed eager to cross the fence and go back to work at KPA for lower wages but less work. A symmetrical question to union leaders on the other side of the fence yielded the same sentiment. Their big complaint was that they had arbitrarily been denied the boon granted to their former colleagues. They advocated divestiture of the rest of the port and had recently advised Thai unions to support divestiture there.

Asked how the increased productivity was to be explained (beyond more work for more pay), the KCT union officials offered the following reasons, in order:

- Much more labor input into decisionmaking
- Improved marketing leading to new business
- A new feeling of belonging, resulting in less loitering and absenteeism
- Incentive bonuses
- New technology.

KCT management made the same points, with particular emphasis on worker participation and morale, but also emphasized two other points. The first was work force restructuring. KCT took over only the wharf personnel. It turned some of them into higher-paid administrative workers; higher-paid workers were upgraded to foremen and managers, and their span of control (number of direct workers per supervisor) was reduced from fifty-five to twenty; and unskilled workers were trained and upgraded to mechanics, equipment operators, and so on.[9] The second point concerned work force flexibility. Workers were now doing whatever jobs needed doing, rather than only those specific to their job classification. Fewer repair and maintenance tasks were being contracted out; instead these were being done by the workers themselves when berths were idle.

In sum, it is difficult to argue with KCT's in-house assessment (*Straits Shipper* 18 March 1991c, p. 15) that, "A new work culture now prevails in KCT. That is probably the most significant achievement as far as the impact of privatization at KCT is concerned."

OTHER INPUTS. Other inputs may be dealt with more briefly, since the important changes are derived from the labor changes above. Figure 15-9, which presents real unit costs,[10] reveals the following:

- The costs of energy, working capital, and rentals are relatively small and exhibit no important changes over the period (except for the nominal jump in energy costs in 1984 and the real jump in 1987, which we are unable to explain except as data discrepancies).
- The real action comes in other intermediate inputs, which are largely repairs and maintenance and administration. There was a one-time jump in the first year of divestiture due to the costs of setting up a new administrative infrastructure. In the ensuing four years these costs were more than halved in real terms, falling at an astounding annual rate of 18.4 percent. This compares with an annual average rate of increase of 0.2 percent in the period before divestiture.
- Nominal unit costs of labor follow a pattern that is strikingly similar to that of intermediate inputs, although the one-time jump in 1986 is due to price (wage) effects rather than to quantity effects. At

Figure 15-9. Unit Costs at Constant Market Prices, Kelang Container Terminal, 1981–90

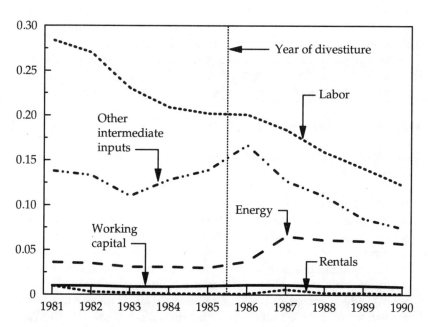

Note: Costs are expressed as a ratio to output.
Source: Authors' calculations from KCT data.

first blush, the steady decline in the real unit cost of labor is disconcerting, because it seems to contradict the story of suddenly improved labor productivity. The explanation, however, is simple. Labor was diverted from wharf operations to repairs, maintenance, and administration, so its true contribution to efficiency is measured not just in its relation to output, but also in terms of its substitution for other intermediate inputs. As always, partial productivity indicators can be dangerously misleading if considered independently of other inputs.

This last warning takes us back full circle to the total performance indicators of figure 15-1, whose explanation we have now completed.

INPUT COUNTERFACTUAL. It remains to specify the input counterfactuals. In terms of real unit costs (technical coefficients), we assume that, under continued KPA operation from 1986 through 1990, labor, energy, rental, and working capital requirements would not have differed from those under KCT operation, but that intermediate input requirements would have held constant at their 1985 level.

In terms of projections beyond 1990, we hold energy, rental, and working capital coefficients constant at their 1990 level in both regimes; reflect diminishing returns by letting labor and intermediate inputs continue to decrease at a decreasing rate to zero after five years under continued KCT operation; let labor coefficients proceed as above with intermediate coefficients constant at the 1985 level under continued KPA operation; let wages grow relative to the consumer price index at the 1986–90 rate for KCT and KPA for five years, with KCT dropping to the KPA rate thereafter; and let relative (to the consumer price index) prices of all other inputs proceed at their historic rate under both regimes.

What Is It Worth?

Given these assumptions, the welfare impact is summarized in table 15-3. Note the following:

- World welfare is enhanced considerably, by a net present value of M$505 million. Relative to the size of the enterprise, this is the second-largest improvement among the twelve divestitures examined in this volume.[11]
- The single largest winner is the government (whose revenue increments include those of KPA, which is wholly owned by the government), which comes out M$357 million ahead. It gives up a profit stream worth M$378 million in return for a modest sale worth M$57 million and a substantial tax gain (including the lease rental agreement, discussed below) of M$683 million.

Table 15-3. *Distribution of Gains and Losses from Divestiture,*
Kelang Container Terminal
(millions of ringgit)

Economic actor	Private operation	Public operation	Gains from divestiture
Domestic			
Consumers	1,539	1,481	58
Government			
Taxes	1,650	967	683
Net quasi rents	185	563	−378
Share sales (less transaction costs)	52	0	52
Debt subsidy or takeover	0	0	0
Other	0	0	0
Total	1,887	1,530	357
Shareholders			
Diversified	0	0	0
Concentrated	109	0	109
Employees	0	0	0
Total	109	0	109
Miscellaneous			
Employees (as inputs)	66	0	66
Competitors	217	330	−113
Providers	0	0	0
Citizens	0	0	0
Total	284	330	−47
Total domestic	3,818	3,341	477
Foreign			
Consumers	770	740	29
Shareholders	27	0	27
Competitors	54	83	−28
Others	0	0	0
Total foreign	851	823	28
Total	4,669	4,164	505

Note: All figures are 1985 present values.
Source: Authors' calculations.

• Buyers (domestic and foreign) also do rather nicely, paying M$57 million for a stream worth M$193 million, for a net gain of M$136 million.
• Employees also gain from higher wages, by an amount estimated at M$66 million.

- Consumers also gain from improved service, by an estimated M$88 million.
- As usual, there are losers: competitors lose M$141 million. However, the bulk of this (M$113 million) is incurred by conventional operations at KPA (and to a much smaller extent by other government-owned ports). Since this is more than made up for by KPA's share in the enhanced profits and the lease rental payments, even KPA comes out well ahead. As a result, the only net losers identified are foreign competitors (principally the Singapore Port Authority), who lose business worth an estimated M$28 million.

In sum, the divestiture of KCT is an unqualified success, whether from a domestic or a world welfare perspective.

Sources of Gains

Where did these gains come from? Table 15-4 answers this question by showing the impact of each of our major assumptions. It also provides a first-order sensitivity analysis, which will permit critical readers to make adjustments where they find particular assumptions overly conservative or liberal. As an aid to understanding the table, note the following structural points:

- The right-hand column gives the bottom-line results just reported, the left-hand column assumes that behavior after divestiture is unchanged from public operation, and the intervening columns explain the differences by introducing one major assumption at a time.
- The change in world welfare is reported in the fifth row from the bottom. Entries in the first five columns are an identical -5. This means that none of the assumptions has any aggregate welfare impact, other than the transaction cost (-5) incurred in the sale. Even so, the distribution of welfare can be substantially altered.
- Moving down the table from the world welfare row and deducting net benefits accruing to foreigners yields the domestic welfare change. This is identical to the difference between the value to society under private and public operation (V_{sp} - V_{sg}), whose composition is given in the middle of the table. Note that the V_{sg} rows are identical across regimes, because behavior under continued public operation is held constant.
- The top set of numbers gives the net present value of the stream of returns to private buyers (V_{pp}) or their maximum willingness to pay.

We now interpret each of the columns in turn, proceeding from left to right:

Table 15-4. *Regime Comparisons, Kelang Container Terminal*
(millions of ringgit)

	Lease rental = *Price =* *Investment =* *Wages =* *Output =* *Intermediates =* *Value*							
	Public *Public* *Public* *Public* *Public* *Public*	*Private* *Public* *Public* *Public* *Public* *Public*	*Public* *Private* *Public* *Public* *Public* *Public*	*Public* *Public* *Private* *Public* *Public* *Public*	*Public* *Public* *Public* *Private* *Public* *Public*	*Public* *Public* *Private* *Public* *Private* *Public*	*Public* *Public* *Public* *Private* *Public* *Private*	*Private* *Private* *Private* *Private* *Private* *Private*
V_{pp}								
Production	412	181	412	412	319	479	554	336
Financial	−139	−139	−139	−139	−138	−166	−181	−144
Total	273	43	273	273	181	312	372	193
V_{sp}								
Production	3,520	3,520	3,520	3,520	3,541	3,566	3,709	4,050
Financial	−222	−222	−222	−222	−225	−257	−274	−227
Total	3,298	3,298	3,298	3,298	3,316	3,309	3,435	3,823
V_{sg}								
Production	3,585	3,585	3,585	3,585	3,585	3,585	3,585	3,585
Financial	−244	−244	−244	−244	−244	−244	−244	−244
Total	3,341	3,341	3,341	3,341	3,341	3,341	3,341	3,341
$V_{sp} - V_{sg}$								
Production	−65	−65	−65	−65	−44	−20	124	465
Financial	22	22	22	22	19	−13	−30	17
Total	−48	−48	−48	−48	−30	−37	89	477

(Table continues on the following page.)

Table 15-4 (continued)

	(1)	(2)	(3)	(4)	(5)	(6)	(7)	(8)
Lease rental =	Public	Private	Public	Public	Public	Public	Public	Private
Price =	Public	Public	Private	Private	Public	Private	Public	Private
Investment =	Public	Public	Public	Public	Private	Private	Public	Private
Wages =	Public	Public	Public	Public	Public	Public	Public	Private
Output =	Public	Public	Public	Public	Private	Private	Public	Private
Intermediates =	Public	Public	Public	Public	Public	Public	Private	Private
Value								
Distribution								
Consumers	0	0	0	0	0	52	0	88
Government	-221	9	-221	-221	-433	-141	29	357
Buyers	216	-14	216	216	124	256	315	136
Employees	0	0	0	0	304	-88	-150	66
Competitors	0	0	0	0	0	-59	-54	-141
World welfare change	-5	-5	-5	-5	-5	19	141	505
Less foreign:								
Consumers	0	0	0	0	0	17	0	29
Buyers	43	-3	43	43	25	51	63	27
Competitors	0	0	0	0	0	-12	-11	-28
Equals domestic welfare change	-48	3	-48	-48	-30	-37	89	477

Note: All figures are 1986 present values.
Source: Authors' calculations.

362

- **Identity regime (column 1).** If divestiture produced no behavioral change but only continued business as usual, then private buyers paid only M$57 million for a stream worth M$273 million ($V_{pp}$), netting M$216 million in the process. As no real change took place, this all came about at the expense of the seller, who lost an offsetting M$221 million (including the transaction cost). Because some of the benefits accrued to foreign buyers, domestic welfare suffered a considerable decline ($V_{sp} - V_{sg} = -48$).
- **Lease rental regime (column 2).** A critical provision of the Kelang divestiture was that KCT would pay KPA an annual rental payment plus a variable payment based on throughput. As shown in the second column, with no behavioral change this would have been sufficient to reduce private willingness to pay to M$43 million, a figure remarkably close to the M$57 million actually paid. While this near identity is presumably accidental, it does have an interesting incentive interpretation: to gain an above-normal return, the new management had to improve efficiency. Furthermore, given the dominance of the variable lease rental over the fixed lease rental (the two were roughly equivalent by 1990, but the variable charge is projected to rise to five times the fixed by the mid-1990s), a considerable portion of the impact of increased efficiency is taxed away. It is this provision that explains the majority of the benefits ultimately accruing to the government, dominating other taxes and the sale price.
- **Pricing regime (column 3).** As with Malaysian Airline Systems (chapter 14), we build in a higher target profit band for price setting under private operation. However, unlike at the airline, this has absolutely no impact on prices or welfare. The reason is that KCT really is a gold mine, and adequate profit levels are maintained throughout with no real price increases.
- **Investment regime (column 4).** The investment regime also has no welfare impact, but this is the result of our assumption that investment is accommodating. Investment does not rise until output exceeds existing capacity, so this variable has an impact only in conjunction with the output assumption discussed below.
- **Wage regime (column 5).** If wages are raised with no change in work levels, then workers are better off and owners are worse off by an equivalent amount, with no net change in welfare. Because the increased wages are tax deductible, the government (which also incurs a share of the cost as owner) pays the bulk of the cost.[12] If, on the other hand, workers are somehow impelled to work harder and smarter without extra wages, then they lose because of the disutility of the extra effort. This explains the negative entries for employees in the next two columns. When they realistically work harder for more pay, the net effect is positive (see the section on "Wages, Effort, and Welfare" below).

- **Output regime (column 6).** One manifestation of enhanced efficiency is increased speed and convenience for users, resulting in greater output for KCT, and the first real welfare gain for the country and the world. Note, however, that this comes at the expense of other transport modes, with competitors losing after tax and after incremental investment quasi rents. Therefore, the gain does not result—as one would think at first—primarily from gains to consumers as such. Roughly half the gain is listed for convenience as consumer surplus, but in fact it is distributed between consumers, middlemen, and producers of tradables (all both foreign and domestic) depending on the degree of competition in the relevant markets. The other half of the gain comes from the switch from higher-cost to lower-cost provision of a given tonnage of service; KCT gains more than competitors lose. Finally, the bulk of the efficiency gains are offset by the uncompensated disutility of the workers' extra effort.
- **Intermediate input regime (column 7).** Finally, we come to the largest single source of welfare gain, which follows from the impact of increased efficiency on unit costs. This also has an output effect, because there is an increase in capacity utilization.[13]
- **Interaction effects (column 8).** The last column gives the impact of all the changes taken together. These interaction effects are considerable, particularly among the output and intermediate input regimes: lower unit costs are applied to greater output, and higher capacity utilization is applied to greater capacity. Furthermore, the pure distribution effects rearrange the surplus considerably: greater effort is more than offset by higher wages, and much of the surplus is transferred to the government by the lease rental provision.

In sum, it is the package of policies that matters. The foregoing piecemeal breakdown helps us see the forces at work, but one would never get the efficiency gains without the wage policy.[14]

Wages, Effort, and Welfare

In previous sections we emphasized that a critical consequence of divestiture at Kelang was rising wages *and* labor productivity. Evaluation of this change hinges on the answer to the following question: If an employer doubles wages but makes employees work twice as hard or twice as smart, how much better off are they? Possible answers include the following:

- The neighbor's wife: "Six years ago my husband and my neighbor's husband had the same job and the same wage. Now they still have the same job description, but her husband earns twice as much, she has twice as many nice things, and their welfare has doubled."

- The unionist: "Yes, but don't forget how much harder I have to work now. My wife may be better off, but I'm worse off from the increased effort."
- The Vince Lombardi School of Management: "Whaddya mean, effort makes you worse off? You're better off! Work is ennobling, and more work is more ennobling. Furthermore, if a new manager (or coach) introduces reforms that turn losers into winners by motivating and focusing effort, employees gain satisfaction through increased self-esteem and pride in their organization."
- The efficient market advocate: "All three effects are valid, but irrelevant, because through the miracle of the market they net out to precisely zero. The losses of the husband exactly and precisely balance the gains of the wife, and the couple's welfare is unchanged.[15] We know this has to be true, because a smart manager (profit maximizer) won't pay more than the minimum necessary to induce the extra effort, and that minimum is the amount that just compensates the worker (and his wife) for that effort."
- The more sophisticated viewer of human nature (this point is paraphrased—we hope without injustice—from Leibenstein 1978, pp. 26–38): "It is utter balderdash to assume a stable, negative relationship between utility and effort. You don't need to be a Vince Lombardi to accept a positive relationship. Most people would be very unhappy simply sitting on their butts for eight hours a day. Avoidance of boredom, if not the need to maintain a positive self-image of productivity, means that, initially, increasing effort actually increases welfare. Eventually, of course, as workers work harder and harder, things become so intense that further effort brings pain and not pleasure.[16] Accordingly, if previously I hadn't been working very hard, doubling my effort and my wages can actually more than double my welfare."

We conclude that the relationship between effort, welfare, and wages depends on whether the worker is initially at a low level of effort, where extra work enhances or at least does not diminish utility, or at a high level, where extra effort incurs disutility and must be compensated by higher wages. Where are the KCT workers? Our answer is in two parts.

At the beginning, we argue, they were at a low level of effort. A weak argument in support of this contention is the widespread assumption that there is slack in public enterprises in general, and that KPA was no exception. A strong—make that conclusive—argument is that all the workers at KPA reportedly would like to move to KCT, and no one at KCT wants to move back to KPA. This can only mean that the improvement in wages and job satisfaction together more than compensate for any disutility associated with increased effort. That is, for inframarginal units the relationship between effort and utility is negative or zero.

At the end, the workers are operating at a high level of effort. KCT is trying to make money, and in later negotiations with the union the efficient market argument holds at the margin.

In sum, marginal utility of income equals marginal disutility of effort at the margin, but exceeds it for inframarginal units. We therefore feel comfortable that the doubling of wages at Kelang resulted in a real welfare gain, but by less than the full amount of the wage increase. We feel uncomfortable specifying precisely how much less. Given that management likely drove workers to the wall, the offset is likely to be significant; given the unanimity and intensity of the workers' preference for the new package, it is unlikely to be very close to the total. Reflecting these two judgments, we arbitrarily and illustratively assume that two-thirds of the wage increase is offset by the decreased utility from increased effort, and that the balance is a real welfare gain.

Summary and Lessons

The facts of the KCT case, interpreted through the twin lenses of theory and judgment, have led us to the following conclusions about the consequences of the KCT version of divestiture:

- If the government sold a gold mine, then divestiture made it into a diamond mine. Domestic welfare from the terminal increased by around 50 percent per year (as measured by the perpetuity equivalent of the welfare change over sales in the base year) as a result of the change in behavior.
- This alchemy was accomplished not primarily through external changes in pricing and investment constraints as at Malaysian Airline Systems, but through internal management changes.
- The most striking manifestation of the internal changes was in the use of labor. Succinctly put, workers were given more pay for more work. Less succinctly, but more accurately, the new management provided incentives, training, and participative decisionmaking. Workers responded by working a little longer, a lot harder, and considerably smarter. The results were not manifest in an accelerated rate of growth of output per worker, but in lower costs for administration and for repairs and maintenance: labor was substituted for other intermediate inputs, and total productivity growth soared.
- The other major manifestation of improved management was accelerated output growth, as improved efficiency lowered costs (especially turnaround time), increasing the quality of service and raising output. Although the resulting gains were impressive for KCT, the bulk of the gains came at the expense of competing transportation modes (especially conventional operations at KPA), so the welfare impact was considerably less. Nonetheless, real gains did accrue to both the

port and its users from the acceleration in switching to lower-cost containerization.
- Only a small portion of the gains leaked to foreign shareholders, consumers, and competitors, so that domestic welfare gains were more than 90 percent of the total. In particular, foreign buyers netted only about 6 percent of the gains, but their management know-how made a substantial (although unquantified) contribution to improved performance. KCT is a clear case of successful use of foreign buyers, in marked contrast to other divestitures where foreigners captured so much of the gain that domestic welfare actually declined (see chapter 23 for an elaboration).
- The government itself received the bulk of the gains, not from the sale price but through three profit-sharing mechanisms. In addition to the usual corporate tax mechanism, the government retained a 49 percent share in the company through KPA, and—most important—imposed a variable (per incremental TEU) lease rental scheme that captured a substantial share of marginal efficiency gains.
- A unique feature of the KCT divestiture was its impact on labor, which was induced to work considerably harder but was more than compensated by increased wages. As a result, unions at both KCT and KPA have become advocates of divestiture, urging the divestiture of KPA itself and advising a Thai port union to support the sale of its own organization.
- Finally, the KCT divestiture came close to being Pareto-improving (no losers). Competitors did lose, but the main loser was KPA, whose losses as a competitor were more than compensated by its gains as a shareholder and rent collector. The only net loser was a foreigner (Singapore Port Authority), and this by a relatively small amount.

The following hypotheses on divestiture are consistent with the KCT case but are, of course, not proved by it:

- Divestiture can dramatically improve welfare by initiating a shift toward efficiency-oriented goals and incentives.
- The short-run potential for such gains in welfare (in percentage terms) is much larger in small organizations, which are unencumbered by the inertia of large size.
- The divestiture of enterprises with market power can be effectively controlled by a regulatory regime that sets prices while paying attention to the public interest.

None of this is particularly earthshaking. What may be surprising about the KCT case, however, is that all this was accomplished by a decidedly *partial* divestiture in which only 10 percent of the shares were divested, with the balance going to other public enterprises. Accordingly:

- Partial divestiture need not be merely cosmetic if the introduction of private shareholders shifts the exercise of government discretion in the direction of more economically rational decisions. The fact that these same decisions *could* have been taken without divestiture is irrelevant if they *would* not have been taken.

Although an economic case can be made for partial divestiture, the motivation at KCT was largely political.[17] Malaysian society is particularly sensitive to the ethnic distribution of entrepreneurial income, and partial divestiture kept the bulk of the gains in Bumiputra hands. Thus, partial sale can be an essential element of divestiture strategy where political consensus building requires that the bulk of the benefits accrue to nationals or to some subset thereof.

In sum, the KCT model of divestiture is one to be emulated and deserves the attention of proponents and opponents alike.

Notes

This chapter was written by Leroy Jones and Fadil Azim Abbas. In addition to those acknowledged at the beginning of this volume, the authors would like to thank the following individuals for superb cooperation at the enterprise level: Abdul Samad Mohamed (chief executive officer, KCT), Gan Chong Kiat (assistant general manager, KPA), Mohamed Abdul Hamid (company secretary, KPA), Tan Chin Koon (chief accountant, KPA), S. C. Wong (senior accountant, KPA), and M. Taib Hashim (Administration Department, KPA).

1. Of a 1985 KPA work force of 6,227, 797 were transferred to Kelang Container Terminal according to KPA, but according to the terminal itself this figure was 801.

2. The New Economic Policy was a fundamental element of Malaysian policy designed to increase the participation of ethnic Malays in all spheres of national activity (see chapter 13 for details).

3. The background to, and mechanics of, the KCT divestiture are well described elsewhere, and we provide only an overview. For further details see Leeds (1989), Levy and Menendez (1989), Havelka and Havelka (1990, pp. 196–209), and Salleh (n.d.). This section also draws on ASEAM Bankers Malaysia Berhad (1984).

4. The current board does not include KCT's chief executive officer. This was not the case in the first year of its operations (1986). At that time, its chief executive officer, who was from P & O Australia, sat on the board. The following year another P & O Australia staff member took over as chief executive officer but was not invited to the board. However, the former chief executive officer continued to be a board member. Since then KCT's chief executive officers have not been board members.

5. Public profitability here is measured by total return to fixed factors (quasi rents) divided by the assets that generated those returns (land plus fixed operating assets). See chapter 2 for a more detailed explanation.

6. Since only a portion of the port was sold, it is necessary to decompose predivestiture accounts so as to extract the container component. Fortunately, KPA accounts allow this to be done in a reasonable way. Separable costs and

revenues are readily identifiable, and the potential errors in allocating joint costs are small enough not to materially affect our conclusions.

7. Inherited capacity was constrained by yard capacity. Berth capacity was increased to 420,000 TEUs in 1987 or 1988 by a fifth crane already ordered by KPA prior to divestiture.

8. Subsequently, KCT found it feasible to add a fourth wharf and associated equipment, bringing maximum capacity to 750,000 to 800,000 TEUs. This project was under way in 1991 (*Straits Shipper*, 18 March 1991a, p. 11).

9. This upgrading of skills presumably explains the gap between our finding that average compensation went up 83 percent and the common interview assertion that compensation (for the same job) rose 50 percent.

10. Since output prices do not change significantly, average variable costs are almost identical to nominal unit costs in the KCT case, and we save trees by not displaying both.

11. The perpetuity equivalent of the change in welfare divided by sales in the base year is 53 percent. The only larger relative improvement in our sample was that for CHILGENER (chapter 9), an electricity generation plant in Chile.

12. Evidence for this assertion does not follow from the levels of benefits flowing to the government and buyers (M$29 million versus M$315 million), but from the changes from column 1 (+M$250 million for the government, but only +M$99 million for the buyers). This should be borne in mind when interpreting similar statements.

13. There is, however, no corresponding increase in consumer surplus because our model rather arbitrarily forces all consumer surplus into the output category where quality of service is located.

14. For this reason in chapter 18, for comparison purposes, we report the output and intermediate gains incorporating a proportionate share of the wage increment.

15. The husband must be a net loser (disutility of effort exceeds utility of becoming a winner), because otherwise an employer would not have to pay him any more to exert the effort.

16. Graphically, then, the total utility of effort first rises and then falls. The law of diminishing returns operates in the usual fashion to ensure that the extra utility of extra effort first increases at a decreasing rate and then decreases at an increasing rate. Leibenstein further assumes a "flat top," representing a range of effort over which workers are indifferent. Although it is not critical to our argument, the commonsense explanation for such an area is that it allows good managers (or coaches, or generals, or chairmen) to improve performance by better motivating workers, and without pay increases.

17. The economic case can be based on maximizing government returns by first establishing a market value for the enterprise by partial sale, and then selling the balance at a higher price.

16. Sports Toto Malaysia

Opium, alcohol, tobacco, and gambling are some of the products traditionally chosen as revenue monopolies because they are good places to
raise money for government coffers.[1] They are good for this purpose for
two distinct reasons. First, as commodities they are not "goods" but
"bads," so that raising the price does not necessarily decrease consumer
welfare, and may actually enhance it. Second, and less intuitively, the
best place to raise a given amount of revenue with minimum welfare loss
is in markets where demand is unresponsive to price (this is what gives
rise to the inverse elasticity rule, or Ramsey pricing; see any standard
public finance text). These economic characteristics of the output market
constitute the first distinguishing characteristic of Sports Toto Malaysia
Berhad, a Malaysian enterprise that provides a variety of numbers
wagering opportunities. As a result, our quantitative focus in this case
will be on the impact of divestiture on government revenues, with
consumer surplus of, at best, tertiary importance.

On the institutional side, Sports Toto is also unique because it is the
only case of complete divestiture among our Malaysian cases. In each of
the other cases the government retained substantial shareholdings, directly or indirectly. The interesting question is whether or not 100 percent
divestiture led to more dramatic behavioral change than in the other
cases.

The divested enterprise is so private, in fact, that absolutely no data
are available other than those required for any publicly listed company.
The managing director maintains that no further information is provided even to the parent holding company, because any leakage would
compromise Sports Toto's competitive position. Be that as it may, the
shortage of facts meant that we could not conduct a full case study.
Nonetheless, the case's unique features make it important enough that
we will present it, but in a more limited way than the other cases.
Fortunately, this is less constraining than it might appear, because the
focus is on government revenue—which we do have data on—and not

on pricing, efficiency, or consumer surplus, where we are in empirical darkness. In any event, the third distinguishing characteristic of this case is that it is a mini-case.

The fourth and final feature of the case has to do with its distributional impact. As far as consumers are concerned, out of ignorance we shall have little to say. In terms of the buyers, however, although a majority of the shares were initially sold to a Bumiputra firm, resale left the majority of the company's shares (57 percent according to Sports Toto's 1989 annual report) in the hands of the Berjaya Corporation, an enterprise in which Bumiputra held a minority stake.

Background

History

Sports Toto was incorporated as a government-owned enterprise in 1969 with the objective of generating funds for sports development in Malaysia by selling numbers betting tickets. Ten percent of the before-tax profits were to be channeled to the National Sports Council through the Ministry of Finance. In addition, although this was not announced officially, it was generally understood that the creation of Sports Toto was designed to curb the incidence of illegal gambling and the crime associated with it.

Institutional Characteristics

Sports Toto was incorporated as a private limited company, and from its inception it largely operated as such, even when fully owned by the government. It geared itself toward making profits, and its employees, of which there were about 400 in 1985, were not part of the civil service. The government exercised its influence by appointing the board of directors, who were usually senior treasury officials. Their main concern was to see that the enterprise stayed within the framework of its objectives and that it paid due regard to broader government policies and to the public interest in general. This watchdog role was, however, coupled with that of a facilitator for the enterprise's dealings with the government bureaucracy, especially the treasury. The enterprise's day-to-day operations were left very much in the hands of the management team and staff.

Sports Toto seems to have played down its connections with the government, at least publicly. For its part the government likewise avoided publicizing its ownership of the enterprise, because of political and religious sensitivities concerning gambling in Malaysia. Most of the electorate are Muslims, and a considerable proportion of them are against gambling.

Market Characteristics

Malaysia's legal gambling market consists of Sports Toto numbers games, other three- and four-digit numbers games, lotteries and sweepstakes, betting on horse races, and casino gambling at Genting Casino. The first three cater to the ordinary gambler, while the last two are directed to a more select clientele. Sports Toto is thus in close competition with the operators of three- and four-digit betting games and lotteries and in more distant competition with the other legal, as well as illegal, forms of gambling. The size of the overall market and relative market shares will be considered in more detail later in this study.

Divestiture

No documents are available to explain the government's specific reasons for selling off its shares in Sports Toto. Nevertheless, it is useful to examine how Sports Toto fit into the overall goals of divestiture as explained in chapter 13.

Clearly the divestiture of Sports Toto was not geared toward the first objective, that of relieving the government's financial and administrative burden, because the company was financially and administratively autonomous, and was profitable to boot. Nor was divestiture aimed at the second objective (facilitating economic growth), given the nature of Sports Toto's business. Thus, the divestiture was probably meant to achieve the other three objectives, namely, improving efficiency and productivity, reducing the size and presence of the public sector in the economy, and increasing the Bumiputra share of corporate equity.

It is also possible that Sports Toto's divestiture was linked to the government's (unwritten) policy of disassociating itself from legalized gambling. It began this process in the late 1970s, when Malaysian Muslims were banned from entering Genting Casino (Malaysia's only casino), and since 1991 has taken the form of dissolving the Social Welfare Lotteries Board.

The divestiture of Sports Toto was carried out through direct negotiations between B&B Enterprise (a private Bumiputra-owned firm) and a treasury-led government working committee following a bid by the former. The government did not call for competitive bids.

By 2 May 1985 the two parties had reached agreement on the terms and conditions of the sale of Sports Toto. The agreement was effected on 1 August 1985 and had the following features:

- The government sold 70 percent of its equity share in Sports Toto to B&B for M$28 million (for a price-earnings ratio of 3.1). During this period the exchange rate was about M$2.3 per U.S. dollar.

- B&B resold 10 percent of the Sports Toto shares to Melewar Corporation and retained 60 percent.
- The treasury issued a betting license to Sports Toto, to be renewed annually.
- If the betting license were not renewed every year for the first ten years following the sale, the government would repurchase Sports Toto at total cost less 5 percent for each year short of the ten years.
- Sports Toto was to pay an annual royalty of 3 percent of its gross sales to the government.
- Sports Toto was to pay the National Sports Council 10 percent of its pretax profits or M$5 million (whichever was higher) annually; this was a continuation of predivestiture practice.
- A redeemable special share was to be issued to the government, giving it the power to ensure that the company's major decisions were consistent with government policies; to approve or disapprove any substantial takeover, asset disposal, amalgamation, or merger; and to appoint three company directors.
- The same employment terms were to remain in effect as before divestiture.

Once in control of Sports Toto, the new owners streamlined its operations. In 1987 they sold 5.251 million ordinary shares to the public. The par value of each share was M$1, but the sale price was fixed at M$2. The offer received a tremendous public response, attracting bids of about M$666 million—that is, it was oversubscribed by about eighty-eight times. It is not only public enterprises that underprice their new issues!

Sports Toto was listed on the Kuala Lumpur stock exchange on 29 July 1987, and during the first six months its shares traded in a range from M$5.50 to M$11.50. In November 1987 Berjaya Corp. acquired a majority interest. Finally, in 1988 the government sold its remaining shares through a private placement to Raleigh Berhad for M$85 million (for a

Table 16-1. Shareholders in Sports Toto Malaysia
(percentages of total)

Shareholder	After privatization	Before listing on stock exchange	After listing on stock exchange	After second sale
B&B Enterprise	7.0	60.0	45.0	45.0
Malaysia government	30.0	30.0	30.0	0.0
Raleigh Berhad	0.0	0.0	0.0	30.0
Berjaya Corp.	0.0	0.0	0.0	52.0
Others	0.0	10.0	25.0	18.0

Source: Malaysia, Government of (1989, p. 23), modified to include Berjaya Corp.

price-earnings ratio of 9.9, and net assets per share of M$1.61). Table 16-1 summarizes the changes in Sports Toto's ownership structure.

What Happened?

Welfare change can be decomposed into the impacts on profit and on consumer surplus. In the case of Sports Toto, the former effect is as clear as crystal, while the latter is as clear as the nature of God. We discuss the two effects in turn.

Profit Changes

SALES AND PROFITS. Table 16-2 and figure 16-1 present the trends in sales and public profits.[2] From 1985 to 1989:

- Nominal sales nearly tripled, while public profits nearly quadrupled.
- As inflation was moderate during this period, real increases were nearly as impressive, with sales up 2.7 times and public profits up 3.7 times.
- Profits rose not only because of the increase in sales volume, but also because of an increase in the spread of profits: from 1978 to 1985 profits ranged from 17 to 25 percent of sales; in 1988 and 1989 they were 29 and 30 percent, respectively.
- How much of the improvement was caused by price effects and how much by quantity effects is unknown because of data limitations. On the basis of these results, divestiture clearly correlates with a dramatic surge in activity.

FISCAL FLOWS. The government's share of the increased profits is even more impressive, as shown in table 16-3 and figure 16-2. The government's fiscal flow from Sports Toto's operations consists of:

- Sports betting duty, which is an indirect tax on gambling
- Income tax on corporate profits (winners do not have to pay income tax on their winnings)
- Annual contributions to the National Sports Council of 10 percent of before-tax profits or M$5 million, whichever is greater[3]
- The government's share of dividends
- All unclaimed prizes, which are estimated at 1 percent of sales[4]
- Income taxes on the private share of dividends
- Royalties of 3 percent of sales.

The first five categories existed prior to divestiture (the contribution to the National Sports Council was added only in 1983), the sixth was an automatic (although often neglected) accompaniment to divestiture, and the last was added as a condition of sale. As shown in figure 16-2, the

Table 16-2. *Production and Distribution Accounts, Sports Toto Malaysia, Fiscal 1978–89*
(millions of ringgit)

Category	1978	1979	1980	1981	1982	1983	1984	1985	1986	1988	1989
Nominal											
Sales (at market price)	26.1	28.2	38.9	51.5	63.0	75.5	86.8	76.0	94.6	186.1	214.5
- Betting duty	2.6	2.8	3.9	5.2	6.3	7.5	8.7	7.6	9.5	18.6	21.4
- Other expenses	21.3	23.4	29.9	39.2	48.5	57.1	65.1	59.6	75.4	132.2	150.2
= Operating profit	2.2	2.0	5.0	7.2	8.2	10.9	13.0	8.8	9.8	35.4	42.8
+ Interest/dividends	1.0	1.3	1.9	2.1	2.6	2.6	3.0	2.0	1.0	2.3	4.0
+ Miscellaneous nonoperating costs	0.0	0.0	0.0	0.0	0.0	0.4	0.3	-0.8	0.0	0.0	5.1
- Taxes											
Income tax	1.5	1.6	3.4	4.3	5.1	3.9	5.7	2.3	3.9	13.4	15.9
Royalty	0.0	0.0	0.0	0.0	0.0	0.0	0.0	1.0	2.8	5.6	6.4
Sports Council	0.0	0.0	0.0	0.0	0.0	5.0	3.5	4.8	0.8	3.2	4.1
= Private profit	1.7	1.7	3.6	4.9	5.7	4.9	7.0	1.9	3.2	15.5	25.5
- Dividends	0.0	0.0	0.0	0.0	0.0	0.0	0.0	36.2	2.4	4.1	17.6
= Retained earnings	1.7	1.7	3.6	4.9	5.7	4.9	7.0	-34.3	0.8	11.4	7.9
Memoranda											
Public profit	4.8	4.8	8.9	12.3	14.5	18.4	21.7	16.4	19.3	54.0	64.3
As a percentage of sales	0.18	0.17	0.23	0.24	0.23	0.24	0.25	0.22	0.20	0.29	0.30
Real (constant 1980 prices)											
Public profit	5.6	5.2	8.9	11.2	12.5	15.3	17.3	13.1	15.2	42.3	48.9
Sales (at market prices)	30.7	30.5	38.9	47.0	54.3	62.7	69.4	60.6	74.9	194.5	163.3

Note: Fiscal 1988 was an interim fiscal year encompassing all of 1987 plus the first four months of 1988. The figures reported here are on an annualized twelve-month basis.

Source: Authors' calculations from Sports Toto data.

376

Figure 16-1. Sales and Public Profit, Sports Toto Malaysia, Fiscal 1978–89

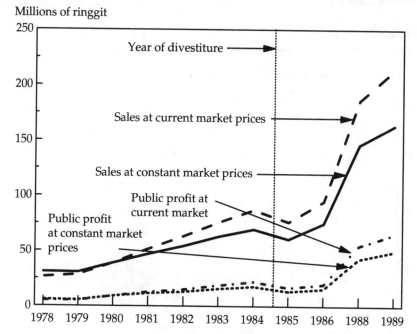

Millions of ringgit

Year of divestiture

Sales at current market prices

Sales at constant market prices

Public profit at current market

Public profit at constant market prices

Source: Authors' calculations from Sports Toto data.

bulk of the fiscal flow comes from corporate and indirect taxes on operations (68 percent in 1989), with special levies contributing 19 percent, and dividends and taxes thereon only 13 percent.

The sum of these flows to the government was 3.3 times larger in real terms in 1989 than in 1985. To be sure, this is less than the overall increase in either revenues or public profits, but in the meantime the government had relinquished all equity in the enterprise. It sold the first 70 percent of its holding in 1985 for M$28 million and the remaining 30 percent in 1988 for M$88 million. Thus, after selling 100 percent of the enterprise, the government was still garnering 85 percent of the quasi rents. As a share of sales, the government's deal looks even better: before divestiture 16 to 22 percent of sales flowed into the treasury; after divestiture (in 1989, the only year in which there was zero government equity) the treasury was getting 26 percent.

To evaluate this arrangement fully we must, of course, take into account the counterfactual and projections. As a rough and ready guide to a preliminary judgment, however, consider how the owner of a private firm might react to the following offer: we'll take over your company, allowing you to retire or devote your energies to other entrepreneurial activities; in return, we'll pay you five times your current

Figure 16-2.   Fiscal Flows at Constant Market Prices, Sports Toto Malaysia,
Fiscal 1978–89

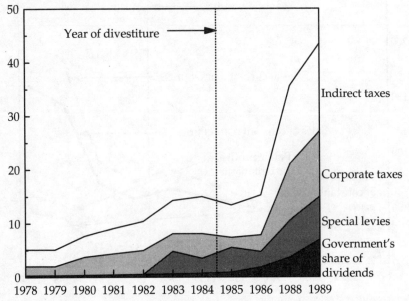

Source: Authors' calculations from Sports Toto data.

annual return from the firm *and* ensure that you continue to receive an
increased share of a greatly increased annual sales volume. The government seems to have done very well for itself.

FINANCIAL RESTRUCTURING. The government does even better when we
take into account the financial restructuring done prior to divestiture.
Such restructuring is quite common internationally. What was unique
at Sports Toto was that the government restructured the enterprise by
taking money out of it rather than by pouring money in. In 1985, prior
to divestiture, Sports Toto paid a special dividend of M$35.5 million. This
payment is, of course, not directly attributable to divestiture, because it
represented retained earnings accumulated under public operation. It is
nonetheless noteworthy in that it is one of the few such negative restruc-
turings we know of.

Consumer Surplus Changes

The question with regard to consumer surplus changes is whether profits
rose:

Table 16-3. *Fiscal Flows, Sports Toto Malaysia, Fiscal 1978–89*
(millions of ringgit, except where otherwise noted)

Category	1978	1979	1980	1981	1982	1983	1984	1985	1986	1988	1989
Nominal											
Betting duty	2.6	2.8	3.9	5.2	6.3	7.5	8.7	7.6	9.5	18.6	21.4
Income tax	1.5	1.6	3.4	4.3	5.1	3.9	5.7	2.3	3.9	13.4	15.9
Uncollected prizes	0.3	0.3	0.4	0.5	0.6	0.8	0.9	0.8	0.9	1.9	2.1
Royalties	0.0	0.0	0.0	0.0	0.0	0.0	0.0	1.0	2.8	5.6	6.4
Sports Council	0.0	0.0	0.0	0.0	0.0	5.0	3.5	4.8	0.8	3.2	4.1
Dividends											
Public share	0.0	0.0	0.0	0.0	0.0	0.0	0.0	0.2	0.7	1.2	0.0
Private tax	0.0	0.0	0.0	0.0	0.0	0.0	0.0	0.2	0.7	1.6	7.0
Total	4.3	4.7	7.6	10.0	12.0	17.2	18.8	16.8	19.3	45.4	57.1
Memoranda: Fiscal flows											
As percentage of public profit	0.91	0.98	0.85	0.81	0.83	0.94	0.87	1.03	1.00	0.84	0.89
As percentage of sales	0.17	0.17	0.20	0.19	0.19	0.23	0.22	0.22	0.20	0.24	0.27
Real (1980 prices)											
Betting duty	3.1	3.1	3.9	4.7	5.4	6.3	6.9	6.1	7.5	14.6	16.3
Income tax	1.7	1.7	3.4	3.9	4.4	3.3	4.6	1.8	3.1	10.5	12.1
Uncollected prizes	0.3	0.3	0.4	0.5	0.5	0.6	0.7	0.6	0.7	1.5	1.6
Royalties	0.0	0.0	0.0	0.0	0.0	0.0	0.0	0.8	2.2	4.4	4.9
Sports Council	0.0	0.0	0.0	0.0	0.0	4.2	2.8	3.8	0.6	2.5	3.1
Dividends											
Public share	0.0	0.0	0.0	0.0	0.0	0.0	0.0	0.2	0.6	1.0	0.0
Private tax	0.0	0.0	0.0	0.0	0.0	0.0	0.0	0.1	0.5	1.3	5.3
Total	5.1	5.1	7.6	9.1	10.4	14.3	15.0	13.4	15.3	35.6	43.5

Note: Fiscal 1988 was an interim fiscal year encompassing all of 1987 plus the first four months of 1988. The figures reported here are on an annualized twelve-month basis.

Source: Authors' calculations from Sports Toto data.

- At consumers' expense through higher prices
- At competitors' expense through increased market share
- At no one's expense through more efficient production
- At other industries' expense through demand shifts induced by advertising, or
- Some combination of the above.

In a full case study we would be obliged to answer these questions, but this is a mini-case study precisely because we cannot. The reasons for our ignorance are nonetheless important for evaluating how much we are losing as a result.

DATA LIMITATIONS. Sports Toto staff would reveal nothing about the company's cost structure. Accordingly, we can say nothing about changes in the cost efficiency of production. This is not too serious an omission, as even the managing director does not claim great gains here.

Much more serious, we have no information about the company's revenue structure, which here includes the payout rate. That is, a customer who pays one dollar for a ticket in a random lottery that pays out 60 percent of its revenues as prizes is paying forty cents for the thrill of the game (or, equivalently, one dollar in return for 60 cents and the thrill of the game). Matters become more complicated with numbers games and sports betting, but at a minimum we need to know the revenue structure and the payout rate by game. Without a time series of these data we can say little about whether or not consumers were being exploited.

One can argue that because Sports Toto has a small share of the formal gambling market and an even smaller share of the total market, competitive theory tells us that the potential for consumer exploitation is low. This conclusion, however, assumes perfect consumer information. Did consumers switch to Sports Toto from its competitors because Sports Toto offered a better product for the price (to the extent that they switched from other gambling rather than from general consumption)? Or did they switch because television advertisements convinced them to switch to an inferior product? Or was it really inferior if they thought it was superior and decided to switch? This brings us to the interpretation of advertising-induced change.

ADVERTISING. Even if we did have all the above data we would still be in a quandary, because Sports Toto staff plausibly claim that the major reason for their success was improved marketing: introducing new games, expanding the quantity and quality of advertising, and adding flashy outlets. The problem is that economists do not really know how to interpret welfare changes accompanying endogenous demand shifts caused by marketing (on the economics of advertising see Dixit and

Norman 1978, pp. 1–17). If someone on television convinces you to spend your money on one product rather than another, are you better off? Or are you merely getting the same amount of utility in a different way, with advertising expenditures a deadweight loss? This is a deep question that we will not even attempt to answer, as we do not have the requisite numbers in the first place.

CONSUMER SOVEREIGNTY. Assume that we had complete data and an analytical framework that showed a change in consumer surplus; then we would still have the problem of deciding whether the change was good or bad. Is more gambling good? Those who respect consumer sovereignty would argue in the affirmative. Those arguing in the negative would not be confined to moral or religious fundamentalists, but would include those appealing to the negative externalities allegedly accompanying gambling, including family disintegration, increased crime, and time lost from work. Even if one accepts these latter concerns, one would have to know what the true opportunity cost was. Does more gambling mean less money for the children or less alcohol consumed (a question posed by Mary Shirley)?

CONCLUSION. In sum, we don't know very much here. We will therefore have to conclude that what we do not know cannot hurt us, as we could not, in any event, place an unambiguous interpretation on the results. Either way, we will conclude by ignoring consumer surplus in the balance of the chapter and focusing on the fiscal impact. Even if this is not the whole story, it is a major part of it.

Why Did It Happen?

Did divestiture cause the impressive gains of 1988 and 1989, or would they have happened anyway under continued public ownership? The quantitative record can be read in two quite different ways, depending on how one interprets the dip in sales in 1985 and 1986 (figure 16-1).

The first way to read the record is to say that divestiture took place in May 1985, but it takes a while for new management to have an impact, so the predivestiture period should be taken as 1978 through 1985 and the postdivestiture period as 1986 through 1989. During the former period, nominal annual sales growth averaged only 16 percent, compared with 41 percent in the latter (table 16-4). Even from the parochial view of the government, the fiscal flow grew 51 percent per year after divestiture compared with only 22 percent before. Divestiture accomplished dramatic changes: the growth rate of sales, public profit, and fiscal flows all considerably more than doubled.

The second way to look at the record is to argue that, although divestiture occurred in May 1985, its announcement in 1984 disillu-

Table 16-4. Average Annual Compound Growth Rates, Sports Toto Malaysia, Fiscal 1978–89
(percentage)

Period	Real			Nominal		
	Revenue	Public profit	Fiscal flow	Revenue	Public profit	Fiscal flow
For divestiture						
1978–85	0.10	0.13	0.15	0.16	0.19	0.21
1985–89	0.39	0.55	0.48	0.41	0.58	0.50
Against divestiture						
1979–84	0.18	0.27	0.24	0.25	0.35	0.32
1984–89	0.24	0.30	0.30	0.25	0.31	0.32
Strongly for divestiture						
1984–86	0.16	0.18	0.20	0.24	0.26	0.28
1986–89	0.48	0.79	0.69	0.51	0.83	0.72

Source: Authors' calculations from Sports Toto data.

sioned a lame-duck management, causing a fall in 1985 output, which then must be attributed to divestiture. Thus the pre- and postdivestiture periods are 1979 to 1984, and 1985 to 1989, respectively (one has to argue that 1978 is somehow atypical). During the former period, nominal annual sales growth averaged 25 percent, exactly the same as in the latter. Even from the parochial view of the government, the growth in the fiscal flow was identical in both periods at 32 percent. Divestiture thus accomplished nothing: growth was equally rapid under both public and private management.

We are, of course, exaggerating a bit to emphasize the point that not all the growth since divestiture can be attributed to divestiture: growth was rapid prior to divestiture, and 1985 and 1986 are in some way atypical. The balance of this section attempts to determine how much of the change was due to divestiture itself, considering quantitative and qualitative information in turn.

First, however, note that the right-hand side hypothesis above (no divestiture effect) posits a negative announcement effect. This is in marked contrast to the conventional wisdom, best articulated with respect to the U.K. experience. There it was widely argued that the announcement of divestiture had a positive impact, as managers either strove to impress the new owners and thereby keep their jobs, or tried to enhance earnings in their role as actual or potential shareholders. It is difficult to disentangle this effect from the simultaneous impact of other policy reforms that enhanced the macroeconomic environment.

Be that as it may, some positive announcement effect certainly seems plausible in the U.K. case. Why might the Malaysian case, or at least the

Sports Toto case, be different? The answer might lie in the institutional nature of the divestiture transactions. The U.K. divestitures were largely sales to diversified shareholders, meaning that postdivestiture owner- ship would be divorced from control.[5] Sports Toto was completely different, with a controlling interest sold via private placement to a single private entity (recall that listing on the stock exchange did not follow until 1987). In the former environment it might well be reasonable for public managers to hope to be retained, while in the latter such an expectation would be foolish. That, at least, is the hypothesis to be explored.

Quantitative Evidence on Causation

As the quantitative record is sparse, our quantitative explorations will be brief. Only two explanatory variables are taken into account: inflation and the impact of the macroeconomic growth rate on demand. These are explored at both the enterprise and the industry level.

THE ENTERPRISE LEVEL. The role of inflation is straightforward. Inflation was more rapid before divestiture, so moving to constant prices means taking more away from the public growth rate than from the private, thereby enhancing the latter relative to the former. As shown on the left-hand side of table 16-4, in real terms even the least favorable com- parison (1979–84 versus 1984–89) shows a 6 percent advantage to private operation (24 percent versus 18 percent in sales, and 30 percent versus 24 percent in fiscal flows). In the more favorable comparisons (using 1985 or 1986 as the break point) real growth rates are three to four times as high after divestiture.

The relationship between real macroeconomic growth and sales is somewhat more complicated. A variety of regressions with and without a selection of divestiture dummies add little to the visual impression of figure 16-3 (table 16-5 presents the data). The data are consistent with the following story:

- During the public period, demand expanded as a declining multi- ple of aggregate demand (income elasticity of 3.4 in 1980 declining smoothly toward unity [1.4] in 1985).
- The recession of 1985 caused a decline in sales that was a several- fold multiple of what would have been expected historically. There is, of course, no reason for the elasticity to be symmetrical around zero, but the multiple is consistent with the hypothesis of a negative announcement effect.
- The 1986 rebound is consistent with a postrecession return to steady state, or with a recovery from the negative announcement effect.

Figure 16-3. Year-to-Year Changes in Real Sales, Sports Toto Malaysia, and in Real Gross Domestic Product, Malaysia, Fiscal 1979–89

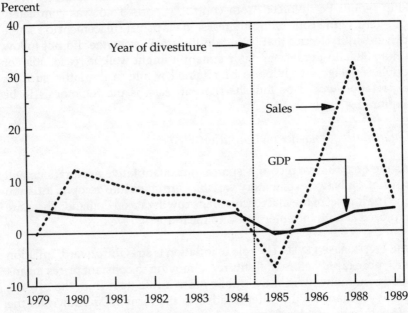

Source: Authors' calculations from Sports Toto data.

- The 1988 peak is hard to explain except as a dramatic one-time burst of innovation accompanying divestiture.
- The 1989 performance represents a return to historic growth rates, maintaining the 1988 gains but adding nothing more.

MARKET SHARE. Table 16-6 sets out available market share data for the Malaysian gambling sector. The figures for the formal market are calculated indirectly by applying tax rates to treasury tax collections at the company level and then aggregating. The estimate for the

Table 16-5. Year-to-Year Changes in Sales, Sports Toto Malaysia, and in Gross Domestic Product, Malaysia, Fiscal 1979–89
(percentages)

	1979	1980	1981	1982	1983	1984	1985	1986	1988	1989
Sales	-0.4	12.1	9.4	7.2	7.2	5.1	-6.8	10.6	32.2	5.6
GDP	4.5	3.6	3.4	2.9	3.0	3.7	-0.5	0.6	3.7	4.4

Source: Authors' calculations from Sports Toto data; GDP from National Income Statistics of Malaysia, various issues.

Table 16-6. *Market Shares, Sports Toto Malaysia, Fiscal 1982–90*
(millions of ringgit, except where otherwise noted)

Category	1982	1983	1984	1985	1986	1987	1988	1989	1990
Nominal									
Formal									
Sports Toto	84	93	88	80	93	174	213	220	261
Other numbers and lottery	1,403	1,380	1,372	1,429	1,347	1,208	1,028	1,451	1,924
Casinos and slot machines	82	96	112	131	244	293	344	439	688
Subtotal	1,569	1,569	1,572	1,640	1,684	1,676	1,584	2,111	2,873
Informal gambling							5,000	5,000	
Total							6,584	7,111	
Real									
Formal									
Sports Toto	73	77	70	64	74	137	163	163	193
Other numbers and lottery	1,208	1,146	1,097	1,139	1,065	953	790	1,073	1,423
Casinos and slot machines	71	79	89	105	193	231	265	325	509
Subtotal	1,352	1,303	1,256	1,307	1,332	1,321	1,219	1,561	2,125
Informal gambling							3,846	3,698	
Total							5,065	5,259	
Memoranda:									
Sports Toto market share (of percentage):									
Total gambling								3.23	3.10
Total formal gambling	5.37	5.92	5.59	4.86	5.53	10.37	13.42	10.43	9.10
Formal numbers and lotteries	5.66	6.31	6.02	5.28	6.46	12.57	17.14	13.17	11.96

Source: Authors' calculations from various sources.

informal sector is based on a verbal report of the bottom line of a police study. These data therefore need to be interpreted with caution. Note that Sports Toto's market share dropped in 1984 and 1985, which is consistent with a negative announcement effect. However, it doubled in 1987 and increased almost another one-third in 1988, but then declined in 1989 and 1990. This is consistent with a one-time burst in innovation.

In sum, the quantitative record strongly suggests a major gain from divestiture in fiscal 1988 and weakly supports a negative announcement effect in 1984 and 1985.

Qualitative Evidence

Senior managers at Sports Toto believe that the growth in sales after divestiture was due to the following:

- The success of its more aggressive and varied marketing strategies. These included not only campaigns directly aimed at attracting more customers, but also campaigns that sought to project Sports Toto as a responsible corporate citizen. Among the programs and activities initiated to achieve the latter was the "Giving Something Back to Society Program," which involved distributing some of Sports Toto's net profits from gaming operations to the poor and needy. This included making donations to the elderly on festive occasions; to social organizations such as the Cancerlink Foundation and PEMADAM, an antidrug organization; to the Girl Guides Association; to BAKTI, an association of ministers' wives that helps the poor and needy; and to individuals affected by tragedies or ill health. Sports Toto also contributed to the promotion of sports development in Malaysia by making donations to sports bodies and providing cash incentives to outstanding athletes.
- Introduction of new games. The divested enterprise introduced three new games during 1987–88.
- Increased number of sales outlets. Between 1987 and April 1989 Sports Toto opened 330 new outlets, bringing the total to 678.
- Revision to legislation on illegal gaming. The revised legislation, which introduced mandatory jail sentences and heavier fines for illegal gaming operators, has helped to discourage gamblers from placing their bets with such operators.

Gains at Whose Expense?

If divestiture caused an increase in Sports Toto's sales, where did this increase come from? Even though we are ignoring consumer surplus, this question is critical because of the impact on government revenues. There are three relevant possibilities:

- If it came at the expense of other formal gambling, then the gain in fiscal revenue from Sports Toto was offset by losses elsewhere, and the government netted nothing from the shift.[6]
- If it came at the expense of the informal gambling sector, then the entire amount is a fiscal gain.
- If it came at the expense of other consumer expenditures, then again the government gain approaches 100 percent.[7]

Note that the critical factor is how much came from the formal sector, because the fiscal impact of the other two possibilities is quite similar.

One way to approach the problem is to look at industry trends and attribute any deviations to the actions of Sports Toto. Recall from table 16-6 that, from 1982 to 1988, industrywide real numbers and lottery sales declined at 5 percent per year before taking off in 1989 and 1990. From 1986 to 1987, the deviation from trend almost exactly matches Sports Toto's growth, suggesting that the entire gain came from outside the formal sector. For 1987 to 1988, in contrast, the deviation is opposite in sign to Sports Toto's gain and twice as large, suggesting that either Sports Toto's advertising caused a reduction in formal gambling, or that the approach is missing something. We conclude that something is missing. Attributing the marginal change in a large industry to a small player makes little sense when many other things are changing. In particular, the approach ignores the causes of major trends in the sales of other large gambling concerns (which are not reported for reasons of confidentiality). These dropped dramatically from 1986 to 1988 but then took off. Without an industrywide study we have no idea what is going on, but we find it ludicrous to assume that at the margin the changes can be all attributed to Sports Toto.

An alternative approach is to look not at the margin but at averages. That is, formal gambling amounts to about one-third of informal gambling, which implies that one-quarter of any gains at Sports Toto would come from the formal sector and three-quarters from the informal sector. Furthermore, gambling is a small fraction of total consumption, so the bulk of Sports Toto's gains would come at the expense of nongambling expenditures. This, of course, ignores the fact that the margin is likely to be quite different from the average and, in particular, that closer substitutes would be likely to change the most (that is, that more of the gain would come from other formal gambling).

Where does this leave us? We really do not know very much and do not know how to know more without a detailed and difficult study of gamblers' consumption functions. As our base counterfactual, therefore, we will adopt a plausible guess that closer substitutes were affected more than the average, and arbitrarily use the following case assumption: equal thirds of the gain came from formal gambling, informal gambling, and general consumption. Readers with different priors can easily adjust our results for alternative scenarios, as we do in our sensitivity analysis below.

Conclusion: The Counterfactual

We conclude that in the absence of divestiture:

- Because of a negative announcement effect, the 1985 fall in sales would have been smaller (arbitrarily, half as large), and the 1986 recovery would have been correspondingly smaller.

Figure 16-4. Actual and Projected Public Profit at Constant Prices, Sports Toto Malaysia, Fiscal 1978–93

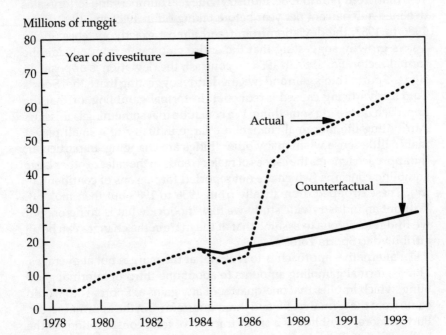

Millions of ringgit

Source: Authors' calculations.

- The 1988 surge would not have occurred, with sales growth continuing at the historic multiple of the GDP growth rate.
- Profits as a share of sales would have continued at 1984 levels.
- The changes were equally distributed at the expense of formal gambling, informal gambling, and general consumption.

In sum, our basic counterfactual is a continuation of 1984 performance, adjusting for inflation and the macroeconomic impact. Figure 16-4 presents the real fiscal effects that follow from these assumptions.

What Is It Worth?

We are now in a position to answer our fundamental question, under the following base assumptions:

- Divestiture is credited with a one-time surge of innovation in 1988.
- Divestiture is debited with a negative announcement effect in 1985.
- Changes in consumer surplus are valued at zero.

- Sports Toto's sales gains come equally at the expense of other formal gambling, informal gambling, and general consumption.
- Sales under both public and private operation are projected to grow at the historic multiple of the overall economic growth rate, with other variables projected from 1989 ratios for private operation and from 1984 ratios for continued public operation.[8]

Under these assumptions, table 16-7 shows who wins, who loses, and by how much. Note the following:

- Divestiture was beneficial, with society gaining M$121 million (at 1985 present values). This is roughly 10 times 1985 profits and 1.5 times 1985 sales.
- The private buyers do very well on the deal, netting M$112 million (M$207 million in future earnings less the sale price of M$95 million), or more than double the opportunity cost of the capital invested.
- The government does even better, netting about M$147 million.
- The losers are the formal and informal gambling sectors, which together are about M$138 million (M$69 million each) worse off.

As always, these figures should be taken only as orders of magnitude. As explained earlier, our most suspect assumption concerns the source of Sports Toto's increased sales. To put boundaries on the implications, table 16-7 also reports the impact of using two extreme alternative assumptions.

Table 16-7. Valuation of Divestiture, Sports Toto Malaysia
(millions of ringgit at 1985 present values)

Category	Base estimate	Maximum (all from consumers)	Minimum (all from formal gambling)
Value of the firm			
To private of private (V_{pp})	207	207	207
To public of private (V_{sp} - V_{sg})	121	409	0
Strike price (Z)	95	95	95
Distribution of gains to society (V_{sp} - V_{sg})			
Government	147	297	95
Buyer	112	112	112
Consumers (by assumption)	0	0	0
Competitors	–138	0	–207
Total gains to society	121	409	0

Source: Authors' calculations.

One extreme posits that all the gains were at the expense of formal gambling. The buyer's gains are unaffected by the assumption, but competitors lose an equal offsetting stream of profits. Similarly, the government's fiscal gains are all offset by losses elsewhere except for the sale price of the firm. In sum, under this extreme assumption, social welfare is not changed, only redistributed. The sale transfers surplus to Sports Toto worth M$207 million, of which the government gets M$95 million and the buyer keeps M$112 million.

The opposite extreme occurs if all the change comes from consumption in perfectly competitive markets. Now society gains M$409 million, with the government the big winner at M$297 million and the buyer receiving the same M$112 million.

This is obviously a very wide margin of error, but our judgment is that something in the vicinity of our base run is most likely. Others may differ. Other sources of error not noted here pale by comparison and are not reported.

Summary and Lessons

The primary conclusions in the Sports Toto case are as follows:

- Divestiture correlated with a lagged but dramatic surge in nominal sales and public profits, which tripled and quadrupled, respectively.
- Even after allowing for the impacts of inflation and recession, there was at minimum a one-time surge that nearly doubled sales brought about by innovative marketing.
- On the debit side, there is evidence of a small negative announcement effect, with public management dispirited by the expected transfer of ownership.
- Consumer surplus can be ignored because the industry is competitive, changes due to advertising are ambiguous, and gambling is as likely to be a "bad" as a "good."
- It is particularly difficult to ascertain where Sports Toto's gains came from. We assume that equal thirds came from formal gambling, informal gambling, and general consumption.
- Our best estimate is that, as a result of the divestiture, Malaysia is M$127 million better off, with the government gaining M$147 million, the private buyer gaining M$112 million, and other gambling operations losing M$138 million.

As we stressed in previous chapters, obviously one cannot generalize internationally from a single case study. Nonetheless, the Sports Toto case is consistent with the hypotheses that dramatic change is more likely where:

- The organization is small and can be changed rapidly.
- The enterprise is completely divested.
- The industry requires skills or attitudes that are particularly hard to provide under public operation (a company producing a standardized product in a stable environment—say, cement or fertilizer—is likely to suffer less from mechanistic public management than one producing in a dynamic market requiring effervescent marketing and advertising, such as gambling or exporting women's clothes to New York City).

At the same time, dramatic change is likely to be beneficial to society where the output market is competitive, or where one does not particularly care about consumer welfare because the product is exported or because it is a "bad." In addition, the U.K. phenomenon of a positive announcement effect can be reversed, perhaps where there is complete divestiture of a small enterprise.

In sum, for the first three reasons, divestiture led to dramatic change at Sports Toto; for the second two reasons, that change had major benefits for Malaysian society. The international implication is that these characteristics might make other revenue monopolies particularly attractive candidates for divestiture. This might apply to cigarettes in Nepal, ginseng in the Republic of Korea, and alcoholic beverages in New Hampshire.

Notes

This chapter was written by Leroy P. Jones and Fadil Azim Abbas. In addition to those acknowledged at the beginning of this volume, the authors would like to note that, on behalf of Sports Toto, selected data were provided by Ng. Foo Leong (senior general manager) and M. Tahir Taib (general manager).

1. Other revenue monopolies—for example, salt and ginseng—have only the second property described below.

2. Public profits are quasi rents or the total return to fixed capital. For Sports Toto, these are approximated by operating profit plus indirect taxes (the betting pool duty) plus depreciation. The opportunity cost of working capital should be deducted, but it is not, because data are not available for the public period (reserves were held in a commingled treasury account), and because in the private period the rapidly growing nonoperating acquisitions mean that some liquid assets are held for speculative purposes and make it difficult to apportion cash and other monetary assets meaningfully.

3. The National Sports Council finances Malaysian teams in international competition. We treat this as an implicit flow to the government on the grounds that in its absence the treasury would have footed the bill. As for the payment of 10 percent of before-tax profits or M$5 million, note that, except in 1983, table 16-3 suggests that the lower rather than the higher of the two figures was actually paid. We are unable to explain the discrepancy. In addition, Sports Toto annually makes a large number of charitable donations to support individual sporting

events. Time-series data are not available, but Sports Toto claims that these have also risen dramatically.

4. We have the actual figures, but they are not part of the public record. The 1 percent figure is an excellent approximation, however.

5. National Freight was the exception of sale to employees, where there is obvious motivation for improvements upon announcement.

6. We have calculated the government's share from data for the market leader (Magnum), which pays the 5 percent betting duty, relevant income taxes, and uncollected prizes, but also a 23 percent levy on sales less the betting duty. The latter charge more or less compensates for the various other charges on Sports Toto. We therefore assume that as a first approximation it does not matter where people gamble, as long as it is in the formal gambling sector.

7. We will arbitrarily use 90 percent, assuming expenditures would otherwise have been on commodities yielding the normal 5 percent sales tax and another 5 percent of sales in direct taxes.

8. Real economic growth is projected at 4 percent and Sports Toto sales at 1.25 times that, or 5 percent. Recall that the historic elasticity was declining steadily and had reached 1.34 by 1984.

17. Summary: Malaysia

The other three countries in this volume are the superstars of the divestiture world. The United Kingdom's leading role in privatization is well known. Chile and Mexico are somewhat less widely renowned but have an even stronger claim to fame. The most comprehensive list of worldwide divestitures identifies 2,100 cases in developing countries between 1980 and 1991 (Kikeri, Nellis, and Shirley 1992, p. 7). Of these, more than half (1,300) were in Mexico and Chile, leaving a low, single-digit average for all other developing countries. Malaysia, with eighteen divestitures, is thus far more typical of the developing world, where problems of political consensus building and implementation have resulted in a measured rather than a wholesale approach to divestiture.[1] The Malaysian case may thus be particularly relevant to conditions in other developing countries.

Saying that Malaysia is not an extreme outlier in terms of the scale of its divestiture program is not to suggest that it is average. Indeed, it is well ahead of the curve. Malaysia was included in this study precisely because—apart from Chile and Mexico—it had one of the widest, if not the widest, selection of divestitures in the developing world in the 1980s. Nonetheless, with divestitures in the teens rather than the hundreds, it was far closer to the mean than to the extreme cases of Mexico and Chile.

Malaysia closely resembles the other countries in this volume in two other respects. First, and more important, all the cases studied were very successful in terms of improving welfare. Second, like Mexico and Chile, Malaysia is among the wealthier developing countries: all three had per capita GDPs of around US$2,000 in the mid-1980s. Among other things this means that all three had reasonably well developed markets to divest into, and the stocks of human capital and functioning institutions to manage the divestiture process effectively and, where necessary, to control the exercise of monopoly power after divestiture. Given these advantages, one cannot necessarily extrapolate from success in these countries to success in less well endowed countries such as those in Sub-Saharan Africa.

Welfare Gains

The second of Malaysia's five goals of divestiture was to improve efficiency (see chapter 13). The primary aim of this volume is to quantify the extent to which all the countries studied have achieved this goal, where "efficiency" is defined broadly to include gains to consumers, workers, and competitors as well as to the buyer and the government seller. The results are decidedly favorable.

To allow international comparisons, it is convenient to express the magnitude of the gains not in ringgit but as the annual component of the perpetuity equivalent relative to predivestiture sales. That is, a gain in this ratio of 10 percentage points would mean that the present value of the gains we attribute to divestiture is equivalent to 10 percent of predivestiture sales received annually and indefinitely.

Thus measured, the gains are impressive in absolute terms, amounting to 22 percent of predivestiture sales at Malaysian Airline Systems (MAS), 53 percent at Kelang Container Terminal (KCT), and 11 percent at Sports Toto Malaysia. They are also impressive compared with the gains recorded in the other countries in this study: the Malaysian enterprises rank second, fifth, and seventh out of the twelve (see table 23-1) in terms of world welfare change.

Although the gains are all substantial and positive, their sources are quite different. At KCT the gains came through internal management changes that resulted in reduced costs or enhanced X-efficiency (improving the ratio of real output to inputs). At MAS, in contrast, there were no discernible internal improvements, but external changes in pricing and investment decisions led to welfare gains. Finally, Sports Toto followed a quite different route, relying primarily on improved marketing to expand its market share. Potential gains from divestiture clearly take a multitude of forms.

Partial Divestiture

A somewhat surprising feature of these positive results is that they were achieved largely by partial divestiture. Full divestiture is the transfer of 100 percent of ownership and control to the private buyer; partial divestiture is anything less. A particularly important case occurs when the government sells shares to the private sector but retains a controlling interest.[2] We call this partial financial divestiture to emphasize that while the distribution of the financial benefits or burden of the enterprise necessarily changes as a result, its behavior need not. Precisely because behavior need not change, partial financial divestiture is commonly derided as merely cosmetic. A cynical variant of this view is that the government is merely yielding to national or international pressures by giving the appearance of change without actually altering anything fundamental in the way the enterprise is run.

A competing view is that partial financial divestiture can result in the *best* of both worlds, combining the strengths of public and private operation (for more on mixed enterprises see Musolf 1972; for a contemporary mixed-enterprise divestiture model see Bos 1988, pp. 339–62). Bringing in private shareholders introduces pressures for efficient operation, while the government shareholders ensure that the public is not exploited in the process.

One can also argue that mixed public and private ownership combines the *worst* features of both partners. Private ownership creates pressures for profit, and government ownership allows this to be achieved by granting special privileges, licenses, and credits rather than by encouraging greater efficiency.

A priori theorizing can thus predict zero, positive, or negative change in the wake of partial financial divestiture. What do the Malaysian cases tell us?

Partial Divestiture in Malaysia

The three Malaysian cases were all partial divestitures but took three quite different forms. At Sports Toto the government initially ceded a controlling interest but retained a substantial (30 percent) minority financial interest for two more years. At KCT the government sold only 10 percent of the equity to the private sector; however, the balance was held by the government not directly but indirectly through other public (or quasi-public) enterprises. At MAS the government sold 48 percent, largely to diversified private shareholders, but retained a direct controlling interest. While all three divestitures were thus partial in one form or another, the results were nonetheless positive. How was this accomplished?

The Sports Toto case provides an important lesson for helping to solve one of the major difficulties of divestiture. When one is selling a previously unlisted company, there is no market price for the shares, and in the absence of a large number of bidders, setting a fair price is difficult: witness the widespread phenomenon of underpricing of new issues, be they public or private. The problem of underpricing is particularly acute for public enterprises, where the normal uncertainty the buyer faces is exacerbated by the change in management and the credibility of government commitment to the enterprise's future. Might the next government renationalize? Might it intervene through tax or regulatory policy to expropriate part or all of the potential surplus? In such an environment, selling part of the shares initially, letting the market observe the results and set a price over time, and later selling the rest can increase government revenues. The first government offering of Sports Toto yielded M$28 million for 70 percent of the enterprise, but the second yielded M$85 million for 30 percent, or seven times as much on a per share basis (inflation accounts for only about 4 percent of the increment). Temporary partial divestiture thus has much to recommend it as a mechanism for increasing the government's share of the gains from divestiture.

At KCT the government did not relinquish the right to control the enterprise, but it substantially altered the way in which it chose to exercise that right. The mechanism was the conversion of a direct government holding to an indirectly held one, where the government owned or controlled the companies that in turn held 90 percent of the shares. The Kelang Port Authority (with 49.0 percent of KCT shares) is wholly owned by the government, and Kontans Nasional (with 40.8 percent of KCT shares) is a quasi-public enterprise owned by other government-owned or-controlled enterprises. Such indirect control has the automatic advantage of freeing the enterprise from many intrusive government regulations. However, this very freedom has elsewhere operated to allow more rather than less inefficiency. In the case of KCT, the government chose to exercise its rights very much as a private shareholder would, thereby allowing KCT to achieve the remarkable gains in efficiency described in chapter 15.

MAS is an example of an even more partial form of divestiture, in which the company retained its status as a directly government-held enterprise. The Malaysian federal government retained 42 percent of the shares itself, and state governments held another 10 percent. Given that the balance of the shares was on the whole widely distributed among small private investors, this alone should have been more than sufficient to ensure government control, but a golden share provided insurance by allowing the government to appoint the chairman, the managing director, and six members of the eleven-member board of directors. The result was to a large extent what opponents of partial divestiture would have predicted: no *internal* management changes. However, important *external* changes did take place. Faced with potential pressures from private investors, or because the presence of such investors gave the government the excuse to do what it had wanted to do before, it relaxed inefficient constraints on investment and pricing. Before partial divestiture the airline was precluded from making commercially sound investments in capacity because of general government fiscal and balance of payments problems. After divestiture commercial logic applied. Similarly, though less certainly, we have argued that the same factors will lead to more economically efficient pricing policies. Relaxation of both these external constraints enhanced welfare significantly.

Although our limited number of case studies does not allow generalization to other countries, they can be taken as broadly reflecting Malaysia's experience. Part of this statement is strong, because of the nine official divestitures completed as of 1991, six were partial (Aircraft Repair and Overhaul, Cement Sarawak, KCT, Malaysian International Shipping Corporation, MAS, and Tradewinds), and only three small companies in competitive markets were fully divested (Sports Toto, a sugar company, and a printing plant). In addition, plans for two major divestitures currently in progress (electricity and telecommunications) call for the sale of only a minority of the shares. Divestiture in Malaysia is thus predominantly of the partial financial form. To assert that the other partial divestitures have been as successful as the Malaysian cases examined in this volume is considerably more problematic, but we do have some evidence on this issue. At the outset of our research we included Malaysian International Shipping Corporation in our sample, and while we did not conduct a complete quantitative analysis, we concluded that the enterprise was too much like the MAS case to warrant inclusion in the volume. That is, partial divestiture resulted in no observable internal management changes, but relaxation of the investment constraint yielded real efficiency gains. Similarly, a preliminary investigation of Syarikat Telekom Malaysia Berhad suggested that the management reforms accompanying corporatization are likely to have generated gains.

The Japanese Model of Partial Financial Divestiture

Is the success of partial financial divestiture in Malaysia an anomaly? Not necessarily. If the United Kingdom provides the model for full divestiture, then Japan provides the model for partial financial divestiture. The divestitures of Nippon Telegraph and Telephone Corp. (NTT), Japanese National Railways, and the tobacco monopoly are some of the more prominent industrial-country divestitures of the 1980s. What is sometimes forgotten, however, is that these were all cases of partial financial divestiture, with the government retaining control. Much of Singapore's public-enterprise sector has for years operated under a similar structure, with an autonomous government body holding the controlling interest and private owners holding substantial noncontrolling shares. Singapore Airlines is but the best-known example of the general success of these mixed public and private enterprises.

To take a broader perspective, the use of mixed enterprises is consistent with an East Asian mode of government-business relationships characterized by sometimes intimate government involvement in business affairs, as opposed to the arm's-length relationship often espoused in the West. Malaysia's prime minister has officially endorsed this model in his call for a "Malaysia Incorporated." We can find no written linkage between partial divestiture and the Malaysia Incorporated concept, or indeed any reference to partial divestiture as an element of the country's privatization strategy. Nonetheless, privatization has been extensively discussed in the context of Malaysia Incorporated (see Ghani and others 1984), and partial divestiture is consistent with that linkage.

Alternatives and Sustainability

In sum, divestiture in Malaysia has been largely partial, but also largely successful in generating welfare gains. This has been accomplished through a process of commercialization: making managers more responsive to market pressures. The conclusion is that partial divestiture need not be merely cosmetic if the introduction of private shareholders shifts the exercise of government discretion in the direction of more economically rational decisions.

This raises the obvious question of whether or not the same results could have been achieved without any divestiture whatsoever. Why could the government not have simply converted its enterprises to joint stock companies, thereby relieving them of some government regulations, and instructed them to pursue profits (subject, in monopoly cases, to a price constraint)? Logically, there is no necessary reason why the government could not have done this. However, the fact that these same decisions *could* have been taken without divestiture is irrelevant if they *would* not have been taken. If the introduction of private shareholders brings pressures to bear for a more commercial orientation, this is a positive step.

Even if the same results could have been achieved without partial divestiture, the question of sustainability remains. All too often, wise public-enterprise reforms under one government are negated by the next. One can argue that the presence of private shareholders reduces the probability of such a reversal.

Distribution and the New Economic Policy

As explained in chapter 13, Malaysia's divestiture program must be seen in the context of the New Economic Policy (NEP), whose goal is to increase the share of ethnic Malays (Bumiputra) in corporate ownership. To what extent have the divestitures studied here contributed to this goal? The answer is not as straightforward as it might seem. Let us first consider the case of Sports Toto.

Sports Toto

Recall the distributional facts. The government sold the first 70 percent of Sports Toto directly to B&B Enterprises (60 percent Bumiputra owned) and the remaining 30 percent to Raleigh Berhad (26 percent Bumiputra owned). A later private placement transferred 10 percent from B&B to

Melewar Corporation (also predominantly Bumiputra owned). Subsequent to these private placements, Sports Toto was listed on the Kuala Lumpur stock exchange and its shares were freely traded. Some shares were disbursed widely among the public, but by the end of fiscal 1990–91, Berjaya Corporation (the holding company of B&B Enterprises) had acquired almost 56 percent of Sports Toto's shares. Bumiputra owned about 42 percent of Berjaya's equity.

How are these facts to be interpreted in the light of the NEP? One approach is to look at the ending distribution. For example, Bumiputra held 24 percent of Sports Toto via their share in Berjaya alone, and so they almost certainly held a total that equaled or exceeded the NEP target of 30 percent. Does this make divestiture at least a limited success? The answer is, not necessarily, because we must first be more precise in formulating the counterfactual.

Assume that these ending Bumiputra shares were all bought on the open market. If Bumiputra had not bought these shares, then presumably they would have bought some other shares, and the Bumiputra share of corporate assets would not be changed but only redistributed. Accordingly, ending shares (and any shares bought in a free market) are irrelevant in judging whether divestiture furthered the goals of the NEP.

What *is* relevant is the value of any subsidy given to Bumiputra buyers through privileged access. To the extent they received an underpriced asset, their wealth increased, and some of this would go to increased investment. How much? One would ordinarily think that the marginal propensity to invest out of extra wealth would be considerably less than one. However, in this case it could actually be greater than one if a belief in potential subsidized profits led investors to invest money they would otherwise have spent on consumption. In sum, the NEP's objective of redistributing corporate assets is accomplished only to the extent that Bumiputra buyers gain more than their opportunity cost from the investment, and then to the extent that the gain is invested.

In the present instance, the sales to Raleigh and Melawar as well as the public offering were at or near the market price, so there was no significant impact on NEP goals. However, 60 percent of the initial sale to B&B accrued to Bumiputra. Since this was double the NEP target and perhaps triple the existing level, the Bumiputra share of corporate assets rose. By how much? As the buyers were wealthy, it is reasonable to assume that they would have saved a considerable portion of any incremental wealth. Illustratively using a marginal propensity to invest of 0.8, and using our base estimate of buyer gains, Bumiputra corporate assets rose by about M$54 million and non-Bumiputra corporate assets by about M$35 million. Given the small size of Sports Toto relative to total corporate assets, this is a minuscule gain, but projected over the realm of potential divestitures it would be significant.

MAS and KCT

With the basic principles established, we can deal with the other cases more briefly. At MAS the initial domestic offering was reserved for Bumiputra institutions and individuals. Their share of the total gain (M$473 million) is reduced to the extent that some of the original buyers were acting as fronts for non-Bumiputra interests, and to the extent that they resold some of their shares before realizing the full gains. The first effect is real but probably small; the second is undoubtedly substantial but unquantifiable. The gain in corporate asset holdings is further reduced to the extent that some of the increment in wealth goes to consumption rather than investment. Given the limitation on the number of shares bought, the bulk of the buyers were middle class, with modest marginal propensities to save, but given privileged access to shares this could have been considerably higher. Putting these various uncertainties together, the most that we can say is that the gain in Bumiputra shareholdings as a result of the MAS divestiture was on the order of a few hundred million ringgit.

At KCT the Bumiputra Investment Foundation ultimately held one-third of the shares, and so received that proportion of the buyers' share of the benefits, or about M$45 million. Given that the shares were held in trust, the marginal propensity to save could have approached unity. If so, then the bulk of the money represented a fulfillment of the NEP. Furthermore, the bulk of the benefits went to the government and could be used in part to further other Bumiputra interests. Finally, efficiency gains were obtained without transferring control to foreign or non-Bumiputra interests.

Bumiputra Control

Although the NEP's goals are usually stated in terms of enhancing Bumiputra shareholdings, they could also be evaluated in terms of transferring control to private Bumiputra interests. In this regard, nothing has been accomplished, because in one of our cases control remained with the government, in another it was transferred to other public enterprises, and in the third it initially went to private Bumiputra interests but was thereafter sold to non-Bumiputra interests.

Summary

The NEP's shareholding goals are furthered only to the extent that the Bumiputra end up with a greater share of Malaysian corporate assets than they would have had without divestiture. Simply selling them shares of former public enterprises when they would have otherwise bought shares in other firms accomplishes nothing. In the three cases considered here, increased Bumiputra shareholding was nonetheless achieved because their wealth was enhanced by the purchases, and a portion of this presumably went to increased investment in shares. This increase in wealth, in turn, was made possible by the gains in efficiency. The initial share offerings were not particularly underpriced relative to their value under the enterprises' traditional management, so that, in the absence of behavioral change, there would have been little or no gain in Bumiputra wealth and shareholding. Divestiture increased the value of the shares, and sales to Bumiputra allowed them to capture a significant portion of this gain.

Functional Distribution

At the outset of the privatization program in Malaysia, Prime Minister Mahathir Mohamad asserted, "Privatization will not be allowed to take place unless we can be assured that employees will not lose by it. Indeed, it is quite possible that employees will be better off through Privatisation" (Mohamad 1984, p. 5). Given labor's widespread opposition (around the world, not just in Malaysia), this is a statement of some importance. However, the prime minister went on to make an even stronger statement: "Privatisation is not formulated for the benefit of any group or political party. Everyone should benefit from it, or at the very least should not lose by it" (Mohamad 1984, p. 6). Given the difficulty of finding pure Pareto-improving policies in the real world, this is indeed an optimistic claim. How did things turn out in our cases?

Labor

In the case of labor, the prime minister proved to be correct. Our study suggests that workers did not lose at MAS and gained substantially at KCT.[3] This was not an accident but the result of a concrete policy. At KCT there were to be no layoffs for five years, and workers were given the options of taking early retirement, staying with the Port Authority, or joining the new company on terms no less favorable than those they had previously enjoyed. As KCT was Malaysia's first divestiture, it set a precedent for dealing with labor, and similar or identical terms have been given to labor in other major divestitures.

At Kelang, virtually all the workers chose to join the new company and were rewarded with higher compensation (a 60 percent gain in real hourly compensation from 1985 to 1990) in return for working a little longer (6 percent) and a lot harder and smarter. As a result they produced about 75 percent more output. In addition, unions at both KCT and its parent Kelang Port Authority have become advocates of divestiture, urging the divestiture of the parent itself and advising a Thai port union to support the sale of its own organization.

There is an important lesson here for divestiture policy in other countries. Workers are widely perceived to be potential losers from divestiture, and their opposition can be a deal breaker. Buying them off with employment guarantees is not the best solution, but it may well be preferable to no divestiture, so long as management is allowed to introduce flexible work rules that allow efficiency gains. With those gains, natural attrition plus expanded capacity utilization can soak up excess workers in a relatively brief period.

Other Actors

The assertion that no one will lose also holds up quite well, but not perfectly. We project that domestic consumers will eventually lose a small amount from higher prices charged by MAS on internal routes, but overall this is a step toward the right prices and thus enhances efficiency. The other group of losers is competitors. At Kelang, the Port Authority loses revenues as containerization is accelerated by increased efficiency due to divestiture. Overall, however, the Kelang Port Authority's losses as a competitor are more than offset by its gains as an owner. Competitors of Sports Toto are clearly net losers, as they lose market share to the divested enterprise with its newly aggressive management. This, of course, is hardly a criticism of the divestiture policies, because increased efficiency is exactly what one wants divestiture to accomplish, and in a competitive market this is bound to hurt someone else.

With these (generally positive) exceptions, the prime minister's no-loser policy was confirmed in our cases. Once again, what made this possible was the gains in efficiency that created a positive-sum game in which appropriate policies could make nearly everyone better off.

Lessons from Malaysia

Divestiture in Malaysia has been partial in two respects. First, as in the vast majority of developing countries, the government has disposed of only a small fraction of the public sector during the first decade or so of the process. Second, in most of the larger cases, only a fraction of the shares have actually entered private hands. Nonetheless, the divestitures studied here have been quite successful, both in enhancing welfare and in achieving a relatively broad distribution of the resulting gains. The Malaysian privatization program thus deserves the attention of other countries.

Notes

This chapter was written by Leroy Jones and Fadil Azim Abbas.

1. The eighteen divestitures include nine carried out by the Economic Planning Unit under the official privatization plan, plus nine sales of small enterprises by the Unit for Monitoring Government Agencies and Enterprises (UPSAK) in the course of exercising its mandate of reforming ailing state enterprises. It excludes a large number of other forms of privatization (build-operate-transfer arrangements, contracting out, and leasing) by the Economic Planning Unit.

2. Operationally, the test of a controlling interest is whether or not the government effectively appoints the chief executive officer. Holding a majority of the voting shares is sufficient, but not necessary, to this end.

3. Recall that we did not have enough information to make a definitive statement about Sports Toto, but informal discussion suggests that workers probably gained there as well, and at least did not lose.

PART V

Mexico:
Divestiture as an Instrument
of Stabilization

18. Divestiture in Mexico

The Mexican divestiture program began in 1983 as part of the macroeconomic stabilization program of that period. Following a rapid buildup during the 1970s (under presidents Luis Echeverría and José López Portillo), the Mexican state-owned sector consisted in 1982 of 1,155 enterprises, producing 12.6 percent of GDP and accounting for 38 percent of investment.[1] In that year the overall government budget deficit was nearly 17 percent of GDP, as rising interest rates and a decline in oil prices combined to push public revenues down and expenditures up. The Mexican government's early response to the crisis was to suspend payments on the external debt and to nationalize the banks.

In 1983, however, the government adopted a package of policies sponsored by the International Monetary Fund aimed at stabilizing the economy. The stabilization program contained several elements designed to reduce the budget deficit. These included reductions in government expenditures, primarily through investment cuts and moderation of wage increases; tax increases; divestitures; and increases in public sector prices. Thus the divestiture program was part of this larger deficit reduction package.

By 1985 the economy was showing signs of improvement, with GDP growing at about 3 percent and inflation down to about 60 percent per year. However, the economy was at this point subjected to two additional shocks. First, Mexico City was hit by a massive earthquake in September 1985, causing damage estimated at US$4 billion. Second, oil prices plunged in 1986 to levels less than half those in 1985. As a result, GDP fell from US$177 billion in 1985 to US$127 billion in 1986 and inflation took off again, with prices rising 106 percent in 1986 and a further 159 percent in 1987.

The government's response to the latest crisis was to embark on a complete transformation of the Mexican economy. The divestiture program, which had previously concentrated on small, relatively insignificant enterprises, began to tackle the large ones, eventually reaching some of the behemoths of the public sector. But the government went well beyond divestiture. Thoroughgoing trade liberalization transformed Mexico from a highly protected economy into one of the most open in the world. Mexico joined the General Agreement on Tariffs and Trade and reduced tariffs to an average of 10 percent by the late 1980s. There was also liberalization and deregulation at home, as market forces were unleashed in transport (except for rail), steel, fertilizers, and many other sectors. Agreement was also reached on the external debt through the Brady Plan, under which US$45.8 billion of Mexico's debt was rescheduled.

The response of the economy to this policy regime has been dramatic: inflation has been brought down below 20 percent, GDP growth is between 3 and 4 percent per year, and interest rates have fallen dramatically. Thus the divestiture program must be seen as part of a highly successful package of reform policies. How important a part it was is a question we will examine later in this chapter.

Size and Scope

Table 18-1 summarizes the extent and pace of the divestiture program. By any account it has been a massive program: the number of public enterprises fell from 1,155 in 1982 to just over 200 in 1991. Of the enterprises divested, only 346 were sold, whereas 594 fall in the "other" category—mostly liquidations. The program can be clearly divided into two stages, from 1983 to 1988, and from 1989 to the present, corresponding to the six-year terms of presidents Miguel de la Madrid and Carlos Salinas de Gortari. Whereas the earlier period was characterized by the divestiture of large numbers of small enterprises, with liquidation the most common method, the later period has seen a big jump in the average size of enterprise, and sale is now the more frequently chosen divestiture option. As table 18-2 shows, the average price (in U.S. dollars) received for those enterprises that were sold tripled from 1988 to 1989, nearly doubled again in 1990, and then increased nearly sixfold in 1991. In the period since 1989 some of the largest public enterprises in the country, including the telephone monopoly Teléfonos de México (Telmex), all the largest commercial banks, the steel conglomerate Sidermex, and the fertilizer monopoly Fertimex, have been sold. This second phase of divestitures seems to have been driven by the desire to raise very large sums of money as part of the macroeconomic stabilization program.

Special Features

Certain elements of the divestiture process, particularly after 1988, deserve special attention.

Table 18-1. Public Enterprises Sold and Otherwise Disengaged, Mexico, 1982–91

Year	Number of enterprises sold	Other disengagement	Number of enterprises remaining at end of year
1982	n.a.	n.a.	1,155
1983	4	77	1,074
1984	3	22	1,049
1985	32	76	941
1986	28	176	737
1987	21	99	617
1988	66	139	412
1989	37	0[a]	379
1990	90	9	280
1991	65	—[b]	215[b]
Total	346	594	n.a.

n.a. Not applicable.

a. Not meaningful. The number of sales exceeds the decline in the number of enterprises, indicating a data incompatibility problem.

b. For this year, "Other disengagement" is assumed to be zero for purposes of calculating the number of enterprises remaining.

Source: Numbers of enterprises sold and remaining are from the Secretariat of Finance and Public Credit. "Other disengagement" (liquidations, mergers, transfer to nonfederal entities) is calculated as the residual.

The Proposal Mechanism

Although formally the ministry with administrative responsibility for the sector in which an enterprise operates "proposes" it for disengagement, the assumption now is that in principle all enterprises are to be disengaged, unless the ministry is able to justify retaining it in the public sector. This subtle change in underlying attitude is partly responsible for the fact that very large numbers of enterprises have been disengaged.

The Privatization Unit

In most cases, administrative responsibility for an enterprise slated for sale is transferred to the privatization unit in the Secretariat of Finance and Public Credit. This unit was created in 1988, and therefore none of its key officials has any strong vested interests in the status quo. Its head, known as the Coordinador General, is assisted by six officials of director-general rank. Their job is to manage the specific sales, but they do so in a supervisory capacity only, as the details are delegated to so-called agent banks (see below). Thus the divestitures are carried out in a manner recalling arm's-length market transactions. The idea is to use these commercial banks' expertise in business valuation and mergers and acquisitions, but to do so at arm's length so that competition among the banks for the government's business ensures good performance. The business is indeed desirable since the government typically pays the agent bank a commission of 1 percent of the final sale price. The disadvantage in relying on the commercial banks is that their expertise is in valuing companies from the private, not the social, point of view. Whether this contributed to the Mexican government's clear reliance on commercial criteria in the divestiture program is unclear.

Agent Banks

The agent bank performs several important functions. The first is to prepare a prospectus for the sale. Bids are then invited. The bidders are often prescreened for financial viability, and deposits are required before the prospectus is released to them. A second crucial function is to perform a technical valuation of the enterprise, to arrive at a reservation price below which it will ostensibly not be sold. The reservation price is not derived from any simple formula; rather it is based on the agent bank's judgment after various methods have been employed to estimate the value of the enterprise. The valuation methods include discounted

Table 18-2. Public Enterprises Sold and Sale Receipts, Mexico, 1983–91

Year	Number of enterprises Nominal[a]	True[b]	Total receipts Millions of pesos	Millions of U.S. dollars	Average dollar price (millions)
1983	4	2	4,847	40.3	20.2
1984	3	1	208	1.2	1.2
1985	32	10	29,180	113.5	11.4
1986	28	14	61,593	100.6	7.2
1987	21	16	229,379	167.9	10.5
1988	66	51	1,180,750	524.8	10.3
1989	37	25	1,798,549	730.8	29.2
1990	90	59	9,017,209	3,196.5	54.2
1991	65	37	32,656,544	10,813.4	292.3
Total	346	215			

a. Number of legally separate companies sold.

b. Number of discrete sale transactions. For example, the sale of the Telmex was one transaction and therefore one true sale, but in fact eighteen legal entities (companies under control of the Telmex holding company) were transferred.

Source: Authors' calculations based on data from the Secretariat of Finance and Public Credit.

cash flow, book value, liquidation value, and market value. Obviously the reservation price remains a closely guarded secret.

Selection Criteria

The sale itself is conducted as a sealed-bid first-price auction. The bids of the prescreened bidders are received simultaneously in the presence of public notaries (who certify the bids), representatives of the finance and comptroller secretariats, and the media. The agent bank examines and homogenizes the bids in order to make them comparable. The stated investment plans and labor policies of each bidder are taken into account, but the primary criterion at this stage is the offer price. The clarity of this criterion (which is a reasonable one given that bidders were prescreened) further assures the transparency and fairness of the sale process.

The Mexican government did not use stock market sales to divest its public enterprises, for several reasons. First, most of the enterprises were not already quoted on the stock exchange and therefore did not have established prices. Second, in almost all cases it was perceived that the management of the enterprises needed to be changed. This would normally not be achieved (at least not immediately) through a stock market placement. Third, and perhaps most important, offers to well-identified investors were likely to yield the highest price—a key goal of the government.

Labor Relations

An important feature of the Mexican divestiture program has been the absence of any serious opposition from labor. It is true that the trade union movement in Mexico has traditionally been closely allied with the Partido Revolucionario Institucional, the party that has held power since the revolution. Nevertheless, if labor felt that its interests were likely to be severely threatened by divestiture (as many believe is inevitable), surely some opposition would develop. Yet it has not, and indeed this lack of opposition has been a necessary condition to allow the divestiture program to proceed smoothly and quickly.

In fact, labor's interests have been protected throughout the program. This protection has taken three forms. First, the unions have, by law, a right of first refusal at each sale. That is, once the bids are known, the union can acquire the enterprise by matching the highest bid. Many enterprises have been sold to their labor unions under this provision—a total of sixteen in the period 1989–91 alone. They have included enterprises in various sectors including fishing, sugar, food products, fertilizers, mining, and auto parts. The largest sale has been the Bajío plant of Fertimex, sold to the union in December 1991 for over US$31 million. A key measure to prevent abuse of this provision is the prohibition of resale. This prevents an outside bidder from making a deal with the union to buy the enterprise after the union has exercised its right, thereby obviating the need to bid in the first place.

The second form of protection for labor has been the understanding that layoffs are not to occur. Thus labor efficiency is expected to improve only gradually as the work force is reduced through attrition or as output expands and the existing number of workers is more fully utilized. In an early study of the effects of divestiture, Perez Escamilla (1988) found at most a 5 percent reduction in the number of workers. At Telmex, for example, despite evidence of massive labor redundancy (the number of workers per line is twice as high as for American telephone companies), no significant layoffs have occurred; instead, the company plans to retrain its workers and to allow growth to absorb the redundancy. This prohibition against worker layoffs has in some cases impeded sales. For example, as detailed in chapter 21, no buyer could be found willing to pay an adequate price for Mexicana de Aviación at the first two attempts to sell the enterprise, because buyers wanted the right to lay off workers or for the government to reach a settlement with labor to reduce the work force. The government did not accommodate these demands. No doubt the bar against layoffs must have reduced the price buyers have been willing to pay for enterprises, although it is difficult to estimate the size of this effect. This may be a small price to pay, however, to ensure labor's cooperation with the divestiture process.

Third, in some instances employees have been sold shares in the enterprise in order to encourage their cooperation. For example, the Telmex union was sold 4.4 percent of that enterprise for US$325 million; the money for the purchase was lent to the union by a government bank. At the enterprise's market price as of 16 April 1992, this shareholding was worth US$1.37 billion, for a gain of over US$20,000 per worker. It is not surprising that workers have not opposed divestiture in this case.

Apart from the protection labor has received, some observers believe that labor's cooperation has been induced partly by the drastic decision by the government to declare Aeroméxico bankrupt (see chapter 20). In 1988, in response to a strike, the government shut down the airline, fired the entire work force (nearly 12,000 workers), and sold the enterprise's assets. Aeroméxico today has about 6,000 workers. The copper enterprise Minera de Cananea suffered through a similar process. The fear of job losses may therefore be keeping labor quiescent as divestiture proceeds.

Foreign Participation

As part of its policy of liberalizing and opening up the economy to international trade, the Mexican government liberalized the rules applying to foreign ownership of Mexican companies. Minority ownership up to 49 percent was made permissible, and majority or even full ownership is now possible under certain circumstances. As a result, there has been some foreign participation in the divestiture program, although less than one might expect given the massive capital flows involved.

According to a document of the finance ministry (Mexico, Secretaría de Hacienda y Crédito Público 1991), 98 percent of 156 enterprises sold from January 1987 to August 1991 were purchased by Mexican investors. Indeed, only three outright sales to foreign companies took place, and all were relatively small (this does not include the sale in January 1992 of the Sicartsa steel complex to Caribbean Ispat Ltd., an Indian-controlled company based in Trinidad). But there were several other important sales in which foreigners played a minority, but key, role as major sources of funds or of technical expertise. For example, 15 percent of Telmex was sold to Southwestern Bell and France Télécom (desired for their know-how), and another 18.7 percent was sold in international stock markets. Because 22 percent of Telmex stock was foreign owned even before divestiture began, foreigners now own 55.7 percent of the company (see chapter 19 for details).

Another example in our sample is Mexicana, where the controlling group that acquired 25 percent of the enterprise is itself 49 percent foreign. Among the foreign owners is Chase Manhattan Bank, which exchanged part of its debtholdings for 9 percent of the equity. This is one of the few cases of divestiture in Mexico that involved a debt-equity swap, a practice that has not been very significant since the debt rescheduling operation.

Successes and Failures

There can be little doubt that the Mexican divestiture program has been a great success. Probably its greatest achievement, and the reason it is widely admired, is its magnitude—as noted above, more than 900 public enterprises were divested between 1982 and 1991. Nor were the divestitures merely cosmetic. The government has sold a number of huge enterprises: the telephone monopoly, the two major airlines, all the large commercial banks, mining enterprises, the entire steel sector, and the fertilizer sector, among others. There has been a partial or even complete withdrawal from an array of sectors that arguably should not have had a government presence in the first place—for example, textiles, fishing, sugar, hotels, and auto parts. Even though the reduction in assets or value added is much smaller proportionately (the state petroleum enterprise Pemex alone constituted about half the public-enterprise sector in terms of contribution to GDP), this nevertheless constitutes a significant reduction in the government's presence in the economy.

Role of Divestiture in Macroeconomic Stabilization

The divestiture program has also generated substantial revenues for the government, thereby fulfilling a key role in the economic stabilization program. As table 18-2 shows, the proceeds from public-enterprise sales in the two years 1990–91 were around US$14 billion, which is three to five times the various estimates of the benefits to Mexico from the debt rescheduling operation.[2] Although the sales were mostly to Mexicans, the Telmex sale brought in US$4.7 billion in foreign capital, and it is safe to say that much of the rest of the revenue from divestiture was probably returning flight capital. World Bank staff have estimated that there was some US$2 billion in new portfolio inflows in 1990 and about US$9 billion in 1991. Although the Mexican stock market boom and the related liberalized rules on foreign ownership of shares have encouraged capital inflows, all of the capital inflows in 1990–91 can be implicitly accounted for by the divestiture program.

Thus there is little doubt that revenues from the divestiture program have played an important role in macroeconomic stabilization. In terms of short-term revenue impact, it could be argued that the program has been even more important than the Brady deal. Further, the proceeds from the divestitures have explicitly not been mingled with other sources of government revenue; rather, they were set aside in a so-called stabilization fund and used to retire a portion of the domestic debt. This has had an immediate favorable impact on interest rates.

Economywide Efficiency Improvement

A third expected benefit from the divestiture program is increased efficiency of the economy as a whole, as major firms operate more on market principles. It is still too early to assess the size of this impact. At the microeconomic (i.e., enterprise) level, our cases provide some mixed evidence. For example, the two divested airlines present contrasting outcomes, with Aeroméxico performing well and Mexicana not so well.

Factors Contributing to Success

A series of factors contributed to the success of Mexico's divestiture program.

Commitment

The key to success was commitment to the program at the highest levels of the Mexican government. This commitment was at most only partly ideological. Rather, it was driven primarily by the perception that divestiture could play a crucial role in the stabilization of the economy.

Transparency

The process of divestiture has been clearly defined and transparent. No deviations are made from the announced rules. To avoid bargaining after a bid is accepted, the government draws up the legal contract of sale *before* calling for bids and permits potential buyers to question (and even modify) aspects of the contract before bidding commences. The key element ensuring transparency is the system of checks and balances established through the inclusion of several different actors in the process: sector ministries, the privatization unit, and the agent banks. The use of bidding rather than negotiation also creates a more transparent situation for all buyers.

Administrative Separation

As was mentioned above, administrative control of enterprises in the process of divestiture was generally transferred from the secretariat with sectoral authority to the privatization unit at the finance secretariat. Thus, for example, when Telmex was being readied for divestiture, control over the enterprise was moved from the communications secretariat to the privatization unit. This policy had three advantages: actions deemed necessary precursors to divestiture could be taken quickly and without dilution or delay; any potential conflict of interest between divestiture and entrenched bureaucracies was avoided; and the management of the divestitures was concentrated into a few capable hands at the privatization unit, allowing benefits from learning and from specialization to be realized.

Selection Criteria

A fourth innovation that probably was important in the scale of divestiture was the way in which enterprises were selected for sale. In the early years of the program a more "normal" process was followed, in which sector ministries were invited to offer those enterprises for sale that were considered to be in nonpriority sectors. The approach was to present an argument why particular enterprises were appropriate for divestiture. As the program developed, however, the presumption became that all enterprises would be sold, and sector ministries then had to argue why particular enterprises were *not* suitable for divestiture if they were to be kept off the list. This change in emphasis may have been instrumental in maintaining the momentum of the divestiture program even after the obvious candidates had been sold.

Notes

This chapter was written by Pankaj Tandon. Many people have contributed to our understanding of Mexico and its divestiture program. Among them we would particularly like to mention Shyamadas Banerji, Bernardo Gomez Palacio, Paul Knotter, Santiago Levy, Inder Ruprah, Manuel Sanchez, Jorge Silberstein, and Aaron Tornell. Able secretarial assistance was provided by Charlene Arzigian and Patricia Regan. To all these individuals goes our gratitude.

1. It is difficult to get precise, comprehensive data on the Mexican public-enterprise sector. Some of the available series contain data for all public enterprises, while others include only "directly controlled" public enterprises, leaving out many large enterprises such as the telephone monopoly Telmex, the state airline Mexicana de Aviación, and the commercial banks. The figures presented here for GDP and investment share include only directly controlled public enterprises.

2. Van Wijnbergen (1991) estimates that the Brady deal reduced Mexico's annual interest bill by US$1.3 billion and total payments (including amortization) by US$4 billion per year.

19. *Teléfonos de México*

Consider the following scenario. A company with about 50,000 employees has annual sales of about US$1.5 billion. Productivity, however, is low and declining, and the stock price has been languishing at about 25 cents per share, setting the market value of the firm at about US$1 billion. Management decides to take action. Three years later, sales are well over US$4 billion and the stock has soared to over US$7 per share, placing the market value of the firm at nearly US$30 billion. The company has been named "Company of the Year" by the country's leading business weekly. Surely this would be the turnaround story of the decade, shining proof that the "action" management took deserves to be studied and emulated.

This story is not fiction. It is the story of Teléfonos de México S.A. de C.V. (Telmex), the period is from 1989 to 1991, and the action taken in 1989 was the commencement of the enterprise's divestiture. It is not hard to see why Telmex is regarded as one of the great success stories of the privatization revolution, why the people involved are invited to give seminars on it all over the world, and why practically every major investment house has done an in-depth analysis and report on the enterprise.

This chapter takes a close look at the divestiture of Telmex and analyzes the factors behind its success. We will argue that the success lies not so much where the popular perception would put it, but rather in the contribution of the Telmex divestiture to the overall economy. In particular, it is tempting to assume that the big runup in the stock price of Telmex reflects the market's estimate of the huge productivity and other efficiency improvements that the new (private) management of the company will bring to fruition. We will argue, however, that this assumption would be only partly correct. Rather, much of the big stock price jump stems from large price increases granted to Telmex by the Mexican government as part of its divestiture concession. Thus the rise in the stock market value of the company has come largely at the expense of the consumer. At the same time, however, we believe that the divestiture of Telmex has played a crucial role in the overall stabilization of the Mexican economy—in the "Mexican economic miracle." The benefits so conferred on Mexico may far outweigh any gains or losses measured at the level of the firm.

After a brief look at the historical background of the enterprise, we examine in detail the last ten years of public ownership. We then look at the period leading up to and including the sale of the enterprise, examining the steps taken to prepare it for sale, the sale transactions themselves, and the regulatory environment created around the enterprise. We look at Telmex's performance in its first year after divestiture. Finally, we present our projections for the future course of Telmex and draw our conclusions for what this has all meant for the Mexican economy.

Background

Teléfonos de México is the principal supplier of telecommunications services in Mexico. It has a monopoly on the provision of local and long distance services. Private networks, cellular communications, and equipment sales and rentals are subject to competition. Long distance and international services are slated to be opened to competition in 1996.

History

Telmex was a private company until 1972.[1] At that time the company was struggling to bear the cost of integrating two different telephone companies, created originally by ITT Corp. and Ericsson, and this turned out to be too expensive, despite large borrowings from the government. To carry the integration to completion, the Mexican government assumed control of the company, converting its loans to stock and then buying additional stock (2 percent of the company) to assure itself of majority (51 percent) ownership. At the time of divestiture, in 1990, it owned 56 percent of the enterprise's stock.

Divestiture

It is unclear what motivated the divestiture of Telmex. Telmex had not been in any financial trouble. It was embarking on an ambitious investment program, and it could be argued that the government may not have wanted to assume the liability of the necessary major expenditures. However, we shall see that Telmex has tremendous ability to generate investible resources internally, so this is not a particularly strong argument. We speculate that Telmex was chosen partly for its symbolic importance and partly as a potential source of a sizable amount of revenue. It is the largest company on the Mexican stock exchange. It was still 44 percent privately owned. And obviously it served a large and important clientele. The divestiture of Telmex would dramatically serve notice that Mexico was serious about divestiture and the development of the private sector. Further, as the country's telephone monopoly, it could be expected to command a high sale price.

The intention to divest Telmex was announced in September 1989. Administrative control of the enterprise was at that time transferred from the Secretariat of Communications and Transport to the Secretariat of Finance and Public Credit, which was overseeing all divestitures. Preparations for divestiture then began in earnest. The decision was made to restructure the capital of the enterprise so that only 40 percent of the shares would have voting rights. The government then offered for sale 20.4 percent of the stock (which was 51 percent of the voting stock and hence a controlling share). Bids were received in November 1990. The winning bidder was a consortium consisting of Mexican investors led by Grupo Carso (a holding company controlled by Carlos Slim Helu), Southwestern Bell, and France Cable et Radio. The sale took place in December 1990.

Regulation

The Secretariat of Communications and Transport has regulatory authority over Telmex. The regulatory mechanism adopted after divestiture is an RPI - X price cap system similar to the one used in the regulation of British Telecom (see chapter 4). Specifically, a basket of services—installation and rental charges, metered local calls, and domestic and international long distance calls—is subject to price controls. The average price of this basket, using the previous year's quantities as weights, can rise at a rate no higher than RPI - X, where RPI is the retail price index and X is a factor to be set in advance by the regulators. For the period 1991–96, X has been set at zero, and for 1997–98 at 3 percent. Thereafter it will be reset every four years based on incremental costs. Services not included in the basket (cellular telephony, yellow pages, private circuits, etc.) are unregulated.

An innovative feature of the regulatory environment for Telmex is that, apart from the price regulation, the company also faces certain quantity constraints and competitive conditions. Under the title of concession, the company has been granted a monopoly on all fixed-link telephone services until August 1996. After that date other firms may be given permission to offer long distance services. Telmex must then provide interconnection to these other firms. Local services will remain the sole franchise of Telmex.

To preserve its monopoly, however, Telmex must meet certain network expansion targets. The function of this feature of the regulation is to ensure that the company is not content with serving its existing client base but continues to expand aggressively. The targets it must meet are the following:

- The number of lines in service must expand at a minimum of 12 percent per year until 1994.
- All towns with populations of 500 or more must have telephone service by the end of 1994.
- The number of public telephones must be increased from 0.8 per 1,000 population to 2 per 1,000 in 1994 and 5 per 1,000 in 1998.
- In towns with automatic exchanges, the maximum waiting time for a new connection must be reduced to six months by 1995 and one month by 2000.

In addition, Telmex is required to meet certain standards in terms of the speed with which repairs are carried out.

Although the penalty for failure to meet these targets is termination of the concession, it is unlikely that the government would exercise that right except in extreme circumstances. Thus Telmex has an effectively secure monopoly on fixed-link local services at least until 2026 (when the concession runs out), and on long distance services until 1996. Further, it is subject to a rather generous price cap on its basic telephone services, with considerable freedom to set prices within the basket.

What Happened?

In this section we examine the performance of Telmex in the ten years leading up to divestiture and then in its first year as a private company. Because the divestiture is so recent, we cannot meaningfully compare performance before and after divestiture. However, we can study whether or not there was an announcement effect on performance and whether there was a substantial "cleaning up" of the company to prepare it for sale. Because the divestiture was announced in September 1989, and certain actions were taken in early 1990 that we believe to have been directly connected to the pending divestiture, we will treat 1990 as the first year under the new regime.

Profit and Profitability

The simplest measures of performance are private after-tax profits and profitability. For the latter we need information on the fixed capital of the enterprise. These simple measures are examined in this section.

PROFITS. Telmex's nominal profits have been growing rapidly, practically doubling every year since 1981. However, in a high-inflation environment such as Mexico was in the 1980s, it is unclear how much we learn from this. Deflating by the consumer price index yields a real profit series that looks quite different (figure 19-1). Real private profit was stagnant or declining during 1981–87, taking a sharp drop in 1986 and standing in 1987 at half the 1981 level: 59 billion pesos (Mex$) versus Mex$120 billion (all peso figures are in "old," that is, pre-1993, pesos; 1 new peso equals 1,000 old pesos). Between 1987 and 1990, private profit in real terms more than doubled each year. In 1991, the first full year after divestiture and the first year under price regulation, real private profit grew "only" about 35 percent.

Why this has happened is not difficult to figure out. Output prices were falling in real terms until 1987 (in a trend stretching back to 1970), but they rose in the period 1988–91. Telmex implemented major price increases on 1 January 1988, perhaps as a reaction to the 159 percent inflation experienced in 1987. Further increases followed. Thus the "terms of trade" were moving against the enterprise until 1987 but have moved in its favor since then. Also, output quantities have been rising rapidly since 1987, perhaps partly because of the improved performance

Figure 19-1. Public and Private Profit at Constant Market Prices, Teléfonos de México, 1981–91

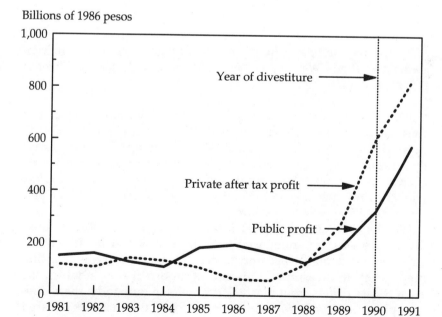

Billions of 1986 pesos

Source: Authors' calculations based on Teléfonos de México annual reports (various years).

Figure 19-2.   Gross Fixed Capital Formation, Teléfonos de México, 1981–91

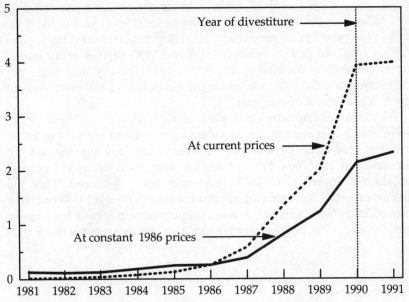

Source: Authors' calculations from Telmex data.

of the economy and partly in response to the major investment program started by Telmex. We examine this explanation in greater detail later in the chapter.

FIXED CAPITAL. Gross fixed capital formation, both at current and at constant prices, rises slowly up to 1987 and then seems to explode upward (figure 19-2), leveling off in 1991 (net capital formation follows the same pattern). The similarity between this pattern and that of private after-tax profits, with the sharp discontinuity in 1987, is unmistakable. Thus the price increases in 1988 might be seen as motivated by a perceived need for investible resources.

The discontinuity in capital formation occurs in 1987. Because divestiture was not announced until 1989, it would be difficult to attribute this change to any announcement effect or even as an action preparatory to divestiture. This is one important way in which the Telmex case differs from most of the others in our study: there does not appear to have been an investment constraint that was released by divestiture; rapid growth in investment started well before even the announcement of divestiture.

PROFITABILITY. Because profitability is obtained by dividing the profit level by the capital stock, its trend can be seen as a combination of the previous two sets of trends. Private profitability followed a declining trend through 1987, and a rising trend thereafter. The kink in the series thus occurs in 1987, a date that, again, cannot seriously be associated with divestiture or even its announcement. Rather, there appears to have been a change in government policy. Price increases were consistent both with the need for greater investible funds and with the need to keep the central budget deficit under control. These price increases were in turn reflected in profits and profitability.

UNIT COSTS. In general, the pattern of nominal unit costs (figure 19-3) shows a broadly upward trend to 1987 with a declining trend since then. Although it is tempting to believe that this reflects productive efficiency trends, it is possible that it instead reflects declining "terms of trade" (that is, output prices relative to input prices) for Telmex up to 1987, with an improving trend since then.

To eliminate these terms-of-trade effects we look at real unit costs, which are remarkably different (figure 19-4). For labor we see the broadly

Figure 19-3. Nominal Unit Costs, Teléfonos de México, 1981–91

Pesos per peso of output

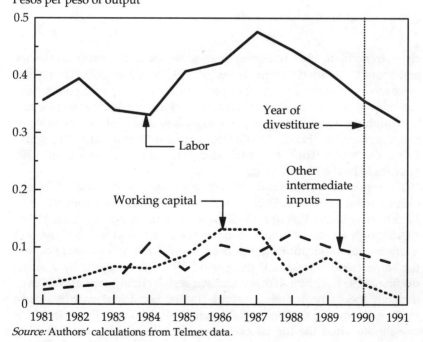

Source: Authors' calculations from Telmex data.

Figure 19-4. Real Unit Costs, Teléfonos de México, 1981–91

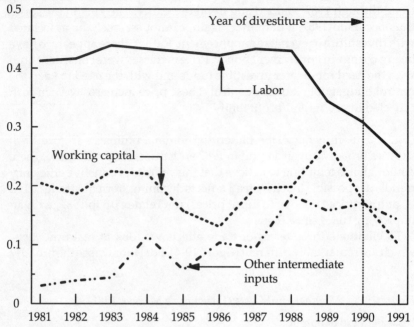

Source: Authors' calculations from Telmex data.

rising trend up to 1987 disappear. Instead we see a rather stagnant series just above 0.4, with dramatic drops in 1989, 1990, and 1991. Thus there seems to have been substantial improvement in labor productivity during these three years. The real cost of working capital meanwhile has been highly variable but appears basically trendless.[2] Intermediate input costs, on the other hand, show a strong upward trend until 1988, stabilizing thereafter. Thus, for both labor and intermediate inputs, 1988 appears to be the pivotal year.

The sum of the various real unit costs gives an idea of how the different elements come together. This series shows some variability but seems to have a rising trend during 1981–88, with declines in the next three years.

Although we do not report the results here, we found that the real average capital-output ratio has been steadily rising with more or less the same trend throughout the period 1981–90, followed by a small decline in 1991. Although this might suggest declining capital efficiency through the early period, it might also be consistent with a steady movement toward a more capital-intensive technology. For example, it is estimated that the digital exchanges that Telmex is now installing require fewer than one-sixth the number of operators that the old analog exchanges required. Thus it would be difficult to conclude whether Telmex is using capital more or less efficiently. The decline in 1991, although it cannot be taken as a trend, does suggest improved capital utilization by the divested enterprise.

SUMMARY OF PERFORMANCE. A series of partial measures of Telmex's performance during the period 1981–91 shows a declining trend in profits and profitability until 1987, with a positive trend thereafter. The primary force behind the kink seems to be the large upward revisions in output prices of 1988 (which were followed by further increases in 1990). We find some decline in unit labor and intermediate costs during 1989–91, although this is somewhat countered by a rising average capital-output ratio during the first two years of that period. The analysis of the productive efficiency of the enterprise as indicated by its unit costs therefore suggests deteriorating efficiency up to 1988, with some improvement thereafter. We turn next to a more comprehensive analysis of efficiency—total factor productivity (TFP)—to confirm this hypothesis.

Total Factor Productivity

The calculations leading to the TFP measure are displayed in table 19-1, and the series itself is plotted in figure 19-5. These figures show how the various conflicting elements of unit costs sort themselves out, and they tell a dramatic story, confirming the hypothesis postulated just above. Through the period 1981–88, Telmex was simply becoming less efficient. The TFP index (with 1986 as 1.00) fell from 1.31 in 1981 to 0.87 in 1988—an astonishing 43 percentage-point drop in productive efficiency! There was then a slight recovery to 0.93 in 1989 and 0.94 in 1990, followed by a more substantial jump to 1.08 in 1991. This is suggestive that, as preparations for divestiture began, the decline in productivity was arrested, and that productivity took off after divestiture took place. The growth in TFP in that first year of private operation was 15.3 percentage points.

These results need to be taken with a measure of caution. Table 19-1 shows clearly a fact that we all know to be true: that fixed capital is the dominant element of cost in telecommunications. In 1986, for example, capital cost accounts for 82.6 percent of total cost. Thus the rising trend we saw in the average capital-output ratio in the previous section is dominating the productivity calculations. And we have already argued that this rising trend may be due at least in part to the capital expansion currently taking place in Telmex. We see another important piece to the puzzle in table 19-1. Note the sharp drop in the opportunity cost of fixed capital in 1989 as compared with 1988. This was due to a sharp drop in interest rates, which in turn was due to the moderating of inflation. Now although the TFP calculation is supposed to be free of price effects

Table 19-1. Total Factor Productivity, Teléfonos de México, 1981–91

Item	1981	1982	1983	1984	1985	1986	1987	1988	1989	1990	1991
Values (billions of pesos)											
Outputs	32	54	108	173	264	565	1,490	3,408	5,246	9,099	13,666
Intermediate inputs	1	2	4	19	16	59	135	422	529	791	941
Labor	11	21	37	57	107	238	710	1,515	2,127	3,243	4,376
Rentals	0	0	0	0	0	0	0	0	0	0	0
Working capital	1	3	7	11	22	74	195	171	437	323	160
Fixed capital	24	78	173	247	472	1,767	5,280	5,061	2,988	4,012	3,978
Total inputs	37	104	221	334	618	2,138	6,319	7,169	6,081	8,369	9,454
Prices (1986 = 1.00)											
Outputs	0.075	0.122	0.249	0.370	0.514	1.000	2.466	5.000	6.273	9.592	12.021
Intermediate inputs	0.063	0.098	0.203	0.346	0.531	1.000	2.356	3.360	3.968	4.865	5.790
Labor	0.065	0.116	0.192	0.283	0.489	1.000	2.710	5.173	7.379	11.094	15.351

Rentals	1.000	1.000	1.000	1.000	1.000	1.000	1.000	1.000	1.000	1.000	1.000
Working capital	0.013	0.031	0.073	0.106	0.275	1.000	1.638	1.266	1.907	1.945	1.402
Fixed capital	0.024	0.071	0.141	0.178	0.283	0.952	2.606	1.976	0.949	1.022	0.890
Total inputs (divisia: price explicit)	−0.031	0.077	0.150	0.197	0.323	1.000	2.679	2.420	1.779	2.186	2.377
Quantities											
Outputs	420	442	434	469	513	565	604	682	836	949	1,137
Intermediate inputs	13	17	19	54	30	59	57	126	133	162	163
Labor	173	184	190	203	220	238	262	293	288	292	285
Rentals	0	0	0	0	0	0	0	0	0	0	0
Working capital	86	82	98	104	81	74	119	135	229	166	114
Fixed capital stock	995	1,110	1,225	1,391	1,669	1,857	2,026	2,562	3,149	3,925	4,470
Total inputs (divisia)	1,219	1,343	1,469	1,696	1,911	2,138	2,359	2,962	3,418	3,828	3,978
TFP index (divisia)	1.306	1.245	1.118	1.047	1.017	1.000	0.970	0.871	0.927	0.938	1.082
TFP: Annual percent change	−0.047	−0.047	−0.102	−0.063	−0.029	−0.016	−0.030	−0.102	0.063	0.013	0.153

Note: TFP: total factor productivity.
Source: Authors' calculations from Telmex data.

Figure 19-5.   Total Factor Productivity and Public Profitability,
Teléfonos de México, 1981–91

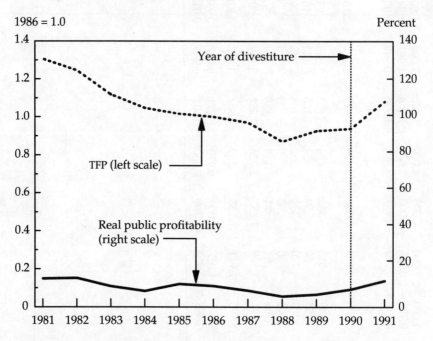

Source: Authors' calculations from Telmex data.

(witness that the fixed capital stock *quantity*, the key variable used in the calculation, rises in 1989 as we would expect), nevertheless the sharp drop in the opportunity cost of capital means a sharp drop in the *weight* given to the capital input in the TFP calculations. In 1989 the share of fixed capital in total input cost dropped to 49 percent, in 1990 to 47.3 percent, and in 1991 it was down to 41 percent. Thus the upward turn in productivity in these three years could be partly explained by the sharp drop in the capital share.

The fact remains that Telmex's TFP was declining during 1981–88 but has since turned upward. The decline could have been due to capital building, it could have been a side effect of the massive inflation (and high interest rates) that Mexico experienced during the early to mid-1980s, or it could reflect some deterioration in efficiency. The improvement since 1989 could reflect the declining share of fixed capital in total cost. Nevertheless, it is clear that productivity has been improving during the past three years, with 1991 showing a quite substantial 15 percent increase. Table 19-1 shows that output rose in 1991 by nearly 20 percent, while intermediate inputs remained essentially unchanged and labor use actually declined. Therefore there can be no ambiguity about this productivity improvement in the first year of private operation.

Fiscal Effects

Telmex has been an important contributor to the Mexican treasury, both through annual tax flows and through the proceeds from its divestiture. We consider each of these components of the fiscal impact in turn.

ANNUAL FLOWS. The primary source of annual fiscal flows to the government from Telmex has been indirect taxes. In addition, the government receives direct (income) tax payments and dividends as a partial shareholder. We have excluded interest payments from Telmex to government-owned banks from our measure of fiscal impact.[3]

The upper panel of table 19-2 shows the fiscal flows, in current pesos, received by the government during 1981–91. The dominant position of indirect taxes (the telephone tax and the value added tax) is clearly seen; they account for about 90 percent of all taxes in most years. The government was receiving an extraordinarily high proportion of Telmex's total revenue. From a high of 42 percent in 1981, this proportion stabilized in a range of 32 to 38 percent for 1982–89, followed by a sharp drop to 26 percent in 1990 and 24 percent in 1991. As we will see below, this decline was due to a substantial reduction in tax rates as a prelude to divestiture. Thus the sharp drop in fiscal inflows as a percentage of total revenue in 1990 and 1991 can be attributed to divestiture.

The bottom panel of table 19-2 shows the same fiscal inflows in real terms, deflating by the consumer price index to 1986 prices. The resultant series are then plotted in figure 19-6. In real terms the government's fiscal receipts stayed more or less constant during 1981–87, jumped dramatically in 1988 and 1989, and were again relatively stable in 1990 and 1991. The stability during 1981–87 may seem strange, given that the real prices of Telmex's services were actually declining during this period. Thus stability was in fact achieved through upward adjustment of the tax rates (see table 19-5). The big price adjustment in 1988 and the large quantity increase in 1989 account for the large increase in tax revenues in those years. Finally, the small decline in 1990 can be attributed to divestiture— specifically, the change in the price and tax structure in January 1990, discussed below. The slight rise in 1991 was entirely driven by higher income tax payments as the company's profits rose.

The bottom line is that throughout the 1980s Telmex contributed substantially to government revenue, with big real increases in 1988 and 1989 followed by a drop in 1990 and recovery in 1991. We believe that the drop and recovery were related to divestiture, but the increases of 1988–89 were not. Of course in 1990 and 1991 the government also

Table 19-2. Fiscal Flows, Teléfonos de México, 1981–91

Flow	1981	1982	1983	1984	1985	1986	1987	1988	1989	1990	1991
Billions of current pesos											
Dividends	1	2	2	3	5	7	10	19	27	42	27
Direct taxes	4	6	11	3	12	21	58	329	271	182	674
Indirect taxes	13	20	39	73	106	225	614	1,504	2,400	2,920	3,286
Total	19	28	52	79	123	253	682	1,852	2,697	3,144	3,987
Flows as percentage of total Telmex revenue	0.42	0.37	0.35	0.32	0.33	0.32	0.32	0.38	0.35	0.26	0.24
Billions of constant 1986 pesos											
Dividends	24	16	12	10	9	7	4	5	6	7	14
Direct taxes	83	57	57	9	26	21	22	84	58	30	95
Indirect taxes	256	193	209	247	219	225	237	382	510	490	463
Total	363	267	278	266	254	253	263	471	573	527	562

Source: Teléfonos de México (various years), and authors' calculations.

Figure 19-6. Fiscal Flows at Constant Prices, Teléfonos de México, 1981–91

Billions of Pesos

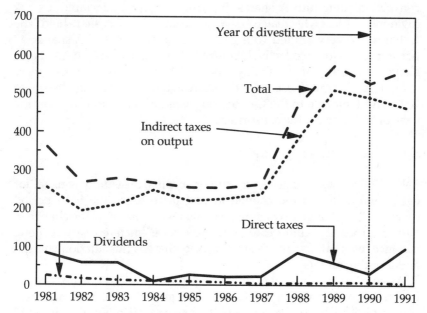

Source: Authors' calculations from Telmex data.

received a substantial fiscal inflow in the form of the Telmex sale price. We examine this next.

THE SALE TRANSACTION. Telmex was divested on 20 December 1990, through the sale of a controlling block of stock to a consortium headed by Grupo Carso. The method of sale was a sealed-bid auction for the entire controlling block of shares. The winning consortium is 51 percent Mexican owned, with the remaining 49 percent divided equally between Southwestern Bell Corp. and France Cable et Radio. The purchase price for 20.4 percent of the enterprise was US$1.67 billion.[4] In addition, the buyers were sold options to buy a further 5.1 percent, and employees were sold a 4.4 percent share. On 15 May 1991 a further 16.5 percent of the company's stock was sold for approximately US$2.37 billion. And in May 1992 the government sold an additional 4.7 percent of the enterprise for US$1.4 billion. In all, the government has sold 51.1 percent of Telmex for a total (in May 1991 dollars) of over US$6.2 billion. Details of our calculations and of the structure of the sale are spelled out in Tandon and Abdala (1992).

One interesting aspect of the sale is the capital stock restructuring carried out just prior to the sale. Before divestiture the enterprise had two classes of stock: AA shares could be owned only by the government, and A shares were unrestricted as to ownership. The government first reduced the number of AA shares (from 55.9 percent to 51 percent) by converting some into A shares. Next the enterprise declared a stock dividend of 1.5 newly created L shares[5] for each A or AA share held. The L shares had very limited voting rights. Thus the AA and A shares (40 percent of the stock) collectively controlled the enterprise. The AA shares alone (51 percent of the voting stock, 20.4 percent of the total) were enough for control; these were the shares offered for sale in December 1990, and their sale to the Carso group was sufficient to turn over the control of Telmex to the consortium.

Effects on Consumer Welfare

Table 19-3 shows changes in consumer surplus, measured as usual for each commodity as the change in real price times the base period quantity. The change in consumer surplus is calculated as the change in surplus from all calling categories of service (metered service, long distance, etc.) minus any change in fixed charges (installation charges and monthly rentals).

We see the same overall pattern that is now familiar: consumers were generally gaining through 1987 but then got hit with price increases during 1988–91. Were consumers better or worse off in 1991 than in 1981? Because the consumer surplus changes are expressed as real price changes, it is meaningful to sum up all the changes. We see that the gains made by consumers during 1981–87 were more than wiped out by the losses in 1988, with additional losses during 1989–91 making matters worse. This would suggest that consumers were indeed worse off by the end of 1991. This conclusion is borne out in the next section, where we examine the changes in real prices more carefully.

Macroeconomic Effects

The announcement that Telmex was to be divested was made in September 1989, the same month that Mexico's external debt rescheduling agreement under the Brady Plan was reached. Thus we might speculate whether the sale of Telmex had anything to do with the subsequent dramatic economic recovery.

We think it did. The argument goes as follows. First, one of the key ingredients of Mexico's macroeconomic stabilization has been to stem and even reverse the tide of massive capital outflows in the form of external debt service and capital flight. This was, after all, the basic premise behind the need for the debt rescheduling agreement: that the capital drain was making investment in the economy impossible.

Table 19-3. Changes in Consumer Surplus, Teléfonos de México, 1981–91

Service	1981	1982	1983	1984	1985	1986	1987	1988	1989	1990	1991
Rentals											
Real Price	74.1	47.9	40.7	37.6	29.7	26.4	28.8	49.4	49.8	47.0	51.2
Change in price	n.a.	-26.2	-7.2	-3.1	-7.9	-3.3	2.4	20.6	0.4	-2.9	4.2
Change in revenue (to be subtracted)	n.a.	-67.5	-17.2	-3.0	-21.5	-6.5	14.4	92.1	19.6	9.0	52.7
Metered service											
Real price	2.3	1.6	2.8	3.2	2.6	2.2	2.2	4.2	4.0	19.3	17.9
Change in price	n.a.	-0.7	1.1	0.5	-0.7	-0.4	0.1	2.0	-0.2	15.2	-1.4
Change in consumer surplus (1986 pesos)	n.a.	0.0	-7.2	-3.1	4.6	3	-.8	-15.6	1.9	-256.7	34.8
Long distance											
Real price	0.2	0.1	0.1	0.1	0.1	0.1	0.1	0.1	0.1	0.2	0.2
Change in price	n.a.	-0.1	0.0	0.0	0.0	0.0	0.0	0.0	0.0	0.0	0.0
Change in consumer surplus (1986 pesos)	n.a.	153.8	-12.8	6.9	79.9	29.2	-10.6	-125.7	-140.4	-145.5	-86.4
International outgoing calls											
Real price	0.9	0.9	1.0	1.2	1.1	1.2	1.1	1.1	1.0	0.7	0.6
Change in price	n.a.	0.0	0.1	0.2	-0.1	0.2	-0.2	0.0	0.0	-0.3	-0.1
Change in consumer surplus (1986 pesos)	n.a.	0.2	-14.6	-24.8	18.6	-25.7	27.2	1.4	11.7	105.6	35.5
International incoming calls											
Real price	0.3	0.5	0.8	0.5	0.5	0.6	0.5	0.5	0.4	0.4	0.3
Change in price	n.a.	0.2	0.3	-0.2	0.0	0.0	-0.1	0.0	-0.1	-0.1	-0.1
Change in consumer surplus (1986 pesos)	n.a.	-40.7	-66.2	59.9	5.4	-12.5	28.3	-9.8	32.1	42.7	92.6

(Table continues on the following page.)

Table 19-3 (continued)

Service	1981	1982	1983	1984	1985	1986	1987	1988	1989	1990	1991
Other local services											
Real price	0.0	0.0	0.0	0.3	0.2	0.1	0.1	0.4	0.3	0.2	0.2
Change in price	n.a.	0.0	0.0	0.3	0.0	-0.1	0.0	0.3	0.0	-0.2	0.0
Change in revenue (to be subtracted)	n.a.	0.0	0.0	57.7	-2.9	-28.1	1.1	81.8	63.2	-64.0	30.9
Miscellaneous											
Real price	24.6	19.7	22.0	22.9	22.0	20.0	17.8	25.2	25.2	25.2	25.9
Change in price	n.a.	-4.9	2.3	0.9	-0.8	-2.1	-2.1	7.3	0.0	0.0	0.7
Change in consumer surplus (1986 pesos)	n.a.	0.0	0.0	0.0	0.0	0.0	0.0	0.0	0.0	0.0	0.0
Total change in consumer surplus (1986 pesos)	0.0	180.7	-83.6	-16.0	132.9	28.6	28.6	-323.7	-177.5	-198.9	-7.1
Memorandum: Consumer price index (1986 = 1.0)	0.1	0.1	0.2	0.3	0.5	1.0	2.6	3.9	4.7	6.0	7.1

n.a. Not applicable.
Source: Authors' calculations from Telmex data.

Second, Telmex has been a source of very large capital inflows, over US$6 billion in a period of a year and a half.[6]

By comparison, the debt rescheduling reduced Mexico's interest payments by US$1.3 billion a year and reduced total capital outflows (interest plus principal) by US$4 billion a year. Thus the sale of Telmex had the same direct fiscal impact on the government in the same time period as did the debt rescheduling. Third, we would argue that Telmex was a catalyst for the highly successful divestitures that followed. Recall from chapter 18 that divestiture revenues in 1991 totaled US$10.8 billion (including US$2.4 billion from Telmex). The high prices commanded by the commercial bank divestitures in particular have been widely commented on: the banks sold for as much as 3.7 times book value, compared with a more "normal" multiple of between 1 and 2. To what extent, if at all, the very successful[7] divestiture of Telmex contributed to this is a matter of speculation; many observers feel it played a very important role.

What does this all mean for the analysis of the Telmex divestiture? Given these very large external effects from the sale, we would argue that the sale revenues need to receive a weight greater than one when the welfare calculations are done. As Jones, Tandon, and Vogelsang (1990) have argued, money in the government's hands may be worth more than money in private hands in a situation of disequilibrium or nonoptimal taxation. Mexico was certainly in disequilibrium at this time, suffering from severe fiscal constraints. The revenues from divestiture played a particularly crucial role in that they were set aside and used to retire domestic debt, thereby encouraging the sharp drop in domestic interest rates that followed.

What then was the marginal value to society of these sale revenues? Van Wijnbergen (1991) has attempted to estimate the value to Mexico of the Brady deal, and because the divestiture revenues were used for a very similar purpose (debt reduction), his calculations are suggestive for our purposes. Van Wijnbergen's calculations suggest that the Brady deal had the effect of reducing Mexico's capital outflow by about US$4 billion per year over the period 1989–94. Correspondingly, he estimates that the positive effect on Mexico's GDP from this operation will be to raise the annual growth rate on the order of about 2 percent (with a low estimate of 1.5 percent and a high of around 2.5 percent). Since Mexican GDP in 1989 was US$200 billion, this suggests an increase in GDP of about US$4 billion. If we completely ignore any persistence effects and assume the increase is only a one-time gain, this would argue for a shadow value of the sale revenues of 2; this would be a lower bound. Estimates of the shadow value of government funds in developing countries are routinely above 2 (Jones, Tandon, and Vogelsang 1990, p. 29), and therefore this estimate appears to be at the low end of the true value.

Summary

We can divide our summary of what happened into two categories: what happened in terms of behavior or performance outcomes, and what happened in terms of the sale transaction.

Telmex was a moribund, poorly performing public enterprise until 1987. Both private profitability and productivity were on a declining trend. But there seems to have been a turnaround over the past few years:

- Private profits and profitability were declining until 1987, but have been growing rapidly since then.
- TFP was declining until 1988 but has been rising since then, with a notable 15 percent improvement in 1991, the first postdivestiture year.
- Labor productivity, after stagnating from 1981 to 1988, rose rapidly over the next three years.
- Real fiscal revenues were fairly stable during 1981–87 but then jumped in 1988 and 1989 to reach a new plateau at approximately double the previous level.
- Consumers enjoyed falling real prices during 1981–87 but have faced steep price increases since then.

The sale of Telmex has been an extremely complex transaction, and indeed it is still not entirely complete. Several key features need to be stressed:

- Because of the size of the sale (a total of over US$6 billion has been received so far), it has been carried out in stages or tranches.
- Through a capital restructuring, effective control of the enterprise was transferred with the original sale of 20.4 percent of the shares.
- The government gained from the rising stock market value through higher per share sale revenues on successive tranches.
- The sale of Telmex clearly signaled the Mexican government's commitment to private sector development.
- The sale revenues played an important role in stabilizing the macroeconomy.

Why Did It Happen?

We next examine to what extent the behavioral changes we observed can be attributed to the divestiture of Telmex. This will then permit us to construct our projections and our counterfactual to divestiture. We will focus on three classes of changes: changes in the price structure and taxation, changes in the investment level, and changes in productivity.

Changes in Prices and Taxation

We believe a key element in explaining what was happening at Telmex through the 1980s was changes in the pricing and taxation regime. We argue that the price increases of 1988 were not attributable to divestiture, but that the price and tax changes of 1990 were.

THE 1981–87 PERIOD. Table 19-4 shows, for 1980–91, the prices of the principal services provided by Telmex,[8] in constant pesos of 1986. For each category of service, the table reports the net price received by the enterprise, the indirect tax (consisting of the telephone tax and the value added tax), and the total price paid by the consumer. Table 19-5 presents the indirect tax rates for each service.

Prices for rentals, metered service, and national long distance declined slowly until 1987 and then recovered in 1988 to close to the 1980–81 level.[9] Connection charges also declined slowly from 1981–87, but the "adjustment" in 1988 was a massive fivefold real increase. There was no discernible trend in the price of international calls.

The slow decline in real prices during 1981–87 partially masks the fact that the prices received by Telmex were declining somewhat faster, because the tax rates on services were rising slightly, as can be seen from table 19-5. The average indirect tax on local service went up from 70 percent in 1981 to 90 percent in 1987, and for national long distance the tax went from 44 percent to 58 percent. According to a study of world-wide telecommunications rates in 1988 (Siemens 1988, quoted in World Bank 1990) Mexico had by far the highest telephone tax rates in the world.

Why were real prices allowed to decline through most of the 1980s? The normal explanation is that there was a regulatory lag, and inflation was accelerating. This seems reasonable, except that there is evidence that the general declining trend stretches back through the 1970s also, when inflation was not as high (World Bank 1990, p. 88). This suggests that low prices were a reflection of government social policy. At the same time, the enterprise was an important source of revenue for the government. We have already seen (see "Fiscal Effects" above) that real fiscal revenues stayed roughly constant from 1982 to 1987. Tax rates were adjusted in a way that stabilized the returns to the government. Thus it appears that the enterprise was used as a source of government revenue *and* that prices were kept low for social purposes. The government obtained its return from the enterprise in the form of indirect taxes, and consumers were kept happy with low prices; the losers were the private shareholders, who received next to no return. Thus, although Telmex remained profitable, it was unable to generate sufficient funds for investment. Both the low level of capital formation and the low stock price of the enterprise throughout this period are thereby explained.

Table 19-4. *Output Prices, Teléfonos de México, 1980–91*
(constant 1986 pesos)

Service	1980	1981	1982	1983	1984	1985	1986	1987	1988	1989	1990	1991
Rent (annual)[a]												
Residential	14,284	13,411	7,560	7,462	4,687	6,443	4,872	5,181	12,879	10,759	14,267	21,335
Tax	9,143	8,584	4,839	5,333	3,350	4,604	4,092	4,352	10,818	9,038	2,140	3,200
Total	23,427	21,995	12,399	12,795	8,037	11,047	8,964	9,532	23,697	19,797	16,407	24,535
Business	25,889	24,047	14,538	14,345	9,011	12,367	9,372	9,963	24,760	31,028	42,137	57,555
Tax	19,676	18,275	11,049	12,050	7,569	10,388	9,166	9,744	24,215	30,346	6,320	8,633
Total	45,565	42,322	25,588	26,396	16,580	22,755	18,538	19,707	48,974	61,374	48,457	66,188
Metered service (per minute)												
Residential	2.98	2.31	1.65	1.55	1.82	1.44	1.13	1.17	2.21	1.85	16.77	15.69
Tax	1.90	1.48	1.05	1.11	1.30	1.03	0.95	0.99	1.86	1.55	2.52	2.35
Total	4.88	3.79	2.70	2.67	3.12	2.47	2.08	2.16	4.07	3.40	19.28	18.04
Business	2.98	2.31	1.65	1.55	1.82	1.44	1.13	1.17	2.21	2.77	16.77	15.69
Tax	2.26	1.76	1.25	1.31	1.53	1.21	1.11	1.15	2.16	2.71	2.52	2.35
Total	5.24	4.07	2.90	2.86	3.35	2.65	2.24	2.32	4.37	5.48	19.28	18.04
Installation charges												
Residential	31,022	96,861	62,893	72,788	45,721	57,275	43,374	56,901	226,114	188,900	150,922	150,039
Business	38,636	146,188	81,783	94,660	59,460	75,763	57,269	75,307	371,059	309,991	261,597	257,350

Domestic long distance
(per minute)

Residential	124	116	78	75	71	56	46	48	70	89	141	162
Tax	48	45	30	34	32	25	24	25	36	46	21	24
Total	172	161	108	109	103	81	70	73	106	135	162	186
Business	124	116	78	75	71	56	46	48	70	89	141	162
Tax	60	56	38	41	39	31	29	31	44	56	21	24
Total	184	172	115	117	110	86	75	79	114	146	162	186

International long distance
(per minute)[b]

Residential	372	366	426	499	448	411	466	406	459	429	299	265
Tax	145	143	166	226	203	187	211	184	185	173	45	40
Total	517	509	593	725	651	598	677	591	644	601	343	304
Business	372	366	426	499	448	411	466	406	459	429	299	265
Tax	180	178	207	275	247	227	257	224	185	173	45	40
Total	552	544	633	774	695	639	723	631	644	601	343	304

a. Per telephone line.
b. On outbound calls to the United States, net of settlement.
Source: Telmex data.

Table 19-5. *Indirect Rates on Telephone Services, Mexico, 1980–92*
(percentages)

Year	Telephone tax			Value added tax	Total tax[a]		
	Local service	National long distance	Inter-national		Local service	National long distance	Inter-national
1980	54.22	30.90	30.90	10.00	69.64	43.99	43.99
1981	54.22	30.90	30.90	10.00	69.64	43.99	43.99
1982	54.22	30.90	30.90	10.00	69.64	43.99	43.99
1983	54.22	30.90	30.90	15.00	77.35	50.53	50.53
1984	54.22	30.90	30.90	15.00	77.35	50.53	50.53
1985	54.22	30.90	30.90	15.00	77.35	50.53	50.53
1986	65.63	37.23	30.90	15.00	90.48	57.82	50.53
1987	65.63	37.23	30.90	15.00	90.48	57.82	50.53
1988	65.63	37.23	22.00	15.00	90.48	57.82	40.30
1989	65.63	37.23	22.00	15.00	90.48	57.82	40.30
1990	0.00	0.00	0.00	15.00	15.00	15.00	15.00
1991	0.00	0.00	0.00	14.32[b]	14.32	14.32	14.32
1992	0.00	0.00	0.00	10.00	10.00	10.00	10.00

a. The value added tax is applied to the price *plus* the telephone tax to arrive at the total tax.

b. Weighted average of a value added tax of 15 percent prior to and 10 percent after 11 November 1991.

Source: Telmex data.

THE 1988 REFORMS. In 1988, however, most prices were raised significantly. It seems reasonable to suppose that this price increase was induced by the rapid inflation of the previous two years and the need for investment capital. The consumer price index had doubled in 1986 and then risen another 159 percent in 1987. Also, the rebuilding of the Telmex system following the 1985 earthquake was proceeding very slowly, partly because of a lack of funds.[10] That the need for funds may have been important is also suggested by the fact that the biggest price increases were for services with the lowest demand elasticities: connection charges, rentals, and metered service, in that order.

THE 1990 PRICE AND TAX REFORM. The pricing and tax regime was drastically reformed in January 1990. The key change was the elimination of the telephone tax, leaving only the 15 percent value added tax, which the enterprise was permitted to absorb partially or wholly into its price. This was true for rentals, metered local calls, and domestic long distance calls. Connection charges had never been taxed. The only exception was international calls, where the nominal price fell. Thus the price reform moved prices more in line with international prices.

Metered local calls underwent the most dramatic increase, from Mex$16 per minute (less than 1 U.S. cent) to Mex$115 per minute (about 4 cents).

At the same time, a new telephone services tax was introduced. This was a charge of 29 percent on Telmex's revenues from rental charges, local calls, and national long distance. Why was 29 percent chosen as the new tax rate? One reason could be that the proportion of indirect tax revenues to Telmex revenues averaged exactly 29 percent for the period 1981–89! Is the "new" telephone services tax nothing but the "old" telephone tax in a different guise?

We do not think so, for two reasons. First, the new tax is applied only on certain selected revenues, as mentioned earlier, so that its proportion of total revenue will now be lower than that of the old tax. Second, the government has permitted Telmex to offset 65 percent of the tax against investment.[11] Because the company is investing heavily (and in fact will have to in order to meet other conditions of its concession), it will certainly get the full benefit of this option. Further, *all* of the notional tax (that is, including the 65 percent investment subsidy) will be deductible for corporate income tax purposes. The effect of these provisions is to reduce the effective indirect tax to zero, as long as investment is high enough to take advantage of the investment subsidy, and as long as income is high enough to take advantage of the income tax offset.[12]

We see therefore that the 1990 reforms provided a substantial boost to Telmex by essentially transferring to it a large proportion of what the government had previously derived from the enterprise. On 1990 base revenues of US$3,413 million, we have calculated this transfer to be US$643 million—a pure transfer from the government to the company![13]

Was the 1990 price-cum-tax reform, coming as it did eleven and a half months before divestiture, "due" to divestiture? Or was it simply a continuation of the process begun in 1988? We believe that the two reforms were quite distinct, and that the 1990 reforms were very much a part of the divestiture process. There are several reasons to believe so.

First, the decision to sell Telmex was not made until some time during the 1988 presidential election campaign, and it was not announced until September 1989. Thus it is safe to assume that the reforms of January 1988 were in no way connected to divestiture. The 1990 reforms, on the other hand, occurred *after* the intention to sell Telmex had been announced.

Second, after the September 1989 announcement, administrative control over Telmex was transferred from the communications secretariat to the finance secretariat, which was managing the divestiture program. This suggests that all major subsequent actions would probably have been taken in light of their impact on the divestiture.

Third, the character of the 1990 reforms was quite different from the price reforms of 1988 or previous years. The abolition of the telephone tax was an obvious major difference. Also, the dramatic change in the price of metered calls was unlike anything seen before. These changes, we contend, were motivated by the need for a "successful" sale, which was the biggest attempted in Mexico and one of the biggest yet attempted in any country. A failure to receive reasonable bids would not only be undesirable in itself but would also have repercussions on future divestitures such as those of the banks. Thus the enterprise needed to be made an attractive buy, and the 1990 reforms certainly did that. Further, by transferring tax revenues to the enterprise, the government was able to render Telmex more attractive to potential buyers while minimizing the adverse impact on consumers.

In summary, it is our contention that the 1990 price reforms were largely (if not solely) motivated by the forthcoming divestiture and would not have occurred otherwise. Even if the government had reformed prices in order to reflect costs more closely, it is very unlikely that the telephone tax would have been abolished; the government had little incentive to do so and, given the atmosphere of fiscal austerity, would probably have been unwilling to give up a solid source of revenue. Thus our counterfactual scenario will not be characterized by such a price-tax reform.

Changes in Investment

As we have seen, the level of investment in Telmex rose slowly up to 1987 and then began to increase rapidly (figure 19-2). In several of our other cases (British Telecom, Malaysian Airline Systems, Compañía de Teléfonos de Chile) the release of an investment constraint has played a key role. It is natural to ask whether the same phenomenon is at work in Telmex.

We think not. Like the price increases of 1988, the investment growth that began in 1988 commenced well in advance of even the announcement of divestiture. Thus it appears that the investment program was part of the Mexican government's overall strategy of economic development, in which telecommunications were seen as an important part of the infrastructure. Some of the impetus for the rise in investment might even be traced back to the 1985 earthquake and the resultant opportunity to upgrade some of the network in the process of rebuilding it.

There is also the issue of how the investment was financed. We have seen (in the section on "Annual Flows" and in table 19-2 and figure 19-6) that real fiscal flows to the government actually rose quite sharply in 1988 and moved even higher subsequently. Thus the investment boom starting in 1988 was not financed, either directly or indirectly, by the government. Rather, two key internal sources of finance were exploited. The first was the higher revenues following the big price increase of January 1988. The second was an innovative scheme to sell future receivables,[14] under which Telmex received US$208 million in 1988, US$256 million in 1989, and US$438 million in 1990.

In summary, the ambitious investment program Telmex undertook in 1988 can be explained by a combination of two sets of forces: a heightened perception of the need for investment and a greater ability to finance that investment.

Changes in Productivity

We saw earlier that TFP at Telmex was declining rather alarmingly during 1981–88, then recovered slightly in 1989 and 1990, and finally took a big jump in 1991, the first year after divestiture. There were three specific points to note. First, real labor productivity stayed constant from 1981 to 1988 and then rose sharply each year from 1989 through 1991. Second, the real unit cost of intermediate inputs rose somewhat sporadically up to 1988 and then declined over the next three years. Third, the average real capital-output ratio kept rising fairly steadily throughout the period.

Of these three factors, certainly the most interesting is the trend in labor productivity. Since 1989 was Telmex's first "good" year, it is tempting to ask whether the improvement was at all related to divestiture. We think it might have been, at least in part because of improved relations with the enterprise's union. When the possibility of a Telmex divestiture began to be discussed, the telephone workers' union (STRM) supported the idea almost unanimously. Then, in April 1989, a landmark agreement was reached with the unions. The agreement replaced fifty-seven different labor contracts with a single one to be negotiated once a year, permitted the enterprise more discretion in moving workers from one job to another, and made provision for layoffs. In exchange, the government awarded workers substantial salary increases (average labor cost per worker rose 43 percent in 1989 and 50 percent in 1990), greatly increased spending on worker retraining and skill development, and later sold the union a 4.4 percent share of the enterprise.

Against this backdrop, the improvement in labor productivity in 1989 and 1990 could be seen as an indication of labor's increased commitment to the enterprise as it prepared for divestiture and as a consequence of management's ability to reduce the work force through attrition and labor mobility within the enterprise (the number of workers at Telmex actually declined in 1989 from 49,995 to 49,203). The alternative hypothesis would be that the labor force reductions were simply a normal reform and that the willingness of the union to make concessions may in part reflect the general decline in the strength of the unions in recent years.[15] We believe that both these sets of forces have been at work, so that part of the improvement in labor productivity might reasonably be attributed to the prospect of divestiture.

The increase in labor productivity in 1991, however, bears all the hallmarks of a classic cost-cutting reorganization by the new private owners. Management has set ambitious productivity goals: there is an active policy of layoffs through attrition; there have been some layoffs as part of reorganization efforts; and an attempt is being made to retrain workers to adapt to more modern, labor-saving technology, thereby obviating the need to hire more workers as the network expands.

There is no sharp kink in the other components of factor productivity. The average capital-output ratio has been trending upward over the entire period under study, and this seems to have been caused by a shift to a more capital-intensive technology. And while real unit intermediate costs trended downward slightly during 1981–91, the movement can hardly be thought definitive. There is insufficient information here to attempt any kind of conclusion on trends or kinks, although the experience of 1991 suggests some possible effect from divestiture.

Summary

We have argued that the divestiture of Telmex led to two important changes affecting the enterprise:

- In an attempt to make the enterprise more attractive to a potential buyer, the government undertook a major price and tax reform in January 1990 in which the telephone tax was scrapped and prices were permitted to rise substantially.
- Labor productivity has risen dramatically.

These changes will play an important part in the construction of our counterfactual to divestiture and the consequent estimate of the long-term impact of the sale of Telmex.

What Will Happen?

In this section we discuss the assumptions and procedures underlying our projections. There are two differences from the other cases. First, because we do not have a substantial postdivestiture span within our data period, we have chosen to project only to a ten-year horizon. Second, the projections are in real terms, in light of Mexico's highly volatile inflation experience.

Revenue

In order to project revenues for Telmex we must first make certain assumptions about future demand and prices.

DEMAND. We assume that demand for telephone services depends upon the country's income and on the size of the system. We assume that the number of lines in service will grow at 12 percent per year, as required in the title of concession. Telmex had already been increasing the number of lines at rates between 11 and 14 percent per year in the 1970s; the 12 percent growth rate therefore appears feasible.[16] Further, because of the huge unmet demand at present, and a projected growth in demand consequent to economic growth, it seems fairly certain that the market will actually absorb all the lines that Telmex does install. That is, we assume there will still be excess demand for telephones in the year 2000.

The assumed growth rate in lines gives us projections of the number of installations per year and the number of customers paying rental charges, both important revenue sources. The projected number of lines is also instrumental in determining the demand for calls. For each class of call, we assume that the growth rate in the level of demand is given by:

$$\text{growth rate} = (\text{GDP growth rate} \times \text{income elasticity})$$
$$+ (\text{line growth rate} \times \text{line elasticity}).$$

We assumed a GDP growth rate of 3.5 percent, based on a variety of macroeconomic projections we have seen. Our other assumptions and the final growth rate for each type of service were then as follows:[17]

	Income elasticity	Line elasticity	Demand growth (percentages)
Metered service	1.2	1.2	18.6
National long distance	1.4	1.2	19.3
International long distance	1.7	1.0	18.0

Note that any effects due to the *price* elasticity of demand are captured in our simulation methodology; they do not require separate treatment at this point. International incoming call volume was assumed to grow at the same rate as outgoing volume. Finally, the "miscellaneous" category was assumed to grow at an arbitrary and very conservative 10 percent per year. This is a small component of total output, and consequently the "big picture" is insensitive to this assumption.

We assumed that the levels of demand in the counterfactual scenario would be identical to those in the projection.

PRICES. Our price projections are largely determined by the regulatory environment. For 1992–96 the company is constrained to hold its average prices constant in real terms, and there are further conditions and allowances on specific services. We took 1991 prices as they actually were. We then assumed that rental prices and set installation charges would be raised to the maximum levels allowed by the concession; the rates for metered calls were assumed to stay constant in real terms, and international call prices were assumed to fall at 4 percent per year, consistent with the global trend toward lower prices (see chapter 4). National long distance prices were used as the clearing price.[18] We assumed these to fall by just the right amount to ensure compliance with the price cap. International incoming prices were assumed to decline at 4 percent per year, and the real price of miscellaneous services was assumed to stay constant.

For 1997 and 1998 the concession specifies that the average price of the basket must actually fall at 3 percent per year in real terms. For 1999 and beyond the regulators will specify the price cap, calculated so as to assure the company an adequate rate of return. We assumed that the same 3 percent per year reduction would be required for 1999 and 2000 and that all prices within the basket would fall at that rate. International incoming and miscellaneous service prices were assumed to stay constant.

For the counterfactual scenario we assumed that 1990 would be the first year of difference, because we believe that the 1990 price-tax reform is attributable to divestiture. Based on the experience of 1981–89, we assumed that the government would hold real prices constant and that the telephone tax would remain as it was in 1989. Thus the prices at factor cost would be quite different between the divestiture and the counterfactual projections because of the wedge created by the telephone tax. International incoming calls were assumed to follow the same trend as in the projection for divestiture.

RESULTS. Under the assumptions just outlined, real revenues at market cost are projected to rise from Mex$15 trillion in 1991 to nearly Mex$64 trillion in 2000, a growth rate of 17.6 percent per year. Growth is almost entirely driven by output increases; after the rise in output prices in 1991, output prices are actually slowly declining because of a combination of the price cap and a decline in the price of international incoming calls.

In the counterfactual case, revenues start lower in 1991 at Mex$9.6 trillion because of lower prices for local calls and domestic long distance. They rise to Mex$41 trillion by 2000, for an annual growth rate of 17.4 percent. This growth rate, which is only slightly lower than that for the divestiture projection, further confirms that the growth rate is output driven. On the other hand, the lower *level* of revenues in the case of continued public ownership reflects the lower average prices.

Costs

Much speculation has surrounded the ability of Telmex to cut costs. Some analysts have projected huge labor savings, claiming that Telmex might lay off around 10,000 operators as it modernizes the system.

Others have estimated that the total number of employees might stay constant for several years. In fact, in its first year as a private company, Telmex achieved a 23 percent increase in labor productivity, compared with increases of 1.0, 24.6, and 11.9 percent in the previous three years. For our projections we assume a growth rate in labor productivity of 15 percent per year. This implies a slight rise in employment over time and an increase in the number of lines per employee to 234 in the year 2000.[19]

For our counterfactual case we assumed a labor productivity growth rate of 5 percent per year. We believe some productivity improvement would have occurred even in the absence of divestiture (see "Changes in Productivity" above). The assumption of a 5 percent labor productivity growth rate implies that the number of lines per employee will remain stable at just over 100.

Consider next the capital spending program. Under its new owners, Telmex is being more aggressive in negotiating favorable terms from suppliers of its capital equipment. It is doing this in three ways. First, the company is simply negotiating harder. In light of its capital program, the company knows it has considerable leverage with its suppliers. Second, it is reportedly coordinating its purchase decisions with its owners (Southwestern Bell and France Télécom) to enhance this leverage even further. And third, it is seeking new sources of supply, such as AT&T, to intensify competition among its traditional suppliers, Ericsson and Alcatel NV.[20] Estimates of cost savings range as high as 20 to 25 or even 50 percent. Once again, in an effort to be conservative, we have assumed in our projections that Telmex will realize a 5 percent saving in its investment spending over the budgeted amounts (which are used in the counterfactual scenario). It turns out that the results are not very sensitive to this assumption.

Thus the divestiture projection differs from the counterfactual projection in two ways: labor productivity is taken to rise at 15 percent per year instead of 5 percent, and a savings of 5 percent in capital spending is posited.

Profits

With higher revenues and lower costs, it is not surprising that we project higher profits under divestiture than in the counterfactual. Quasi rents are projected to rise from Mex$8,300 billion in 1991 to Mex$46,000 billion in 2000, for an annual growth rate of 21 percent. For the counterfactual, quasi rents rise from Mex$2,800 billion to Mex$18,500 billion over the same period.

What Is It Worth?

Table 19-6 and figure 19-7 summarize our basic conclusions on the impact of the Telmex divestiture. The key points are as follows:

- Mexico's welfare will rise by Mex$7,844 billion. This is equivalent to approximately 10 percent of the present market value of Telmex, or to a perpetual annuity equal to 5.3 percent of Telmex's 1991 sales.
- Consumers lose Mex$92 trillion (US$33 billion).
- The government gains an extra Mex$16 trillion in revenues.
- Domestic shareholders (the new buyers and those holding shares prior to divestiture) gain Mex$43 trillion.
- Telmex's employees are better off by Mex$23.5 trillion.
- World welfare improves by Mex$75 trillion because foreign shareholders gain Mex$67 trillion.

In what follows, we decompose our estimates of this overall change in various ways in order to understand the sources of the changes and how they are distributed. The sources of the changes are to be found in the key differences between our projections for divestiture and the

Table 19-6. *Distribution of Gains and Losses from Divestiture,*
Teléfonos de México
(billions of pesos)

Economic actor	Privatized operation	Public operation	Gain from divestiture	Perpetual annuity equivalent as share of 1991 sales
Government				
Taxes	148,164	132,492	15,672	
Net quasi rents	8,255	25,323	−17,068	
Net sales proceeds (cash)	17,093	0	17,093	
Total government	173,512	157,816	15,696	10.60
Employees	29,131	5,620	23,512	15.88
Domestic shareholders	34,773	9,649	25,124	16.96
Domestic buyers	22,489	4,221	18,268	12.34
Foreign shareholders	37,151	10,329	26,822	18.11
Foreign buyers	53,686	13,263	40,423	27.30
Providers	0	0	0	0.00
Citizens (via shadow increments)	17,093	0	17,093	11.54
Subtotal	367,834	200,897	166,937	
Consumers	1,568,346	1,660,194	−91,848	−62.02
Total	1,936,180	1,861,090	75,089	50.70
Private value	163,132	45,301	117,831	79.57
Net change in welfare			7,844	5.30

Source: Authors' calculations.

Figure 19-7. Distribution of Welfare Gains and Losses from Divestiture, Teléfonos de México

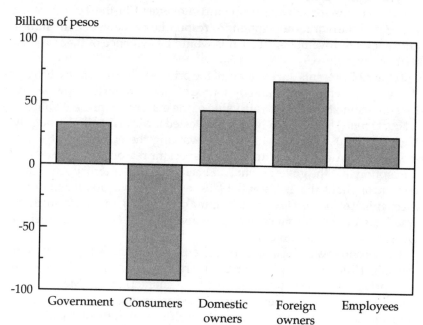

Billions of pesos

Source: Authors' calculations.

counterfactual: the cost savings of 5 percent in capital outlays, labor productivity growth of 15 percent as opposed to 5 percent, and the new price-tax regime. We will study the effect of each of these three differences in the various values of the firm.

Private Value of Telmex

Perhaps the most dramatic change brought about by the divestiture of Telmex is that in its stock market value, which is the capital market's assessment of the private value of the firm. The illustrative list of key dates and the related stock market valuation of Telmex below drives home the point:

Event	Date	Stock market value of Telmex (US$ billions)	Bolsa index
Predivestiture	Late 1988	1.2	215
Divestiture announcement	September 1989	3.3	420
Actual sale	December 1990	7.6	640
Combined offering	May 1991	14.5	1,010
Public offering	May 1992	29.8	1,785

The stock has risen twenty-five-fold in the past four years compared with only an eightfold increase in the Bolsa index of the Mexican stock market. What accounts for the sharp upward movement in the Telmex stock price? Was the market anticipating or responding to news of tremendous efficiency improvements? If so, this would be evidence of the market's faith in divestiture.

Table 19-7 presents our estimate of the private value of Telmex, broken down by ownership class and by source of value. In the first row we see that our estimate of the private value of the enterprise (present value of all quasi rents) had Telmex not been divested is Mex$45 trillion (roughly US$15 billion). Why was the market valuing the enterprise at much lower levels prior to divestiture? We suspect the reason was the market's perception that the government had been using the enterprise as a cash cow throughout the 1970s and 1980s, extracting surplus through the mechanism of indirect taxes and keeping dividends at a token level; there was therefore no assurance of private investors ever receiving much of a return on their investment.

The second row of the table shows the distributional realignment from the sale of Telmex. The government has relinquished 51.1 percent of the enterprise, which was worth (in the base counterfactual) Mex$23 trillion.[21] That amount has been redistributed according to the new ownership shares. The net effect of the sale itself is shown therefore as zero. The next three rows show the incremental effects of the three key changes in the projections. The saving of 5 percent in capital costs raises the value by only Mex$1,354 billion, which is only 1.1 percent of the total gain.[22] Raising the growth rate of labor efficiency from 5 percent (in the counterfactual) to 15 percent (in the projection) raises the private value of Telmex by Mex$20 trillion, which is 17.5 percent of the total gain. This

Table 19-7. Composition of Change in Private Value by Owner,
Teléfonos de México
(billions of pesos)

Source of value	Govern- ment	Domestic owners	Employees	Foreign owners	Total
Value under public operation	25,323	9,649	0	10,329	45,301
Effect of ownership change	−23,140	6,223	1,991	14,926	0
Effect of capital saving	65	474	60	755	1,354
Effect of improved labor efficiency	996	7,241	908	11,521	20,666
Effect of price-tax change	4,618	33,570	4,211	53,413	94,811
Value under private operation	7,862	57,157	7,170	90,943	163,132

Source: Authors' calculations.

gain is fairly sensitive to the achieved growth rate in labor productivity, rising rapidly as the productivity growth rate goes up. By far the bulk of the gain in private value (over 80 percent) comes from the change in the price-tax regime. The gain from this factor is Mex$96 trillion (roughly US$30 billion). There are two ways in which Telmex benefits from the changed price-tax regime: higher prices mean higher total revenues, and, with the abolition of the telephone tax, the company gets to keep a larger proportion of its revenues.

The bottom row shows the estimated value of the firm under the projection. The net increment in the private value of the enterprise brought about by divestiture is nearly Mex$120 trillion (US$40 billion). Thus our estimate of Telmex's private value is considerably higher than the market's assessment; indeed, the market value is more than accounted for by the value under public operation plus the effects of the price-tax change. It seems that the market is *not* anticipating any huge efficiency improvements; rather it is anticipating almost no efficiency improvements and perceives some risk in the stock.

Social Value of Telmex

In table 19-8 we present estimates of the change in the social value of Telmex. In the base counterfactual (first row), as we saw earlier, the private value of the enterprise is Mex$45 trillion. In addition, the government receives a present value of Mex$132 trillion in tax revenues, and employees receive Mex$5.6 trillion in profit-sharing payments. The number for consumer welfare should be ignored; its only significance is to remind us that consumers enjoy substantial amounts of surplus.

Successive rows show the impact of divestiture. The private value rises by just under Mex$120 trillion, taxes on balance rise by Mex$15 trillion, employees receive an additional Mex$16 trillion in profit-sharing payments, and consumers are worse off by Mex$92 trillion because of higher prices. Interestingly, the price-tax changes are almost exactly neutral in their fiscal impact. Finally, the macroeconomic impact is valued at Mex$17 trillion. On balance, consumers are the only losers, with the gains sprinkled among the government, shareholders, and employees. Thus the divestiture of Telmex has the result of "taxing" consumers—a rather diffuse, unorganized group—and distributing the gains among the better defined groups. Within the consumer group, it is of course in local charges that the damage is done, with users of long distance service gaining.[23]

This finding can be, and has been, criticized on the ground that the big price increase of 1990—occurring as it did *prior* to divestiture—should not be attributed to divestiture. We have already argued why the 1990 reform should in fact be associated with divestiture. But to focus on this

Table 19-8. Composition of Change in Social Value, Teléfonos de México
(billions of pesos)

Source of value	Private value of enterprise	Taxes	Employees	Consumers	Total
Value under public operation	45,301	132,492	5,620	1,660,194	1,843,607
Effect of capital saving	1,354	1,280	175	0	2,809
Effect of improved labor efficiency	20,666	14,611	2,716	0	37,993
Effect of price-tax change	95,811	–219	13,450	–91,848	17,194
Effect on macroeconomy	n.a.	n.a.	n.a.	n.a.	17,093
Value under private operation	163,132	148,164	21,961	1,568,346	1,901,603
Net change	117,831	15,672	16,341	–91,848	75,089

n.a. Not applicable.
Source: Authors' calculations.

matter would be to lose sight of the main point. No one can deny that the 1990 price reform was a major departure from past practice and an attempt to modernize the telecommunications sector by bringing prices more in line with the costs of providing different types of services. Divestiture was another out-of-the-ordinary step to transform the sector. The reader who is convinced that the two policies were not linked should then view our results as analyzing the impact of the government's modernization program of 1990 rather than of divestiture alone. It is not our purpose to criticize the price reform. Table 19-8 shows clearly that the net effect of the price reform was a *rise* in social welfare of Mex$17 trillion—this was a welfare-improving reform. But the summary figure masks a very large distributive effect of the reform, as it cost consumers Mex$92 trillion in present value while raising the value of the firm by Mex$96 trillion.

Finally, it is important to note that none of our calculations reflects any welfare effects from quality improvements. We omit this partly because the measurement of such effects is notoriously difficult, and partly because information on this aspect is relatively sparse; that is, there is no specific information to suggest that quality has in fact improved.

Conclusion

The divestiture of Telmex was accompanied by a major overhaul of its price-tax regime. Our analysis of this price restructuring shows several things:

- The impact of the price reform is massive. It alone accounts for an increase in the private value of the firm by Mex$96 trillion (US$30 billion). It will cost consumers Mex$92 trillion. Employees will receive an extra Mex$13 trillion in profit-sharing payments.
- The fiscal impact of the reform is essentially zero—government revenues change only marginally; reductions in indirect taxes are compensated by increased corporate income tax payments.
- The net welfare impact of the price reform is positive, indicating that Telmex was not charging welfare-maximizing (Ramsey) prices prior to divestiture.

In addition, productivity—particularly labor productivity—has grown rapidly. Our estimate is that this will raise welfare by Mex$38 trillion, of which Mex$20.7 trillion accrues to the shareholders, Mex$14.6 trillion to the government in the form of taxes, and Mex$2.7 trillion to workers in higher profit-sharing payments.

In sum, the divestiture of Telmex can be regarded as highly successful. The Mexican government sold 51.1 percent of the country's largest publicly traded company (its third largest company overall) at a respectable price, especially when compared with the price at which the shares had been trading for years prior to divestiture. Further, the stock price quadrupled in the first year and a half after divestiture. The government has been able to capitalize on the stock price increases by selling the shares in tranches, thereby realizing higher and higher prices on successive rounds. Thus the sale process has been managed very skillfully.

If there is one negative with regard to the Telmex sale, it is that, because such a high proportion of the ownership is foreign, a large fraction of the total benefits have leaked abroad. By our estimate, foreign shareholders have gained Mex$67 trillion, or nearly 90 percent of the total welfare gain of Mex$75 trillion. Even if our estimates of the private value of the firm are too high, the leakage abroad is substantial. At June 1992 prices the market value of Telmex is around US$30 billion. The foreign shareholding is now 55.7 percent, which is therefore valued at US$16.6 billion. The new foreign buyers paid a total of US$4.6 billion for their shares, and there was preexisting foreign ownership of some 22.8 percent of the enterprise. Thus foreign owners have unquestionably realized a gain of US$12 billion (approximately Mex$37 trillion at the current exchange rate—compared with our estimate of Mex$67 billion based on a higher valuation of the firm).

Was this leakage unavoidable? Because the prices at which successive tranches have been sold have been market determined, first through a sealed-bid auction and then successively at prevailing stock market prices, it could be argued that the government must have received full value for its shares each time. This would suggest that the big runup in the stock price has been due to news about improvements in the firm's profit prospects.

Our calculations, however, suggest that the stock price increase can be fully accounted for by the price-tax reform of 1990 and the subsequent regulatory reform. That the stock price did not fully reflect this information suggests that the market viewed Telmex stock as risky. This perceived risk has been slowly declining over time. What might this risk have been? We would argue that, because the government had so clearly used the enterprise as a cash cow up until 1988, it had difficulty credibly committing to the market that Telmex would truly be permitted to be independent and profitable. In this light, the decision to sell Telmex cheaply, and largely to foreign investors, can be seen as a signaling device to make this commitment credible.

In addition to this signaling function, the Telmex divestiture played an important role in Mexico's macroeconomic stabilization. The sale revenues themselves were used to reduce the national debt, thereby reducing interest rates and helping create a more positive investment climate. We estimate that a lower bound on the value of this to Mexico is Mex$17 trillion, or nearly US$6 billion, and it could be much higher.

It is in this larger context that, ultimately, the divestiture of Telmex must be seen, and where its true success lies.

We are left with the following lessons from our analysis of the Telmex case:

• It is possible, through innovative financial restructuring and sales in successive tranches, to sell very large enterprises in developing countries.
• Even very large organizations can realize large productivity improvements relatively rapidly.
• Worker commitment to divestiture can be enhanced through making them shareholders in the enterprise.
• Regulation can be used effectively to ensure that expansion and quality targets are met.

Notes

This chapter was written by Pankaj Tandon with Manuel Abdala. Special thanks go to Inder Ruprah for close collaboration on many aspects of this research. Jorge Silberstein of the Mexican privatization office was very helpful on many counts and was our partner in many fruitful discussions. Many people at Telmex were extremely helpful, including Carlos Cassasus, Adolfo Cerezo, Jose Cervantes, and especially Carlos Rebolledo, who was not only extremely helpful at every turn but also commented in detail on an earlier version of this paper. We have also had helpful discussions with or comments from Carlos Mier y Teran, Ricardo Halperin, and Mark Correll. Boyd Gilman provided expertise in the production of graphs and Patricia Regan and Charlene Arzigian provided invaluable assistance in the preparation of the manuscript.

1. For further details about the history of Telmex see chapter 45 of Hyman, Toole, and Avellis (1987).

2. The substantial fall in 1991 may reflect a data problem. Because of an accounting change at Telmex, it was difficult to establish exactly the company's 1991 use of working capital. Our procedure for allocating the short-term assets may have slightly underestimated the requirements for working capital.

3. We do so because the banks retained separate accounts throughout this period, and because the banks themselves were nationalized only in 1982, and most have now been returned to the private sector.

4. The figure normally quoted is US$1.76 billion. However, most of the difference (approximately US$75 million) consisted of payment for certain options granted by the government. See the discussion in Tandon and Abdala (1992) for details.

5. The "L" stands for "limited," referring to the fact that the L shares have limited voting rights. L shareholders can vote on the following three matters: changes in the company's line of business, merger with another company, and withdrawal of the company from the Mexican stock exchange. The last two items are particularly interesting, in that they provide a barrier to the acquisition of Telmex by an outside company or a private leveraged buyout.

6. Although only US$4.6 billion of the sale price was formally received from the international capital market, it is not unreasonable to suppose that, in effect, most of the remainder was reverse capital flight.

7. Success from the point of view of investors was evidenced by the rapid runup in the stock price after divestiture.

8. The data were supplied to us by Telmex. Mark Correll has pointed out that they do not agree in every detail with prices quoted in the prospectus for the initial public offering of Telmex stock in May 1991. This sort of data incompatibility problem has plagued the research at many points. Nevertheless, we constructed price series that, when combined with series on quantities of services, yielded the revenue figures reported in the Telmex annual reports. These price series tell exactly the same story as the one we tell in this section.

9. In national long distance there were price increases in 1988 and 1989; the level in 1989 was still lower than that of 1981, although it was roughly comparable.

10. Government receipts from Telmex, however, stayed at about the usual level in real terms.

11. This percentage applies from 1991 onward. For 1990 the percentage was 46 percent. As a result, the following argument does not completely hold for 1990.

12. For a demonstration of this point, along with an illustrative example of how the new indirect tax works, see Tandon and Abdala (1992).

13. This number illustrates only the general size of the continuing subsidy. In 1990 itself the subsidy was only 46 percent of the telephone tax, or US$455 million. The new rate of 65 percent is valid for 1991–95. After that the telephone services tax is completely eliminated. For details see Tandon and Abdala (1992).

14. This was actually a form of debt financing, except that it was cheaper than conventional debt. Telmex would sell rights to receive future settlement charges that would be paid to Telmex by American Telephone and Telegraph Corp. (AT&T) as its share of U.S.-originated long distance calls to Mexico. Obviously

these receivables were sold at a discount to reflect the time value of money, but there was essentially no risk premium attached since the payer was AT&T. The implicit interest rate used on such transactions was therefore typically one or two percentage points lower than the rate at which Telmex could borrow on its own account.

15. The strong actions by the government with regard to the unions, such as Aeroméxico's 1988 declaration of bankruptcy (discussed in chapter 20) and the similar bankruptcy of the copper company, Minera de Cananea, may have proved a powerful inducement to labor to cooperate.

16. The company's own plans actually call for a somewhat higher growth rate; in fact, a 12.5 percent growth in lines in service was achieved in 1991, and the increase in the number of lines installed was 14.8 percent. (See the prospectus for the public stock offering of May 1992.)

17. Elasticities were largely guesstimates based on previous empirical work. For a review of this work, see Taylor (1980).

18. There are three reasons why this clearing role was assigned to national long distance prices. First, international prices are driven by conditions in the international market and are outside the control of Telmex. Second, the elasticity of demand for rentals and installation fees is very low, and hence profit maximization would argue for very high prices in these categories. Therefore it seemed likely that the firm would try to maximize these within the concession. Third, because the national long distance market would be opened to competition in 1996, it would be in Telmex's interest to keep prices here relatively low in order to preempt entry or to lay the groundwork for successful competition.

19. A 20 percent growth rate in labor productivity would have entailed a rise in the number of lines to well over 300 per employee in 2000, which is probably unsustainable.

20. Apart from putting pressure on Ericsson and Alcatel to improve their terms, this strategy also begins to preempt the possibility of AT&T entering the Mexican long distance telephone market in 1996, when competition will be permitted.

21. The government received about Mex$17 trillion, or US$6 billion; this is not reflected in the table.

22. This result is not very sensitive to the level of cost saving assumed. The relationship is linear; that is, for every 1 percent saving in capital costs, the private value rises by Mex$270 billion. At a higher discount rate the effect of the assumed saving in capital costs is lower.

23. After 1995 we expect national long distance prices to be lower under the projection, as Telmex prepares for potential competition. Outgoing international calls are projected to be cheaper throughout the period. Incoming international calls and miscellaneous services are assumed to have the same prices in both the divestiture and counterfactual projections.

20. Aeroméxico

The divestiture of Aeroméxico is an extremely interesting case study with several unique features:

- The enterprise had been a consistent money loser for three decades before divestiture.
- Its unions had a reputation for militancy.
- The government chose a radically different method to divest the enterprise, first placing it into bankruptcy, thereby quelling the principal union and making possible the liquidation of the enterprise.
- The sale price was essentially zero.
- Partners in the buying consortium had major disagreements among themselves after divestiture, creating fears that the firm was heading for bad times.
- Nevertheless, the divested enterprise is now regarded as a major success.
- The government has meanwhile deregulated the airline industry and has also divested Aeroméxico's major competitor, Mexicana de Aviación (discussed in chapter 21).

Many of these features are important to the analysis that follows. Thus this case study might have something to teach us about how to handle the divestiture of an extremely unprofitable enterprise and about deregulation coupled with multiple divestitures in an industry.

Background

Aeroméxico was started as a private sector company in 1934; its first route was between Mexico City and Acapulco.[1] Over the next several decades the company grew steadily, largely by acquiring smaller airlines in financial difficulty. Although this may have seemed a cheap way to expand, it had a serious unanticipated cost: the airline accumulated a hodgepodge of aircraft that were therefore expensive to maintain. In

1940 Pan American World Airways acquired 40 percent of the company's shares but did not take control. Pan Am eventually sold its holding to a group of Mexican investors in 1957.

In July 1959, in response to a strike by the pilots' union and a perceived need to keep the airline operating, the Mexican government nationalized Aeroméxico by acquiring all the shares of the company. For the next three decades, until its divestiture in 1988, Aeroméxico was a consistent money loser, turning a profit in only three years (1979–81). In each of the years 1982–87 the enterprise received government subsidies equal to about 15 percent of its revenues. Although these subsidies were officially listed as capital subsidies (contributions of capital or absorption of debt), there was in fact a close correspondence between the size of the subsidy and the net loss of the enterprise for that year. In a period of fiscal austerity, with Mexico facing pressure from its creditors to reduce its deficit, the continued drain of resources to Aeroméxico was clearly undesirable.

Divestiture

The opportunity to end the hemorrhage came in April 1988. Ironically, just as a strike had precipitated its nationalization, it was another strike that led to Aeroméxico's divestiture. In a contract dispute over wages and working conditions, the airline's ground workers went out on strike on 12 April.[2] A few days later, on 18 April, Aeroméxico was placed in bankruptcy. Under Mexican law, workers are entitled to job security, but if a company goes into bankruptcy, its workers can be discharged. This is what happened to Aeroméxico's workers. They were, however, paid compensation according to the legal requirement (three months' pay plus another twelve days' pay for each year of service).

Aeroméxico—or, rather, the enterprise that owned it, Aeronaves de México S.A.—was placed in the hands of a trustee for administration during its bankruptcy. The trustee was a government bank, Banobras (Banco Nacional de Obras y Servicios Públicos); it moved rapidly to liquidate all of the enterprise's contracts, except for its aircraft rental agreements, and to restart operations on a skeleton basis.

The airline recommenced operations in early May. Initially only five aircraft were used (four owned and one rented DC-10s) to fly on ten routes. The routes selected were the key routes between Mexico City and other destinations not served by any other airline. Sharp cuts were made in personnel requirements. The ground crew for each flight at each airport was reduced from sixty to thirteen, and the flight crew from eight to four. Passenger occupancy rate in these early weeks was a little higher than 50 percent. As the situation stabilized, the flight schedule was slowly expanded, so that by mid-June eleven aircraft were serving twenty-one destinations. At this point the airline was operating with a total of 118 employees per aircraft, compared with 292 employees per aircraft in 1987.

Buoyed by the success in temporarily operating Aeroméxico at a much reduced staffing level, the Mexican government announced its decision to divest the airline. However, Aeronaves was in bankruptcy, and to resurrect it would mean also restoring the labor union's contracts. The legal way out of this quandary was to create a new company—dubbed Aerovías de México S.A. de C.V.—and to divest that (technically, Aerovías was never a public sector enterprise). Accordingly, Aerovías was created on 7 September with a capital stock of Mex$100 million (approximately US$44,000), of which 35 percent was contributed by the pilots' union, ASPA, and the rest (temporarily) by Banobras.

The new company quickly reached contractual agreements with its workers. Partly because they had been given a large equity share in the company, the pilots agreed to a 10 percent reduction in salaries, longer working hours, and other changes allowing the airline greater flexibility and efficiency. Similar efficiency-enhancing agreements were signed with ASSA, the flight attendants' union, and a new union for ground crew (the National Union of Workers of Airlines and Related Companies, dubbed "Independencia"). The old ground workers' union no longer represented any of Aeroméxico's workers.

Aerovías took formal control of Aeroméxico on 10 October. Ownership of the assets of Aeronaves, however, stayed in the hands of the bankruptcy trustee pending their sale. These assets were offered for sale to the private sector by the trustee. Legally speaking, therefore, the privatization of Aeroméxico was not a divestiture (the sale of a going concern) but rather a liquidation involving the sale of assets.

The offer to sell these assets was made on 26 September. Potential buyers were offered two options:

- To buy all the fixed assets of Aeronaves, including all flight equipment and rental contracts, for a minimum price of Mex$770 billion (US$337 million), or
- To buy all the assets except the aircraft and engines owned by the enterprise, for a minimum price of Mex$370 billion (US$162 million).

The sale process for Aeroméxico was therefore very different from the usual method of divestiture in Mexico. Another unusual feature was the step of preannouncing the minimum price, which was set as the *higher* of two different measures of value: the liquidation value of the assets, and the present discounted value of future cash flows.[3] Of these, the so-called liquidation value turned out to be the higher, and this was used to set the minimum bids.

The offer to sell Aeroméxico's assets was announced on 11 September 1988. Bidders had until 19 September to express interest; nine such expressions of interest were received. On 26 September the minimum

Table 20-1.   Selected Airfares, United States and Mexico, 1989

Route	Fare (U.S. dollars)	Distance (miles)	Fare per mile (U.S. dollars)
Boston-Newark	178	206	0.864
Mexico City-Acapulco	52	191	0.273
New York–Cleveland	296	417	0.710
Guadalajara-Monterrey	75	410	0.182
Seattle–Los Angeles	472	1,133	0.417
Mexicali-Guadalajara	142	1,113	0.128

Source: Ruprah (1992).

prices were announced. To continue further, potential buyers were required to deposit Mex$500 million (just over US$200,000), which would not be refunded if no bid was made. Only three buyers chose to continue; of these, only two actually made bids.

One bid was by a large investment brokerage firm, Operadora de Bolsa S.A. The firm offered to buy all the assets for a total of US$245.5 million, 28 percent less than the minimum set by the government. Operadora de Bolsa further required favorable tax treatment for lease expenses, permission to sell up to 49 percent of the enterprise to foreigners, and renegotiation of various aspects including routes, tariffs, and financial structure.

The second, winning bid was that of a consortium of investors under the corporate name of Dictum S.A. de C.V. This was a joint venture of Bancomer, a government-owned (but since divested) commercial bank, and Icaro Aerotransportes, a holding company formed to hold shares of Aerovías. Icaro in turn was owned directly and indirectly by a number of different Mexican investors, among whom Gerardo de Prevoisin Legorreta, who controls Mexico's largest reinsurance company, eventually emerged in a dominant position.[4] Dictum offered the minimum required price (US$337 million) for all the assets, subject to their valuation and approval. The company reserved the right to review all the assets and to reject those it deemed unnecessary. Further, the offer was for only 75 percent of Aerovías stock (leaving 25 percent for the pilots' union). Of the 75 percent, Bancomer was to own 20 percent and Icaro 55 percent.

Upon subsequent evaluation, Dictum did reject some of the assets (about half the parts and inventories and two DC-10-15 aircraft), and the price was accordingly adjusted down by about Mex$114 billion. The net price therefore was Mex$655.2 billion (approximately US$285 million).[5] The sale contract was signed on 25 November 1988. Payments were made over a period of time (Mex$600 billion plus interest was paid by August 1989) as a series of complicated transactions for formalizing the transfer were carried out. Nevertheless, Aeroméxico began its operation as a private company at the end of November 1988.

The Mexican Air Transport Market

Mexico has a medium-sized market for air transport services. In 1987, the last full year before the divestiture of Mexico's airlines began, a total of 13.5 million passengers were carried on 189,000 scheduled departures. Mexico's market is larger than that of Chile, Malaysia, or Argentina, but less than half the size of the U.K. market. Mexico City's Benito Juárez Airport (which has about six times as much activity as the next largest Mexican airport, Acapulco) is comparable in terms of traffic to that of New Orleans.

Air transport is growing in importance within Mexico's overall transportation system, surpassing rail in terms of number of passengers in 1989. Air freight remains relatively unimportant as a mode for transporting goods, but the passenger market is growing fairly steadily.

THE DOMESTIC MARKET. A little over 50 percent of the traffic is domestic. This market is dominated by the two major airlines, Aeroméxico and Mexicana.[6] Together they carry over 80 percent of passengers and account for over 90 percent of passenger-kilometers traveled.

Through most of the period under study, the domestic market was tightly regulated. Entry, both of new airlines and of new routes or schedules by existing airlines, was strictly controlled. Any fare increases also required prior approval of the Secretariat of Communications and Transport (SCT). Domestic fares were held at low, uneconomic levels, and increases generally lagged inflation. A sample of 1989 fares, matched with fares for similar distances in the United States, is shown in table 20-1. They demonstrate how much lower Mexican fares are. Although the lower fares could be explained partly by lower costs, the cost differential is not as large as the difference in fares. According to International Civil Aviation Organization (ICAO) statistics, the average operating cost per available seat-kilometer for the two Mexican airlines was 4.7 cents in 1989, compared with an average of 5.4 cents for the nine largest U.S. carriers. Thus the low, regulated domestic airfares can account at least in part for the poor financial performance of Mexico's state-owned airlines, particularly Aeroméxico, which was more dependent on domestic services. Because both the trunk airlines were state owned, there was little pressure to raise fares any faster. Competition was essentially nonexistent. A clear manifestation of this occurred during Aeroméxico's bankruptcy in 1988, when Mexicana did not change its flight offerings at all in a bid to take advantage of Aeroméxico's troubles. Deregulation of the airline market (discussed below) took place in July 1991, well after the divestiture of the two major airlines.

Figure 20-1. Public and Private Profit at Current Market Prices,
Aeroméxico, 1981–91

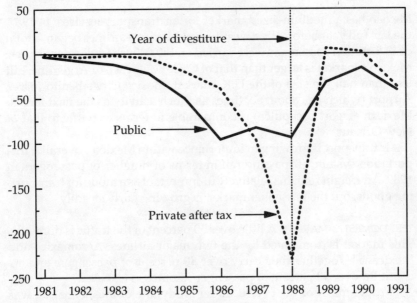

Source: Authors' calculations from Aeroméxico data.

THE INTERNATIONAL MARKET. The market for air transport in and out of
Mexico, although smaller in volume than the domestic market, was
growing more rapidly during the 1980s. The number of passengers on
international flights to and from Mexico grew by about 50 percent
between 1980 and 1991, compared with just over 7 percent for domestic
traffic. From 1981 to 1987 the Mexican airlines steadily raised their share
of this market, to a peak of 55.4 percent in 1987. In 1988, particularly with
Aeroméxico's bankruptcy, the Mexican share fell dramatically, and it has
not yet recovered. According to SCT data, the Mexican share in 1990 was
around 46 percent; Pizzimenti (1992) estimates that in 1991 the Mexican
share was only 40 percent.

The bulk of Mexico's international air traffic is with the United States,
which accounts for almost 90 percent of the passengers. Several major
airlines compete in this market, including the big three American airlines—American, Delta, and United.[7] Because of the bilateral nature of
international air traffic arrangements, the Mexican carriers have substantially the same number of flights as the foreign airlines and so have close
to a 50 percent market share. Aeroméxico, which flies to only six U.S.
cities, has a relatively small share compared with Mexicana. The only

other international destinations of any significance to Aeroméxico are Paris and Madrid, but in these markets it is far behind Air France and Iberia, respectively, and it has only about 10 percent of the passenger traffic between Mexico and Europe. Mexicana does not fly to Europe.

Summary

Aeroméxico is one of two major airlines in Mexico, a country with a medium-sized air transport market where the sustainability of two major airlines may be questionable. The enterprise has a long history of losses, and the government chose to stem the tide in dramatic fashion, by placing the enterprise in bankruptcy and liquidating it. A unique feature of the liquidation process was the preannouncement of a minimum price. The government obtained and accepted a bid at the minimum price but subsequently agreed to renegotiate the price downward.

What Happened?

In this section we examine the performance of Aeroméxico in the eleven-year period 1981–91 to study its pre- and postdivestiture experience.

Figure 20-2. Fixed Operating Assets, Aeroméxico, 1981–91

Billions of pesos

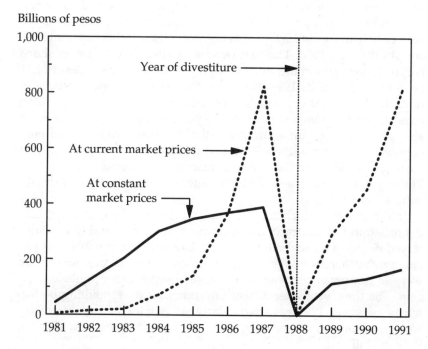

Source: Authors' calculations from Aeroméxico data.

However, there are problems with including data for the unusual year 1988 in the analysis: 1988 was the year of the strike and eventual divestiture of Aeroméxico, and during much of the year the airline was operating on a sharply reduced schedule. Apart from the unsettled operating conditions, there are severe problems with the data from this period, as Aeronaves filed some reports and Aerovías others, and the periods covered by the data are unclear. Further, the balance sheet at the end of 1988 was in a state of flux because final agreement on the sale had not yet been reached, and thus it was undecided exactly which assets would be bought. The year-end balance sheet therefore lists zero fixed capital. For these reasons data for 1988 should be disregarded in the analysis: we will take the years 1981–87 to represent the predivestiture years and 1989–91 the postdivestiture period. The goal is to see if the performance or behavior of the enterprise was radically different on any dimension between the two periods.

Profit and Profitability

We begin, as usual, with an analysis of the profitability of the airline.

PROFITS: PRIVATE AND PUBLIC. As already mentioned, Aeroméxico was a consistent money loser in its entire predivestiture history, 1959–87, with the exception of the three years 1979–81. Thus our data period starts with a small profit of Mex$220 million in 1981, but, as can be seen clearly in figure 20-1, profits became negative thereafter and fell steeply through 1988. The first two years after divestiture, in sharp contrast, were profitable, even though profits were small (less than 1 percent of sales). In 1991, however, the company saw a return to unprofitability.[8] At constant prices (not shown), the steep negative trend is not so dramatic, because the years of very large losses were also years of high inflation. Nevertheless, Aeroméxico performed significantly worse in 1985, 1986, and 1987 than in previous years, hit a trough in 1988, and then became marginally profitable in 1989–90. The loss in 1991 was considerably smaller in real terms than the losses suffered in 1985–87.

Public profit—which adds to private profit taxes, interest, and depreciation but subtracts the opportunity cost of working capital—stayed negative throughout the period. Examination of public and private profits therefore suggests that the first two years after divestiture were an improvement over the last several years under public ownership. The third year after divestiture showed a disappointing performance; however, 1991 was a particularly bad year for the airline industry worldwide because of the sharp drop in demand during and after the Persian Gulf war.[9]

Table 20-2. *Size and Composition of Fleet, Aeroméxico, 1981–91*

Year	Total fleet	Owned	Rented	Type of aircraft			
				DC-8	DC-9[a]	DC-10	Boeing 767
1981	39	33	6	5	30	4	0
1982	38	25	13	5	29	4	0
1983	40	25	15	5	30	5	0
1984	42	26	16	5	32	5	0
1985	43	27	16	5	33	5	0
1986	43	24	19	6	32	5	0
1987	43	24	19	6	32	5	0
1988	29	2	27	0	24	5	0
1989	32	2	30	0	26	6	0
1990	39	2	37	0	33	6	0
1991	45	2	43	0	35	6	4

a. Includes MD-82 and MD-88 aircraft.
Source: Secretariat of Communications and Transport and Aeroméxico data.

FIXED CAPITAL. The operating assets of Aeroméxico underwent a dramatic change with divestiture. As we can see from figure 20-2, the fixed operating assets of the airline rose throughout the predivestiture period—steeply at current prices, gradually at constant prices. The divestiture year of 1988 saw a collapse to zero because, technically, at the end of the year all the assets were owned by a trust. The postdivestiture years saw a resumption of an upward trend in fixed assets, but at a far lower level. Assets in 1991 were well below half their 1987 level at constant prices. Thus, in marked contrast to the other cases in our sample, Aeroméxico dramatically *shrank* its capital stock after divestiture.

This is not to say that the airline itself became smaller. Table 20-2 shows that, at the end of 1991, the fleet size was the largest it had ever been. The notable change was that almost the entire fleet was now leased, not owned. In 1987, with a fleet size of forty-three aircraft, Aeroméxico owned twenty-four aircraft and leased nineteen. But in 1991 only two aircraft were owned, while forty-three were leased. Further, the 1991 fleet was more modern, the older, less efficient aircraft such as the DC-8s and DC-9-15s having been completely eliminated. Finally, the capital stock was further reduced because the company needed to hold far less in parts and inventories. Thus divestiture was accompanied by a dramatic reduction in fixed operating assets—achieved through a reduction in inventories and a new strategy of leasing rather than owning the bulk of the airline's operating flight equipment.

PROFITABILITY. Because of the sharp reduction of Aeroméxico's operating assets in 1988, it is not clear whether profitability is very meaningful in

Table 20-3. *Nominal and Real Unit Costs, Aeroméxico, 1981–91*
(pesos per peso of revenue)

Category	1981	1982	1983	1984	1985	1986	1987	1988	1989	1990	1991
Nominal											
Working capital	0.298	0.353	0.295	0.313	0.332	0.313	0.089	0.187	0.053	0.020	0.016
Rentals	0.077	0.088	0.084	0.085	0.082	0.096	0.087	0.061	0.218	0.202	0.191
Labor	0.468	0.532	0.253	0.252	0.280	0.294	0.295	0.333	0.232	0.241	0.246
Energy	0.124	0.145	0.132	0.143	0.198	0.194	0.189	0.118	0.135	0.185	0.188
Other intermediate inputs	0.272	0.299	0.473	0.497	0.529	0.495	0.470	0.492	0.396	0.362	0.377
Total	1.239	1.416	1.238	1.290	1.421	1.391	1.130	1.192	1.033	1.010	1.017
Real[a]											
Working capital	0.342	0.486	0.464	0.376	0.301	0.313	0.080	0.197	0.111	0.045	0.040
Rentals	0.039	0.066	0.083	0.083	0.082	0.096	0.094	0.225	0.220	0.201	0.211
Labor	0.293	0.347	0.296	0.276	0.270	0.294	0.296	0.356	0.169	0.159	0.165
Energy	0.215	0.275	0.158	0.162	0.190	0.194	0.193	0.114	0.167	0.228	0.247
Other intermediate inputs	0.474	0.568	0.567	0.562	0.507	0.495	0.480	0.477	0.491	0.445	0.496
Total	1.363	1.743	1.568	1.458	1.351	1.391	1.143	1.370	1.157	1.078	1.159

a. At 1986 prices.
Source: Authors' calculations from Aeroméxico data.

this case. It might be that the appropriate normalizing variable is not the owned fixed operating assets but the fleet size. In either event, however, the story will be the same. Private profitability was about -10 percent during the predivestiture period, became marginally positive during 1989 and 1990, and turned slightly negative in 1991. Public profitability (see figure 20-3) remained negative throughout but shows an improving trend, although it worsened in the last year of the period. Because of the problems of interpretation associated with the large capital stock changes, we will rely more on the total factor productivity calculations below.

UNIT COSTS. We begin our analysis of profit performance by looking at unit costs: first nominal variable costs, then real variable costs, and finally capital-output ratios.

The upper panel of table 20-3 shows unit costs—the cost of generating one peso of revenue—broken down by input. Because we include the opportunity cost of working capital in our cost breakdown, we find the unit cost to be above one peso in every year of the period, corresponding to the negative public profit discussed earlier. But we also see that unit costs were considerably lower in the postdivestiture than in the pre-divestiture period. Labor costs were sharply lower; against these, how-ever, were sharply higher rental costs, reflecting the increased reliance on aircraft leasing. But because labor constitutes a higher proportion of costs, the net effect is a reduction in unit costs.

Real unit costs, shown in the lower panel of table 20-3, also show a decline after divestiture, although in this case this decline appears to be a continuation of a trend. There was a sharp decline in labor require-

Table 20-4. *Intensity of Use of Flight Equipment, Aeroméxico, 1981–91*

| Year | Fleet size | Available seat-kilometers | | Revenue passenger-kilometers (millions) | Load factor |
		Millions	Per aircraft		
1981	39	10.64	0.272	6.66	0.63
1982	38	11.20	0.295	6.19	0.55
1983	40	11.83	0.296	7.36	0.62
1984	42	13.34	0.318	8.05	0.60
1985	43	13.47	0.313	8.30	0.62
1986	43	12.56	0.292	7.77	0.62
1987	43	12.50	0.291	7.83	0.63
1988	29	6.15	0.212	4.10	0.67
1989	32	7.89	0.247	5.46	0.69
1990	39	10.35	0.265	6.79	0.66
1991	45	12.77	0.284	7.54	0.59

Sources: Secretariat of Communications and Transport; International Civil Aviation Organization.

Table 20-5. Labor Productivity, Aeroméxico, 1981–91

Year	Labor productivity
1981	22.02
1982	19.46
1983	21.81
1984	23.70
1985	24.08
1986	22.16
1987	22.10
1988	13.70
1989	28.68
1990	44.39
1991	42.21

Note: Figures are calculated by dividing the Divisia index of output by the number of employees.
Source: Authors' calculations from Aeroméxico data.

ments, with labor unit costs almost halving from about 0.3 to around 0.16. Rental requirements slightly more than doubled: recall from table 20-2 that the number of aircraft rented more than doubled from 1987 to 1991.

CAPITAL-OUTPUT RATIOS. The conventional capital-output ratio is misleading in the case of Aeroméxico because of the shift to leased rather than owned aircraft; we need an alternative measure. A standard measure of capacity utilization for airlines is the load factor: the number of available seats, on average, occupied by paying passengers. We see from table 20-4 that Aeroméxico's load factor was higher than normal during 1988–90, but slightly lower than normal in 1991. Further, by comparing the available seat-kilometers with fleet size, we see that the aircraft were being used somewhat less intensively after 1988 than in the predivestiture period. During 1988–90, as the airline was building back up to its normal flight schedule, it was operating less frequently on given routes, and accordingly its aircraft utilization was probably lower. By 1991 things were probably back to something approaching the predivestiture equilibrium.

It is worth noting here one dramatic effect accompanying divestiture, namely, the sharp drop in output. In table 20-4 this is visible in the decline in revenue passenger-kilometers to 4.10 million in 1988 from 7.83 million in 1987. Output has been rising steadily as the airline's full flight schedule has been restored.

PRODUCTIVITY. Partial productivities are simply the inverse of the real unit costs we have already discussed, and therefore they do not need

Figure 20-3. Total Factor Productivity and Public Profitability, Aeroméxico, 1981–91

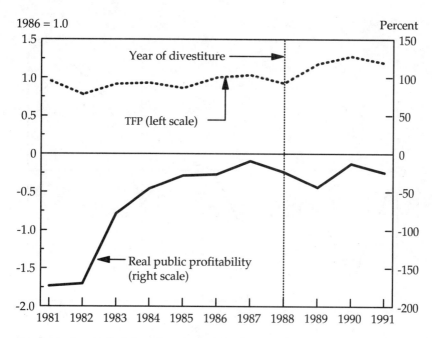

Source: Authors' calculations from Aeroméxico data.

much additional elaboration. For ease of interpretation, nevertheless, we provide in table 20-5 a labor productivity series, obtained by dividing our Divisia index of output by the average number of employees. The approximate halving of unit labor costs is here reflected in an approximate doubling in labor productivity after divestiture.

In figure 20-3 we see the marked rise in total factor productivity (TFP) for Aeroméxico in the postdivestiture period.[10] The simple average of TFP in the seven predivestiture years 1981–87 was 0.933. By comparison, the three postdivestiture years 1989–91 had an average TFP of 1.154, some 23.7 percent higher. This appears to be a significant difference. The difference is apparent in figure 20-4, which shows TFP in logarithms. Whereas during the entire predivestiture period the logarithm of TFP was at or below zero (indicating a TFP less than or equal to 1; 1986 TFP was normalized to unity), for the three postdivestiture years the logarithm of TFP was clearly positive.

In summary, then, TFP at Aeroméxico has been significantly higher in the postdivestiture period than before. It appears, however, that this may be a one-time jump rather than the beginning of an improving trend.

Figure 20-4.   Total Factor Productivity, Logarithmic Scale, Aeroméxico, 1981–91

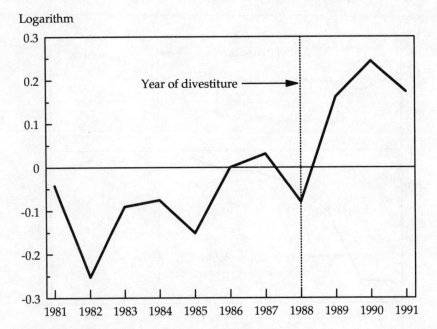

Logarithm

Source: Authors' calculations from Aeroméxico data.

Fiscal Effects

There are two key fiscal effects to consider: the financial transfer to the government as part of the sale, and the annual flows. We consider these in turn.

THE SALE TRANSACTION. As already mentioned, the sale of Aeroméxico was, technically, a liquidation of the assets of Aeronaves. The contractual price was Mex$656 billion (US$285 million). This amount, more or less, was paid by the buying group to Banobras, the bankruptcy trustee. It was not, however, the amount received by the Mexican government. Recall that the buyers inherited a clean balance sheet—that of Aerovías; they did not acquire any of the liabilities of Aeronaves. The purchase price of Mex$656 billion became an asset of Aeronaves, with which its liabilities could be discharged.

What exactly was the amount paid out in the discharge of Aeronaves' liabilities, and what was the residual amount received by the Mexican government? We do not know the precise answers to these questions because the process is not yet complete. And because the bankruptcy proceeding is ongoing, the bankruptcy trustee was unwilling to release the relevant information to us. We can, however, construct our own estimates.

Table 20-6 summarizes our estimate of the net liabilities. We start with the liabilities of Aeronaves on the date it ceased operating: Mex$670.7 billion. This figure includes Mex$87.8 billion in liabilities connected with aircraft lease contracts. Because most of the leases were taken over by Aerovías, we assume that only Mex$10 billion in liabilities was retained by Aeronaves.[11] That leaves about Mex$593 billion in liabilities that Aeronaves needed to discharge.

Further, Mexican bankruptcy law required severance payments to the airline's workers. According to Genel (1988) and to conversations with staff of the bankruptcy trustee, total payments to Mexican workers were about Mex$165 billion, those to U.S.-based workers some Mex$15 billion, and those to workers in France and Spain roughly Mex$9 billion, for a total of approximately Mex$189 billion. This matches exactly the airline's 1987 wage bill of Mex$189 billion.

Finally, Aeronaves retained some assets. It had cash and deposits of just over Mex$60 billion, receivables of over Mex$19 billion, and other assets of Mex$12 billion, for a total of about Mex$92 billion. We have left out inventories, worth Mex$50 billion, and prepayments of Mex$30

Table 20-6. Net Liabilities of Aeronaves at Bankruptcy

Item	Billions of pesos
Balance sheet liabilities	
Bank credits	219.1
Providers	160.6
Lease contracts	10.0
Prepaid services	31.7
Other liabilities	171.5
Subtotal	592.9
Severance payments	
Mexican workers	165.0
U.S. workers	15.0
French and Spanish workers	9.0
Subtotal	189.0
Less net retained assets	
Cash and bank deposits	60.2
Receivables	19.4
Other assets	12.2
Subtotal	91.8
Net liabilities	690.1

Source: Authors' estimates.

billion on the assumption that these were handed over to Aerovías. Subtracting these liquid assets from the liabilities, we get a figure for net liabilities of about Mex$690 billion.

Before a final comparison can be made with the sale price of Mex$656 billion, some additional considerations should be noted (all peso values in this chapter are in "old," that is, pre-1993, pesos; 1 new peso equals 1,000 old pesos). First, recall that Icaro chose not to buy certain inventories and parts with a book value of Mex$90 billion. If we arbitrarily assume that it was possible to sell these items for half their book value, the total sale price of assets becomes about Mex$700 billion. Second, there are costs associated with the bankruptcy proceeding itself. Banobras had to set up an elaborate organizational structure to manage the bankruptcy. Initially some 450 people were working full time on this; the number has been declining over time, but even in early 1992 some 200 individuals were still working on the bankruptcy. Banobras will receive a fee varying from 2 to 4 percent of the value of assets sold, which will receive priority in the payment order. Third, an annuity to ensure pension payments to the retired workers of Aeronaves is to be set up. No estimate is available for the cost of this annuity. However, these considerations suggest that the total net liabilities are well in excess of Mex$700 billion.

The liabilities therefore seem to be greater than the assets. Many of the creditors have already settled at a rate of 70 percent of their claim. Those waiting to be paid at the completion of the bankruptcy proceeding are obviously hoping for more, but the bankruptcy trustee estimates (and our calculations confirm) that they will not receive full payment. We therefore estimate that the government will receive no payment from the sale of Aeroméxico, since—as the shareholder—the government has lower priority than the creditors. Further, we estimate that the creditors will receive only 70 percent of their original claims: Mex$386 billion on claims of Mex$551 billion.

ANNUAL FLOWS. The government will not receive any revenue from the sale of Aeroméxico, but there is a discernible effect of the divestiture on annual flows. As we have seen, Aeroméxico received substantial transfers from the government in the predivestiture period 1982–87. The enterprise paid no taxes. Since divestiture, however, some small tax payments have been made. Figure 20-5 shows the effect clearly; from being a large net drain on the treasury, Aeroméxico became a small contributor to public revenue after divestiture.

Market Value Effects

Aeroméxico stock was closely held during the initial period after divestiture; accordingly there was no formal market for the stock until 1991.[12]

Figure 20-5.   Fiscal Flows, Aeroméxico, 1981–91

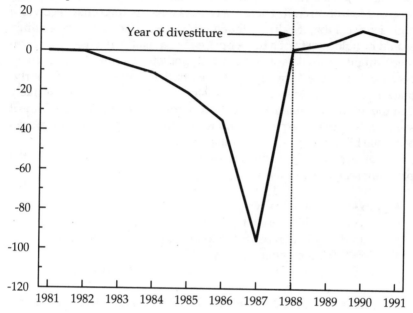

Billions of pesos

Note: Negative flows are subsidies from the Mexican treasury to Aeroméxico.
Source: Aeroméxico data.

The sale transaction itself was so complex that it is difficult to discover exactly what the buyers paid, and for what. In what follows, we summarize what we know or estimate with regard to the market valuation of Aeroméxico.

THE PURCHASE TRANSACTION. In the previous section we discussed the sale transaction and estimated that the government would receive nothing from the sale of Aeroméxico. Here we examine the same transaction from the buyers' perspective in order to estimate what the buyers paid for Aeroméxico. The contracted price of Mex$656 billion is only the tip of the iceberg, as we will see.

The first point to note is that, although Dictum contracted to buy the assets of Aeroméxico, the firm never took possession of the aircraft, except for two DC-9s. The rest of the aircraft were sold to international aircraft leasing companies, and then some were leased back by Aeroméxico. Thus what Dictum paid was the contractual price minus what the firm received from the sale of the aircraft.

Although we were unable to learn the terms of the sale-leaseback transaction, we do know that, prior to divestiture, the government had arrived at a valuation of the airline's flight equipment of Mex$398 billion, based on bids they had received from international leasing companies (see note 3). This furnishes us with a lower bound for what Dictum received for the aircraft. There are two reasons to expect they received a higher price. First, it is likely that a private seller, in actual bargaining, would be able to extract a higher price than a relatively passive government might receive as a bid for a hypothetical transaction. Second, because Aeroméxico was going to lease back twenty-seven of the forty-one aircraft, and was likely to be a customer in the future also, it is likely that the leasing companies were more accommodating to them. Thus it seems reasonable to expect that Dictum would have received more than Mex$400 billion from the sale of the aircraft.

In their account of the sale transaction, Sales and Gomez describe the payment schedule as follows:

- Mex$72.2 billion upon signing
- Mex$442.2 billion upon transfer of the aircraft, after January 1989
- Mex$51.5 billion in reference to the furniture and fixtures
- Mex$34.0 billion after January 1989
- Mex$55.3 billion in reference to parts and accessories.

The figure of Mex$442.2 billion stands out as a suggestive number for the price received by the buyers for the sale of the aircraft. Further, of the Mex$51.5 billion paid for the furniture and fixtures, 50 percent was to be paid upon the transfer of ownership to those deemed by Icaro, suggesting another sale-leaseback arrangement. We therefore assume that the buyers were able to recover Mex$442.2 billion by selling the aircraft and Mex$25.75 billion (half of Mex$51.5 billion) by selling some furniture, leaving a purchase price for the ongoing enterprise of Mex$188 billion.

In addition to the price paid to the Aeronaves bankruptcy trustee, the buyers must also have made a cash equity infusion into the company. We calculate this to have been about Mex$152 billion,[13] yielding a total cash expenditure on the part of the buyers of Mex$340 billion. Because this gave them 75 percent of the company's stock, it implies a total value for the company of about Mex$450 billion, or US$197 million.

THE INITIAL PUBLIC OFFERING. In November 1991 Aeroméxico made an initial public offering of its stock in the Mexican stock market and to foreign institutional investors. The company, which had 167.4 million shares outstanding prior to the offering, offered 43.5 million new shares, thereby raising the total number of shares to about 211 million. In addition, the two principal owners of the company, Gerardo de Prevoisin Legorreta and Maria Pia Hirmas Said, each sold about 70 percent of their shareholding (each sold just under 25 million shares, from an initial holding of 35.6 million shares).

The price of the public offering in the United States was US$1.35 per share, implying a market value for the company of US$285 million, or about Mex$870 billion. In peso terms, therefore, the implicit value of the company had almost doubled, although in U.S. dollar terms the increase was only about 45 percent. By comparison, during the same period the Bolsa index (the Mexican stock market index) had risen by a factor of more than seven (in peso terms). Thus Aeroméxico has lagged behind the general stock market by a wide margin.

In May 1992 Aeroméxico stock was trading at around US$1.50 per share, implying a market value of about US$325 million, or Mex$1 trillion, some 15 percent higher than six months previously (in dollar terms the rise was 14 percent). This is slightly less than the rise in the stock market index during the same period.

OWNERSHIP STRUCTURE. There have been three stages in the evolution of Aeroméxico's ownership structure. At divestiture, ASPA (the pilots' union) owned 25 percent, Bancomer 20 percent, and Icaro 55 percent. Icaro was a consortium of large Mexican investors, who ultimately divided into two groups—what we have termed the "de Prevoisin group" and the "other group." The de Prevoisin group, consisting of Gerardo de Prevoisin Legorreta, Maria Pia Hirmas Said, and various insurance and reinsurance companies controlled by de Prevoisin, collectively owned 20.5 percent of the company. In September 1990 the de Prevoisin group bought out the other group of investors—who had owned 34.5 percent of Aeroméxico—in settlement of a dispute over strategy for the airline. Terms were not disclosed. At this point, therefore, the de Prevoisin group's ownership was 55 percent.

The public offering was a way for the de Prevoisin group to reduce its exposure in the company, and simultaneously for Aeroméxico to raise fresh equity capital. A total of 44 percent of the company was sold (20.6 percent by Aeroméxico as new shares and 23.4 percent by de Prevoisin and Hirmas). Net of transactions costs, the company received US$55.3 million (about Mex$169 billion), and the selling shareholders received US$62.7 million (about Mex$191 billion). Of the 44 percent sold, 33.5 percent went to foreign investors and 10.5 percent were sold in the Mexican stock exchange. The de Prevoisin group's shareholding is now just over 20 percent, but they retain control of Aeroméxico: de Prevoisin is chairman of the board and chief executive officer of the company.

Summary

We summarize below what happened at Aeroméxico during the period surrounding divestiture, dividing the events into two broad categories: changes in behavior or outcomes, and the divestiture transaction itself.

CHANGES IN BEHAVIOR OR OUTCOMES. The most obvious change following divestiture was that the company broke even for two years instead of being the heavy money loser and fiscal drain it had been during the predivestiture period. There were several underlying key changes in behavior:

- There was a dramatic fall in the fixed assets of the company, reflecting a changed strategy emphasizing leasing rather than owning of flight equipment. Correspondingly, the rental cost per unit of output doubled in real terms.
- There was a sharp reduction in labor cost per unit of output; correspondingly, labor productivity doubled.
- As a consequence, TFP rose by over 20 percent. However, this may have been a one-time jump in productivity rather than the start of a rising trend.
- Output fell dramatically, as a corollary of the airline's bankruptcy, but then recovered steadily, so that by 1991 it was close to the pre- divestiture level.

THE SALE TRANSACTION. In effect, the sale price of Aeroméxico was zero, because the government will not, in our estimation, receive anything after repayment of the airline's creditors. Thus the "sale" was equivalent to handing over the enterprise gratis. The buyers then took the liquid assets of the enterprise, along with most of the fixed assets (which they sold and then leased back), combined with some Mex$188 billion of their own money to discharge substantially all the enterprise's liabilities. In the process, the airline's creditors were forced to absorb a substantial loss, which we estimate at Mex$165 billion (about US$70 million). Subsequently, the buyers made equity infusions of Mex$72 billion in 1988 and Mex$95 billion in 1989 to provide operating funds for the airline. Finally, in 1991 the buyers sold 23 percent of the company for Mex$191 billion, thereby getting substantially all of their investment in the company back, and the company raised additional equity capital of about Mex$169 billion through a dilutive stock offering. As a result, some 33.5 percent of the company is now owned by foreigners.

Why Did It Happen?

We examine now to what extent the behavioral or outcome changes we observed can be attributed to divestiture. This then permits us to form a basis for our counterfactual to divestiture.

Sale-Leaseback Strategy

Consider first the dramatic cut in fixed assets and the related doubling of rental cost per unit of output. This change was clearly a consequence of divestiture, reflecting the buying group's strategy of relying on leased rather than owned aircraft. Pizzimenti (1992, p. 15) attributes this strategy to the management's "belief that its competitive advantage lies in being the operator, not the owner of the asset." He points out further that a leasing strategy permits Aeroméxico greater flexibility.

This may be true, and given the glut in the airliner market, the strategy appears to have paid off handsomely for Aeroméxico. Nevertheless, we suspect that the dominant reason for this strategy was that it permitted the buyers of the airline to reduce their exposure substantially.[14] As was pointed out in the previous section, the principal investors have now substantially recovered all their investment, while still owning 20 percent of the company and retaining control. This does not, of course, negate the positive effects this strategy might have on the company.

Having argued that the sale-leaseback strategy and reliance on leasing were definitely related to divestiture, we will assume in our counterfactual scenario a continuation of the previous strategy of relying on both owned and leased aircraft.

Labor Productivity

A second dramatic change was the approximate doubling of labor productivity. Once again, this was clearly caused by divestiture. When Aeronaves was placed into bankruptcy, the entire work force was laid off. As Aeroméxico resumed skeleton operations, the bankruptcy administrators were free to hire whomever they wanted, and labor inputs were held at levels considerably lower than before (recall the section titled "Divestiture" above). When Aerovías was created and Aeroméxico began growing back to its original size, the number of employees was kept to a minimum.

Table 20-7 shows the dramatic cut in employment that accompanied divestiture. Immediately following divestiture, employment was only one-third of its previous level, although output was also significantly lower. The table shows a crude total output measure: the number of revenue passenger-kilometers flown. We see that in 1991 Aeroméxico was still somewhat short of its peak output by this measure. Nevertheless, employment was only a little more than half its peak, with the result that output per employee was considerably higher. Clearly, this sharp reduction in employment would have been impossible without divestiture. Indeed, it may be argued that it would have been impossible without bankruptcy. As we will see in the next chapter, Mexicana has been unable to realize anything like this work force reduction since its divestiture.

We therefore conclude that the dramatic increase in labor productivity is definitely due to divestiture. Our counterfactual scenario will assume

Table 20-7. Employment and Passenger Traffic, Aeroméxico, 1981–91

Year	Number of employees		Revenue passenger-kilometers	
	At end of year	Average for year	Millions	Per employee
1981	10,532	9,448	6,658	705
1982	10,301	10,417	6,190	594
1983	10,624	10,463	7,363	704
1984	10,957	10,791	8,048	746
1985	11,062	11,010	8,298	754
1986	11,366	11,214	7,766	693
1987	11,644	11,505	7,832	681
1988	3,752	7,015	4,101	585
1989	4,683	4,218	5,462	1,295
1990	5,524	5,104	6,785	1,329
1991	6,484	6,004	7,540	1,256

Source: Secretariat of Communications and Transport, International Civil Aviation Organization, and Aeroméxico estimates.

a continuation of employment levels and labor productivity from their predivestiture pattern.[15]

Other Productivity Changes

By themselves, the two major changes so far discussed—improved labor productivity and increased reliance on leasing of flight equipment—can explain the bulk of the productivity improvement, because labor costs represent a higher proportion of total costs than do rental expenses.[16] Nevertheless, other unit input costs have also declined slightly, and they account for a small part of the productivity improvement. Nominal unit intermediate costs varied between 0.47 and 0.53 during 1983–87; the range was 0.36 to 0.42 in the postdivestiture years. Because of the very drastic change Aeroméxico went through, and because this category of inputs showed no declining trend in the predivestiture period, we have assumed slightly higher unit "other intermediate inputs" requirements in our counterfactual scenario, following the pattern established in the data period.

Output

We observed that Aeroméxico's output level fell dramatically during the divestiture year and has since been rising rapidly. Clearly these events are associated with the bankruptcy of the airline. The question is, To what extent are the bankruptcy and divestiture related? We hypothesize that the decision to place the enterprise into bankruptcy was intimately related to its divestiture, in that the government would not have chosen the bankruptcy option had a decision not been made to divest the airline. Thus the hypothesis is that bankruptcy was chosen as the method of divestiture. Governments are not apt to place into bankruptcy enterprises they intend to continue operating, nor do we believe the Mexican government wanted to shut Aeroméxico down permanently.

The consequence of this hypothesis is that the sharp drop in Aeroméxico's output in 1988 must be viewed as having been "caused" by divestiture, in that there would have been no corresponding output reduction absent the decision to divest. Thus in our counterfactual we assume higher output levels than those actually observed in 1988–91. Specifically, we assume that, for domestic traffic, output would have stayed constant in 1988 (because of the labor troubles) and then would have grown linearly between the 1987 level and the 1991 level. The implicit assumption is that by 1991 the divested Aeroméxico has "caught up" with where it would have been had it not been divested (see table 20-8). This assumption is consistent with a growth rate of demand of between 4 and 5 percent per year, which seems reasonable in light of previous experience. For international passengers we have arbitrarily assumed that output would have remained constant during 1987–91 at the 1987 level. Although this is not per se justifiable, it seems a reasonable approximation to the fluctuating demand that it is likely would have been seen.[17]

Table 20-8. *Domestic and International Passenger Traffic, Aeroméxico and Mexicana de Aviación, 1981–91*
(millions of revenue passenger-kilometers)

	Domestic			International		
		Aeroméxico			Aeroméxico	
Year	Mexicana	Actual	Counter-factual	Mexicana	Actual	Counter-factual
1981	3,161	3,877	3,877	4,819	2,782	2,782
1982	3,791	3,473	3,473	3,302	2,717	2,717
1983	4,093	4,619	4,619	4,339	2,744	2,744
1984	4,032	4,668	4,668	5,034	3,380	3,380
1985	4,390	5,449	5,449	5,004	2,849	2,849
1986	3,842	5,289	5,289	5,277	2,478	2,478
1987	3,296	4,630	4,630	6,440	3,202	3,202
1988	3,706	3,205	4,630[a]	7,064	896	3,202[a]
1989	4,005	4,253	4,826[a]	6,532	1,209	3,202[a]
1990	4,291	4,694	5,021[a]	7,156	2,091	3,202[a]
1991	4,715	5,217	5,217[a]	6,028	2,323	3,202[a]

a. Counterfactual assumptions.

Source: International Civil Aviation Organization company reports, and authors' estimates.

Summary

We have argued that all the substantial changes we observed in association with the divestiture of Aeroméxico were in fact causally related to divestiture and therefore form the basis for the differences between what we observe and our counterfactual. In summary, therefore, our counterfactual differs from the observed behavior of the firm in the following ways:

- The firm now operates almost exclusively with leased aircraft. We assume that an undivested Aeroméxico would have operated a mix of owned and leased aircraft, as before.
- Labor productivity is sharply higher, following a massive reduction in the work force. Our counterfactual assumes no change in labor productivity.
- Other inputs are being used more efficiently, as reflected by a rise in TFP. The counterfactual assumes no change in the productivity of other inputs.
- Output levels fell sharply because of the bankruptcy but thereafter grew rapidly. The counterfactual assumes that output levels would have remained at higher levels during and immediately after divestiture, but that the growth rate would have been slower, so that the divested airline is assumed to "catch up" in a few years.

What Will Happen?

In this section we discuss our projections for the divested Aeroméxico, along with projections for our counterfactual scenario: what would have happened had the airline stayed in the public sector. We begin with a discussion of a major policy change: deregulation.

Deregulation

Recall that Mexico's airline market was tightly regulated. The government made no regulatory changes prior to or simultaneously with the divestiture of Aeroméxico or, for that matter, the divestiture of Mexicana in late 1989. Nevertheless, because the government was so vigorously pursuing deregulation in many other parts of the economy, it was clear that deregulation of airlines would also come eventually. What was not clear was the particular form that deregulation would take. Thus the newly divested airlines were in a state of limbo, wondering and waiting for deregulation to arrive.

Deregulation of the airlines was announced in July 1991, and the bylaws were published in September. The reform was far reaching. Entry of new airlines is now free, airlines may add new routes and new flights on existing routes freely, and setting of fares is almost free. On routes served by more than one airline, or on regional routes where intermodal competition is strong, fares are totally unregulated. On trunk routes served by only one airline, fares continue to be regulated; however, carriers must now simply notify the secretary of communications and transport of their intention to raise prices. The secretary must then decide whether to object; if there is no objection, the fare increases go through. At the time of deregulation only 12 percent of Aeroméxico's revenues came from the so-called monopoly routes where there is even nominal fare regulation. And entry into these routes will reduce this proportion further. Thus most of the market is deregulated.

Because the deregulation is so recent, our data have not picked up any effects from it. But clearly deregulation is going to have a major impact on the industry. The key question is what that impact will be. On the one hand, it might be expected that domestic fares would rise, because they have been so uneconomic in the past. On the other hand, the Mexican industry might follow the example of deregulation in the United States, which was followed by a prolonged period of intense competition as new, no-frills airlines such as People Express and New York Air entered the market and the major carriers were forced to respond. In fact, both sets of forces seem to be at play in Mexico.

There have been substantial fare increases, as can be seen in table 20-9. December 1991 prices were about 45 percent higher in nominal terms, or about 30 percent higher in real terms, than prices in June, before deregulation. At the same time, there appears to be intense competition in certain markets. Aeroméxico may have touched off a price war in January 1992 by entering two markets hitherto served only by Mexicana, namely, Mexico City–Veracruz and Mexico City–Tampico. Mexicana responded by aggressively expanding its service from Mexico City to Monterrey, an Aeroméxico stronghold. There have also been some new entries. The last column of table 20-9 shows some aggressively marketed one-way promotional fares advertised in Mexican newspapers in January 1992.

Thus it appears that deregulation is so far having a mixed impact in Mexico. On the one hand, full-fare economy class ticket prices are going up substantially. At the same time, however, competition is intensifying, with heavy discounting on certain routes. In other words, price discrimination is growing. The bottom line on prices is yields—revenues per passenger-kilometer. Aeroméxico reported that its yields were 7 percent higher in real terms in the first quarter of 1992 than in the same quarter a year earlier. Thus it seems that the net effect of deregulation has been to raise real prices slightly. Real prices are still well below U.S. levels, however. Table 20-10, which compares selected prices in each of the five largest Mexican markets with fares on U.S. routes covering the same distances, shows that Mexican prices in the winter of 1991–92 were still

Table 20-9.   Airfares in Selected Markets before and after Deregulation, Mexico, 1991–92

| Market[a] | Number of passengers, 1990 | Full Y fare (pesos) | | | Promotional fares, January 1992 |
		Before deregulation (June 1991)	After deregulation (December 1991)	Ratio of post- to pre- deregulation fare	
Guadalajara	995,265	160,370	239,360	1.49	167,550[b]
Monterrey	813,031	232,850	341,230	1.47	198,000[c]
Acapulco	751,242	143,620	214,370	1.49	
Tijuana	476,271	485,910	712,090	1.47	300,000[d]
Cancún	466,007	399,490	585,440	1.47	
Tampico	—	125,600	180,820	1.44	130,620[b]
Veracruz	—	143,020	205,910	1.44	150,000[b]
Minatitlán	—	173,130	242,590	1.40	190,000[d]

— Not available.

Note: The first five markets listed are the largest domestic markets in Mexico.

a. All markets are to and from Mexico City.

b. Advertised by Aeroméxico.

c. Advertised by Mexicana.

d. Advertised by Saro, a new entrant.

Source: Mexicana data; price office, Secretariat of Communications and Transport; newspaper advertisements from the period.

less than half the corresponding U.S. prices.[18] Therefore we believe that indeed the net effect of deregulation will be to raise real prices in the domestic market. Our base assumption will be for a 10 percent real price increase, with alternative scenarios looking at larger increases. The reason we do not expect real prices to rise substantially more is that there is a capacity overhang in the industry, because Mexicana is expanding its fleet through a major purchase program. The effect of this is already visible: load factors dipped below 60 percent in early 1992. We discuss this aspect of the market in greater detail when we consider the Mexicana case (chapter 21). For the counterfactual scenario we assume no real price change, following the past practice of regulated prices.

Revenue

We approach the calculation of revenue projections by first specifying assumptions for future air transport demand and prices.

DEMAND. As in other cases, we assume the same demand growth in our projections for the postdivestiture and the counterfactual cases. In line with recent history, we assume growth in demand at 5 percent per year; this may be conservative for the domestic market, and possibly optimistic for the international market. To assess the sensitivity of our base projections to changes in assumptions, we also look at the case where demand grows at 8 percent per year.

For the demand projections we also need assumptions on the elasticities of demand. Again, based on the literature, and as discussed in the cases on British Airways (chapter 5) and Malaysian Airline Systems (chapter 14), we assume price elasticities of demand of 1.1 for the domestic market, 1.2 for the international market, and 1.0 for freight and miscellaneous services. The assumption for the domestic market is particularly troubling. Ideally we would want to divide the market into two segments—business and pleasure travel—with a much lower elasticity for the former and a higher one for the latter, who tend to be discretionary flyers. However, the available data do not allow us to divide the market in this way. We performed sensitivity analysis by changing the assumed demand elasticity and found our results to be insensitive to this factor.

PRICES. We have already discussed the basis for our assumption that domestic prices will experience a one-time 10 percent real price increase and remain constant in real terms subsequently.

As was discussed in chapter 5, international airfares are the subject of bilateral negotiations. We assume therefore that international prices will be the same under the divestiture and the counterfactual scenarios and that real prices will remain constant over time.

Table 20-10. Airfares in Selected Domestic Markets, Mexico and United States, 1991–92

Market	Approximate distance (miles)	Full one-way fare (U.S. dollars)
Mexico City–Acapulco	200	70
New York–Boston	200	142
Mexico City–Guadalajara	300	78
New York–Buffalo	300	238
Chicago-Nashville	300	371
Mexico City–Monterrey	450	112
Chicago-Buffalo	450	384
Mexico City–Cancún	800	191
Chicago-Dallas	800	468
New York–Atlanta	800	429
Mexico City–Tijuana	1,400	233
New York–Houston	1,400	534
New York–Dallas	1,400	542

Source: For Mexican fares, price office, Secretariat of Communications and Transport, December 1991; for U.S. fares, telephone calls to travel agents, March 1992.

PROJECTIONS. Putting demand and prices together, we get revenues. Our assumptions for the divestiture scenario lead to a real growth in private revenues at the rate of 5.6 percent per year, while revenues in the counterfactual rise slightly slower at 5.4 percent per year, reflecting the absence of the initial price increase.

Costs

For our base scenario, we assume that input requirements per unit of output remain fixed over time. Because of the dramatic restructuring of Aeroméxico via bankruptcy, the cut in its work force by at least 40 percent, and the complete change in strategy with regard to aircraft leasing, it is likely that most of the potential efficiency gains from divestiture are already reflected in the observed data. Indeed, Aeroméxico's TFP declined slightly in 1991.

Regarding the counterfactual, the public Aeroméxico showed little ability to improve productivity. Although TFP was at a peak in 1987 (the last full year before divestiture), it had grown at less than 1 percent per year since 1981. Unchanged productivity therefore seems reasonable for the base counterfactual scenario; we also perform sensitivity analysis on this variable.

The key effect of the unchanged-productivity scenarios is that, while the quasi rents of the private Aeroméxico are positive, those of the public Aeroméxico are not. This is a reflection of the markedly improved profit performance of Aeroméxico since divestiture, and it naturally casts a favorable light on the divestiture scenario.

Summary

The revenue and cost projections drive the entire ex ante valuation exercise. As expected, the private Aeroméxico is expected to be profitable, whether profit is measured by the accountant (net income on the income statement) or by the economist (quasi rents). The public Aeroméxico could have been expected to be a money loser as it traditionally had been.

What Is It Worth?

The basic results can be seen in table 20-11 and figure 20-6 and summarized as follows:

- Mexico's welfare rises in present value terms by Mex$5,195 billion (at 1988 prices, equivalent to US$2.28 billion) with the divestiture of Aeroméxico. World welfare rises by Mex$4,761 billion (US$2.09 bil-

Table 20-11. Distribution of Gains and Losses from Divestiture, Aeroméxico
(billions of pesos)

Stakeholder	Private operation	Public operation	Gains from divestiture	Perpetual annuity equivalent as share of 1989 sales
Government				
Taxes	2,619	0	2,619	
Net quasi rents	0	–3,496	3,496	
Net sales proceeds (cash)	0	0	0	
Total government	2,619	–3,496	6,115	62.33
Employees	235	0	235	2.40
Private domestic shareholders				
Diverse	125	69	56	0.57
Concentrated	428	44	383	3.91
Foreign shareholders	397	219	178	1.82
Competitors	0	0	0	0.00
Providers	386	551	–165	–1.69
Citizens (via shadow increments)	0	0	0	0.00
Subtotal	4,190	–2,613	6,803	
Foreign consumers	5,724	6,336	–613	–6.24
Domestic consumers	13,355	14,784	–1,429	–14.57
Total	23,269	18,505	4,761	48.53
Net change in welfare			5,195	52.95

Source: Authors' calculations.

lion). The perpetual annuity equivalents of these amount to 53 percent and 48.5 percent, respectively, of Aeroméxico's 1989 net sales—a very substantial gain.

• Foreigners, because they consume a large proportion of Aeroméxico's services, are made worse off by the rise in prices. Foreign consumers are worse off by Mex$613 billion (the annuity equivalent is 6 percent of sales), but foreign shareholders gain Mex$178 billion.

• Domestic consumers are also worse off, to the tune of Mex$1,429 billion.

• Domestic shareholders gain Mex$449 billion; the bulk of these gains go to the controlling de Prevoisin group.

• The big winner is the government, despite the fact that we estimate that it received nothing from the sale itself. It got rid of a money-losing enterprise that would have cost it nearly Mex$3,500 billion in losses and converted it to a tax-paying company that will contribute over Mex$2,600 billion (in present value terms) in tax revenues. The net gain to the government, then, is Mex$6,115 billion, or US$2.12 billion, equivalent in annuity terms to 62 percent of Aeroméxico's 1989 sales.

- Providers—in this case, the creditors of the bankrupt Aeronaves—are estimated to lose Mex$165 billion.
- "Workers" (here the pilots, as part owners of the firm) gain Mex$235 billion, equivalent in annuity terms to 2.4 percent of sales.[19]

Sources of the Welfare Changes

Here we will express all the welfare changes in their annuity equivalents as a percentage of the enterprise's 1989 net sales. We wish to explain the welfare gain, which is equal to an annual flow of 48.5 percent of 1989 sales (the gain to domestic actors is 53 percent and the loss to foreigners is 4.5 percent). A summary of gains and losses by major group affected and by source is provided in table 20-12.

Figure 20-6. Distribution of Welfare Gains and Losses from Divestiture, Aeroméxico, 1981–91

Billions of pesos

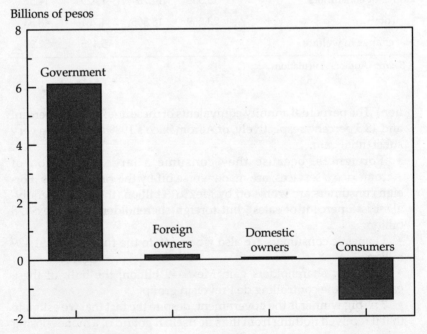

Source: Authors' calculations.

Table 20-12. *Sources of Welfare Change, Aeroméxico*
(annuity equivalents as percentage of 1989 sales)

Source	Government	Buyers	Creditors	Consumers Domestic	Consumers Foreign	Total
Transaction	35.7	–39.0	–1.7	–0.1	0.0	–5.1
Increased labor productivity	13.3	38.9	0.0	0.0	0.0	52.2
Price increase	13.3	7.8	0.0	–14.5	–6.2	0.4
Other productivity changes	0.0	1.0	0.0	0.0	0.0	1.0
Total	62.3	8.7	–1.7	–14.6	–6.2	48.5

Source: Authors' calculations.

THE TRANSACTION. The divestiture transaction in the Aeroméxico case causes a loss equal to an annual flow of 5.1 percent of 1989 sales. Three different kinds of costs are reflected in this figure. First, the creditors of the airline suffer a loss in that they will receive less than they were due. Second, consumers suffer small losses due to the curtailment of service during the bankruptcy process. Third, the new owners of the firm had to make equity infusions into the company. In table 20-12 this last is reflected in the fact that the buyers suffer a loss of -39.0 percent of 1989 sales as compared with the government gain of 35.7 percent. This "gain" of course offsets most of the loss of the buyers, reflecting the fact that the government transferred a losing enterprise to the private sector.

INCREASED LABOR PRODUCTIVITY. The increase in labor productivity is by far the biggest source of welfare change. It results in a net welfare increase of over Mex$5 trillion, or about US$2.26 billion; this is equivalent to an annual flow of 52.2 percent of 1989 sales. This gain is shared between the new owners of Aeroméxico, who gain a flow worth 38.9 percent of sales, and the government, which gains a flow of 13.3 percent of sales because of higher tax payments. Note that the labor productivity increase just about compensates the buyers for their "loss" in the transaction. This conforms with our observation that the firm broke even in the first few years following divestiture, when prices were still regulated but the productivity improvements were in place.

PRICE INCREASE. The assumed 10 percent price increase due to deregulation turns out to be almost welfare neutral: there is a small welfare increase of Mex$33 billion (less than 0.4 percent of 1989 sales on a flow basis). This neutrality masks some real distributional effects of the price increase, however. Consumers (domestic and foreign) lose the equivalent of 20.8 percent of sales per year because of the higher prices; this is slightly outweighed by the increased profits and tax payments. The small size of the welfare effect here suggests that the price is very close to the welfare-optimizing one.

One necessary caveat is that the methodology for calculating welfare changes was changed for this case and that of Mexicana. In all other cases we have calculated the welfare impact on competitors, and consumer surplus calculations have reflected the effect on *all* the consumers in the industry, whether customers of the divested enterprise or of its competitors. In the case of Aeroméxico, however, we have excluded all effects on competitors' profits and on most of the customers of competitors. The reason is that the bulk of the competition is from Mexicana, which was also divested. In that case we again assume a 10 percent real price increase in the domestic market and study its impact on the airline. To avoid double counting, we have therefore divided up the impact of the price change between the two cases according to Aeroméxico's and Mexicana's market shares. In 1991, Aeroméxico's share of the domestic market was 50 percent and that of Mexicana 44 percent. We have therefore included 53 percent of the impact of rising prices on consumers in the Aeroméxico study and 47 percent of the effect in the computations for Mexicana. Finally, we have ignored any impact on the profits of other competitors because their share is so small; implicitly, this assumes that their marginal cost is equal to their price.

OTHER PRODUCTIVITY CHANGES. Other productivity changes have a marginal impact, leading to a small annual welfare improvement equivalent to 1 percent of 1989 sales. All of this accrues in the form of higher profits. The small size of this effect suggests that the decision to lease rather than buy aircraft may not have a very large long-term impact. Indeed, this finding was reassuring, because it implies that the aircraft lease markets are sufficiently competitive to ensure that neither mode (lease or buy) strongly dominates the other. Rather, our result lends support to the argument made earlier that the primary motivation for this decision may have stemmed from the financial decisions of the buyers.

Alternative Scenarios

To examine the sensitivity of our results to some of our assumptions, we looked at various alternative scenarios and their impact on the welfare outcomes. The results are summarized in table 20-13.

PRICE INCREASES. We implicitly discussed what would happen if prices do not rise when we considered the effect of the assumed 10 percent price increase. If prices remain unchanged in real terms, the divestiture impact will still be an annual benefit of 48 percent of 1989 sales. Basically, with

Table 20-13. Welfare Gains and Losses in Alternative Scenarios, Aeroméxico
(annuity equivalents as percentage of 1989 sales)

Scenario	Govern- ment	Buyers	Creditors	Consumers Domestic	Foreign	Total
No price increase	49.1	0.9	–1.7	–0.1	0.0	48.2
Price increase of 15 percent	67.9	12.0	–1.7	–21.2	–9.1	47.9
Price increase of 20 percent	72.6	14.8	–1.7	–27.4	–11.7	46.6
Demand growth at 8 percent	90.7	18.0	–1.7	–21.7	–9.3	76.0
Public labor efficiency improvement of 5 percent	32.0	8.7	–1.7	–14.6	–6.2	18.2
Base scenario	62.3	8.7	–1.7	–14.6	–6.2	48.5

Source: Authors' calculations.

no price increase the firm will just about be breaking even, so the government would receive the benefit of not suffering the large losses it would otherwise suffer.

If competition after deregulation proves less intense than we assumed in our base scenario, prices may rise more than 10 percent. We have looked at scenarios with price increases of 15 percent and 20 percent. Each of these results in a slight welfare reduction from the base scenario, as the consumer surplus losses outweigh the gains to the firm and to the government. This conforms to the idea that the 10 percent price increase may be close to the welfare-maximizing one, and that further price increases might result in welfare losses. The net effect of these increases is, however, small in total, although with some distributional significance. Further, domestic Mexican welfare would be rising in each case because the share of the loss borne by foreign consumers is greater than the share of the gain accruing to foreign shareholders.

FASTER DEMAND GROWTH. We assumed for our base case a 5 percent rate of growth in demand, which may be conservative. If demand were to grow at 8 percent, the welfare impact of divestiture would be much bigger—equivalent to an annual flow of 76 percent of 1989 sales as compared with 48.5 percent. These gains would accrue to the buyers and the government.

PUBLIC LABOR EFFICIENCY IMPROVEMENT. Finally, we consider an alternative counterfactual scenario in which we permit some labor efficiency improvement to take place under continued public ownership.

Mexicana had experienced improved labor productivity during its last three years as a public enterprise, and clearly there was room for similar improvement at Aeroméxico. In out alternative counterfactual scenario we assume that labor productivity improves at the rate of 5 percent per year for five years. This considerably weakens but does not eliminate the benefit of divestiture: from an annual flow of 48.5 percent of 1989 sales to one of 18.2 percent. Aeroméxico would still have been a loss maker (to the tune of Mex$525 billion in present value), and so the gain from divestiture would still have been substantial.

Summary and Lessons

The divestiture of Aeroméxico has been highly successful, resulting in a substantial welfare improvement. The key points are as follows:

- Welfare improved dramatically: we estimate an annual flow of 48.5 percent of 1989 sales as the welfare gain.
- The Mexican government is the big winner: its annualized gain is 62 percent of 1989 sales. The buyers experience a more moderate gain (8.7 percent), while consumers lose.
- The primary source of the government's gain is elimination of the deficit caused by Aeroméxico; the gain from this source is equivalent to an annuity of 36 percent of 1989 sales.
- The overall welfare improvement is driven largely by the dramatic increase in labor productivity, which in turn stems from the massive labor force reductions following the airline's bankruptcy.
- The welfare gains will be more substantial if demand grows more rapidly than we postulated.

Surviving Hypotheses

We are left with the following possible conclusions from our analysis of the case:

- Legal restructuring of an enterprise through bankruptcy prior to divestiture can be a highly effective way to ensure subsequent welfare gains.
- By absorbing liabilities (or, in this case, paying them off through the bankruptcy trustee), governments can achieve a politically necessary positive "price" even for a money-losing enterprise.
- Even if the government receives no net revenue from the sale of an enterprise, it can still receive a substantial fiscal benefit.
- Worker opposition to divestiture can be preempted by strong action on the part of the government.

Notes

This chapter was written by Pankaj Tandon. The author acknowledges particularly helpful discussions with Arturo Rangel of Banobras and helpful discussions with Luis Mestre and David Pizzimenti. Thanks go to Inder Ruprah for assistance in obtaining data for the predivestiture years, to Brian Maddox for providing information on 1991, to Manuel Abdala for research assistance during the very early phases of this work, and to Patricia Regan and Charlene Arzigian for cheerful and capable secretarial assistance under extreme time pressure.

1. Much of this discussion on the history of Aeroméxico and its divestiture is based on Genel (1988), Sales and Gomez (1989), and Carrera (1990). Interestingly, the first two papers are virtually identical. Because the Genel paper has an earlier date, credit has generally been given to that paper in what follows.

2. The wage demand was reportedly for a 30 percent increase, which may not appear excessive in light of the 159 percent inflation Mexico had experienced in 1987. However, according to our estimates, average wages had already risen by a factor of two and a half in 1987.

3. The methods used to calculate these were rather unsophisticated and probably yielded serious underestimates. For a brief discussion, see Tandon and Abdala (1992). One key component of the liquidation value, however, was determined fairly accurately: the value of the owned aircraft was estimated at Mex\$398 billion (US\$174 million) on the basis of actual offers.

4. In September 1990, following a dispute over the strategic direction of Aeroméxico, de Prevoisin and companies controlled by him or his associates bought all the other investors' shares of Icaro. These amounted to 62.7 percent of Icaro's shares.

5. In fact, it appears that the owners of Aerovías achieved a further price reduction in negotiations over the valuation of parts and inventories. The 1991 income statement reports an extraordinary gain of Mex\$62 billion for "amortization of surplus on business acquired," which we believe to have been a settlement of some outstanding issues on the purchase price. It is possible that the final price paid was lower than Operadora de Bolsa's offer, although we were unable to establish this definitively.

6. There have been a varying number of smaller niche airlines, ranging from five or six in the mid-1980s to fourteen in 1991, and a larger number of regional air companies providing unscheduled service. The smaller airlines had been declining in importance, except that in the last three years there appears to have been a resurgence in this category.

7. United is a small but rapidly growing presence in this market. Its 1990 share was 2.7 percent, up from 1.5 percent in 1989 and 1.2 percent in 1988.

8. All 1991 data are an extrapolation from data for the first eight months of the year, which was all the information available at the time of the analysis.

9. The problems caused to U.S. airlines by the war-related reduction in demand are well known: several major airlines went bankrupt, and many of those that survived suffered large losses. Even as late as the first quarter of 1992 American Airlines (AMR Corp.) was the only major U.S. airline to turn a profit, which was an anemic US\$20 million.

10. Note, however, that real public profitability does not capture the same effect. Real public profitability is calculated by dividing real public profit by fixed operating assets. But in the case of Aeroméxico fixed operating assets fell dra-

matically as the company shifted to a leasing strategy. The TFP index solves this problem by calculating the input index using all inputs (including fixed capital), including the opportunity cost of the fixed assets, thus providing a more comprehensive view of performance.

11. Recall from table 20-2 and the associated discussion that fourteen aircraft were eliminated from the Aeroméxico fleet in 1988. These were its six DC-8 aircraft and its eight DC-9-15s—the fourteen oldest aircraft in its fleet. Most of these were owned by Aeroméxico, but three of the DC-8s were leased. We assume that the lease liabilities for these three aircraft totaled Mex$10 billion.

12. In contrast, the two other enterprises we studied in Mexico had stock exchange listings even through their parastatal periods.

13. The initial capital stock was a token Mex$100 million, but at the end of 1988 a capital stock of Mex$72 billion appears in the balance sheet. A further equity increase of Mex$95 billion is recorded in 1989. If we discount this by 20 percent (the 1989 inflation rate), we get a present value of Mex$80 billion in 1988. These two numbers sum to Mex$152 billion.

14. In fact, one of the differences of opinion that led to the split of Icaro and the buyout by the de Prevoisin group was apparently related to the question of leasing versus buying, with the de Prevoisin group preferring leasing and the other investors favoring a purchase program.

15. The manner in which the labor productivity gains were realized, through confrontation with a "troublesome" union and bankruptcy of the enterprise, may have had major implications for the rest of Mexico's divestiture program. In a country with powerful and militant unions, the almost total absence of effective worker opposition to divestiture has often been noted. Some observers point to the Mexican government's strong stand on Aeroméxico (and similarly in 1989 in connection with the bankruptcy of the copper enterprise Minera de Cananea) as critical to preempting labor's opposition to divestiture. We have not included any such "external" benefits in our calculations of the welfare impact of Aeroméxico's divestiture.

16. Although the gap has narrowed. Labor costs have stayed at just under one-quarter of total costs, but rental expense has risen from about 8 percent of costs to nearly 20 percent.

17. This was a period of great turmoil in the international airline market, as a result of which demand growth was curbed by events such as the crisis in Kuwait and the subsequent war in the Persian Gulf. Mexicana, whose experience may be taken as something of a proxy for Aeroméxico's, actually saw its international passenger traffic decline from 1988 to 1991 (table 20-8).

18. Although this may have changed consequent to the steep price reductions in the United States, and the reported fare increases in Mexico in May 1992.

19. We have not calculated a welfare loss or gain to the other workers. It might well be argued that the workers who suffered the loss of their jobs did suffer a welfare loss. However, we estimate this loss to be negligible because of the sizable severance payments. We calculated earlier that total severance payments were only slightly smaller than the annual wage bill.

How much the workers lost in wages depends on how soon they could have obtained an alternative job. Mexico's unemployment rate was officially about 5 percent at the time. Although this is surely an understatement, the Aeroméxico prospectus of 1991 talks of a shortage of skilled workers and of the airline's efforts to train new workers. Thus it is likely that Aeroméxico's workers could have gotten new jobs fairly easily. If we take the probability of getting a new job to be

0.9, then the expected earnings of a fired worker would be $0.9w$ (where w is the annual wage), and the wage loss would be $0.1w$ per year. The present value of this infinite stream at a 10 percent discount rate would be the annual wage w. Further, the welfare loss to the worker is not the full wage loss, because he or she has additional leisure. Because severance payments close to the annual wage bill were paid, it seems that this was approximately full compensation to the workers.

Finally, one could use a revealed preference argument that, because this was the compensation called for under the law, this was *society's* estimate of the welfare loss to workers, and therefore no net gain or loss in social welfare took place.

21. *Mexicana de Aviación*

When Mexicana de Aviación was divested in September 1989, hopes were running high. This was the first sale of a major public enterprise in the term of President Carlos Salinas de Gortari, and it marked a major change in that the buying group was 49 percent foreign owned. Savvy investors such as Chase Manhattan Bank and British takeover artist Sir James Goldsmith were putting down substantial sums to buy a piece of Mexico's flagship airline, at a price twice the enterprise's prevailing stock market value. The new management promised an ambitious US$3 billion investment program that would capitalize on the expected boom in the Mexican tourism industry. *Forbes* magazine ran a profile (King 1989) of the Mexican industrialist who headed the buying consortium, Pablo Brener. Articles in the media of the day painted nothing but a rosy future for the enterprise.

What makes the study of the Mexicana divestiture so interesting is that that rosy future has, so far at least, failed to materialize. *Forbes* followed up its admiring profile two years later with an account of "that sinking feeling" (Poole 1991) at Mexicana. The airline has been losing market share to its chief rival, Aeroméxico. And the stock price is one-third the level at which the divestiture transaction took place.

In this chapter we will analyze the factors that explain this dismal performance. We will see that not all divestitures are successful, and not all private sector managers transform the enterprises they buy. Sometimes there are failures. This is not a condemnation of divestiture. It is merely a reminder that sometimes private firms fail. Indeed the way of the market is that, when bad decisions are made, evolutionary forces start cutting back on the sources of those bad decisions. Whether by the replacement of present management policies with new, more successful ones, or by the overthrow of existing management by takeover or merger, or, finally, by the extinction of the enterprise itself, Mexicana will not be allowed to continue to perform as it has been performing. How the forces of the market will work this out remains to be seen.[1]

Background

Mexicana de Aviación,[2] founded in 1921, is the oldest airline in Latin America and the fourth oldest in the world. In its early years it was based in the port of Tampico. In 1926 all of the airline's shares were acquired by Pan American World Airways. Pan Am obtained a concession from the U.S. Postal Service to transport mail between the United States and Mexico and inaugurated Mexicana's first international flight (Mexico City–Los Angeles) in 1935. Over the next three decades Mexicana steadily expanded its system. In 1967 Pan Am sold its interest in the airline to a group of Mexican investors led by Cresencio Ballesteros, a construction industry figure.

The airline then embarked on a program to modernize and rapidly expand its fleet, relying exclusively on the acquisition of Boeing 727 aircraft. Starting with seventeen aircraft in 1970, the airline's fleet grew to forty-four by 1980, and all of these were 727s. In 1981 the first three DC-10s were added. This expansion program was funded largely by debt.

In 1982, when rising interest rates and falling oil prices led to the Mexican debt crisis, Mexicana—reflecting its country's fortunes—had a debt crisis of its own. The enterprise was unable to meet its obligations and turned to the government for help. The government elected to acquire a 51 percent shareholding (the terms were not disclosed), thereby making Mexicana a parastatal enterprise.

Divestiture

Mexicana's tenure as a parastatal was short, however. The government decided in October 1986 to divest it,[3] which was early for such a relatively large enterprise. Banamex was appointed the agent bank.

The first attempt to sell the enterprise ended in July 1987. Two bids had been received but were deemed inadequate. A second attempt followed. The government declared it wanted Mex$225 per share plus a minimum equity investment of US$75 million. Letters of intent were received from a number of potential buyers, including Gerardo de Prevoisin Legorreta, who later that year bought control of Aeroméxico (this was in March 1988, before Aeroméxico filed for bankruptcy); the Lanzagorta group, which owned Avemex, a small private air carrier; Grupo Protexa, owner and operator of another small airline; and Roberto Hernandez of the brokerage firm Acciones y Valores, who some years later bought control of Banamex.

Despite all the interest, Mexicana remained unsold. Each potential bidder was willing to pay the government's price and to guarantee investment, but each had a list of requirements to be satisfied, and it was these that were the stumbling block. Two important conditions reappeared again and again:

- Mexicana was severely overstaffed, and the prospective buyers insisted that the work force be cut *before* the divestiture. One bidder specifically mentioned the need to cut 3,000 workers from the payroll, at an estimated severance cost of Mex$100 billion (about US$45 million; all peso values are in "old," that is, pre-1993, pesos; 1 new peso equals 1,000 old pesos).
- Mexicana was too heavily indebted, and the government had to restructure or take over the debt before the sale.[4]

Negotiations over these and other preconditions for sale led nowhere, and eventually, in October 1988, the government declared the sale attempt a failure and closed the proceedings.

In May 1989 the government switched agent banks, appointing Banco Internacional. Now a new scheme to divest Mexicana was announced. The government would not sell its share, but rather was searching for an equity infusion into the enterprise. It was willing to dilute its shareholding in exchange and to permit the new controlling group to be up to 49 percent foreign owned. Letters of interest were sought in June, and by August seven formal offers had been received.

The winning bid was filed by Grupo Falcon, a consortium of Mexican and foreign investors. The Mexican investors owned 51 percent of the consortium, of which 33 percent was held by the brothers Pablo and Israel Brener, through their holding company, Grupo Xabre. Of the foreign investors, Chase Manhattan Bank held 35.7 percent of Falcon, Drexel Burnham Lambert owned 7.1 percent, and Sir James Goldsmith 6.1 percent. The consortium was put together primarily by the Breners, the sons of Lithuanian immigrants who had made a fortune in the 1980s by buying assets when everybody else in Mexico was trying to get their money out of the country. Their investments had included the Camino Real Hotel chain and the Las Hadas resort in Manzanillo, tourist properties that they regarded as synergistic with Mexicana. The foreign investors were largely passive: business associates of Pablo Brener, they had faith in his ability to make profitable investments.

The Falcon bid proposed a US$140 million equity infusion in exchange for 20 percent of the enterprise's stock, implying a value for Mexicana of US$700 million. They were also required by the terms of the agreement to buy an additional 5 percent of the shares in the open market. The ownership structure of the enterprise therefore evolved as follows (figures are percentage shares):

	Predivestiture	*Postdivestiture*
Government	50.83	40.60
Domestic shareholders	49.17	34.40
Domestic buying group	0.00	12.75
Foreign buyers	0.00	12.25

The government placed another 25 percent of the shares in a trust over which Falcon had voting control until September 1992, thereby assuring the group control over the enterprise for a period of three years. Falcon had the option to buy this block of shares at any time during this three-year period, at a price implying the same valuation as the original bid plus interest at the London interbank offer rate plus 2 percent. Finally, Falcon promised an ambitious US$3 billion, ten-year investment program, of which US$1.1 billion would be spent in Mexico, creating an estimated 21,500 new jobs.

The winning bid was announced on 22 August 1989, and the transfer of Mexicana took place shortly thereafter, in September.

The Mexican Air Transport Market

Since we reviewed the Mexican air transport market in the previous chapter, no comprehensive review is necessary here. We simply note the following (see table 21-1 for details):

- In terms of employment or output measures such as passenger-kilometers flown, Mexicana is only slightly larger than its main rival Aeroméxico.
- Mexicana has historically been more oriented to international service than Aeroméxico, with domestic service generally accounting for less than 50 percent of its revenues. As a result, Mexicana was less affected by adverse regulatory conditions (i.e., low domestic prices) than was Aeroméxico.

Table 21-1. Employment and Revenues, Mexicana de Aviación and Aeroméxico, 1981–91

Year	Average employment (number of workers)		Revenues (billions of pesos)		Share of revenues from domestic passengers	
	Mexicana	Aeroméxico	Mexicana	Aeroméxico	Mexicana	Aeroméxico
1981	10,212	9,448	15	12	39	62
1982	11,031	10,417	22	19	40	59
1983	11,910	10,463	61	48	40	53
1984	12,158	10,791	96	75	41	54
1985	12,980	11,010	162	120	39	56
1986	13,373	11,214	334	246	35	57
1987	13,906	11,505	867	640	33	52
1988	13,540	7,015	1,703	492	37	75
1989	12,783	4,218	1,881	981	39	76
1990	11,974	5,104	2,525	1,624	42	71
1991	11,289	6,004	2,668	2,323	50	66

Source: Company reports and Secretariat of Communications and Transport.

Figure 21-1. Public and Private Profit, Mexicana de Aviación, 1981-91

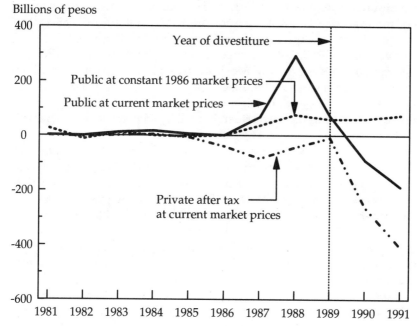

Billions of pesos

Source: Authors' calculations from Mexicana data.

What Happened?

This section reviews the performance of Mexicana during the eleven-year period 1981–91, to study its pre- and postdivestiture experience. At the time of our research, final figures for 1991 were not available for all items. Therefore some figures are extrapolations based on data up to the third quarter of 1991 (September), others on data up to November, and still others are the final figures for the year.

Profit and Profitability

We begin, as usual, with an analysis of the profitability of the airline.

PROFITS: PRIVATE AND PUBLIC. The first step is an analysis of private profit. Through most of the predivestiture period Mexicana was approximately breaking even, with a small dip into somewhat more significant losses in the three years 1986–88 (see figure 21-1). Recall from chapter 20 that Aeroméxico was doing steadily worse in successive years of this period and found its profits plunging in 1986 and 1987. Mexicana showed a similar but much more moderate decline in these years.

The reason for the decline surely was reduced air travel due to Mexico's severe recession. According to data from the Secretariat of Communications and Transport, the number of passengers transported on domestic flights fell 20 percent, from 14.4 million in 1985 to 11.6 million in 1986, and a further 13 percent to 10 million in 1987. Aeroméxico, with its greater dependence on the domestic market, felt this dramatic decline deeply. Mexicana was a little more insulated from the effects of this decline because its international traffic continued to grow at a healthy rate, but it too felt the effects of the downturn in domestic travel: its domestic ridership fell by 15 percent and 13 percent in these two years.

The following year saw a recovery for Mexicana. As Aeroméxico suffered through its bankruptcy and divestiture, Mexicana enjoyed some spillover benefits. Mexicana did not, however, try to capitalize on Aeroméxico's woes—rather than try to steal passengers from Aeroméxico it retained its normal flight schedule. Nevertheless, on routes served by both airlines, Mexicana naturally received additional customers. Its load factor for 1988 rose to 67.6 percent, compared with a normal level for the airline of about 60 percent.[5] Thus the profitability picture in 1988 improved considerably.

In fact, the loss posted in 1988 (figure 21-1) is partly an accounting artifact caused by taxes on phantom gains. Mexican accounting practice requires enterprises to adjust their accounts for the effects of inflation by including an item called "gain or loss from monetary position." This item forces the firm to recognize on its income statement the net increase or decrease in the value of its monetary assets and liabilities (whether realized or unrealized) due to inflation and exchange rate movements. These changes affect reported income, can convert an actual loss to a paper gain, and thereby cause the firm to incur a tax liability.

In our presentation of private profits we have excluded the gain or loss from monetary position on the grounds that it is an accounting artifact. No money actually changed hands, and, indeed, these gains or losses are removed when companies report their cash flow reconciliation. For 1988 we therefore report a pretax profit of Mex$48 billion. But because of the inflation accounting, Mexicana had a tax liability of Mex$91 billion. Our reported post-tax income is therefore a loss of Mex$43 billion, even though the enterprise would have been profitable if the tax had been applied only on the realized gain. The upshot of this discussion is that 1988 should be seen as a profitable year for Mexicana. The next year shows a similar pattern, although at a reduced order of magnitude.

The big surprise in the private profit history of the enterprise is the rapidly deteriorating position in the two postdivestiture years 1990 and 1991. Here the inflation accounting plays no role—the firm was genuinely unprofitable, unable even to cover its operating costs. This sharp drop in private profits is unique among all our cases, and requires explanation.

Turning to public profit, however, we get a somewhat more accurate view of the trends. At current prices, 1988 shows up as the best year, followed by steep declines into negative territory by 1990 and 1991. But at constant prices, public profit more or less levels off after 1988. This indicates that the terms of trade were moving against the enterprise, which could well have been happening. Recall from the discussion in chapter 20 that airline prices were regulated, and that real prices were being allowed to drift lower.

FIXED CAPITAL. To be able to discuss the airline's profitability we must look next at what happened with fixed capital. Looking at fixed operating assets (figure 21-2), we see that not much change was taking place throughout 1981–90, but that there was a big jump in 1991 (see the pronounced kink in fixed operating assets at constant prices). The figure also illustrates the strong inflation effects in 1986 and 1987, as the series at current prices rises rapidly even though that at constant prices is moving rather slowly in its normal trend.

Figure 21-2. Fixed Operating Assets, Mexicana de Aviación, 1981-91

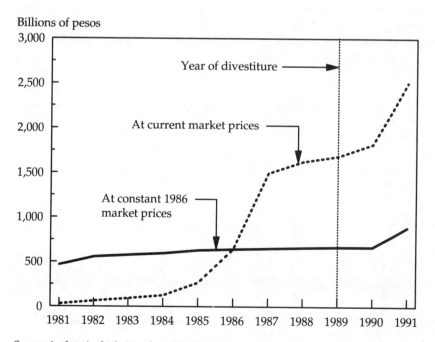

Billions of pesos

Source: Authors' calculations from Mexicana data.

In fact, if we look simply at Mexicana's fleet, these effects are fully captured (table 21-2). The fleet did not grow during 1986–89. In 1990 there was an increase of two aircraft, but both were rented and therefore do not appear in the measure of fixed assets. There was, however, a substantial jump in fixed assets in 1991.

PROFITABILITY. The three profitability series in figure 21-3 reflect our previous findings. Private profitability varied around zero through most of the period, then dropped to a loss of about 15 percent in the last two years. Public profitability at current prices was variable but positive until 1990, when it became negative. Public profitability at constant prices rose to a high in 1988 and then stayed roughly constant.

UNIT COSTS. Real unit costs declined from a plateau around 1 until 1986 to 0.9 in 1987 and 0.8 in 1988. They then stayed roughly constant at this lower level. The primary force behind the trend seems to be labor unit costs, which declined from around 0.25 to around 0.18 (figure 21-4). "Other intermediate inputs" also shows a declining trend from close to 0.5 to around 0.43. This is suggestive of some productivity improvement at Mexicana.

Productivity

Data on labor productivity (table 21-3) do provide evidence of some productivity improvement. We see that Mexicana experienced no real labor productivity improvement during 1981–87, but there is only a mild increase in the last four years.

Table 21-2. *Size and Composition of Fleet, Mexicana de Aviación, 1981–91*

Year	Total fleet	Aircraft	
		Owned	Rented
1981	45	36	9
1982	45	38	7
1983	43	36	7
1984	44	36	8
1985	46	38	8
1986	45	34	11
1987	45	34	11
1988	45	34	11
1989	44	31	13
1990	46	31	15
1991	52	34	18

Note: Figures are as of the end of the year.
Source: Secretariat of Communications and Transport and Mexicana de Aviación data.

Figure 21-3. Private and Public Profitability, Mexicana de Aviación, 1981–91

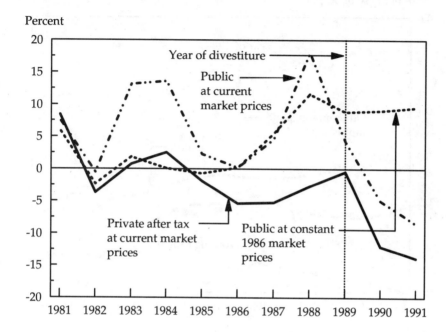

Percent

Source: Authors' calculations from Mexicana data.

The total factor productivity (TFP) picture for Mexicana (figure 21-5) reflects what we saw with real unit costs and labor productivity. There was a slight declining trend up to 1985, when a mild upturn took place. TFP then hit a peak in 1988 and stayed only slightly below that level for the remaining three years. The average TFP for the years 1981–88 was 1.075, while that for the divestiture years of 1989–91 was 1.20, nearly 12 percent higher. The real public profitability series displays a similar pattern.

In summary, productivity at Mexicana has been slightly higher in the postdivestiture period, but the trend toward improved productivity started earlier. Thus the matter of attribution seems somewhat ambiguous.

Fiscal Effects

Fiscal effects are not an important part of the Mexicana story. Because the sale took the form of a dilutive equity infusion, the government received no revenue from it. The government does still own a 40 percent share of the company and could realize revenues by selling that shareholding any time after September 1992.

Figure 21-4.   Real Unit Costs, Mexicana de Aviación, 1981–91

Pesos per peso of output

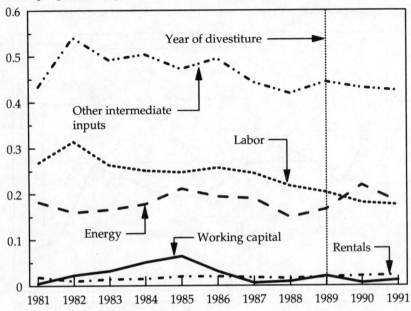

Source: Authors' calculations from Mexicana data.

Annual fiscal flows are also insignificant. Mexicana, unlike Aeroméxico, was not a recipient of government subsidies. In some years it
paid some taxes, but these were relatively minor.

Market Value Effects

As already mentioned, the price paid by Falcon for control of Mexicana
was roughly double the prevailing stock market price of the airline. It is
interesting to see what has happened to the stock price since. The sale
price at divestiture was US$140 million, or Mex$358.8 billion, for a 20
percent share, which works out to approximately Mex$6,330 per share.
A month later the stock was trading below Mex$4,000 per share, and a
year later it was well below Mex$3,000 per share—the 1989 closing price
was Mex$2,662 per share. The share price later fell below Mex$2,000 in
1991 before recovering to trade at roughly Mex$2,200 in May 1992. This
implies a market value for the company at that time of Mex$649 billion,
or just over US$200 million. The value of the US$140 million investment
was then down to about US$40 million. Clearly the market has not been
impressed by Mexicana's performance. The Mexican stock market index

Table 21-3. Labor Productivity, Mexicana de Aviación, 1981–91

Year	Labor productivity
1981	24.02
1982	20.56
1983	24.59
1984	25.81
1985	26.24
1986	25.36
1987	26.68
1988	29.21
1989	30.61
1990	34.35
1991	35.26

Note: Figures are calculated by dividing the Divisia index of output by the number of employees.
Source: Authors' calculations from Mexicana data.

in the meantime rose from 420 in September 1989 to 1,785 in May 1992—a 325 percent increase.

Summary

We can summarize our discussion thus far as follows:

• From roughly breaking even in every year of the predivestiture period, Mexicana became highly unprofitable in its first two years as a private airline.
• Capital formation, which had stagnated through much of the period, suddenly took off in 1991.
• Productivity improved slightly over the period, in a trend that started around 1985; it peaked in 1988 and has stayed only slightly below that peak in subsequent years.

Why Did It Happen?

In this section we analyze the specific factors that might explain the observed behavioral and performance changes, to see to what extent they can be attributed to divestiture. This then will suggest a counterfactual for our simulation exercise.

The Investment Plan

The first and obvious factor underlying the changes at Mexicana is the massive investment program upon which the company has embarked.

*Figure 21-5.   Total Factor Productivity and Public Profitability,
Mexicana de Aviación, 1981–91*

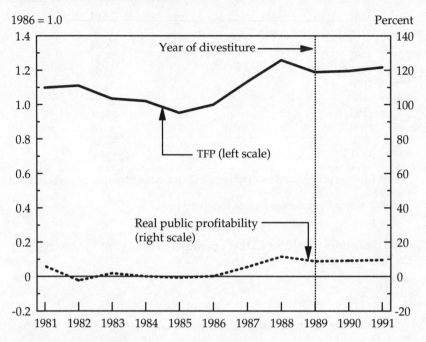

Source: Authors' calculations from Mexicana data.

Recall that, at the time of divestiture, the government was specifically looking for a buyer willing to commit to a substantial investment program.[6] The Falcon group did commit to a US$3 billion investment program, although this commitment was in the nature of an assurance and was not legally binding.

Nevertheless, Falcon was true to its word, and in August 1990 the airline placed a sizable order for twenty-two Airbus A320 aircraft, with options to buy fourteen more. Delivery was to be spread over a period of seven years, from 1991 to 1997, and the total price (undiscounted) was US$1.6 billion. Because the program of aircraft retirement was considerably slower, this order constituted a commitment to expand the airline rapidly. Mexicana also leased four more Boeing 727 aircraft, raising the size of its fleet from forty-four in 1990 to fifty-two in 1991. Besides investments in fleet expansion, the new management undertook major investments in other areas, such as a US$15 million to US$20 million investment in computer systems and unspecified other expenditures to expand and modernize terminals and maintenance facilities.

The expansion of investment surely explains the jump in capital formation in 1991, as Mexicana took delivery of its first four Airbus aircraft. The other investments and expenditures associated with the Airbus acquisition, such as training and creation of facilities, must also surely have had something to do with the poor profitability performance. And certainly it seems reasonable to suppose that such a massive investment program would not have been undertaken had Mexicana stayed in public hands.

In our projections for the company, therefore, we assume that it will follow the expansion plan outlined in its announcements. For the counterfactual we assume fleet expansion in conformity with past practice, so that the load factor for the airline stays fairly steady around 60 percent.

Strategic Decisions

A key factor underlying Mexicana's postdivestiture performance has been the strategic decisions of its new managers. We have already discussed management's decisions regarding the investment program. There is also the question of what kind of strategy the company was following for business development. A number of mistakes were made that affected the bottom-line performance of the company.

One important decision regarded the strategic direction of the company. Either because of Grupo Xabre's close association with other segments of the tourist industry (notably hotels and resorts), or simply because it was their estimate of the direction in which the market was developing, the new managers decided to concentrate their attention on tourist traffic. Of course, such traffic is highly discretionary and has a high elasticity of demand. This proved to be a costly mistake for Mexicana. Particularly because of the crisis in Kuwait, the Persian Gulf war, and the consequent worldwide decline in air travel, tourist traffic did not grow at the rate the company had been expecting. In contrast, Aeroméxico chose to concentrate on business travelers. The low elasticity of this demand, its nondiscretionary character, and the Mexican economic boom combined to make this the winning strategy.

Mexicana's problems were compounded by other management decisions. At one point in 1990 Mexicana decided to try to start direct booking of tours, cutting out the tour agents who had supplied much of their tourist business. The attempt proved a disaster, and Mexicana has been trying to repair its bridges to the tour operators ever since. Early in 1990 Mexicana expanded its service to certain U.S. cities, such as Baltimore, Philadelphia, Tampa, Orlando, and Seattle (Poole 1991), but abruptly canceled them when they proved to be losers. One notorious extravagance that apparently cost the director general (that is, the chief executive officer) his job was the decision to spend US$32 million to paint twenty aircraft with a new design. Apparently not only was this money spent on a cosmetic improvement, but the paint used was so heavy as to raise fuel consumption substantially.

Thus management performance at Mexicana has been less than satisfactory. Clearly this is attributable to divestiture. However, because the chief executive was changed in the spring of 1991, after all the major blunders had already been made, we did not postulate any effect from this in the projection as compared with the counterfactual. A simple way to include some effect of poor management would have been to lower the market share of Mexicana. From the social point of view, however, there would be little welfare impact from this, because losses to Mexicana would be balanced by gains to its rivals, notably Aeroméxico. In the interest of simplicity we have ignored this factor in our simulations. Thus the only negative impact of management that we explicitly include is the increased investment plan.

Productivity Increases

We observed above, through an analysis of real unit costs, labor productivity, and TFP, that Mexicana's productivity improvement was more rapid after divestiture than before, although the improving trend started in 1985 or 1986, depending on which series one looked at. Further, the peak in TFP at least was achieved in 1988. Labor productivity continued an improving trend throughout.

We must first explain what was special about 1988. This was the year of Aeroméxico's bankruptcy and sale; thus it was a year of severe disruption in service for Mexicana's key competitor. As already noted, Mexicana benefited from this disruption on many domestic routes where it competed with Aeroméxico, raising its load factor from around 60 to 68 percent. Thus Mexicana's output measure for 1988 was unusually high, and this is what caused TFP to peak and other productivity measures to show considerable improvement.

Clearly this phenomenon is an aberration. It is certainly not attributable to the Mexicana divestiture, nor can it be considered representative of predivestiture performance. Accordingly we adjust for this by simply looking at the labor productivity improvement from 1986–89 and comparing it with the postdivestiture period. We find a slight difference in the rate of growth of labor productivity—6 percent per year since divestiture.

Is this difference attributable to divestiture? We think it is. Since divestiture, Mexicana's management has been working hard to try to improve productivity and has been cutting the work force in an attempt to do so. But the public sector managers were doing the same thing. We see from table 21-1 that average employment reached a peak in 1987 and has been declining ever since. An argument could even be made that the decline in 1987 and 1988 was an "announcement effect," as the government tried to make the enterprise more attractive to potential buyers.

We conclude that divestiture has led to some productivity improvement, although this trend had started some years prior to sale. We use for our base case 7 percent productivity growth in the projection and 6 percent in the counterfactual; we then check for sensitivity by varying the assumptions.

Deregulation and Its Impact on Prices

As discussed in detail in chapter 20, we associate the deregulation of Mexico's airline industry with the divestiture of the airlines. In conformance with the Aeroméxico case, we adopt a postulated 10 percent real price increase on domestic flights as a result of deregulation, and we assume no real price change in the counterfactual.

Summary

We have argued that some of the changes we observed in the behavior of Mexicana can be attributed to its divestiture, while others cannot. Thus the following list characterizes the differences between our projections and our counterfactual:

- The new management adopted a massive investment and fleet expansion program, involving the purchase of twenty-two aircraft and increased leasing. Absent divestiture, we assume fleet expansion would have continued at a rate compatible with previous experience.
- We assume labor productivity growth of 6 percent per year in the counterfactual and 7 percent per year in the projection.
- Following deregulation, domestic real fares will rise by 10 percent. In the counterfactual, real prices remain unchanged.

What Will Happen?

In this section in other cases, we normally discuss the specific assumptions we make in order to perform the simulation exercise, and then discuss our projections of revenues, costs, and profits. However, because the basic model assumptions are identical to those we made for Aeroméxico, we need not repeat them here. Our simulations then find revenue growing at the rate of 5.9 percent per year in the divestiture projection, and at 6.4 percent per year in the counterfactual. Output is growing an average of 5.4 percent per year in the projection, and at 6.4 percent per year in the counterfactual. The reason for the difference is of course the price increase in the projection scenario. Because demand elasticity is greater than one, revenue falls as a result of the price increase, as does its growth rate. Then output grows more slowly as demand grows more slowly in the projection.

What Is It Worth?

The basic results on the welfare impact of the Mexicana divestiture can be seen in table 21-4 and figure 21-6 and summarized as follows:

- Mexico's welfare falls by Mex\$450 billion at 1989 prices. This is equivalent to US\$170 million or an annual flow equal to 2.4 percent of Mexicana's 1989 sales.
- World welfare falls by Mex\$1,319 billion (about US\$500 million), equivalent to an annual flow of 7 percent of Mexicana's 1989 sales.
- Government comes out ahead by Mex\$657 billion, mainly by avoiding losses it would otherwise have suffered as the majority shareholder of the airline.

Table 21-4. Distribution of Gains and Losses from Divestiture, Mexicana de Aviación
(billions of pesos unless stated otherwise)

Economic actor	Private operation	Public operation	Gains from divestiture	Perpetual annuity equivalent as share of 1989 sales
Government				
Taxes	45	0	45	
Net quasi rents	−126	−739	612	
Total government	−82	−739	657	3.49
Employees	0	0	0	0.00
Private domestic shareholders				
Diverse	−383	−715	333	1.77
Concentrated	0	0	0	0.00
Foreign shareholders	−251	0	−251	−1.34
Competitors	0	0	0	0.00
Providers	0	0	0	0.00
Citizens (via shadow increments)	0	0	0	0.00
Subtotal	−715	−1,454	739	
Foreign consumers	5,223	5,841	−617	−3.28
Domestic consumers	12,188	13,628	−1,440	−7.66
Total	16,696	18,015	−1,319	−7.01
Net change in welfare			−450	−2.39

Source: Authors' calculations.

Figure 21-6. Distribution of Welfare Gains and Losses from Divestiture, Mexicana de Aviación

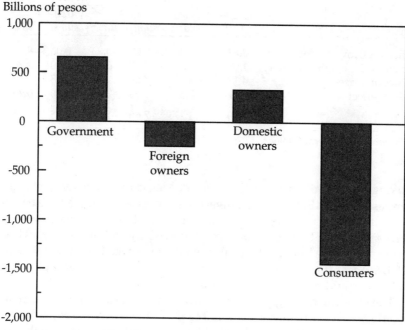

Source: Authors' calculations.

- Foreigners lose Mex$868 billion, of which the buyers lose Mex$251 billion and consumers Mex$617 billion.
- Domestic consumers are worse off by Mex$1,440 billion because of the rise in real domestic airfares.
- Domestic shareholders of Mexicana gain by reducing their losses to the tune of Mex$333 billion.

Sources of the Welfare Changes

In this section we consider the sources of the welfare changes in the Mexicana case. As in the previous chapter, it is convenient to present the welfare effects of each of the sources in terms of annual flows generated as a percentage of Mexicana's 1989 sales. We consider each of the key effects in turn. Details are provided in table 21-5.

RELEASE OF THE INVESTMENT CONSTRAINT. In all the other cases we have studied, the release of an investment constraint faced by an enterprise has invariably led to welfare improvement, presumably because the investment constraint had been preventing the enterprise from under-

Table 21-5. Sources of Welfare Change, Mexicana de Aviación
(annuity equivalents as percentage of 1989 sales)

| | | Domestic | | Foreign | | |
Source	Govern-ment	Share-holders	Con-sumers	Buyers	Con-sumers	Total
Increased investment	−3.62	−4.38	0.00	−0.86	0.00	−8.85
Increased labor productivity	1.07	1.39	0.00	0.35	0.00	2.80
Price increase	4.17	5.33	−7.66	1.26	−3.28	−0.17
Other effects	1.87	−0.57	0.00	−2.09	0.00	−0.79
Total	3.49	1.77	−7.66	−1.34	−3.28	−7.01

Source: Authors' calculations.

taking worthwhile projects. The case of Mexicana, however, yields an opposite result. Releasing the investment constraint allowed the enterprise to adopt an excessively ambitious investment program, with a present value of US$1.43 billion, compared with a counterfactual investment program whose present value would have been US$840 million (in 1989). According to our estimates, the added investment brought little by way of additional revenue or profit.

The investment program leads to an annual welfare loss equivalent to nearly 9 percent of Mexicana's 1989 sales. This is shared between the government, the domestic shareholders, and the foreign buyers (that is, among all shareholders) in rough proportion to their shareholdings.

INCREASED LABOR PRODUCTIVITY. Evidence suggests that the divested Mexicana is slightly more productive than it would have been absent divestiture. We estimate that this increased labor productivity raises social welfare annually by 2.8 percent of Mexicana's 1989 sales of Mex$1,881 billion (US$725 million). The gain is shared, as before, by the various shareholding groups.

PRICE INCREASE. As in the Aeroméxico case, the assumed 10 percent price increase due to deregulation turns out to be almost welfare neutral, but, unlike with Aeroméxico, the welfare effect here is mildly welfare reducing instead of welfare increasing. The small net welfare effect again masks more substantial distributive effects: consumers lose an annual flow of 11 percent of sales, and the firm gains almost that much. These results are quite comparable to those we found for Aeroméxico. The numbers here are slightly smaller, reflecting the fact that Mexicana's 1989 sales were greater than those of Aeroméxico.

The fact that the welfare effect of the price increase is negative in the Mexicana case and positive in the Aeroméxico case might appear odd, because it implies that the price is greater than Mexicana's marginal cost but lower than Aeroméxico's. But Aeroméxico is the more efficient producer now. The solution to this conundrum is that the model is using Aeroméxico's long-run marginal cost (that is, including the capital cost), but Mexicana's short-run marginal cost (excluding the capital cost). The reason why this is appropriate is that Mexicana is committed to its investment program; any small output changes can be accommodated within the preplanned capital stock. Aeroméxico, on the other hand, is free to optimize its capital stock. Thus Aeroméxico's marginal cost is implicitly higher than that of Mexicana.

The Airline Divestitures as a Package

It is interesting to think of the divestitures of Aeroméxico and Mexicana as a package, because the government could not logically divest one without divesting the other. If the two sets of results are therefore added up (with appropriate adjustment for the size difference between the two enterprises; Aeroméxico's 1989 sales were about 58 percent of Mexicana's), one could arrive at the net welfare effect of the airline divestitures as a whole. Doing so yields the following results: the airline divestitures have together yielded net welfare benefits of nearly Mex\$4,000 billion, equivalent to an annual flow of 12.5 percent of combined airline industry 1989 sales. Mexico has enjoyed a benefit of Mex\$5,250 billion, equivalent to an annual flow of nearly 20 percent of 1989 airline industry sales. In short, this was a highly successful package of divestitures.

Summary and Lessons

The divestiture of Mexicana has been unsuccessful, in the sense that social welfare (whether of Mexico or the world) has fallen from where it would have been had the airline not been divested. The key points are as follows:

- The main factor behind the welfare loss is the adoption by the company of an overambitious investment program.
- The welfare loss would be considerably greater if we projected a continuation of the mismanagement that has been characteristic of the two and a half years since divestiture.
- The government has, nevertheless, managed to come out ahead through reducing its exposure in the money-losing enterprise.
- Mexicana has been unable to realize the productivity improvements achieved by Aeroméxico.
- If the divestitures of Aeroméxico and Mexicana are considered as a single package, airline divestiture-cum-deregulation has been highly successful.

We are left with the following possible conclusions from our analysis of the case:

- A divested enterprise cannot realize labor productivity gains as great as it might if labor restructuring took place prior to divestiture.
- Sometimes divested enterprises will not perform well, just as some firms that were in the private sector from the beginning do not perform well.
- The ability of the capital market to play its watchdog role is hampered if the management of a divested enterprise has voting control, thereby precluding the possibility of hostile takeover.

Notes

This chapter was written by Pankaj Tandon with Inder Ruprah. We have had helpful discussions with Luis Mestre, Carlos Moreno, Enrique Servin, Federico Sierra, Jorge Silberstein, and David Treitel. Manuel Abdala served as research assistant for much of the research. Able secretarial assistance was provided by Charlene Arzigian and Patricia Regan.

1. Indeed, well after our research was complete, Mexicana was taken over by Aeroméxico. We have been unable to incorporate this event into any of our discussion.

2. Much of this historical background is based on the Mexicana sale prospectus.

3. The following discussion on the divestiture of Mexicana is based on conversations with various individuals at Mexicana and at the Mexican privatization office, on official documents of the sale process, and on two papers: Echegaray (1990) and a preliminary case study on Mexicana done at the Centro de Analisis e Investigación Económica (CAIE) done by Luis Herrera (1993) under the supervision of Manuel Sanchez.

4. Interestingly, one bidder suggested allowing Mexicana to default on its loans and go into bankruptcy as a way of forcing a debt restructuring. Only two months later, the government did just that with Aeroméxico, although the primary motive there was a labor restructuring.

5. Mexicana's load factors were 58 percent in 1985, 56 percent in 1986 (an extraordinarily bad year), 60.3 percent in 1987, and 62.7 percent in 1989.

6. The government was projecting huge investment requirements for the Mexican airline industry over the decade of the 1990s. Reportedly this projection had been prepared by Boeing Co., which hardly appears to be an unbiased source for this kind of information.

22. Summary: Mexico

Mexico is widely regarded as one of the great success stories of the privatization wave. In a period of ten years over 80 percent of Mexico's public enterprises were liquidated, sold, or otherwise disposed of, including some of the very largest,[1] three of which we have examined here. In the period 1980–91 gross receipts from divestiture were higher in Mexico (US$15.6 billion) than in any other developing country—Chile's US$3.4 billion was a distant second.[2] Further, of the twenty-eight divestitures in developing countries during 1988–91 that were valued at over US$100 million, Mexico accounted for fourteen (Kikeri, Nellis, and Shirley 1992, p. 26). For countries wanting to divest in a hurry, perhaps Mexico has some lessons to offer. In this chapter we will see what some of these lessons might be.

From the point of view of our research, however, the most important aspect of Mexico's divestiture program was not that it was large in scale, but that it was part of a much wider, comprehensive economic reform program. Not only was a massive divestiture program in motion, but simultaneously there was a tremendous liberalization of the trade regime, relaxation of rules governing foreign and domestic investment, and deregulation. In many ways, it was precisely this interlinkage of the divestiture program with other economic reforms that contributed to its success.

Although this sort of policy coordination makes for a sound program, it creates a problem for our research. Because our methodology calls for comparing the actual and projected performance of the divested enterprise with a counterfactual—how the enterprise would have performed absent divestiture—we are forced to construct a counterfactual in a rapidly changing economic environment. This was a problem in each of our cases. Along with the airline divestitures there was implemented, with a slight lag, a major deregulation. Should the counterfactual be constructed with a deregulation occurring at around the time it actually did? It is quite possible, given the overall attitude of the government, that, had divestiture not occurred, some sort of change in the regulatory environment (say, with regard to pricing rules) might have. Similarly, the divestiture of Telmex was preceded by a major price restructuring. Would this have occurred if divestiture had not been on the horizon? Once again, some sort of price restructuring might well have taken place, but exactly what its magnitude and pattern might have been is quite unclear. Our strategy here has been to consider these major changes in the policy environment as linked to the divestitures, and we have made our welfare calculations accordingly. In each case, however, we have separated out the effects of each major policy change, to allow readers to make their own judgments as to what the effects of the divestiture itself really were. In this sense, our calculations should be seen as measures of welfare change induced by the whole policy package, rather than divestiture per se; our contention, however, is that the divestiture program was so integrated into the overall reform that it is risky at best to try to separate the effects of divestiture from those of other economic reforms.

With this caveat in mind, we discuss in the rest of this chapter the major lessons other countries might learn from the Mexican experience, as typified by our three case studies. A more complete synthesis of cases and the findings of the research will be presented in chapter 23.

Welfare Gains

The primary purpose of this research was to measure the gains and losses from divestiture. We begin our summary by considering the Mexican experience in this regard.

Two of the cases studied (Telmex and Aeroméxico) showed substantial welfare gains from divestiture. Telmex's divestiture produced a gain equivalent to about 51 percent of its 1991 sales, in perpetuity. The figure for Aeroméxico was 49 percent of 1989 sales. The third case, however, Mexicana de Aviación, showed a welfare loss equivalent to 7 percent of 1989 sales in perpetuity. This was the only case in our entire sample that resulted in a welfare loss. The lesson to be learned is that, whereas divestiture is normally successful in bringing about welfare improvements, there are sometimes failures. Indeed, the real strength of the market system is that the damage from such failures is minimized, because the market will not permit failed policies to be perpetuated. One way or another, either through extinction, reform, or takeover, the market will correct the Mexicana failure.[3]

The key sources of welfare change were different in each case. The gains at Telmex came partly from improvements in labor productivity, partly from desirable price changes, and partly from stabilization effects on the macroeconomy. The gains at Aeroméxico were almost entirely from labor productivity improvements, achieved through a massive reduction in the number of employees. The losses at Mexicana were largely led by an overinvestment program that created severe overcapacity problems. In all cases, labor productivity improvements were realized; this was the one general result to which we can point.

Divestiture, Fiscal Effects, and Stabilization

We have argued that the primary motive of Mexico's divestiture program was the need to cut the budget deficit and stabilize the economy. Recall from chapter 18 that divestiture was first undertaken in 1983 as part of a stabilization program sponsored by the International Monetary Fund, and that it gained steam after the crisis of 1985–87. In many other countries also, divestiture of public enterprises is discussed at such times of crisis, but there is frequently skepticism about the government's ability to raise truly large sums from a (generally) moribund public sector. What does the Mexican experience teach us?

The first lesson is that divestiture can play a very large role in macroeconomic stabilization. Mexico's success in this area was nothing short of spectacular. Recall that US$15.6 billion was raised during 1983–91, US$14 billion of that in the last two years. These were the first two years after the announcement of the celebrated Brady Plan, under which the bulk of Mexico's external debt was renegotiated. The Brady agreement has often been seen as one of the key factors behind Mexico's highly successful macroeconomic stabilization. But, as we argued in chapter 19, the divestiture program was probably even more significant, because the amount of money raised through divestitures far exceeded the savings realized under the debt rescheduling.[4] The divestiture proceeds were used largely to retire domestic public debt and were thereby crucial in bringing interest rates down.[5] Although we have not attempted to measure its impact precisely, the divestiture program clearly played a central role in Mexico's economic recovery.

To what extent can other countries reproduce Mexico's success? We feel that some features may have been rather unique to Mexico, but that others are more universal, and, indeed, other countries such as Argentina have successfully followed a similar strategy. Two of the features unique to Mexico were the availability of flight capital and the expectation of eventual ratification of the North American Free Trade Agreement (NAFTA).

As we mentioned in chapter 18, the Mexican economic crisis of 1982, which prompted the government to nationalize the banks, led to a considerable amount (estimates range as high as US$50 billion) of capital flight. When, in 1989, the government started divesting in a big way, this flight capital represented a large pool of potential investment funds. Mexico thus enjoyed a ready source of demand for the securities of its divested enterprises. Many other countries probably have similar pools of capital waiting for the right investment climate, although many others may not. The announcement of NAFTA also clearly created considerable investor interest in Mexico. This must have made it somewhat easier for Mexico to divest its public enterprises. Not every country has the advantage of sitting on the southern border of the United States.

That said, other countries can enjoy some of the same successes achieved by Mexico. NAFTA itself is the epitome of something more fundamental that the Mexican government was doing, namely, deregulating and liberalizing the economy. Joining the General Agreement on Tariffs and Trade, making the trade regime one of the most open in the world, deregulating at every turn, liberalizing rules for foreign investors—all of these policies signal a real commitment to a market-oriented development strategy. It is this whole constellation of policies, rather than just divestiture, that created investor confidence and led to the success of the divestiture program. Further, although Mexican flight capital may have been important, there is clearly a large enough pool of investment capital available in the now relatively unified world capital market that any country pursuing a sincere policy of liberalization and public-enterprise divestiture is likely to have its efforts rewarded. To this extent, the Mexican example does show a way for others to consider.

The second lesson is that large sums can be raised from a relatively moribund public sector. Within our sample, Telmex is the obvious example. Prior to the divestiture announcement, Telmex was 44 percent privately owned and had an actively traded stock. At that time the market value of Telmex was under US$1 billion, so that the government's 56 percent share was worth only about half that. Yet within the next two years the sale of 51 percent of Telmex raised for the government US$6.2 billion, and its remaining 5 percent share is still worth another US$1.5 billion!

How did the government achieve this seemingly impossible result? As we saw in chapter 19, the engine that drove the Telmex stock price up was the price-tax regime established along with divestiture.[6] To make Telmex attractive to investors, it was rendered a much more profitable enterprise through the abolition of indirect telephone taxes[7] and the establishment of a very favorable price regime. The raising of many prices, in turn, was itself a welfare-improving move, because prices were at artificially low levels. Thus this case provides strong evidence of a contention much discussed throughout the world, namely, that many public enterprises in developing countries need price "reform" (i.e., price increases) to render them much more efficient.

Some may argue that, by abolishing indirect taxes and then selling Telmex, the Mexican government was simply selling a stream of future returns, exchanging an indefinite stream of indirect tax revenues for a sale price up front. But, as we saw, this was not the case. In fact, the annual tax flows from Telmex remain basically unaffected by the divestiture, as the indirect taxes are replaced by corporate income tax payments from (the now much more profitable) Telmex. Thus the government suffered no reduction in the annual flows; the sale revenues of US$6.2 billion were just gravy!

One final point worth noting about Telmex is the fact that the stock was sold in three tranches, with successive offerings yielding higher prices. On the one hand, this could be praised as an effective strategy to capitalize on a rising stock price and to manage the placement of such a large offering without swamping the capital market. On the other hand, because the interval between the offerings was so short, one could argue that the government could have done better in the early rounds by waiting longer. There are three comments to be made, however. First, all tranche sales were at market prices, so it is difficult to argue that the known true value was higher. Second, because even the first divestiture sale took place at a value eight times the previous market valuation of Telmex, it is difficult to argue that the government could have anticipated the huge stock price runup. Third, even if it could have done so, the strategy of selling some stock cheaply up front might still have been desirable as a "loss-leader" strategy. By permitting early investors to achieve astronomical returns on their investments, the government created huge investor interest in Mexico and its future divestitures. This may have greatly contributed to the success of the subsequent divestitures, which raised even larger amounts than the sale of Telmex.

A third, related lesson is that the fiscal impact of divestiture need not operate through multibillion-dollar sales. As we saw in chapters 20 and 21, neither the sale of Aeroméxico nor that of Mexicana raised even a penny of sale revenue for the government. Yet the fiscal effects of both these sales were still very substantial. Our estimate (see table 20-11) is that the net fiscal impact of the Aeroméxico divestiture was a positive Mex$6.12 trillion (equivalent to US$2.68 billion), consisting of a reduction in ongoing losses worth US$1.53 billion in present value and US$1.15 billion in future tax payments. This net fiscal impact was the equivalent of 62 percent of the company's 1989 sales in perpetuity. The Mexicana divestiture was less dramatic, but it too had a positive fiscal impact of some US$250 million, consisting almost entirely of avoided future losses.

The Aeroméxico story particularly makes the case that a moribund, loss-producing public enterprise can make a huge positive contribution to the fiscal situation of the government, even if it cannot command a positive sale price. It is worth emphasizing how this was done. In many countries it is often thought that money-losing enterprises cannot fetch a positive price, and that therefore it is politically impossible to sell them. By absorbing all of Aeroméxico's liabilities and selling only the assets, the Mexican government was able to create the appearance of a positive sale price. Although we have postulated that the sale price was zero (with creditors absorbing the loss), it is possible that in fact the Mexican government will end up with a negative sale price. Nevertheless, the fiscal impact of the sale is highly positive.

In sum, the Mexican experience in general, and our case studies in particular, suggest that seemingly unattractive, money-losing, or marginally profitable public enterprises can be sold; that indeed they can be sold for large sums of money; that even if they do not sell for large sums they can still make a substantial positive contribution to the fiscal situation; and that the aggregate sums can be large enough to make a real difference at the macroeconomic level.

Divestiture and Regulation

A second broad theme is the interrelationship between divestiture policy and the need for regulatory regimes. A major fear in many countries considering divestiture is that consumers could be hit hard as divested enterprises seek to use their market power to their advantage. The obvious antidotes to this problem are to ensure that competitive forces are given play wherever possible, thereby controlling the firms' market power, or to introduce regulation where it seems competition is unlikely to emerge (particularly in natural monopolies). What does the Mexican experience teach us?

The Mexican government in fact adopted both these strategies, and there have been some problems. In the case of tradable goods, reliance has been placed on liberalizing imports, and, in principle, this ought to be adequate. The key sectors in this regard are steel and fertilizers, in which enterprises have only just been divested, so it is too early to tell whether trade will do the job. The divestiture of sugar mills was a problem case because the complicated regulatory structure and low prices hampered the ability of the newly private sugar mills to make adequate profits. The terms on the loans the mills had been granted had to be renegotiated. Details of this case are difficult to uncover; however, the limited evidence suggests that the Mexican economy paid a price for the government's decision not to completely deregulate this market.

Our case studies were all concerned with nontradable goods—telecommunications and air transport. In the case of telecommunications, a regulatory structure was put in place prior to the divestiture of Telmex, and while this mechanism does provide some structure to the market, officials in the Mexican communications secretariat are quick to concede that their regulatory capability at this time is rather limited. As a result, the regulations embody quantity targets that were already in Telmex's own strategic plans and a price regulation patterned after the United Kingdom's RPI - X formula (see chapter 19 for details), but that has already been compromised more than once by agreement between the company and the government.[8]

One key test of the regulatory regime, of course, is whether consumers have been protected. Our results show that consumers have been hit hard by the changes in Telmex's price-tax regime, and this might tempt one to conclude that the regulatory regime has failed. This, however, would be unwarranted. Our calculations showed that the price changes were welfare improving, indicating that the previous prices were uneconomically low. Thus, even though consumers were adversely affected, the change was desirable. Simply put, the subsidies that consumers were previously enjoying were taken away. The real test of the regulatory regime, therefore, will be whether the network expands rapidly, whether quality improves, and whether prices decline rapidly over time because of technological improvements. More time needs to pass before any real judgment can be made on these points.

In the case of the airline industry, a strict regulatory structure was in place prior to divestiture, and no regulatory changes were made for several years thereafter, causing severe disruption of (or at least uncertainty in) the airlines' strategic planning. Aeroméxico was sold in September 1988 and Mexicana in September 1989; yet it was only in July 1991 that the air transport market was largely deregulated. In the meantime the airlines had to live with controlled domestic airfares that were too low, and they had no clear idea what entry regulations were going to be. This cost the industry two years at a time when the market was already unsettled because of the Persian Gulf war. Time will tell how the deregulation will work out; early results suggest a pattern similar to that followed by the United States after deregulation, with bruising price wars and brisk entry that are likely to result eventually in consolidation. Even in the United States it is unclear whether consumers are better or worse off as a result of deregulation—even more so for Mexico.

On the whole, therefore, we can say little that is definitive about Mexico's experience with the regulation of divested enterprises, mainly because the time since divestiture has been too short. Our cases do indicate, however, that Mexico probably paid a price for the speed with which the divestiture program was carried out. There was not enough time to develop and properly coordinate the installation of appropriate regulatory regimes, particularly in the airline industry. This may have been a small price to pay, however, to achieve success on other dimensions.

Other Issues

We mention here two other pitfalls that other countries may wish to avoid as they seek to emulate Mexico's divestiture successes. The first relates to the government's policy of selling enterprises to well-identified buyers rather than to a diffuse set of buyers in the stock market. Frequently a particular individual can be identified as "the buyer." Thus it may be said, even though the shares were actually bought by consortia, that Carlos Slim Helu bought Telmex or that Roberto Hernandez bought Banamex. Whereas this type of sale might be thought desirable because it gives the buyers greater freedom of action (and hence might raise their willingness to pay), it potentially reduces the ability of the capital market to police the divested enterprise as the threat of takeover disappears. This, for example, may have played a role in prolonging the agony at Mexicana.[9]

The second point is special to the case of Telmex. It could be argued that, because a large proportion of the stock was sold to foreign investors, too much rent from the sale was dissipated abroad. Calculations show that, whereas foreign investors paid the Mexican government a total of US$4.7 billion for about 35 percent of the stock, they had gained US$5.5 billion by June 1992 through stock appreciation. In fairness, the government sold at market prices, and therefore this argument could be dismissed as twenty-twenty hindsight. Nevertheless, the question remains whether the government could have anticipated the eventual rise in share prices because of its intimate knowledge of the enterprise. The point is discussed in greater detail in chapter 19. One lesson to be drawn here is that, if a government does follow a "loss-leader" strategy, perhaps more effort could be made to increase the share of domestic shareholders, so that they are the primary beneficiaries of the windfall.

Conclusion

In reviewing the Mexican experience, this chapter has perhaps taken a critical tone, highlighting the pitfalls and problems that occurred. These problems, however, are all minor compared with the successes achieved by the divestiture program. Much as an emerald, by its very nature, has imperfections within it, no divestiture program will be perfect. Many of the key factors behind Mexico's success were discussed at length in chapter 18. Some more have been identified here, in particular the skillful coordination of divestiture with other policies conducive to the development of the private sector. It is clear that Mexico provides an example of outstanding success to other countries considering or carrying out programs of divestiture. Perhaps the discussion in this chapter can help them do even better.

Notes

This chapter was written by Pankaj Tandon.

1. The most notable exception, of course, is Pemex (Petroleos Mexicanos), the government oil monopoly, which is required to be state owned under the Mexican constitution.

2. See figure 18-2 and, for Chile, Kikeri, Nellis, and Shirley (1992, p. 30). The US$3.4 billion figure for Chile actually covers a longer period, from 1973 to 1991.

3. As noted in chapter 21, well after our research was complete, Mexicana was taken over by Aeroméxico, and we have been unable to incorporate this event into any of our discussion.

4. The Brady deal is estimated to have saved Mexico US$1.3 billion a year in interest payments, and another US$2.7 billion a year in postponed principal payments.

5. The Banco de México average cost of funds fell from 67.6 percent in 1988 to 21.8 percent in June 1991.

6. This is an example of the confounding of divestiture with regulatory changes that we mentioned above. Some observers see the January 1990 price reform as independent of divestiture. Whether it was or was not is really moot. The Mexican government was moving on several fronts, and we are evaluating the coordinated set of policies.

7. Recall that in chapter 19 we argued that the new telephone services tax is effectively a zero tax.

8. Specifically, price changes specified in the concession have been renegotiated, sometimes at the initiative of the government and sometimes at the initiative of Telmex.

9. As noted above, Mexicana was in fact acquired by Aeroméxico in early 1993, when the Mexicana management's controlling window of three years expired. This takeover might have occurred earlier had the government not awarded the Breners such complete (albeit temporary) control of Mexicana.

PART VI

Cross-Country and Cross-Enterprise Comparisons and Conclusions

23. Synthesis of Cases

Did divestiture make the world a better place, or not? In our twelve cases this question is answered with a surprisingly uniform and resounding "yes." As summarized in the far right-hand column of table 23-1, the net world welfare change was positive in eleven of twelve cases; only Mexicana de Aviación shows a net loss. Furthermore, the magnitudes of the gains were substantial: the annual component of the perpetuity equivalent of the gains averaged 30 percent of predivestiture annual sales;[1] in more than half the cases the gain in welfare exceeded 10 percent; in the single negative case the loss was only 7 percent.

Some will find vindication in these results, others consternation, but our only concern is edification. What caused these positive results? How could policy tools have further enhanced them? What modifications to the results are necessary because of selection bias in our small sample and the limitations of our methodology? We address these questions in this chapter.

In the first section of this chapter we confine ourselves to evidence from the cases themselves. We first take the analysis one step deeper by decomposing the net welfare change in two ways: by its distribution (winners and losers), and by its sources (for example, rising productivity or higher prices). We then summarize the limitations of our sample and our methodology.

Recognizing these limitations, in the balance of the chapter we combine the case evidence with informed speculation to explain the observed outcomes. The causal form of the question is, What determines the degree of success in divestiture? The policy form of the question, taken up in the concluding chapter, is, What strings can the government pull to maximize the net benefits?

Table 23-1. Winners and Losers from Divestiture in the Twelve Case Studies
(percentages)

Country and enterprise	Domestic						Foreign			World net welfare change
	Government	Buyers	Consumers	Workers[a]	Others	Net welfare change	Buyers	Consumers	Others	
United Kingdom										
British Telecom	2.7	3.1	4.9	0.2	-0.1	10.8	1.2	0.0	0.0	12.0
British Airways	0.9	1.4	-0.9	0.3	0.0	1.7	0.4	-0.5	0.0	1.6
National Freight	-0.2	0.8	0.0	3.7	0.0	4.3	0.0	0.0	0.0	4.3
Chile										
CHILGENER	-1.4	2.0	0.0	0.1	0.0	0.7	1.4	0.0	0.0	2.1
ENERSIS	-1.6	7.6	2.2	3.9	-7.4	4.6	0.6	0.0	0.0	5.2
CTC	8.0	1.0	131.0	1.0	4.0	145.0	10.0	0.0	0.0	155.0
Malaysia										
Malaysian Airline Systems	5.2	2.0	-2.9	0.4	0.0	4.6	0.8	0.8	15.8	22.1
Kelang Container Terminal	37.6	11.5	6.2	7.0	-11.9	50.4	2.9	3.1	-3.0	53.4
Sports Toto Malaysia	13.6	10.7	0.0	0.0	-13.0	10.9	0.0	0.0	0.0	10.9
Mexico										
Teléfonos de México	13.3	11.4	-62.0	15.6	28.3	6.6	25.1	0.0	17.9	49.5
Aeroméxico	62.3	3.9	-14.6	2.4	-2.3	52.9	1.8	-6.2	0.0	48.5
Mexicana de Aviación	3.5	-1.4	-7.7	0.0	3.2	-2.4	-1.3	-3.3	0.0	-7.0

Note: All figures are the annual component of the perpetuity equivalent to the welfare change, expressed as a percentage of annual sales in the last predivestiture year.

a. Includes workers both in their role as wage earners and as buyers of shares.

Source: Authors' calculations.

528

Net Welfare Changes

The Negative Case

Let us begin by examining the outlier in our sample: Mexicana, the only case where welfare declined because of divestiture. Was this a failure of divestiture? The source of the loss was not, as might be thought, producer exploitation of consumers, with the latter's losses outweighing the former's gains. Rather, the buyer also lost because of a series of mistaken business decisions (especially the decision to expand capacity at a time of stagnant or declining demand). Clearly, private managers, just like public ones, can make mistakes, and to expect all buyers to be infallible is to apply an overly stringent standard. Rather, one might hope that the bulk of buyers will make intelligent decisions and, even more important, that when they do make mistakes, there are mechanisms to reverse them. That there are such mechanisms was apparent in the case of Mexicana, when the large losses in the first few years after divestiture were reversed thereafter. In asking whether or not this was a failure of divestiture, one must ask how quickly bad decisions in public enterprises are turned around. Our view is that both sectors make mistakes, but that it is much more likely that public sector errors will be allowed to persist.

Winners and Losers

Even when the net benefits are overwhelmingly positive, might not this conceal the fact that certain groups lose from divestiture? The answer is an emphatic yes: in only one case, that of Compañía de Teléfonos de Chile (CTC) were we unable to identify any losers.[2] Room for Pareto-efficient reallocations (reallocations that make no one worse off) is as regrettably but inevitably absent in divestiture as in other policy realms. In all other cases there is a mix, with benefits accruing to some and costs to others. Who then are the winners and the losers? As summarized in table 23-1 they include:

- **Workers.** Given widespread union opposition to divestiture, it will surprise some to find that we found no case of workers *as a class* losing from divestiture, and ten cases where workers gained. Workers benefited substantially from share appreciation at the United Kingdom's National Freight Corporation, Teléfonos de México (Telmex), and Chile's electricity distributor ENERSIS, and from higher wages at Malaysia's Kelang Container Terminal. Individual workers could of course be made worse off, especially where layoffs or reduced hiring were involved. In the cases analyzed, however, there was substantial severance pay and reasonably full employment, so these losses were minimal (we elaborate on this point below). One important result of our study is that divestiture *can* be managed so as to make workers no worse off. To some extent, however, there is a selection bias here, because workers may often be powerful enough to block divestitures where they stand to lose. If efficiency gains are realized as a result of divestiture, workers can be bought off with a share of the increased profits.

- **Consumers**. The other group that might be expected to lose in some cases is consumers. Here our priors are at least partially fulfilled: five of the cases resulted in losses to consumers. However, in only three of these were the losses substantial. Note that the major consumer losses were all in Mexico. An important question is whether these losses occurred because prices were raised to an exploitative level, or because prices rose to an economically efficient level. In both cases consumers lose, but only in the former is it a bad thing. As we will see in the next subsection, the welfare impact of the price changes was strongly positive in one case and near neutral in the other two, indicating that the consumer losses were due primarily to movement toward efficiency prices. In the four cases where consumers gained, this was largely the result of increased investment and the resulting expansion of service.

- **Government and buyers**. One very general result in our sample is that, in all cases, profits (in the broad definition of quasi rents) rose, as evidenced in table 23-1 by the positive totals for the government and for domestic and foreign buyers. However, the distribution of these gains is considerably less uniform. Whereas *both* domestic and foreign buyers came out ahead in every case except Mexicana, governments lost in three cases, albeit by small amounts. Overall, however, the fiscal impact was positive in nine of twelve cases.

- **Foreigners versus nationals**. When foreigners are involved, they generally do quite well, but nationals do even better. There are only three cases where foreigners lose on balance—British Airways, Mexicana, and Aeroméxico—and in the case of British Airways the losses are minuscule (less than 1 percent). In contrast, domestic groups gain on balance in all cases except Mexicana. In two cases—Malaysian Airline Systems and Telmex—domestic groups gain on balance, but more than three-quarters of the gains go to foreigners. In contrast, at CTC and Kelang Container Terminal foreigners gain substantially, but domestic actors gain many times as much.

- **Competitors**. Given that most of the enterprises we studied were near or complete monopolies, there was little opportunity for competitors to gain or lose. One major exception is Sports Toto Malaysia, where dramatic management changes brought major improvements in profits, about half of which, according to our estimate, came at the expense of lost market share by competitors (shown in the "Others" column in table 23-1).[3] The other major exception is CTC, whose dramatic expansion benefited the competing company that provides long distance services.

Behavioral Changes

Distributional changes follow from behavioral changes at the enterprise and its supervisory bodies. Selected manifestations of these changes are summarized in table 23-2. The bulk of the table is devoted to primary changes affecting the operating performance of the enterprise, but additional columns are provided for secondary changes affecting nonoperating performance and macroeconomic, fiscal, and other shadow effects. Operating performance is further decomposed into price and quantity changes. Quantity effects include both those stemming from productivity gains and those following from changes in output levels. Output can increase as a result of any or all of several factors: an increase in capacity utilization; a reduction in excess demand (this appears in the table as part of the rise in productivity); an exogenous rise in demand (which does not appear in the table, because it is not a change attributable to divestiture); endogenous shifts in demand induced by improved advertising or product quality; expansion of capacity that reduces excess demand (rather than accommodating expanded demand) by releasing an investment constraint; or by improvements in product quality or product differentiation. All changes are listed only in the column where they originate: for example, if falling prices trigger increased demand and investment, the welfare effect is listed only under the output price. Finally, a separate column is provided for interaction or cross-product terms: when both output prices and productivity rise together, the net effect (listed in the world welfare change column) will differ from the pure individual effects (listed in the other columns) by the amount of the interaction effect.

The more important patterns apparent in table 23-2 include the following:

- **Productivity**. When poorly managed public enterprises are converted to well-managed private firms, major productivity gains should follow. In general, our results support this expectation: productivity grew in three-quarters of our cases and declined in none. Furthermore, in four of the nine positive cases—Kelang Container Terminal, the Chilean electricity generating enterprise CHILGENER, National Freight, and Telmex—the rise in productivity was largely due to better management with more or less the same work force.

Table 23-2. *Primary Sources of Welfare Gains and Losses from Divestiture in the Twelve Case Studies*
(percentages)

	Welfare changes in operating performance						Nonoperating performance	Fiscal and other macro shadow effects	Interaction effects	World net welfare change
	Due to quantity changes			Due to price changes						
	Output									
Country and enterprise	Endogenous demand	Investment	Productivity	Outputs	Indirect taxes	Wages				
United Kingdom										
British Telecom	0.0	5.1	9.0	7.2	0.0	0.0	0.0	0.0	−9.3	12.0
British Airways	0.0	0.0	2.4	−1.5	0.0	0.0	0.0	0.0	0.7	1.6
National Freight	0.0	0.5	4.0	0.0	0.0	0.0	0.2	0.0	−0.4	4.3
Chile										
CHILGENER	0.0	0.0	2.1	0.0	0.0	0.0	0.0	0.0	0.0	2.1
ENERSIS	1.5	0.0	0.0	3.7	0.0	0.0	0.0	0.0	0.0	5.2
CTC	48.2	97.3	9.6	0.0	0.0	0.0	0.0	0.0	0.0	155.1
Malaysia										
Malaysian Airline Systems	0.0	22.7	0.0	3.4	0.0	0.0	0.0	0.0	−3.7	22.1
Kelang Container Terminal	15.8	0.0	28.2	0.0	0.0	(6.9)	0.0	0.0	9.3	53.3
Sports Toto Malaysia	10.9	0.0	0.0	0.0	0.0	0.0	0.0	0.0	0.0	10.9
Mexico										
Teléfonos de México	0.0	0.0	19.8	16.3	0.0	1.9	0.0	11.5	0.0	49.5
Aeroméxico	0.0	0.0	48.1	0.4	0.0	0.0	0.0	0.0	0.0	48.5
Mexicana de Aviación	0.0	−8.9	2.8	−0.2	0.0	0.0	0.0	0.0	−0.7	−7.0

Note: All figures are the annual component of the perpetuity equivalent to the welfare change, expressed as a percentage of annual sales in the last predivestiture year. Figures may not sum to totals because of rounding. The welfare impact is indicated solely under the initiating variable and not under the accommodating variable. For example, if price changes were accommodated by greater capacity utilization or investment, the whole welfare impact is listed in the price column. Interaction or cross-product effects appear in the next to last column, so the world net welfare change is the sum of the other columns. The sign (positive or negative) refers to the direction of the price changes, not the change in the variable. For example, a positive price effect means that welfare improved as a result of the price changes, not that prices rose. Parentheses indicate that the variable changed significantly in the indicated direction, but with negligible net welfare impact.

Source: Authors' calculations.

532

However, in three of the nine—British Telecom, British Airways, and Aeroméxico—the bulk of the gains in productivity were largely the result of work force reductions.[4]

- **Investment constraint**. If the first surprise is fewer gains where more might have been expected, the second surprise is significant gains where many might not have expected them. Relaxing an investment constraint, and thereby reducing excess demand, had a significant positive impact in three cases. For example, at CTC capacity doubled in five years, yielding the largest percentage welfare change in our sample. On the other hand, the same increase in autonomy at Mexicana led the private buyer to overinvest, thereby reducing welfare.

- **Output prices**. It is unsurprising that significant output price changes accompanied divestiture in seven of our cases. It may, however, be surprising that there were no such changes in five cases, and that where they did occur they tended to be overwhelmingly welfare enhancing—due to movements toward efficiency prices. Only in the cases of British Airways and Mexicana did price changes modestly reduce welfare because of increased exploitation of market power.[5] A special case is Chile's ENERSIS, where better management substantially reduced electricity theft, thereby effectively raising the price per unit of production, (but not the price per unit sold).

- **Input prices**. The only significant input price changes we could identify were the wage increases at Malaysia's Kelang Container Terminal. These, however, were judged to be welfare neutral (as indicated by the parentheses in table 23-2), with employee gains largely offset by profit reductions. However, when workers also work harder, productivity rises and there are net gains, which appear in the cross-product column.

- **Endogenous demand expansion**. Under this rubric we include a variety of market-expanding activities, such as marketing, advertising, product development, and product quality and service. Surprisingly, only four such welfare-improving cases were identified: Kelang Container Terminal, Sports Toto Malaysia, ENERSIS, and CTC.

- **Nonoperating performance**. There was only one case of improved nonoperating performance, and this was minor (National Freight).

- **Fiscal and other macroeconomic shadow effects**. Macroeconomic effects were not deemed important in the United Kingdom, Chile, or Malaysia, whose economies were not significantly in disequilibrium during the periods in question. Mexico, however, was characterized by external debt and a domestic fiscal crisis at the time of divestiture. Accordingly, the government revenue multiplier at the time of sale was set at 2. This had no impact on the airline sales, because no net revenue accrued to the government. The divestiture of Telmex, however, had a substantial positive impact on the domestic economy.[6]

Two very important and surprising patterns emerge from these results. First, the bulk of the gains followed from divestiture-induced changes that were external to the enterprise rather than internal to it. Roughly three-quarters of the welfare improvements from divestiture[7] came from just three sources: revised output prices and increased flexibility in hiring and in investment decisions. To be sure, given that our results are based on differencing the actual and the counterfactual, both types of changes would not, in our judgment, have taken place without divestiture. Second, the origin and distribution of the welfare effects of divestiture vary substantially across cases. As will be explained below, these variations reflect the initial conditions of each enterprise, its sector and policy characteristics, and the nature of the sale transaction.

This summary of welfare changes by recipient and by source raises more questions than it answers. What caused these patterns of results? The balance of this chapter attempts to answer this question in terms of the relevant environmental and policy variables.

Methodological and Selection Biases

The results of this study, like those of any other, are due in part to the world being studied and in part to the way in which it was studied. Accordingly, our search for explanations of our results begins with introspection. To what extent were our results biased by limitations of our study?

DEFINING SUCCESS. Our definition of divestiture success is a positive welfare change coupled with an acceptable distribution thereof. Some (for example, Leeds 1991, p. 113) would argue that this is a secondary criterion and that divestiture can be successful even in the absence of positive welfare changes. This is not simply the view of a merchant banker, whose idea of success is limited to getting the deal done and getting on to the next deal. Rather, it points to a limitation in our case studies, which confine themselves to the boundaries of the industry and thus ignore broader atmospheric implications. As a tangible manifestation of government commitment to market forces, divestiture can, among other things:

- Unleash additional private entrepreneurial activity on the part of domestic and foreign investors
- Stimulate remaining public enterprises to become more efficient
- Demonstrate government commitment to liberalizing policies
- Foster capital market development in general and people's capitalism (the broader distribution of corporate ownership) in particular.

Atmospheric factors such as these clearly bring additional benefits to the divestiture transaction (although they must be set against additional atmospheric costs such as increased concentration of wealth and economic power). We doubt, however, that they are sufficient to make divestiture a success. If all these benefits were realized but the welfare impact of divestiture was significantly negative, then there would be a lot of significant losers, who might be expected to exert sufficient political power to bring divestiture to a screeching halt. We would conjecture that this is what has happened to divestiture programs in several countries. The implication is that welfare change is necessary for continued atmospheric gains. Be that as it may, our study omits these effects. Bringing them in would reinforce our already positive results.

METHODOLOGICAL BIAS. Methodological problems can arise in either conception or execution. One potential conceptual problem of our analysis is that we do not deal with uncertainty in a serious way. Other than this, however, we can only say that, if we knew of any such problems, we would have fixed them. We leave it to others to expose us.

With regard to execution, we can only plead guilty to error. Because we are making quantitative counterfactual projections into an unknown and unknowable future, both the charge and the plea are self-evident. The question is whether the errors are systematic enough to bias our results. Our use of counterfactual differencing substantially reduces many forms of projection error, but here, too, we can only say that if we knew of any biases we would have eliminated them. We look forward to seeing what others feel we have missed.

SELECTION BIAS. We are less sanguine when it comes to selection bias. Our cases are by no means a random sample of public enterprises around the world, and the biases are systematic. There are two distinct sources of bias. The first is imposed by the world, because:

- The countries that had divested significant numbers of public enterprises by the mid-1980s are different from those that had not.
- Within those countries, the enterprises that were divested first were different from those divested later or not at all.

The second source of bias results from limitations on our selection from that sample:

- The countries and enterprises that allowed us access are different from those that denied us access.
- Even among those countries and enterprises where access might have been possible, we chose a nonrandom sample.

Such biases—which are common to any case study approach—do not mean that we cannot learn from our sample, but only that we must be cautious in generalizing therefrom. That is, as we attempt to explain our results, the sample characteristics must be taken into account.

PERSONAL BIAS. In a study of this sort, innumerable choices of parameter values and other assumptions are made on the basis of judgments or educated guesses. This obviously leaves a lot of room for subjectivity. In general, we have tried to be conservative in the sense of underestimating the gains accruing to divestiture. This does not mean that we have taken the extreme approach of lowballing every estimate, but simply that, when confronted with a range of reasonable doubt, we have generally taken the conservative end of the spectrum.

PRECISION OF RESULTS. Finally, as we explained in the methodology chapter (chapter 2), our attempt at measuring the effect of divestiture involves attributing certain benefits and costs to divestiture, projecting these effects into the future, and hypothesizing a complete counterfactual scenario for the enterprise had it remained under public ownership. In the process, we make several assumptions and educated judgments. Some of these assumptions may not hold, or the reader may disagree with us. In either case, our consolation is that we make our assumptions explicit so that others may contradict us. In addition, we provide a range of estimates in the cases themselves, so that each reader may net out those counterfactual assumptions he or she deems unbelievable. In this chapter, however, we refer only to our point rather than to our range estimates.

The implications of the various biases will be detailed in the balance of this chapter. Here we only note that their existence means that we cannot generalize from our sample without incorporating information exogenous to our cases. This leap is taken at this point as we now attempt to explain our results.

Determinants of Success: A Verbal Regression

We now wish to explain why the results described above followed from divestiture. The standard problem is to avoid mistaking correlation for causation because of omitted variables. For example, is it really divestiture in the sense of ownership changes that caused the welfare gains cited above? Or were there contemporary changes in market structure that caused the gains? Or do the two factors interact, with some forms of ownership change having positive effects only with some market structures? The standard solution to the standard problem is to run a regression, with welfare change (or its distribution) as the left-hand (dependent) variable and a variety of independent explanatory factors as right-hand variables.

We of course cannot attempt this because we lack a sufficient number of observations relative to the number of possible explanatory factors. Nonetheless, we find it useful to structure our investigation of causation as a verbal regression. The goal is to explain welfare changes as a function of a set of independent variables, with full awareness of the potential for interaction effects on the right-hand side.

INDEPENDENT VARIABLES: MARKETS AND INSTITUTIONS. At the most basic level we distinguish between two sets of independent variables. Enterprise behavior is hypothesized to be subject to (or controlled by, or a result of) both the markets in which it operates and the institutional superstructure that lies above it. Inefficiency can result from lack of competition in the markets in which the enterprise sells. Or it can result from imperfections in the hierarchy of principal-agent relationships, including imperfect incentives, goal setting, a poor allocation of decisionmaking power, impacted information, or other causes. We examine these two sets of explanatory factors in turn.

SHIFT VARIABLES: COUNTRY CHARACTERISTICS. Market characteristics are largely specific to an industry, and institutional characteristics are largely specific to the enterprise, but another set of possible explanatory factors is specific to the country. Does success vary with the level of economic development? with macroeconomic circumstance? with some vaguely defined set of social-cultural-political factors? The first two can be thought of as additional independent variables, and the last as a country-specific shift factor.

SALE STRUCTURE. Country characteristics are wholly beyond the control of divestiture decisionmakers, and market structure partly so, but the way the sale is structured can be varied to cope with the exogenous circumstances. Should ownership and control be wholly transferred to the private sector, or can gains be had through partial divestiture? Does prior restructuring help? How should buyers and price be determined? Who should do all this? To what extent do systematic rules and guidelines emerge from our results, and to what extent does it all depend on the enterprise and country in question?

TOWARD A GENERAL THEORY OF DIVESTITURE. In sum, we now wish to explain the level and distribution of welfare change as a function of a set of market, institutional, country, and sale characteristics. A general theory of divestiture would answer this question definitively and comprehensively, asserting that welfare change is a quantified function of certain well-defined variables. Given our limited sample, we have no such ambitions, but we hope to make a contribution toward the development of such a general theory.

Market Determinants of Success

In this section we consider a range of market factors that might explain our results. Divestiture places great faith in the ability of markets to work well. In general, divestiture involves shifts in the environment of the enterprise from a relatively government-controlled toward a market-dominated setting. In pure divestiture, the control mechanism for the enterprise is transformed from a command to a market mechanism. Also, the enterprise's relationship with its output markets may be quite different, going in some cases from administered to market price setting. Therefore, the market setting of the divested enterprise is an obvious place to start when studying the factors that influence the degree of success achieved by divestiture. Generally, if divestiture is to succeed, either the markets in which the enterprise operates must work reasonably well, or certain mechanisms that substitute for or regulate the market must work well.

Here we examine the extent to which these factors played a role in explaining the outcomes observed in our cases. We focus first on output market structure and then consider technology, labor, and capital markets.

Output Market Structure: Level

Are divestiture outcomes invariant to market structure? It is widely believed (see, e.g., Vernon 1988) that public enterprises in competitive markets are obvious candidates for divestiture because in such markets there is generally no strong argument for public ownership in the first place. Theory would therefore predict that welfare could only rise with divestiture in such industries, with productivity gains being a key source of the improvements.

In contrast, as explained in chapter 1, in monopoly industries there is not such a clear-cut prediction as to the beneficial impact of divestiture. Although the fact that divested enterprises will pursue profit-maximizing strategies suggests that they will be more cost efficient, the countervailing facts that they do not face competitive pressures and that, under regulation, they face a different mechanism for cost recovery suggest that their incentives to minimize costs might be weak or possibly even perverse.[8] Thus the key feature of the monopoly cases would be what we have termed elsewhere the "fundamental trade-off" of divestiture (Jones, Tandon, and Vogelsang 1990, chapter 5). The trade-off is that against any efficiency improvements must be weighed the possibility of increased exercise of monopoly power. This alerts us to expect a negative welfare impact from divestiture on consumers in monopoly industries, unless the government takes steps to protect them.

What about the magnitude of the gains from divestiture? For enterprises in competitive industries, welfare improvement might be expected, but this may be small because public enterprises in competitive industries may already be fairly efficient precisely because of the competitive pressures they face. In monopoly industries there may be greater potential improvement, but the possibility of market power exploitation creates a possibility of welfare losses also. In such cases the outcome depends on balance upon the quality of regulation introduced. Thus we would expect competitive enterprises to show positive, albeit moderate, welfare gains from divestiture, while monopoly enterprises would have much greater variance, with potentially large gains or losses.

Between the two extremes of perfect competition and monopoly lie various degrees of imperfect competition and oligopoly. Here the outcome will depend on the number of firms and their strategic behavior. However, in general, if the process of divestiture brings about or is accompanied by the introduction of more competition, productivity gains are likely to be strengthened. In the opposite case, if divestiture is coupled with reduced competition, we might expect productivity actually to decline (we explore the changes in output market structure more fully below).

Turning to the evidence from our sample, we present in table 23-3 the weighted market share[9] of each enterprise in our sample as an indicator of the market structure in which the enterprise operates. To facilitate the comparison we also present the welfare change associated with divestiture. The key observation here is that, for enterprises with market power, we find high variance in the welfare outcome and no evidence of welfare losses even in the pure monopoly cases (British Telecom, Telmex, ENERSIS, and CTC). This may be an indication of the effectiveness of the regulation that has been introduced in all the monopoly cases. At the more competitive end of the spectrum, the welfare changes tend to be more moderate, although positive.

Thus, we do not have much evidence in support of the fundamental trade-off. Although consumers are worse off in a number of cases (Telmex, British Airways, Malaysian Airline Systems; see table 23-1), the effects are strong in only one (Telmex),[10] and this was a case where prices were raised explicitly as part of the introduction of regulation. This was done to bring prices more in line with international norms and to enable the enterprise to finance a major investment program. The point here is that, in anticipation of the possible exercise of monopoly power, governments have introduced regulation, and it appears that by and large such regulation has succeeded in protecting consumers: prices rose to the vicinity of efficiency prices, but not above.

Table 23-3. Market Factors in the Twelve Case Studies

Country and enterprise	Market share [a] (percentages)	Change in market structure [b] Endogenous	Change in market structure [b] Exogenous	Number of employees [c]	Impact of regulation [d]	Z/V_{PP} [e]	World net welfare change [g]
United Kingdom							
British Telecom	97	0	+	235,000	+	50	12.0
British Airways	39	−	+	40,800	+	53	1.6
National Freight	10	0	0	24,300	n.a.	19	4.3
Chile							
CHILGENER	13	0	0	791	0	65	2.1
ENERSIS	95	0	0	2,495	0	29	5.2
CTC	95	+	0	7,240	0	51	155.1
Malaysia							
Malaysian Airline Systems	60	0	0	10,600	0	39	22.1
Kelang Container Terminal	55	+	+	800	0	30	53.4
Sports Toto Malaysia	5	0	0	400	0	46	10.9
Mexico							
Teléfonos de México	99	+	+	50,000	+	41	49.5
Aeroméxico	38	+	+	11,500	0	—[f]	48.5
Mexicana de Aviación	39	+	+	12,700	0	0	−7.0

n.a. Not applicable.
a. Revenue-weighted market share of the enterprise in the year prior to divestiture.
b. Change in the intensity of competition, not in market share.
c. In the year prior to divestiture.
d. Effect of the postdivestiture regulatory environment on welfare, relative to that before divestiture.
e. Price at which the enterprise was sold (Z) divided by the estimated discounted stream of profits (V_{PP}).
f. Not meaningful because V_{PP} is negative.
g. Figures are from table 23-1.
Source: Company data and authors' calculations.

Divestiture in competitive industries thus leads to some welfare improvement. In monopoly industries, where the potential exercise of monopoly power might be welfare reducing, governments can and have forestalled this by introducing efficient regulation. In some monopoly cases, however, large welfare improvements are possible if effective regulation combines with a situation where the predivestiture enterprise was performing poorly or faced critical constraints that divestiture removed. These are the circumstances where the greatest potential payoff to divestiture lies.

Output Market Structure: Changes

A large body of economics literature argues that, after market structure has been corrected for, there is no difference between public and private ownership.[11] That is, what is wrong with public enterprise is not its public ownership but the fact that it usually operates in monopoly markets, and in such markets all enterprises—whether public or private—tend to be inefficient. The implication for divestiture is straightforward: if you do not change market structure, you do not change anything (see Heald 1984a, 1984b; Heald and Steel 1982).

To what extent were the welfare changes we found caused by alterations in the structure of output markets? The answer is simple: very little. The reason is not that market structure has not changed, or that market structure does not matter, but partly that our methodology attempted to correct for the way in which changes in market structure matter. That is, our base counterfactuals (with which we compared the actual cases to calculate welfare gains) assumed identical market structures, except where market structures changed *as a result of* divestiture. For example, we argue that the merger of British Airways and British Caledonian would most likely not have been allowed had British Airways remained in public hands; thus, this merger was an endogenous (and adverse) market structure change. As a result, domestic passengers suffered from higher prices on some routes after divestiture, and this explains the negative welfare effects for British Airways consumers in table 23-1 and the negative price effects in table 23-2. In contrast, the technological changes taking place in the telecommunications industry have created competitive possibilities that we regard as exogenous market structure changes. Similarly, predivestiture public-enterprise reforms that change market structure (e.g., those in Chilean electricity, described below) are also regarded as exogenous.

When reforms of market structures have already taken place, the benefits to divestiture may be reduced compared with a situation where they have not. The most dramatic example is in Chile, where reform of the electricity industry provides a model that, in our view, should be studied and emulated by developing and industrial countries alike (a summary is provided below). Why, then, do the Chilean electricity generation and distribution firms show comparatively modest gains in tables 23-1 and 23-2? The answer is simply that competitive restructuring and regulatory reform took place while the sector was still under public ownership, and there was therefore comparatively less to gain from divestiture. Another example is that of British Telecom, where market liberalization was decided on in 1981, one year before the divestiture decision. These examples suggest that many of the gains commonly associated with divestiture could also be achieved in theory through the effective implementation of public sector reforms, with an emphasis on the application of market principles to the public enterprises. The question here is, To what extent are governments capable of introducing and implementing such reforms? Most countries have been less successful than Chile with their public-enterprise reforms, and those that have been successful under one regime often see the gains reversed under a subsequent regime. The case for divestiture then rests on its sustainability and credibility of commitment to reforms.

An interesting case of a market structure change is that of the Mexican airlines. Before divestiture the Mexican air transport industry was basically a duopoly of two public enterprises; after divestiture it was a duopoly of two private enterprises. Does this constitute a change in market structure? In principle, since the predivestiture enterprises had the same owner, it could be argued that competition has increased and one might expect prices to decline. In fact, however, prices in the predivestiture period were held to low (money-losing) levels, and therefore it might be reasonable to expect prices to rise.[12] So far, the Mexican airlines are partly behaving according to theory, but partly reliving the early days of U.S. airline deregulation. Although nominal fares have risen sharply, some major routes are characterized by intense competition and discounting. But only time will tell how this particular market will evolve.

Price Regulation

The issue of monopolistic market structure is closely related to that of price regulation. Here two questions seem relevant. First, does divestiture lead to an increase in prices? and if it does, is that necessarily welfare reducing? Second, given that price regulation can be implemented in any of several ways, is there any evidence to support the notion that one scheme is better than another in terms of enhancing the potential gains from divestiture?

First, let us identify the potential gains and losses from changes in prices. In the public-enterprise literature it is often noted that government-owned monopolies receive lower prices than they might under private ownership. The reasoning is that governments tend to use pricing of utilities to attempt to control inflation, redistribute income, and/or buy votes. Under these conditions, enterprises are likely to make relatively low rates of return, and at times of fiscal stringency they may be unable to expand sufficiently to meet demand. Accordingly, it can be expected that divestiture will give governments an opportunity to raise prices, which should improve welfare. However, if that increase is excessive because of monopolistic behavior, it can have negative allocative and distributional consequences. In sum, the goal is to get prices up to efficiency levels, but not beyond.

How is the goal achieved under various regulatory schemes? In theory, the RPI - X approach (applied by the United Kingdom and Mexico to telecommunications) and the rate-of-return approach based on an efficient firm (of the variety applied by Chile, in telecommunications and in electricity) have some superior cost-saving properties compared with other types of regulation, such as rate-of-return regulation with fully distributed cost pricing. Under RPI - X regulation, the average price level of the regulated services is independent (in the short run) of the enterprise's own costs. This means that, for a period of typically three to five years, the enterprise can retain as profit all cost savings realized from superior performance. By the same token, the enterprise bears all the costs of inferior performance.[13]

Against its superior properties with regard to cost efficiency, RPI - X regulation may be characterized as less favorable to some consumers, because it permits firms flexibility within the overall basket of services. Thus firms are free to raise prices on services with lower elasticity.

Under Chile's rate-of-return regulation, the regulators set maximum prices for each service and zone on the basis of the long-run marginal cost of an efficient (model) firm. This is yardstick regulation against ideal performance. It shares some of the advantages of the RPI - X formula. In particular, because the firm's price is set against that of an ideal firm, it can retain as profit (for the five years between revisions) all cost savings realized from superior performance, and it bears all the costs of inferior performance. In addition, the Chilean approach offers the firm an ex ante rate of return derived from future costs, which may induce expansion in situations characterized by excess demand.

Against these advantages, however, the Chilean type of regulation has some disadvantages. Most important, it is quite demanding in that it requires regulators to be experts who are willing to subject the firm to a tough test. Further, it can lead to disputes over the definition of the ideal firm.

What does our evidence show? Where prices were kept too low under public ownership, divestiture gave governments the opportunity to bring them closer to their economic values, with positive welfare implications for society. The most illustrative example here is Telmex. Mexico started the postdivestiture regulatory process for Telmex with a price-tax reform that increased the starting levels above what they would have been without divestiture. In contrast, the divestiture of Chile's electricity enterprises CHILGENER and ENERSIS did not cause prices to change, because these enterprises operated under the same pricing regime before their divestiture.

While our evidence also supports the notion that the regulation of monopolies was effective in preventing exploitation of consumers, it shows that firms facing RPI - X reduced cross-subsidization as expected by theory. For example, British Telecom raised monthly rentals and the price of local calls (where it had a monopoly) while reducing prices of long distance calls (where it faced competition). Telmex drastically raised its prices for metered local calls. In contrast, this behavior was not observed in Chile, because the price of each service was regulated.[14]

In sum, although our evidence favoring a particular form of regulation is weak, our evidence is strong that regulation is important and worked in most of our cases. Consumers were generally protected from the exploitation of market power. Where consumers lost—as at Telmex—this was not because of exploitation but because of a reduction in inefficient subsidies. That is, prices were brought up to economic levels from the subsidized levels of the past, and although consumers lost, society as a whole benefited. How the regulation of prices was accomplished is explained in more detail later in this chapter.

Technology

In the standard industrial organization paradigm, a basic determinant of market structure is technology, especially minimum efficient scale. The question here is whether any technological characteristic serves to increase or decrease the probable gains from divestiture, beyond its impact on market structure.

One such characteristic is absolute size. Huge organizations are difficult to change, at least quickly, because of the inertia of entrenched people, fiefdoms, and processes. Our results provide some support for this hypothesis. As table 23-3 shows, we have only three small enterprises in the sample, employing only a few hundred people rather than the several thousand in each of the others. How did their welfare changes compare with those of larger enterprises? As table 23-3 also reveals, there is no apparent correlation between size and overall welfare change.

However, the picture changes if we ignore divestiture-induced changes in external constraints (on pricing, investment, and labor levels) and focus on manifestations of internal organizational changes—other productivity and endogenously generated demand shifts. The sum of these two sources is higher for smaller than for larger enterprises. The sample is again much too small to allow conclusions to be drawn but supports the conjecture that potential percentage welfare gains from private management are inversely related to the size of the firm, at least in the short run. If so, this helps explain the otherwise limited evidence of dramatic internal efficiency gains.

Related to its size is the capital intensity of an enterprise. If an enterprise is highly capital intensive, with technology embodied in its capital, then it is naturally difficult to raise productivity rapidly. For example, Telmex has approximately 12,000 telephone operators (out of a total work force of about 50,000), whereas the company estimates that, were it to transform itself into a modern network, it would need only 2,000! Here the need is to switch from mechanical to digital exchanges, a process that naturally will take time. Productivity improvements therefore might be expected to appear only after there has been enough time to implement the capital restructuring necessary.

A further related characteristic is the extent of scale economies. Although the effects of scale economies ought, in principle, to be captured by market structure, an interesting interaction arises when the enterprise faces an investment constraint before divestiture. In that case, divestiture would allow the enterprise to fully exploit scale economies as the investment constraint is removed. An example of this phenomenon is the Chilean telephone company, CTC, which effectively doubled capacity in the five years following divestiture.

Finally, we may look at the effect of the rapidity with which either markets or technology are changing. It has been hypothesized that public enterprises are slow, mechanistic organisms with risk-evading incentives, at less of a disadvantage when operating in markets that change only slowly, where innovation and creativity are less important, and where marketing and advertising are inconsequential (Jones and Vogelsang 1983). This has been used to explain, for example, why public enterprises have often dominated a country's exports of raw and intermediate goods but almost everywhere have played a negligible role in manufactured exports, especially consumer goods. Accordingly, one would expect greater gains from divestiture in industries where tastes are changing rapidly (making them advertising- and marketing-intensive) or where technological change is progressing rapidly. This may help to explain the dramatic changes at Sports Toto Malaysia, where the introduction of new products and advertising led to a surge in revenues and profits after divestiture.

The Labor Market

One stereotype about public enterprises throughout the world is that they are overstaffed. Frequently they serve as havens for political patronage, the vehicles of government "job creation" programs. Even if this is not the problem, it is widely believed that the lack of market discipline allows public enterprises to grow fat. Competitive private enterprises of course cannot afford to be fat. An expected result of divestiture would then be a trimming of the work force of the enterprise, a loss of welfare to workers, and opposition from the labor unions. The strength and effectiveness of this opposition could then have a direct effect on the success of divestiture (or the lack thereof).

One of the surprising features of the divestiture cases we have examined is the marked absence of effective opposition from labor. On the contrary, we observed above that workers gained in ten of the twelve cases analyzed, and lost in none. In the Chilean cases and Telmex, the gains accrued to workers in their capacity as buyers of shares. In only one case—Aeroméxico—was there any kind of labor trouble, and it is clear that the Aeroméxico strike was not at all motivated by opposition to the proposed divestiture, which had not even been announced. Rather, the strike was due to more standard labor grievances. In fact, it can be argued that the strike *caused* divestiture to take place, as the labor problem was dealt with summarily by the government through liquidation and sale of the enterprise. In none of our cases has there been any serious labor trouble after divestiture.

When might labor oppose divestiture? Obviously, if workers thought they were going to be very much worse off as a result of divestiture, they would oppose it. However, in none of our cases were workers on balance worse off as a result of divestiture. But what might explain the fact that workers were not hurt by divestiture?

First, as already noted, there is quite likely a self-selection bias in our sample. Our sample consists of enterprises that *have* been divested. If a particular divestiture was going to hurt labor badly, it is quite likely that labor's opposition would be clear well before divestiture took place. There would then be three possible outcomes:

- The opposition might be fierce enough to prevent divestiture from taking place at all.[15]
- Labor could be bought off by being offered enough of the gains from divestiture to more than compensate for any welfare losses they might suffer.
- Divestiture could be rammed through despite opposition from labor.

We are unlikely to see the third type of outcome because of the political cost involved, and because buyers are going to be naturally leery of buying an enterprise whose employees oppose the transaction. We do not observe the first type of outcome in our sample because we are looking only at divested enterprises. Therefore the enterprises in our sample are going to be of two types: those where labor is not hurt by divestiture, and those where labor has been compensated for the welfare losses they suffer.

In considering the first type, we need to clarify what we mean when we say "labor is not hurt by divestiture." In defining labor's welfare gains or losses, we have restricted our analysis to the employees of the enterprise at the time of divestiture. Arguably, these workers were receiving rents prior to divestiture, from above-market wages or low effort requirements, or both. Absent divestiture, they would have continued receiving those rents. We generally assume that, as long as the workers retain their jobs, they suffer no loss in these rents. More important, we assume that this is the only group we need consider. We do not include in our calculations workers who would have gotten jobs in the enterprise (with the attendant rents) but do not because it has now been divested. In most of our cases, we project lower employment levels under divestiture than under our counterfactual. But frequently the lower level of employment is achieved through attrition of employees or through slower growth in the work force rather than through layoffs. In such cases we have generally ignored the rents that would have been received by workers who would have been hired in the counterfactual. Falling into this category of cases then are Telmex and Mexicana. In the case of Kelang Container Terminal, however, we took into account, through a shadow wage multiplier, the adverse effect on workers of increased effort and reduced rents (see chapter 15).

Several of our cases appear to be of the second type, that is, where workers received compensation for potential welfare losses from divestiture. Indeed, workers were compensated fairly substantially in many of our cases, both through generous severance payments for workers who were laid off (British Telecom, British Airways, Aeroméxico) and through special allocations of shares at discount prices (British Telecom, British Airways, National Freight, Telmex, CTC). One interesting observation here is that many of the cases we studied were highly capital-intensive. It is reasonable to suppose that, when labor accounts for a relatively small proportion of total cost, it is not too costly to buy its cooperation. We may speculate, for example, that the high labor cost in the railroad and postal sectors might account for the almost complete lack of divestiture in those sectors anywhere in the world.[16]

Another important issue related to these compensation schemes is whether employee share programs or other facets of labor relations contribute to improved labor productivity. The argument here would be that, by creating ownership rights for workers, companies may be able to induce them to exert increased effort. Another manifestation would be to permit management greater flexibility in setting work assignments. If that argument were to hold, one would observe a positive correlation between improved labor relations and improved labor productivity.

We do see some evidence of improved labor productivity and improved labor relations in our sample. For example, British Telecom and Telmex made provisions for employee share ownership, and both were able to win concessions from labor about work rules. At Aeroméxico, the government singled out the pilots as a key employee group with significant influence on performance, and awarded them shares in the enterprise. National Freight is a clear example of dramatic improvements in labor productivity following, in this case, takeover of the enterprise by its employees. In contrast, Mexicana made no provision for employee participation in ownership and has not experienced any improvement in its labor relations. At ENERSIS, management and employees took over the control of the enterprise, but productivity did not improve beyond its historical level, because the enterprise was relatively efficient to begin with.

In sum, labor has not been hurt because it generally had sufficient power to negotiate predivestiture agreements that made them no worse off. Subsequent productivity gains were then shared, in some cases making them better off. Gains to workers as buyers were also significant in some cases.

The Capital Market

In theory, the nature of the country's capital market could be expected to have an important influence on the divestiture transaction and on the success of divestiture itself. For the market to induce efficient transactions and to effectively exercise its control function on the enterprise once divested, it must be relatively well developed and efficient, and it ought to be possible for takeovers to take place.

For example, where the capital market is small or relatively undeveloped and the enterprise being sold is relatively large, it may be deemed necessary to bring in foreign buyers. In this event, along with the benefits to the economy from the inflow of foreign capital, some leakage abroad of the positive welfare impact of divestiture is to be expected. Indeed this happened to a substantial extent in two of the cases we studied: Telmex and CTC;[17] in the case of Telmex the gains to foreigners were great, but Mexico realized tremendous gains from a higher sale price, greater investor confidence, and macroeconomic stabilization. Without these gains, the leakage to foreigners would have outweighed the net world welfare change. In the case of CTC foreign participation created a positive-sum game in which foreigners and Chileans were left better off.

The sophistication of the stock market might also be a factor in determining whether it is possible to use stock market-determined prices, which might distribute the gains more toward the seller (the government). We examine this by comparing the ratio of the actual sale price Z to our calculation of the private value V_{pp} in table 23-3. Our evidence shows that stock market divestitures offer the prospect of higher prices to the government, but there is considerable variance within our sample. For example, in the United Kingdom, which no doubt has the most sophisticated stock market in our sample, two stock market sales (British Telecom and British Airways) yielded the government about half the private value of the enterprises. Similarly, in Chile, the government sold CHILGENER and CTC in part on the stock market and got over 50 percent of the enterprise's private value. In contrast, non-stock market sales in Malaysia and Mexico[18] yielded prices to the government that were significantly less than half of V_{pp}, and close to the lower end of the range experienced for stock market sales in our sample.

Apart from its role as a transaction mechanism, the capital market might influence divestiture outcomes too. Since private, widely held companies are posited to be controlled by the capital market, the efficiency of that market as compared with the efficiency of the government's control mechanisms is crucial to the outcome of the divestiture program. In this regard, although we observed no takeovers in our sample, we have some interesting observations to make. First, it is worth noting that almost all the firms in our sample are quoted on stock exchanges (the exception is Kelang Container Terminal), so that in principle the control mechanism of the capital market can function. Second, even in our limited data period we have seen two ownership transfers. The Chilean telephone enterprise CTC was sold first to Bond Corporation of New Zealand. Bond Corp. later sold its share to Telefónica de España. The dominant share in Sports Toto Malaysia was resold to a firm with more experience in the gambling industry and thus, through synergies, willing to pay more than the company was worth to the original owner. Third, in the one case where divestiture has led to a welfare loss, that of Mexicana, the divestiture process actually prevented the capital market from exerting its control function. The buying consortium, Grupo Xabre, was *required* by the terms of the divestiture agreement to retain 25 percent ownership of the company for three years after the sale (until September 1992). The Mexican government placed another 25.1 percent of the company in a trust over which Xabre has voting control and which it has an option to buy within the same period. Thus it was impossible for an outside group to gain control over Mexicana at the time. The fact that Mexicana has performed so poorly and that the capital market has not played its usual controlling role can therefore be explained as a failure not of the capital market but of the structure of the divestiture itself.[19]

In sum, stock market divestitures seem to offer the prospect of yielding higher prices to the government, but they show considerable variance within our sample. The capital market can influence divestiture outcomes through takeovers. Although this mechanism was not observed in our sample, we find that in two cases resales did occur and led to improved outcomes. In a third case, a resale or even a takeover seemed desirable but was preempted by the structure of the divestiture sale. Finally, where enterprises are large relative to the domestic capital market, the inflow of foreign capital can be critical to the distribution of the gains from divestiture between foreign and domestic nationals.

Other Input Markets

Although it was not a major issue in any of our cases, we feel it is important to mention the possible redistributive effects of elimination of rents to suppliers of inputs. In many public enterprises, the prices paid for inputs can be higher than their market level, either because of explicit government policies such as domestic sourcing[20] or because negotiated prices are too high because of lack of adequate incentives or simple corruption. There is some evidence from Telmex that the divested enterprise has been able to lower the prices it pays foreign equipment suppliers through harder bargaining. In general, this is an area where it is difficult to get solid evidence, both because of the level of detail required and because of the sensitive nature of the information; we expect that in many cases this may be an important factor in the redistribution of welfare from divestiture.

Summary

Market factors can, in sum, influence divestiture outcomes in several ways:

- If the divested enterprise operates in a competitive industry, welfare gains are likely to be positive, but small.
- In monopoly industries welfare gains are more variable, with large gains possible. Effective regulation plays a crucial role in ensuring positive (and preventing large negative) outcomes.
- Divestiture can induce changes in market structures, and the effects of these can be positive or negative.
- Internal changes in efficiency cannot be effected overnight, particularly in large and capital-intensive enterprises.

- Workers may not be hurt by divestiture, perhaps because of their strong bargaining power, which largely allow them to get a share of the gains from divestiture.
- An efficient capital market can increase government revenues from the sale of enterprises, and it may improve divestiture outcomes through the resale mechanism. Further, while the inflow of foreign capital can expand the set of large enterprises for which divestiture is feasible, some of the gains may leak abroad.

Institutional Determinants of Success

In theory, divestiture replaces bureaucrats and politicians whose utility function is multivariate with motivated and profit-minded private owners, and it removes the institutional rigidities associated with public ownership. On the other hand, when the divested enterprise is a natural monopoly, divestiture also leads to the creation of new regulatory rules, processes, and institutions, all managed by a new set of civil servants. Failure of the resulting regulatory institutions can also be costly. Thus the net gains from divestiture depend in part on whether or not the benefits from reducing the institutional problems of public ownership outweigh the costs of failing to regulate private monopolies effectively.

Accordingly, in exploring the role of institutional factors in determining welfare outcomes, we examine how divestiture altered the relationship between the principals (the owners) and their agents (the managers) and that between the regulators and the regulated firms. Under the principal-agent rubric we explore three sets of changes: in enterprise goals, in the autonomy to pursue those goals, and in the motivation provided by accountability and incentives. In studying regulatory institutions we explore the nature of the relationship between the regulatory agencies and the regulated enterprises, and how conflicts between them are resolved. Throughout, we illustrate how these changes may have contributed to the change in welfare.

The Principal-Agent Relationship

Stereotypically, public enterprises suffer from an array of institutional problems.[21] Their objectives are often numerous and ill defined, ranging from profit maximization to regional development and employment. Frequently they report to several principals, including both politicians and bureaucrats. Management incentives are seldom linked to performance, and performance itself is seldom evaluated. As a result, a public enterprise operates much like a soccer game in which no score is kept and there is neither goal nor referee.

The divested enterprises in our sample fit this description, albeit to varying degrees. Even in the United Kingdom, where one would expect public ownership to impinge the least on the operation of state-owned enterprises, the 1978 White Paper stated that public enterprises "should pursue" or "in fact pursued" noncommercial objectives in addition to their so-called financial targets. It allocated greater power to government ministers at the expense of enterprise boards, reversing the arm's-length approach that had been followed since 1967. Preoccupied with macroeconomic considerations, the paper reinstated the limits on public-enterprise borrowing.[22]

In contrast, before divestiture the Chilean public enterprises were probably managed as well as any in the world. After getting rid of excess labor and freeing prices in the 1970s and early 1980s, the government instructed the enterprises under its authority to maximize profit. And it gave managers the autonomy in operational decisionmaking to do so. CORFO, the government holding company, held them responsible for achieving this outcome. Most unique to Chile, public-enterprise monopolies operated under regulatory rules that applied equally to public and privately owned monopolies, for example in the electricity sector.

In further contrast, the institutional setup of the Malaysian and Mexican cases is not atypical for developing countries. One example from Malaysia will illustrate. The government provided Malaysian Airline Systems with a set of conflicting objectives, which included the commercial objective of providing efficient and profitable provision of air transport systems, as well as the noncommercial objectives of contributing to the economic and social integration of the country's eastern and western regions, to trade and tourism, and to forwarding national aspirations. The government (appropriately as the owner) appointed the airline's board members, chairman, and managing director, but it drew them largely from a pool of civil servants rather than from the business sector.

In theory, divestiture is expected to ameliorate or remove these institutional constraints. In particular, it is expected to narrow the objective of the enterprise to profit maximization. Private owners, even if multiple, are expected to pursue this objective. For the same reason, they are expected to better monitor and provide incentives to management to do so. Finally, management itself is expected to face fewer political and bureaucratic constraints in pursuing profit maximization.[23] As a result, firm efficiency is likely to be enhanced.

A second implication concerns the magnitudes of the gains from divestiture. One may expect that the more binding the initial institutional constraints facing a public enterprise, the greater the gains that can result from their removal by divestiture. Accordingly, one would expect the gains to be more substantial in Mexico and Malaysia than in the United Kingdom and Chile.

What institutional changes did divestiture bring about in our sample? Table 23-4 shows the main institutional changes in each of our cases, but first some explanation is needed. The table is designed to capture the changes in enterprise goals and the pattern of managerial autonomy and incentives in order to see whether these changes contributed to divestiture outcomes. We do not attach specific values to the institutional changes because of the difficulty involved. Instead, we indicate the direction of the change and its importance for the outcome: a plus sign indicates increased goal specificity, autonomy, or incentives, with positive effects on divestiture outcomes; a negative sign indicates the contrary; and a zero indicates either no change or a change that made no difference to the outcome. We note the following:

- **Enterprise goals**. Divestiture concentrated the managerial mind on commercial objectives in all but the Malaysian Airline Systems case (the only case where the government retained control). It did not bring about changes in noncommercial objectives, in part because the enterprises in our sample pursued few to begin with, and in part because they were embodied in the operating license (e.g., the quantity targets on telephone provision set for Telmex).
- **Managerial autonomy**. Divestiture increased managerial autonomy, especially in the areas of finance and investment (in ten of the twelve cases), but also in personnel matters (in more than half the cases). Although the new owners replaced top management in seven cases, as expected, it is surprising that they left management unchanged in five: ENERSIS, National Freight, British Telecom, Malaysian Airline Systems, and British Airways.[24] This may suggest that the problem in some cases is not the quality of public-enterprise managers but their motivation. Finally, apart from the layoffs preceding divestiture, the new owners seldom made significant changes in the labor force. This can be explained in part by constraints in labor relations and in part by the specialized nature of the work forces in many of our cases.
- **Motivation and incentives**. Divestiture improved incentives not only for management but also for workers in virtually all cases, the exception being Malaysian Airline Systems. In the Chilean cases (especially CHILGENER), compensation was explicitly linked to firm profitability and individual performance. In other cases it was sometimes explicit and sometimes implicit, but generally effective.

In sum, divestiture reduced or eliminated the role of the government as owner in every case, even where the sale was only partial. But, as can be expected, the regulatory role of the government became stronger in the monopoly cases. We will discuss this strengthened role after first considering the results of the changes.

Table 23-4. *Changes in Principal-Agent Relationships with Divestiture in the Twelve Case Studies*

Country and enterprise	Goals		Autonomy					Incentives	World net welfare change[a]
	Commercial	Noncommercial	Personnel	Finance	Production	Marketing	Investment		
United Kingdom									
British Telecom	+	+	+	+	0	0	+	+	12.0
British Airways	(+)	0	(+)	+	0	0	+	+	1.6
National Freight	+	0	+	+	+	0	+	−	4.3
Chile									
CHILGENER	+	0	+	+	0	0	0	+	2.1
ENERSIS	+	0	0	+	+	0	+	+	5.2
CTC	+	0	0	+	+	0	+	+	155.1
Malaysia									
Malaysian Airline Systems	0	0	0	+	0	0	+	0	22.1
Kelang Container Terminal	+	0	+	0	0	0	0	+	53.4
Sports Toto Malaysia	+	0	+	0	+	+	0	+	10.9
Mexico									
Teléfonos de México	+	0	+	+	0	0	+	+	49.5
Aeroméxico	+	0	+	+	+	0	+	+	48.5
Mexicana de Aviación	+	0	0	+	+	0	+	+	−7.0

Notes: Plus (minus) signs indicate increased (decreased) importance of the goal, increased (decreased) autonomy, or increased (decreased) incentives. Signs in parentheses indicate a slight impact.

a. Figures are from table 23-1.

Source: Authors' calculations from enterprise data.

Goal specificity, increased autonomy, and performance-based compensation seem to have contributed to the gains in welfare in all cases where gains were realized, as reflected in the last column of table 23-4. But the source of the change varied from case to case, as can be seen from the first five columns of the table. In the Chilean cases, where the institutional constraints were least binding, X-efficiency hardly improved beyond its historical trend (at ENERSIS), or improved modestly (at CHILGENER and CTC). However, at ENERSIS the drive to maximize profit by the same but better-motivated management led to a significant diversification of output, reduction of losses of electricity from theft, and investment in profitable companies elsewhere. At CHILGENER, management diversified its coal supplies, used them more efficiently, and utilized its port facility to serve third parties. CTC expanded its basic network, diversified its activities into value added services, and aggressively tried to penetrate the market for long distance services.

In the U.K. cases, the greater freedom enjoyed by private managers resulted in an increase in fixed capital in all the divested enterprises and acquisition of other firms in some cases. National Freight and (somewhat less successfully) British Telecom acquired large foreign equity holdings. British Airways merged with its principal domestic rival. British Airways and National Freight also engaged in extensive off-balance sheet financing.

In the Malaysian cases, the experience was diverse. At one extreme, Sports Toto Malaysia moved to pure private ownership with pure profit motives and autonomy. The result was manifested primarily in a surge of innovation, with new products and extensive and creative marketing resulting in a tripling of sales. At the other extreme, very little changed at Malaysian Airline Systems. The airline was reasonably well run to begin with, and no internal changes were identifiable as a result of divestiture. Gains came only from external changes—in the way the government exercised its right to set prices and approve investment decisions. At Kelang Container Terminal, although, like the airline, it was only partially divested, there were dramatic changes in autonomy and incentives and equally dramatic changes in performance, manifested primarily in efficiency gains rather than product differentiation and marketing.

Mexico provides the one case where the greater autonomy accorded to management (at Mexicana) led to a major investment decision that appears to have been a mistake. Both Telmex and Aeroméxico aggressively pursued profit opportunities successfully.

In sum, divestiture can reduce the principal-agent problems associated with public ownership, which in our sample meant greater focus on profit maximization and improved managerial autonomy and incentives. The fact that the gains from divesting a reformed public enterprise are modest means that reforming public enterprises can of itself be beneficial, but even then divestiture can still be beneficial. This proposition is best demonstrated by the Chilean cases.

Regulatory Institutions

Replacing public monopolies with regulated private monopolies rids enterprises of the organizational failure associated with public ownership, but at the same time it gives rise to potential regulatory failure. One reason why regulated firms do not "behave" is that they often capture regulatory agencies and thereby control the regulation they face. Short of capture, the regulated firms obviously exercise pressure and influence on regulatory authorities. For example, when firms are doing poorly financially, as the Mexican airlines were in 1989 and 1990, the pressure for the regulatory authority to loosen its regulation so as to enhance profits naturally becomes quite intense. This is true under public and private ownership alike. However, with private shareholders, the intensity of profit-oriented pressures is considerably greater. It is this feature that explains the hypothesized welfare gains from getting prices "righter" at Malaysian Airline Systems.

Entry and pricing policies aside (they are analyzed above under market determinants of success), regulatory failure may follow from unclear regulatory formulas, lack of conflict resolution mechanisms, and weak institutional capacity to enforce regulations. Under these circumstances, divestiture may mean that buyers will offer the government a discounted price for the enterprise, and, following divestiture, may refrain from investing further, fearing expropriation of quasi rents. Therefore, the effectiveness of the regulatory institutions in enforcing clearly spelled out regulatory rules, as well as the ability of governments to provide a credible commitment to safeguard against expropriation of assets, is critical to the success of divestiture.[25]

Finally, the potential for regulatory failure will vary by industry, mainly because industries differ in such characteristics as speed of technological progress, sunkness and jointness of costs, and interdependence of demands between services. Thus, while credibility of government commitment is critical for the private sector to invest in such asset-specific activities as electricity and telecommunications, this issue is less critical for the airline industry, for example. On the other hand, liberalization and deregulation are critical for the airline industry but are precluded in electricity distribution because of economies of scale.

In general, then, success at divesting monopolies can be traced in part to the effectiveness of regulatory institutions and the credibility of government commitment. In our sample, nine cases fall in just three industries in which regulation plays a major role: telecommunications, airlines, and electric power. Given the importance of the regulatory institutions in the telecommunications and electric power sectors, we take them up first. We then consider the airline industry, focusing on liberalization and deregulation.

THE TELECOMMUNICATIONS AND ELECTRIC POWER SECTORS. The divestitures of the telecommunications enterprises and the electric utilities in our sample enhanced domestic consumer welfare in the United Kingdom and Chile. It hurt consumers in Mexico, but that was because prices were too low to begin with. In addition, divestiture led to significant private investment at British Telecom and at CTC. At Telmex, investment is continuing at a high level, as envisaged in the government's plans. Divestiture did not increase investment in the power sector in Chile beyond its historical trend, because there was no excess demand. Thus, it seems that the three countries were able to pursue reasonable regulatory arrangements, which the private sector perceived to be credible.

What are the main features of the regulatory institutions in the three countries? The following points are noteworthy:

- **Timing of regulation and divestiture**. The United Kingdom created OFTEL (the Office of Telecommunications) and introduced the RPI - X regulation shortly before divestiture. Chile did even better: it introduced its regulatory laws for telecommunications and electricity in 1982. It had already set up the National Commission of Energy (CNE) as an autonomous regulatory agency for electricity in 1978 and created a department in the Ministry of Transport to oversee implementation of telecommunications regulation in 1977, both well before divestiture. In Mexico the Secretariat of Communications and Transport only changed from discretionary price regulation to the RPI - X rule, introducing the latter concurrently with divestiture.
- **Clarity of regulations**. The regulation of the electric power sector in Chile clearly spelled out the basis for tariff formulation, entry, coordination of operation, access to transmission lines and dispatch load centers, and technical standards. The rules have been applied to all enterprises in the sector, irrespective of ownership. On the regulatory rules in telecommunications, all three countries provided clearly stated tariff formulas and conditions for entry and exit. Mexico's tariff formulas were actually modeled after the United Kingdom's RPI - X formula.
- **Conflict resolution mechanisms and arbitration**. The United Kingdom and Chile provided clear procedures for settling regulatory disputes. In Chile disputes over telecommunications tariffs are settled by a three-person arbitration committee: a neutral party plus one representative of each of the two sides. In Mexico the situation is still too new to be evaluated.

- **Capacity of regulatory institutions**. The United Kingdom and Chile had already accumulated some experience in regulating private monopolies before the enterprises in our sample were divested. Also, Chile empowered the CNE board with ministerial-level members and staffed it with qualified personnel. Although it is working strenuously to rectify the situation, the Mexican secretariat of communications still lacks this kind of expertise and therefore may be at a disadvantage when it comes to negotiations with Telmex.

How did these institutional changes affect divestiture outcomes? To summarize, we find in the telecommunications sector in Chile that the combination of marginal cost pricing, competition where possible, and clear conflict resolution mechanisms provided the private sector the confidence necessary to double capacity in a relatively short period of time. In the electric power sector, the effective institutional framework has similarly contributed to the reliable provision of electricity at reasonable cost to consumers. The savings from reduced losses to theft, although temporarily internalized by the distribution companies, are likely to be transmitted to consumers the next time tariffs are revised.

In the United Kingdom, OFTEL has been able to restrain British Telecom from exploiting consumers and has put pressure on the company to be more efficient. The X in the *RPI* - X formula was increased from 3 percent to 4.5 percent in 1989 and again to 6.25 percent in 1991, but the latter now includes international calls. The position of director general of OFTEL has become politically highly visible as that of an advocate for consumer protection and competition.

The Mexican experience has been too short to demonstrate the functioning of its regulatory institutions in the resolution of conflicts. However, the reduction in domestic consumer welfare we found is entirely due to the government's choice for a tax-cum-price change at the time of the divestiture of Telmex. This change brought most of Telmex's prices in line with international levels. Connection charges were increased to an extent that clearly has reduced nonprice rationing and boosted Telmex's ability to finance future expansion. All these changes, however, are not the result of ongoing regulation within the new institutional structure. It should also be mentioned that the regulations applicable to Telmex call for stringent and specific targets on network expansion and on quality, thereby preempting any backsliding on these counts.

In sum, we observe no regulatory capture in any of our cases. Rather, we observe significant investment by the private sector in such an asset-specific sector as telecommunications. This massive investment reflects not only the private sector's commitment to the sector, but also the credibility of regulatory contracts in all three countries.

Summary

Our attempt to explore causality between the welfare effect of divestiture and its institutional determinants suggests that:
- Divestiture generally reduces political and bureaucratic intervention, promotes profit-maximizing behavior, enhances managerial autonomy, and improves motivation through incentives.
- Combined with effective and credible regulatory institutions, divestiture can improve welfare even in noncompetitive markets.
- Where divestiture leads to the first but not the second, its welfare impact can be negative.

Country Determinants of Success

Might some of the factors leading to successful divestiture be country specific? In the language of statistical regression analysis, might country dummy variables be significant in explaining the size of the welfare change associated with divestiture? This is the question we address next, focusing on economic factors.[26]

Level of Development

We begin by considering whether the level of development of a country might have any impact on the success of divestiture. Our starting point is that the success of divestiture requires (among other things) that market failures associated with private ownership be in some sense smaller or more controllable than the organizational failures associated with public ownership. Here it could be argued that market failures are likely to be smaller in more industrial countries, which would suggest more successful divestitures there. One relevant argument, which has been made elsewhere (Jones, Tandon, and Vogelsang 1990, chapter 9), is that a key factor explaining divestiture is the changing relationship between market size and cost structure. To illustrate the idea in a very simple way, suppose the demand for a particular good is 100 units and the plant size at which the cost of producing it is minimized is 90 units. In such a case, competition is unlikely to emerge, and, indeed, if it did it might not be desirable. There would be a case for public intervention. If, over time, demand expands to 500 units and the minimum efficient scale simultaneously falls to 50 units, the case for public intervention disappears and a market solution becomes desirable. In such cases divestiture would be successful. Thus the larger the market (compared with minimum efficient scale), the more likely it is that divestiture will have a positive welfare effect. Although this set of factors is heavily dependent on the industry under consideration, it does suggest that divestiture is also likely to have a positive effect in larger and wealthier economies.

On the other hand, it could be argued that organizational failures might be smaller in industrial countries as well. Industrial countries typically possess better-educated populations, among them people with substantial managerial experience, than do developing countries. This would then suggest that public enterprises in industrial countries would be relatively well managed, which would mean less impact from divestiture. On balance, therefore, in an industrial (developing) country context, the outcome of divestiture would depend on the relative weight of modest (large) gains from removing the organizational failure of public ownership and modest (large) losses from correcting market failures. The relative magnitude of the net effects in both instances is difficult to predict. It hinges on which type of failure, market or organizational, declines more rapidly in the process of development, which is difficult to ascertain.

All three of the U.K. cases in our sample exhibited positive welfare changes, as did all the cases in Chile and Malaysia. The one negative welfare change is seen in Mexico (Mexicana). Therefore there is no discernible pattern in our sample as to the sign of welfare change and the level of development. On the other hand, it bears emphasizing that the changes in welfare seem smaller in the U.K. cases than in those of Malaysia and Mexico. The Chilean cases fall closer to the U.K. cases, largely because of the significant public-enterprise reforms undertaken prior to divestiture. This suggests that the magnitude of the welfare gains can be more substantial in developing economies, especially where public enterprises are not reformed. Note finally that divestiture outcomes are more varied within each of our developing countries than in the U.K. cases. This suggests that in developing countries it matters even more how each sale is concluded.

These conclusions have to be extrapolated with caution to other countries. And nowhere does this cautionary note apply more than to the very poor countries of the world, which are at a different level of development than any in our sample and therefore lack some of the institutions and markets our sample countries possess. The same point applies to the former socialist countries, whose standards of living are comparable to those of our sample countries, but which almost completely lack private sector institutions and the kind of market mechanisms taken for granted in mixed economies. In both these groups of countries, the experience with divestiture could well be quite different from what we have observed in this study.

Fiscal Stringency

Obviously a major driving force behind divestiture in many countries has been fiscal stringency. The first effect of such stringency might be to "force" or catalyze divestiture in the first place. This seems, for example, to have been one of the primary forces behind the divestiture program in Mexico. Divestiture can ease fiscal crises in several ways. At a minimum, the government can rid itself of enterprises whose borrowing needs worsen the public deficit (British Telecom, for example).[27] The sale proceeds themselves can also play a role in reducing the short-run deficit. Finally, if the problem of external debt is particularly severe, the sale of public enterprises in part to foreigners can be viewed as a way to earn foreign currency.

Given that fiscal stringency may play a role in "causing" divestiture, the question is, Does the fact that enterprises were sold in an atmosphere of stringency affect the outcome? There are two important ways in which these fiscal considerations can and do affect divestiture outcomes. First, where the fiscal constraint is truly binding (British Telecom, Malaysian Airline Systems, CTC, Mexicana), one of the primary effects of divestiture is to permit a rapid increase in investment, which generally—Mexicana being the one exception—leads to a substantial welfare improvement. Thus divestiture seems to pay off in the presence of fiscal stringency in cases where large investments are desirable.

Second, where there is a serious external debt problem and the enterprise is sold at least in part to foreigners (Telmex, the Mexican airlines, Kelang Container Terminal) to obtain foreign exchange, substantial benefits leak out of the country, given that buyers generally do well from divestiture (recall table 23-1). The key is for the government to ensure that the overall gains outweigh these leakages so that the domestic economy nevertheless gains.

The Business Cycle

Is the success of divestiture at all dependent upon the point in the business cycle at which it was effected? To some extent the effect of the business cycle is bound up with the level of fiscal stringency: if the economy is in a trough, the fiscal situation is more likely to be strained. But are there any other effects of the business cycle on divestiture outcomes? There are two points to be noted.

First, it is natural to expect more divestitures to occur after than during a recession because of the reduced uncertainty about the private profitability of the enterprise. For example, the U.K. government was unable to sell British Airways at the height of the recession in the early 1980s. On the face of it, this would tend to make divestitures that did occur at such times look rather successful, because the years after divestiture would correspond with upswings in the economy, whereas the last years of public ownership would be periods of recession. However, our methodology corrects for this potential problem. Because we compare the performance of the divested enterprise with the counterfactual performance of the same enterprise had it not been divested, the pure effects of the business cycle are conceptually eliminated. Thus, for example, both Mexican airlines were divested just before a difficult time for the airline industry, but this by itself did not adversely affect our estimate of their performance.

Second, to the extent that divestitures do occur during recessions, we might expect that the sale price would be depressed. The ratio of the realized sale price to our calculated value (V_{pp}) ought to be low for these cases. Indeed, National Freight was sold at an unfavorable time, and the U.K. government received a low price. Similarly, the Mexican government sold Mexicana and Aeroméxico while the economy was still early in the recovery phase and received disappointingly low bids for the enterprises.

The Policy Environment

Yet another important country characteristic is the policy environment in which divestiture is carried out, including the way in which divestiture policy itself is designed and executed. The first point is explored below under "Sale Structure," but a general argument can be made that when governments liberalize their markets (domestic and foreign) and generally pursue sound macroeconomic management, divested and undivested enterprises alike face greater pressure to operate more efficiently. Conversely, where governments follow restrictive and unsound macroeconomic policies, all enterprises are likely to capitalize on market distortions by engaging in rent-seeking activities, possibly reducing welfare. The issue is whether our sample can tell us something about this.

All the countries in our sample were, in this regard, "institutionally strong." We have not uncovered cases involving egregious policy mistakes. On the contrary, a number of potential problems were avoided because of preemptive actions taken by the government. For example, the introduction of appropriate regulation in monopoly industries effectively eliminated excessive market power where it threatened to be a problem in our cases. Labor opposition to divestiture was deflected by choosing largely capital-intensive enterprises for divestiture and by including labor in the ranks of gainers by offering workers shares and other benefits. In these and other ways, our sample countries have managed to contain potential problems, and this is naturally reflected in largely positive outcomes. The extension of these kinds of results to other countries will depend at least to some extent on their ability to anticipate and clear potential roadblocks to successful divestiture.

Summary

In general, country characteristics exhibit little variance in our sample and hence play a limited role in our verbal regression. However:

- Divestiture is associated with positive changes in welfare in the one industrial country (the United Kingdom) and the three developing countries (Mexico, Malaysia, and Chile) in our sample, which suggests that gains are possible across countries at different levels of development.
- The gains are relatively modest in the U.K. and Chilean cases (when CTC is excluded). This suggests that the potential gains from divestiture can be more substantial in developing economies with unreformed public enterprises, but that remains an open question.
- Divestiture outcomes in the U.K. cases varied less than those of Chile, Mexico, and Malaysia. This suggests that countries at earlier stages of development can influence divestiture outcomes significantly.
- Finally, caution must be exercised in extrapolating our results to very poor countries, which lack some of the institutions and markets our sample countries possess. The same caution applies to the former socialist countries, which do have levels of living comparable to our sample but almost completely lack private sector institutions and the kind of market mechanisms taken for granted in mixed economies. In both instances, divestiture outcomes may differ from those found here.

Sale Structure

We now turn to our final set of determinants of divestiture outcomes, namely, those relating to the way in which the sale itself was conducted. This includes such policy choices as the following. Should the government relinquish ownership and/or control? Should it invest in enterprises prior to selling them? How should the government sell the enterprise? To whom should it sell it? How long should the process take?

Our starting point is that the sale structure itself could enlarge or shrink the welfare pie and determine the winners and losers. For example, some authors (e.g., Kikeri, Nellis, and Shirley 1992) have hypothesized that divestiture enhances welfare more when the deal entails no special exemptions; when the government relinquishes control to the private sector (or exercises control better); when only appropriate prior restructuring is undertaken; when the process is conducted in a timely and transparent fashion; and when foreign participation is carefully handled. Do our findings support these assertions? In terms of our verbal regression, this is equivalent to asking whether the sale structure achieves significance as an independent variable.

Ownership versus Control

The argument for selling a majority holding in a public enterprise is that the government thereby relinquishes control, thus setting in train the behavioral changes expected of private sector ownership and relaxing the constraints associated with public ownership. If this is so, it follows that the sale of a minority holding would be cosmetic, inducing no behavioral change and no aggregate welfare impact—a merely financial exchange. The counterargument is that it is entirely possible for the government to transfer effective control without selling a majority of its shares; conversely, it may retain effective control even after it has sold a majority of its stake; and it may exercise control differently even if it has only sold a minority of its holding to the private sector. Therefore, there is no one-to-one relationship between ownership and control. Accordingly, we expect that ownership changes alone primarily affect the distribution of welfare changes, while it is change in control that affects the level of any welfare increment—often the two change together, but they may not.

To explore these issues, table 23-5 profiles how ownership and control changed in the wake of divestiture in our sample:

- In ten of the twelve cases analyzed, governments relinquished more than 50 percent of the shares in the enterprises—the two exceptions were Malaysian Airline Systems and Kelang Container Terminal. In all ten cases, the government also relinquished control, albeit with some variations in implementation.[28] Here ownership and control work together.
- In the other two cases, the government relinquished ownership but retained control. In the case of Malaysian Airline Systems, the government retained more than 50 percent of the shares and thus retained direct control of the enterprise. In the case of Kelang Container Terminal, the government sold 100 percent of the shares, but 90 percent went to other public enterprises; thus the government effectively retained indirect control.[29]

How do these configurations relate to divestiture outcomes? In eight of the ten cases where governments relinquished both ownership and control, domestic welfare improved. However, our findings also suggest:

- That the divestiture of a majority holding and relinquishing of control do not constitute sufficient conditions for domestic welfare to improve; other determinants of success matter. This is evident from the case of Mexicana.
- Even the sale of a minority holding or of a majority holding to other public entities can be beneficial to society. This is evident from the cases of Malaysian Airline Systems and Kelang Container Terminal.

How may the second set of results be explained? In the case of Malaysian Airline Systems, the sale of 48 percent of the enterprise to the private sector led to no identifiable change of behavior. However, it changed the

Table 23-5. *Features of the Divestiture Process in the Twelve Case Studies*

Country and enterprise	Prior restructuring[a]	Method of sale[b] Stock market — Market price	Method of sale[b] Stock market — Initial public offering	Bids	Direct sale	Duration of sale (months)	Government	Public enterprises	Domestic Diverse	Domestic Concentrated[c]	Employees	Foreigners	Control after divestiture
United Kingdom													
British Telecom	Le, F	No	Yes	No	+	28	49[d]	0	33	0	3	14	Pr
British Airways	Le, L, M	No	Yes	No	+	93	0	0	74	0	10	16	Pr
National Freight	Le, F	No	No	No	Yes	33	0	0	0	18	83	0	Pr
Chile													
CHILGENER	No	Yes	No	No	+	30	0	0	28	26	5	41	Pr
ENERSIS	No	Yes	No	No	+	26	0	0	34	30	27	10	Pr
CTC	No	+	No	Yes	+	44	0	0	26	12	3	59	Pr
Malaysia													
Malaysian Airline Systems	N	+	Yes	No	No	24	52	10	15	0	5	18	G
Kelang Container Terminal	Le	No	No	+	Yes	28	0	90	0	10	0	10	PE
Sports Toto Malaysia	–F[e]	No	No	No	Yes	18	0	0	0	100	0	0	Pr
Mexico													
Teléfonos de México	F	+	No	Yes	+	15	10	0	24	10	4	56	Pr
Aeroméxico	I, Le	No	No	Yes	+	6	0	0	0	80	20	0	Pr
Mexicana de Aviación	Le	No	No	Yes	No	36	40	0	35	13	0	12	Pr

Note: P, physical; L, labor; Le, legal; M, managerial; F, financial; N, none; Pr, private; G, government; PE, other public entities.

a. Between the sale announcement and consummation of the deal.

b. A "Yes" refers to the predominant method of sale, a "+" refers to secondary methods, and a "No" indicates that that method was not used.

c. Concentrated domestic shareholders have 51 percent or more of the voting stock.

d. Further sale of shares in November 1991 reduced the government's share to 21.8 percent.

e. Negative financial restructuring; the government took retained earnings out of the enterprise prior to sale.

Source: Authors' calculations from enterprise data.

way the government exercised its control over the enterprise, the effect of which was to relax the external investment and price constraints. In the case of Kelang Container Terminal, indirect control meant that the government *could* intervene as before, but that power was exercised very much as a private owner would exercise it, resulting in a desirable change in goals, autonomy, and incentives.

More generally, the correlation between the sale of a majority state holding and domestic welfare improvement lends support to the hypothesis that the benefits from divestiture are likely to materialize under such conditions. However, our results warn against believing that such action is necessary or sufficient to make divestiture welfare enhancing. Other determinants of success (discussed in previous sections) are as important if not more important. In addition, partial divestiture and the sale of enterprises to other public entities can be more than cosmetic changes; these transactions can alter the attitude of the government toward the enterprise, with attendant positive effects on welfare.

Prior Restructuring

It is widely believed that physical, labor, financial, managerial, or legal restructuring of a public enterprise before selling it enhances government revenue and increases salability.[30] Our view is that physical restructuring is likely to be a wash at best, and at worst may reduce government revenue. However, other types of restructuring may be necessary for practical rather than theoretical reasons, to facilitate sale. We elaborate on both arguments below.

The case for major physical restructuring rests on the grounds that buyers are then likely to offer a price that more than covers the incremental investment. However, given that governments have proved to be less than perfect investment decisionmakers in the past, it is entirely possible—if not likely—that buyers may offer a price that is less than the cost of physical restructuring.

The case for other types of restructuring is more persuasive. Labor restructuring can ease the social cost of divestiture and may reduce labor opposition. Coupled with managerial restructuring, it may improve the efficiency and competitiveness of the enterprise now and ready it for sale sooner.[31] Legal restructuring may be necessary to permit the sale of the enterprise or make managerial and labor restructuring possible (imagine even the most dynamic chief executive trying to fire workers in a departmental enterprise, where workers are guaranteed their jobs by law). Cleaning up the balance sheet (i.e., adjusting the debt-equity ratio and settling arrears) may be desirable, especially where it involves a mere cancellation of mutual debts between the government and public enterprises or among enterprises.[32]

Our cases seem to support the above views. Table 23-5 reveals the following patterns:

- In none of our cases was physical restructuring undertaken prior to divestiture. On the contrary, in selling the telephone enterprises in Chile and Mexico, the two governments explicitly left that task to the new owners, insisting that they commit themselves to massive investment programs to meet pending demand.
- Only sporadically did we observe instances of legal, labor, or financial restructuring. This point is illustrated by a few examples below.

Legal restructuring was common to all three of our U.K. enterprises, dictated by the fact that public enterprises had to be made limited companies before they could be sold. In Malaysia, the government had to change the legal status of the Kelang Container Terminal before selling it, because the terminal was part of a larger public enterprise.

As for labor restructuring, the case of Aeroméxico provides the most dramatic example. Facing a massive strike as the government was preparing to divest the enterprise, the government chose to declare it bankrupt, liquidated it, and then sold its assets. Thus, the new owners of Aeroméxico were free to hire whomever they chose, which turned out to be a fraction of the previous work force. At the end of 1987 Aeroméxico had 12,524 workers; at the end of 1988 there were only 3,752 (the number rebounded to 6,321 at the end of 1991). But Aeroméxico is not the only case. Labor and managerial restructuring took place at British Airways, following the appointment of Sir John King. Even though the Chilean enterprises underwent no restructuring of any kind immediately before divestiture, there was in the 1970s and early 1980s a major restructuring of all public enterprises, including those in our sample.

Finally, the only case of financial restructuring in our sample is that of Sports Toto Malaysia, which is quite unusual. Rather than putting in money, the government actually extracted some of the enterprise's accumulated retained earnings before selling it.

In sum, in our sample, major investment by the government prior to divestiture played no role in improving divestiture outcomes. Instead, where there was an important demand gap, governments insisted that buyers bring in fresh capital to finance needed expansion, and this expansion brought about significant positive welfare effects. Our cases also suggest that some legal, labor, and managerial restructuring can be useful if it speeds up the process of reform, reduces the social cost of divestiture, and improves the efficiency of public enterprises in the interim.

Methods of Sale and Buyers

How the enterprise is sold and to whom may or may not affect the change in welfare and its distribution. On the distribution front, selling the enterprise on perfectly developed stock markets or through transparent public bids with no concessions and perfect information should not affect the initial distribution of wealth. Where these conditions are not present, however, an imperfect sale structure can have a deleterious impact, for example by leaking national wealth abroad to such an extent that nationals are worse off.

What about the welfare increment? Here the key points are whether or not the divestiture process leaves the enterprise with a buyer (or a small group of buyers) whose stake in the enterprise is high enough to worry about the outcome, and whether the buyers have the capacity and motivation to change the enterprise. A subsidiary issue is whether selling enterprises to workers improves welfare or not.

In table 23-5 we summarize the methods of sale employed and the buyers of the enterprises in our sample. We find that:

- The United Kingdom and Chile combined various methods of sale, even for a single enterprise; these methods included stock market flotation, bidding, and direct sale to workers. Mexico relied largely on bidding, even though Telmex and Mexicana were already quoted on the Mexican stock market. Malaysia relied on direct placement and the stock market. Thus our countries concluded the deals using whatever vehicles were available.
- The United Kingdom and Malaysia fixed the price of their initial public offerings. In Chile that was not necessary because the shares of the divested enterprises were already being traded on the stock market.
- Mexico, Chile, and the United Kingdom allowed foreign participation in public bids for their telecommunications enterprises, primarily because these enterprises were large relative to domestic capital markets. In addition, foreign participation, together with share dispersion, may have been intended to reduce the probability of renationalization.
- Workers gained a significant share in the equity of National Freight in the United Kingdom, ENERSIS in Chile, and Aeroméxico (where the pilots' union acquired a 20 percent stake), sometimes at an explicit or implicit discount.[33] In most of the remaining cases workers purchased relatively modest percentages of the shares, ranging between 3 percent and 10 percent.
- Foreigners acquired a significant percentage of the shares in the majority of our cases in Mexico and Chile, but not in the United Kingdom or Malaysia. In the United Kingdom domestic savings were

probably high enough to absorb the sale of large enterprises. But in Malaysia sensitivity to foreign participation may have played a role.
• Finally, no case in our sample involved a divestiture transaction in which ownership was fully dispersed with no controlling interest.

Can these patterns explain some of the findings reported in table 23-1? With the customary caution that the sample is limited, we note the following:

• No correlation seems to exist between the method of sale and the distribution of welfare gains between nationals and foreigners. For example, public bids were used in selling both Telmex in Mexico and CTC in Chile, but domestic welfare improved more in Chile than in Mexico.
• Nor does selling the shares in the stock market seem to guarantee that the fiscal effect of divestiture will be positive. The two electricity enterprises in Chile (CHILGENER and ENERSIS) are examples.
• Finally, no correlation seems to exist between the change in welfare and the nature of the buyers. In fact, in the two cases (National Freight and ENERSIS) where workers gained significant shares, welfare also improved.

Duration of the Sale

Finally, does the duration of the sale transaction make a difference in the price received, and ultimately in the net fiscal impact of divestiture (defined as the sum of the sale price and taxes under private operation minus the dividends and taxes that would have accrued to the government had it kept the enterprise publicly owned)? A priori, the answers to both questions are less than obvious. On the one hand, if the government expects share prices to go up over time at a rate greater than its discount rate, it would pay off to sell gradually. On the other hand, if share prices are expected to go down because the government is dragging its feet, the treasury would be better off selling the enterprise in one shot.

We plotted duration of sale against net fiscal impact for our sample and found only a weak correlation. This result lends support to the idea that the duration of sale is not the most critical factor in determining the sale price or in determining the fiscal impact of divestiture. Rather, the sale price depends, perhaps to a larger extent, on buyers' perceptions of the enterprise's potential and their expectations of future government policies: price regulation, the trade regime, labor policies, corporate taxes, and so on. In addition, the fiscal impact of divestiture depends critically on the difference in profitability between private and continued public operation.

Summary

Sale structure can enhance welfare under several circumstances:

- If the government relinquishes control to the private sector—which is not necessarily equivalent to selling more than 50 percent of the shares
- Or if it retains control but exercises it better (for example, regarding pricing and investment), which could follow from partial divestiture
- If the government agrees with the buyers to invest to meet an existing demand gap, provided it has established a reasonable regulatory framework if the enterprise is a monopoly
- And, if the sale is concluded, irrespective of the method, given that the latter depends on the size of the enterprise relative to domestic capital market, and on the state of development of the capital market.

Prediction versus Prescription

What can we conclude from this discussion of case results and their causation? The most important conclusion is that ownership matters. It has implications for the size of the welfare pie and for its distribution. In our cases taken as a whole, divestiture overwhelmingly enhanced domestic and world welfare.

The second main conclusion involves bad news and good news. The bad news is that we cannot use the fact that our cases were on balance overwhelmingly successful to *predict* comparable success elsewhere. Success was caused, not by the simple act of divestiture alone, but by divestiture in combination with a set of intelligent accompanying policies, most notably regulation and sale conditions. The governments of the countries in the sample were generally doing a lot of things right in the economic arena and were divesting into relatively well developed markets. Where conditions are not comparable, results may differ.

The good news comes from the fact that considerable gains are possible when accompanied by good policy. This means that the case experiences can be used to *prescribe* measures for attaining equivalent or superior success elsewhere. It is to this topic we turn in the concluding chapter.

Notes

1. To allow comparisons of these gains across enterprises and countries, we need to calculate a ratio of welfare change to some measure of the size of the firm. As a measure of size we take annual sales in the last year prior to divestiture. This, however, is a single year's flow, whereas our net welfare change is a stock—the present value of multiple years' flows. To aid comparison, we therefore convert the stock to an equivalent flow—the annual component of a perpe-

tuity with an equivalent present value. For example, if the net welfare change were 1,000, computed using a real discount rate of 10 percent, then its perpetuity equivalent would be 100, because, at that discount rate, an annual flow of that magnitude forever also has a present value of 1,000.

2. This is true, at least, at the level of aggregation we used to report our results. Further disaggregation yields greater variance: for example, consumers as a whole may win, but some subsets of consumers may lose, or all may gain over the long haul while losing in some subperiods.

3. Kelang Container Terminal also shows a loss to competitors, but this was primarily at the expense of conventional cargo at Kelang Port Authority, and was more than offset by the port's gains as a recipient of dividends and rent.

4. These companies improved management in the adaptive sense of adjusting to the smaller work force, but it is difficult to show major independent improvements.

5. This generalization, as with several others in this broad-brush overview, will need to be modified when we look at individual markets. For example, at British Telecom, connection charges and monthly rentals increased in real terms, while long distance calls became substantially cheaper.

6. For another case where macroeconomic effects were central see Abdala (1992).

7. As measured by the sum of investment, output, and 80 percent of the productivity price columns over the sum of all the columns, excluding interaction effects.

8. One possible perverse outcome is the Averch-Johnson effect, according to which a profit-maximizing monopolist subject to rate-of-return regulation will adopt an excessively capital-intensive technology because this investment will expand its rate base. For more details see Averch and Johnson (1962), Wellisz (1963), and Kahn (1988).

9. This is defined as the weighted average of market shares for each commodity the firm produces, the weights being the revenue shares, measured at the time of divestiture.

10. A similar worsening of consumer welfare is being seen in the Argentine telephone company ENTel (Abdala 1992).

11. For example, see Caves and others (1982). For a survey see Borcherding and others (1982). For theoretical arguments see DeAlessi (1982), Borcherding (1983), and Vickers and Yarrow (1988). For empirical evidence see Boardman and Vining (1989) and Millward and Parker (1983).

12. In empirical work on U.S. routes served by two airlines, Brander and Zhang (1990) find prices to conform roughly to Cournot levels, suggesting again that we might expect Mexico's airfares to rise.

13. For further details see Symposium on Price-Cap Regulation (1989).

14. The institutional side of regulation, with some emphasis on the issue of regulatory capture, is further discussed below.

15. An example is provided by Scooters, India Ltd., a public sector motor scooter manufacturer. A buyer had been found for the enterprise, but opposition from the labor unions scared him off and the deal was never consummated.

16. For example, labor costs constitute about 80 percent of the operating cost of Mexico's state-owned railroad, Ferrocarriles Nacionales de México, and there has been little talk of divesting that enterprise.

17. ENTel Argentina displayed a similar situation (Abdala 1992).

18. Note that the figure of 41 percent for Telmex is actually too high for the analysis here because it includes the effect of the second tranche sale. If we take the ratio of the sale price at the divestiture sale of December 1990 to V_{pp}, we get a figure of 31 percent.

19. Well after the case study had been written, the Xabre group in fact acquired control of 50 percent of Mexicana in September 1992, through purchases on the stock market and a further purchase from the government's shareholding.

20. For example, the Deutsche Bundespost is claimed to have paid substantially higher than world market prices to the domestic suppliers of telecommunications equipment.

21. These problems are discussed in detail elsewhere. To cite but a few examples, see Aharoni (1990), Jones and Vogelsang (1983), Shirley and Nellis (1991), and Galal (1991).

22. In the years following the 1978 White Paper, attention in the United Kingdom has shifted to divestiture, overshadowing the performance of enterprises that were not divested. Interestingly, nondivested enterprises have improved their productivity significantly, especially since 1982. But these improvements may have been helped by the government's emphasis on financial constraints and cost savings plus its willingness to back labor force reductions if deemed necessary.

23. To be sure, non-profit-maximizing behavior on the part of management can arise in large public and private corporations alike. However, the management of a public enterprise has fewer incentives and faces greater constraints on maximizing profit.

24. At ENERSIS, top management remained the same, but they are now part owners of the company. In Mexico, ironically, the general director (the chief executive officer) of Mexicana appointed in March 1991 is a well-known ex-public figure, the former head of the government social welfare agency.

25. The underpinning of a government's capacity to write and enforce credible regulatory contracts in telecommunications is currently being explored in a World Bank research project covering five countries: Chile, the United Kingdom, Jamaica, the Philippines, and Argentina. For further details see Spiller (1991).

26. We take as exogenous what Davis and North call "the set of fundamental political, social, and legal ground rules that establishes the basis for production, exchange, and distribution (in a society)" (1971, p. 6).

27. British Telecom was an interesting case in that, just prior to divestiture, it won approval to raise money in the bond market despite the public sector borrowing requirement restrictions. Nevertheless, it had been constrained prior to that time and, in fact, never issued the so-called Buzby bonds because divestiture rendered them unnecessary.

28. In the British Telecom case, the government reserved a "golden share" and veto power over certain decisions, such as whether to allow a foreign takeover. In the case of Telmex, the government created two classes of stock: voting (40 percent) and nonvoting (60 percent). It then sold 51 percent of the voting stock (20.4 percent of the enterprise) to the controlling shareholders—a consortium of investors led by a leading Mexican businessman and including Southwestern Bell and France Télécom. In the case of Mexicana, the controlling shareholders acquired only 25 percent of the stock, but the government placed an additional block of shares in a trust voted by the controlling shareholders, thereby guaranteeing them control over the company.

29. The limited number of divestiture cases in our sample where government retained a majority holding is no accident. Since we were interested in measuring

the effect of the change of ownership on welfare, we deliberately selected our sample from a set of cases in which governments relinquished majority holdings. In the Malaysian cases the choice was dictated by the absence of such cases, which we did not mind because we also wanted to explore the very issue now being addressed.

30. By physical restructuring we mean the rehabilitation or replacement of capital; by labor restructuring optimization of the labor-capital ratio; by financial restructuring the removal from the balance sheet of excessive debt and arrears; by managerial restructuring the replacement of top management; and by legal restructuring changes in corporate form. Some authors include competition policy under restructuring, but we treat this as a change in the market environment, and here we only consider changes internal to the enterprise. Restructuring of enterprises in the sense of splitting them into smaller units, allowing entry, and so forth, before selling them, to create more competitive markets, was discussed above.

31. In Lawrence H. Summers' terminology, this is equivalent to evicting the tenant before selling your apartment.

32. The main issue for government is the fiscal cost of labor and financial restructuring. But this is essentially an intertemporal problem, which needs to be addressed anyway.

33. For example, in the case of Telmex, the government arranged a loan for workers of US$325 million for their 4.4 percent share and is holding the shares in a trust until the loan is paid off. In contrast, workers in Chile were only allowed in most cases to use their legal severance payments in advance to purchase shares.

24. *Policy Summary*

The fundamental goal of this book has been to contribute to the divestiture debate by presenting and analyzing the evidence from comprehensive empirical case studies. That task is complete. The remaining task is to integrate whatever knowledge has been generated into concrete policy recommendations. Many readers will judiciously decide to quit reading at this point, for either of two quite different reasons:

- This chapter adds no further research or analysis. What is added is opinion—informed, we hope, but opinion nonetheless—to fill in the gaps in existing research. There is nothing left to learn for those whose interest is limited to that which can be demonstrated, or at least argued, with some attempt at rigor.
- Others will recognize that policy must be made today, regardless of the state of research. Those readers with practical real-world experience may well conclude that they rather than we have comparative advantage in drawing policy conclusions from the evidence we have presented.

For what it is worth, however, we offer our own synthesis of fact, theory, intuition, and wishful thinking. We warn the reader that in the process we take off our policy-oriented research hats and put on our policy adviser hats, with an attendant diminution of confidence in our assertions. Our suggestions have at least the merit of being largely derived from empirical observation; that is, they are arrived at inductively, using a bottom-up approach.

Goals and Motivations

To provide a framework for this policy discussion, let us assume that a mixed-economy developing country is considering including public-enterprise divestitures in an economic reform package and has asked us for guidance based on international experience (again, we do not

presume to extend our results to the former centrally planned economies, where the problem is to create a market to divest into). In formulating our response, we understand that:

- The goal is enhanced domestic economic welfare. Many pressing
economic goals—such as responding to a fiscal crisis, if one exists—
are subsumed here, but the achievement of one target must be
balanced against costs imposed elsewhere. Further, foreigners are
not part of the relevant constituency; their interests must be considered, but they are a means rather than an end. Finally, political
considerations are not our specialty, but we trust that domestic
economic gains, if dramatic, will enhance political goals, however
defined.

How dramatic are the gains that might reasonably be expected?
This depends in large part on how much room there is for improvement. If the country's public enterprises are run as well as Singapore
Airlines, the Republic of Korea's Po Hang Iron and Steel, or other
world-class public enterprises, then the potential gains are small.
However, for a typical developing country, international experience
suggests that:

- *If wisely implemented,* divestiture is perfectly capable of producing
annual welfare gains in the vicinity of 5 to 10 percent of predivestiture
annual sales,[1] or a return whose present value is equivalent to 50 to
100 percent of sales (discounting at 10 percent).
- In a typical developing country the public-enterprise sector generates about 10 percent of GDP, and annual sales are 2.5 times that. If half
the sector were to be divested, the annual gains would amount to
something like 1 percent of GDP.[2] This is a small percentage, but of a
large number, which produces substantial absolute gains, as can be
seen by multiplying nearly any country's GDP by 0.01. Alternatively,
in a typical developing country it would be equivalent to 7.6 percent
of government consumption.[3] Note that these are annual gains that
will accrue year after year, so that one may arrive at the present value
of the stream of these annual returns by multiplying each of the above
figures by 10.
- Additional economic benefits might follow from unleashed private
entrepreneurial activity, accelerated capital market development, better use of scarce administrative resources, heightened productivity on
the part of remaining public-enterprise managers and workers chas-
tised by the divestiture of their peers, and other indirect effects. These
atmospheric effects are clearly potentially important, but to our
knowledge they are nowhere substantiated by empirical work.

If these benefits are sufficiently large to warrant expenditure of the scarce time and political capital of decisionmakers, then what must be done to achieve them? Alas:

- There is no simple, internationally applicable recipe for divestiture. What *should* be done will vary with the country's economic circumstances as summarized in the relative development of market forces, the civil service, and the capitalist-managerial class. What *can* be done is further constrained by sociopolitical circumstances, including the strength of the government and the prevailing attitude toward capitalism in the society.

Accordingly, in what follows we do not provide a single set of recommendations. Rather, we identify a series of decisions to be made and the factors that influence each.

What Is to be Sold?

Logically, the first decision is what to sell:

- Divestiture "triage" is the act of trifurcating the public-enterprise sector into those enterprises that will be allowed to die, those that will be divested, and those that will be retained in the public sector. Done exhaustively, this requires answers to all the subsequent questions and will consume a year or more of time and a lot of consultant resources.[4] If the government's needs include deferring pressure from international lending agencies, then such a study might be a first priority. If, on the other hand, it wishes to proceed expeditiously, then it should form a committee whose initial assignment is to identify within a few weeks a selection of enterprises that clearly belong in the second category. A comprehensive study can be commissioned at the same time to thresh out difficult boundary cases.

A category of enterprises whose selection for divestiture should be virtually automatic consists of those whose presence in the public sector has no economic justification whatsoever. For example:

- Competitive enterprises that are small relative to *both* their product and their factor markets should be among the first to be sold. Because they are small relative to domestic sales (including imports), there is no danger of their exploiting market power, and the difficult problems of postdivestiture regulation are avoided. Because they are small relative to the factor market, competitive bidding is feasible and the difficult problems of price setting and negotiation are avoidable.

Because they are small in absolute size, rapid changes in performance are possible.

This was the strategy followed in Mexico, where hundreds of enterprises in competitive sectors such as hotels, auto parts, and textiles were sold early in the divestiture program.

As usual, however, the scope for taking the easy way out is limited. Although the number of such enterprises is likely to be large, their aggregate contribution to GDP will necessarily be small, and even large percentage gains are unlikely to produce a noticeable impact on the overall growth rate of the economy. Further, it may be deemed politically desirable to establish the credibility of the program by selling one or more highly visible enterprises. Accordingly, many governments may wish to include some larger noncompetitive enterprises in the initial set. How are they to be selected?

- It is tempting to sell the best-run enterprises first, because they are seen to be the easiest to find buyers for. This makes political sense if the goal is to get started quickly and show that the government is serious about the program. Economically, however, these enterprises are a lower priority because the potential gains are smaller where the enterprise is already relatively well run. If a government does decide to sell such a cash cow, it should be careful to appropriate a substantial share of the returns, through mechanisms described later.[5]
- Conversely, the greatest potential economic gains come from divesting the worst-run enterprises (as distinguished from those with the worst economic prospects, whatever the character of management). Here the problem is to find a buyer; price is of secondary importance. The opportunity cost of *not* selling is very high, because the potential gains from changes in performance are great. Gains from the sale price itself become secondary economically, and the quest for short-term fiscal transfers should not be allowed to impede progress toward getting the best buyer quickly.
- Particularly large gains are also possible in industries where public autonomy constraints are especially damaging. Public enterprises do particularly badly where quick and decentralized decisions are required or where large amounts of "frivolous" expenditures on travel, entertainment, or advertising are required. Accordingly, enterprises selling differentiated consumer goods (especially abroad) or requiring heavy marketing efforts are likely to benefit disproportionately from divestiture. The extreme case is revenue monopolies such as gambling, alcohol, or tobacco.

This is a short list, and some may find it disappointingly so. The reason for the brevity is that:

- It is not so much *what* one divests as *how* that makes a difference. Successful divestitures have occurred across a wide spectrum of industries, enterprise sizes, and competitive environments. It is the policies that accompany divestiture that matter.

Competition Policy

The first such set of policies involves divesting enterprises where competition can be induced. Many economists argue that the real problem with public enterprise is not its ownership but the noncompetitive markets in which it operates, and that if one corrects for market structure there is no demonstrable difference between public and private operation. Whether or not one accepts this assertion in full, it is an essential truth that trading a public monopolist for its unregulated private equivalent is not guaranteed to enhance either the enterprise's efficiency or the government's chances of being kept in office by satisfied consumers. One implication is that governments must worry profoundly about price regulation when they divest a monopoly or an oligopoly. We will discuss how to deal with this problem next, but first let us try to make the problem go away through competition policy:

- For producers of tradable goods, the solution is simple: announce a strict timetable for phased reduction and eventual elimination of import restrictions on competing goods. For example, in conjunction with divestiture, Mexico liberalized competing imports in a number of industries, including fertilizers, auto parts, steel, and chemicals.[6]

Unfortunately, we also know of cases where the exact opposite has been tried:

- Under pressure to get the deal done, it is tempting to provide concessions to the buyer. In Togo, a steel mill was granted monopoly import rights on noncompeting imports, guaranteeing profits even if domestic production activities were unchanged. In an undocumented and hence unnamed Pacific country, profits at a canning plant soared after divestiture, but closer inspection showed that this was due to a ban on competing imports. There are of course good political reasons to sweeten the deal, but there are less costly, nondistorting ways to do so, as we shall see when we discuss financial restructuring below.

Potential competition can also have an impact on pricing behavior. A policy of free entry into the markets of divested enterprises should be adopted.

For nontradables such as telecommunications and electricity, the problem is considerably less amenable to solution, because it is rooted in technology rather than policy. As a result, the problem cannot be made to disappear, but it can be ameliorated:

- Many natural monopolies have been granted unnatural monopolies in ancillary goods and services. The clearest example is in the telecommunications industry, where competition is perfectly feasible in such markets. Other examples include new services such as cellular systems. A significant addition to the gains from the divestiture of British Telecom came from allowing private entry into these markets.
- In the case of electric power, a quite different opportunity presents itself, because while the core grid is necessarily a monopoly, the separate generating plants are not. The model here is Chile, where prior to divestiture the electricity monopoly was carved up into a core grid plus a number of independent generating and distribution units. The generating units were then made to engage in price competition for supplying power to larger customers. The separate distribution units, although noncompetitive, at least gave regulators a comparative basis for regulating prices and costs.
- More generally, breaking up large enterprises prior to sale (competitive restructuring) is desirable where it promotes competition and is technologically feasible. We included no such cases in our sample, but the former socialist countries offer particularly abundant opportunities. Romania converted 2,000 of its public enterprises into 6,000 prior to divestiture. The importance of the technological feasibility constraint (economies of scope and scale) is illustrated by the case of Mongolia, where the telephone company was broken up into twenty-three separate operating companies on the U.S. model. The wisdom of this is open to question in a country of 2 million with low telephone density.

Another form of predivestiture breakup can also be helpful, even when it does not foster competition:

- The Kelang Container Terminal in Malaysia was split off from general port activities prior to sale, but this did not, nor was it intended to, promote competition. Rather, it was done to create a profitable unit that could be sold quickly. In other cases this would have the further advantage of creating a smaller unit more appropriate for sale on the local capital market and hence more likely to attract a larger number of competitive bidders.

Regulation

Even if competition policy is taken to its maximum extent, it will remain necessary to continue to regulate the prices of some large divested enterprises if one is going to significantly reduce the size of the public-enterprise sector. Price regulation has two quite different tasks:

- First, *given costs*, one needs to set a price that is low enough to preclude exploitation of consumers yet high enough to allow a fair return on capital. There is a large distributional impact and a small welfare impact of failure to achieve such allocative efficiencies.
- Second, one needs to motivate producers to keep those costs as low as possible. Failure to accomplish this means exploitation of everybody, because there is a large negative welfare impact of costs stemming from X-inefficiencies.

Accomplishing these two goals is not easy, either before or after divestiture. If it were, then there would be little economic debate over the scope of the public-enterprise sector. Accordingly:

- The single most important task to ensure welfare enhancement in large-scale divestitures is to see that achievement of *both* price-setting goals is improved.
- International divestiture experience to date yields clear cases where the first goal has been achieved. British Telecom established the model: it was allowed to raise prices only at a discount from the general rate of price inflation (the RPI - X formula), the discount ostensibly accounting for the rate of technological progress. Other countries followed either more (Chile) or less (Malaysia) sophisticated price-setting methodologies. In each case this generated sufficient enterprise revenues to allow expansion without subsidies or consumer exploitation.
- In contrast, success with the second goal has been less obvious. In none of the cases of large-scale monopoly divestitures have major cost-saving productivity improvements been convincingly demonstrated. This may be in part because it takes time to turn a large ship around. In Chile it may have been because these improvements had been largely accomplished prior to divestiture.[7] Elsewhere, it may also be in part because there is simply no perfect incentive mechanism for motivating cost containment and eliminating the ratchet effect when regulating prices. For example, it is sometimes argued that because the RPI - X formula is independent of costs (unlike the traditional U.S. cost-plus regulatory formula), enterprises reap any gains from cost cutting and thus are fully motivated to do so. This ignores the fact that X will be reset in a few years, and when it is, higher profits due to lower costs are likely to mean a lower future X. Between such adjustments, cost-cutting incentives remain but are far from complete, as U.S. regulatory experience shows. This is not to say that the RPI - X formula is not an improvement, but only that it remains imperfect.

- The basic problem is how to get information on best-practice costs. Here the breakup of Chile's electricity sector has a further advantage in providing multiple independent accounting units whose cost structures can be tested against one another.

Specifying exactly how to regulate prices is well beyond our current mandate. We only stress that it is not easy, but it is critical and major resources should be committed to it. Other regulatory issues are also important:

- Specifying a responsible regulatory regime in advance does not confer a burden on the buyer, but rather a blessing. Few governments will not respond to consumer pressures for lower prices in monopoly markets in the presence of excess profits; if the present government is permissive, the next one may not be. In the absence of a prespecified regulatory regime, there is a greater danger of unfair appropriation of earnings in the future, and a concomitant reluctance of potential buyers to bid for the enterprise and make necessary investments after the purchase.

Foreign Participation

A decision needs to be made early on whether to permit foreign buyers. If foreign buyers are allowed to participate, then it is also necessary to decide whether to permit direct investment (including participation in management) or only indirect (portfolio only) investment. The advantages of foreign participation are largely economic:

- Foreign participation expands the opportunities available, and thus increases the potential yields from divestiture to the government. The more bidders there are, the more likely it is that the government can extract a maximum price and thus increase its share of the divestiture gains.
- Indirect foreign participation can also raise the level of divestiture gains through macroeconomic activation effects: bringing in capital, increasing domestic investment, and reducing balance of payments constraints. However, material benefits of this sort are confined to countries—such as Mexico and Argentina—where foreign participation in capital markets is presently controlled or where there is some other capital market distortion. Where capital markets are already open—as in Malaysia and the United Kingdom—increased foreign participation (at the expense of domestic participation) in the divested enterprise is unlikely to bring net economic gains.
- Foreign direct participation brings the further advantage of motivated technical and managerial know-how. Foreign expertise can always be hired by wholly domestic enterprises, public or private, but

it is difficult to write a contract that motivates full foreign effort without equity incentives. This was a key element at Telmex, where Southwestern Bell and France Télécom took major equity positions and provided technical advice.

The disadvantages of foreign participation are both economic and political:

- On the economic side, some of the buyers' gains accrue to foreigners rather than benefiting domestic actors.
- Popular antipathy to foreign participation can help derail a divestiture program. Turkey was hailed as a divestiture model in the mid-1980s, but the first major sale,[8] that of five cement enterprises, was to a foreign buyer. The subsequent blockage of this transaction through court proceedings led to a government announcement that no more foreign sales would be allowed; meanwhile the entire divestiture program suffered a multiyear hiatus.

Political problems are in part a function of how the deal is structured:

- When empirical work suggests—as in the cases of the Mexican and Argentinian telecommunications monopolies—that foreigners reap huge gains from divestiture while some domestic participants lose, it is not unreasonable to expect heightened political tensions. In marked contrast, at Malaysia's Kelang Container Terminal foreigners were given a mere 10 percent direct stake but helped contribute to welfare gains that overwhelmingly benefited the citizens and the government of the country. At Compañía de Teléfonos de Chile (CTC) foreigners took 59 percent of the enterprise, yet the domestic welfare gain was the largest in our sample.

In sum, if the government can handle the political flak, it should certainly use foreign participation to enhance the net domestic benefits of divestiture.

Partial versus Full Divestiture

Full divestiture is the transfer of 100 percent of ownership and control to the private buyer or buyers; partial divestiture is anything less. Partial divestiture in turn reflects a continuum of choice on the ownership scale but a discontinuity on the control scale, depending on whether or not a controlling interest is sold:[9]

- The decision to relinquish control should be separated from that of how much of the ownership to sell. At first blush it might be thought that there is a simple correlation: selling a majority of shares relinquishes control; selling a minority does not. In fact, holding a majority of shares is neither necessary nor sufficient to retain control. It is not necessary for the obvious reason that a 20 percent stake or less is sufficient to control a company if the remaining shares are widely dispersed.[10] It is not sufficient because the government can retain nonvoting stock—as in the cases of Telmex and Mexicana[11]—and thus receive the financial benefits of ownership while ceding control.

Should full or partial divestiture be chosen? If the latter, what percentage of the shares should be sold, and should control be relinquished?

- Partial divestiture is often derided as a merely cosmetic transaction. It can be accomplished by selling a noncontrolling interest to diversified private shareholders or by transferring ownership to another public enterprise. In either case, effective government control over the internal decisionmaking process of the enterprise is retained even though the official list of public enterprises (which typically excludes indirectly held and minority stakes) is shortened. Appearances of course matter in politics, and the government may well benefit from the altered face of the public sector, even if its behavior does not change.

However, behavior *can* change under partial divestiture, and real economic gains are possible, even if control is not ceded. How can this happen?

- What matters is not the government's right to intervene, but how it intervenes, and partial divestiture can alter this. One surprising result of our empirical work is that the largest divestiture gains resulted from relaxation of an investment constraint, where a fiscally strapped government refused to allow rational investments. In the case of CTC, release of the constraint followed complete divestiture, but in the cases of British Telecom and Malaysian Airline Systems it accompanied partial divestitures, because the firms no longer fell under public sector borrowing rules. Similarly, partial divestiture allowed redundant managers to be laid off at British Telecom, and more rational prices to be charged by Malaysian Airline Systems.
- The same principle can apply to internal operating efficiency. Divestiture is supposed to dramatically enhance productivity by improving incentives and increasing the autonomy of managers and workers. The most dramatic case of such change that we documented was at Malaysia's Kelang Container Terminal. Efficiency was enhanced despite the fact that the government still both owned and

controlled the two enterprises that owned about 80 percent of Kelang's shares, and Kelang's board of directors still included three government officials, five representatives of other public enterprises, and only one private sector participant. Clearly, partial divestiture can be more than cosmetic.

Valid though these possibilities may be, they remain possibilities, and in any case they at best allow partial divestiture to be as good as full divestiture. Further, even if partial divestiture works as well as it possibly can under the divesting government's enlightened guidance, the potential remains for quick reversal under its successor. There are, however, additional strong reasons why partial divestiture may often be superior as a first step:

- The first economic argument for partial divestiture follows from the difficulty of determining a fair price for the enterprise in an uncertain environment. The second economic argument follows from the difficulty of actually obtaining a fair price for the enterprise, even if it can be determined, when the offering is large relative to the existing capital market. Selling part of the shares initially, letting the market set a price over time, and later selling the rest can thus increase government revenues. At the time of sale of the first tranche of Telmex shares, the market valued the enterprise at US$8 billion; at the second sale six months later it was worth US$14 billion; and a year later, when the third tranche was sold, the value was US$30 billion.
- The political argument for partial divestiture is that, in the presence of contending political forces, the alternative to the compromise of partial divestiture may be no divestiture, at least for the time being.

In sum, partial divestiture need not be cosmetic, and in some circumstances it may improve both the country's economic welfare and the government's political well-being. Particular attention should be given to the Mexican option of relinquishing control (to achieve behavioral change) while retaining majority ownership (to maximize the government's share of the results of the changed behavior).

Internal Restructuring

It is quite common, especially in Africa, to "prepare an enterprise for sale" by internal restructuring. Most commonly this takes the form of a financial restructuring, in which the government makes the enterprise more attractive by taking some debt off the enterprise's balance sheet. Other types of restructuring include changing the legal corporate form, laying off workers, making new investments, or completely reforming internal management. Should this pattern be followed?

- There is a fundamental inconsistency in the concept of restructuring for divestiture. If one really believes that private management is better in this industry, then why think that public management can accomplish reform more effectively? If restructuring costs 1 million and the enterprise can then be sold for 3 million, then all parties would generally be better off if it were sold for 2.2 million as is and the private buyer made the changes. This view is supported by two cases in Mexico[12] where potential private buyers were reported to be considering terminating ongoing restructuring projects. Accordingly, one should treat all restructuring proposals with skepticism and ask whether the government really has a comparative advantage at reform.

There are legitimate affirmative answers to this question:

- Restructuring by the government may be desirable because it is supported by foreign aid or low-interest loans that would not otherwise be available.
- A necessary precondition to sale may be a legal restructuring, for example, conversion of a departmental enterprise (subject to government legal statues) or public corporation (operating under special law) into a joint stock or limited liability corporation (operating under general corporate law).
- If workers need to be fired, or if a particularly obstreperous union needs to be tamed, it may make future management's life easier if the previous management assumes the role of the villain. The ultimate model is Aeroméxico, where the government legally terminated the old public enterprise (thereby abolishing the unions and worker tenure) and then reconstituted it as a new legal entity, which was sold free of the encumbering labor relations of its predecessor. This restructuring resulted in an immediate two-thirds reduction in the work force (although employment rose substantially thereafter).
- Financial restructuring is a first-round, zero-sum economic game that can have positive-sum second-round consequences by achieving a politically acceptable price for the enterprise. Many enterprises can and should be sold at a price that is low (or even negative—see below) relative to book value or some other popular perception of worth. This, however, leaves the government open to charges of "giving away the national patrimony," if not of outright corruption. Accordingly, it is often desirable to structure the deal so as to get the price up to a politically acceptable level. There are many costly and a few cheap ways to do this. The costly ways include promises of protection from imports and entry. A cheap way to accomplish the same goal is for the government to take some debt off the books—every dollar of debt removed should make the buyer willing to pay a dollar more. The

result is an economic wash for both parties, but a political gain.[13] An example is Aeroméxico, whose assets (but not its liabilities) were sold for less than the value of the liabilities, forcing the creditors of the bankrupt enterprise to take a loss.

• Finally, government reform *now* may dominate private reform *later*. If there is some legitimate reason why the sale cannot take place in the near future, then it may be better to start reform now rather than delay it until after the sale. Note the fundamental distinction, however: it is legitimate to initiate reform until the sale can be accomplished, but it is illegitimate to delay the sale until reform can be accomplished. For example, by bankrupting Aeroméxico, the government was able to eliminate redundant labor, something that the divested Mexicana has still not been able to do.

How Should the Enterprise Be Sold?

How the enterprise is sold also makes a difference:

• Even in the simplest case of the sale of a small enterprise, success in the sense of sustainability is not guaranteed. In marked contrast to its successful second wave of divestitures, Chile's first attempt in the 1970s was largely unsuccessful, resulting in bankruptcies and the eventual return of most of the divested enterprises and banks to effective public control in the early 1980s. Bangladesh's mid-1980s divestitures of many small and medium-sized enterprises had much the same result.

What sale mechanisms can be utilized to ensure sustainability and maximize welfare benefits?

• Be sure that the buyer puts up sufficient equity. The failures in Bangladesh and early on in Chile were in part attributable to buyers being loaned money to buy enterprises based on the collateral ostensibly provided by the highly indebted enterprises themselves. In many cases it then proved easier to make a large profit by asset stripping and transfer pricing than by turning the firms around. Welfare-diminishing leveraged buyouts are not confined to the United States.

• To ensure sustainability, be sure that the political opposition cannot support a charge that "the government sold the national patrimony for a song." In part the plausibility of this charge is a function of the sale price, but various forms of postdivestiture profit sharing have proved quantitatively superior in many cases. Income taxes are an automatic form of profit sharing—so long as the government has avoided giving away tax breaks as a condition of sale. Other mechanisms include keeping some of the shares initially and imposing special taxes, rents, or levies that take effect only after some target level of performance has been reached.

- Select the buyer through competitive bidding where possible, but do not necessarily accept the highest bidder. The highest bidder may simply be the most foolish—or the most clever, offering terms and conditions in fine print that do not yield the highest economic gain. Instead, governments should evaluate *dis*investment alternatives just as they would investment alternatives, through a present value calculation.

Who should manage the sale? A single centralized body, the enterprises themselves, or multiple intermediary organizations? Which supraenterprise organizations should be involved? Organizational questions such as these are largely country specific, and the answers will vary depending on where the best people in the country in question are to be found. However, two general principles apply:

- To minimize waste and corruption, *centralize policy*. To maximize speed and take advantage of self-interest and competition, *decentralize execution*. One model is Mexico, where a small staff of seven supervised the decentralized sale of 193 enterprises in just three years.

Finally, when should one sell? Some would say "yesterday," which is impossible. Others would say "tomorrow," hoping that tomorrow never comes. We would say "it depends":

- Sell only when the necessary accompanying policies are in place to make the divestiture a success. Violating this rule will bring a quick end to one's divestiture program, if not one's tenure. Compare the failed Chilean divestitures of the 1970s with the successes of the 1980s.

Conclusion

Some may be distressed at the length of our list of lessons (and it could well be longer). Be not faint of heart. The fact that substantial gains from divestiture are possible, but by no means guaranteed, means that policy can make a difference. In government there is no magic wand; *policy matters*.

Notes

1. In our sample, the change in net domestic welfare ranged from -2 to +145 percent of the enterprise's predivestiture annual sales, with a mean of 24 percent

and a median of 5 percent. Additional gains accrued to foreigners, some portion of which could be captured domestically under different policies. Finally, if we net out gains in consumer surplus—which we view as economically and politically important, but others view as hairy-fairy—the variance in the domestic results is significantly reduced: the range is then from 1 to 68 percent, with the mean at 20 percent but a median of 6 to 7 percent. We conclude that the empirical evidence supports a target of 5 to 10 percent as perfectly reasonable in typical cases.

2. Assuming an intermediate 8 percent gain: 8 percent of half of 25 percent equals 0.01. This assumes that our partial-equilibrium, enterprise-level results are not substantially undermined by general-equilibrium considerations when a significant portion of the economy is divested.

3. For ninety-five low- and middle-income countries general government consumption averaged 13 percent in 1987 (World Bank 1989, p. 181).

4. For example, in Turkey it took Morgan Guaranty Trust Company from June 1985 to June 1986 to complete a master plan for privatization. This is only one of many delays that in that country resulted in only 0.5 percent of public-enterprise assets being divested by 1991.

5. In contrast to the following case, the net welfare gains from changes in the firm's performance are small, so any overall gains come from the sale price (in our notation, if $V_{sp} - V_{sg}$ is small, then the change in welfare is heavily dependent on Z, assuming λ_g exceeds λ_p.

6. Using tariff policy to control monopoly power in the wake of divestiture is of course not a substitute for a broader trade liberalization scheme. Consideration must also be given to the price competitiveness of the enterprise's inputs: moving toward world prices for outputs may not be feasible without a similar move for inputs.

7. Chile uses a considerably more sophisticated price-setting mechanism for electricity regulation. It starts with a cost-plus formula, which in itself is neither superior or inferior. However, the Chilean regulators establish costs not through legal negotiation as in the United States, but through outer-bound cost functions based on best-practice firms, and they use a capital asset pricing model to establish the "plus" factor.

8. We view as minor the earlier sales of a 20 percent stake in a telephone equipment firm and 100 percent sale of a bridge.

9. The minimum condition for a controlling interest is that the private sector effectively appoints the chief executive officer.

10. For statistical purposes, the U.S. Bureau of Economic Analysis considers a mere 10 percent ownership of a U.S. firm by a foreign party a "direct" investment (implying a measure of control).

11. In the case of Mexicana, nonvoting shares were not created, but the same thing was accomplished by putting voting shares into a trust voted by the controlling minority block.

12. These were the fertilizer manufacturing enterprise Fertimex and the Ahmsa steelmaking operation. We were unable to confirm that any of these projects were actually cancelled.

13. In a few countries governments and public enterprises have historically avoided paying their bills to one another, leading to the accumulation of accounts receivable and payable. In such cases, mutual debt cancellation is not quite an economic wash because it reduces future transaction costs and uncertainty, thus increasing the buyers' willingness to pay.

Bibliography

Abdala, Manuel. 1992. "Distributional Impact Evaluation of Divestiture in a High-Inflation Economy: The Case of ENTel Argentina." Ph.D. diss., Boston University, 1992.

Adam, C. S., W. Cavendish, and P. S. Mistry. 1992. *Adjusting Privatization: Case Studies from Developing Countries.* London: J. Curry; Portsmouth, N.H.: Heinemann.

Aharoni, Yair. 1986. *The Evolution and Management of State-Owned Enterprises.* Cambridge, Mass.: Ballinger.

———. 1990. "On the Measurement of Successful Privatization." In Ravi Ramamurti and Raymond Vernon, *Privatization and Control of State-Owned Enterprises.* EDI Development Studies. Washington, D.C.: World Bank.

Ahlbrandt, R. 1973. "Efficiency in the Provision of Fire Services." *Public Choice* 16:1–15.

Alé, Jorge, and others. 1990. "Estado Empresario y Privatización en Chile." Cuadernos Universitarios, Serie Investigación 2. Universidad Andres Bello, Santiago.

Al-Haj, Radin Soenarno, and Zainal Aznam Yusof. 1988. *The Experience of Malaysia in Privatization: Policies, Methods and Procedures.* Manila: Asian Development Bank (April).

Arellano, J. P. 1983. "De la Liberalización a la Intervención: El Mercado de Capitales en Chile: 1974–83." Colección Estudios CIEPLAN 11. CIEPLAN, Santiago (December).

ASEAM Bankers Malaysia Berhad. 1984. *Privatization of the Port Kelang Container Terminal: Final Report.* Kuala Lumpur: Lambaga Pelabuhan Kelang (December).

Atkinson, S. E., and R. Halvorsen. 1986. "The Relative Efficiency of Public and Private Firms in a Regulated Environment." *Journal of Public Economics* 29: 281–94.

Averch, Harvey, and Leland Johnson. 1962. "Behavior of the Firm Under Regulatory Constraint." *American Economic Review* 52 (December):1052–69.

BA (British Airways). 1973. *Annual Report.* London.

———. 1978. *Annual Report.* London.

———. 1987. *Prospectus of British Airways plc: Offer for Sale by Hill Samuel & Co. Limited on Behalf of the Secretary of State for Transport.* London: Hill Samuel & Co. Ltd.

———. Various years. *Annual Report.* London.

Beesley, M. E., and B. Laidlaw. 1989. *The Future of Telecommunications.* London: Institute of Economic Affairs.

Bennett, James T., and Manuel H. Johnson. 1979. "Public versus Private Provision of Collective Goods and Services: Garbage Collection Revisited." *Public Choice* 34:55–64.

Bernstein, Sebastian. 1988. "Competition, Marginal Cost Tariffs and Spot Pricing in the Chilean Electric Power Sector." *Energy Policy* (August):369–77.

Bishop, M., and J. Kay. 1988. *Does Privatization Work? Lessons from the UK.* London: London Business School, Centre for Business Strategy.

———. 1991. "The Impact of Privatisation on the Performance of the UK Public Sector." Paper presented at the CEPR/IMPG Conference, Milan, May 24–25.

Bishop, M., and D. Thompson. 1990. *Peak-Load Pricing in Aviation—The Case for Charter Air Fares.* London: London Business School, Centre for Business Strategy.

———. 1991. *Privatization in the UK: Internal Organization and Firm Performance.* London: London Business School, Centre for Business Strategy.

Boardman, Anthony E., and Aidan R. Vining. 1989. "Ownership and Performance in Competitive Environments: A Comparison of the Performance of Private, Mixed, and State-Owned Enterprises." *Journal of Law and Economics* 32 (April):1–36.

Borcherding, T. E. 1983. "Toward a Positive Theory of Public Sector Supply Arrangements." In R. Prichard, ed., *Public Enterprises in Canada.* Toronto: Butterworth.

Borcherding, T. E., W. W. Pommerehne, and F. Schneider. 1982. "Comparing the Efficiency of Private and Public Production: The Evidence from Five Countries." *Zeitschrift für Nationalökonomie* 2:127–56.

Borenstein, S. 1989. "Hubs and High Fares: Dominance and Market Power in the U.S. Airline Industry." *RAND Journal of Economics* 20:344–65.

Borins, Sanford F., and Barry E. C. Boothman. 1985. "Crown Corporations and Economic Efficiency." In Donald W. McFetridge, ed., *Canadian Industrial Policy in Action.* Toronto: University of Toronto Press.

Bös, Dieter. 1988. "Welfare Effects of Privatizing Public Enterprises." In Dieter Bös, M. Rose, and C. Seidel, eds., *Welfare and Efficiency in Public Economics.* Berlin: Springer-Verlag.

Boycko, Maxim, Andrei Shleifer, and Robert W. Vishny. 1993. "A Theory of Privatization." Harvard University, Boston.

Boyd, Colin W. 1986. "The Comparative Efficiency of State-Owned Enterprise." In Ananth Negandhi, Howard Thomas, and K. L. K. Rao, eds., *Multi-National Enterprises and State-Owned Enterprises: A New Challenge in International Business.* Greenwich, Conn.: JAI Press.

Bradley, K., and A. Nejad. 1989. *Managing Owners: The National Freight Consortium in Perspective.* Cambridge, England: Cambridge University Press.

Brander, J., and A. Zhang. 1990. "Market Conduct in the Airline Industry: An Empirical Investigation." RAND Journal of Economics (Winter):567–83.

Brittan, Samuel. 1984."The Politics and Economics of Privatisation." *Political Quarterly* 55 (2):109–28.

———. 1986. "Privatisation: A Comment on Kay and Thompson." *Economic Journal* 96:33–38.

Bulow, Jeremy, and Kenneth Rogoff. 1991. "Sovereign Debt Repurchases: No Cure for Overhang." *Quarterly Journal of Economics* 11:1219–36.

Campbell-Smith, D. 1986. *The British Airways Story: Struggle for Take-Off.* London: Hodder and Stoughton.

Carrera Cortes, Emilio. 1990. "Case Study on Aeronaves de México." Instituto Nacional de Administración Pública, Programa Avanzado en Dirección de la Empresa Pública, Mexico City.

Caves, D. W., and L. R. Christensen. 1980. "The Relative Efficiency of Public and Private Firms in a Competitive Environment: The Case of the Canadian Railroads." *Journal of Public Economy* 88:958–76.

Caves, D., Laurits R. Christensen, Joseph A. Swanson, and Michael W. Tretheway. 1982. "Economic Performance of U.S. and Canadian Railroads: The Significance of Ownership and the Regulatory Environment" In W. T. Stanbury and Fred Thompson, eds., *Managing Public Enterprise.* New York: Praeger.

Caves, R. E. 1990. "Lessons from Privatization in Britain: State Enterprise Behavior, Public Choice, and Corporate Governance." *Journal of Economic Behavior and Organization* 13:145–69.

CHILGENER. 1990. *Annual Report.* Santiago.

———. Various years. *Annual Report.* Santiago.

Christensen, L. 1981. Testimony filed in *United States v. American Telephone and Telegraph Co.* (C.A. 74-1698).

Christiansen, R., and Stackhouse, L. 1987. "Privatization of Agricultural Trading in Malawi." Working paper, Harvard University, John F. Kennedy School of Government, Center for Business and Government, Cambridge, Mass.

CNE (National Energy Commission). 1986. "Demanda de Electricidad en Chile." Santiago.

———. 1989. *The Energy Sector in Chile* (in Spanish). Santiago.

CORFO (Corporación de Fomento de la Producción). 1978. *Privatización de Empresas y Activos 1973–1978.* Santiago.

———. Various years. *Memoria Anual.* Santiago.

Crandall, R. 1989. "Efficiency Gains from Divestiture." Brookings Institution, Washington, D.C.

CTC (Compañía de Teléfonos de Chile). 1990. *Statistical Yearbook of Development in Telecommunications, 1960–89.* Santiago.

———. Various years. *Annual Report.* Santiago.

Danker, Millicent, ed. 1981. *Information Malaysia 1980–91.* Kuala Lumpur: Berita Publishing.

Davies, D. G. 1971. "The Efficiency of Public versus Private Firms: The Case of Australia's Two Airlines." *Journal of Law and Economics* 14:149–66.

———. 1977. "Property Rights and Economic Efficiency—The Australian Airlines Revisited." *Journal of Law and Economics* 20:223–26.

Davis, Lane E., and Douglass C. North. 1971. *Institutional Change and American Economic Growth*. Cambridge, England: Cambridge University Press.

DeAlessi, L. 1982. "On the Nature and Consequences of Private and Public Enterprises." *Minnesota Law Review* 67:191–209.

Dixit, A., and V. Norman. 1978. "Advertising and Welfare." *Bell Journal of Economics* (Spring):1–17.

Duch, W. M. 1991. *Privatizing the Economy—Telecommunications Policy in Comparative Perspective*. Ann Arbor: University of Michigan Press.

Echegaray, Gabriela. 1990. "Caso Final: Companía Mexicana de Aviación." Instituto Tecnológico Autónomo de México (ITAM), Mexico City, August.

The Economist. 1991. "A Survey of Telecommunications." (5 October).

Elixmann, D. 1989. "An Econometric Analysis of Total Factor Productivity Gains of the German Telecommunications Carrier." Paper presented at the joint ITS/EARIE Conference, Budapest, 29 August–1 September.

Encaoua, D. 1991. "Liberalizing European Airlines: Cost and Factor Productivity Evidence." *International Journal of Industrial Organization* 9 (1):109–24.

ENDESA. 1989. *Annual Report*. Santiago.

———. Various years. *Production and Consumption of Energy in Chile* (in Spanish). Santiago.

Farrell, J., and C. Shapiro. 1990. "Horizontal Mergers: An Equilibrium Analysis." *American Economic Review* 80:107–26.

Foreman-Peck, J., and D. Manning. 1986. "Productivity Growth in the British Telecommunications Network." University of Newcastle, Department of Economics, Newcastle-upon-Tyne, England.

———. 1988. "How Well is BT Performing? An International Comparison of Telecommunications Total Factor Productivity." University of Newcastle, Department of Economics, Newcastle-upon-Tyne, England.

Foxley, A. 1988. *Experimentos Neoliberales en América Latina*. Mexico City: Fondo de Cultura Económica.

Galal, Ahmed. 1990. "Does Divestiture Matter?" PRE Working Paper 475. World Bank, Washington, D.C.

———. 1991. "Public Enterprise Reform: Lessons from the Past and Issues for the Future." World Bank Discussion Paper 119. Washington, D.C., March.

———. 1994. "Regulation and Commitment in the Development of Telecommunications in Chile." World Bank Policy Research Working Paper Series 1278. Washington, D.C.: World Bank.

Genel Garcia, Julio Alfredo. 1988. "Aeroméxico: Metamorfosis Creativa." Secretaría de Hacienda y Crédito Público and Banobras, Mexico City, November.

Ghani, Mohd. Nor Abdul, Bernard T. H. Wang, Ian K. M. Chia, and Bruce Gale, eds. 1984. *Malaysia Incorporated and Privatisation*. Kuala Lumpur: Malaysian

Administrative Modernization and Manpower Planning Unit, Prime Minister's Department.

Green, F., ed. 1989. *The Restructuring of the* UK *Economy*. Hertfordshire, England: Harvester-Wheatsheaf.

Green. J. H. T. 1978. *United Kingdom Air Traffic Forecasting*. London: Department of Trade.

Grout, P. 1987. "The Wider Share Ownership Programme." *Fiscal Studies* 8:59–74.

Hachette, D. 1988. "Aspects of Privatization: The Case of Chile 1974–85." Report No. IDP17, Internal Discussion Paper, Latin America and the Caribbean Region Series. World Bank, Washington, D.C.

Havelka, Zdenek, Sr., and Zdenek Havelka, Jr. 1990. *Privatization of Transport in Developing Countries*. Eschborn, Germany: Deutsche Gesellschaft für Technische Zusammenarbeit.

Hawley, W. D., and D. Rogers, eds. 1974. *Improving the Quality of Urban Management*. Urban Affairs Annual Review 8. Beverly Hills, Calif.: Sage.

Hayashi, P. M., M. Sevier, and J. M. Trapani. 1987. "An Analysis of Pricing and Production Efficiency of Electric Utilities by Mode of Ownership." In M. V. Crew, ed., *Regulating Utilities in an Era of Deregulation*. New York: St. Martin's Press.

Heald, David. 1984a. "Privatization: Analyzing Its Appeal and Limitations." *Fiscal Studies* 5 (February):36–49.

———. 1984b. "Will the Privatization of Public Enterprises Solve the Problem of Control?" *Public Administration* 63:7–22.

Heald, D. A., and D. R. Steel. 1982. "Privatising Public Enterprises: An Analysis of the Government's Case." *Political Quarterly* 53:333–49.

Herrera, Luis. 1993. "Mexicana." Centro de Analisis e Investigación Económica, Mexico City.

Hurdle, G. J., R. L. Johnson, A. S. Joskow, G. J. Werden, and M. A. Williams. 1989. "Concentration, Potential Entry, and Performance in the Airline Industry." *Journal of Industrial Economics* 38:119–39.

Hutchinson, G. 1991. "Efficiency Gains through Privatization of UK Industries." In A. F. Ott and K. Hartley, eds., *Privatization and Economic Efficiency*. Aldershot, Gower, England: Edward Elgar.

Hyman, Leonard S., Richard C. Toole, and Rosemary M. Avellis. 1987. "The New Telecommunications Industry: Evolution and Organization." Public Utilities Report, Inc., Washington, D.C.

International Airline Statistics. Various years.

Johnson, L. L. 1989. "Price Caps in Telecommunications Regulatory Reform." RAND Note N-2894-MF/RC. RAND Corp., Santa Monica, Calif., January.

Jones, Leroy, and Ingo Vogelsang. 1983. *The Effects of Markets on Public Enterprise Conduct: and Vice Versa*. Ljubljana: IPCE.

Jones, Leroy P., Pankaj Tandon, and Ingo Vogelsang. 1990. *Selling Public Enterprises: A Cost-Benefit Methodology*. Cambridge, Mass.: MIT Press.

Kahn, Alfred. 1991. *The Economics of Regulation: Principles and Institutions*. Cambridge, Mass.: MIT Press.

Kay, J. A., and D. Thompson. 1986. "Privatisation: A Policy in Search of a Rationale." *Economic Journal* 96:18–32.

Keeler, T. E. 1989. "Deregulation and Scale Economies in the U.S. Trucking Industry: An Econometric Extension of the Survivor Principle." *Journal of Law and Economics* 32:229–53.

Kikeri, Sunita, John Nellis, and Mary Shirley. 1992. "Privatization: The Lessons of Experience." World Bank, Country Economics Department, Washington, D.C.

King, M., and D. Fullerton. 1984. *The Taxation of Income from Capital*. Chicago: University of Chicago Press.

King, Ralph, Jr. 1989. "Mexican Constraints." *Forbes* (4 September).

Kontans Nasional Sendirian Berhad and P & O Australia Ltd. 1985. *A Proposal for the Privatisation of the Port Kelang Container Terminal*. Kuala Lumpur, February.

KPA (Kelang Port Authority). 1983. *Annual Report*. Kuala Lumpur.

Kwoka, John E., Jr. 1990. "Policy and Productivity in the US and UK Telecommunications Industries." George Washington University, Washington, D.C.

Laffont, J. J., and J. Tirole. 1993. *A Theory of Incentives in Procurement and Regulation*. Cambridge, Mass.: MIT Press.

Larraín, Felipe. 1988. "Public Sector Behavior in a Highly Indebted Country: The Contrasting Chilean Experience, 1970–1985," revised draft. Universidad Católica de Chile, Santiago, September.

Larrañaga, O., and J. Marshall. 1990. "Ajuste Macroeconómico y Finanzas Públicas, Chile: 1982–1988." Serie Investigación I-22. ILADES/Georgetown University, Postgraduate Program in Economics, June.

Larroulet, C. 1984. "Reflexiones en Torno al Estado Empresario en Chile." *Estudios Públicos* 14 (Fall).

Leeds, Roger. 1987. "Turkey: Implementation of a Privatization Strategy." Working paper, Harvard University, John F. Kennedy School of Government, Center for Business and Government, Cambridge, Mass., December.

———. 1988. "Privatization in Jamaica: Two Case Studies." Working paper, Harvard University, John F. Kennedy School of Government, Center for Business and Government, Cambridge, Mass.

———. 1989. "Malaysia: Genesis of a Privatization Transaction." *World Development* 17 (5):741–56.

———. 1991. "Privatization through Public Offerings: Lessons from Two Jamaican Cases. In Ravi Ramamurti and Raymond Vernon, *Privatization and Control of State-Owned Enterprises*. EDI Development Studies. Washington, D.C.: World Bank.

Leibenstein, Harvey. 1976. *Beyond Economic Man*. Cambridge, Mass.: Harvard University Press.

———. 1978. "General X-Efficiency Theory and Economic Development." New York: Oxford University Press.

Levy, Brian, Hadi Salehi Esfahani, Ahmed Galal, and others. 1994. "Regulatory Institutions and the Performance of Private Telecommunications: A Comparative Analysis of Five Country Studies." Working paper, Policy Research Department, Finance and Private Sector Division, World Bank, Washington, D.C.

Levy, Herman, and Aurelio Menendez. 1989. "Privatization in Transport: The Case of the Port Kelang (Malaysia) Container Terminal." EDI Working Paper. World Bank, Economic Development Institute, Washington, D.C., July.

Littlechild, S. C. 1983. *Regulation of British Telecommunications Profitability*. London: Her Majesty's Stationers Office.

Lorch, K. 1988. "The Privatization Transaction and Its Longer Term Effects: A Case Study of the Textile Industry in Bangladesh." Working paper, Harvard University, John F. Kennedy School of Government, Center for Business and Government, Cambridge, Mass.

Luders, R. 1993. "Privatization in Chile: Objectives, Economic Environment, and Results." Paper presented at the meetings of the Eastern Economic Association, Washington, D.C., 19–21 March.

Mackie, P. J., D. Simon, and A. E. Whiting. 1987. *The British Transport Industry and the European Community*. Aldershot, Gower, England: Edward Elgar.

Malaysia, Government of. 1984. *Mid-Year Review of the Fourth Malaysia Plan 1981–1985*. Kuala Lumpur: National Printing Department.

———. 1985. *Malaysia's Economic Report 1984/85*. Kuala Lumpur: National Printing Department.

———. 1989. *Privatisation Master Plan: Review of Past Experiences*. Kuala Lumpur: National Printing Department.

———. 1991. *Privatisation Master Plan*. Kuala Lumpur: National Printing Department.

Malaysian International Merchant Bankers Berhad. 1985. *Prospectus MAS*. Kuala Lumpur.

Marcel, M. 1989. "La Privatización de Empresas Públicas en Chile: 1985–88." Notas Técnicas CIEPLAN 125. Santiago, January.

Marshall, J., and F. Montt, 1988. "Privatization in Chile." In P. Cook and C. Kirkpatrick, eds., *Privatization in Less Developed Countries*. Sussex, England: Wheatsheaf Books.

Martínez, J. 1985. "La Trayectoria Empresarial del Estado en Chile." Master's thesis, Universidad de Chile, Department of Economics.

MAS (Malaysian Airline Systems). Various years. *Annual Report*. Kuala Lumpur.

Maynard, G. 1989. *The Economy Under Mrs. Thatcher*. Oxford: Basil Blackwell.

McLachlan, S. 1983. *The National Freight Buy-Out*. London: Macmillan.

Megginson, W. L., R. C. Nash, and M. Van Radenborgh. 1992. "Efficiency Gains from Privatization: An International Empirical Analysis." University of Georgia, Department of Banking and Finance, Athens.

Mexico, Secretaría de Hacienda y Crédito Público. 1991. *The Divestiture Process in Mexico*. Mexico City, August.

Millward, R. 1982. "The Comparative Performance of Public and Private Ownership." In Lord E. Roll, ed., *The Mixed Economy*. New York: Macmillan.

————. 1988. "Measured Sources of Inefficiency in the Performance of Public and Private Enterprises in LDCs." In P. Cook and C. Kirkpatrick, eds., *Privatization in Less Developed Countries*. Sussex, England: Wheatsheaf Books.

Millward, R., and D. M. Parker. 1983. "Public and Private Enterprise: Comparative Behavior and Relative Efficiency." In R. Millward, D. M. Parker, L. Rosenthal, M. T. Summer, and N. Topman, eds., *Public Sector Economics*. London and New York: Longman.

Mohamad, Mahathir. 1984. "Malaysia Incorporated and Privatisation: Its Rationale and Purpose." In Mohd. Nor Abdul Ghani, Bernard T. H. Wang, Ian K. M. Chia and Bruce Gale, eds., *Malaysia Incorporated and Privatisation*. Kuala Lumpur: Prime Minister's Department, Malaysian Administrative Modernization and Manpower Planning Unit.

————. 1970. *The Malay Dilemma*. Kuala Lumpur: Federal Publications.

Mohamed, Abdul Samad. 1990. *Privatization of Public Enterprises: The KCT Experience*. Kelang, Malaysia: Kelang Container Terminal, November.

Moore, Thomas G. 1970. "The Effectiveness of Regulation of Electric Utility Prices." *Southern Economic Journal* 36 (4):365–75.

Morrison, S. A., and C. Winston. 1987. "Empirical Implications of the Contestability Hypothesis." *Journal of Law and Economics* 30:53–66.

Musolf, Lloyd. 1972. *Mixed Enterprise*. Lexington, Mass.: D. C. Health.

Myer, R. A. 1975. "Publically Owned Versus Privately Owned Utilities: A Policy Choice." *Review of Economics and Statistics* 57:391–99.

National Freight Consortium. 1974. *Annual Report*. London.

————. 1976. *Annual Report*. London.

————. Various years. *Annual Report*. London.

Oks, Daniel F. 1992. "Stabilization and Growth Recovery in Mexico." World Bank Policy Research Working Paper. Washington, D.C., January.

Organization for Economic Cooperation and Development. 1988. "The Telecommunications Industry." Paris.

Parker, D., and K. Hartley. 1991. "Status Change and Performance: Economic Policy and Evidence." In A. F. Ott and K. Hartley, eds., *Privatization and Economic Efficiency*. Hants, England: Edward Elgar.

Peltzman, S. 1971. "Pricing in Public and Private Enterprises: Electric Utilities in the United States." *Journal of Law and Economics* 14:109–48.

Perez Escamilla Costas, Juan Ricardo. 1988. "El Redimensionamiento del Sector Público en México, 1982–88." Secretaría de Hacienda y Crédito Público, Mexico City.

Pescatrice, D. R., and J. M. Trapani. 1980. "The Performance and Objectives of Public and Private Utilities Operating in the United States." *Journal of Public Economics* 13:259–76.

Pizzimenti, David J. 1992. *Research Report on Aerovías de México, S.A. de C.V.* New York: Nomura Research Institute America, January.

Poole, Claire. 1991. "That Sinking Feeling." *Forbes* (9 December):83–86.

"Privatization Threatens Workers and Consumers." 1989. In K. S. Jomo, ed., *Mahathir's Economic Policies*. Petaling Jaya, Malaysia: INSAN.

Pryke, R. 1982. *The Nationalised Industries—Policies and Performance since 1968*. Oxford, England: Martin Robertson.

Ramírez, G. 1989. "Política Bancaria y Legislación Financiera: La Experiencia Chilena de los Años 1980." *Revista Información Financiera*. Santiago: Superintendencia de Bancos, June.

Ruprah, Inder. 1992. "Privatization: Case Study Companía Mexicana de Aviación." CIDE, Mexico City.

Saez, Raul. 1990. "The Transaction Cost of Divestiture." CIEPLAN, Santiago.

Sales Gutierrez, Carlos, and Ismael Gomez Gordillo. 1989. "Aeromexico." C395-AD-INAP. Instituto Nacional de Administración Pública, Mexico City, August.

Salleh, Ismail. n.d. *Port Klang: A Privatization Case Study*. Kuala Lumpur (source unknown).

Savas, E. S. 1974. "Municipal Monopolies vs. Competition in Delivering Urban Services." In W. D. Hawley and D. Rogers, eds., *Improving the Quality of Urban Management*. Urban Affairs Annual Review 8. Beverly Hills, Calif.: Sage.

———. 1977. "Policy Analysis for Local Government: Public vs. Private Refuse Collection." *Policy Analysis* 3 (Winter):49–74.

Shirley, Mary, and John Nellis. 1991. *Public Enterprise Reform: The Lessons of Experience*. EDI Development Studies. Washington, D.C.: World Bank, Economic Development Institute.

Siemens AG. 1988. "Study on National Telephone Tariffs Worldwide: A Detailed Comparison, Status in January 1988." Munich.

Sigmund, Paul E. 1990. "Chile: Privatization, Reprivatization, Hyperprivatization." In Ezra N. Suleiman and John Waterbury, eds., *The Political Economy of Public Sector Reform and Privatization*. Boulder, Colo.: Westview Press.

Spiller, Pablo. 1991. "Regulation, Institutions and Economic Efficiency: Promoting Regulatory Reform and Private Sector Participation in Developing Countries." University of Illinois, Champaign, February.

Stevens, B. J. 1978. "Scale, Market Structure, and the Cost of Refuse Collection." *Review of Economics and Statistics* 60 (3):438–48.

Straits Shipper. 1991a. "Advertising Section. Kelang Container Terminal." (March).

———. 1991b. "Extending a Positive Environment for Growth." *Straits Shipper* (5 March):5.

———. 1991c. "The Flag Bearer of Efficiency." (18 March):7.

Symposium on Price-Cap Regulation. 1989. RAND *Journal of Economics* 20 (Autumn):369–472.

Tandon, Pankaj, with Manuel Abdala. 1992. "Teléfonos de México." Paper presented at the World Bank Conference on the Welfare Consequences of Selling Public Enterprises, Washington, D.C., 11–12 June.

Taylor, L. 1980. *Telecommunications Demand: A Survey and Critique*. Cambridge, Mass.: Ballinger.

Teléfonos de México. Various years. *Annual Report*. Mexico City.

Teeples, R., and D. Glyer. 1987. "Cost of Water Delivery Systems: Specification and Ownership Effects." *Review of Economics and Statistics* 69:399–408.

Thompson, P. A. 1990. *Sharing the Success*. London: Collins.

United Kingdom, Central Statistical Office. Various issues. *Annual Abstract of Statistics*. London.

United Kingdom, Civil Aviation Authority. 1978. *Criteria for Licensing Airlines on Short-Haul Routes*. CAA Official Record Series 2, no. 316. London.

———. 1984. *Airline Competition Policy*. CAP 500. London.

———. 1985. *Statement of Policies on Air Transport Licensing*. CAP 501. London.

United Kingdom, Department of Transport. 1984. *Airline Competition Policy*. Cmnd 1366. London: Her Majesty's Stationers Office.

———. 1985. *Airports Policy*. Cmnd 9542. London.

———. Forthcoming. *Transport Statistics Great Britain 1980-1990*. London.

United Kingdom, Her Majesty's Treasury. 1967. *Nationalised Industries: A Review of Economic and Financial Objectives*. White Paper. Cmnd 3437. London: Her Majesty's Stationers Office.

United Kingdom, Her Majesty's Treasury. 1978. *The Nationalised Industries*. White Paper. Cmnd 7132. London: Her Majesty's Stationers Office.

United Kingdom, Monopolies and Mergers Commission. 1987. *British Airways plc and British Caledonia Group plc—A Report on the Proposed Merger*. CM 247. London.

United Kingdom, National Audit Office. 1987/88. "Department of Transport: Sale of the Government Shareholding in British Airways plc." Session 1987/88, HC 37. London.

Valenzuela, M. 1989. "Reprivatización y Capitalismo Popular en Chile." *Estudios Públicos* 33 (Summer).

Van Wijnbergen, Sweder. 1991. "The Mexican Debt Deal." *Economic Policy* (April):13–56.

Varian, H. R. 1984. *Microeconomic Analysis*, 2nd ed. New York: W. W. Norton.

Vernon, Raymond. 1988. *The Promise of Privatization: A Challenge for American Foreign Policy*. New York: Council on Foreign Relations.

Vickers, J., and G. Yarrow. 1988. *Privatization: An Economic Analysis*. Cambridge, Mass.: MIT Press.

Vincent, D., and D. Stasinopoulos. 1990. "The Aviation Policy of the European Community." *Journal of Transport Economics and Policy* 24:95–100.

Vogelsang, Ingo. 1988. "Price Cap Regulation of Telecommunications Services: A Long-Run Approach." RAND Note N-2704-MF. RAND Corp., Santa Monica, Calif., February.

Vuylsteke, C., Nankani, H., and Candoy-Sekse. 1988. "Techniques of Privatization of State-Owned Enterprises." World Bank Technical Paper 88-90. World Bank, Washington, D.C.

Wahab, Haji Yahya Abdul. 1987. "Investment Opportunities in Government Privatization Projects." Speech to the Malaysia-Arab Trade and Investment Conference, Kuala Lumpur, November.

Wellisz, Stanislaw H. 1963. "Regulation of Natural Gas Pipeline Companies: An Economic Analysis." *Journal of Political Economy* 71 (February):30–48.

Willig, R. D. 1991. "Merger Analysis, Industrial Organization, and Merger Guidelines." In M. N. Baily and C. Winston, eds., *Brookings Papers on Economic Activity: Microeconomics*. Washington, D.C.: Brookings Institution.

Wilson, E. 1987. "Privatization in the Ivory Coast: Three Case Studies." Working paper, Harvard University, John F. Kennedy School of Government, Center for Business and Government, Cambridge, Mass.

World Bank. 1988. *Malaysia: Matching Risks and Rewards in a Mixed Economy.* Washington, D.C.

———. 1989. *World Development Report 1989.* New York: Oxford University Press.

———. 1990. *Mexico, Industrial Policy and Regulation.* Report No. 8165-ME. Washington, D.C., August.

———. 1993. "The World Bank Role in the Electric Power Sector: Policies for Effective Institutional, Regulatory, and Financial Reform." Washington, D.C.

Yarrow, G. 1986. "Privatization in Theory and Practice." *Economic Policy* 2 (April):324–77.

Yunker, James. 1975. "Economic Performance of Public and Private Enterprise: The Case of U.S. Electrical Utilities." *Journal of Economics and Business* 28 (1):60–67.

Index

Adam, C. S., 15

Advertising. *See* Marketing and promotion

Aeroméxico: acquisition of Mexicana de Aviación by, 514 n1, 523 n3, 523 n9; bankruptcy of, 412, 457, 458, 472, 478, 508; capital-output ratio at, 468; counterfactual scenario for, 479–84, 489; employee share purchases at, 459, 548, 568; financial and labor restructuring at, 519, 586, 587; fiscal flows at, 472–73, 519; fixed capital formation at, 465; fleet size of, 458, 465, 467, 492 n11; foreign participation in ownership of, 476; intermediate input costs at, 478; labor productivity at, 468, 469, 476–78, 480, 487, 489–90, 516; labor relations at, 457–59, 546; leasing by, 465, 473–74, 476–77, 480, 488; load factors at, 468, 482; market structure and market share of, 461–63, 481, 488; ownership structure of, 475; predivestiture history of, 457–61; price received by government for, 457, 472; prices charged by, 481, 487–89; private and public profit at, 462, 464–65; private and public profitability of, 467, 491 n10; projections for, 480–84; regulation of, 461, 480–82; sale transaction of, 459–61, 470–76, 487; sensitivity analyses for, 483–84, 488; stock market valuation of, 472–75; taxes paid by, 472; total factor productivity at, 469, 470, 476, 478, 484, 492 n10; unit costs at, 466–68; welfare effects of divestiture of, 484–90, 492 n19, 516; work force reductions at, 458, 477, 567

Aeronaves de México, S.A., 458, 470, 471

Aerovías de México, S.A. de C.V., 459

Agent banks, 410

Aharoni, Yair, 12, 14

Ahmsa, 589 n12

Airfares. *See* Prices and pricing policy

Airline industry: economics of, 111–14; in Malaysia, 309–10; in Mexico, 457, 461–63, 521, 542; regulation of, 114–15; in United Kingdom, 111–14, 114, 133–34

Alcatel NV, 456 n20, 447

Alfalfal hydroelectric plant (Chile), 194, 200, 205, 215

Allende, Salvador, 224

Allied Van Lines, 165, 166, 172 nn12–13

American Telephone and Telegraph Co. (AT&T), 73, 87–91, 447, 456 n20

Announcement effect: absence at Teléfonos de México of, 420, 422; at British Airways, 107, 131, 139, 140; at British Telecom, 64; at Compañía de Teléfonos de Chile, 261, 282 n5; at Malaysian Airline Systems, 312, 316; at Mexicana de Aviación, 508; at National Freight, 164, 170; at Sports Toto Malaysia, 381–83, 385, 387–88, 390–91

Annual component of the perpetuity equivalent, calculation of. *See* Perpetual annuity equivalent of the change in welfare

Atkinson, S. E., 13

Averch-Johnson effect, 18 n12, 571 n8

B&B Enterprises, 373, 398

Banamex, 496

Banco Internacional, 497

Bancomer, 460, 475

Bangladesh, 587